Inside Delphi® 2006

Ivan Hladni

Wordware Publishing, Inc.

Library of Congress Cataloging-in-Publication Data

Hladni, Ivan.
    Inside Delphi 2006 / by Ivan Hladni.
        p.   cm.
    Includes index.
    ISBN-13: 978-1-59822-003-2
    ISBN-10: 1-59822-003-9 (pbk., companion cd-rom)
    1. Delphi (Computer file)   2. Windows (Computer programs)   I. Title.
    QA76.76.W56H58 2005
    005.265--dc22   2005029722
                                                          CIP

© 2006, Wordware Publishing, Inc.

All Rights Reserved

2320 Los Rios Boulevard
Plano, Texas 75074

No part of this book may be reproduced in any form or by
any means without permission in writing from
Wordware Publishing, Inc.

Printed in the United States of America

ISBN-13: 978-1-59822-003-2
ISBN-10: 1-59822-003-9
10 9 8 7 6 5 4 3 2 1
0510

All inquiries for volume purchases of this book should be addressed to Wordware Publishing,
Inc., at the above address. Telephone inquiries may be made by calling:

(972) 423-0090

To Borland and the entire Delphi community.

Code long and prosper! :)

Contents

Acknowledgments

First and foremost, I'd like to thank Wes Beckwith of Wordware Publishing for accepting this book in the first place, for being patient, and for answering my incessant emails, even while he was on vacation. You're really the best acquisitions editor an author could hope for.

I'd also like to thank Beth Kohler for liking the smileys, for making the book much more readable, and for spotting several errors that would've undoubtedly removed at least one star from the book's rating.

The final thank you for Wordware goes to Alan McCuller for making a great cover. Thumbs up!

I am greatly honored that Anders Ohlsson agreed to technically review this book. This allowed me to quicken the pace and worry less about the accuracy of the stuff I write. I knew I'd have been slapped behind the ear if I did something wrong. ;) Thank you.

Many thanks to Karen Giles from Borland for sending me such cool stuff. And just last year I stopped believing in Santa Claus!

There are a lot of people back home who helped me complete this book, either directly or by accident. :)

Thanks to Hrvoje Lovrekovic, for being a great friend and for solving my software problems while I was busy typing.

Many thanks to Snjezana Grgic, for making sure I was always typing and for allowing me to use her photographs (http://www.rdcentar.com) in the book. To be quite honest, Snjezana, I don't always think kindly of you, especially when it's 3 A.M. and you're saying things like "You know, Wes is going to kill you if you don't finish this chapter today." :)

Finally, I'd like to thank the members of my family, most notably my parents, aunt and uncle, and my grandmother, simply for being such a great bunch of people.

Introduction

Delphi, now in its 10th version, provides us with four programming languages: Delphi for Win32 and C++ for building Windows applications, and Delphi for .NET and C# for building applications that target the .NET platform. This book focuses on teaching you how to build applications using all four programming languages.

Generally speaking, this book is meant to be read from cover to cover because each chapter builds on the previous ones. But, since you may not have the time or the need to read the entire book, I've divided the material into three distinct sections to help you focus on what you want to learn:

■ Delphi for Win32 and C++ languages (Chapters 1 to 10)

■ VCL framework programming (Chapters 11 to 28)

■ .NET programming (Chapters 29 and 30)

The reasons for covering both C++ and Delphi in the first part of the book are pretty simple:

■ The Delphi IDE includes both C++ and Delphi for building Win32 applications, so why not have a book that describes both languages?

■ Delphi for Win32 and C++ use the same VCL framework for building Win32 applications. Why get two books that cover exactly the same topics, when you can have one book that describes a certain topic and provides both Delphi and C++ code examples?

■ The majority of Win32 source code on the web that is not written in Delphi is written in C/C++, so even if you're a Delphi-only developer, it might be prudent to learn how to read, if not write, C++ code.

■ The book also covers, albeit not in great detail, C#, the "default" language of the .NET framework. Since C# borrows from both Delphi and C++, the first two parts of the book teach you C# programming, although it is never mentioned.

The VCL part of the book shows how to build Windows applications using the VCL framework. The majority of the material in this part is written in Delphi, because it would serve no purpose — except to bore you to death — to show all examples in both Delphi and C++. C++ is explicitly covered only when there are large differences between Delphi and C++. C++ material is also, in almost all cases, placed at the end of a chapter, so you can skip those sections if you're not interested in learning C++.

Another reason why Delphi is the preferred language in this part of the book is that Delphi VCL projects can be easily converted to VCL.NET projects. This means that you can have a single code base that can be used to produce both standard Win32 and managed .NET applications.

Finally, the last two chapters of the book cover .NET related topics and the C# language, but not exclusively. These two chapters also describe Win32 topics, especially those that relate to .NET topics or were introduced in Delphi for Win32 because of .NET.

Recommendations for How to Read the Book

The following table outlines different approaches for reading this book.

You are	You want to	Recommendation
New to programming	Learn everything you can	Read the entire book.
New to programming	Learn Delphi	Read chapters 1 to 28 and skip the C++ sections.
New to programming	Learn C++	Read chapters 1 to 28. You'll have to read the Delphi and C++ sections of each chapter, because the Delphi sections tell you why and how something works, and the C++ sections tell you how the same thing works in C++.
New to programming	Learn C#	Read the C++ sections of all chapters in the book, check the chapter's Delphi section if you don't understand a particular topic, and finally read Chapters 29 and 30.
Delphi developer	Learn Delphi	Read chapters that cover topics you're interested in, and also read Chapters 4, 5, 29, and 30 to learn about cool new things added to the Delphi language.
Delphi developer	Learn C++	At least skim the Delphi section of each chapter and more thoroughly read the C++ section.
Visual Basic developer	Learn everything	At least skim through the first six chapters to learn Delphi and/or C++ syntax, then read the rest of the chapters thoroughly to learn about sets, file I/O, and OOP. Skim the VCL chapters to learn about the differences between Visual Basic's intrinsic controls and Delphi's VCL controls, and pay special attention to Chapters 24 to 27 to learn how to build your own components.

You are	You want to	Recommendation
C/C++ developer	Learn C++	If you already know C/C++, you can start reading the book from Chapter 11 to learn about the VCL framework and the reserved words and constructs specific to Borland's C++Builder.
C/C++ developer	Learn Delphi	Skim the Delphi sections of each chapter and read the C++ sections more carefully since the C++ sections usually point out the differences between the two languages.

Using the CD

The companion CD contains all the examples from the book plus two additional applications — the Autorun and Example Browser applications. Both applications come with full source code, and you're free to use this source code in your applications.

I've created the Example Browser application for three reasons:

1. To show how to use the TTreeView component

2. To show how to create a VCL/VCL.NET application that can be compiled as a native Win32 application and a managed .NET application

3. To give you a user-friendly way of browsing and accessing the book's examples

The Autorun application was created to help you browse the CD and to show you how to build odd-shaped windows. The Autorun application's source code contains a very useful function that creates window regions from a bitmap, so you'll be able to create great-looking applications in no time.

I hope you'll have fun reading the book, and that you'll find the examples informative and useful.

Chapter 1

Getting Started with Delphi

This chapter serves primarily as an introduction to the Delphi IDE and the basics of creating a console application. This chapter doesn't provide you with a detailed overview of all IDE elements but rather describes only those elements that are needed to get you on the right track. Other IDE elements are described later in the book.

The Delphi IDE

The Delphi IDE (integrated development environment) appears when you start Delphi. The Delphi IDE is made up of a number of tools that are used to design, build, and test applications. Figure 1-1 shows the Delphi IDE.

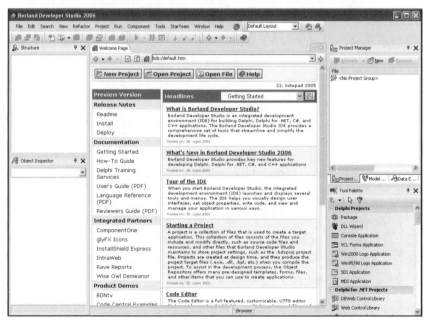

Figure 1-1: The Delphi IDE

Elements of the Delphi IDE

Even though Delphi contains a vast number of tools for developing applications, only a small number of these are shown at startup. The most significant tools of the Delphi IDE are:

- Tool Palette
- Designer Surface
- Object Inspector
- Structure View
- Code Editor
- Project Manager
- Main menu and the toolbars

Tool Palette

The Tool Palette (previously known as the Component Palette) is a window in the bottom-right corner of the IDE. The Tool Palette is an enhanced version of the Component Palette. It displays a collection of components or files and projects you can create in Delphi. If you are new to programming, it will suffice for now to know that components are the basic building blocks of Windows-based applications.

To see the default collection of components used to build Windows applications, we have to create a new Windows application project. To create a new project, select File ≻ New ≻ VCL Forms Application - Delphi for Win32 or double-click the VCL Forms Application item in the Delphi Projects category on the Tool Palette window.

Figure 1-2: The Tool Palette

Designer Surface

The Designer Surface (previously known as the Form Designer) is the central portion of the Delphi IDE. The Designer Surface (see Figure 1-3) is actually the main window of the new application, but at design time, it is used as a drawing canvas to create the application user interface.

To build a user interface in Delphi, you use the Designer Surface in unison with the Tool Palette and the Object Inspector. Using these three tools, the process of creating a user interface is reduced to three simple steps:

1. Select the component on the Tool Palette.
2. Drop the selected component onto the Designer Surface.
3. Customize the component with the Object Inspector.

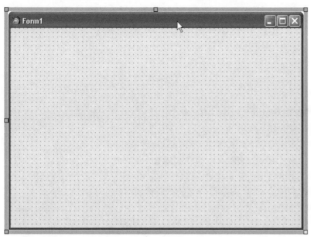

Figure 1-3: The Designer Surface

The dots displayed on the Designer Surface are the Designer Grid. The Designer Grid is only visible at design time and is a very useful tool for helping maintain a consistent spacing between components on the form. If you don't need the Designer Grid, you can hide it or disable it in the Options dialog box. To do this, select Tools ➤ Options, expand the Environment Options and the Delphi Options nodes, and select VCL Designer. Finally, uncheck the Display grid and Snap to grid options.

Object Inspector

The Object Inspector, just like the Designer Surface, is an invaluable tool in the Delphi repertoire. The Object Inspector is used to display and modify properties of the selected form or the selected component(s) on the form. Component properties are various values that define a component. Many of the properties displayed in the Object Inspector define how the component looks on the screen.

When a new project is created, the Object Inspector automatically displays properties of the main form. In previous versions of Delphi, the Object Inspector displayed component properties alphabetically, but in versions 8.0 and later, the default style has been changed and the properties are displayed in categories. To display properties alphabetically, right-click the Object Inspector and select Arrange ➤ By Name on the pop-up menu.

The Object Inspector consists of two parts. The drop-down list at the top is known as the instance list. It lists all components on the selected form (including the form itself) and shows the currently selected component. Below the instance list are two tabs. The Properties tab displays the properties of the selected

Figure 1-4: The Object Inspector

component, and the Events tab displays the events to which the component can respond. An event is a section of code that gets executed when something happens in your application, and that something is usually a mouse click or a keypress.

Structure View

The Structure View displays the hierarchy of components on the form and enables us to change hierarchy relations between components using simple drag and drop techniques. The Structure View is an especially valuable tool in larger applications. Figure 1-5 shows the hierarchical representation of a form with a large number of components.

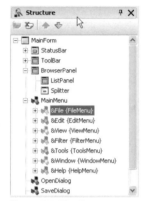

Figure 1-5: The Structure View

    The Structure View has replaced two tools from previous Delphi versions: the Object TreeView and the Code Explorer. While you're designing the user interface, the Structure View displays the component hierarchy (like the Object TreeView in previous versions). When you switch to the Code Editor, the Structure View shows the hierarchy of various source code segments (like the Code Explorer in previous versions).

Code Editor

The Code Editor is a very sophisticated tool for entering the code for the application. To display the Code Editor, click on the Code tab in the status bar of the Delphi IDE.

```
unit Unit1;

interface

uses
  Windows, Messages, SysUtils, Variants, Classes, Graphics, Controls, Forms,
  Dialogs;

type
  TForm1 = class(TForm)
  private
    { Private declarations }
  public
    { Public declarations }
  end;

var
  Form1: TForm1;

implementation

{$R *.dfm}

end.
```

Figure 1-6: The Code Editor

TIP   The fastest way to display the Code Editor is to press the F12 key on the keyboard. The F12 key is used to switch between the Designer Surface and the Code Editor.

After a better look at the Code Editor, we can see two things: The editor supports syntax highlighting and we can see that because there is already a decent amount of code in the editor. The first is a really good thing, and the second only seems bad if you're a beginning programmer.

The Code Editor in Delphi 2006 is an absolute beauty. Besides syntax highlighting, it has the extremely useful Sync Edit ability, which enables you to simultaneously edit duplicate identifiers in the selected portion of code.

Project Manager

The Project Manager is a window in the upper-right corner of the Delphi IDE that displays the files that make up the current project. The Project Manager also enables us to perform various project-related tasks such as adding/ removing files and compiling. This tool will be really useful when we start building our own components and packages.

Main Menu and Toolbars

The main menu is your door into the Delphi world. As in all other Windows applications, the main menu contains all options available in the application. The options that you are likely to use often can also be found on the toolbars. Toolbars are used to provide a faster way to access often-used options, and they never contain an option that cannot be found on the main menu.

Toolbars can be easily configured to better suit your needs. You can customize a toolbar by using the Customize dialog box.

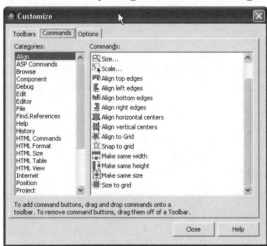

Figure 1-7: Customizing toolbars

To display the Customize dialog box, right-click on a toolbar and then select Customize from the pop-up menu.

Creating a Console Application

This section describes how to create a console application and introduces you to various files created by the IDE.

Creating a New Project

A project is simply a collection of files used to build an application. Delphi has an immense selection of different projects and a lot of ways to create them. In previous versions of Delphi, the only way to create a console application was by using the New Items dialog box. To display the New Items dialog box, select File ➢ New ➢ Other. The New Items dialog box displays all project types available in Delphi.

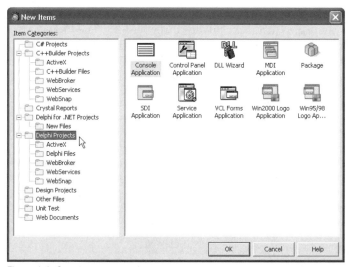

Figure 1-8: Creating a new project

To create a new console application project, you have to select the Delphi Projects node in the Item Categories tree and then double-click the Console Application icon on the right.

NOTE   Delphi automatically closes the open project when you create a new one, but if you want to close the open project yourself, the fastest way to do so is to select File ➢ Close All.

When you create a console application project, all visual design tools will be disabled because console applications do not have a visual user interface. Console applications are Windows applications that are displayed in the console window and look like DOS applications.

Figure 1-9: A simple console application

A faster way to create a console application project in Delphi 2005 and newer versions is to select the Delphi Projects category in the Tool Palette window and double-click the Console Application item.

Project Files

To review files that make up the console application project, we have to save the project to disk. The fastest way of saving the entire project to disk is to use the File ➤ Save All option or click the corresponding button on the Standard toolbar (the icon with two overlapped floppy disks).

TIP   Always save projects into separate directories. If you save more than one project into a directory, you may inadvertently rewrite a file that belongs to another project and that will render the other project useless.

When you select the File ➤ Save All option, Delphi asks you to enter the name for your project. To simplify things, accept the name Delphi suggests and click Save after you've created and/or selected an empty folder.

The important files that define a console application have the extensions .dpr, .bdsproj, and .cfg. The most important file in every project is the .dpr file — the Delphi project file. The project file contains the essential portions of code that define the project and make it work. When you create a console application project, Delphi automatically displays the project's source code in the editor, as shown in Figure 1-10 on the following page.

Like .dpr files, both .cfg and .bdsproj files are text files, but unlike the .dpr file, they contain project settings rather than code. The .cfg file contains project configuration settings and the .bdsproj file contains various settings like compiler directives, search paths, and a link to the .dpr file. The .bdsproj file is the new XML-based project file that contains project settings that can be viewed and changed in the Project Options dialog box.

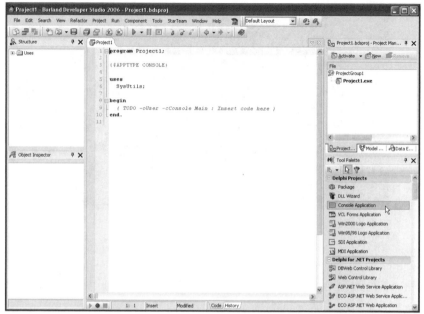

Figure 1-10: Project source code

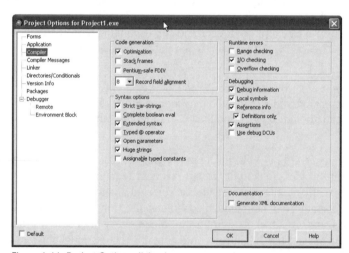

Figure 1-11: Project Options dialog box

Compiling Projects

Compilation is the process of creating an executable file from one or more files containing source code. To compile a project in Delphi, select Project ➤ Compile or Project ➤ Build. After you select either option, Delphi compiles the project file into an executable file with the project name and the extension .exe and places the executable file into the project directory.

Currently, it makes no difference whether you use Compile or Build to create the executable file. But there is a difference in larger projects that have more than one unit (source code module). When you use the Compile option, only the units that were changed since the last compilation are recompiled. When you use the Build option, however, all units are recompiled, regardless of their last compilation status.

To test the application, run it from the IDE using the Run ➤ Run option. When you run the application from the IDE, the application is first compiled and then run. When the application starts, all designer windows except the Code Editor are hidden and are replaced by debug windows. If you want to run the application without bringing up the debug windows, select Run ➤ Run Without Debugging.

The executable file Delphi created in the compilation process is a fully functional standalone Windows application that can be distributed and run on other machines. The only problem with this application is that it doesn't do much — it actually does nothing. To see how to create an application that does something, turn the page to Chapter 2.

Chapter 2

Delphi and C++ Language Basics

This chapter deals with the basics of Delphi and C++ programming. It first explains the general structure of a Delphi application by dissecting the source code of the automatically generated console application. After this overview, the chapter shows how to work with variables and how to achieve basic input/output. Finally, the chapter covers the basics of the C++ language.

Structure of a Delphi Application

The best way to learn about the basic structure of every Delphi application is to create a console application project. Create the console application project and take a look at the source code (see Listing 2-1). (If you've skipped the first chapter, select File ➤ New ➤ Other on the main menu, select the Delphi Projects node on the New Items dialog box, and double-click the Console Application icon.)

Listing 2-1: Console application

```
program Project2;

{$APPTYPE CONSOLE}

uses
  SysUtils;

begin
  { TODO -oUser -cConsole Main : Insert code here }
end.
```

Even though the source code generated for the console application is quite short, the basic skeleton of a Delphi application is actually much shorter. To function properly, a Delphi application needs only two lines of code:

```
begin
end.
```

These two words are known as reserved words.

Reserved Words

Reserved words are an essential part of the programming language, and every reserved word has a special meaning. Reserved words are very easy to spot in Delphi, since they are boldfaced by default. Delphi reserved words are displayed in Table 2-1.

Table 2-1: Delphi reserved words

and	array	as	asm
begin	case	class	const
constructor	destructor	dispinterface	div
do	downto	else	end
except	exports	file	finalization
finally	for	function	goto
if	implementation	in	inherited
label	library	mod	nil
not	object	of	or
out	packed	procedure	program
property	raise	record	repeat
resourcestring	set	shl	shr
string	then	threadvar	to
try	type	until	uses
var	while	with	xor

The reserved words begin and end followed by a period represent the main block of the application. All statements that we want to execute when the application starts have to be written inside the main block.

Besides the reserved words that define the main block, the generated console application uses two more reserved words: program and uses.

The reserved word program is used to define the application's name. To properly define an application's name, the word program has to be followed by the application name and a semicolon. The application name defined by the word program should match the project file name (program Asterix = Asterix.dpr).

The reserved word uses represents a list of units that the application needs to successfully compile. Units contain various code segments that we can use in our applications. A more detailed discussion on units can be found in Chapter 5 in the "Creating Units" section.

Comments

Comments are simply segments of source code in which the programmer writes plain text that describes a piece of code. Comments are completely ignored by the compiler, meaning that they aren't compiled into and don't increase the size of the executable file.

There are two types of comments in Delphi — block comments and single-line comments. A single-line comment is written using two slashes:

```
// begin
```

A single-line comment is the text between the two slashes and the end of the line. In this example, the Delphi compiler no longer sees the word begin as a reserved word but as a comment.

The single-line comment can be written anywhere in a line, but only the text to the right of the slashes is interpreted as a comment.

The block comment can be written in two ways. One way of writing block comments can be seen in the main block of the generated console application as shown in Listing 2-1. The text between the left and right braces is a block comment. A block comment can even stretch over multiple source code lines:

```
begin
  { TODO -oUser
    -cConsole Main :
    Insert code here }
end.
```

Another way of writing a block comment is to use the asterisk-parenthesis combination. Use the left parenthesis followed by an asterisk to open the block comment and an asterisk followed by a right parenthesis to close the block comment:

```
(*
uses
  SysUtils;
*)
```

You can even nest block comments, but you can only nest comments of different types:

```
// The following comment is OK.
(*
begin
  { TODO -oUser -cConsole Main : Insert code here }
end.
*)

// This syntax is illegal - "end." is not commented.
{
begin
  { TODO -oUser -cConsole Main : Insert code here }
end.
}
```

In addition to using comments as a means of source code documentation, Borland developers opted to use comments for several other tasks. One of these tasks is to maintain a to-do list for the project. You can see this specialized comment in the main block of the console application.

All to-do comments can be viewed in the To-Do List dialog box. To display the To-Do List dialog box, select View ➤ To-Do List (see Figure 2-1).

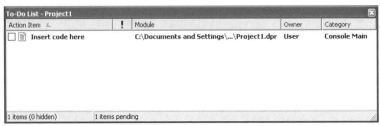

Figure 2-1: The To-Do list

You can add your own to-do comments by typing them directly into the source code, using the To-Do List dialog box, or right-clicking the Code Editor and selecting Add To-Do Item (see Figure 2-2).

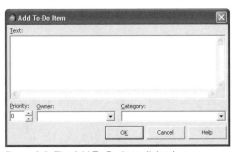

Figure 2-2: The Add To-Do Item dialog box

Another specialized comment type has the ability to change the behavior of the Delphi compiler. This type of comment is known as a compiler directive.

Compiler Directives

Compiler directives are special comments that can be used to change the default compiler behavior. Compiler directives are written as block comments but with the addition of the dollar sign as the first character inside the braces:

```
{$APPTYPE CONSOLE}
```

The $APPTYPE compiler directive is used to tell the compiler to generate a console application or a GUI (windows-based) application. If the $APPTYPE directive is omitted, Delphi compiles the application as a GUI application.

Basic Output

Now that we have covered the structure of the console application, we can deal with the more tangible realm of input and output.

The WriteLn Statement

To output a piece of data to the console screen, you can use the WriteLn statement.

Listing 2-2: Basic text output

```
program Project1;

{$APPTYPE CONSOLE}

uses
  SysUtils;

begin
  WriteLn('Hello from Delphi!');
end.
```

To test the application, simply press F9 on the keyboard. This is what happens when you run an application:

1.   The execution starts at the beginning of the main block.

2.   All statements inside the main block are sequentially executed.

3.   When all statements finish executing and the end of the main block is reached, the application terminates.

In this case, the console window appears on screen for a very short amount of time and immediately closes. In that time, it successfully executes the WriteLn statement and displays our message to the screen. But, in order to see that it really works, we have to add one more statement to the application: the ReadLn statement.

Although not its primary job, the ReadLn statement can be used to delay the termination of the console application. When used anywhere in a console application, the ReadLn statement defers further execution until the user presses Enter on the keyboard.

Listing 2-3: The updated console application

```
program Project1;

{$APPTYPE CONSOLE}

uses
  SysUtils;

begin
  WriteLn('Hello from Delphi!');
  ReadLn;
end.
```

If you run the application now, the WriteLn statement displays the "Hello from Delphi!" message and the ReadLn statement keeps the console window visible until you press the Enter key.

Figure 2-3: The updated console application

To display more than one line, simply use the WriteLn statement again and add the text enclosed in single quotation marks:

Listing 2-4: Displaying several lines of text

```
program Project1;

{$APPTYPE CONSOLE}

uses
  SysUtils;

begin
  WriteLn('Hello from Delphi!');
  WriteLn('Want to learn more?');
  ReadLn;
end.
```

NOTE   You have to add a semicolon to the end of every statement. Delphi uses semicolons to separate one statement from another. The only time you don't have to add a semicolon to the end of a statement is when it's the only or the last statement in a block.

Listing 2-5: Exception to the semicolon rule

```
program Project1;

{$APPTYPE CONSOLE}

uses
  SysUtils;

begin
  WriteLn('Hello from Delphi!');
  WriteLn('Want to learn more?');
  ReadLn
end.
```

Omitting the semicolon elsewhere will make Delphi present a cute little compiler error, like the one in Figure 2-4.

Delphi shows compilation errors in the Messages window, which is at the bottom of the Code Editor. The Messages window displays all errors found in the source code, but the Code Editor highlights only the first one.

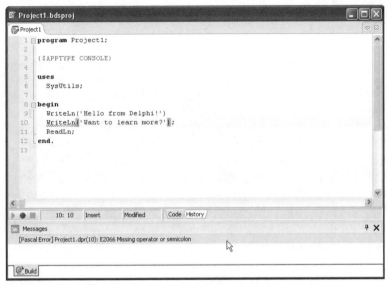

Figure 2-4: A compiler error

The Messages window provides you with all necessary information about the error — the name of the unit where the error is located, the line number, and a short description of the error. You can also get a more detailed description of the error by selecting the error in the Messages window and pressing F1 on the keyboard.

TIP When trying to fix the error, first examine the source code line specified in the Messages window. If you can't find the error in that line, try looking for the error in one of the preceding lines.

The Write Statement

In addition to the WriteLn statement, Delphi has the Write statement for displaying data in a console application. The only difference between the two statements is that the WriteLn statement writes data in separate lines and the Write statement writes data in the same line.

Listing 2-6: Write and WriteLn text output

```
program Project1;

{$APPTYPE CONSOLE}

uses
  SysUtils;

begin
  Write('This is ');
  Write('the first ');
  Write('line.');
  WriteLn('This is the second line.');
```

```
  ReadLn;
end.
```

Don't be fooled by the text inside the Write and WriteLn statements. When you run the above application, everything will be displayed in the same line. The reason is that the Write statement always writes text in the same line and the WriteLn statement first writes the user-defined data and then moves the cursor to a new line.

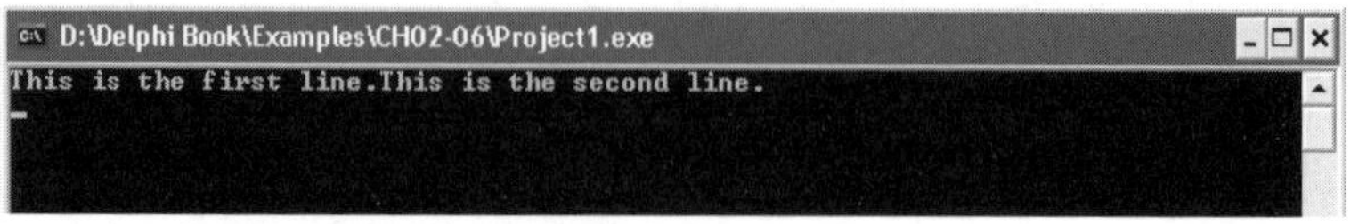

Figure 2-5: Output of the Write statement

To correct this situation, we have to move the cursor to a new line before we display the second text message. To do that, use the WriteLn statement without any additional data.

Listing 2-7: Displaying an empty line

```
program Project1;

{$APPTYPE CONSOLE}

uses
  SysUtils;

begin
  Write('This is ');
  Write('the first ');
  Write('line.');

  { Write an empty line. }
  WriteLn;

  WriteLn('This is the second line.');
  ReadLn;
end.
```

Data Types

When working with data in Delphi, you usually don't work with memory segments where any kind of data can be found or stored. Instead, you usually work with segments of memory that are strictly defined by a data type. A data type can be regarded as a name for a specific type of data — a string, character, integer, etc. A data type defines not only the name but also the memory size, value range, and operations that can be performed on the data.

Delphi has a plethora of data types (the more the merrier), but a vast majority of these are user-defined types. Basic data type categories in Delphi are string, integer, real, character, and Boolean.

String Data Types

We use the string data type when we want to work with a sequence of characters. The default string data type we use in Delphi is called the AnsiString or long string. The Delphi string can be used to hold very long strings up to 2 GB. That's a lot of text! The string data type is actually the only data type you've used so far. A string in Delphi is any value enclosed in single quotation marks.

Along with the AnsiString type, Delphi supports two other string types: the ShortString and the WideString. The ShortString is an old string type used in DOS and Win 3.x, but there are a few of situations where this type can still be utilized. The ShortString cannot hold more than 255 characters, while the WideString can hold a 2 GB string, just like the default AnsiString. The difference between the AnsiString and WideString data types is that the WideString works with 16-bit Unicode characters.

The string data type defines several operators, including the concatenation operator (+) that can be used to concatenate any number of characters and string parts into a final string:

```
WriteLn('This ' + 'is ' + 'a ' + 'concatenated ' + 'string.');
```

Integer and Real Data Types

Table 2-2 shows the Delphi integer types. The Integer and Cardinal types give the best performance results.

Table 2-2: Integer types

Type Name	Range
Integer	−2147483648..2147483647
Cardinal	0..4294967295
Shortint	−128..127
Smallint	−32768..32767
Longint	−2147483648..2147483647
Int64	$-2^{63}..2^{63-1}$
Byte	0..255
Word	0..65535
Longword	0..4294967295

You can display integer values by passing them directly to the Write/WriteLn statements:

```
WriteLn(65);
WriteLn(-165 + 35);
```

Real types are used to store floating-point values. Table 2-3 displays the list of real types. The Double data type gives the best performance results.

Table 2-3: Real types

Type Name	Range
Double (Real)	$5.0 \times 10^{-324}..1.7 \times 10^{308}$
Single	$1.5 \times 10^{-45}..3.4 \times 10^{38}$
Extended	$3.6 \times 10^{-4951}..1.1 \times 10^{4932}$
Comp	$-2^{63+1}..2^{63-1}$
Currency	$-922337203685477.5808..922337203685477.5807$

When displaying integer data, you can specify the display width of the value. This is useful when you want to display a simple table or format the output. To specify the width, append the display value with a colon and an integer value that defines the width in characters:

```
Write(1:5); WriteLn(12:5);
Write(123:5); WriteLn(1234:5);
```

The result of this code is displayed in Figure 2-6.

Figure 2-6: Result of the Write/WriteLn width parameter

When displaying real data, you can add another parameter, DecPlaces, to define how many characters should be displayed. The decimal places parameter is also defined by appending a colon and an integer value that specifies the width in characters. When specified, the decimal spaces value is a portion of the entire width value; thus, writing 8:2 results in the width of six spaces and two decimal places (see Figure 2-7):

```
WriteLn(123.4687:8:2);
WriteLn(90.1:8:2);
WriteLn((33.34 + 66.66):8:2);
```

Figure 2-7: Formatting real values

Character and Boolean Types

There are two basic character types in Delphi: AnsiChar and WideChar. The default character data type is Char, which is identical to AnsiChar. Characters are usually enclosed in single quotation marks, just like strings:

```
WriteLn('A');
```

Since characters are really integer values that map to a specific position in the character table (ANSI or Unicode), they can be represented by integers, but we have to insert the number symbol (#) in front of the integer value:

```
WriteLn(#65);
```

Now that we know how to write character values using their integer representation, we can display text in a new line without using the WriteLn statement. To do that we have to use characters 10 and 13, which are better known as linefeed and carriage return, respectively:

```
Write('a');
Write(#10#13);
Write('b');
```

Another way of writing these characters is to combine them into a string and display them with only one Write statement (making sure there are no spaces between the text in single quotation marks and the character values):

```
Write('a'#10#13'b');
```

The Boolean data type is used to represent two logical values: True and False. Boolean values can also be represented as an integer where False is 0 and True is 1.

Variables

Variables are a fundamental programming concept that you have to master before you can start writing useful applications. Simply put, a variable is a name for a segment of memory that we can read data from and write data to. The primary job of a variable is to enable the programmer to work with a piece of data while the application is running.

Before we can use a variable in a Delphi application we have to declare it.

Declaring Variables

There are three steps that you need to complete in order to properly declare a variable:

1. Use the reserved word `var` to let Delphi know that you are declaring one or more variables.
2. Specify a name for the variable.
3. Specify a data type for the variable.

The basic syntax for a variable declaration is:

```
var VariableName: DataType;
```

Here is an example declaration of a variable that can hold a string value:

```
var s: string;
```

If you want to declare more than one variable, you don't have to place the reserved word `var` in front of every variable declaration. Here is the preferred way of declaring several variables at once:

```
var
  s: string;
  I: Integer;
  c: Char;
```

If you need to declare more than one variable of the same type, you can declare them all in one line:

```
var
  str1, str2, str3: string;
  I, I2: Integer;
```

The most important thing to note about variables in Delphi is that they have to be declared before they are used. Delphi doesn't allow implicit variable declarations like Visual Basic or declarations inside of a block like C++. The variable declaration block must be written before the block in which we wish to use our variables. In a console application, the var block must precede the main block.

Listing 2-8: Variable declarations

```
program Project1;

{$APPTYPE CONSOLE}

uses
  SysUtils;

var
  str1, str2, str3: string;
  I, I2: Integer;

begin
  ReadLn;
end.
```

Delphi has two flavors of variables: global and local. All variables in the var block in Listing 2-8 are global variables. There are some differences between the two types of variables, but these are described in more detail in Chapter 5 in the "Local and Global Variables" section.

Identifiers

An identifier is a word that is used to name certain elements of an application — variables, constants, units, and others. For a word to qualify as an identifier it must follow these simple rules:

- Can be of any length, but only the first 255 characters are significant
- Can contain letters, numbers, and underscores
- Must begin with an underscore or a letter but never a number
- Cannot contain spaces

- Normally, an identifier cannot be the same as one of the reserved words; to use a reserved word as an identifier, you need to prefix the identifier with &:

```
var
   &begin: string;
```

Delphi identifiers are not case sensitive like identifiers in C++, so you cannot declare two variables with identical names but different capitalization:

```
{ The following two declarations result
  in a compiler error - Identifier redeclared. }
var
   str: string;
   STR: string;
```

The Assignment Operator

The assignment operator in Delphi is the symbol ":=" (a colon followed by the equal sign). The assignment operator is used in an assignment statement to write a new value to a variable. The syntax of the assignment statement is:

```
Variable := Value;
```

or

```
Variable := Expression;
```

The following example shows how to write simple assignment statements. Notice how easy it is to display the contents of a variable using the WriteLn statement.

Listing 2-9: Simple assignment statements

```
program Project1;

{$APPTYPE CONSOLE}

uses
   SysUtils;

var
   x: Integer;
   xSquared: Integer;

begin
   x := 3;
   xSquared := x * x;
   WriteLn(xSquared);
   ReadLn;
end.
```

When you run the above code, the application will display 9, which is the correct result of this simple assignment.

Arithmetic Operators and Expressions

Delphi has six binary and two unary arithmetic operators.

Binary Arithmetic Operators

Binary arithmetic operators in Delphi are:

- Addition (+)
- Subtraction (–)
- Multiplication (*)
- Integer division (div)
- Real division (/)
- Remainder (mod)

Delphi has two different operators for division. The div operator is meant to be used with integer values and the / operator is meant to be used with floating-point values. The div operator returns an integer value rounded toward the smaller value, and the / operator always returns a real value, as shown in Listing 2-10.

Listing 2-10: Real and integer division

```
var
  x: Integer;
  d: Double;
begin
  x := 11 div 2;
  d := 11 / 2;
  WriteLn(x);      { Displays 5 }
  WriteLn(d:0:2);  { Displays 5.50 }
  ReadLn;
end.
```

The mod operator is used to return the remainder of an integer division (see Listing 2-11). If you're a beginning programmer you may not find this operator interesting, but there are a number of situations where it helps significantly. For example, you can use the mod operator when you want to do something after a specific interval or to easily find out if a specific year is a leap year.

Listing 2-11: The mod operator

```
var
  x: Integer;
  y: Integer;
  start: Integer;
begin
  start := 17;
  x := start div 3;
  y := start mod 3;
  WriteLn(x);  { Displays 5 }
  WriteLn(y);  { Displays 2 }
  ReadLn;
end.
```

Unary Arithmetic Operators

Delphi has two unary operators: unary + and unary –. The unary plus is not used very much (if at all) since its usage always results in the original value (see Listing 2-12).

Listing 2-12: The unary plus operator

```
var
  x: Integer;
begin
  x := 20;
  WriteLn(+x);

  x := -20;
  WriteLn(+x);
  ReadLn;
end.
```

On the other hand, the unary minus operator always changes the selected value (inverts the sign) and can sometimes be very handy and result in pretty clean and fast code.

Expressions

Each operator in Delphi has its own precedence — the precedence of execution in an expression. Arithmetic operators that have the highest precedence are *, /, div, and mod. Arithmetic operators with lower precedence are the + and – operators.

When Delphi reads an expression, it reads the expression from left to right but evaluates operators according to operator precedence. When Delphi reads the expression 10 + 20 * 5, it will first multiply the numbers 20 and 5 and then add the resulting value to the first operand. If the expression only contains operators of the same precedence, they will be evaluated as they appear in the expression.

You can override the precedence of an operation by enclosing it in parentheses. In the expression (1 + 2) * 3, the operation in parentheses will be evaluated first.

Listing 2-13: Arithmetic operator precedence

```
var
  x: Integer;
  y: Integer;
begin
  x := 20 * 9 + 3;
  y := 20 * (9 + 3);
  WriteLn(x);  { Displays 183 }
  WriteLn(y);  { Displays 240 }
  ReadLn;
end.
```

Constants

A constant is an identifier whose value is defined by the programmer and cannot be changed at run time. Constants are declared using the reserved word `const`. Declarations of constants differ somewhat from variable declarations. When you declare a constant, you don't have to (but you can) specify the type. If you don't specify the data type, the Delphi compiler will automatically align the constant value to the most appropriate data type. Delphi uses the smallest data type that is sufficient to hold the desired constant value. For instance, if we define a constant with the value 128, Delphi will mark the constant as a Byte constant.

In Delphi, we can declare two types of constants: true and typed. True constants are declared like this:

```
const
  Z = 10;
  Z2 = Z + 5;
```

Typed constants are constants with an explicitly defined data type:

```
const
  XX: Integer = 100;
```

The difference between the two types of constants is that true constants can be used in other constant declarations while typed constants cannot:

```
const
  Z = 10;
  Z2 = Z + 5; { OK to use the true constant Z. }
```

```
const
  XX: Integer = 100;
  XX2 = XX + 20; { This is illegal. XX is a typed constant. }
```

You should declare a constant when you repeat the same value in two or more places in the source code. If you start using constants from the start, you will save yourself a lot of headaches later on. To easily discern variables from constants in your source code you should always write constants using uppercase letters.

Basic Input

There is only one statement that you need to use in console applications to get input from the user: the ReadLn statement. So far, we have used the ReadLn statement to pause the execution of the application. This works perfectly because the ReadLn statement waits until the user presses Enter on the keyboard. When the user presses Enter, the ReadLn statement finishes and subsequent statements get executed.

To actually read a piece of data that we can work with, we have to put whatever the user enters into a variable. The syntax for reading a value into a variable is the same as when we are displaying the value of the variable. The only difference is that for reading we use the ReadLn statement instead of WriteLn.

Listing 2-14: Reading values with ReadLn

```
program Project1;

{$APPTYPE CONSOLE}

uses
  SysUtils;

var
  UserName: string;

begin
  Write('Enter your name: ');
  ReadLn(UserName);
  WriteLn;
  WriteLn('Hello, ', UserName, '!');
  ReadLn;
end.
```

The application in Listing 2-14 illustrates two things: how to read values using the ReadLn statement and how to display multiple values with one WriteLn statement. When you display multiple values with the WriteLn statement, you have to separate each item with a comma.

The last example in the Delphi portion of the chapter is a small application that calculates the full price of a product — the original product price plus shipping and handling. In this example, shipping and handling always costs 15% of the original product price. The user only has to enter the original product price and the application does the rest (see Figure 2-8).

Listing 2-15: Working with user data

```
program Project1;

{$APPTYPE CONSOLE}

uses
  SysUtils;

var
  Price: Double;
  FullPrice: Double;

begin
  Write('Product price: ');
  ReadLn(Price);
  FullPrice := Price + (Price * 15 / 100);
  WriteLn('Price with shipping: $', FullPrice:0:2);
  ReadLn;
end.
```

```
D:\Delphi Book\Examples\CH02-16\Project1.exe              _ □ ✕
Product price: 134.28
Price with shipping: $154.42
```

Figure 2-8: Calculating the total cost

There are a couple of details that can be enhanced in this code. First, we can remove the uses list since we don't use anything from the SysUtils unit (this removes some 25 KB from the executable). Second, the percentage value should be placed into a constant if we plan to do more calculations with it. Third, this simple calculation can be performed inside the WriteLn statement, so we can remove the FullPrice variable. This shorter version of the application is displayed in Listing 2-16.

Listing 2-16: A shorter version of the total cost application

```
program Project1;

{$APPTYPE CONSOLE}

var
  Price: Double;

const
  SHIPPING = 1 + (15 / 100);

begin
  Write('Product price: ');
  ReadLn(Price);
  WriteLn('Price with shipping: $', (Price * SHIPPING):0:2);
  ReadLn;
end.
```

C++ Language Basics

To learn about the basics of the C++ language, you should first create a C++Builder console application project. To do so, select File ➤ New ➤ Other to display the New Items dialog box, select the C++Builder Projects node in the Item Categories tree, and double-click the Console Application item on the right (see Figure 2-9). C++Builder projects, like all other projects, can also be created by double-clicking the appropriate item on the Tool Palette.

After you click OK on the New Items dialog box or double-click the Console Application item in the C++Builder Projects category on the Tool Palette, the IDE displays the New Console Application wizard, which allows you to choose between a C and a C++ console application project (see Figure 2-10).

Since a basic C console application (at least the way basic output is achieved) is syntactically more similar to a Delphi console application than a C++ console application is, let's first create a C console application. To do so, select the C radio button in the Source Type group box and uncheck all but the Console Application check box in the group box on the right. When the IDE finishes creating the project files and opens them in the IDE, select File ➢ Save All to save all project files to disk.

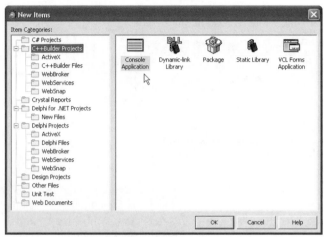

Figure 2-9: Creating a C++Builder console application project

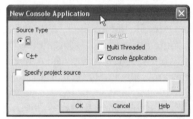

Figure 2-10: The New Console Application wizard

C/C++ Project Files

The IDE creates four files with the extensions .bdsproj, .bpf, .c, and .res. The .bdsproj, .bpf, and .res files are created for both C and C++ console application projects, and the .c source file is created when you create a C console application project. If you create a C++ console application project, the IDE creates a .cpp source file.

Although it contains no source code or configuration settings, the .bpf file, displayed in the IDE automatically after you create a new console application project (see Figure 2-11), is the most important file, because it alone gives us the ability to compile the console application project inside the IDE.

Figure 2-11: The .bpf file

The .bdsproj file in a C/C++ project is the same as in a Delphi project. It's an XML file that contains project configuration settings. The .res file is a resource file that contains the main icon for the application (see Figure 2-12). The .c file is the main source code file.

Figure 2-12: Delphi and C/C++ console applications

If you compile the application now, the IDE will create three more files: an .obj, a .tds, and finally the .exe file. The .obj file is the compiled version of the .c or .cpp source file, the .tds file contains debugger symbol information used for debugging, and the .exe file is of course the final executable.

Before we move on, you should note that Delphi console applications can also have a custom application icon, just like C++ console applications do. To add a custom application icon to a Delphi console application, you need to create or otherwise acquire a .res file that contains an icon resource called MAINICON (this is explained later in the book) and link it to the application using the $R compiler directive. For now, you can simply copy the Project1.res file from a C++Builder console application project to your Delphi console application project and add the following line of code before the uses list:

```
{$R Project1.res}
```

Listing 2-17 shows the entire Delphi console application that uses the default C++Builder icon.

Listing 2-17: Delphi console application with the C++Builder icon

```
program Project1;

{$APPTYPE CONSOLE}
{$R Project1.res}

uses
  SysUtils;

begin
  WriteLn('Delphi Console Application with the C++Builder icon.');
  ReadLn;
end.
```

The Structure of a C/C++ Console Application

After you create a new C++Builder console application project, the IDE stores the necessary code that makes the application work in a .c or a .cpp file. In this case, the source code of the console application is stored in the Unit1.c file. You can see this code in Listing 2-18. When you start typing this example (and others), remember that both C and C++ are case sensitive and that most of the identifiers you'll encounter in these languages are lowercase.

Listing 2-18: The source code of a C console application

```
//---------------------------------------------------------------------

#include <stdio.h>
#pragma hdrstop

//---------------------------------------------------------------------

#pragma argsused
int main(int argc, char* argv[])
{
   return 0;
}
//---------------------------------------------------------------------
```

Comments

Like Delphi, C++ supports both single-line and block comments. As you can see below, a single-line comment is written exactly the same in Delphi and C++, using two adjacent slashes:

```
// This is a Delphi/C++ single-line comment.
```

C++ also supports block comments. A block comment in C++ begins with the slash/asterisk combination and ends with the asterisk/slash combination:

```
/* This is a C++ block comment */

/* It can also stretch
   through several lines. */
```

Preprocessor Directives

Preprocessor directives in C/C++ start with the symbol # and are usually placed at the beginning of the source code file. The most useful preprocessor directive, which can be seen at the beginning of the source code, is the #include directive.

The #include directive is the C/C++ version of Delphi's uses list. It enables us to reuse existing code that resides in another source code file. Each #include directive only includes a single file. So, if you want to use routines that reside in several source code files, you must add an #include directive for each file:

```
#include <stdio.h>
#include <conio.h>
```

```
#include <stdlib.h>
```

There are two more preprocessor directives in the source code: #pragma hdrstop and #pragma argsused. You should always use the #pragma hdrstop directive because it boosts compiler performance, especially in large projects that consist of a large number of source code files and include a large number of common header files.

The #pragma hdrstop directive terminates the list of header files that should be precompiled. All header files above the #pragma directive are compiled once and then stored to disk. These precompiled headers drastically increase the speed of compilation because the compiler no longer has to parse the headers but simply loads the already parsed headers from disk. For best compiler performance, you should place common header files before the #pragma hdrstop directive and project-specific source code files (the ones you're working on) after it.

The only, and not so serious, downside of precompiled headers is the fact that they use a bit more disk space. In C++Builder 2006, all precompiled headers are, by default, cached to the vcl100.csm file located in the InstallDir\ lib directory, so you can check how much disk space the precompiled headers use on your machine. If you really miss the several megabytes used by the precompiled headers, you can completely disable the creation of precompiled headers in the Project Options dialog box (see Figure 2-13).

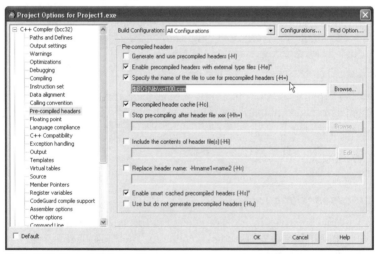

Figure 2-13: Precompilation settings

The #pragma argsused directive is automatically generated by the IDE to remove the warning message that tells us that we're not using the argc or argv parameters in the main function (see Figure 2-14). The directive is placed immediately above the main function because it only affects a single function, the one that follows in the source code. You can read more about functions and parameters in Chapter 5.

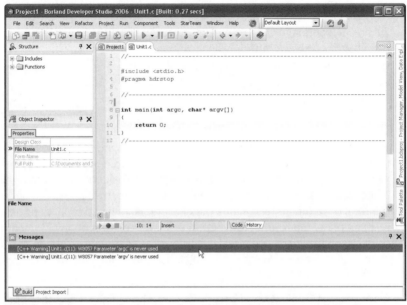

Figure 2-14: A console application compiled without the #pragma argsused directive

Note that, by default, you won't get the above warning messages even if you remove the #pragma argsused directive. You won't get the "Parameter is never used" warning because it is disabled in Project Options. To receive this and other warning messages, open the Project Options dialog box, select the Warnings node on the left, and then select the Enable all warnings radio button in the Warnings area to have the IDE display all warning messages.

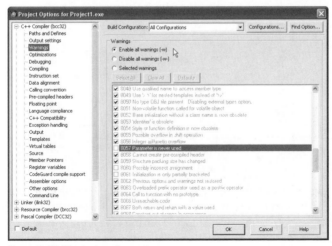

Figure 2-15: Displaying all warning messages

The main Function

The main function in C/C++ console applications is the equivalent of the main begin-end block in Delphi applications — it's the place where C/C++ console applications begin executing:

```
int main(int argc, char* argv[])
{
   return 0;
}
```

To execute a statement when the application starts, place it after the left brace (which denotes the beginning of a block in C/C++) and before the return statement. Although the main function's block ends with the right brace, you must place your statements before the return statement because the return statement terminates the execution of a function. In the case of the main function, the return statement terminates the execution of the entire console application. If you place a statement after the return statement, your statement will never be executed, and in fact, the compiler will issue a warning to notify you of this.

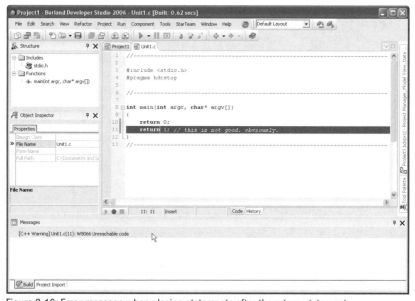

Figure 2-16: Error message when placing statements after the return statement

The value 0 that follows the reserved word `return` is the return value of the function. The main function returns 0 to indicate that it executed successfully. To notify the system that an error occurred during execution, you can return a non-zero value.

Standard C Output with printf

To output a piece of data to the console window in a C console application, you can use the printf statement, which is declared in the stdio.h header file. Note that strings in C and C++ are surrounded by double quotes, not by single quotes as in Delphi.

The following listing shows how to output a simple text message using the printf statement. (Note that redundant comments have been removed from the listing to save space.)

Listing 2-19: Basic text output with the printf statement

```
#include <stdio.h>
#pragma hdrstop

#pragma argsused
int main(int argc, char* argv[])
{
    printf("Hello from C++Builder!");
    return 0;
}
```

If you run the application now, you'll undoubtedly notice that this console application too, like the basic Delphi console application, immediately closes after all statements in the main function have executed. In order to keep the console window visible, we need to use a statement similar to the ReadLn statement used in Delphi console applications.

To pause the execution of a C/C++ console application until the user presses a key, we can use the getch() function, which reads a character from the keyboard but doesn't display it on screen. To use the getch() function in your application, you have to include the conio.h header file using the #include directive. Don't forget to include it before the #pragma hdrstop directive.

The following listing shows the complete console application that remains on screen until the user presses a key to close it. The getch() function works better in this case since it finishes after the user presses any key, unlike ReadLn, which finishes only when the user presses the Enter key.

Listing 2-20: Using the getch() function to pause application execution

```
#include <stdio.h>
#include <conio.h>
#pragma hdrstop

#pragma argsused
int main(int argc, char* argv[])
{
    printf("Hello from C++Builder!");
    getch(); // wait until the user presses a key on the keyboard
    return 0;
}
```

Standard C++ Output with cout

Now that you understand the structure of a C/C++ console application, we can start creating C++ console applications and output data to the screen the C++ way — using the cout object. Don't forget to select the C++ radio button on the New Console Application wizard to create a new C++ console application project. By selecting the C++ radio button, the IDE will generate a .cpp source file and will not automatically include the stdio.h header file, since it's not required in a C++ console application.

The following listing shows a very simple C++ console application that uses the cout object to output the string "Hello from C++Builder!" to the screen.

Listing 2-21: A simple C++ console application

```
#include <iostream.h>
#pragma hdrstop

#pragma argsused
int main(int argc, char* argv[])
{
   cout << "Hello from C++Builder!";
   return 0;
}
```

Although the way text is displayed with the cout object is a bit awkward at first, there's not much to it. To display text or other data using the cout object, you have to remember only two things:

■ The cout object is declared in the iostream.h header file, so this is the header file you need to include in your source code.

■ You need to use the insertion operator (<<, two less-than characters) to pass data to the cout object.

The cout object normally works like the Write statement in Delphi — it displays text in the same line. To move the cursor to a new line, like Delphi's WriteLn statement does, you need to assign the endl (end line) manipulator to the cout object (this is much easier than it sounds).

The following code shows how to output text using the cout object and how to use the endl manipulator to move the cursor to a new line. Figure 2-17 shows the result of the code.

Listing 2-22: Displaying several lines of text with cout

```
#include <iostream.h>
#include <conio.h>
#pragma hdrstop

#pragma argsused
int main(int argc, char* argv[])
{
   cout << "This is the ";
   cout << "first line.";

   // use the endl manipulator to write an "empty line"
```

```
    cout << endl;

    // simulate the WriteLn statement by writing the text first
    // and then the newline character to move to a new line
    cout << "This is the second line." << endl;
    cout << "This is the third line." << endl;

    cout << endl << endl;
    cout << "Press any key to continue...";

    getch();
    return 0;
}
```

Figure 2-17: Displaying text with the cout object

Fundamental Data Types

As you've already read earlier in this chapter, data types are used to define the memory size, value range, and allowable operations of a variable. Table 2-4 lists integer types, matching Delphi types, and their memory size and value range. Table 2-5 lists the real types, their memory size, and their range.

Table 2-4: C++ integer types

C++ Type	Delphi Type	Memory Required (bytes)	Range
bool	Boolean	1	true/false
char	Shortint	1	−128..127
unsigned char	Char	1	0..255
short	Smallint	2	−32768..32767
unsigned short	Word	2	0..65535
long	Integer	4	−2147483648..2147483647
unsigned long	Cardinal	4	0..4294967295
int	Integer	4	−2147483648..2147483647
unsigned int	Cardinal	4	0..4294967295
__int64	Int64	8	$-2^{63}..2^{63-1}$

Table 2-5: C++ real types

C++ Type	Memory Required (bytes)	Range
float	4	$1.18 \times 10^{-38}..3.4 \times 10^{38}$
double	8	$2.23 \times 10^{-308}..1.79 \times 10^{308}$
long double	10	$3.37 \times 10^{-4932}..1.18 \times 10^{4932}$

Variables

Variable declaration in C++ is somewhat different from that in Delphi. There are five basic differences:

■ When declaring a variable in C++, you first specify the data type and then the variable's name, and you don't have to type the colon between the variable's type and name.

■ You don't have to use a special reserved word, like var in Delphi, to declare a variable.

■ You have to declare variables before you can use them, but you don't have to declare them in a special variable declaration section like in Delphi.

■ Variables in C++ can be automatically initialized at the point of declaration (it is also possible to automatically initialize global variables in Delphi; you can read more about local and global variables in Chapter 5).

■ Identifiers in C++ are case sensitive, which means that cpp, CPP, cPp, and Cpp are four different identifiers that can be used to name four different variables.

The following example shows how to declare two variables for use in the main function.

Listing 2-23: Declaring variables in C++

```
#include <iostream.h>
#include <conio.h>
#pragma hdrstop

#pragma argsused
int main(int argc, char* argv[])
{
   // declare two variables
   int x;
   float f;

   // display the values of x and f variables
   cout << "x = " << x << endl;
   cout << "f = " << f << endl;

   getch();
   return 0;
}
```

If you run this application, you'll learn an important thing about Delphi and C++ variables: When a variable is declared, it is assigned a random value from memory (see Figure 2-18). So, before using a variable in either language, you should initialize the variable to a valid value.

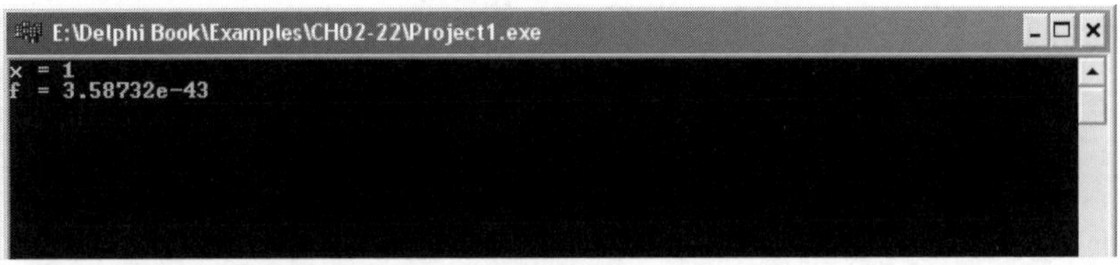

Figure 2-18: Variables containing random values

The previous example shows how to declare variables the semi-Delphi way — at the beginning of a block — before all other statements. The following example, however, shows that it's valid to declare a variable anywhere in a block, as long as you don't try to use the variable before it's declared.

Listing 2-24: Declaring variables in C++, revisited

```
#include <iostream.h>
#include <conio.h>
#pragma hdrstop

#pragma argsused
int main(int argc, char* argv[])
{
    int i;
    cout << "i = " << i << endl;

    float f;
    cout << "f = " << f << endl;

    double d;
    cout << "d = " << d << endl;

    getch();
    return 0;
}
```

Initializing Variables

There are two ways a variable can be initialized in C++ (the first way is used most often):

```
data_type variable_name = initial_value;
data_type variable_name (intial_value);
```

The example in Listing 2-25 illustrates both ways of variable initialization.

Listing 2-25: Initializing variables in C++

```
#include <iostream.h>
#include <conio.h>
#pragma hdrstop

#pragma argsused
int main(int argc, char* argv[])
```

```
{
  int i = 5;
  int j(10);

  cout << "i = " << i << " & j = " << j << endl;

  getch();
  return 0;
}
```

Assignment Operators

Even though the title suggests that C++ has more than one assignment operator, C++, like Delphi, only has one real assignment operator. Other assignment operators available are not pure assignment operators since they do more than just assign a value to a variable. The assignment operator in C++ is the equal sign:

```
int i;
i = 2;
```

Another notable difference between Delphi and C++ is that the assignment operator can be used to assign a common value to multiple variables at once. Here's how you can assign the number 5 to four different variables (and how to declare several variables of the same type in the same source code line):

```
int a, b, c, d;
a = b = c = d = 5;
```

Other available assignment operators are actually a mix of the main assignment operator and arithmetic operators (see Table 2-6). These are known as compound assignment operators.

Table 2-6: Basic compound C++ assignment operators

Operator	Meaning	Abbreviated Form	Standard Form
+=	Add and assign	a += 2;	a = a + 2;
−=	Subtract and assign	a −= 2;	a = a − 2;
*=	Multiply and assign	a *= 2;	a = a * 2;
/=	Divide and assign	a /= 2;	a = a / 2;
%=	Get division remainder and assign	a %= 2;	a = a % 2;

The example in Listing 2-26 fully illustrates how to use compound assignment operators.

Listing 2-26: Using compound operators

```
#include <iostream.h>
#include <conio.h>
#pragma hdrstop

#pragma argsused
int main(int argc, char* argv[])
{
```

```
int i = 1;

// increment i by 2 using the += compound operator
i+=2;
cout << i << endl; // i = 3

getch();
return 0;
}
```

Arithmetic Operators

Table 2-7 shows both C++ and Delphi arithmetic operators and two minor differences between arithmetic operators in these two languages: C++ has only one division operator for integer and floating-point numbers and it has two operators not available in Delphi. Actually, the increment and decrement operators exist in Delphi, but as the Inc and Dec procedures (more on these procedures in Chapter 5).

Table 2-7: Arithmetic operators

C++ Operator	Delphi Operator	Description
+	+	Addition
–	–	Subtraction
/	div	Integer division
/	/	Floating-point division
%	mod	Modulo (remainder)
++	N/A	Increment
--	N/A	Decrement

The increment and decrement operators can be used to increment or decrement the value of a variable by one. The following example shows all three ways of incrementing a variable by one:

```
#include <iostream.h>
#include <conio.h>
#pragma hdrstop

#pragma argsused
int main(int argc, char* argv[])
{
   int a = 0;
   // the following statements do exactly the same thing,
   // increment the value of variable a by one

   a = a + 1; // a = 1
   a += 1;    // a = 2
   a++;       // a = 3

   cout << "a = " << a << endl; // 3
   getch();
   return 0;
}
```

The ++ operator in the above example is also known as the postincrement operator since it is written after the identifier. If the ++ operator is written before the identifier, it is known as the preincrement operator:

```
int a = 0;
a++; // postincrement, a = 1
++a; // preincrement, a = 2
a--; // postdecrement, a = 1
--a; // predecrement, a = 0
```

When the increment or decrement operators are used in a simple statement, as they are in the above code, there's no difference between the two. But the difference is clearly visible in an expression because the preincrement and predecrement operators change the value before the entire expression is evaluated, and the postincrement and postdecrement operators modify the value after the entire expression is evaluated. This means that when you use the postincrement or the postdecrement operator in an expression, it doesn't affect the expression at all.

Here's an example that shows the result of using the postincrement operator in an expression:

```
int b = 2;
int sum = 0;

sum = a + b++; // sum = 3 because a = 1, b = 2
// now b equals 3
```

But if we change the postincrement operator to the preincrement operator, the sum will be 4 because the preincrement operator will first increase the value of the b variable to 3, then add the value of the b variable to the a variable, and finally assign the sum of a and b to the left side, the sum variable:

```
int a = 1;
int b = 2;
int sum = 0;

sum = a + ++b; // sum = 4 because a = 1, b = 3
```

Believe it or not, the space in the above substatement is extremely important. If you remove the space from the statement, you'll get an incorrect result and a bug in your code. Here's the statement without a space:

```
sum = a+++b;
```

You'll get an incorrect result because the C++ compiler no longer sees this statement as the variable plus the preincremented b variable but as the postincremented a variable plus the b variable:

```
// this is what the compiler thinks you want when you omit whitespace
sum = a++ + b;
```

If you don't want to worry about the space in this statement, enclose the preincrement operator and the variable in parentheses:

```
sum = a+(++b);
```

Constants

There are two ways to define a constant in C++: with the #define prepro-cessor directive and with the reserved word const. Although both ways are valid, you're better off using the const reserved word since type-checking can be performed on such constants.

The syntax of the #define directive is:

```
#define identifier value
```

The syntax of the const reserved word is:

```
const data_type identifier = value;
```

Here's a simple example that shows how constants are declared using both the #define preprocessor directive and the reserved word const:

```
#include <iostream.h>
#pragma hdrstop

#define MAGIC_NUMBER 20
#define ANOTHER_NUMBER 101

const int MY_SECRET_NUMBER = 1000;
const float SPEED = 2.66;

#pragma argsused
int main(int argc, char* argv[])
{
    return 0;
}
```

Constants declared using the #define preprocessor directive aren't real con-stants because the C++ preprocessor replaces the defined identifier with the defined value (for instance, the MAGIC_NUMBER with 20) in the source code and then provides the C++ compiler with the modified source file. The object file generated by the C++ compiler actually doesn't contain a single reference to the MAGIC_NUMBER identifier or any other defined identifier.

Standard C++ Input with cin

The cin object, declared in the iostream.h header file just like the cout object, makes basic input in C++ as simple as it is in Delphi. To get input from the user using the cin object, you need to use the extraction operator (>>, two greater-than characters). Here's how you use the cin object to store user input to a variable:

```
cin >> variable;
```

Finally, here's the C++ version of the application that calculates the total cost of a product (the Delphi version of this example is displayed in Listing 2-16).

Listing 2-27: Working with user data

```
#include <iostream.h>
#include <conio.h>
#pragma hdrstop

const double SHIPPING = 1.15;

#pragma argsused
int main(int argc, char* argv[])
{
   double price;
   cout << "Product price: ";
   cin >> price;
   cout << "Price with shipping: $" << price * SHIPPING << endl;

   getch();
   return 0;
}
```

Chapter 3

Conditions

When developing applications, we have to make sure that the user enters valid values and selects the appropriate options before executing a portion of code that uses these user-defined values. The programmer's job is to expect an error, secure the application against it, and show the user how to properly use the application.

Conditions are used not only to test user-defined values but also to add depth and functionality to the application by providing conditional execution — the ability to execute various portions of code depending on the state of the condition.

In this chapter, you'll first learn about the if and case statements in Delphi, and then you'll see how to test for a condition using the C++ language.

The if-then Statement

The if-then statement is used to test an expression and see if the expression evaluates to True or False. Subsequent execution depends on the result of the if-then statement. If the expression evaluates to True, the statement or statements that follow are executed, and if the expression evaluates to False, the statement or statements that follow are skipped.

The syntax of the if-then statement is:

```
if expression then
    statement;
```

To create a valid expression that can be used with the if-then statement, you usually have to use one or more relational operators. Table 3-1 contains the relational operators available in Delphi.

Table 3-1: Relational operators

Relational Operator	Meaning
=	Equality
<>	Inequality
<	Less than
>	Greater than

Relational Operator	Meaning
<=	Less than or equal to
>=	Greater than or equal to

The final result of all relational operators is a Boolean value, and thus the expression used in the if-then statement can be either an expression built with relational operators or a simple Boolean value.

Let's first see how to create an application that tests if the user has entered the correct value. The application will spell out a number and the user has to enter the correct numerical value. To keep things simple, the application always spells out the number three and successfully executes if the user enters 3 (see Figure 3-1).

Listing 3-1: A simple if-then statement

```
program Project1;

{$APPTYPE CONSOLE}

uses
  SysUtils;

var
  TheNumber: Integer;

begin
  WriteLn('The application selected number three.');
  Write('Enter the numerical value of the selected number: ');
  ReadLn(TheNumber);

  if TheNumber = 3 then
    WriteLn('You entered the correct value.');

  WriteLn('Press any key to exit...');
  ReadLn;
end.
```

The if-then statement is used to test the value the user entered into the TheNumber variable. If the user entered 3, the expression TheNumber = 3 evaluates to True and the application executes the line that displays the "You entered the correct value." message. If the user enters any other number, the application skips this line and executes the line that displays the "Press any key to exit..." message.

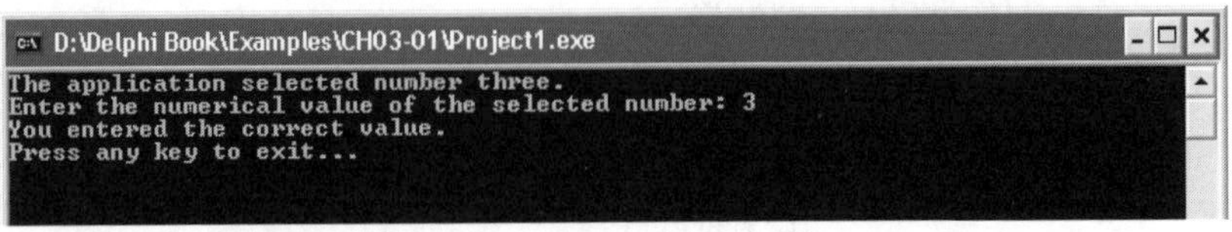

Figure 3-1: The result of the if-then statement

If you indent code properly, it's really easy to see which lines are executed depending on the result of the if-then statement. You should always try to follow the standard Borland formatting style since it is used in the Delphi documentation, in this book, and by the vast majority of Delphi programmers. Even with a superficial look at the source code in Listing 3-1, you can easily see the lines that belong to the main block since they are indented. The conditional WriteLn statement is also easy to spot since it is indented even more.

This example only executes one line of code if the expression evaluates to True. If you want to execute more than one line, you have to write them inside a block. All blocks begin with the reserved word begin, but only the main block ends with the reserved word end followed by a period. Other blocks have to end with the reserved word end followed by a semicolon:

```
if TheNumber = 3 then
begin
  WriteLn('You entered the correct value.');
  WriteLn('Thank you for using this application.');
end;
```

When the if-then statement is followed by a block, all statements in the block are executed if the condition in the if-then statement evaluates to True.

If we want the application to display a message when the user enters an invalid value, we can use another if-then statement but with the opposite relational operator. In this case, we have to use the inequality (< >) operator to see if the user entered anything but the requested number 3.

Listing 3-2: Two if-then statements

```
program Project1;

{$APPTYPE CONSOLE}

uses
  SysUtils;

var
  TheNumber: Integer;

begin
  WriteLn('The application selected number three.');
  Write('Enter the numerical value of the selected number: ');
  ReadLn(TheNumber);

  if TheNumber = 3 then
    WriteLn('You entered the correct value.');

  if TheNumber <> 3 then
    WriteLn('Sorry. You entered the wrong value.');

  WriteLn('Press any key to exit...');
  ReadLn;
end.
```

In this example, we have manually inverted the relational operator to execute a piece of code if the user enters the wrong value. Although you can write two if-then statements to cover both the True and False results of the desired condition, this is usually done with another version of the if-then statement: the if-then-else statement.

The if-then-else Statement

The if-then-else statement is a shorter and more elegant way of testing two logically opposite conditions. Using the if-then-else statement, the if-then section enables us to execute a piece of code if the expression evaluates to True, and the else section enables us to execute a piece of code if the same expression evaluates to False. The syntax of the if-then-else statement is:

```
if expression then
  statement
else
  statement;
```

If you want to execute more statements, write them inside a block:

```
if expression then
begin
  statement1;
  statementN;
end else
begin
  statement1;
  statementN;
end;
```

NOTE: The statement or block that precedes the reserved word else doesn't end with a semicolon. If you add a semicolon, you will get a compiler error.

A simple example of the if-then-else statement is an application that asks for a user name. The if-then section tests if the user entered a valid user name, and the else section is used to display a message if the user failed to enter a valid user name.

Listing 3-3: The if-then-else statement

```
program Project1;

{$APPTYPE CONSOLE}

uses
  SysUtils;

var
  UserName: string;

begin
  Write('Please enter your name: ');
```

```
ReadLn(UserName);
if UserName <> '' then
  WriteLn('Hello, ', UserName, '!')
else
  WriteLn('Invalid user name!');

ReadLn;
end.
```

The if-then-else statement in this example assumes the user name is valid if the value entered in the UserName variable is not an empty string. In Delphi, an empty string is denoted by two single quote marks. The UserName variable in this example can be an empty string if the user presses the Enter key without entering the user name. Since an empty string isn't a valid user name, the if-then-else statement evaluates to False and executes the WriteLn statement in the else section.

Using Code Templates

Writing an if-then-else statement can be time-consuming since it can consist of many lines of code. To speed up the typing process, the developers at Borland added code templates to Delphi.

If you want to use the code template for the if-then-else statement, type the shortcut "ifeb" (without the quotation marks) in the Code Editor and press Ctrl+J. When you press Ctrl+J, the shortcut is replaced with the appropriate code template, and in this case it's an if-then-else statement with blocks, as shown in Figure 3-2.

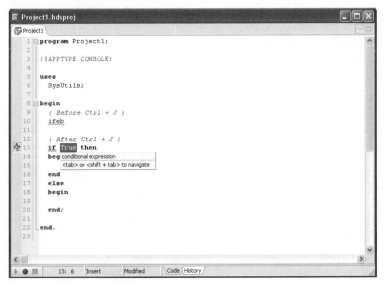

Figure 3-2: Using code templates

Another way of using code templates is to press Ctrl+J without typing a shortcut. This displays a list of all code templates available.

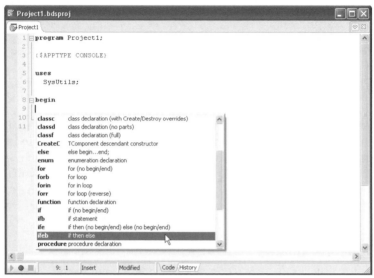

Figure 3-3: The code template list

Nested if-then Statements

If you need even more control over application execution, you can write
nested if-then statements. Nesting if-then statements enables you to define
very specific conditions under which your code can successfully execute. A
very simple example of a nested if-then statement is an application that tells
the user if a number is odd or even, but only if the user enters an integer
value larger than 0.

Listing 3-4: A nested if-then statement

```
program Project1;

{$APPTYPE CONSOLE}

uses
  SysUtils;

var
  Num: Integer;

begin
  Write('Enter a number: ');
  ReadLn(Num);

  if Num > 0 then
    if Num mod 2 = 0 then
      WriteLn('An even number.')
    else
      WriteLn('An odd number.')
  else
```

```
  WriteLn('The number has to be larger than zero!');

  ReadLn;
end.
```

This simple application illustrates a somewhat hard-to-read nested if-then statement that uses the mod operator to see if the number is odd or even. If not for the indentations in the code, these two else reserved words could cause a lot of trouble for an unwary programmer. A much better (read: recommended) solution is to write the inner if-then statement in a block:

```
if Num > 0 then
begin
  if Num mod 2 = 0 then
    WriteLn('An even number.')
  else
    WriteLn('An odd number.');
end else
  WriteLn('The number has to be larger than zero!');
```

Multiple if-then Condition Testing

If we have to test multiple conditions, we need to use yet another version of the if-then statement: the if-then-else-if statement. The syntax of the if-then-else-if statement looks like this:

```
if expression1 then
  statement1
else if expression2 then
  statement2
else if expression3 then
  statement3;
```

The following application asks the user to enter a number and then writes the textual representation of the number if the user entered a number from 1 to 5.

Listing 3-5: Multiple if-then statement

```
program Project1;

{$APPTYPE CONSOLE}

uses
  SysUtils;

var
  Num: Integer;

begin
  Write('Please enter a number: ');
  ReadLn(Num);

  if Num = 1 then
    WriteLn('One')
  else if Num = 2 then
    WriteLn('Two')
```

```
else if Num = 3 then
  WriteLn('Three')
else if Num = 4 then
  WriteLn('Four')
else if Num = 5 then
  WriteLn('Five');

ReadLn;
end.
```

The multiple if-then statement can have an else section, just like the single if-then statement. In a multiple if-then statement, the else section executes only if all previous conditions evaluate to False. The application in Listing 3-5 functions properly only if the user enters a valid number, and does absolutely nothing if the user errs. To display an error message, you can add an else section to the end of the multiple if-then statement:

```
if Num = 1 then
  WriteLn('One')
else if Num = 2 then
  WriteLn('Two')
else if Num = 3 then
  WriteLn('Three')
else if Num = 4 then
  WriteLn('Four')
else if Num = 5 then
  WriteLn('Five')
else begin
  WriteLn('You''ve entered an unsupported number.');
  WriteLn('Try again next year.');
end;
```

Boolean and Bitwise Operators

Delphi has four Boolean operators: not, and, or, xor. Boolean operators are used to create more complex conditions. All Boolean operators work with Boolean values and return a Boolean value as the result. Bitwise operators work with integer values and return an integer value as the result. Delphi has six bitwise operators: not, and, or, xor, shl, shr.

The not Operator

The Boolean not operator is a unary operator used to invert a Boolean value. The following table shows the results of the not operator.

Table 3-2: Boolean not operator

Expression	not Expression
True	False
False	True

Listing 3-6: Using the Boolean not operator

```
program Project1;

{$APPTYPE CONSOLE}

uses
  SysUtils;

var
  Test: Boolean;
begin
  WriteLn('Default Boolean Value: ', Test);
  WriteLn('Inverted Boolean Value: ', not Test);
  ReadLn;
end.
```

The first WriteLn statement always displays False because Delphi automatically initializes global Boolean variables to False.

The Boolean not operator is often used in an if-then statement as a more elegant way of testing whether the expression evaluates to False:

```
var
  B: Boolean;

begin
  if B = False then
    WriteLn('Not OK');

  if not B then
    WriteLn('Not OK');

  ReadLn;
end.
```

The same elegance can be used when testing whether the expression evaluates to True:

```
var
  B: Boolean;

begin
  B := True;

  if B = True then
    Writeln('OK');

  if B then
    WriteLn('OK');

  ReadLn;
end.
```

The bitwise not operator is used to perform a bitwise negation of an integer value. The following table shows the results of the bitwise not operator.

Table 3-3: Bitwise not operator

Bit	not Bit
1	0
0	1

The and Operator

The Boolean and operator is a binary operator that returns True only if both tested expressions evaluate to True. The following table shows the result of using the and operator.

Table 3-4: Boolean and operator

Expression1	and Expression2	Result
True	True	True
True	False	False
False	True	False
False	False	False

Let's say that we need to write a piece of code that can only work properly if the user enters a number in the –10 to 10 range. To make sure the entered value is in this range, we can use either two nested if-then statements or one if-then statement that uses the Boolean and operator.

Listing 3-7: Using the Boolean and operator

```
program Project1;

{$APPTYPE CONSOLE}

uses
  SysUtils;

var
  Num: Integer;

begin
  Write('Enter a number from -10 to 10: ');
  ReadLn(Num);

  if (Num >= -10) and (Num <= 10) then
    WriteLn('Range Test OK.')
  else
    WriteLn('You''ve entered an invalid value!');

  ReadLn;
end.
```

NOTE: Both expressions must be separated from the reserved word and by parentheses. This is necessary because the Boolean and operator has higher precedence than the relational operators. If you forget the parentheses, you will get an "Incompatible types" compiler error. Delphi generates this error because, without the parentheses, the compiler interprets the and operator as the bitwise and operator. Things go awry because the bitwise and operator returns an integer and the if-then statement expects a Boolean value.

The following table shows the results of the bitwise and operator.

Table 3-5: Bitwise and operator

Bit1	and Bit2	Result
0	0	0
0	1	0
1	0	0
1	1	1

The or Operator

The Boolean or operator is used to test whether at least one expression evaluates to True. The only time the or operator returns False is when both expressions evaluate to False. The following table shows the results of the or operator.

Table 3-6: Boolean or operator

Expression1	or Expression2	Result
True	True	True
False	True	True
True	False	True
False	False	False

Listing 3-8: Using the Boolean or operator

```
program Project1;

{$APPTYPE CONSOLE}

uses
  SysUtils;

var
  c: Char;

begin
  Write('Format C: (Yes/No): ');
  ReadLn(c);

  { See if the user selected yes }
  if (c = 'y') or (c = 'Y') then
    WriteLn('Formatting... ;)')
```

```
    else if (c = 'n') or (c = 'N') then
      WriteLn('Too bad...')
    else
      WriteLn('You have to type "y" for yes and "n" for no.');

    ReadLn;
end.
```

The following table shows the results of the bitwise or operator.

Table 3-7: Bitwise or operator

Bit1	or Bit2	Result
0	0	0
1	0	1
0	1	1
1	1	1

The xor Operator

The xor (exclusive or) operator is used to test whether only one expression evaluates to True. If both expressions evaluate to either True or False, the xor operator returns False. The Boolean xor operator isn't used often, but the bitwise xor operator is used by some programmers to optimize code. The following table shows the results of both Boolean and bitwise xor operators.

Table 3-8: Boolean and bitwise xor operators

Expression1 (Bit1)	xor Expression 2 (Bit2)	Result
True (1)	True (1)	False (0)
True (1)	False (0)	True (1)
False (0)	True (1)	True (1)
False (0)	False (0)	False (0)

The shr and shl Operators

The shr (shift right) and shl (shift left) operators shift bits in integer values. The shr and shl operators are often used as a substitute for division or multiplication by 2^n since both operations tend to execute slightly faster than ordinary multiplication and division.

To fully understand how the shl and shr operators function, we have to take a brief look at the binary representation of numbers. For example, let's multiply and divide the number 4 by 2. The binary representation of 4 is 0100. To multiply 4 by 2, we shift its bits one place to the left using the shl operator (4 shl 1). The result is 1000, or decimal 8. To divide 4 by 2, we shift its bits one place to the right using the shr operator (4 shr 1). The result is 0010, or decimal 2.

Listing 3-9: Using the shr and shl operators

```
program Project1;

{$APPTYPE CONSOLE}

uses
  SysUtils;

begin
  WriteLn('4 / 2 = ', 4 shr 1);
  WriteLn('4 * 2 = ', 4 shl 1);
  WriteLn('8 / 4 = ', 8 shr 2);
  WriteLn('8 * 8 = ', 8 shl 3);
  ReadLn;
end.
```

Boolean Evaluation

Delphi supports two modes of Boolean evaluation: complete and short-circuit. The default evaluation mode is the short-circuit mode since it results in faster code execution and smaller code size. The Boolean evaluation mode only alters the behavior of the Boolean or and Boolean and operators.

```
x := 8;
if (x > 10) and (x < 20) then
begin
end;
```

In this example, the if-then statement tests whether the number x is in the 11 to 19 range. If we use the short-circuit evaluation mode, only the x > 10 part of the statement is evaluated. Since x > 10 evaluates to False, there is no need to evaluate the statement any further.

In complete evaluation mode, the entire statement is evaluated, regardless of the fact that the result is known immediately after the first part of the statement is evaluated. In this case, complete evaluation is absolutely unnecessary, but there are situations where short-circuit evaluation can result in random and erroneous behavior. (You can read more about this in Chapter 5 in the "Creating Functions" section.)

You can change the Boolean evaluation mode for specific code sections by using the $B or $BOOLEVAL compiler directives. To switch to complete Boolean evaluation, use the $B+ or $BOOLEVAL ON directives. Use $B- or $BOOLEVAL OFF to switch to short-circuit evaluation.

You can also change the Boolean evaluation mode for the entire project in the Project Options dialog box.

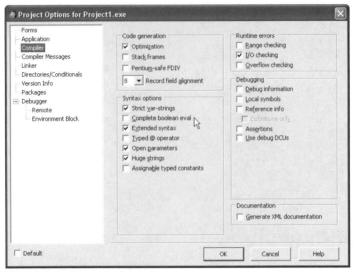

Figure 3-4: Boolean evaluation option

The case Statement

The case statement is a Delphi language construct that can be used to test
multiple conditions. In fact, the if-then statement is suitable only for a small
number of tests because it soon becomes hard to both read and write. This is
especially true for nested if-then statements or multiple if-then statements
that involve Boolean operators. The case statement is more structured and
more readable and tends to execute a bit faster than if-then statements.

Let's say that we have to make an application that outputs the name of
the month depending on user input. Writing this test using the if-then statement is really time-consuming and long, as shown in Listing 3-10.

Listing 3-10: A long if-then statement

```
var
  monthNum: Integer;

begin
  Write('Enter a number from 1 to 12: ');
  ReadLn(monthNum);

  if monthNum = 1 then
    WriteLn('January')
  else if monthNum = 2 then
    WriteLn('February')
  else if monthNum = 3 then
    WriteLn('March')
  else if monthNum = 4 then
    WriteLn('April')
  else if monthNum = 5 then
    WriteLn('May')
```

```
  else if monthNum = 6 then
    WriteLn('June')
  else if monthNum = 7 then
    WriteLn('July')
  else if monthNum = 8 then
    WriteLn('August')
  else if monthNum = 9 then
    WriteLn('September')
  else if monthNum = 10 then
    WriteLn('October')
  else if monthNum = 11 then
    WriteLn('November')
  else if monthNum = 12 then
    WriteLn('December');

  ReadLn;
end.
```

Simple case Statements

The syntax of the case statement is:

```
case expression of
  case_1: statement_1;
  case_2: statement_2;
  case_n: statement_n;
end;
```

If you want to execute more statements in response to a condition, you have to write them inside a block. The syntax of the case statement that can execute more than one statement in response to a certain condition is:

```
case expression of
  case_1: begin
    statement_1;
    statement_2;
    statement_n;
  end;
  case_2: begin
    statement_1;
    statement_n;
  end;
  case_n: begin
    statement_1;
    statement_n;
  end;
end;
```

The application in Listing 3-10 that displays the names of the months is noticeably smaller and more readable when written using the case statement.

Listing 3-11: A simple case statement

```
var
  monthNum: Integer;

begin
```

```
Write('Enter a number from 1 to 12: ');
ReadLn(monthNum);

case monthNum of
  1: WriteLn('January');
  2: WriteLn('February');
  3: WriteLn('March');
  4: WriteLn('April');
  5: WriteLn('May');
  6: WriteLn('June');
  7: WriteLn('July');
  8: WriteLn('August');
  9: WriteLn('September');
  10: WriteLn('October');
  11: WriteLn('November');
  12: WriteLn('December');
end;

ReadLn;
end.
```

Value Ranges

The case statement can also be used to test a range of values. The syntax for testing a range of values is:

```
case expression of
  x_low..x_high: statement;
  y_low..y_high: statement;
end;
```

Listing 3-12: Testing a range of values

```
var
  x: Integer;

begin
  Write('Enter a number from 0 to 200: ');
  ReadLn(x);

  case x of
    0..99: WriteLn('Less than 100.');
    100: WriteLn('100');
    101..200: WriteLn('More than 100.');
  end;

  ReadLn;
end.
```

Value Lists

You can use the case statement to test a list of values. The syntax for testing a list of values is:

```
case expression
  value_1, value_2, value_n: statement;
  value_3, value_4, value_n: statement;
```

```
end;
```

Listing 3-13: Testing a list of values

```
var
  x: Integer;

begin
  Write('Enter a number from 1 to 10: ');
  ReadLn(x);

  case x of
    1, 3, 5, 7, 9: WriteLn('Number ', x, ' is odd.');
    2, 4, 6, 8, 10: WriteLn('Number ', x, ' is even.');
  end;

  ReadLn;
end.
```

Case Statement Comparison

There are two major differences between the Delphi case statement and case statements in other popular programming languages, such as C++ and Visual Basic. The difference between Delphi and C++ is that the C++ switch statement enables the application to fall through conditions (for more details on fall-through, see "The switch Statement" section at the end of this chapter).

The difference between the Delphi case statement and the Visual Basic/VB.NET select statement is that the Delphi case statement uses only ordinal types, whereas the Visual Basic select statement can also use string values. Since Delphi uses only ordinal values, the execution of the Delphi case statement is much faster than that of the Visual Basic select statement. To see how you can use string values in the Delphi case statement, see Chapter 6.

The case-else Statement

Just like the if-then statement, the case statement can have the else section to cover any condition not tested before. The syntax of the case-else statement is:

```
case expression of
  case_1: statement_1;
  case_n: statement_n;
  else
    else_statement;
end;
```

The else section can also have its own block:

```
case expression of
  case_1: statement_1;
  case_n: statement_n;
  else begin
    else_statement;
  end;
end;
```

The syntax requirements of the else keyword are different in the if-then-else and case-else statements. In the if-then-else statement, the semicolon is not allowed before the else keyword, while in the case-else statement it is.

Listing 3-14: The case-else statement

```
var
  x: Integer;

begin
  ReadLn(x);

  case x of
    1: WriteLn('Gold');
    2: WriteLn('Silver');
    3: WriteLn('Bronze');
    else
      WriteLn('No medal for you.');
  end;

  ReadLn;
end.
```

You can also nest case statements and, if you do so carefully, you can increase the speed of your application even further. We can modify the application that displays the names of the months by using two case statements. The outer case statement checks if the number is in the 1 to 12 range, and the inner case statement displays month names. This solution is displayed in Listing 3-15.

Listing 3-15: Nested case statements

```
program Project1;

{$APPTYPE CONSOLE}

uses
  SysUtils;

var
  monthNum: Integer;

begin
  Write('Enter a number from 1 to 12: ');
  ReadLn(monthNum);

  case monthNum of
    1..12: begin
      case monthNum of
        1: WriteLn('January');
        2: WriteLn('February');
        3: WriteLn('March');
        4: WriteLn('April');
        5: WriteLn('May');
        6: WriteLn('June');
        7: WriteLn('July');
```

```
   8: WriteLn('August');
   9: WriteLn('September');
  10: WriteLn('October');
  11: WriteLn('November');
  12: WriteLn('December');
  end;  // inner case
 end;   // 1..12
 else
    WriteLn(monthNum, ' is not a valid number.');
 end;       // outer case

 ReadLn;
end.
```

C++ Conditions

Like Delphi, C++ has two statements for testing conditions: the if statement for testing a small number of conditions and the switch statement for testing a larger number of conditions. Unlike Delphi, the C++ language has a special operator, the conditional (or ternary) operator, which can also be used to test for a condition.

The if Statement

To write an if statement in C++, or in any language for that matter, you need to know which relational operators exist and how they are written. The following table lists all C++ relational operators. Note that the first two operators are also known as equality operators since they are used to test for equality or inequality.

Table 3-9: Relational operators

Relational Operator	Meaning
==	Equality
!=	Inequality
<	Less than
>	Greater than
<=	Less than or equal to
>=	Greater than or equal to

Remember that the equality operator in C++ is written with _two_ adjacent equal signs (==), not one. If you use Delphi's equality operator (=) in a C++ expression, you'll be able to compile the application, but you'll also have a bug in your code.

The syntax of the if statement in C++ differs from that in Delphi. The differences are that the condition must always be enclosed in parentheses and that there is no then reserved word that follows the expression:

```
if (expression)
   one_statement;
```

If you want to execute more statements in case the expression evaluates to True, place them inside a block:

```
if (expression)
{
    statement_1;
    statement_2;
    statement_n;
}
```

The following listing shows a simple example that tests whether the user entered the number 1.

Listing 3-16: A simple if statement

```
#include <iostream.h>
#include <conio.h>
#pragma hdrstop

#pragma argsused
int main(int argc, char* argv[])
{
    int i;

    cout << "Please enter 1: ";
    cin >> i;

    if (i == 1)
        cout << "Thank you." << endl;

    cout << "Press any key to continue...";
    getch();
    return 0;
}
```

The if-else Statement

The if-else statement in C++ is different from the Delphi if-then-statement in that it allows the statement before the reserved word else to end with a semicolon. Here's the syntax of the if-else statement:

```
if (expression)
    one_statement_if_true;
else
    one_statement_if_false;

if (expression)
{
    statement_1;
    statement_n;
}
else
{
    statement_1;
    statement_n;
}
```

The following listing shows the updated version of the previous example. The updated version uses the if-else statement to output a sad smiley if the user fails to enter the correct value.

Listing 3-17: A simple if-else statement

```
#include <iostream.h>
#include <conio.h>
#pragma hdrstop

#pragma argsused
int main(int argc, char* argv[])
{
   int i;

   cout << "Please enter a number larger than 0: ";
   cin >> i;

   if (i > 0)
      cout << "Thank you." << endl; // note the semicolon
   else
      cout << ":(" << endl;

   cout << "Press any key to continue...";
   getch();
   return 0;
}
```

Nested and Multiple if Statements

Multiple if statements in C++ are written exactly as in Delphi, by appending additional if statements after the else statement:

```
if (expression_1)
   statement;
else if (expression_2)
   statement;
else if (expression_3)
   statement;
else
   statement_if_nothing_above_is_true;
```

The following listing contains a simple example that illustrates nested and multiple if statements in C++.

Listing 3-18: Nested and multiple if statements in C++

```
#include <iostream.h>
#include <conio.h>
#pragma hdrstop

#pragma argsused
int main(int argc, char* argv[])
{
   int i;

   cout << "Please enter a number from 1 to 5: ";
```

```
cin >> i;

if (i >= 1) {
    if (i <= 5) {
        if (i == 1)
            cout << "One." << endl;
        else if (i == 2)
            cout << "Two." << endl;
        else if (i == 3)
            cout << "Three." << endl;
        else if (i == 4)
            cout << "Four." << endl;
        else if (i == 5)
            cout << "Five." << endl;
    } else
        // this is called when i > 5
        cout << "You entered an invalid value." << endl;
} else {
    // this is called when i < 1
    cout << "You entered an invalid value." << endl;
}

cout << "Press any key to continue...";
getch();
return 0;
}
```

The Conditional (Ternary) Operator

The conditional operator (?:) allows us to perform an if-else test without writing either the `if` or the `else` reserved words. Here's the syntax of the conditional operator:

```
condition ? expression_if_true : expression_if_false;
```

The conditional operator works by testing the condition and executing the expression_if_true part if the condition evaluates to True. If the condition evaluates to False, only the expression_if_false expression is executed.

The following example shows how to use the conditional operator to find the larger of two numbers.

Listing 3-19: The conditional operator

```
#include <iostream.h>
#include <conio.h>
#pragma hdrstop

#pragma argsused
int main(int argc, char* argv[])
{
    int i, j;
    cout << "Enter the first number: ";
    cin >> i;
    cout << "Enter the second number: ";
    cin >> j;
```

```
//              true : false
int max = i > j ?   i  :  j;
cout << "The larger number is " << max << "." << endl;

getch();
return 0;
}
```

The conditional operator in the above example replaces the following if-else statement:

```
int max;
if (i > j)
   max = i;
else
   max = j;
```

Logical (Boolean) and Bitwise Operators

In Delphi, bitwise and Boolean operators are written the same, and the compiler determines which ones we want to use from context. In C++, however, logical and bitwise operators are written differently. The following two tables list the logical and bitwise operators in the C++ language, respectively.

Table 3-10: Logical operators

Syntax	Operator
!	not
&&	and
||	or

Table 3-11: Bitwise operators

Syntax	Operator
&	Bitwise and
|	Bitwise or
^	Bitwise exclusive or
~	Complement (bitwise not)
>>	Shift right
<<	Shift left

When you use the logical operators to construct more complex if statements, don't forget the main pair of parentheses:

```
int x = 5;

if ((x >= 1) && (x <= 10))
{
   // x is in the 1..10 range
   cout << "OK" << endl;
}
```

If you need to perform a shift left or a shift right operation in the assignment to the cout object, enclose the operation in parentheses. If you don't enclose the shift left operation ($<<$) in parentheses, the compiler will treat it as the insertion operator ($<<$) and you'll get an incorrect result:

```
int x = 2;
cout << x << " shl 3 = " << x << 3 << endl; // wrong (23)
cout << x << " shl 3 = " << (x << 3) << endl; // OK (16)
```

The switch Statement

The switch statement is the C++ version of Delphi's case statement and enables you to test multiple conditions. Here's the syntax of the switch statement:

```
switch (expression)
{
  case constant_1: statements;
  case constant_2: statements;
  default: default_statements;
}
```

The default case serves the same purpose as the else reserved word does in Delphi's case statement: It allows us to execute statements when none of the specific conditions evaluate to True. Like the else part of the case statement in Delphi, the default statement is optional.

In addition to syntax differences, the behavior of the C++ switch statement differs from that in other popular programming languages (except C, of course). The difference lies in the fact that, by default, the C++ switch statement allows execution to fall through all subsequent cases after one of the cases evaluates to True.

To see what fall-through is, take a look at the following example. If it were written in Delphi, it would only display the string "One". In C++, however, the following code displays all three strings because the first case statement evaluates to True, and the execution then falls through all other case statements.

Listing 3-20: Fall-through

```
#include <iostream.h>
#include <conio.h>
#pragma hdrstop

#pragma argsused
int main(int argc, char* argv[])
{
   int x = 1;

   switch(x) {
      case 1: cout << "One" << endl;
      case 2: cout << "Two" << endl;
      case 3: cout << "Three" << endl;
   }
```

```
    getch();
    return 0;
}
```

To disable fall-through, which is rarely useful and rarely used, end each case statement with the reserved word break, which exits the entire switch statement, and thus effectively skips other case statements:

```
#include <iostream.h>
#include <conio.h>
#pragma hdrstop

#pragma argsused
int main(int argc, char* argv[])
{
    int x = 1;

    switch(x) {
        case 1: cout << "One" << endl;
            break;
        case 2: cout << "Two" << endl;
            break;
        case 3: cout << "Three" << endl;
            break;
    }

    getch();
    return 0;
}
```

Chapter 4

Iterations

This chapter describes three Delphi statements that enable you to repeatedly execute one or more statements. Delphi loops are the for loop, the repeat loop, and the while loop.

The chapter ends with a description of loops in C++.

The for Loop

The for loop is probably the most used of all loop constructs. Unlike other loop constructs, the for loop is used when you already know how many times you have to repeat a statement.

The syntax of the for loop is:

```
for counter := startValue to endValue do
  statement;
```

The counter is an ordinal (usually integer) value used by the loop to keep track of the number of iterations. startValue and endValue define the total number of iterations. Listing 4-1 shows a basic for loop that displays the user's name several times. You can see the result of the for loop in Figure 4-1.

Listing 4-1: A simple for loop

```
program Project1;

{$APPTYPE CONSOLE}

uses
  SysUtils;

var
  userName: string;
  displayCnt: Integer;
  i: Integer;

begin
  Write('User name: ');
  ReadLn(userName);
  Write('How many iterations: ');
  ReadLn(displayCnt);
```

```
WriteLn('--------------------');

for i := 1 to displayCnt do
  WriteLn(i, ') ', userName);

ReadLn;
end.
```

Figure 4-1: Result of the for loop

Although it's pretty easy to write the for loop, the loop itself is pretty complex and a lot of things happen behind the scenes. First, the for loop tries to execute endValue – startValue + 1 iterations. If endValue is less than startValue, the for loop executes nothing. If startValue and endValue are the same, the for loop executes only once. For instance, the following for loop displays the message "Hello":

```
var
  i: Integer;

begin
  for i := 0 to 0 do
    WriteLn('Hello');
end.
```

If startValue is less than endValue, the loop first executes the statement(s) and then increments the counter variable. When the counter variable reaches the endValue limit, the for loop executes the statement(s) once more and then finishes.

Since the for loop can utilize any ordinal variable as the counter, you can, for instance, use a Char variable to loop through all lowercase letters of the alphabet. You can see the result of this for loop in Figure 4-2.

Listing 4-2: Char counter

```
program Project1;

{$APPTYPE CONSOLE}

uses
  SysUtils;

var
  ch: Char;
```

```
begin
  for ch := 'a' to 'z' do
  begin
    case ch of
      'b': WriteLn('borland');
      'd': WriteLn('delphi');
      else
        WriteLn(ch);
    end;    // case
  end;    // for

  ReadLn;
end.
```

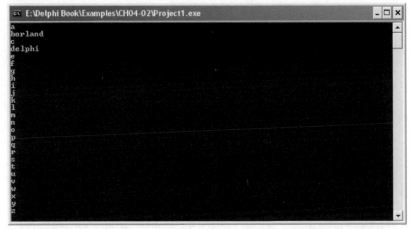

Figure 4-2: Char counter output

With a little more code, you can even display the entire ASCII character table using only one for loop. The ASCII (American Standard Code for Information Interchange) table contains numerical values of characters. It defines 256 characters (including letters, punctuation, numbers, and other characters).

Listing 4-3: Displaying the ASCII character table

```
program Project1;

{$APPTYPE CONSOLE}

uses
  SysUtils;

var
  ch: Char;
  newLine: Integer = 1;

begin
  { Display the entire ASCII table }
  for ch := #0 to #255 do
  begin
    { Skip CR and LF characters }
```

```
    if (ch <> #10) and (ch <> #13) then
      Write(ch:2);

    newLine := newLine + 1;
    { Limit to 16 characters per row }
    if newLine = 16 then
    begin
      newLine := 1;
      WriteLn;
    end;    // if newLine
  end;      // for ch

  ReadLn;
end.
```

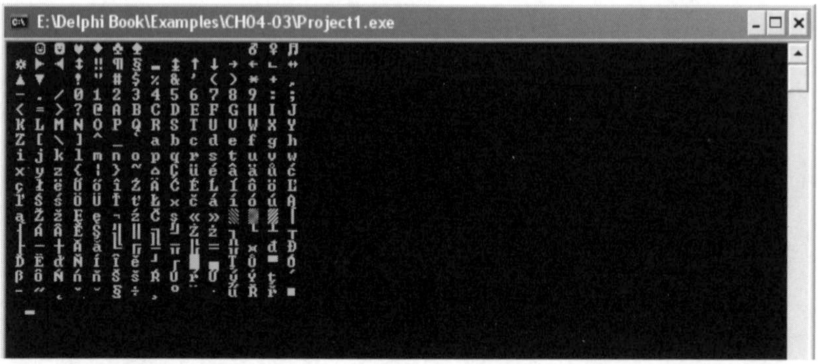

Figure 4-3: The ASCII table

The newLine variable is used to limit the number of characters per row to 16. Limiting the number of characters per row without using the newLine variable can be accomplished by typecasting (converting a variable to another data type) the ch variable to an integer. The code that converts a Char variable to an integer variable is listed here, but implicit and explicit typecasting is explained in more detail in Chapter 5.

Listing 4-4: For loop with typecasting

```
program Project1;

{$APPTYPE CONSOLE}

uses
  SysUtils;

var
  ch: Char;

begin
  { Display the entire ASCII table }
  for ch := #0 to #255 do
  begin
    case ch of
      #10, #13:
```

```
      else begin
        if (ch <> #0) and (Integer(ch) mod 16 = 0) then WriteLn;
        Write(ch:2);
      end;  // else
    end;    // case
  end;      // for

  ReadLn;
end.
```

In this example, the if-then test for the CR and LF characters has been replaced with the case statement to illustrate another possible use of the case statement. Since there is no code after the colon where we check for characters #10 and #13, iterations 10 and 13 are skipped. The result of this code is the same as the code in Listing 4-3.

Like the if-then and case statements, the for loop can also be nested. Nested for loops can be very helpful in a number of situations. For instance, you can use a nested for loop to easily display the multiplication table, as shown in Listing 4-5 and Figure 4-4.

Listing 4-5: Displaying the multiplication table

```
program Project1;

{$APPTYPE CONSOLE}

uses
  SysUtils;

var
  i, j: Integer;

begin
  WriteLn('Multiplication Table:');
  WriteLn;

  for i := 1 to 10 do
  begin
    for j := 1 to 10 do
    begin
      Write((i * j):4);
    end;   // for j
    WriteLn;
  end;     // for i
  ReadLn;
end.
```

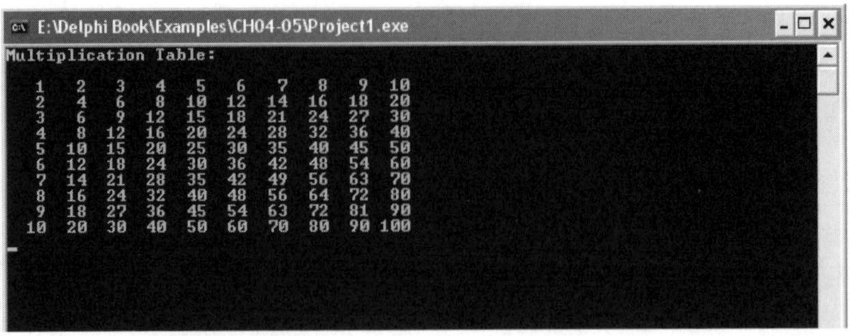

Figure 4-4: The multiplication table

The for-downto Loop

Another flavor of the for loop is the for-downto loop, where the counter variable is decremented rather than incremented. The syntax of the for-downto loop is:

```
for counter := startValue downto endValue do
  statement;
```

The for-downto loop fails to execute if endValue is greater than startValue. If both values are the same, the loop executes only once. The for-downto loop can, for instance, be used to implement a countdown.

Listing 4-6: The for-downto loop

```
program Project1;

{$APPTYPE CONSOLE}

uses
  SysUtils;

var
  i: Integer;

begin
  for i := 10 downto 1 do
  begin
    if i > 1 then
      WriteLn(i, ' seconds')
    else
      WriteLn(i, ' second');
  end;

  WriteLn;
  WriteLn('Lift-off');
  ReadLn;
end.
```

The for-in Loop

The for-in loop is the youngest flavor of the for loop; it was added to the Delphi language in version 2005. The for-in loop is used to iterate through elements in a collection. Its syntax is:

```
for element in collection do
   statement;
```

The simplest collection supported by the for-in loop is the string type (a collection of characters). The iteration variable (element) used in the for-in loop has to be of the same type as the elements in the collection. Since a string is a collection of Char values, you have to use a Char variable to iterate through a string with the for-in loop. The following example uses the for-in loop to display each character in a string on a separate line.

Listing 4-7: The for-in loop

```
program Project1;

{$APPTYPE CONSOLE}

uses
  SysUtils;

var
  UserName: string;
  c: Char;

begin
  Write('Username: ');
  ReadLn(UserName);

  for c in UserName do
    WriteLn(c);

  ReadLn;
end.
```

The for loop (any flavor) is usually the fastest and most straightforward way of iterating through a number of items. But, in certain circumstances, the for loop may not be the best solution because of two basic characteristics: The value of the iteration variable cannot be changed in the loop, and the iteration variable is always incremented or decremented by one.

If you need to change the iteration variable in the loop or change the value of the iteration variable by more than one, you have to use the repeat-until or the while loop.

The while Loop

The while and repeat-until loops are different from the for loop because they don't use an iteration variable to perform the iteration. Unlike the for loop, which iterates a specific number of times, the while and repeat-until loops are used when we don't know how many times to perform the iteration.

Both while and repeat-until loops use a condition to determine how many times to perform the iteration. In essence, the while loop continues to execute statements while the condition is True. The syntax of the while loop is:

```
while condition do
  statement;
```

When working with the while loop, you have to remember to modify the condition inside the loop or else the loop will continue executing forever and the application will become unresponsive. When this happens, the user will probably have to terminate the task (on an NT/2000/XP-based computer) or restart the computer (Windows 95/98/ME).

Let's start with an example that simply displays a couple of numbers and doesn't hang the computer.

Listing 4-8: A simple while loop

```
program Project1;

{$APPTYPE CONSOLE}

uses
  SysUtils;

var
  i: Integer;

begin
  i := 1;

  { Display numbers 1 to 10. }
  while i <= 10 do
  begin
    WriteLn(i);
    i := i + 1;
  end;

  ReadLn;
end.
```

The while loop tests the condition before it starts executing statements in the loop block. If the condition evaluates to False at the beginning, the while loop will not execute at all. You can test this by simply setting the i variable to 11 or any other value larger than 10.

If the condition evaluates to True, the while loop executes all statements in the block. Once it has finished executing the statements in the block, the loop reevaluates the condition to see if it should iterate again. If the condition evaluates to True, the loop is continued until it finally evaluates to False. If the condition evaluates to False, the loop terminates.

The repeat-until Loop

The repeat-until loop, like the while loop, uses a condition to determine the number of times it needs to execute a group of statements. One difference between the while and repeat-until loops is that the while loop executes statements while the condition is True, and the repeat-until loop executes statements while the condition is False (until the condition is met).

The syntax of the repeat-until loop is:

```
repeat
  statement_1;
  statement_n;
until condition;
```

Let's see how to display the numbers 1 to 10 using the repeat-until loop.

Listing 4-9: A simple repeat-until loop

```
program Project1;

{$APPTYPE CONSOLE}

uses
  SysUtils;

var
  i: Integer;

begin
  i := 1;
  { Display numbers 1 to 10. }
  repeat
    WriteLn(i);
    i := i + 1;
  until i > 10;

  ReadLn;
end.
```

Another major difference between the while and repeat-until loops is that the repeat-until loop tests the condition after it executes the statements in the block. This means that the repeat-until loop executes the statements at least once, regardless of the condition. This can lead to subtle errors in your applications (see Listing 4-10 and Figure 4-5).

Listing 4-10: An erroneous repeat-until loop

```
program Project1;

{$APPTYPE CONSOLE}

uses
```

```
SysUtils;

var
  i: Integer;

begin
  i := 25;
  repeat
    WriteLn('Number ', i, ' is smaller than number 10.');
    i := i + 1;
  until i >= 10;

  ReadLn;
end.
```

Figure 4-5: An erroneous repeat-until loop

Unlike other loop constructs, the repeat-until loop acts as a block, so you can automatically write a larger number of statements inside the repeat-until loop without having to define a block.

Controlling Loop Execution

Loop execution is normally governed by the condition of the while and repeat-until loops or the start and end values of the for loop. In case we have to exit from the loop earlier, we can use the Break procedure (you can read more about procedures in Chapter 5). The following example shows how to exit from a loop after it executes five times.

Listing 4-11: Breaking out of a loop

```
program Project1;

{$APPTYPE CONSOLE}

uses
  SysUtils;

var
  i: Integer;

begin
  for i := 1 to 1000 do
  begin
    WriteLn(i);
    if i = 5 then Break;
  end;   // for i
```

```
  ReadLn;
end.
```

Infinite Loops

As the title suggests, you can write loops that continue to execute forever. In Delphi, only the while and repeat-until loops can be infinite, but in C++ and C# the for loop can also be infinite.

Infinite loops are really easy to write. Since a while loop continues to execute as long as the condition evaluates to True, a simple infinite while loop looks like this:

```
while True do
  WriteLn('This is an infinite while loop.');
```

An infinite repeat-until loop is equally easy to write since it continues to execute as long as the condition evaluates to False:

```
repeat
  WriteLn('This is an infinite repeat-until loop.');
until False;
```

NOTE: Actually, as you will see in Chapter 23, all Windows applications are based on infinite while loops that are terminated with the Break procedure or other similar procedures.

The following example utilizes an infinite while loop to read user names. To exit from the loop, the user has to enter the word "end."

Listing 4-12: An infinite while loop

```
program Project1;

{$APPTYPE CONSOLE}

uses
  SysUtils;

var
  UserName: string;
  UsrCount: Integer;

begin
  UsrCount := 0;

  while True do
  begin
    Write('Username: ');
    ReadLn(UserName);

    if UserName = 'end' then
    begin
      WriteLn('Thank you.');
      ReadLn;
      Break;
```

```
      end else
      begin
        UsrCount := UsrCount + 1;
        WriteLn(UsrCount, '. ', UserName);
      end;    // if
    end;      // while
end.
```

Another way of controlling loop execution is by skipping certain iterations. To skip an iteration, you can use the Continue procedure. The Continue procedure causes the loop to skip to the next iteration without executing the statements that follow it in the block. The following example displays only odd numbers by skipping even iterations.

Listing 4-13: The Continue procedure

```
program Project1;

{$APPTYPE CONSOLE}

uses
  SysUtils;

var
  i: Integer;

begin
  i := 0;
  while i < 20 do
  begin
    i := i + 1;
    { Skip even numbers. }
    if i mod 2 = 0 then Continue;
    WriteLn('Number ', i, ' is odd.');
  end;

  ReadLn;
end.
```

The WriteLn statement is only called when the variable i contains an odd number. If the variable i contains an even number, the Continue procedure executes and returns to the first line of the while loop that increments the i variable, thus skipping an iteration.

C++ Loops

The following table lists C++ loops and shows how they relate to Delphi loops. Notice the C++ for loop.

Table 4-1: C++ and Delphi loops

C++ Loop	Works Like Delphi Loop
while	while
do-while	repeat-until
for	for, while

The while Loop

The while loop in C++ works exactly as it does in Delphi: It executes a statement or a block of statements as long as the condition is True. The while loop tests the condition before executing its statements, and if the condition evaluates to False at the beginning, the statements never get executed.

The only notable difference between the two languages lies in syntax. Here's the syntax of the C++ while loop:

```
while (condition) statement;
while (condition) {
    statements;
}
```

The following example shows how to display the first 20 numbers with the while loop.

Listing 4-14: The while loop

```
#include <iostream.h>
#include <conio.h>
#pragma hdrstop

#pragma argsused
int main(int argc, char* argv[])
{
    int x=0;
    while(++x <= 20)
        cout << x << endl;

    getch();
    return 0;
}
```

The do-while Loop

The do-while loop in C++ is the equivalent of the repeat-until loop in Delphi, which means that it executes its statements at least once and continues to do so until the condition is met. The syntax of the do-while loop is:

```
do
    statement
```

```
while (condition);

do {
   statements;
} while (condition);
```

The following example uses the do-while loop to display the first 20 numbers.

Listing 4-15: The do-while loop

```
#include <iostream.h>
#include <conio.h>
#pragma hdrstop

#pragma argsused
int main(int argc, char* argv[])
{
   int x = 0;

   do
      cout << ++x << endl;
   while (x < 20);

   getch();
   return 0;
}
```

The for Loop

Depending on how it is written, the for loop in C++ can work like a for or a while loop in Delphi. The syntax of the for loop is:

```
for (initialization; condition; condition_update)
   statement;
```

The initialization part is used to initialize the loop's counter. The condition is an expression that gets evaluated before the statements are executed, which means that the statements of the for loop are not executed if the condition evaluates to False at the beginning. The condition_update part is an expression called after each iteration to update the loop's counter.

For instance, the for loop in Listing 4-16 displays all lowercase letters of the alphabet. The loop works by setting the letter 'a' (characters in C++ are written inside single quote marks, as they are in Delphi) as the beginning letter in the initialization section and by setting the char <= 'z' condition in the condition part to make the for loop iterate as long as the Char variable contains any of the lowercase letters of the alphabet. The condition_update part updates the condition by incrementing the Char variable by one at each iteration.

Listing 4-16: A simple for loop

```
#include <iostream.h>
#include <conio.h>
#pragma hdrstop

#pragma argsused
```

```
int main(int argc, char* argv[])
{
    char ch;
    for(ch = 'a'; ch <= 'z'; ch++)
        cout << ch;

    getch();
    return 0;
}
```

Unlike the Delphi for loop, which allows you to increase or decrease the value of the counter variable by 1, the for loop in C++ allows you to increase or decrease the counter variable by whatever you like. For instance, the for loop in Listing 4-17 outputs only odd numbers to the console by setting the counter to 1 in the initialization part and then incrementing the counter variable by 2.

Listing 4-17: Using compound operators in the for loop

```
#include <iostream.h>
#include <conio.h>
#pragma hdrstop

#pragma argsused
int main(int argc, char* argv[])
{
    int i;
    for(i=1; i<20; i+=2)
        cout << i << endl;

    getch();
    return 0;
}
```

The for-downto Loop

To create a for-downto loop in C++, you only have to rewrite the condition_update part of the loop to decrement the counter variable. Listing 4-18 shows how to write a for-downto loop in C++.

Listing 4-18: A C++ for-downto loop

```
#include <iostream.h>
#include <conio.h>
#pragma hdrstop

#pragma argsused
int main(int argc, char* argv[])
{
    int i;
    for(i=20; i>0; i--)
        cout << i << endl;

    getch();
    return 0;
}
```

The while-like for Loop

The for loop in C++ can very easily be written to act just like the while loop — to repeat statements as long as a condition is True. For instance, the following for loop enables the user to enter an integer value and calculates the square of the entered number. The loop repeats this action until the user enters 0.

This for loop has only the condition part. Both the intialization and condition_update parts are empty. The initialization part is empty because the counter variable is initialized in the declaration, and the condition_update part is empty because the counter variable (the condition) is updated in the loop's block.

Listing 4-19: A weird-looking for loop

```
#include <iostream.h>
#include <conio.h>
#pragma hdrstop

#pragma argsused
int main(int argc, char* argv[])
{
   int i=1;
   for(; i!=0; )
   {
      cout << "Enter a number (or 0 to exit): ";
      cin >> i; // this reads the user input and updates the condition
      if(i != 0)
         cout << "The square of your number is " << i*i << endl << endl;
   }

   cout << "Thank you. Press any key to continue..." << endl;
   getch();
   return 0;
}
```

The Infinite for Loop

To write an infinite for loop in C++, simply omit all three parts of the for statement. To terminate the loop, use the reserved word break. The following example shows how to display numbers from 1 to 10 with an infinite loop.

Listing 4-20: An infinite for loop

```
#include <iostream.h>
#include <conio.h>
#pragma hdrstop

#pragma argsused
int main(int argc, char* argv[])
{
   int i = 1;
```

```
for( ; ; ) {
   cout << i << endl;
   if (i++ == 10) break;
}

getch();
return 0;
}
```

The Strange for Loop

The for loop in the C++ language has two more characteristics:

- It supports multiple expressions in the initialization, condition, and condition_update parts (the expressions must be comma delimited).

- Because of the aforementioned characteristic, it can perform useful tasks without having to execute additional statements in its block.

The example that follows is an updated version of the example in Listing 4-19, which allows the user to enter integer values and displays these values squared until the user enters 0. The initialization part of the for loop is empty, the condition part keeps the loop working as long as i != 0, and everything else (input and output of values) is done in the final section of the loop.

Note the semicolon with which the for loop is ended. When a semicolon is placed immediately after the loop, without additional statements, it means that the loop should do nothing.

Listing 4-21: A pretty unusual for loop

```
#include <iostream.h>
#include <conio.h>
#pragma hdrstop

#pragma argsused
int main(int argc, char* argv[])
{
   int i=1;
   cout << "Enter 0 to exit..." << endl << endl;

   for( ; i != 0; cout << "Number: ",
    cin >> i, cout << "Squared = " << i*i << endl) ;

   cout << "Finished. Press any key to continue...";
   getch();
   return 0;
}
```

Figure 4-6: The result of the strange loop from Listing 4-21

Declaring a Dedicated Counter Variable

In Delphi you can only use a simple local variable as the counter variable in a for loop. In C++, you can use a local variable for the counter, as we've done, or you can declare the counter variable inside the for loop. Such a variable only exists as long as the for loop is executing and can only be used by the for loop and the statements in the for loop's block. The counter variable is declared in the initialization part of the for loop:

```
for(data_type var_name = init_value; condition; condition_update)
```

Listing 4-22 shows how to declare a counter variable in the for loop and shows where this variable can and cannot be used.

Listing 4-22: Declaring a counter variable in the for loop

```
#include <iostream.h>
#include <conio.h>
#pragma hdrstop

#pragma argsused
int main(int argc, char* argv[])
{
    /* i cannot be used before the loop */
    for(int i=0; i<20; i++)
    {
        cout << i+1 << endl;
    } // i is destroyed here

    /* i cannot be used after the loop */
    getch();
    return 0;
}
```

Chapter 5

Procedures and Functions

Procedures and functions represent the most important material that you have to master before you can call yourself a programmer. Object-oriented programming, and Delphi programming in general, relies heavily on procedures and functions.

We have already used procedures in previous chapters, two of them very frequently: ReadLn and WriteLn. Every procedure or function is essentially a group of statements that hide behind a common name. For instance, the ReadLn procedure is made up of a number of statements that ask the user to enter a value and then transfer that value to a variable.

Procedures and functions are extremely useful because they enable us to write a piece of code once and then reuse it as many times as we need to. For example, Borland developers created the WriteLn procedure for displaying text in the console window, so now we don't have to rewrite the code for displaying text, but simply call the WriteLn procedure.

This chapter shows how to use existing procedures and functions and how to create new ones. You'll also read about several advanced topics related to procedures and functions, such as overloading and inlining.

The chapter ends with a description of how to create procedures and functions using the C++ language.

Using Procedures

Using the Write and WriteLn procedures is really simple because they are built into the Delphi compiler. Only a small number of procedures are built into the compiler. The vast majority of procedures and functions can be found in separate source code files called units. All Delphi units have the extension .pas.

Before we can use a procedure in our application, we have to know three things about it: its name, the unit where the procedure is declared, and the parameters the procedure takes. The name of the procedure and the parameter list are parts of the procedure header. A simple procedure header looks like this:

```
procedure ProcedureName;
```

The reserved word `procedure` is always followed by a procedure name, which is any valid identifier. This procedure has no parameters. A procedure header with a parameter list looks like this:

```
procedure ProcedureName(ParameterList);
```

The parameter list is a mechanism for passing values to procedures (and functions). The parameter list can contain one or more parameters. If the parameter list contains more than one parameter, they are separated by semicolons. Here is the header of a procedure that accepts a single string value:

```
procedure DisplayString(s: string);
```

The procedure DisplayString has a single string parameter. As you can see, the parameters are declared almost exactly like variables. When we use procedures, the parameter name is not that important, but the parameter data type is. When we create procedures, parameters act like variables, so both the parameter name and data type are important.

Delphi has an enormous number of standard functions that you can use in your applications. Among these are two procedures that are really simple, extremely useful, and often used to optimize code: Inc and Dec. The Inc procedure can be used to increment any ordinal value by one or more, and the Dec procedure can be used to decrement any ordinal value by one or more. Their headers are:

```
procedure Inc(var X [ ; N: Longint ]);
procedure Dec(var X [ ; N: Longint ]);
```

Both procedure headers are a bit complicated to read at first, but the only thing that you have to know right now is that Delphi documentation uses brackets to show which parameters are optional. This means that both Inc and Dec can be called with one or two parameters.

Listing 5-1: Inc and Dec procedures

```
program Project1;

{$APPTYPE CONSOLE}

uses
  SysUtils;

var
  x: Integer;
  c: Char;
begin
  x := 10;
  Inc(x); { faster way of writing x := x + 1; }
  Dec(x); { faster way of writing x := x - 1; }
```

```
Inc(x, 5); { faster way of writing x := x + 5; }

Write(x);

c := 'a';
Inc(c);
Write(c); { c := 'b'; }
ReadLn;
end.
```

Not only is it faster to write Inc(x) than x := x + 1, the Inc procedure also executes faster. It is recommended that you use the Inc and Dec procedures whenever you can.

If you take a closer look at the code in Listing 5-1, you will notice that you can use the Inc procedure to increment a character value and that there is no comment that shows how to do this manually. If you wanted to increment a character value manually, you would have to write something like this:

```
var
  c: Char;

begin
  c := 'a';
  c := Chr(Integer(c) + 1);
end.
```

This code increments a character value by performing two separate typecasts, one explicit and one implicit. It first converts the character to an integer, increments it by one, and then converts it back to a character value. Note that this code shouldn't be used in an application since there are much better ways of working with characters. You can read more about this and typecasting later in this chapter.

Using Functions

The main difference between procedures and functions is that functions have a return value. When you call a procedure in an application, the procedure executes and that's about it. When you call a function, the function executes and returns a value to the caller application.

Here is a simple function header:

```
function SomeFunction(ParameterList): ReturnValue;
```

Functions are more versatile than procedures. While procedures can only be called as standalone statements, functions can be called as standalone statements and can also be used in expressions.

Let's take a look at the Chr function that we used earlier. The Chr function can be used to convert an integer value to an ASCII character. The header of the Chr function looks like this:

```
function Chr(X: Byte): Char;
```

The example in Listing 5-2 uses the Chr function to illustrate both function call methods.

Listing 5-2: Function calls

```
program Project1;

{$APPTYPE CONSOLE}

uses
  SysUtils;

var
  c: Char;

begin
  { standalone call }
  Chr(65);

  { function call in an expression }
  c := 'A';
  if c = Chr(65) then
    WriteLn('ASCII 65 = A');

  ReadLn;
end.
```

Note that calling functions as procedures (outside of an expression) defeats the very purpose of functions. When you call a function as you would a procedure, the return value of the function is discarded. The return value is usually the reason that you call a function in the first place, but there are situations in which you only need the function to execute without giving you a result. For instance, you can call a function that copies a file without needing to know how many bytes have actually been transferred.

There are three more standard functions that you can use in your application. All three functions are extremely fast and versatile. The first one is Ord, which can, for instance, be used to convert a character value to an integer.

The other two functions operate on all ordinal values and return the predecessor (the Pred function) or the successor (the Succ function) of a value. These functions are pretty special because Delphi doesn't even treat them as functions, instead computing their result at compile time. These functions can also be used in constant declarations.

```
const
  X = Succ(19);  { 20 }
  Y = Pred(101); { 100 }
  Z = Ord('A');  { 65 }
```

Typecasting in Delphi

Typecasting is the process of converting a value or a variable from one data type to another. There are two types of typecasting: implicit and explicit. Explicit typecasting is also called conversion.

The difference between implicit and explicit typecasting is that implicit typecasting is lossless, whereas explicit typecasting can result in data loss. Implicit typecasting is only possible with compatible data types, usually only ordinal types. For instance, implicit typecasting is automatically done by Delphi when you assign an integer value to a Double variable.

```
var
  i: Integer;
  d: Double;

begin
  i := 2005;
  d := i;
end.
```

An automatic typecast is possible because a Double variable can hold larger values than an integer value. When you assign an integer value to a Double variable (or any other variable that can hold an integer value), the integer value is expanded and assigned to the destination variable.

If you have to perform an implicit typecast manually, the syntax is:

```
DataType(Expression)
```

We have already performed implicit typecasts earlier in this chapter, usually to convert character values to integers:

```
var
  c: Char;
  i: Integer;

begin
  c := 'X';
  i := Integer(c);
end.
```

If you try to assign a large value to a variable that cannot hold it, the compiler will give you the "Constant expression violates subrange bounds" or "Incompatible types: 'Type' and 'Type'" error. If you get one of these errors, you'll have to perform either an implicit or an explicit typecast.

```
var
  b: Byte;

begin
  b := 255;         { OK }
  b := 1000;        { Error, subrange bounds violation }
  b := Byte(1000);  { OK }
end.
```

When you get a subrange bounds violation error, you should think about selecting another data type that supports larger values. What do you think the value of the variable will be after the implicit typecast to Byte(1000)? It can't be 1000 because the value 1000 occupies 2 bytes of memory, and a Byte variable occupies only 1 byte of memory. When we convert the number 1000 (hexadecimal 03E8) to a Byte value, the low-order byte (hexadecimal E8) is written to the Byte variable. The value of the Byte variable after the implicit typecast is 232.

Assigning a Double value to an integer variable also results in a compiler error because integer variables cannot hold real numbers. When you have to assign a real value to an integer, you always have to perform an explicit typecast. You can convert a real value to an integer using either the Round or the Trunc standard functions. The Trunc function strips the decimal part of the number, and the Round function takes the decimal part of the number into account; they usually give different results. Round and Trunc can also be used in constant declarations.

```
var
  i: Integer;
  d: Double;

begin
  d := 12.8;
  i := Round(d); { i = 13 }
  i := Trunc(d); { i = 12 }
end.
```

In Delphi, you can differentiate a constant value typecast and a variable typecast. A value typecast is actually the implicit typecast we've used so far. A value typecast can only be written on the right side of the assignment statement.

A variable typecast can be written on both sides of the assignment statement, as long as both types are compatible.

```
var
  b: Byte;
  c: Char;

begin
  b := Byte('a'); { value typecast }
  c := Char(b);   { variable typecast }
  Byte(c) := 65;  { temporary variable typecast }
end.
```

Typecasting in C++

To typecast a variable in C++, you can use the standard Delphi syntax for an implicit typecast or the C++ syntax. Here are both:

```
(new_data_type)expression;
```

or

```
new_data_type(expression);
```

Here's how to perform both explicit and implicit typecasts in C++:

```
#include <iostream.h>
#include <conio.h>
#pragma hdrstop

#pragma argsused
```

```
int main(int argc, char* argv[])
{
    /* note that the same syntax works for
    implicit and explicit typecasts */

    float f = 65.20;
    char c = (char)f;

    double d = 12.9;
    int x = int(d);

    cout << c << endl;  // writes "A"
    cout << x << endl;  // writes "12"

    getch();
    return 0;
}
```

Creating Procedures

If you want to be a productive programmer, you have to know how to create your own procedures. Procedures enable you to reuse your own code in one or more projects and to separate application logic into more manageable, smaller pieces of code. They also help minimize the number of errors in the application. If the procedure contains a bug, we only have to repair the bug once, inside the procedure, and the problem is solved in the entire application.

A really simple procedure looks like this:

```
procedure Hello;
begin
end;
```

As you can see, all you have to do to create a simple procedure is to define the name of the procedure in the procedure header and write the procedure block. The problem is where to write the procedure implementation. If you have any doubts as to where you have to write a piece of code, remember that in Delphi everything has to be declared before it can be used. So, since we're going to use this procedure in the main block of the application, it has to be written before the main application block. Actually, it has to be located between the uses list and the main application block, as shown in Listing 5-3.

Listing 5-3: Our first procedure

```
program Project1;

{$APPTYPE CONSOLE}

uses
  SysUtils;

procedure Hello;
begin
end;
```

```
begin
end.
```

To see how procedures actually work, we have to add some code to the Hello procedure:

```
program Project1;

{$APPTYPE CONSOLE}

uses
  SysUtils;

var
  i: Integer;

procedure Hello;
begin
  WriteLn('I ', #3, ' Delphi.');
end;

begin
end.
```

If you run this code, the message from the Hello procedure will not be displayed on screen because we didn't call the Hello procedure in the main block of the application. No matter how many procedures there are in the source code, the execution of the application always starts at the beginning of the main application block.

Listing 5-4: Calling the Hello procedure

```
program Project1;

{$APPTYPE CONSOLE}

uses
  SysUtils;

var
  i: Integer;

procedure Hello;
begin
  WriteLn('I ', #3, ' Delphi.');
end;

begin
  for i := 1 to 20 do
    Hello;

  ReadLn;
end.
```

Creating Functions

When you create a function, you have to define at least two things: the name of the function and the data type of the result. For instance, this is a function that returns a string value:

```
function ReturnString: string;
begin
end;
```

The function header tells Delphi that the function returns a string, but it actually returns nothing. To return a value from a function, we have to assign a value to a special variable called Result. The variable Result is a special variable that is created implicitly in every function. So, to return the string "Delphi" from the function, we have to write the following:

```
function ReturnString: string;
begin
  Result := 'Delphi';
end;
```

Since this function always returns the same value, it is also known as a constant function. Although constant functions might not seem very useful, they actually are, especially in larger projects.

A constant function can be used instead of a variable or a constant in an application to provide a consistent way of reading a value. As the complexity of the application grows, you may have to add more code to the function, perhaps to perform range checking or something similar. In this case, you'll only have to change the implementation of the function, and since you've been using the function from the start, everything works great. If you've used a variable or a constant, you'll waste time by finding and replacing the variable with the function call.

If you finish the project, and the constant function still returns only this constant value, you can replace the constant function with a constant value of the same name to optimize application performance. If you use Delphi 2005 or a newer Delphi version exclusively, a better solution would be to mark the constant function with the inline directive. This directive is described in more detail later in this chapter.

Short-circuit Evaluation

Short-circuit evaluation is the default Boolean evaluation mode that results in faster code execution than complete Boolean evaluation. In the vast majority of cases, short-circuit evaluation works perfectly, but you can get into trouble when you call functions inside the if-then statement that do more than just return a value. The following example has a subtle bug caused by short-circuit evaluation.

Listing 5-5: Short-circuit evaluation bug

```
program Project1;

{$APPTYPE CONSOLE}

uses
  SysUtils;

var
  x: Integer;
  FunctionCall: Boolean;

function MakeTrue: string;
begin
  FunctionCall := True;
  Result := 'Hello';
end;

begin
  FunctionCall := False;
  Write('Enter number 1: ');
  ReadLn(x);

  if (x = 1) and (MakeTrue = 'Hello') then
    WriteLn('Everything works fine.');

  if FunctionCall = False then
    WriteLn('If you can see this, something is wrong.');

  ReadLn;
end.
```

This example features a really simple function called MakeTrue. The purpose of the MakeTrue function is to return the string "Hello" and to change the value of the FunctionCall variable to True.

When the application starts, it initializes the FunctionCall variable to False. It then asks the user to enter the number 1 and writes the user-entered value into variable x. The problem lies in the if-then statement that tests the x variable. If the user entered 1, the first part of the if-then statement evaluates to True, and the function MakeTrue is called in the evaluation process of the second part of the if-then statement. The function changes the FunctionCall variable to True and the application works as planned. In this case, you never see the message "If you can see this, something is wrong."

If the user enters anything but 1, the first part of the if-then statement fails. When the first part of the if-then statement fails, the entire statement fails, and the MakeTrue function is never called because the second part of the if-then statement is never evaluated. The FunctionCall variable remains False, and the error message that should never be displayed is displayed as shown in Figure 5-1.

Figure 5-1: Short-circuit evaluation bug

If you only have one function call in the if-then statement, you can solve this problem by testing the function result first:

```
if (MakeTrue = 'Hello') and (x = 1) then
  WriteLn('Everything works fine.');
```

Another solution is to temporarily enable complete Boolean evaluation. You should do this if you have multiple function calls that affect the application globally:

```
{$B+}
if (x = 1) and (MakeTrue = 'Hello') then
  WriteLn('Everything works fine.');
{$B-}
```

Creating Units

Our practice so far has been to create functions and procedures in the main Delphi project file. Although this is allowed and is useful in really small projects, you should try to create functions and procedures in separate source code files (units). A unit is a plain text file that contains Delphi source code. Units allow you to reuse functions and procedures in multiple projects.

Delphi allows you to create a new unit even when there are no open projects, but it doesn't allow you to compile the unit. Delphi only compiles projects. So, before we can create a new unit, we have to create a new console application project and save it to disk.

To create a new unit, you can select File ➤ New ➤ Unit - Delphi for Win32, or you can double-click the Unit item in the Delphi Projects/Delphi Files category of the Tool Palette. Delphi automatically adds the new unit to the project (see Figure 5-2) and shows the unit source code in the Code Editor:

```
unit Unit1;

interface

implementation

end.
```

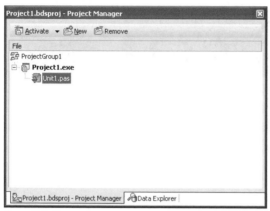

Figure 5-2: New unit

The first line is the unit heading that specifies the unit name. The unit name specified after the reserved word `unit` must match the file name. So, if the unit name is Unit1, the file name must be Unit1.pas.

Every unit is separated into two distinct sections: the interface and implementation sections. The interface section is the public part of the unit that contains declarations that can be used from other units and project files. It begins with the reserved word `interface` and ends with the reserved word `implementation`.

The implementation section of the unit is the private part of the unit that contains declarations and statements that can only be used by other statements in the same unit. This part of the unit starts with the reserved word `implementation` and usually ends at the end of the entire unit.

Using Units

When you add a new unit to the project, Delphi automatically adds the unit reference to the project uses list:

```
uses
  SysUtils,
  Unit1 in 'Unit1.pas';
```

Delphi uses the UnitName in FileName syntax in the uses list when it doesn't know the exact location of the unit or when the unit is not in the search path. The in syntax is also used to differentiate between units that belong to the project and those that don't. In this case, Delphi uses the in syntax because the file hasn't been saved to disk, and therefore it can't determine if the file is in the search path or not. If you save the unit outside of the search path or outside of the project directory, Delphi adds the absolute file path to the uses list:

```
uses
  SysUtils,
  Unit1 in 'C:\Unit1.pas';
```

If you save the unit to the project directory, Delphi only adds the unit file name, but still uses the UnitName in FileName syntax. In this case, the in syntax tells Delphi that the unit is local to the project. The in syntax only changes Delphi IDE functionality. For instance, if the unit is referenced with the in syntax, you can double-click the unit in the Project Manager window and Delphi will open it. If you remove the in syntax, Delphi will treat the unit as an outside unit and you will lose a few IDE options.

If you create units that contain utility functions and procedures that can successfully be reused in multiple projects, you should create a separate directory for all your units and add that directory to the search path.

You can modify the search path in the Project Options or the Default Project Options dialog box. If you're currently working on a project, you can only display the Project Options dialog box, which is accessed by selecting Project ➢ Options. If the IDE is empty, you can display the Default Project Options dialog box by selecting Project ➢ Default Options ➢ Delphi for Win32.

To see the current search path, select the Directories/Conditionals item on the left side of the dialog box (see Figure 5-3). When the search path is empty, you can only use standard Delphi units from the InstallDir\lib directory.

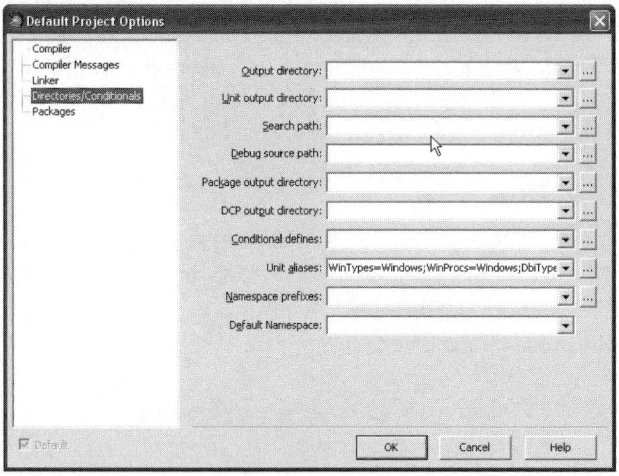

Figure 5-3: Default Project Options dialog box

To add your own units to the search path, click the (…) button to the right of the Search path text box. The Directories dialog box that appears helps you add directories to the search path.

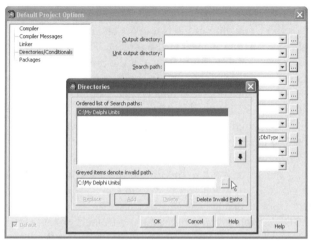

Figure 5-4: Directories dialog box

Once you've added all necessary directories to the search path, you may want to make these options the default for all new projects. If you are modifying options in the Default Project Options dialog box, these settings are already set as the default for new projects. If you are modifying options in the Project Options dialog box and want to set them as the default, you have to select the Default option in the lower-left corner of the dialog box.

Adding Code to the Unit

Units can contain code that is private to the unit or available for public use. If you define a constant or a variable in the interface section, the variable or constant is public and can be used outside of the unit.

Listing 5-6A: Public constants and variables in a unit

```
unit Unit1;

interface

const
  PUBLIC_CONST = 'Hello';

var
  PublicVar: string;

implementation

end.
```

Listing 5-6B: Using public constants and variables

```
program Project1;

{$APPTYPE CONSOLE}

uses
```

```
  SysUtils,
  Unit1 in 'Unit1.pas';

begin
  PublicVar := PUBLIC_CONST;
  WriteLn(PublicVar);
  ReadLn;
end.
```

Unlike constant and variable declarations, you cannot add a procedure to the interface part of the unit. Procedures and functions can only be written in the implementation section of the unit.

```
unit Unit1;

interface

const
  PUBLIC_CONST = 'Hello';

var
  PublicVar: string;

implementation

procedure About;
begin
  WriteLn(PUBLIC_CONST, ' from Unit1.');
end;

end.
```

The About procedure can currently be called only by other procedures in the same unit. If you want to use the About procedure in other units, you have to declare it in the interface section of the unit. To declare a function or a procedure, you only have to copy the procedure or function header to the interface section of the unit.

```
unit Unit1;

interface

const
  PUBLIC_CONST = 'Hello';

var
  PublicVar: string;

procedure About;

implementation

procedure About;
begin
  WriteLn(PUBLIC_CONST, ' from Unit1.');
```

```
end;

end.
```

Delphi units can have a third section, the initialization section. This section gives you the ability to execute procedures or statements at application startup. If a unit has an initialization section, the implementation section ends at the beginning of the initialization section. The initialization section can only be defined after the implementation section.

Listing 5-7: Unit initialization

```
unit Unit1;

interface

procedure About;

implementation

procedure About;
begin
  WriteLn('Made with Delphi.');
end;

initialization
  About;
end.
```

Local and Global Variables

In Delphi, there are two types of variables: local and global. All previous examples in the book have used global variables. Global variables are variables that are declared outside of a function or a procedure. For instance, variables declared in the main Delphi project file or in the interface or implementation sections of a unit are global. Listing 5-8A shows several global variables.

Listing 5-8A: Global variables in the project file

```
program Project1;

{$APPTYPE CONSOLE}

uses
  SysUtils,
  Unit1 in 'Unit1.pas';

var
  globalOne: string;        { global variable }
  globalInt: Integer = 100; { initialized global variable }

begin
  ReadLn;
end.
```

Listing 5-8B: Global variables in a unit

```
unit Unit1;

interface

var
  s: string; { global variable that can be used in other units }

implementation

var
  i: Integer; { global variable, but can only be used in this unit }
end.
```

Global variables are allocated when the application starts, exist as long as the application is running, and are deallocated when the application ends. Not only are they available throughout the lifetime of the application, they are also publicly accessible. Every procedure and function that we create can access a public variable. One exception is when we declare a global variable in the implementation section of the unit. In that case, that variable is still global, but can only be accessed in the unit where it is declared.

Global variables are automatically initialized by the compiler to "empty". Integer values are set to 0, strings to '', and Boolean values to False. Global values can also be initialized manually at the same time they are declared:

```
var
  x: Integer = 101;
```

Local variables are variables that are declared in a procedure or a function. Local variable declaration looks like this:

```
procedure ProcedureName;
var
  localVar_1: DataType;
  localVar_n: DataType;
begin
end;
```

Local variables are pretty different from global variables. Local variables only exist for a short period of time. They are created when the procedure or function is called and are immediately destroyed when the procedure or function finishes. Local variables can only be used in the procedure or function where they are declared. Unlike global variables, local variables are not automatically initialized by the compiler and they can't be initialized at the same time they are declared. You should always manually initialize a local variable in the body of the procedure before you use it because, before initialization, local variables contain random values.

The for loop will actually issue a warning message if you use a global variable as the counter (see Figure 5-5). You should never use a global variable as the counter in a for loop because it diminishes the performance of the loop. When you use a local variable for the for loop counter, the compiler is able to use the CPU registers (the absolutely fastest memory locations on the computer) to perform the counting, which results in better performance.

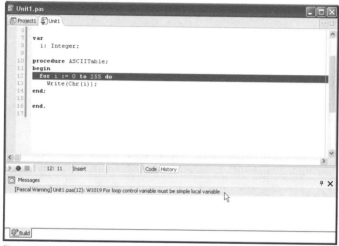

Figure 5-5: The for loop doesn't like global variables

Parameters

The best mechanism for passing user-defined values to functions and procedures is the parameter list. It is also possible to use global variables in procedures, but they should be avoided as much as possible.

There are several parameter types in Delphi: value, variable, constant, and out.

Value parameters are declared like this:

```
procedure ProcedureName(ParamName: DataType);
```

When you call a procedure and pass a value as the value parameter, the procedure receives only a copy of the original value.

Listing 5-9: Value parameter example

```
program Project1;

{$APPTYPE CONSOLE}

uses
  SysUtils;

procedure MakeAbsolute(Num: Integer);
begin
  if Num < 0 then
    Num := -Num;
```

```
   WriteLn('Absolute value = ', Num);
end;

var
  x: Integer;

begin
  MakeAbsolute(10);

  x := -100;
  MakeAbsolute(x);

  ReadLn;
end.
```

Take a look at these lines of code:

```
x := -100;
MakeAbsolute(x);
{ the value of x is still -100 }
```

When you call the MakeAbsolute procedure, the procedure creates the Num parameter and copies the value from the x variable to the Num parameter. The procedure changes the value of the Num parameter, but that change never affects the x variable because the procedure actually doesn't know that you passed a variable as the parameter. Because parameters act like local variables, changes made to the parameters are lost when the procedure finishes.

Variable, Constant, and Out Parameters

If you want to change the value of a variable in the body of the procedure, you have to use a variable parameter. Variable parameters are declared with the reserved word var:

```
procedure ProcedureName(var VarParam: DataType);
```

Value parameters are passed by value, while variable parameters are passed by reference. The difference is that value parameters receive a copy of the value, and variable parameters receive the address of the variable. When you use variable parameters, you work directly with original variables, not their copies. You can only pass variables as variable parameters. If you try to pass a constant value as a variable parameter, you will receive a compiler error.

Listing 5-10: Variable parameter example

```
program Project1;

{$APPTYPE CONSOLE}

uses
  SysUtils;

procedure MakeAbsolute(var Num: Integer);
```

```
begin
  if Num < 0 then
    Num := -Num;

  WriteLn('Absolute value = ', Num);
end;

var
  x: Integer;

begin
// MakeAbsolute(10); { Error. Constant value. }

  x := -100;
  MakeAbsolute(x);    { OK because x is a variable. }
  WriteLn(x);         { x = 100 }

  ReadLn;
end.
```

Constant parameters are similar to value parameters, but they don't allow you to change the value of the parameter in the body of a procedure or function. Constant parameters are declared with the reserved word `const`:

```
procedure ProcedureName(const ConstParam: DataType);
```

Constant parameters are extremely useful when you're passing string values to a procedure or a function. You should always pass string values as constant or variable parameters. If you need to change the string value, use a variable parameter; otherwise, use a constant parameter.

String values should never be passed as value parameters because strings can be very large and constantly creating string copies at every procedure call would decrease application performance.

```
procedure SayHello(const UserName: string);
begin
  WriteLn('Hello, ', UserName);
end;
```

Out parameters are very similar to variable parameters because they are also passed by reference. Out parameters are used to return values from the procedure or function to the caller. Like variable parameters, out parameters only accept variables.

```
procedure GetMeaningOfLife(out Number: Integer);
begin
  { According to Douglas Adams. }
  Number := 42;
end;
```

Multiple Parameters

If you want to pass more than one parameter to the procedure or function, you have to separate the parameters with semicolons.

```
procedure WriteLnEx(const AText: string; ACount: Integer);
var
  i: Integer;
begin
  for i := 1 to ACount do
    WriteLn(i, '. ', AText);
end;
```

If two or more parameters are of the same data type, they can be declared together and separated with a comma.

```
function Max(X, Y: Integer): Integer;
begin
  if X > Y then
    Result := X
  else
    Result := Y;
end;
```

Default Parameters

Default parameters in Delphi are value or const parameters that have a default value. For instance, let's take a look at the following procedure.

```
procedure WriteLnEx(const AText: string; ACount: Integer);
var
  i: Integer;
begin
  for i := 1 to ACount do
    WriteLn(i, '. ', AText);
end;
```

The WriteLnEx procedure is able to output a string value as many times as you pass in the ACount parameter. But, if you need to output the string value twice, you have to pass 2 in the ACount parameter:

```
WriteLnEx('Hello', 2);
WriteLnEx('Something else', 2);
```

Constantly passing 2 in ACount soon becomes both tiresome and unnecessary. This is where default parameters can be used. By specifying a default value in the procedure or function declaration, you won't have to pass the value in the procedure call. The default parameter syntax looks like this:

```
procedure ProcedureName(Param: DataType = Value);
```

Listing 5-11 shows the updated version of the WriteLnEx procedure where the ACount parameter is declared as default.

Listing 5-11: Default parameter example

```
program Project1;

{$APPTYPE CONSOLE}

uses
  SysUtils;

procedure WriteLnEx(const AText: string; ACount: Integer = 2);
var
  i: Integer;
begin
  for i := 1 to ACount do
    WriteLn(i, '. ', AText);
end;

begin
  WriteLnEx('Hello');            { ACount = 2 }
  WriteLnEx('Hello again', 5); { ACount = 5 }
  ReadLn;
end.
```

The only thing that changes when you declare a default parameter is the way you call the procedure or function. Note that you can now call the WriteLnEx procedure without passing a value in the ACount parameter.

```
WriteLnEx('Hello');
```

In this case, the compiler uses the default value specified in the procedure header, and the call to the WriteLnEx procedure actually looks like this:

```
WriteLnEx('Hello', 2);
```

To successfully use a procedure or a function in your code, you have to know what parameters the procedure or function accepts. If you need to take a look at the parameter list of a procedure or function, type the procedure or function name in the Code Editor, open the left parenthesis, and press Ctrl+Shift+ Space. The Code Insight feature of the Code Editor will display the parameter list (see Figure 5-6). Note that the hint displays the value of the default parameter and the entire default parameter is enclosed in brackets.

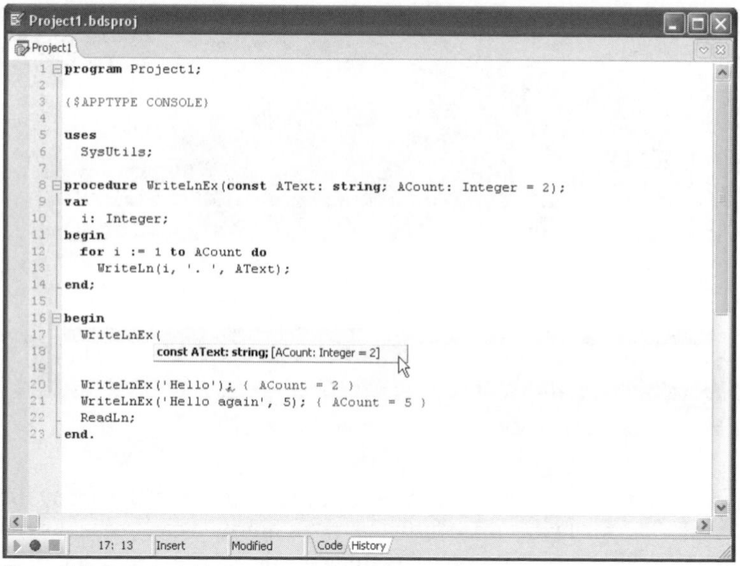

Figure 5-6: Code Insight parameter information

Default parameters must be declared at the end of the parameter list. For instance, the following procedure will not compile because default parameters cannot precede standard parameters. If you declare parameters after a default parameter, they also have to be default.

```
procedure CannotCompile(ADefault: Integer = 5; AValue: Double); { Error }
begin
end;
```

Recursive Procedures and Functions

A recursive procedure is a procedure that can call itself. Actually, all procedures can call themselves, but if the call isn't properly implemented, the result is a bug (an infinite loop), not a recursive procedure. The following shows a poorly written recursive procedure:

```
procedure Bug;
begin
  Bug;
end;
```

Calling the Bug procedure has disastrous results because the procedure will continue calling itself until it has used all available resources, and then it will crash (see Figure 5-7). If you run the application from the Delphi IDE, the Bug procedure will crash both the application and the entire IDE. The point is: Never write something that works like the Bug procedure.

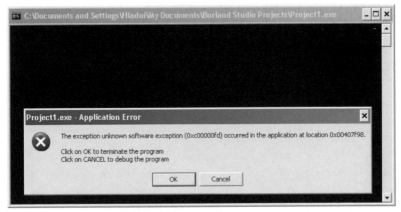

Figure 5-7: The result of infinite procedure recursion

A valid recursive procedure must have a way of controlling how many times it calls itself. The following procedure illustrates how you can use an integer parameter to implement a simple countdown. You can see the result of the CountDown procedure in Figure 5-8.

Listing 5-12: A simple recursive procedure

```
program Project1;

{$APPTYPE CONSOLE}

uses
  SysUtils;

procedure CountDown(AStart: Integer);
begin
  WriteLn('Counter: ', AStart);
  Dec(AStart);

  if AStart = 0 then
    WriteLn('Counting finished.')
  else
    CountDown(AStart);
end;

begin
  CountDown(10);
  ReadLn;
end.
```

Figure 5-8: The result of the CountDown procedure

The CountDown procedure recursively calls itself as long as the AStart parameter is greater than 0.

The most famous recursive function is the function that calculates factorials. The factorial is the product of all numbers in the range from 1 to n. For instance, the factorial of 4 is 24 (1 * 2 * 3 * 4).

Listing 5-13: A recursive function

```
program Project1;

{$APPTYPE CONSOLE}

uses
  SysUtils;

function Factorial(ANumber: Integer): Integer;
begin
  if ANumber = 0 then
    Result := 1
  else
    Result := ANumber * Factorial(ANumber - 1);
end;

begin
  WriteLn('f(5) = ', Factorial(5)); { 120 }
  ReadLn;
end.
```

Forward Declarations

Forward declarations are closely related to the Delphi language rule that everything has to be declared before it can be used. The following application works properly because the MyAbs function is declared before the procedure that uses it.

```
function MyAbs(X: Integer): Integer;
begin
  if X > 0 then
    Result := X
  else
    Result := -X;
end;
```

```
procedure MyWriteAbsolute(X: Integer);
begin
  WriteLn('Abs = ', MyAbs(X));
end;
```

But, if we declare the MyWriteAbsolute procedure before the MyAbs function, the application will no longer compile because the procedure can no longer see the MyAbs function. In large units (actually in any unit), constantly changing the procedure declaration order is neither smart nor useful.

Forward declarations help us bend the "declare before you use" rule. Forward declarations are actually procedure or function headers followed by the forward directive. Forward declarations should always be written before all other declarations. In this case, we have to make a forward declaration of the MyAbs function. With a forward declaration, the function will be usable even if it's located below all other procedures and functions in the unit.

Listing 5-14: Forward declaration

```
program Project1;

{$APPTYPE CONSOLE}

uses
  SysUtils;

function MyAbs(X: Integer): Integer; forward;

procedure MyWriteAbsolute(X: Integer);
begin
  WriteLn('Abs = ', MyAbs(X));
end;

function MyAbs(X: Integer): Integer;
begin
  if X > 0 then
    Result := X
  else
    Result := -X;
end;

begin
  MyWriteAbsolute(-100);
  ReadLn;
end.
```

Overloading

Normally, every function and procedure in the unit must have a unique name. However, you can declare multiple procedures and functions that have the same name if you overload them. Overloaded procedures and functions can have the same name, but they must have parameter lists that differ in the number of parameters, parameter types, or both. To overload a procedure or a function, you have to mark it with the overload directive.

Listing 5-15: Overloaded functions

```pascal
program Project1;

{$APPTYPE CONSOLE}

uses
  SysUtils;

function Max(X, Y: Integer): Integer; overload;
begin
  if X > Y then
    Result := X
  else
    Result := Y;
end;

function Max(X, Y, Z: Integer): Integer; overload;
begin
  Result := X;
  if Y > Result then
    Result := Y;
  if Z > Result then
    Result := Z;
end;

begin
  WriteLn(Max(5, 4, 3));
  ReadLn;
end.
```

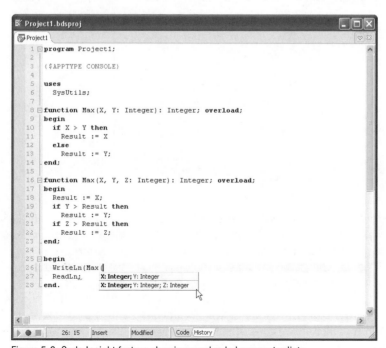

Figure 5-9: Code Insight feature showing overloaded parameter lists

When you call overloaded functions, Delphi determines which one to call by the parameters you pass. If you press Ctrl+Shift+Space in the Code Editor while calling an overloaded function or procedure, Delphi shows you the parameter lists of all overloads.

The Inline Directive

The inline directive, introduced in Delphi 2005, gives you advanced control over procedure and function compiling. The inline directive enables you to increase the speed of small functions and procedures. Inlined procedures and functions are faster, but they increase the size of the executable.

To successfully use the inline directive, you have to know what happens when you call a procedure or a function and what effect the inline directive has on your code.

When a procedure or function is called, it has to allocate memory for all local variables and parameters it has. The memory for local variables and parameters is allocated from the stack, and this allocation is called stack frame creation. The stack is a segment of memory that the application uses when working with variables. The stack is automatically allocated by the application at application startup. By default, all Delphi applications allocate 16 KB and can allocate a maximum of 1 MB of memory for the stack. Although you can change these values, as shown in Figure 5-10, you shouldn't do so unless there is a very good reason.

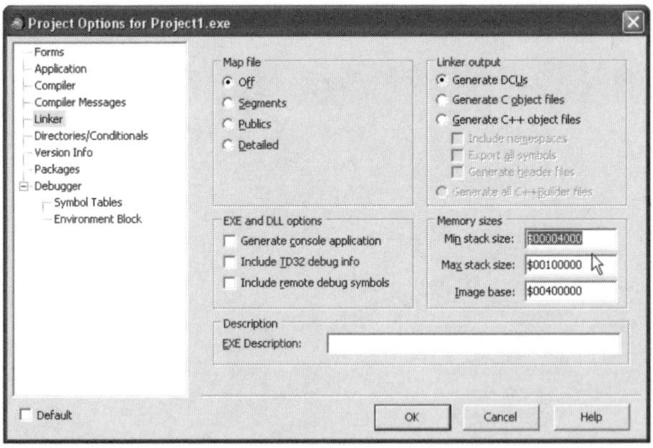

Figure 5-10: Stack size settings

The stack frame is a piece of stack memory where the parameters and local variables of the procedure temporarily exist. When the procedure finishes, the parameters and local variables on the stack frame are automatically deallocated. This is the reason you can't use local variables and parameters outside of the procedure or function in which they are declared.

All these allocations and deallocations aren't done magically. While the process may appear magical from the Delphi programmer's point of view, the Delphi compiler has to generate machine language instructions to do these things at run time. So, when a procedure or a function is compiled, the executable contains not only the machine language version of the procedure's logic but also some entry and exit code that manages these stack allocations and deallocations. Also, for every procedure call we make, Delphi has to generate machine language instructions that do parameter passing and the actual procedure call.

Let's take a look at what machine language instructions are generated for the very simple MyAbs function that returns an absolute value of an integer. The Delphi code of the function is displayed in Listing 5-16.

Listing 5-16: An inlined function

```
function MyAbs(I: Integer): Integer;
begin
  if I < 0 then
    Result := -I
  else
    Result := I;
end;

begin
  x := MyAbs(-20);
end.
```

For the MyAbs call in the main block, Delphi generates the following three instructions (compiler optimizations are turned off):

```
mov eax,$ffffffec
call MyAbs
mov [$0040565c],eax
```

The first instruction moves the number –20 into the eax register. This is necessary because the MyAbs function expects the value for the I parameter to be located in the eax register. The second instruction obviously calls the MyAbs function, and the last instruction copies the result of the function to the x variable. The $0040565c value is the address of the x variable in memory (note that this value isn't constant).

The instructions generated for the MyAbs function are:

```
// begin
push ebp
mov ebp,esp
add esp,-$08
mov [ebp-$04],eax

// if I < 0 then
cmp dword ptr [ebp-$04],$00
jnl $00403a19

// Result := -I
mov eax,[ebp-$04]
neg eax
mov [ebp-$08],eax
jmp $00403a1f

// Result := I;
```

```
mov eax,[ebp-$04]
mov [ebp-$08],eax
mov eax,[ebp-$08]

// end;
pop ecx
pop ecx
pop ebp
ret
```

The first two instructions deal with setting up the stack frame. The third instruction, add esp,-$08, allocates 8 bytes of memory from the stack (enough space to save two integer values). The more logical instruction would be to use sub esp,$08 to allocate the space from the stack, but the developers of the Delphi compiler used a little trick here. Adding a negative value gives you the same result as subtracting a positive value, except adding executes faster. The fourth instruction moves the value of the I parameter to the stack.

The second section of the generated code performs a test to see if the value of the I parameter needs to be converted to a positive value.

```
// if I < 0 then
cmp dword ptr [ebp-$04],$00
jnl $00403a19
```

The first instruction compares the I parameter on the stack with 0. The second instruction is the jump-not-less instruction that determines whether the value of the I parameter needs to be converted to a positive value. If the value of the I parameter is larger than 0, the value doesn't need to be converted and the function copies the original parameter value to the Result function:

```
// Result := I;
mov eax,[ebp-$04]
mov [ebp-$08],eax
mov eax,[ebp-$08]
```

The first instruction moves the value of the parameter to the eax register (in actuality, it moves the parameter value to the function's Result). The second parameter copies the Result value to the other stack location that the function allocated at the beginning. This is needed because the function, in the end, returns the value located at the ebp-$08 memory location.

If the parameter value has to be converted to a positive value, the function executes the third section of the code:

```
// Result := -I
mov eax,[ebp-$04]
neg eax
mov [ebp-$08],eax
jmp $00403a1f
```

The function uses the neg instruction to change the sign of the parameter value and moves the negated value to the ebp-$08 stack location. Then it executes the jmp (jump) instruction that jumps to the end of the function and executes the last instruction that moves the changed value to the Result function:

```
mov eax,[ebp-$08]
```

The last four instructions remove the local variables and parameters allocated on the stack at the beginning of the function. These instructions restore the stack to the state before the function call. This way, the caller's stack is restored, and the caller can continue executing like nothing happened to the stack. The final instruction, ret, returns the control to the caller.

A large number of instructions in the generated code are involved in reading and writing values to the stack. Actually, there are more instructions that deal with reading and writing values to the stack than there are instructions that perform the function logic.

The inline directive completely changes the way Delphi generates code for the function. When we mark a function or procedure with the inline directive, Delphi no longer generates the call for the function but copies the function body to the place of the call. This way, the compiler doesn't have to generate code that creates the stack frame and sets up the stack frame with appropriate values, move values from the stack to the Result, or generate the code that returns to the caller and restores the caller's stack frame.

Using the inline directive on small functions and procedures can drastically increase the speed of the application, especially if these functions and procedures are used in tight loops. When you mark a function with the inline directive, all instructions from the function are always copied to the place of the call, which causes the final executable to be larger. When you mark small functions with the inline directive and turn on compiler optimizations in the Project Options dialog box, this increase is absolutely insignificant.

Here is the inlined version of the MyAbs function:

```
function MyAbs(I: Integer): Integer; inline;
begin
  if I < 0 then
    Result := -I
  else
    Result := I;
end;
```

When the function is inlined, nothing is generated for the function. The instructions are only generated at the call site. If you turn on the compiler optimizations and inline small functions like this one, the compiler will generate first-class, extremely fast code:

```
mov eax,$fffffffec
test eax,eax
jnl $00403a6c
neg eax
mov ebx,eax
```

Normally, you would have three instructions that only call the function, plus many more instructions in the function itself. With inlining and optimizations, you get five instructions that do the whole thing.

Conditional Compilation

Delphi has a nice assortment of compiler directives that can be used to implement conditional compilation. Conditional compilation enables you to keep a single code base and only compile certain sections of the code, based on various conditions. Conditional symbols work like Boolean values. In conditional compilation, you test if a symbol is defined or undefined. This is achieved with the $IFDEF compiler directive. The conditional block has to finish with the $ENDIF directive. The following procedure will display a message only if you run it on a Linux computer:

```
{$IFDEF LINUX}
WriteLn('Linux');
{$ENDIF}
```

If you want to make sure that procedures and functions marked with the inline directive can be recompiled with older Delphi compilers, you should include the inline directive in the compilation process only if you're using the Delphi 2005 compiler or a newer one.

To determine if you're using the Delphi 2005 compiler, write this:

```
{$IFDEF VER170}

// Delphi 2005 specific code

{$ENDIF}
```

The VER180 constant indicates the current compiler, and the VER170 constant indicates the Delphi 2005 compiler. Versions 1.0 to 7.0 are Turbo Pascal versions, 8.0 to 15.0 are Delphi versions 1.0 to 7.0, and version 16.0 is Delphi 8 for the .NET framework.

So, if you want to make sure that the compilation will not fail in older compiler versions because of the inline directive, write something like this:

```
function MyAbs(I: Integer): Integer; {$IFDEF VER170} inline; {$ENDIF}
```

The above line of code will use the inline directive only in Delphi 2005. To use the inline directive in both Delphi 2005 and newer versions, you can also use the RTLVersion constant and the $IF compiler directive (see Listing 5-17).

Listing 5-17: Using the RTLVersion constant to determine the compiler

```
program Project1;

{$APPTYPE CONSOLE}

var
  x: Integer;

function MyAbs(I: Integer): Integer;
  {$IF RTLVersion >= 17} inline; {$IFEND}
begin
  if I < 0 then
    Result := -I
  else
```

```
    Result := I;
end;

begin
  x := MyAbs(-20);

  WriteLn(x);
  ReadLn;
end.
```

Functions in C++

The title of this part of the chapter is not "Functions and Procedures in C++" because C++ doesn't have procedures like Delphi does. In C++, you can only create functions, but these can work like Delphi procedures if you make them return nothing. To make the function return nothing, all you have to do is tell it to return void. The void data type is a special data type that is used to indicate that no value exists.

Here is how you declare a function in C++:

```
return_type function_name(parameter list)
{
  function body
}
```

As you can see, there are some differences between a function declaration in Delphi and C++:

- The return type is specified before the function name, not after the function name and parameter list as it is in Delphi.

- There is no semicolon after the function name, or after the parameter list, if there is one.

The example in Listing 5-18 shows how to create and use a simple procedure in C++.

Listing 5-18: A simple procedure

```
#include <iostream.h>
#include <conio.h>
#pragma hdrstop

void hello()
{
  cout << "Hello from a C++ procedure." << endl;
}

#pragma argsused
int main(int argc, char* argv[])
{
  hello(); // call the hello() procedure

  getch();
  return 0;
}
```

When declaring and calling a function in C++, you have to write the parentheses even when the function has no parameters. To show that a function accepts no parameters, you can also include the reserved word void inside the parentheses:

```
void hello(void)
{
    cout << "Hello from a C++ procedure." << endl;
}
```

Parameters

The parameter list in C++ is a comma-separated list:

```
return_type function_name(data_type first_param, data_type last_param)
{
    function body
}
```

Listing 5-19 features a simple function named add, which accepts two integer values and returns their sum.

Listing 5-19: A simple function

```
#include <iostream.h>
#include <conio.h>
#pragma hdrstop

int add(int first, int second)
{
    return first + second;
}

#pragma argsused
int main(int argc, char* argv[])
{
    int i, j, sum;
    cout << "First number: ";
    cin >> i;
    cout << "Second number: ";
    cin >> j;

    sum = add(i, j); // call the add(int, int) function
    cout << "Sum = " << sum << endl;

    getch();
    return 0;
}
```

To return a value from a function in C++, you have to use the reserved word return. However, you have to be careful how you use it, since it greatly differs from the Result variable in Delphi. Since Result is a variable, it can be used as such without disrupting the normal flow of execution. But the reserved word return breaks execution and immediately exits the function, returning the expression that follows it to the caller function, so you can't write anything after it.

For instance, Listing 5-20 shows the Max3 function implemented in Delphi. As you can see in the listing, the Result variable is freely used throughout the function.

Listing 5-20: Delphi version of the Max3 function

```
program Project1;

{$APPTYPE CONSOLE}

uses
  SysUtils;

function Max3(num1, num2, num3: Integer): Integer;
begin
  Result := num1;      // num1 is the largest?
  if num2 > Result then
    Result := num2;    // num2 is the largest?

  if num3 > Result then
    Result := num3;    // num3 is the largest
end;

begin
  WriteLn('Max = ', Max3(1, 2, 3));
  ReadLn;
end.
```

The C++ version of the function is different — not in logic, but in the way things are done. There are two differences: You have to declare a variable in the function to temporarily store the max value and use the reserved word return after all other statements to return the result to the calling function, as shown in Listing 5-21.

Listing 5-21: The C++ version of the Max3 function

```
#include <iostream.h>
#include <conio.h>
#pragma hdrstop

int max3(int num1, int num2, int num3)
{
   int max_val = num1;  // num1 is the largest?

   if(num2 > max_val)
     max_val = num2;    // num2 is the largest?

   if(num3 > max_val)
     max_val = num3;    // num3 is the largest

   return max_val;
}

#pragma argsused
int main(int argc, char* argv[])
{
```

```
   cout << "Max = " << max3(1, 2, 3) << endl;

   getch();
   return 0;
}
```

There's also another way of implementing the Max3 function — by using the conditional operator — but if you've got a weak stomach, feel free to skip the following listing. Listing 5-22 contains two versions of the Max3 function, called Max3 and Max3_2. The Max3 function is easier to read since it uses a temporary variable to store the max value. The Max3_2 function is something you'd want to do to your worst enemy, but it is nice from a geek's point of view since it returns the max value without using a temporary variable.

Listing 5-22: Two more versions of the Max3 function using the conditional operator

```
#include <iostream.h>
#include <conio.h>
#pragma hdrstop

int max3(int num1, int num2, int num3)
{
   int max_val = num1 > num2 ? num1 : num2;
   return num3 > max_val ? num3 : max_val;
}

int max3_2(int num1, int num2, int num3)
{
   return num3 > (num1>num2 ? num1:num2) ? num3: (num1>num2 ? num1:num2);
}

#pragma argsused
int main(int argc, char* argv[])
{
   cout << "Max = " << max3(10, 20, 30) << endl;
   cout << "Max(again) = " << max3_2(500, 400, 300) << endl;

   getch();
   return 0;
}
```

Before we move on to the topic of parameter passing, you should remember one last thing: You cannot define more parameters of the same type in a comma-separated list, as you can in Delphi:

```
procedure ParamSample(I, J, K: Integer; A, B: Double);
begin
end;
```

In C++, all parameters must be fully defined, with the data type first and then the parameter name:

```
void param_sample(int i, int j, int k, double a, double b)
{
}
```

Passing Parameters By Value and By Reference

When you declare a parameter list as we did earlier (data type first and then the name of the parameter), you declare parameters that receive a copy of the argument's value. (An argument is anything passed to a function parameter, like a constant value or a variable.) Value parameters in C++ work just like Delphi value parameters — the parameter receives only a copy of the value. The value of the parameter can be freely modified in the function's body, but no matter what you do with it, the changes aren't reflected to the world outside the function.

To change the value of a variable passed to the function, you need to declare the function's parameters a bit differently so that they accept the address of the variable instead of a copy of its value. By accepting the address of the original variable, the code in the function's body is able to modify the value of the variable. This is known as passing by reference.

To declare a reference parameter (known as a var parameter in Delphi), you have to use the reference operator (&) after the data type, between the data type and the parameter name, or before the parameter name — it doesn't matter. Here's how to declare a reference parameter (the following declarations differ only in the position of the reference operator):

```
return_type function_name(data_type& param_name);
return_type function_name(data_type & param_name);
return_type function_name(data_type &param_name);
```

Listing 5-23 shows two versions of the my_abs function, which is actually the my_abs procedure, since it doesn't return the absolute value of the argument as the result but changes the argument itself.

Listing 5-23: Passing by value and by reference

```
#include <iostream.h>
#include <conio.h>
#pragma hdrstop

void my_abs(int i)      // passing by value, doesn't work
{
   if (i < 0)
      i = -i;
}

void my_abs_ref(int& i) // passing by reference, works OK
{
   if (i < 0)
      i = -i;
}

// pass normally, by value, since we aren't changing the value of num
void show_int(int num)
{
   cout << num << endl;
}

#pragma argsused
```

```
int main(int argc, char* argv[])
{
    int test = -5;
    my_abs(test);
    show_int(test);    // -5, not good

    my_abs_ref(test);
    show_int(test);    // 5, OK, since test was passed by reference

    getch();
    return 0;
}
```

Default Parameters

Default parameters in C++ are declared the same way as they are in Delphi:

```
void function_name(data_type param_name = default_value);
```

Default parameters in C++ have the same limitation as they do in Delphi —
you cannot declare a non-default parameter after a default one:

```
int default_OK(int i = 5, int j = 20)
{
    return i * j;
}
```

```
int default_ERROR(int i = 5, int j)
{
    return i * j;
}
```

Function Prototypes

In C++ and Delphi, all functions (and procedures) must be declared before
they are used. So far, we've tackled this problem by declaring all functions
above the main function, which made them automatically usable in the program. However, this is not the preferred way of function declaration in C++.
The preferred way of declaring functions, which gives the compiler the ability
to perform stronger type checking, is to declare them below the main function. But when you declare a function below the main function, it cannot be
used in the main function without a function prototype.

A function prototype is similar to a forward declaration in Delphi. In
C++, a function prototype is a function header followed by a semicolon:

```
return_type function_name(parameter_list);
```

To make the function visible in the entire unit, function prototypes are
declared at the top of the unit. The following example shows how to declare
functions below the main function and how to write a function prototype.

Listing 5-24: Function prototypes

```
#include <iostream.h>
#include <conio.h>
#pragma hdrstop

void prototyped_hello();   // function prototype, no body

#pragma argsused
int main(int argc, char* argv[])
{
    prototyped_hello();

    getch();
    return 0;
}

void prototyped_hello()    // function's body after the main function
{
    cout << "function prototype" << endl;
}
```

When you have a function with a parameter list, you can omit parameter names in the function prototype. The following example illustrates how to create a function prototype for a function with a parameter list:

```
// void prototyped_func(int i, char c, double d);
```

or

```
void prototyped_func(int, char, double);

#pragma argsused
int main(int argc, char* argv[])
{
    prototyped_func(0, 'a', 1.0);
    return 0;
}

#pragma argsused
void prototyped_func(int i, char c, double d)
{
}
```

Local, Global, and Static Local Variables

As in Delphi, local variables are variables declared in a function, allocated on the stack, and can only be used inside the function in which they are declared. In C++, you can also declare a "really" local variable inside a block. A variable declared inside a block only exists in the block in which it is declared:

```
void local_variables()
{
    int local_i = 10;

    if(local_i == 10)
    {
```

```
        int block_local_i = 20;
        cout << local_i << endl;
        cout << block_local_i << endl;
    }

    /*
        local_i can be used anywhere in the function
        block_local_i can only be used in the if statement's block
    */
}
```

Global Variables

Global variables are variables declared outside of any function, can be used in any function, and unlike local variables, they exist as long as the application is running. The following example shows how to declare and use a global variable in C++:

```
#include <iostream.h>
#include <conio.h>
#pragma hdrstop

// function prototype
void display_global();

// global variable
int global_i = 101;

#pragma argsused
int main(int argc, char* argv[])
{
    // use the global variable in the main() function
    cout << "global_i in main() = " << global_i << endl;
    display_global();

    getch();
    return 0;
}

void display_global()
{
    // use the global variable in the display_global() func
    cout << "global_i in display_global() = " << global_i << endl;
}
```

Static Local Variables

Both global and local variables can be marked as static, but since there are differences between static local and static global variables, static local variables are described first, and static global variables are described later in this chapter.

To declare a static local variable, use the static storage specifier before the data type:

```
static data_type identifier;
```

Here are the characteristics of static local variables:

■ They are declared inside a function block, like local variables.

■ Because they are declared inside a function, they can only be used inside the function in which they are declared.

■ Unlike ordinary local variables, static local variables aren't destroyed when the function exits. Because of this, static local variables retain their value through multiple function calls.

The code in Listing 5-25 and Figure 5-11 illustrate the difference between local and static local variables.

Listing 5-25: Using static local variables

```
#include <iostream.h>
#include <conio.h>
#pragma hdrstop

void local_var();
void static_local_var();

#pragma argsused
int main(int argc, char* argv[])
{
   int i;
   for(i = 1; i <= 5; i++)
      local_var();

   for(i = 1; i <= 5; i++)
      static_local_var();

   getch();
   return 0;
}

void local_var()
{
   int cnt = 0;
   cout << "local_var() function has been called " <<
        ++cnt << " times." << endl;
}

void static_local_var()
{
   static cnt = 0; // initialized to 0 only the first time the func is called
   cout << "static_local_var() function has been called " <<
        ++cnt << " times." << endl;
}
```

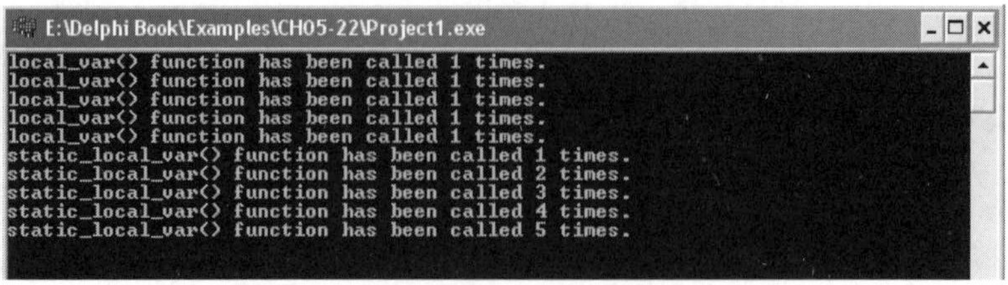

Figure 5-11: Static local variables preserve their value between multiple function calls.

Function Overloading and Inlining

To overload a function in C++ you don't have to mark it with a special directive like you do in Delphi. To create overloaded functions in C++, you only have to declare several functions that have the same name but differ in the number or type of parameters.

The example in Listing 5-26 shows how to create an overloaded function in C++ and how to use data type suffixes to make sure the appropriate overload is called. If you omit the "f" suffix for the float data type, the example will fail to compile because the compiler won't be able to decide if it should call max(int, int) or max(float, float).

Listing 5-26: Overloaded functions

```
int max(int, int);
int max(int, int, int);
int max(float, float);

#pragma argsused
int main(int argc, char* argv[])
{
   max(1, 2);
   max(1, 2, 3);

   /* to make sure that the max(float, float) overload
      is called, append the floating-point type suffix ("f")
      to the 1.0 and 2.0 constant values */
   max(1.0f, 2.0f);
   return 0;
}

int max(int a, int b) {
   return 0;
}

int max(int a, int b, int c) {
   return 0;
}

int max(float a, float b) {
   return 0;
}
```

To inline a function in C++, use the reserved word `inline` at the beginning of function declaration:

```
inline return_type function_name(parameter_list);
```

You can read more about inlined functions earlier in this chapter in the section titled "The Inline Directive."

Units

In Delphi, a unit is a single file with interface and implementation sections. Function and procedure declarations, constants, types, and variables that are to be used from outside the unit are written in the interface part of the unit. Function and procedure implementations, as well as constants, types, and variables that are used only in the unit, are written in the implementation part.

In C++, the interface section is stored in a header file (.h or .hpp) and the implementation section is stored in the standard source file (.cpp).

For instance, let's see how to move the my_abs() function from the following example to a my_math unit:

```
#include <iostream.h>
#include <conio.h>
#pragma hdrstop

int my_abs(int num);

#pragma argsused
int main(int argc, char* argv[])
{
    int n;
    cout << "Enter a number: ";
    cin >> n;
    cout << "The absolute value of " << n <<
        " is " << my_abs(n) << "." << endl;

    getch();
    return 0;
}

int my_abs(int num)
{
    return num < 0 ? -num : num;
}
```

First, you need to create a new .cpp file and save it to the project directory under my_math.cpp. When you've saved the file, move the implementation of the my_abs() function to the my_math.cpp file (see Listing 5-27A).

Listing 5-27A: The my_math.cpp file

```
int my_abs(int num)
{
    return num < 0 ? -num : num;
}
```

The second thing that you have to do is to create a new header file (both the CPP File and Header File items can be found in the C++Builder Files category on the Tool Palette). When you've created a new header file, move the my_abs() function's prototype to it and save the header file to the project directory under my_math.h (see Listing 5-27B).

Listing 5-27B: The my_math.h file

```
int my_abs(int num);
```

Now that you've moved the my_abs() function to the my_math unit, you won't be able to compile the application until you include the my_math header file using the #include directive. However, to include a custom header, you have to do two things differently:

■ Include the header by using the #include "header_name" syntax, not by using #include <header_name>

■ Include the header below the #pragma hdrstop directive

The difference between #include "header_name" and #include <header_name> is in how the compiler searches for header files. The <header_name> syntax is meant to be used with standard headers that are stored in default directories. If you use the <header_name> syntax with your own units, like <my_math.h>, the application will fail to compile. But when you include the header using the "header_name" syntax, the compiler searches in the current directory, the directory of the file that contains the #include directive, or other user-supplied directories.

The following listing shows how to properly include the my_math header file.

Listing 5-27C: Including a custom header file

```
#include <iostream.h>
#include <conio.h>

#pragma hdrstop

#include "my_math.h"

#pragma argsused
int main(int argc, char* argv[])
{
    int n;
    cout << "Enter a number: ";
    cin >> n;
    cout << "The absolute value of " << n <<
        " is " << my_abs(n) << "." << endl;

    getch();
    return 0;
}
```

Static Global Variables and Static Functions

When you declare a variable in the interface section of a Delphi unit, the variable is automatically usable in all other units and the main project file. When you declare a variable in a C++ unit, it is also global and likewise usable in other units, but not automatically. To use a variable declared in another unit, you have to redeclare the variable using the extern modifier in the unit in which you want to use it. When you use the extern modifier on a variable, you are simply telling the compiler that the variable is stored in some other unit.

For instance, the following listing shows an updated version of the my_math.cpp file that now contains an int variable.

Listing 5-28A: An updated version of the my_math.cpp file

```
int unit_integer = 2005;

int my_abs(int num)
{
   return num < 0 ? -num : num;
}
```

To use the unit_integer variable in the main unit, you have to include the my_math header file and you have to redeclare the variable using the extern modifier. When you redeclare a variable using the extern modifier, you can omit the initialization part since you're only telling the compiler to look for the variable elsewhere (see Listing 5-28B).

Listing 5-28B: Using an external variable

```
#include <iostream.h>
#include <conio.h>
#pragma hdrstop
#include "my_math.h"

extern int unit_integer;

#pragma argsused
int main(int argc, char* argv[])
{
   cout << unit_integer << endl; // correctly displays 2005

   getch();
   return 0;
}
```

If you need a global variable that is only visible in the unit in which it is declared, like variables declared in the implementation section of a Delphi unit, you need to mark the variable as static to create a static global variable:

```
static int unit_integer = 2005;
```

If you mark the unit_integer variable in the my_math.cpp file as static, you won't be able to run the application anymore because the extern modifier in the main unit is no longer able to see the unit_integer variable in the my_math.cpp file.

The static directive has the same effect on functions. By default, all functions are globally visible, but when marked as static, they can only be used inside the unit in which they are declared (see Figure 5-12).

Figure 5-12: Static global variables and static functions can't be used outside of the unit in which they're declared.

Chapter 6
Arrays and Strings

This chapter shows how to efficiently work with large numbers of variables, how to manipulate strings using standard Delphi procedures and functions, and how to create your own procedures and functions that work with strings.

Arrays

Arrays are very useful for working with a large number of variables of the same type that are logically related. For instance, imagine that you have to create an application for your local cinema that shows which seats are occupied and which are vacant. Let's say that the entire cinema has 350 seats. To remember the state of every seat in the cinema, you would need 350 uniquely named Boolean variables:

```
var
  seat1: Boolean;
  seat2: Boolean;
  seat3: Boolean;
  seat350: Boolean;
```

Not only is this large number of declarations unacceptable, it leads to even more problems. What if you wanted to update the state of a seat based on what the user enters? There is no way other than to write a huge if-then or case statement that would check the value the user entered and change the corresponding variable. This means that you would have at least 350 lines of code to simply change the state of one seat:

```
var
  seat1: Boolean;
  seat2: Boolean;
  seat3: Boolean;
  seat350: Boolean;
  userSeat: Integer;

begin
  ReadLn(userSeat);
  case userSeat of
    1: seat1 := True;
    2: seat2 := True;
    350: seat350 := True;
```

```
  end;
end.
```

Obviously, there has to be a better way of dealing with large collections of variables. The best way of doing so is to use an array.

An array is simply a collection of variables. All variables in the array share the same name and have the same data type. But unlike individual variables, all variables in an array have an additional property that differentiates them from one another — the index.

The syntax for array declaration is:

```
ArrayName: array[Range] of DataType;
Cinema: array[1..350] of Boolean;
```

To access a variable in the array, you have to specify the name of the array followed by the variable's index. The variable's index must be enclosed in brackets. The syntax for accessing a single element of the array is:

```
ArrayName[Index]
```

If you are using the Cinema array and you need to change the state of seat 265 to vacant, you can write this:

```
Cinema[265] := False;
```

The index of an element doesn't need to be a constant value. It can be a variable or a function result. The important thing is that the index value has to be inside the declared range.

Listing 6-1: Array element access

```
const
  MAX_SEATS = 350;

var
  Cinema: array[1..MAX_SEATS] of Boolean;
  userSeat: Integer;

begin
  ReadLn(userSeat);
  if (userSeat >= 1) and (userSeat <= MAX_SEATS) then
    Cinema[userSeat] := True;
end.
```

The best thing about arrays is that you can access array elements in a loop, which can easily solve a lot of problems. In this case, you can easily set all seats to vacant if the cinema is empty or calculate the percentage of seats occupied. If you take a closer look at the GetPercent function, you will notice that arrays support the new for-in loop.

Listing 6-2: Accessing array elements in a loop

```
program Project1;

{$APPTYPE CONSOLE}
```

```
uses
  SysUtils;

const
  MAX_SEATS = 350;

var
  Cinema: array[1..MAX_SEATS] of Boolean;
  i: Integer;

procedure ClearCinema;
var
  i: Integer;
begin
  for i := 1 to MAX_SEATS do
    Cinema[i] := False;
end;

function GetPercent: Double;
var
  seat: Boolean;
  occupiedCnt: Integer;
begin
  occupiedCnt := 0;

  for seat in Cinema do
    if seat then Inc(occupiedCnt);

  Result := occupiedCnt * 100 / MAX_SEATS;
end;

begin
  { 67 seats occupied }
  for i := 1 to 67 do
    Cinema[i] := True;

  WriteLn(GetPercent:0:2, '% seats occupied.');
  ReadLn;
end.
```

Arrays in Delphi are much more flexible than arrays in other programming languages. For instance, array indexes in C++, C#, and VB.NET are always zero based. In Delphi, you can use index values that best suit your needs:

```
negativeArray: array[-100..100] of Integer;
bigIndex:      array[1000..1020] of Integer;
alphabet:      array[Ord('a')..Ord('z')] of Char;
```

Since arrays in Delphi can have different indexes, it can be difficult to remember the starting and ending indexes of every array you use in an application. Delphi has two functions that get the first and last index of an array: Low and High. If you're not using the for-in loop, the best way to read index values is by using the High and Low functions.

Listing 6-3: Low and High functions

```
program Project1;

{$APPTYPE CONSOLE}

uses
  SysUtils;

var
  alphabet: array[Ord('a')..Ord('z')] of Char;
  i: Integer;

begin
  for i := Low(alphabet) to High(alphabet) do
  begin
    alphabet[i] := Chr(i);
    WriteLn(alphabet[i]);
  end;

  ReadLn;
end.
```

The Low and High functions remove the burden of remembering the exact indexes of an array, are easy to read, and don't slow down the application because the functions aren't called at run time. The compiler replaces the calls to both functions with appropriate values from the array declaration at compile time.

Array Constants

The syntax for array constant declaration is:

```
const
  ArrayName: array[Range] of DataType = (value_1, value_2, value_n);
```

There are times when array constants can drastically reduce the amount of code. One such situation is when using a function that returns the name of the month. The function for returning the month name is pretty long when implemented without an array constant.

```
function GetMonthName(AMonth: Integer): string;
begin
  case AMonth of
    1: Result := 'January';
    2: Result := 'February';
    3: Result := 'March';
    4: Result := 'April';
    5: Result := 'May';
    6: Result := 'June';
    7: Result := 'July';
    8: Result := 'August';
    9: Result := 'September';
    10: Result := 'October';
    11: Result := 'November';
    12: Result := 'December';
```

```
    else Result := '';
  end;
end;
```

A much better solution to this problem is to declare a local array constant. The function that uses the array constant is much smaller and looks more professional.

Listing 6-4: Using array constants

```
function GetMonthNameEx(AMonthName: Integer): string;
const
  MONTH: array[1..12] of string = ('January', 'February',
    'March', 'April', 'May', 'June', 'July', 'August',
    'September', 'October', 'November', 'December');
begin
  if (AMonthName < Low(MONTH)) or (AMonthName > High(MONTH)) then
    Result := ''
  else
    Result := MONTH[AMonthName];
end;
```

The GetMonthNameEx function returns an empty string if the AMonth parameter is out of valid range. You should always check user values to make sure they are valid. If you blindly accept user values, even simple functions like this one can cause an error and produce invalid results. In this case, if the user passes the number 13 as the AMonth parameter, the function returns an empty string.

```
    WriteLn(GetMonthNameEx(13));
```

If you remove the range check, the application will try to read a value that is located outside of the array. If that memory location is empty, the call will probably execute without problems, but if the memory location isn't empty, the call will cause an error.

Array constants also give us the ability to use the case statement with string values. Although we can't use string values directly in the case statement, we can get the index of the value in the array and use that index in the case statement.

Listing 6-5: Using strings with the case statement

```
program Project1;

{$APPTYPE CONSOLE}

uses
  SysUtils;

function MonthIndex(const AMonthName: string): Integer;
const
  MONTH: array[1..12] of string = ('January', 'February',
    'March', 'April', 'May', 'June', 'July', 'August',
    'September', 'October', 'November', 'December');
var
  i: Integer;
```

```
begin
  Result := -1;
  for i := Low(MONTH) to High(MONTH) do
  begin
    if AMonthName = MONTH[i] then
    begin
      Result := i;
      Exit;
    end;     // if AMonthName
  end;       // for i
end;

var
  userEntry: string;

begin
  Write('Enter a month: ');
  ReadLn(userEntry);

  if MonthIndex(userEntry) = -1 then
    WriteLn('Invalid month name')
  else begin
    case MonthIndex(userEntry) of
      4: WriteLn('Easter');
      12: WriteLn('Christmas');
    end;     // case MonthIndex
  end;

  ReadLn;
end.
```

The MonthIndex function returns –1 if the AMonthName parameter isn't a valid month name and the proper index if AMonthName is a valid month name. You should remember this value because a large majority of functions (not only in Delphi) return –1 if something is wrong.

Another thing to note in the MonthIndex function is the use of the Exit procedure. The Exit procedure is used when you want to terminate the procedure or function and immediately return control to the caller. In this case, the use of the Exit procedure ensures optimal execution. If the user passes "January" as the AMonthName parameter, the Exit procedure terminates the loop after the single iteration. You can omit the call to the Exit procedure, but the function will be slower because it will needlessly iterate 11 more times and give the same result.

Multidimensional Arrays

In Delphi, there are two ways of declaring multidimensional arrays:

```
ArrayName: array[Range_1, Range_2] of DataType;
ArrayName: array[Range_1] of array[Range_2] of DataType;
```

Just as one-dimensional arrays make it easier to work with large numbers of variables, multidimensional arrays help us when we have to work with a large number of one-dimensional arrays. For instance, we can use a very simple two-dimensional array to hold the multiplication table and then read appropriate values when we have to.

Listing 6-6: A simple two-dimensional array

```
program Project1;

{$APPTYPE CONSOLE}

uses
  SysUtils;

var
  MultTable: array[1..10, 1..10] of Integer;
  i, j: Integer;

begin
  for i := 1 to 10 do
  begin
    for j := 1 to 10 do
    begin
      MultTable[i, j] := i * j;
      Write(MultTable[i][j]:4);
    end;
    WriteLn;
  end;

  ReadLn;
end.
```

The example in Listing 6-6 illustrates both ways of accessing a value in a multidimensional array:

```
ArrayName[index_1, index_2]
ArrayName[index_1][index_2]
```

Dynamic Arrays

All variables and arrays that we have used so far were static variables and static arrays. They are called static because their size is known at compile time, they are allocated on the stack, and they are automatically created and destroyed.

Dynamic arrays are different from static arrays in many ways:

- Dynamic arrays are manually allocated during run time.
- The first index in a dynamic array is always 0.
- Dynamic arrays are allocated on the heap.

The heap is the main memory area that is only limited by the amount of virtual memory available on the computer. If you need to hold a lot of data in an array, you should use a dynamic array because the size of static arrays is limited by the size of the stack.

The syntax for declaring a dynamic array is:

```
ArrayName: array of DataType;
```

When you declare a dynamic array, it contains no elements and no memory is allocated. To allocate space for the dynamic array, you have to call the SetLength function. SetLength accepts two parameters. When working with dynamic arrays, the first parameter is the dynamic array and the second parameter is an integer value that specifies the new size of the array.

Listing 6-7: Creating a dynamic array

```
program Project1;

{$APPTYPE CONSOLE}

uses
  SysUtils;

var
  students: array of string;
  stNumber: Integer;
  cnt: Integer;

begin
  Write('Number of students: ');
  ReadLn(stNumber);
  SetLength(students, stNumber);

  { Get student names from the user }
  for cnt := Low(students) to High(students) do
  begin
    Write('Student: ');
    ReadLn(students[cnt]);
    if students[cnt] = 'end' then Break;
  end;

  ReadLn;
end.
```

To determine the size of the dynamic array, you can use the Length function, which accepts only one parameter — the dynamic array. The Length function returns the total number of elements in the dynamic array. The index of the last element is Length – 1, which is equal to High.

```
var
  DynArray: array of string;
  i: Integer;

begin
  for i := Low(DynArray) to High(DynArray) do ;
  for i := 0 to Length(DynArray) - 1 do ;
  ReadLn;
end.
```

Both for loops execute the same number of times so it's up to you to decide which syntax you like best. If you want to be consistent, you should use the

High and Low functions in loops like these and the Length function when you have to read the number of elements in the dynamic array. Note that both for loops are terminated with the semicolon. This means that the loops execute absolutely nothing. If your loop doesn't seem to function properly, make sure that you haven't added a semicolon after the reserved word do. Here is an illustration of this bug:

```
program Project1;

{$APPTYPE CONSOLE}

uses
  SysUtils;

var
  i: Integer;

begin
  for i := 1 to 2000 do ;
  begin
    WriteLn('This executes only once!');
  end;
  ReadLn;
end.
```

Delphi also allows you to create dynamic multidimensional arrays. The syntax for declaring a dynamic multidimensional array is:

```
ArrayName: array of array of DataType;
```

The following example shows how to represent a chess table using a dynamic multidimensional array. All the pieces on the table are set to their default positions.

Listing 6-8: Working with a dynamic multidimensional array

```
program Project1;

{$APPTYPE CONSOLE}

uses
  SysUtils;

var
  ChessTable: array of array of Integer;
  i: Integer;
  j: Integer;

const
  PAWN = 1;
  ROOK = 2;
  KNIGHT = 3;
  BISHOP = 4;
  QUEEN = 5;
  KING = 6;
```

```
begin
  { allocate 8 empty arrays }
  SetLength(ChessTable, 8);

  for i := Low(ChessTable) to High(ChessTable) do
  begin
    { define length of every array }
    SetLength(ChessTable[i], 8);

    for j := Low(ChessTable[i]) to High(ChessTable[i]) do
    begin
      { set first line pieces }
      if (i = 0) or (i = 7) then
        case j of
          0, 7: ChessTable[i, j] := ROOK;
          1, 6: ChessTable[i, j] := KNIGHT;
          2, 5: ChessTable[i, j] := BISHOP;
          3: ChessTable[i, j] := QUEEN;
          4: ChessTable[i, j] := KING;
        end;

      { set pawn line }
      if (i = 1) or (i = 6) then
        ChessTable[i, j] := PAWN;

    end;     // for j
  end;       // for i

Finalize(ChessTable);
end.
```

Delphi automatically manages dynamic arrays. The memory allocated for a dynamic array is automatically deallocated when you no longer use the array. You can also manually deallocate the array by passing it to the Finalize procedure. The Finalize procedure deallocates the memory allocated for the ChessTable array.

Array and Open Array Parameters

You can pass arrays as parameters in functions and procedures, but you cannot specify the range of an array parameter. The following example illustrates a procedure declaration that causes a compilation error.

```
procedure WriteStrings(Str: array[1..20] of string);
begin
end;
```

If you need to pass an array of 20 strings to a procedure, you have to create a new data type and then create a procedure that accepts the new data type as the parameter. To create a new data type, you have to use the reserved word type. The syntax for creating a new data type is:

```
type
  TNewDataType = ExistingType;
```

To create a new data type that represents an array of 20 strings, you have to write something like this:

```
program Project1;

{$APPTYPE CONSOLE}

uses
  SysUtils;

type
  TSmallArray = array[1..20] of string;

begin
end.
```

Now that you have a new data type that represents the array, you can successfully pass it as a parameter to a procedure or a function.

```
type
  TSmallArray = array[1..20] of string;

procedure WriteStrings(StrArray: TSmallArray);
var
  item: string;
begin
  for item in StrArray do
    WriteLn(item);
end;
```

There is a drawback to this solution: The WriteStrings procedure can only accept a TSmallArray variable and thus we're limited to an array of 20 strings. If you want to work with arrays of different sizes, you have to define an open array parameter.

The syntax of open array parameters is the same as the syntax for declaring a dynamic array:

```
procedure ProcedureName(ArrayName: array of DataType);
```

Open array parameters enable you to pass arrays of various sizes to the procedure or function. You can easily pass static and dynamic arrays and custom array types.

Listing 6-9: Open array parameters

```
program Project1;

{$APPTYPE CONSOLE}

uses
  SysUtils;

type
  TSmallArray = array[1..20] of string;

var
  SmallArray: TSmallArray;
```

```
DynamicArray: array of string;
StaticArray: array[1..100] of string;

procedure WriteStrings(StrArray: array of string);
var
  item: string;
begin
  for item in StrArray do
    WriteLn(item);
end;

begin
  WriteStrings(SmallArray);
  WriteStrings(DynamicArray);
  WriteStrings(StaticArray);
end.
```

Open array parameters allow you to create an array directly in the procedure or function call. This is also known as passing an open array constructor. An open array constructor is a sequence of values or expressions enclosed in brackets and separated by commas. The syntax of the open array constructor in a procedure call is:

```
procedure ProcedureName([expr_1, expr_2, expr_n]);
```

To create an array of strings inside the WriteStrings procedure call, you can write this:

```
WriteStrings(['Open', 'Array', 'Constructor']);
```

Open array parameters can be very useful when we have to create a utility function or a procedure that can work with a range of values. For instance, if we have to create a function that calculates the average of parameters, the version that can accept an array of values is much more useful than other versions that cannot.

Listing 6-10: Function with an open array parameter

```
program Project1;

{$APPTYPE CONSOLE}

uses
  SysUtils,
  Math;

function Average(num1, num2: Integer): Integer; overload; inline;
begin
  Result := (num1 + num2) div 2;
end;

{ open array functions can't be marked with inline }
function Average(nums: array of Integer): Integer; overload;
var
  n: Integer;
begin
  Result := 0;
```

```
  for n in nums do Inc(Result, n);
  Result := Result div Length(nums);
end;

begin
  WriteLn(Average(2, 4));
  WriteLn(Average([56, 21, 33, 44, 59]));
  ReadLn;
end.
```

Strings

The string data type is the most widely used data type in standard applications. When you have to work with string values, you can use one of the available string types or an array of characters. Delphi allows you to use the assignment operator to assign a string value to a character array.

```
var
  s: array[0..255] of Char;

begin
  s := 'Hello';
end.
```

Since a character array is statically allocated, the size of the array cannot be changed during run time and always uses 256 bytes of stack memory, regardless of how many characters the array actually holds.

Delphi still supports the old Pascal string type, but in Delphi, this string type is called a ShortString. A ShortString, just like a character array, is statically allocated and always uses 256 bytes of stack memory. A ShortString can hold a maximum of 255 characters. The first character, at index 0, contains the length of the string — the actual number of characters the ShortString holds.

The following example shows the length and memory size of a ShortString variable. To find out how many bytes a variable occupies, you can use the SizeOf function.

Listing 6-11: ShortString facts

```
program Project1;

{$APPTYPE CONSOLE}

uses
  SysUtils;

var
  s: ShortString;

begin
  s := 'Borland Delphi';
  WriteLn('ShortString Length = ', Length(s));  { 14 }
  WriteLn('S[0] Length = ', Ord(s[0]));  { 14 }
  WriteLn('ShortString Size = ', SizeOf(s));  { 256 }
```

```
    ReadLn;
end.
```

The ShortString type is superseded by the AnsiString type for many reasons. If we use a lot of short string values, they waste a lot of valuable space. On the other hand, working with a really long string is impossible because the ShortString type limits the length of the string to 255 characters.

To solve the problem of wasting space, Delphi enables us to explicitly define the maximum length of a string. The syntax for a string declaration with an explicitly defined length is:

```
VariableName: string[Length];
UserName: string[15];
```

To declare a string with explicit length, we used the reserved word `string` that is usually used to declare an AnsiString (long string) variable. When we explicitly define the string length, the resulting variable is a ShortString that occupies Length + 1 bytes. This additional byte is the first byte that contains the length of the string. In this case, UserName occupies 16 instead of 256 bytes of memory.

By default, the reserved word `string` represents the AnsiString data type that can hold up to 2 GB of characters. The meaning of the reserved word `string` can be changed with the $H or $LONGSTRINGS compiler directives. Because string is a much better data type than the ShortString, there is no need to change this behavior.

The main difference between ShortString and string data types is that strings are dynamically allocated on the heap. This means that their size can change during run time and that they don't occupy more space than they need to. Even though strings are dynamically allocated, we don't have to worry about the allocation/deallocation part of working with strings because Delphi does that automatically.

Another major advantage of the string data type is that it is reference counted. Each time you assign a ShortString to another ShortString, all 256 bytes are copied. Unlike the ShortString type, when you assign a string to another string, the string isn't copied. After you assign a string to another string, the destination string only points to the first character of the source string and the reference count of the source string increases by one. So, you only have a single copy of the string value in memory, but several variables use it. When you assign one string to another, no matter how large the string is, only 4 bytes of memory are copied. The following example shows two variables that use the same value.

```
var
  orig: string;
  clone: string;

begin
  orig := 'Borland';
  clone := orig;
end.
```

Delphi only makes an actual copy of the string when you change the contents of the string. When you change the contents of the string, the string becomes "standalone" and the reference count of the original string is decremented. When the reference count of a string reaches 0, Delphi automatically deallocates the memory occupied by the string.

```
var
  orig: string;
  clone: string;

begin
  orig := 'Borland';
  clone := orig;

  orig[Length(orig)] := 'D';
  WriteLn(orig); { BorlanD }
  WriteLn(clone); { Borland }

  ReadLn;
end.
```

String Handling

Delphi has a large number of utility procedures and functions that work with strings. This chapter only illustrates the most frequently used procedures and functions. They are:

- function Pos(Substr: string; S: string): Integer;
- function Copy(S; Index, Count: Integer): string;
- function Length(S): Integer;
- function IntToStr(Value: Integer): string; overload;
- function StrToInt(const S: string): Integer;
- procedure Delete(var S: string; Index, Count:Integer);
- procedure Insert(Source: string; var S: string; Index: Integer);
- procedure Val(S; var V; var Code: Integer);
- procedure Str(X [: Width [: Decimals]]; var S);

Searching

String searching can be implemented manually or with the Pos function. The Pos function returns 0 if the substring cannot be found in the string. The following example uses the Pos function to determine if a string contains more than one word.

Listing 6-12: Searching a string with the Pos function

```
program Project1;

{$APPTYPE CONSOLE}
```

```
uses
  SysUtils;

var
  s: string;
begin
  Write('Enter some text: ');
  ReadLn(s);

  if Pos(' ', s) <> 0 then
    WriteLn('You entered a couple of words.')
  else
    WriteLn('You entered only one word.');

  ReadLn;
end.
```

If you only need to search for a single character in a string, you can also implement your own Pos function. The following function returns the index of the character in the string if the character is found or 0 if the character doesn't exist.

Listing 6-13: Manual character searching

```
program Project1;

{$APPTYPE CONSOLE}

uses
  SysUtils;

function CharPos(ch: Char; const s: string): Integer;
var
  i: Integer;
begin
  Result := 0;
  if s <> '' then
  begin
    for i := 1 to Length(s) do
    begin
      if s[i] = ch then
      begin
        Result := i;
        Exit;
      end;     // if s[i]
    end;         // for i
  end;           // if s
end;

var
  testStr: string;
  iPos: Integer;

begin
  testStr := 'BorlaNd Delphi';
  iPos := CharPos('N', testStr);
```

```
  if iPos <> 0 then
    testStr[iPos] := 'n';

  WriteLn(testStr); { Borland Delphi }
  ReadLn;
end.
```

Inserting

The Insert procedure accepts three parameters. The first parameter is the string value that is to be inserted into another string, the second parameter is the destination string, and the last parameter is the index at which the string is to be inserted.

The following example uses the Insert procedure to properly format a string that contains a poorly formatted uses list. The string contains a comma-delimited list of Delphi units, but there are no spaces between the commas and the unit names. The Insert procedure is used to insert spaces after each comma in the string.

Listing 6-14: Using the Insert procedure

```
program Project1;

{$APPTYPE CONSOLE}

uses
  SysUtils;

var
  Units: string;
  i: Integer;

begin
  Units := 'Windows,SysUtils,Forms,StdCtrls,Controls,Classes;';

  i := 0;
  repeat
    Inc(i);
    if Units[i] = ',' then
    begin
      Insert(' ', Units, i + 1);
      Inc(i);
    end;      // if Units[i]
  until i = Length(Units);

  WriteLn(Units);
  ReadLn;
end.
```

We can't use the for loop here because we change the length of the string inside the loop. If you use the for loop, all spaces will be added before or after the first comma. This happens because the for loop only reads the string length at the beginning of the loop. Since both repeat-until and while loops always reevaluate the condition, you can try to write a while loop version of this example.

Deleting

The Delete procedure enables you to delete a certain number of characters from a string. The Delete procedure accepts three parameters: a variable string parameter that is modified, the index where deletion should start, and the number of characters to be deleted.

The following example uses the Delete procedure to remove all spaces from a string. The RemoveSpaces procedure calls the Delete procedure as long as there are spaces in the source string. The parameter must be a variable parameter because that is the only parameter type that allows you to make changes to the original variable.

Listing 6-15: Using the Delete procedure

```
program Project1;

{$APPTYPE CONSOLE}

uses
  SysUtils;

procedure RemoveSpaces(var s: string);
var
  spacePos: Integer;
begin
  spacePos := Pos(' ', s);
  while spacePos <> 0 do
  begin
    Delete(s, spacePos, 1);
    spacePos := Pos(' ', s);
  end;
end;

var
  testStr: string;

begin
  testStr := '  D  el  p  h  i  ';
  RemoveSpaces(testStr);

  WriteLn(testStr); { Delphi }
  ReadLn;
end.
```

Copying

The Copy function accepts three parameters. The first parameter is the source string, the second parameter is the index where the copying starts, and the last parameter defines how many characters are copied.

The following example shows how to use the Copy function to extract the drive and directory portions of a file name.

Listing 6-16: Using the Copy function

```
program Project1;

{$APPTYPE CONSOLE}

uses
  SysUtils;

function GetFilePath(const AFileName: string): string;
var
  i: Integer;
begin
  i := Length(AFileName);

  while i > 0 do
  begin
    if AFileName[i] = '\' then Break;
    Dec(i);
  end;      // while

  if i > 1 then
    Result := Copy(AFileName, 1, i)
  else
    Result := '';
end;

var
  testStr: string;

begin
  testStr := 'c:\windows\system32\kernel32.dll';
  WriteLn(GetFilePath(testStr)); { c:\windows\system32\ }
  ReadLn;
end.
```

This version of the GetFilePath function only works on the Windows operating system because we only search for a backslash. This function doesn't work on Linux because Linux uses slashes to separate directories.

If you know for sure that a function or procedure is specific to a platform and you want to be completely professional, you should mark that procedure or function with the platform directive:

```
function GetFilePath(const AFileName: string): string; platform;
```

When you mark a procedure or a function with the platform directive, you will always receive a compiler warning that the specified function or procedure is specific to a platform.

In this case, it's really easy to make the function platform independent. The SysUtils unit contains a global constant that holds the proper delimiter for each platform:

```
const
  PathDelim = {$IFDEF MSWINDOWS} '\'; {$ELSE} '/'; {$ENDIF}
```

All we need to do to make the GetFilePath function platform independent is to change the if-then statement in the loop:

```
while i > 0 do
begin
  if AFileName[i] = PathDelim then Break;
  Dec(i);
end;      // while
```

Converting

Probably the most frequent of all conversions is the conversion between the string and integer data types. The common way to do these conversions is to use the IntToStr and StrToInt functions declared in the SysUtils unit. These functions are easy to use and really fast.

```
var
  sValue: string;
  iValue: Integer;

begin
  sValue := IntToStr(2005);
  iValue := StrToInt('-24');
end.
```

If you're trying to create a really small application, you'll probably remove the SysUtils unit from the uses list. In this case, you can use the Str and Val procedures that are declared in the System unit.

```
var
  sValue: string;
  iValue: Integer;

begin
  iValue := 42;
  Str(iValue, sValue); { sValue = '42' }
end.
```

The Val procedure accepts three parameters: the string value that needs to be converted to an integer, the destination integer variable, and the error code parameter. If the Val procedure fails to convert the string to an integer, the variable passed as the last parameter will hold the index of the character that cannot be converted.

```
var
  sValue: string;
  iValue: Integer;
  code: Integer;

begin
  sValue := '-250';
  Val(sValue, iValue, code);

  if code <> 0 then
```

```
  begin
    WriteLn('Character ', code, ' is invalid.');
    ReadLn;
  end;
end.
```

Arrays in C++

Array declaration in C++ is completely different from array declaration in Delphi. In Delphi, you specify the index of the first and the last elements in the array, which defines the number of elements in the array. In C++, you specify the number of elements in the array, and get the index of the first and last element from this number. The index of the first element in a C++ array is always 0, and the index of the last element is always declared_number_ of_elements –1.

Here's how to declare an array in C++:

```
data_type array_name[number_of_elements];
```

The following example shows how to declare and use an array of 10 integers.

Listing 6-17: C++ arrays

```
#include <iostream.h>
#include <conio.h>
#pragma hdrstop

#pragma argsused
int main(int argc, char* argv[])
{
    int arr[10];
    int i;

    for(i=0; i<10; i++)
    {
        arr[i] = (i + 1) * 10;
        cout << arr[i] << endl;
    }

    getch();
    return 0;
}
```

Initializing Arrays

In Delphi, you can initialize global arrays by using the standard array declaration syntax followed by an assignment operator and a comma-delimited list of values enclosed in parentheses (the number of values inside the parentheses must match the number of elements in the array):

```
var
  InitArray: array[1..5] of Integer = (10, 20, 30, 40, 50);
```

To initialize an array in C++, you have to do almost the same thing as in Delphi with one difference: The comma-delimited list of values must be surrounded by curly braces:

```
int initialized_array[3] = {1, 2, 3};
```

In C++, you don't have to explicitly define the number of elements in the array if you're initializing it. In this case, the initialization part of the array declaration defines the number of elements in the array:

```
data_type array_name[] = {value_1, value_2, value_n};
```

For instance, the following example shows how you can declare and initialize an array with six elements:

```
int initialized_array[] = {10, 20, 30, 40, 50, 60};
```

When you declare an array without explicitly defining the number of elements, you might need to know how many elements there are. To do so, you'll need to use the sizeof operator. When you pass an array to the sizeof operator, it will return the number of bytes occupied by the entire array. So, to get the number of elements in the array, divide the size of the entire array by the size of its first element. The following example shows how to use the sizeof operator to determine the number of elements in the array.

Listing 6-18: Using the sizeof operator to determine the number of elements in an array

```
#include <iostream.h>
#include <conio.h>
#pragma hdrstop

#pragma argsused
int main(int argc, char* argv[])
{
   int initialized_array[] = {10, 20, 30, 40, 50, 60};

   // display the size of the array
   cout << "The array occupies " << sizeof(initialized_array)
      << " bytes." << endl;

   // display the size of each element
   cout << "Each element occupies " << sizeof(initialized_array[0])
      << " bytes." << endl;

   // display the number of elements
   cout << "Number of elements in the array: "
      << sizeof(initialized_array) / sizeof(initialized_array[0])
      << endl;

   getch();
   return 0;
}
```

Delphi is much stricter when it comes to array initialization because you have to specify the number of elements and initialize all array elements. In C++, if

you explicitly specify the number of elements in the array, you can initialize all
of them or just as many as you need. For instance, the following example
shows how to declare an array of 10 integers and initialize only the first three.
When you initialize only some of the elements in an array, those that aren't
initialized are set to 0 by the compiler (see Figure 6-1).

Listing 6-19: Initializing only some of the elements in an array

```
#include <iostream.h>
#include <conio.h>
#pragma hdrstop

#pragma argsused
int main(int argc, char* argv[])
{
    int semi_init[10] = {1, 2, 3};
    for(int i=0; i<10; i++)
        cout << "semi_init[" << i << "] = " << semi_init[i] << endl;

    getch();
    return 0;
}
```

Figure 6-1: Initializing arrays in C++

Multidimensional Arrays

To declare a multidimensional array in C++, you have to write this:

```
data_type array_name[n1][n2];
```

The first number is the number of one-dimensional arrays and the second
number is the number of elements in each one-dimensional array:

```
// ten arrays with 5 elements each
int multi_array[10][5];
// find out the number of elements in each array
cout << sizeof(multi_array[0]) / sizeof(multi_array[0][0]) << endl;
```

The following example shows how to build a multiplication table and store it
into a two-dimensional array. Listing 6-6 shows the Delphi implementation of
this example.

Listing 6-20: Using a two-dimensional array in C++

```
#include <iostream.h>
#include <conio.h>
```

```
#pragma hdrstop

#pragma argsused
int main(int argc, char* argv[])
{
    int mult_table[10][10];

    for(int i=0; i<10; i++)
    {
        for(int j=0; j<10; j++)
        {
            mult_table[i][j] = (i+1) * (j+1);
            cout.width(4);
            cout << mult_table[i][j];
        }
        cout << endl;
    }

    getch();
    return 0;
}
```

In the Delphi example, the Write(data:width) syntax was used to specify the width of each item displayed on screen. To specify the width of an item in C++, you have to write cout.width(width).

Both Write(data:4) and cout.width(4) result in columns that are four characters wide. Figure 6-2 shows both the Delphi (left) and the C++ (right) multiplication table examples.

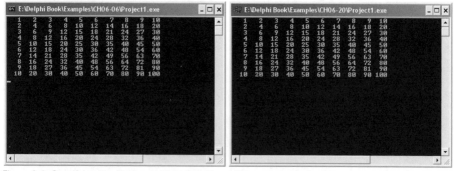

Figure 6-2: Specifying the display width in Delphi and C++ console applications

Initializing Multidimensional Arrays

In Delphi, you can initialize global multidimensional arrays or declare multidimensional constant arrays using the following syntax:

```
ArrayName: array[index_1, index_2] of DataType = (
    (1st_array_val_1, 1st_array_val_2, 1st_array_val_n),
    (2nd_array_val_1, 2nd_array_val_2, 2nd_array_val_n)
    // etc..
);
```

The example in Listing 6-21 shows how to initialize a global multidimensional array in Delphi and display its values on screen.

Listing 6-21: Initializing a multidimensional array in Delphi

```
program Project1;

{$APPTYPE CONSOLE}

uses
  SysUtils;

var
  i, j: Integer;
  MultiInit: array[1..4, 1..3] of Integer = (
    (-10, -20, -30),
    (-1, -2, -3),
    (1, 2, 3),
    (10, 20, 30)
  );

begin
  for i := Low(MultiInit) to High(MultiInit) do
  begin
    for j := Low(MultiInit[1]) to High(MultiInit[1]) do
    begin
      WriteLn('Array[', i, '][', j, ']', ' = ', MultiInit[i,j]);
    end;
    WriteLn;
  end;

  ReadLn;
end.
```

In C++, you can initialize a multidimensional array like you would a one-dimensional array and you can initialize it as you would initialize it in Delphi, with each array's values in separate parentheses (in C++, parentheses are replaced with curly braces).

The following listing shows both ways of initializing multidimensional arrays. Figure 6-3 shows what Delphi and C++ initialized multidimensional arrays look like.

Listing 6-22: Initializing multidimensional arrays in C++

```
#include <iostream.h>
#include <conio.h>
#pragma hdrstop

#pragma argsused
int main(int argc, char* argv[])
{
  // initialize it as you would a one-dimensional array
  // int array1[4][3] = {-10, -20, -30, -1, -2, -3, 1, 2, 3, 10, 20, 30};

  // multidimensional array initialization, more readable
  int array2[4][3] = {
```

```
    {-10, -20, -30},
    {-1, -2, -3},
    {1, 2, 3},
    {10, 20, 30}
};

for(int i=0; i<4; i++)
{
    for(int j=0; j<3; j++)
    {
        cout << "array[" << i << "][" << j << "] = "
            << array2[i][j] << endl;
    }
    cout << endl;
}

getch();
return 0;
}
```

Figure 6-3: Initialized multidimensional arrays

C++ Strings

The C++ language, unlike Delphi, doesn't have a native string type. The closest thing the C++ language has to a string is an array of characters:

```
char array_name[number_of_chars];
```

Even though the C++ language doesn't have a proper string data type, C++Builder has the AnsiString data type, which is equivalent to the Delphi string data type.

In this chapter, and other chapters that deal with the C++ language, we're going to use character arrays. Starting with Chapter 11, which is the first chapter that covers VCL Forms programming for the Win32 platform, we're mainly going to use the string data type in Delphi (as always) and the AnsiString type in C++Builder applications.

Initializing Strings

In C++, you can initialize a character array as you would other arrays, or you can initialize a character array by passing a string literal to it. Here are three different initializations:

```
char str[] = "A simple C++ string.";
char str2[] = {'a', 'b', 'c', 'd'};
char str3[] = {'1', '2', '3', '\0'};
char str4[5];
```

The first way of initializing character arrays is the best way since it involves the least typing and because the compiler implicitly adds the null character at the end of the string. The null character (\0) is absolutely necessary since strings in C++, like the string data type in Delphi, are null-terminated.

The second array is initialized improperly. Although the code compiles perfectly, it will produce errors at run time (see Figure 6-4) since there's no null character at the end of the array.

The str3 array shows how to properly initialize a character array if you really want to initialize it char by char, and the last array illustrates how to explicitly define the length of the character array. Note that the str4 array can only accept four characters. The last element must be reserved for the null character.

The following listing contains code that displays the above character arrays on screen. Notice what happens when you use a character array without a null character at its end.

Listing 6-23: Using character arrays

```
#include <iostream.h>
#include <conio.h>
#include <string.h>
#pragma hdrstop

#pragma argsused
int main(int argc, char* argv[])
{
    char str[] = "A simple C++ string.";
    char str2[] = {'a', 'b', 'c', 'd'};
    char str3[] = {'1', '2', '3', '\0'};
    char str4[5];

    cout << "str[] = " << str << endl
        << "str2[] = " << str2 << "  --> Bug!" << endl
        << "str3[] = " << str3 << endl;

    getch();
    return 0;
}
```

Figure 6-4: Using character arrays

Assigning Values to Strings

To assign a value to a character array, you cannot use the assignment operator. Instead, you have to use the strcpy function declared in the string.h header file. The strcpy function accepts two character array parameters. The first one is the destination array and the second is, obviously, the source character array.

Here's how to assign a value to a character array (string) in C++:

```
char name[15];
strcpy(name, "Santa Claus");
```

If you want to, you can also assign a value to a character array like this:

```
name[0] = 'S';
name[1] = 'a';
name[2] = 'n';
name[3] = 't';
name[4] = 'a';
name[5] = '\0';
cout << name << endl;
```

String Related Functions

Commonly used string manipulation functions are declared in two header files: string.h and stdlib.h. The string.h header file contains manipulation functions, and the stlib.h header file contains functions for converting strings to integers and back.

Table 6-1: Common string manipulation functions

C++ Function	Delphi Equivalent	Header File	Description
strcpy(dest, src)	=, Copy	string.h	Copies src to dest
strcat(dest, src)	+, Concat	string.h	Adds src to the end of dest
strlen(string)	Length	string.h	Gets length of string
strcmp(str1, str2)	=, <>	string.h	Compares two strings
strchr(string, char)	Pos	string.h	Finds char in string
strstr(string, substring)	Pos	string.h	Finds substring in string
int atoi(string)	StrToInt	stdlib.h	Converts string to integer
itoa(int, char[], int)	IntToStr	stdlib.h	Converts integer to string

Listing 6-24 illustrates how to use the common functions listed in Table 6-1.

Listing 6-24: Using common string functions

```
#include <iostream.h>
#include <conio.h>
#include <string.h>
#include <stdlib.h>
#pragma hdrstop

#pragma argsused
int main(int argc, char* argv[])
{
   char test[15] = "ab";
   char name[15];
   strcpy(name, "Santa Claus");

   /* comparing and copying */
   if(strcmp(name, test) == 0)
      cout << "Strings are the same." << endl;
   else {
      cout << "Strings are different." << endl;
      strcpy(test, name);
      if(strcmp(name, test) == 0)
         cout << "Now they're the same." << endl;
   }

   /* finding a substring */
   if(strstr(name, "Santa") != 0) {
      cout << "I found Santa!" << endl;
   }

   /* get length, concatenate, */
   char empty[20] = {'\0'};
   if(strlen(empty) == 0) {
      strcat(empty, "abc");
      strcat(empty, "def");
      cout << empty << endl;
   }

   /* convert string to int */
   char s[] = "101";
   int x = atoi(s);
   cout << "x = " << x << endl;

   /* convert int to string, itoa(int, dest_array, radix)
*/
   int y = 2005;
   char dest[5];
   itoa(y, dest, 10); // 10 for decimal
   cout << "y = " << dest << endl;

   getch();
   return 0;
}
```

Chapter 7

User-Defined Types

Custom data types are used very often in programming because they are more descriptive than standard data types and because their usage results in cleaner code. This is especially true for records. But before we learn how to create and use records, we have to understand how to create and use enumerated types, subrange types, and sets.

Enumerated Types

An enumerated type is an ordered list of identifiers and is a good replacement for a collection of constants. For instance, the following constants can be replaced with an enumeration:

```
const
  PAWN = 1;
  ROOK = 2;
  KNIGHT = 3;
  BISHOP = 4;
  QUEEN = 5;
  KING = 6;
```

The syntax for declaring an enumerated type is:

```
type
  TEnumeratedType = (value_1, value_2, value_n);
  TChessFigure = (cfPawn, cfRook, cfKnight,
    cfBishop, cfQueen, cfKing);
```

By using a TChessFigure variable instead of an integer, the code is easier to read and it enables Delphi to perform type checking. Each identifier in the enumeration gets an ordinal value. The ordinal values in the enumeration start at zero. So, Ord(cfPawn) = 0.

All ordinal procedures and functions can work with enumerated types.

You can also explicitly define the ordinal value of an enumeration element:

```
type
  TOddNumber = (oddFirst = 1, oddSecond = 3,
    oddThird = 5, oddFourth = 7);
```

```
TEvenNumber = (evFirst = 0, evSecond = 2,
   evThird = 4, evFourth = 6);

var
  OddNum: TOddNumber;

begin
  OddNum := oddThird;
  WriteLn(Ord(OddNum));  { 5 }
  ReadLn;
end.
```

Subrange Types

A subrange type represents a part of the base type (any ordinal type). To declare a subrange type, you use the same range syntax as in an array declaration:

```
type
  { enumerated type }
  TDay = (Monday, Tuesday, Wednesday,
     Thursday, Friday, Saturday, Sunday);

  { subrange types }
  TWeekend = Saturday..Sunday;
  TPercent = 0..100;
  TAlphabet = 'a'..'z';
```

Sets

Sets are collections of ordinal values that can have a maximum of 256 elements. To declare a set, you need to create an enumerated type first. Then use the following syntax to declare a set:

```
TNewSet = set of EnumeratedType;
```

Sets are really lightweight and give us the ability to work with a collection of values. A set variable occupies a single byte of memory. The following code shows how to declare a new set based on the TDay enumeration and how to assign an empty set to the ThisWeek set variable:

```
type
  { enumerated type }
  TDay = (Monday, Tuesday, Wednesday,
     Thursday, Friday, Saturday, Sunday);

  { set }
  TDays = set of TDay;

var
  ThisWeek: TDays;

begin
```

```
  ThisWeek := []; // the set contains no values
end.
```

Working with Sets

The assignment operator allows you to assign one or several values to a set in one statement. To assign values to a set, you have to enclose them in brackets. If you're assigning multiple values to the set, the values inside the brackets must be separated with commas:

```
ThisWeek := [Monday];
ThisWeek := [Monday, Tuesday, Friday];
```

The + and – operators can be used to add or remove values from a set:

```
ThisWeek := ThisWeek - [Friday];
ThisWeek := ThisWeek + [Saturday, Sunday];
```

These operators are usually used to add or remove elements from the set. However, if possible, you should use the Exclude and Include procedures instead because the procedures work faster than the operators:

```
Exclude(ThisWeek, Friday);
Include(ThisWeek, Saturday);
Include(ThisWeek, Sunday);
```

The difference between the operators and the Exclude and Include procedures is that operators can work with multiple values ([Saturday, Sunday]), while procedures only accept one value at a time.

Set Membership

The reserved word in can be used to determine if a specified value exists in the set. For instance, to find out if the ThisWeek set contains Wednesday, you can write this:

```
if Wednesday in ThisWeek then
  WriteLn('Have to work on Wednesday.');
```

You can browse through a set using any of the available loops, even the for-in loop, which also requires the least amount of typing and results in the most readable code.

Listing 7-1: Working with sets

```
program Project1;

{$APPTYPE CONSOLE}

uses
  SysUtils;

type
  TDay = (Monday, Tuesday, Wednesday,
    Thursday, Friday, Saturday, Sunday);
  TDays = set of TDay;
```

```
var
  ThisWeek: TDays;
  Day: TDay;

const
  DAY_TEXT: array[TDay] of string = ('Monday', 'Tuesday',
    'Wednesday', 'Thursday', 'Friday', 'Saturday', 'Sunday');

begin
  ThisWeek := [Monday, Tuesday, Friday];

  for Day in ThisWeek do
    WriteLn('I have to work on ', DAY_TEXT[Day], '.');

  { If you need to use a compiler older than Delphi 2005. }
  for Day := Monday to Sunday do
    if Day in ThisWeek then
      WriteLn('I have to work on ', DAY_TEXT[Day], '.');

  ReadLn;
end.
```

Records

A record is a structured data type that consists of a number of elements. Unlike an array, which is merely a group of variables that share the same name and the same data type, a record is a data type that contains elements (fields) of different types. To create a new record, you have to use the reserved word record and declare the fields inside the record block. Field declarations are actually standard variable declarations.

The syntax of a record type declaration is:

```
type
  RecordName = record
    Field_1: DataType;
    Field_2: DataType;
    Field_n: DataType;
  end;
```

After you create a new record type, you can use it after you declare a variable of the same type:

```
type
  TBook = record
    ISBN: string;
    Title: string;
    PageCount: Integer;
    Authors: array[1..4] of string;
  end;

var
  Book: TBook;
```

To access fields in a record, you have to use the dot syntax:

```
Record.Field
```

To fill the Book record with data, you can write something like this:

```
Book.Title := 'Bring Me the Head of Prince Charming';
Book.Authors[1] := 'Roger Zelazny';
Book.Authors[2] := 'Robert Sheckley';
Book.PageCount := 280;
```

Reserved Word with

Normally, you always have to write the record name before you can access its fields. But, if you use the reserved word with, you only have to write the record name once. The reserved word with is used to define a block where you can directly access the fields of the specified record.

The syntax of the with block is:

```
with Record do
begin
  Field_1 := Value;
  Field_2 := Value;
  Field_n := Value;
end;
```

The with block enables you to write less code, especially when the record has a large number of fields or when the record name is really long.

```
with Book do
begin
  Title := 'Bring Me the Head of Prince Charming';
  Authors[1] := 'Roger Zelazny';
  Authors[2] := 'Robert Sheckley';
  PageCount := 280;
end;
```

The following example illustrates how to define record fields in another record and how to use record arrays.

Listing 7-2: Using records

```
program Project1;

{$APPTYPE CONSOLE}

uses
  SysUtils;

type
  TSex = (sxMale, sxFemale);

  TAuthor = record
    FirstName: string;
    MiddleName: string;
    LastName: string;
    Age: Integer;
    Sex: TSex;
```

```
  end;

  TBook = record
    ISBN: string;
    Title: string;
    PageCount: Integer;
    Authors: array[1..4] of TAuthor;
  end;

var
  TownLibrary: array[1..100] of TBook;

begin
  with TownLibrary[1] do
  begin
    Title := 'Starship Troopers';
    with Authors[1] do
    begin
      FirstName := 'Robert';
      MiddleName := 'A.';
      LastName := 'Heinlein';
      Sex := sxMale;
    end;        // with first or only author
  end;          // with first book
end.
```

Passing Records to Procedures

When you create procedures and functions that accept a record as a parameter, that parameter should be declared as a variable parameter or a constant parameter. If you have to change fields in the record, use a variable parameter. If you only have to read field values, use a constant parameter.

If you use a standard value parameter, the procedure has to make a copy of the entire record every time you call it. In this case, if you pass a value parameter, the procedure has to copy 92 bytes (SizeOf(TBook)). For a constant or variable parameter, the procedure call only has to pass the address of the variable, which is only 4 bytes in size.

```
procedure DisplayBook(const ABook: TBook);
begin
  WriteLn(ABook.Title);
  Write(ABook.Authors[1].FirstName, ' ',
    ABook.Authors[1].LastName);
end;

var
  TownLibrary: array[1..100] of TBook;
  i: Integer;

begin
  for i := Low(TownLibrary) to High(TownLibrary) do
    DisplayBook(TownLibrary[i]);
```

```
    ReadLn;
end.
```

As you might have noticed, the names of all custom types start with the capital letter T. This is merely a convention, but since it is so widely and consistently used, you should follow it as if it were a rule.

User-Defined Types in C++

In C++ and in Delphi, you can create either a new data type or an alias for an existing data type. To create an alias in Delphi, you have to use the reserved word type like this:

```
type
    TMyString = string;
```

To create an alias in C++, you need to use the reserved word typedef:

```
typedef existing_type_name new_type_name;
```

For instance, the following listing shows how to create integer and ShortString types in C++.

Listing 7-3: Using typedef to create data type aliases

```
#include <iostream.h>
#include <conio.h>
#pragma hdrstop

typedef long Integer;
typedef char ShortString[256];

#pragma argsused
int main(int argc, char* argv[])
{
    ShortString s;
    cout << "User name: ";
    cin >> s;
    cout << "Hello, " << s << endl;

    getch();
    return 0;
}
```

Enumerations

To create an enumerated type in C++, you have to use the reserved word enum:

```
enum enumerated_type_name {value_1, value_2, value_n};
enum figure {pawn, rook, knight, bishop, queen, king};
```

By default, in both Delphi and C++, the value of the enumeration's first element is 0. To change the value of an element and others that follow it, use the following syntax:

```
enum enumeration_name {element_1 = value_1, element_n = value_n};
```

For instance, in the following enumeration, the value of pawn is 1, the value of rook is 2, and the value of the king element is 11:

```
enum figure {pawn = 1, rook, knight, bishop, queen = 10, king};
```

Structures

Structures are the C++ equivalent of Delphi's records. To declare a new structure, you need to use the reserved word struct followed by a block that contains a list of fields. The structure's block must be terminated with a semicolon:

```
struct name_of_the_structure {
    field_1;
    field_n;
};
```

The following listing shows how to declare a TBook structure that contains both simple fields and a string array field. It also shows how to declare a variable of type TBook and how to access structure members (the same way record fields are accessed in Delphi).

Listing 7-4: Using structures

```
#include <iostream.h>
#include <conio.h>
#include <string.h>
#pragma hdrstop

struct TBook {
    char Title[50];
    int PageCount;
    char Authors[4][40]; // array of four 40-character strings
};

#pragma argsused
int main(int argc, char* argv[])
{
    TBook book;

    strcpy(book.Title, "Delphi Language Guide");
    strcpy(book.Authors[0], "Borland");
    book.PageCount = 249;

    return 0;
}
```

Since C++ is less strict than Delphi, it allows you to declare structure variables when you declare the structure itself. To declare structure variables at the same time you declare the structure, use the following syntax:

```
struct name_of_the_structure {
    field_1;
    field_n;
} variable_1, variable_n;
```

```
struct TBook {
   char Title[50];
   int PageCount;
   char Authors[4][40];
} lang_guide, user_guide, reference; // declare 3 variables
```

Passing Structures to Functions

If you want to pass a structure to a function, declare the parameter as a reference parameter to avoid copying the entire record when you call the function:

```
void ShowBook(TBook& b)
{
}
```

Dynamic Structures

The new and delete operators can also be used to dynamically create and delete structures. When we dynamically create a structure, we can no longer use the dot syntax to access its fields. To access the fields of a dynamically created structure, you have to write this:

```
TBook *book = new TBook;
 (*book).PageCount = 100;
delete book;
```

Although you can use the (*dynamic_structure).field syntax to access fields in a dynamically created structure, there's a more popular operator (especially in OOP) that can be used in this situation, the -> operator (indirect member selector):

```
TBook *book = new TBook;
book->PageCount = 100;
delete book;
```

Chapter 8

Basic File I/O

Every programmer must know how to work with files. This chapter shows how to work with text files, files that contain records, and files that have no structure or are treated as if they have no structure. Text files are covered first since they are the most common file type.

Working with Text Files

To gain access to a text file you have to use a Text type variable:

```
var
  myFile: Text;
```

Before you can start working with a file, you have to assign it to the Text variable using the AssignFile procedure. The AssignFile procedure accepts two parameters: the file variable and the file name.

```
procedure AssignFile(var F; FileName: string);
AssignFile(myFile, 'c:\data.txt');
```

After you assign a file name to the file variable, you have to determine what you want to do with the file. You can prepare the file for reading, writing, or appending.

Writing to a Text File

To prepare a file for writing, you have to use the Rewrite procedure, which always creates a new empty file. If a file with the same file name already exists, the Rewrite procedure first deletes the existing file and then replaces it with the new, empty file. The Rewrite procedure then opens the file and sets the file position to the beginning.

When working with text files, you only have to pass the Text variable to the Rewrite procedure:

```
procedure Rewrite(var F: File [; Recsize: Word ]);
Rewrite(myFile);
```

When the file is opened and ready for writing, you can use the standard WriteLn procedure to write text to the text file. When writing to a text file, the first parameter passed to the WriteLn procedure has to be the file variable:

```
procedure WriteLn([ var F: Text; ] P1 [, P2, ...,Pn ]);
WriteLn(myFile, 'cave canem');
```

Once you're finished with the file, you should always close it to ensure that the file is properly written to the disk and that any memory used in the process is released. To close the file, use the CloseFile procedure, which accepts only one parameter — the file that needs to be closed:

```
procedure CloseFile(var F);
CloseFile(myFile);
```

The entire program for writing a line of text to a text file is shown in Listing 8-1.

Listing 8-1: Writing text to a text file

```
program Project1;

{$APPTYPE CONSOLE}

uses
  SysUtils;

var
  myFile: Text;

begin
  AssignFile(myFile, 'c:\data.txt');
  Rewrite(myFile);
  WriteLn(myFile, 'cave canem');
  CloseFile(myFile);
end.
```

Reading from a Text File

To prepare the file for reading, you have to use the Reset procedure. The Reset procedure, like the Rewrite procedure, only accepts the file parameter. The Rewrite procedure can be considered safe in the sense that everything works fine as long as the drive and/or directory specified in the file name exists. Unlike the Rewrite procedure, the Reset procedure will fail if the file assigned to the file variable doesn't exist.

To read data from a text file, you can use the ReadLn procedure. The first parameter is the file variable and the second parameter is a string variable that will temporarily hold the value read from the file. The following example shows how to read values from a text file and display them on the screen.

Listing 8-2: Reading text from a text file

```
program Project1;

{$APPTYPE CONSOLE}

uses
  SysUtils;

var
  myFile: Text;
  line: string;

begin
  AssignFile(myFile, 'c:\data.txt');
  Reset(myFile);

  ReadLn(myFile, line);
  WriteLn(line);

  CloseFile(myFile);
  ReadLn;
end.
```

This code will work properly as long as the data.txt file exists. If the data.txt file doesn't exist, the program will crash. To ensure that the application doesn't crash when the file doesn't exist, you have to check whether the Reset procedure successfully opened the file.

I/O Errors

To see if an I/O error occurred, you have to call the IOResult function immediately after a call to an I/O procedure like Rewrite or Reset. The IOResult function returns the result of the last I/O operation. If IOResult returns 0, it means that everything went fine.

To check for I/O errors using the IOResult function, you need to disable the automatic I/O error checking first. I/O error checking is enabled and disabled with the $I compiler directive. Usually, automatic I/O checking is disabled before the call to an I/O procedure and automatically re-enabled immediately after that call:

```
{$I-}
I/O procedure call
{$I+}
```

The following example illustrates how to check for I/O errors and read text from the file only if the file was successfully opened.

Listing 8-3: Checking I/O errors

```
program Project1;

{$APPTYPE CONSOLE}

uses
  SysUtils;

var
  myFile: Text;
  line: string;
  fileName: string;

begin
  fileName := 'c:\data.txt';
  AssignFile(myFile, fileName);
  {$I-}
  Reset(myFile);
  {$I+}
  if IOResult = 0 then
  begin
    ReadLn(myFile, line);
    WriteLn(line);

    CloseFile(myFile);
  end else
    WriteLn('Cannot open file: ', fileName);

  ReadLn;
end.
```

Remember that you can call the IOResult function only once after a call to an I/O procedure. This is because the IOResult function resets the result of the last I/O operation to 0. So, if you call the IOResult function twice, the first IOResult call correctly reports an error, but the following call tells you (incorrectly) that everything is okay.

Working with the Entire File

When you want to read an entire text file, you have to read it sequentially until you reach the end of the file. To see if you have reached the end of the file, use the Eof function. The Eof function accepts a single file parameter and returns a Boolean value that tells you if you've reached the end of the file or not:

```
function Eof [ (var F: Text) ]: Boolean;
```

Typically, the best way to read a text file is to use a while loop that continues iterating until the end of file is reached. The following example illustrates how to copy the contents of one text file to another using the while not Eof loop (see Figure 8-1).

Listing 8-4: Copying a text file

```pascal
program Project1;

{$APPTYPE CONSOLE}

uses
  SysUtils;

var
  srcFile: Text;
  destFile: Text;
  line: string;

begin
  { try to open the source file }
  AssignFile(srcFile, 'c:\data.txt');
  {$I-}
  Reset(srcFile);
  {$I+}
  if IOResult = 0 then
  begin
    { try to open the destination file }
    AssignFile(destFile, 'c:\copy.txt');
    {$I-}
    Rewrite(destFile);
    {$I+}
    if IOResult = 0 then
    begin
      { while loop that copies text from source to dest }
      while not Eof(srcFile) do
      begin
        ReadLn(srcFile, line);
        WriteLn(destFile, line);

        WriteLn('Copying: ', line);
      end;    // while not Eof

      CloseFile(destFile);
      WriteLn;
      WriteLn('File successfully copied.');
    end;        // if destFile is OK

    CloseFile(srcFile);
  end;          // if srcFile is OK
  ReadLn;
end.
```

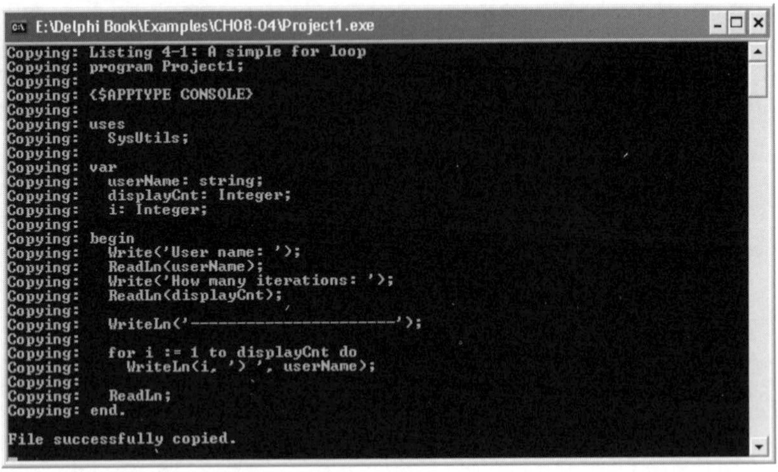

Figure 8-1: Copying a text file

Loading the Text File into a Dynamic Array

If you need to read the entire text file into memory, the easiest way to do so is to read the file into a dynamic array of strings. To do that, you need to know how many lines of text are in the file. Since there are no functions available to do the job for us, we have to create one. To calculate the number of lines in a text file, use the while not Eof loop to count how many lines are in the file and then call Reset to return the position to the beginning of the file.

The following example uses the while not Eof loop in the GetLineCount function to read the number of lines in the text file. The result is then used in the call to the SetLength function to resize the dynamic array.

Listing 8-5: Loading a text file into a dynamic array

```
program Project1;

{$APPTYPE CONSOLE}

uses
  SysUtils;

var
  myFile: Text;
  lines: array of string;
  cnt: Integer;
  fileName: string;

function GetLineCount(var ATextFile: Text): Integer;
begin
  Result := 0;

  while not Eof(ATextFile) do
  begin
    ReadLn(ATextFile);
```

```
    Inc(Result);
  end;

  Reset(ATextFile); { move position to the beginning }
end;

begin
  fileName := 'c:\data.txt';

  AssignFile(myFile, fileName);
  {$I-}
  Reset(myFile);
  {$I+}
  if IOResult = 0 then
  begin
    { resize dynamic array and load the lines into the array }
    SetLength(lines, GetLineCount(myFile));
    for cnt := Low(lines) to High(lines) do
      ReadLn(myFile, lines[cnt]);

    { close file }
    CloseFile(myFile);

    { work with strings in memory }
    for cnt := Low(lines) to High(lines) do
      WriteLn(UpperCase(lines[cnt]));

  end else
    WriteLn('Cannot open file: ', fileName);

  ReadLn;
end.
```

Once the application loads the entire text file into a dynamic array, you can close the file and work with the strings in memory. You can, of course, do whatever you want with the strings in the array, but this code only converts the strings to uppercase (temporarily) using the UpperCase function and displays them on the screen.

Working with Typed Files

Typed files are binary files that contain items of identical size. Typed files are usually files that contain records. To create a typed file, you first have to create a new file data type using the following syntax:

```
type
  NewFileType = file of DataType;
```

The following code illustrates how to create a new file type that can be used to read and write records to a typed file:

```
type
  TPerson = record
    FirstName: string[20];
    LastName: string[30];
```

```
    Age: Integer;
  end;

  TPersonFile = file of TPerson;
```

Notice that string fields in the record declaration have an explicitly defined length. The string length must be explicitly defined because the size of the entire record must be constant. If you want to store the record to a disk file, you cannot use normal strings since their length can change at any time and the compiler cannot determine their length at compile time.

There are several differences between text and typed files:

■ When you reset a typed file you can read and write to the file (you can only read from a text file when you reset it).

■ When you read or write from a typed file, you have to use the Read and Write procedures, not ReadLn and WriteLn.

The following example shows how to work with typed files.

Listing 8-6: Working with typed files

```
program Project1;

{$APPTYPE CONSOLE}

uses
  SysUtils;

type
  TPerson = record
    FirstName: string[20];
    LastName: string[30];
    Age: Integer;
  end;

  TPersonFile = file of TPerson;

procedure ReadRecord(const AFileName: string; var Rec: TPerson);
var
  F: TPersonFile;
begin
  AssignFile(F, AFileName);
  {$I-}
  Reset(F);
  {$I+}
  if IOResult = 0 then
  begin
    Read(F, Rec);
    CloseFile(F);
  end;      // if IOResult
end;

procedure WriteRecord(const AFileName: string; var Rec: TPerson);
var
  F: TPersonFile;
begin
```

```
  AssignFile(F, AFileName);
  Rewrite(F);
  Write(F, Rec);
  CloseFile(F);
end;

procedure DisplayRecord(var Rec: TPerson);
begin
  WriteLn('First Name: ', Rec.FirstName);
  WriteLn('Last Name: ', Rec.LastName);
  WriteLn('Age: ', Rec.Age);
  WriteLn;
end;

var
  TestRec: TPerson;
  ReadRec: TPerson;

begin
  TestRec.FirstName := 'Stephen';
  TestRec.LastName := 'King';
  TestRec.Age := 58;
  WriteRecord('c:\info.dat', TestRec);
  ReadRecord('c:\info.dat', ReadRec);
  DisplayRecord(ReadRec);
  ReadLn;
end.
```

Another major difference between text and typed files is that while text files only allow sequential access, typed files allow you to randomly access records in the file. Random access is possible because every record in the file is the same size, and to read a specific record, procedures only have to skip a certain, easily determinable, amount of bytes.

To determine the number of records in a file, you can use the FileSize function. To move to a specific record in the file, you can use the Seek procedure. The Seek procedure accepts two parameters: the file variable and a zero-based integer that specifies the number of the record to move to.

```
var
  F: TPersonFile;
  RecCount: Integer;

begin
  RecCount := FileSize(F);
  if RecCount = 0 then
    WriteLn('File is empty')
  else
    Seek(F, FileSize(F));
end.
```

Working with Untyped Files

Untyped files are files that have no structure. Basically, untyped files are typed files that use bytes instead of records. The declaration of an untyped file variable looks like this:

```
var
  F: file;
```

The calls to the Reset and Rewrite procedures are a bit different when you're working with untyped files. Normally, both procedures use 128 bytes as the default record size. When you're working with untyped files, you should set this size to 1 byte. You can do this by passing 1 as the second parameter in both calls:

```
Reset(F, 1);
Rewrite(F, 1);
```

To read data from and write data to typed files, you have to use the BlockRead and BlockWrite procedures. Here are the declarations of these procedures:

```
procedure BlockRead(var F: File; var Buf;
  Count: Integer [; var AmtTransferred: Integer]);

procedure BlockWrite(var F: File; var Buf;
  Count: Integer [; var AmtTransferred: Integer]);
```

The first parameter is the untyped file variable that is used to access the file on disk. The second parameter is a buffer that the procedures use to transfer data to and from the file. This buffer is usually a static array of bytes, but it can also be a record. The third parameter specifies how many bytes to transfer. This is usually the size of the array, which can easily be determined with the SizeOf function. The optional AmtTransferred variable parameter can be used to track the exact number of bytes transferred to and from the file.

The application in Listing 8-7 uses the BlockRead and BlockWrite procedures to enable the user to copy files. The application also enables the user to specify the source and destination file names in the command line (see Figure 8-2).

Figure 8-2: Passing parameters to the application

To see how many parameters the user passed to your application, you can use the ParamCount function. ParamCount takes no parameters and returns 0 if the user called the application with no additional parameters.

To read application parameters, you have to use the ParamStr function. The ParamStr function accepts a single Integer parameter: the parameter's index. If you pass 0 to the ParamStr function, it will return the path and file name of your application. Custom parameters, if there are any, start at index 1.

Listing 8-7: Copying files using BlockRead and BlockWrite

```pascal
program Project1;

{$APPTYPE CONSOLE}

uses
  SysUtils;

procedure BlockCopyFile(const SrcPath, DestPath: string);
var
  Src: file;
  Dest: file;
  Buffer: array[1..1024] of Byte;
  BytesRead: Integer;
begin
  if LowerCase(SrcPath) = LowerCase(DestPath) then Exit;

  AssignFile(Src, SrcPath);
  {$I-}
  Reset(Src, 1);
  {$I+}
  if IOResult = 0 then
  begin
    AssignFile(Dest, DestPath);
    {$I-}
    Rewrite(Dest, 1);
    {$I+}
    if IOResult = 0 then
    begin
      BytesRead := -1;

      while BytesRead <> 0 do
      begin
        BlockRead(Src, Buffer, SizeOf(Buffer), BytesRead);
        BlockWrite(Dest, Buffer, BytesRead);
      end;

      CloseFile(Dest);
      WriteLn('File successfully copied.');
    end;        // if Dest Rewrite
    CloseFile(Src);
  end;          // if Source Reset
end;

var
  SourcePath: string;
  DestPath: string;

begin
  { Accept parameters }
  if ParamCount = 2 then
    BlockCopyFile(ParamStr(1), ParamStr(2))
```

```
  else begin
    { if there are no parameters in the command line,
      ask the user to enter filenames here }
    Write('Source path: ');
    ReadLn(SourcePath);

    Write('Destination path: ');
    ReadLn(DestPath);

    if (SourcePath <> '') and (SourcePath <> '') then
      BlockCopyFile(SourcePath, DestPath);
  end;

  WriteLn('Press Enter to exit.');
  ReadLn;
end.
```

The application first checks whether the user passed two parameters in the command line. If the user passed two parameters, ParamStr(1) contains the path of the source file and ParamStr(2) contains the path of the destination file.

The copying is done in the BlockCopyFile procedure. The first line:

```
if LowerCase(SrcPath) = LowerCase(DestPath) then Exit;
```

uses the LowerCase function to temporarily convert both file names to lowercase and tests whether both file names point to the same file. If destination and source are equal, then there is no need to perform the copy and the if-then statement calls Exit to exit from the procedure.

The main part of the BlockCopyFile procedure is the while loop that calls the BlockRead and BlockWrite procedures:

```
while BytesRead <> 0 do
begin
  BlockRead(Src, Buffer, SizeOf(Buffer), BytesRead);
  BlockWrite(Dest, Buffer, BytesRead);
end;
```

The BlockRead procedure reads 1 KB of data at a time from the file, writes the data into the Buffer array, and updates the BytesRead variable, which always holds the exact amount of bytes transferred. The loop will iterate as long as the BlockRead procedure continues reading data from the file. When the BlockRead procedure reaches the end of the file, the BytesRead value will drop to 0, the condition of the while loop will be met, and the copying of the file will finish.

Chapter 9

Pointers

Pointers have a reputation of being a tough nut to crack. In some cases this is true, but on a basic level, they are just a bit more complicated than ordinary variables. You should try to have at least a general idea of what pointers are and how they work because they are one of the most powerful programming tools available.

Declaring Pointers

A pointer is nothing more than a special variable. Unlike an ordinary variable that stores a value of a specific type, a pointer stores an address of a memory location. The name pointer comes from the fact that a pointer doesn't hold a specific value but points to a location in memory where the value is stored.

There are two types of pointers in Delphi: typed and untyped (generic). Typed pointers can only be used with variables of a specific type, while untyped pointers can point to any kind of data.

To declare a typed pointer, you have to write the ^ symbol before the data type identifier:

```
var
  I: Integer;  { ordinary static variable }
  P: ^Integer; { a typed pointer }
```

The P pointer can be used to point to any memory location that contains an integer value.

Initializing Pointers

You shouldn't try to use the P pointer yet because it isn't initialized. When a pointer is not initialized, it points to an invalid memory location. Trying to use a pointer that points to an invalid memory location is like trying to bungee jump with your pockets full of nitroglycerine vials. Not a pleasant experience, to say the least.

To initialize a pointer, you have to assign it a memory address. To read the address of a variable, you can use the @ operator or the Addr function:

```
P := Addr(I);
P := @I;
```

The P pointer now points to the memory location of the I variable. If you want to know the exact memory location of the I variable, typecast the pointer to an integer and display it:

```
P := @I;
WriteLn(Integer(P));
```

Using Typed Pointers

After you assign an address to a pointer, you can use the pointer to change the value of the variable it points to. To access the variable to which the pointer points, you have to dereference the pointer by writing the ^ symbol after the pointer name (see Listing 9-1).

Listing 9-1: Using a simple typed pointer

```
program Project1;

{$APPTYPE CONSOLE}

uses
  SysUtils;

var
  I: Integer;  { ordinary static variable }
  P: ^Integer; { a typed pointer }

begin
  I := 101;
  WriteLn(I);  { 101 }

  P := @I;     { point to I }
  P^ := 202;   { change I to 202 }
  WriteLn(P^); { 202 }

  ReadLn;
end.
```

To change the location to which the pointer points, you have to assign an address to the pointer. But if you want to change the value stored at the memory location to which the pointer points, you have to dereference the pointer. The WriteLn procedure knows what value to display because the P pointer is typed, and when it is derefenced, it is actually an integer value.

The Pointer Type

The other Delphi pointer type is the Pointer. The Pointer is the untyped pointer type that can be used to point to a variable of any data type. To use the value to which an untyped pointer points, you first have to typecast the untyped pointer to another pointer type and dereference it. Casting to another pointer type is simple because every data type in Delphi already has a pointer counterpart. For instance, a pointer to a Char is PChar, a pointer to a string is PString, a pointer to an integer is PInteger, etc.

Listing 9-2 shows how to use the Pointer type and how to typecast it to other pointer types.

Listing 9-2: Using an untyped pointer

```
program Project1;

{$APPTYPE CONSOLE}

uses
  SysUtils;

var
  I: Integer;
  C: Char;
  P: Pointer;    { untyped pointer }

begin
  I := 2004;
  C := 'd';

  P := @I;       { point to I }
  { typecast to an integer pointer, dereference, and increment }
  Inc(PInteger(P)^);
  WriteLn('I = ', PInteger(P)^);

  P := @C;       { point to C }
  { typecast to a char pointer, dereference, and convert to 'D' }
  PChar(P)^ := Chr(Ord(PChar(P)^) - 32);
  WriteLn('C = ', PChar(P)^);

  ReadLn;
end.
```

To be completely safe when using pointers, you should make sure that the pointer references a valid memory location. To see if the pointer references an invalid memory location, you can use the reserved word nil. The reserved word nil is a constant value that denotes an invalid memory location. A nil pointer doesn't reference anything:

```
program Project1;

{$APPTYPE CONSOLE}

uses
  SysUtils;

var
  I: Integer = 2005;
  P: ^Integer = @I; { automatically point to I }

begin
  WriteLn(P^);        { P points to I }
  P := nil;           { P points to nothing }
```

```
  ReadLn;
end.
```

Dynamic Variables

Dynamic variables are variables allocated on the heap (also known as free store). The heap is the main portion of memory excluding the stack. The size of the heap is limited only by the amount of the computer's virtual memory (physical memory plus swap file).

Dynamic variables are allocated with the New procedure, which accepts a single pointer parameter. The New procedure allocates the appropriate amount of memory to store the value and assigns the address of the allocated memory block to the passed pointer. When you allocate memory for the pointer, the pointer doesn't reference another variable but has its own memory:

```
var
  P: PInteger;

begin
  New(P);     { create a dynamic integer }
end.
```

Unlike static variables, dynamic variables aren't automatically managed. This means that you have to manually release the memory allocated for them. To release the memory allocated with the New procedure, use the Dispose procedure. If you forget to call the Dispose procedure to remove the dynamic variable from memory, your code will leak memory. Memory leaks diminish the performance of the application and may even cause it to crash.

You should always delete dynamic variables when you don't need them anymore:

```
var
  P: PInteger;

begin
  New(P);     { create a dynamic integer }

  { use the dynamic variable }
  P^ := 2005;
  WriteLn(P^);

  Dispose(P); { release the memory }
  ReadLn;
end.
```

Strings and Dynamic Arrays

Strings and dynamic arrays are dynamic types allocated on the heap, but Delphi automatically manages their memory. To allocate memory for a dynamic array, use the SetLength procedure. To release the memory used by the array, you can either call the Finalize procedure or assign the nil value to the array.

```
var
  DynArray: array of Integer;

begin
  SetLength(DynArray, 1000);  { resize the array }

  Finalize(DynArray);         { one way of releasing array memory }
  DynArray := nil;            { another way of releasing array memory }
end.
```

When you work with a string variable, memory is allocated when you assign text to the variable. You can also use the SetLength procedure to explicitly set the length of a string variable. To release the memory occupied by the string, assign a null string to the string variable.

```
var
  s: string;

begin
  s := 'Dynamic allocation';

  { release memory }
  s := '';
end.
```

Working with Blocks of Memory

To allocate and work with a custom block of memory, you have to use the GetMem and FreeMem procedures. Both procedures take two parameters: the pointer that is to be associated with the allocated block of memory and an integer that specifies how many bytes of memory to allocate. You don't have to pass the second parameter when you call FreeMem. If you do, you have to make sure that you pass the value that matches the number of bytes allocated with the GetMem call.

The following example shows how to use the BlockRead procedure to read an entire text file into a dynamically allocated block of memory.

Listing 9-3: Loading a file into a dynamically allocated memory block

```
program Project1;

{$APPTYPE CONSOLE}

uses
  SysUtils;

procedure ReadFile(var P: Pointer; const AFileName: string);
var
  Src: file;
  BytesRead: Integer;
  BufferPos: Pointer;
```

```
begin
  AssignFile(Src, AFileName);
  {$I-}
  Reset(Src, 1);
  {$I+}
  if IOResult = 0 then
  begin
    if P <> nil then FreeMem(P);    { release old data }
    GetMem(P, FileSize(Src));       { allocate memory for the file }

    BytesRead := -1;
    BufferPos := P;
    while BytesRead <> 0 do
    begin
      BlockRead(Src, BufferPos^, 1024, BytesRead);
      Inc(Integer(BufferPos), BytesRead);
    end;

    CloseFile(Src);
  end;          // if IOResult
end;

procedure RemoveFile(var P: Pointer);
begin
  FreeMem(P);
  P := nil;
end;

var
  FilePtr: Pointer;

begin
  ReadFile(FilePtr, 'c:\data.txt');
  WriteLn(string(FilePtr));

  RemoveFile(FilePtr);
  ReadLn;
end.
```

The code for loading the file into memory is located in the ReadFile procedure. Before allocating a new memory block, the procedure has to determine if the pointer passed as the P parameter already points to a memory block. If it does, we have to release the old memory block. If we forget to release the old file from memory, we will have a huge memory leak.

```
if P <> nil then FreeMem(P); { release old data }
```

The GetMem procedure uses the FileSize function to determine the exact number of bytes needed to hold the entire file in memory. After the memory is allocated, we can start reading the file into memory.

Probably the strangest part of the procedure is the local BufferPos pointer. Before we start reading the file in the while loop, we assign the P pointer to the BufferPos pointer.

```
BufferPos := P;
```

The BufferPos pointer points to the exact location in memory where the BlockRead procedure has to store the 1,024 bytes it reads from the file.

```
BlockRead(Src, BufferPos^, 1024, BytesRead);
```

After the BlockRead procedure stores the 1,024 bytes to the memory block, we have to update the BufferPos pointer. If we forget to update the pointer, the BlockRead procedure will read the entire file but will also overwrite the old data with the latest 1,024 bytes from the file.

When the BlockRead procedure reads 1,024 bytes, we have to tell the BufferPos pointer to point to the following 1,024 bytes in memory. This is done by typecasting the BufferPos pointer to Integer and by incrementing the address of the pointer with the number of bytes read from the file.

```
Inc(Integer(BufferPos), BytesRead);
```

Without the BufferPos pointer, this procedure wouldn't work. BufferPos enables us to do something that we mustn't do with the variable pointer parameter — modify the location to where the pointer points. If we were to modify the location of the original pointer, each call to BlockRead would leak 1,024 bytes of memory, because the following line would tell the original pointer to point 1,024 farther into the memory block.

To display the entire text file, simply typecast the memory block to a string:

```
WriteLn(string(FilePtr));
```

```
procedure TMainForm.Font1Click(Sender: TObject);
begin
    FontDialog1.Font := Editor.Font;
    if FontDialog1.Execute then
    begin
        Editor.Font := FontDialog1.Font;
        TextPrinter.Font := FontDialog1.Font;
    end;
end;

procedure TMainForm.OpenItemClick(Sender: TObject);
begin
    if OpenDialog1.Execute then
    begin
        Editor.Lines.LoadFromFile(OpenDialog1.FileName);
    end;
end;

procedure TMainForm.ExitItemClick(Sender: TObject);
begin
    if Printer.Printing then Printer.Abort;

    Close;
end;
```

Figure 9-1: Typecast memory block

Accessing Array Elements

Pointers can be used to access array elements. To read the address of the first element in the array (to point to the first element), you can write this:

```
var
  Numbers: array[1..20] of Integer;
  PI: PInteger;
begin
```

```
  PI := @Numbers;
end.
```

To point to another element in the array, simply increment the pointer using the Inc procedure. However, you also need to typecast the pointer to an integer before passing it to the Inc procedure:

```
Inc(Integer(PI)); { move to next element }
```

The Inc procedure doesn't increment the pointer by one but by SizeOf(ElementType). In this case, the Inc procedure increments the pointer by 4 (SizeOf(Integer)), thus moving 4 bytes farther into memory, to the correct address at which the next array element is stored. Listing 9-4 shows how to access array elements through a pointer.

Listing 9-4: Accessing an array through a pointer

```
program Project1;

{$APPTYPE CONSOLE}

uses
  SysUtils;

var
  Numbers: array[1..20] of Integer;
  I: Integer;
  PI: PInteger;

begin
  { standard access }
  for I := Low(Numbers) to High(Numbers) do
  begin
    Numbers[I] := I;
    WriteLn(Numbers[I]);
  end;

  { pointer access }
  PI := @Numbers;          { point to first element in Numbers }
  for I := Low(Numbers) to High(Numbers) do
  begin
    PI^ := I;
    WriteLn(PI^);
    Inc(Integer(PI));      { move to next element }
  end;

  ReadLn;
end.
```

You can also use pointers to access characters in a string. The following code shows the standard way of accessing characters in a string:

```
var
  s: string;
  i: Integer;

begin
```

```
  s := 'Borland Delphi';
  for i := 1 to Length(s) do
    Write(s[i]);
end.
```

When you access characters in a string through a pointer, you don't have to call the Length function to determine the length of the string nor do you have to use the counter variable to index the characters in the string.

Accessing String Characters

Strings can easily be accessed through a pointer (see Listing 9-5) because all strings (except ShortString) are null-terminated. In memory, there is always a #0 character at the end of a string.

Listing 9-5: Accessing the string through a pointer

```
program Project1;

{$APPTYPE CONSOLE}

uses
  SysUtils;

var
  s: string;
  c: PChar;

begin
  s := 'Borland Delphi';
  c := Pointer(s);      { point to s[1] }

  { display the string }
  while c^ <> #0 do
  begin
    Write(c^);
    Inc(c);
  end;

  Readln;
end.
```

Record Pointers

When creating a new record type, the usual practice is to create two types: the record type and the record pointer type. Pointer data types usually start with the capital letter P. The syntax of the pointer type declaration is:

```
PointerTypeName = ^TypeName;
```

The following code shows how to declare a record and a record pointer:

```
type
  TBook = record
    Title: string[200];
```

```
    Author: string[40];
    PageCount: Integer;
  end;

  PBook = ^TBook;
```

When you create a dynamic record, you have to dereference it before you can access its elements. The following example shows how to dynamically create a record and how to dereference the dynamic record to access the record's fields.

Listing 9-6: Dynamically creating records

```
program Project1;

{$APPTYPE CONSOLE}

uses
  SysUtils;

type
  TBook = record
    Title: string[200];
    Author: string[40];
    PageCount: Integer;
  end;

  PBook = ^TBook;

var
  Book: PBook;

begin
  New(Book);
  Book^.Title := 'Roget''s Thesaurus';
  Book^.PageCount := 1254;

  Dispose(Book);
end.
```

Pointers in C++

To declare a pointer in C++, use the indirection operator (*) before the identifier:

```
data_type *pointer_name;
int *i; /* pointer to an int */
```

To initialize the pointer in C++, you have to use the reference operator (&). Here's how you can declare and automatically initialize a pointer in C++:

```
int n = 20;
int *i = &n; /* point to "n" */
```

If you want, you can initialize a pointer to point to nothing. In Delphi, you would use nil for this, but in C++, you use the NULL constant (since C++ is case sensitive, always write NULL):

```
int *p = NULL;
```

You use pointers in C++ the same way as in Delphi. To access the pointer's address, use the pointer name without additional operators, and to access the value to which it points, write the indirection operator (*) before the pointer's name (see Listing 9-7).

Listing 9-7: Pointer basics

```
#include <iostream.h>
#include <conio.h>
#pragma hdrstop

#pragma argsused
int main(int argc, char* argv[])
{
   int n = 20;
   int *i = &n; /* point to "n" */

   cout << i << endl;     // display the pointer's address
   cout << *i << endl;    // display the value of the n variable

   getch();
   return 0;
}
```

void Pointers

Pointers of type void are the C++ equivalent of Delphi's Pointer type, which means that a void pointer is untyped and can be used to point to a variable of any data type. The void pointer in C++ has the same "limitation" the Pointer type in Delphi has: To access the value to which it points, you must first type-cast it to a typed pointer type and dereference it. To do this, use the following syntax:

```
*(typed_pointer)void_pointer_name
```

Listing 9-8 illustrates how to work with void pointers.

Listing 9-8: Void pointers

```
#include <iostream.h>
#include <conio.h>
#pragma hdrstop

#pragma argsused
int main(int argc, char* argv[])
{
   int n = 20;
   char c = 'A';
   float f = 1.45;

   void *ptr = &n;        // declare the pointer and point it to "n"
```

```
cout << *(int *)ptr << endl;

ptr = &c;                    // point to the "c" variable"
cout << *(char *)ptr << endl;   // display A

ptr = &f;                    // point to "f"
cout << *(float *)ptr << endl;

getch();
return 0;
}
```

Accessing Array Elements

To access an array through a pointer, you need to make the pointer point to an element in the array, usually the first one. To get the address of the first element in an array, simply assign the array's name to the pointer:

```
pointer = array;
```

To move to another element in an array, use the + + or -- operators:

```
pointer++;                   // move to the next element
```

The following listing illustrates how to access array elements through a pointer.

Listing 9-9: Accessing array elements through a pointer

```
#include <iostream.h>
#include <conio.h>
#pragma hdrstop

#pragma argsused
int main(int argc, char* argv[])
{
    int arr[5] = {1, 2, 3, 4, 5};
    int *p;

    p = arr;              // point to the first element in the array
    cout << *p << endl;

    p = &arr[0];          // this is the same as p = arr;
    cout << *p << endl;

    p++;                  // move to the 2nd element
    cout << *p << endl;

    p +=2;                // move to the 4th element
    cout << *p << endl;

    getch();
    return 0;
}
```

Pointers to Structures

When you declare a pointer to a structure, you can no longer access the fields using the simple dot syntax (the direct member selector). To access fields in a structure pointed to by a pointer, you have to write this:

```
(*pointer_name).field_name
```

Although you can use the above syntax to access fields in pointers to structures, it is much better to use the indirect member selector, or the -> operator, because it is used in object-oriented programming to access object fields:

```
pointer_name->field_name
```

The following listing shows how to access fields in a structure through a pointer. The example illustrates both ways of accessing fields indirectly.

Listing 9-10: Accessing structure fields through a pointer

```cpp
#include <iostream.h>
#include <conio.h>
#include <string.h>
#pragma hdrstop

struct TBook {
    char Title[50];
    int PageCount;
    char Authors[4][40];
};

#pragma argsused
int main(int argc, char* argv[])
{
    TBook book;
    TBook* bookPtr = &book;

    // access the book structure through the pointer
    strcpy((*bookPtr).Title, "The ANSI C Programming Language");

    // display data by accessing the book structure directly
    cout << "Title: " << book.Title << endl;

    strcpy(bookPtr->Authors[0], "Brian W. Kernighan");
    cout <<"Author: " << book.Authors[0] << endl;

    strcpy(bookPtr->Authors[1], "Dennis M. Ritchie");
    cout <<"Author: " << book.Authors[1] << endl;

    (*bookPtr).PageCount = 238;
    cout << "Page Count: " << book.PageCount << endl;

    getch();
    return 0;
}
```

Dynamic Variables

You create and use dynamic variables the same way in Delphi and C++; the only difference lies in syntax.

To create a new dynamic variable in C++, you need to declare a pointer and allocate it on the heap using the new operator:

```
data_type *pointer_name = new data_type;
int *p = new int;
```

You can also automatically initialize a dynamic variable by including a pair of parentheses containing the initial value of the variable:

```
data_type *pointer_name = new data_type(initial_value);
int *p = new int(1001);
```

When you're done with the dynamic variable, you must release it from memory if you don't want to leak memory. To remove a dynamic variable from memory, use the delete operator:

```
delete pointer_name;
delete p;
```

The short example in Listing 9-11 illustrates how to use a dynamic variable.

Listing 9-11: Dynamic variables in C++

```
#include <iostream.h>
#include <conio.h>
#pragma hdrstop

#pragma argsused
int main(int argc, char* argv[])
{
   int *p = new int(1001);    // create & initialize the dynamic var
   cout << *p << endl;        // use the variable
   delete p;                  // remove the var from memory

   getch();
   return 0;
}
```

Dynamic Arrays

The new operator is used to create both dynamic variables and dynamic arrays. When you want to create a dynamic array, use the following syntax:

```
data_type *array_name = new data_type[num_of_elements];
```

Removing a dynamic variable and a dynamic array from memory is done using the delete operator. The only difference is that when you want to delete an array, you have to use the delete [] syntax:

```
int *dyn_var = new int;
int *dyn_array = new int[20];

delete dyn_var;           // delete one variable
delete [] dyn_array;      // delete an entire array
```

Strings (Dynamic Character Arrays)

Now that you know more about pointers, you can start declaring strings using the following syntax:

```
char * string_name;
```

The difference between char[] and char* is that a char[] string is stored on the stack and the char* string is stored in the heap. Actually, the char* pointer (4 bytes) is stored on the stack and the string's data is stored on the heap.

Chapter 10

Object-Oriented Programming

Object-oriented programming (OOP) is a programming style based on objects rather than on procedures and functions. It is the natural upgrade of the structured programming style we used in the previous chapters.

In structured programming, you have to think about procedures and functions that solve a particular problem. In object-oriented programming, you think in terms of objects — self-contained boxes that contain both data and code that operates on object data.

This chapter gives you an overview of object-oriented programming and explains the following core terms related to it: class, object, encapsulation, inheritance, and polymorphism.

Encapsulation

In structured applications, data is usually stored in records and the application logic is divided between numerous functions and procedures. The application data and the code that uses this data are always separated.

For instance, the following example shows the standard way of working with data in structured applications.

Listing 10-1: Working with records

```
program Project1;

{$APPTYPE CONSOLE}

uses
  SysUtils;

type
  TAnimal = record
    Name: string;
    Age: Integer;
    Hungry: Boolean;
  end;
```

```
procedure ShowInfo(var AAnimal: TAnimal);
const
  HUNGRY_STRING: array[Boolean] of string = ('No', 'Yes');
begin
  with AAnimal do
  begin
    WriteLn('Name: ', Name);
    WriteLn('Age: ', Age);
    WriteLn('Hungry: ', HUNGRY_STRING[Hungry]);
  end;          // with AAnimal
end;

var
  MyDog: TAnimal;

begin
  MyDog.Name := 'Apollo';
  MyDog.Age := 10;
  MyDog.Hungry := False;
  ShowInfo(MyDog);

  ReadLn;
end.
```

To access data stored in the MyDog record, you have to pass the record as a variable parameter to a procedure. Every procedure that needs to work with data stored in a TAnimal type record has to have a parameter that accepts a pointer (variable parameters act like pointers) to the actual data.

This produces three undesirable side effects: You always have to pass the record pointer to a procedure or a function, you have to write code that checks whether the data is valid, and you have to check whether the data even exists.

If you only use static records, the data always exists, but if you opt to use dynamic records, you have to make sure that the record isn't nil because trying to access fields in a nil value always results in an error.

In order to properly use a dynamic record, the code in the procedure has to be changed to accept a real pointer to the record and it has to test whether the pointer references a valid memory location. This is illustrated in Listing 10-2.

Listing 10-2: Accessing records through pointers

```
program Project1;

{$APPTYPE CONSOLE}

uses
  SysUtils;

type
  PAnimal = ^TAnimal; { pointer to a TAnimal record }
  TAnimal = record
    Name: string;
    Age: Integer;
    Hungry: Boolean;
```

```
  end;

procedure ShowInfo(AAnimal: PAnimal);
const
  HUNGRY_STRING: array[Boolean] of string = ('No', 'Yes');
begin
  if AAnimal = nil then Exit;

  with AAnimal^ do
  begin
    WriteLn('Name: ', Name);
    WriteLn('Age: ', Age);
    WriteLn('Hungry: ', HUNGRY_STRING[Hungry]);
  end;          // with AAnimal
end;

var
  MyDog: TAnimal;

  MyDynamicCat: PAnimal;

begin
  MyDog.Name := 'Apollo';
  MyDog.Age := 10;
  MyDog.Hungry := False;
  ShowInfo(@MyDog);

  New(MyDynamicCat);
  ShowInfo(MyDynamicCat);
  Dispose(MyDynamicCat);

  ReadLn;
end.
```

Creating a New Class

The solution to these three problems lies in object-oriented programming, and specifically in encapsulation. To remove both the need for pointers to the actual data and the need for data validation, you can encapsulate the TAnimal record and the ShowInfo procedure into a TAnimal class.

Before we move on, note the use of the word "class." In object-oriented programming, classes are blueprints for objects, just like the human genome is the blueprint for human beings. An object is an instance of a class, a tangible result of the blueprint. Without the blueprint, nature wouldn't be able to instantiate us and the Delphi compiler wouldn't be able to instantiate objects.

Creating a basic class is as simple as creating a basic record. The only difference is that in order to create a class we have to use the reserved word `class`.

```
type
  TAnimal = class
    Name: string;
```

```
  Age: Integer;
  Hungry: Boolean;
end;
```

Now that we have the TAnimal class, we can create an object of type TAnimal and use it in the application. The first step in creating an object is to declare an object variable, that is, to declare a variable of a class type:

```
var
  MyDog: TAnimal;
```

But this is only the declaration of the object. To actually use the MyDog object in the application, we have to create it.

Objects are created with a constructor, which is a special method called Create that is used to create object instances. The syntax for creating an object is:

```
Object := Class.Create;
```

To create the MyDog object, we have to call the TAnimal constructor, because the MyDog variable is declared as TAnimal:

```
MyDog := TAnimal.Create;
```

The constructor allocates the memory on the heap necessary to store the declared fields and sets all field values to empty. The constructor also returns the reference to the new object. After the call, the MyDog variable points to the new object created by the constructor. Yes, objects are actually pointers, but you don't have to dereference objects (you don't have to write the ^ symbol) to access their fields or methods.

```
MyDog.Name := 'Apollo';
WriteLn(MyDog.Name);
```

Because objects are dynamically created on the heap, you have to release the memory occupied by the object once you're finished with it. Releasing the memory occupied by the object is called object destruction.

To destroy the object, you have to call the object's destructor. A destructor is a special method called Destroy that is used to free the object from memory. You should never call the Destroy method directly. Instead, you should call the Free method because the Free method makes sure the object exists before trying to destroy it. An object that doesn't exist references an invalid memory location, and by accessing an invalid memory location you're asking for trouble.

When calling either Destroy or Free, you have to reference the object, not the class:

```
MyDog.Destroy;
MyDog.Free;
```

The following listing shows how to properly use an object.

Listing 10-3: Using an object

```
program Project1;

{$APPTYPE CONSOLE}

uses
  SysUtils;

type
  TAnimal = class
    Name: string;
    Age: Integer;
    Hungry: Boolean;
  end;

var
  MyDog: TAnimal;

begin
  { create the object }
  MyDog := TAnimal.Create;

  { use it }
  MyDog.Name := 'Apollo';
  WriteLn(MyDog.Name);

  { destroy it }
  MyDog.Free;
  ReadLn;
end.
```

Adding Methods to the Class

To completely finish the encapsulation process, we have to encapsulate the ShowInfo procedure. Encapsulating the ShowInfo procedure means to declare it as a part of the TAnimal class:

```
type
  TAnimal = class
    Name: string;
    Age: Integer;
    Hungry: Boolean;
    procedure ShowInfo;
  end;
```

Note that this is only the declaration of the ShowInfo procedure. We still have to write the method implementation. In Delphi, the method implementation has to be written outside of the class block (unlike C++, which allows both inline and external method implementation).

When writing the method implementation (procedures and functions that belong to a class are called methods), you have to specify to which class the method belongs. This requires writing the class name before the method name and separating class and method names with a dot.

```
procedure Class.Method(ParameterList);
function Class.Method(ParameterList);
```

Thus, the implementation of the ShowInfo method looks like this:

```
procedure TAnimal.ShowInfo;
begin
end;
```

The ShowInfo method has no parameter list because the data needed by the ShowInfo method is encapsulated in the class. Here is the full implementation of the ShowInfo method:

```
procedure TAnimal.ShowInfo;
const
  HUNGRY_STRING: array[Boolean] of string = ('No', 'Yes');
begin
  WriteLn('Name: ', Name);
  WriteLn('Age: ', Age);
  WriteLn('Hungry: ', HUNGRY_STRING[Hungry]);
end;
```

The Self Pointer

Since both fields and the ShowInfo method belong to the same class, the method can directly access the fields. Actually, the method can access the fields through an invisible pointer called Self. The Delphi compiler implicitly creates the Self pointer for every object. The Self pointer references the object in which the method is called, which means that by using the Self pointer, the object can reference itself (hence the name). If you want, you can use the Self pointer in the ShowInfo method to reference the fields of the TAnimal class explicitly:

```
procedure TAnimal.ShowInfo;
const
  HUNGRY_STRING: array[Boolean] of string = ('No', 'Yes');
begin
  WriteLn('Name: ', Self.Name);
  WriteLn('Age: ', Self.Age);
  WriteLn('Hungry: ', HUNGRY_STRING[Self.Hungry]);
end;
```

Using the Class

Object-oriented programming is so popular today because using objects in your code results in cleaner and more straightforward code. The call to the ShowInfo method is now simpler and easier to understand than the call to the ShowInfo procedure, because we don't have to worry about superfluous parameter passing.

Listing 10-4: The completed class

```
program Project1;

{$APPTYPE CONSOLE}

uses
  SysUtils;

type
  TAnimal = class
    Name: string;
    Age: Integer;
    Hungry: Boolean;
    procedure ShowInfo;
  end;

procedure TAnimal.ShowInfo;
const
  HUNGRY_STRING: array[Boolean] of string = ('No', 'Yes');
begin
  WriteLn('Name: ', Name);
  WriteLn('Age: ', Age);
  WriteLn('Hungry: ', HUNGRY_STRING[Hungry]);
end;

var
  MyDog: TAnimal;

begin
  { create the object }
  MyDog := TAnimal.Create;

  { use it }
  MyDog.Name := 'Apollo';
  MyDog.Age := 10;
  MyDog.Hungry := True;
  MyDog.ShowInfo;

  { destroy it }
  MyDog.Free;
  ReadLn;
end.
```

Moving the Class to a Unit

The encapsulation of the TAnimal record and the ShowInfo procedure is now complete, but we have done a VBT (very bad thing). We have created a class in the main project file, but classes should always reside in separate units.

To move the class to a new unit, we have to do the following:

■ Create a new unit (called Animal).

■ Move the class declaration to the interface section of the unit.

■ Move the method implementation(s) to the implementation section of the unit.

The resulting Animal.pas unit should look like the one in Listing 10-5.

Listing 10-5: The TAnimal class unit

```
unit Animal;

interface

type
  TAnimal = class
    Name: string;
    Age: Integer;
    Hungry: Boolean;
    procedure ShowInfo;
  end;

implementation

procedure TAnimal.ShowInfo;
const
  HUNGRY_STRING: array[Boolean] of string = ('No', 'Yes');
begin
  WriteLn('Name: ', Name);
  WriteLn('Age: ', Age);
  WriteLn('Hungry: ', HUNGRY_STRING[Hungry]);
end;

end.
```

Inheritance

Classes, like animals and plants in the real world, have the ability to inherit the properties and methods of their parents. Not only do classes have the ability to inherit the functionality of a parent class, they always do so. If you fail to specify the parent class in the class declaration, Delphi implicitly derives your class from the ultimate parent — the TObject class. To explicitly define a parent class, you have to specify the class name after the reserved word:

```
TNewClass = class(TParentClass)
```

For instance, the TAnimal class used earlier implicitly derives from the TObject class. If you want, you can also explicitly define the parent class of the TAnimal class:

```
type
  TAnimal = class(TObject)
    Name: string;
    Age: Integer;
    Hungry: Boolean;
  end;.
```

The only reason we are able to instantiate objects of type TAnimal is because the TAnimal class inherits the necessary methods from the TObject class. The TObject class encapsulates the essential methods necessary to create and destroy objects like Create, Destroy, and Free.

To view the entire list of methods inherited from the TObject (or any other parent class), you can utilize the Code Insight feature of the Code Editor (see Figure 10-1). To display the list of properties and methods that belong to an object, write the object name followed by a period and press Ctrl+Space.

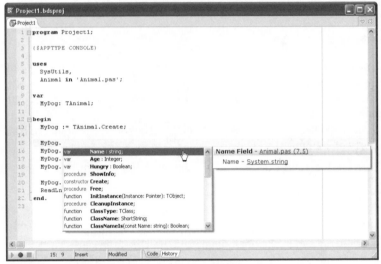

Figure 10-1: Methods inherited from the TObject class

The TAnimal class can also be used as a parent class for other classes. For instance, the TAnimal class can be the parent class of TBird or TFish classes.

```
type
  TAnimal = class
    Name: string;
    Age: Integer;
    Hungry: Boolean;
    procedure ShowInfo;
  end;

  TFish = class(TAnimal)
    Carnivorous: Boolean;
    Length: Integer;
  end;

  TBird = class(TAnimal)
    CanFly: Boolean;
  end;
```

Both TFish and TBird classes inherit the functionality of the TAnimal class but also enhance the original class by introducing new properties like Length and CanFly:

```
var
  F: TFish;

begin
```

```
  F := TFish.Create;
  F.Name := 'Rainbow Trout';
  F.Length := 54;
  F.ShowInfo;
  F.Free;
end.
```

Polymorphism

Polymorphism is somewhat difficult to describe without proper code examples and will be described in more detail later in the book. For now, polymorphism can be described as the ability to access objects of various types through a common ancestor.

For instance, the following procedure can be used to change the Name property of TAnimal type objects.

```
procedure SetAnimalName(AAnimal: TAnimal; const AName: string);
begin
  AAnimal.Name := AName;
end;
```

Along with TAnimal type objects, polymorphism enables you to pass TBird or TFish type objects to the SetAnimalName procedure because both classes descend from the common ancestor — the TAnimal class.

Listing 10-6: Polymorphic calls

```
program Project1;

{$APPTYPE CONSOLE}

uses
  SysUtils,
  Animal in 'Animal.pas';

var
  F: TFish;
  A: TAnimal;
  B: TBird;

begin
  F := TFish.Create;
  A := TAnimal.Create;
  B := TBird.Create;

  SetAnimalName(F, 'Fish');
  SetAnimalName(A, 'Animal');
  SetAnimalName(B, 'Bird');

  A.Free;
  B.Free;
  F.Free;
end.
```

The last thing to note about the SetAnimalName procedure has to do with the AAnimal parameter. The AAnimal parameter is the standard value parameter. Object parameters don't have to be declared as variable in order to change the object's properties. If you declare an object parameter as variable, you'll be passing a pointer to a pointer. That will only slow down the application and unnecessarily complicate your source code.

Object-Oriented Programming in C++

The C++ language, like Delphi, uses the reserved word `class` to create a new class:

```
class ClassName {
   field_1;
   field_n;
};

class TAnimal {
   char Name[20];
   long Age;
   bool Hungry;
};
```

The difference between the C++ TAnimal class and the TAnimal class we created earlier in Delphi is that we cannot use the Name, Age, and Hungry fields of the C++ TAnimal class automatically. If you create an instance of the TAnimal class and try to access any of its properties, the compiler will refuse to compile your code:

```
TAnimal an;
an.Age = 2;    // TAnimal::Age is not accessible
```

The reason you cannot access these fields is visibility. In Delphi, fields are public by default, which means that any code that can use the object can access its fields. In C++, fields are private by default, which means that they can only be accessed inside the methods of the class. Even if a piece of code can use the object, it cannot use its private fields.

In order to have the C++ TAnimal class behave like the Delphi TAnimal class, we have to make these fields public by storing them in the public section of the class. This simply involves writing them after the reserved word `public` followed by a colon (public:), which denotes the beginning of the public section in a C++ class:

```
class TAnimal {
   public:
      char Name[20];
      long Age;
      bool Hungry;
};
```

After you've made the fields public, you'll be able to access these fields in TAnimal objects, as shown in Listing 10-7.

Listing 10-7: Accessing the public fields of the TAnimal class

```
#include <iostream.h>
#include <conio.h>
#pragma hdrstop

class TAnimal {
    public:
        char Name[20];
        long Age;
        bool Hungry;
};

#pragma argsused
int main(int argc, char* argv[])
{
    TAnimal an;       // create an instance of the TAnimal class
    strcpy(an.Name, "ant");
    an.Age = 1;
    an.Hungry = true;

    getch();
    return 0;
}
```

Adding Methods to the Class

To make the C++ TAnimal class work like the Delphi TAnimal class, we still have to do one more thing — create the ShowInfo method for displaying the object data on screen.

To add a method to a C++ class, you have to add the method's header to the public section of the class and write the method's implementation outside the class (in C++ you can also write the method's implementation inside the class block, as you'll see shortly).

Here's how to implement a new method in a C++ class:

```
class ClassName {
    return_type MethodName(parameters);
};

return_type ClassName::MethodName(parameters)
{
    method_implementation;
}
```

Listing 10-8 shows how to add the ShowInfo method to the TAnimal class.

Listing 10-8: The complete C++ TAnimal class

```
#include <iostream.h>
#include <conio.h>
#pragma hdrstop

class TAnimal {
    public:
        char Name[20];
        long Age;
```

```
        bool Hungry;
        void ShowInfo();
};

void TAnimal::ShowInfo()
{
    // declare and initialize an array of strings
    char* HUNGRY_STRING[] = { {"No"}, {"Yes"} };

    cout << "Name: " << Name << endl;
    cout << "Age: " << Age << endl;
    cout << "Hungry: " << HUNGRY_STRING[Hungry] << endl;
}

#pragma argsused
int main(int argc, char* argv[])
{
    TAnimal an;
    strcpy(an.Name, "ant");
    an.Age = 1;
    an.Hungry = true;

    an.ShowInfo();

    getch();
    return 0;
}
```

The this Pointer

The this pointer is the C++ equivalent of the Delphi Self pointer. You can use the this pointer in methods to access the object in which the method is called:

```
void TAnimal::ShowInfo()
{
    char* HUNGRY_STRING[] = { {"No"}, {"Yes"} };

    cout << "Name: " << this->Name << endl;
    cout << "Age: " << this->Age << endl;
    cout << "Hungry: " << HUNGRY_STRING[this->Hungry] << endl;
}

int main(int argc, char* argv[])
{
    TAnimal animal1;
    strcpy(animal1.Name, "one");
    animal1.ShowInfo();     // this in ShowInfo() = animal1

    TAnimal animal2;
    strcpy(animal2.Name, "two");
    animal2.ShowInfo();     // this in ShowInfo() = animal2

    return 0;
}
```

Inline Methods

In both Delphi and C++, standard functions and procedures can be marked with the inline directive to tell the compiler to try to optimize the code. To reduce typing, C++ allows you to add inline methods by simply writing the implementation of the method inside the class block:

```
class ClassName {

    return_type InlinedMethod(parameters)
    {
        method_implementation;
    }
};
```

The following listing shows an updated version of the TAnimal class that has two new methods: Eat and Eat2. These methods illustrate how you can add inline methods to a C++ class.

Listing 10-9: Inline methods

```
class TAnimal {
    public:
        char Name[20];
        long Age;
        bool Hungry;
        void ShowInfo();

        void Eat() {
            Hungry = false;
        }

        void Eat2();
};

inline void TAnimal::Eat2()
{
    Hungry = false;
}
```

Moving the Class to a Unit

In Delphi, a class can be stored in one unit, with the class interface in the interface section and the method implementations in the implementation section. In C++, you have to store the class interface in a header file, and the method implementations in a .cpp source file. You must also include the class header file in its source file to connect the two files. Listings 10-10A and 10-10B show the Animal.h and the Animal.cpp files that make up the TAnimal class.

Listing 10-10A: The Animal.h file

```
class TAnimal {
    public:
        char Name[20];
        long Age;
```

```
        bool Hungry;
        void ShowInfo();

        /* inline method */
        void Eat() {
           Hungry = false;
        }

        void Eat2();
};
```

Listing 10-10B: The Animal.cpp file

```
#include <iostream.h>   // for cout
#pragma hdrstop
#include "Animal.h"

inline void TAnimal::Eat2()
{
   Hungry = false;
}

void TAnimal::ShowInfo()
{
   // declare and initialize an array of strings
   char* HUNGRY_STRING[] = { {"No"}, {"Yes"} };

   cout << "Name: " << Name << endl;
   cout << "Age: " << Age << endl;
   cout << "Hungry: " << HUNGRY_STRING[Hungry] << endl;
}
```

Inheritance

To derive a new class from an existing class in C++, use the following syntax:

```
class NewClass: ExistingClass {
};

class TBird: TAnimal {
};
```

When you declare a new class from an existing one using the above syntax, you won't get the same results as you do in Delphi. In Delphi, when you derive a new class from an existing one, you'll automatically be able to access all fields that are publicly visible in the original class. In C++, all fields will be treated as private, no matter what their visibility in the ancestor class is. To retain original field visibility, use the following syntax to derive a new class in C++:

```
class NewClass: public ExistingClass {
};

class TBird: public TAnimal {
};
```

The AnsiString Class

The AnsiString class is the C++Builder equivalent of the Delphi string type. To use AnsiStrings in your application, you have to include the vcl.h header file, and the easiest way to do that is to check the Use VCL check box in the New Console Application dialog box, as shown in Figure 10-2.

Figure 10-2: Including VCL headers

The difference between the AnsiString class in C++Builder and the Delphi string type is mostly in syntax. The following table shows Delphi string related functions and the corresponding methods found in the AnsiString class. Note that when you include the vcl.h header file, you can use Delphi IntToStr and StrToInt functions to convert AnsiStrings to int and backward.

Table 10-1: Delphi string functions and corresponding AnsiString class methods

Delphi Function	AnsiString Method
Pos(Substring, String)	AnsiString.Pos(AnsiString)
Copy(String, Index, Count)	AnsiString.SubString(Index, Count)
Length(String)	AnsiString.Length()
Delete(String, Index, Count)	AnsiString.Delete(Index, Count)
Insert(SrcString, DestString, Index)	AnsiString.Insert(SrcString, Index)

By default, you cannot display AnsiStrings using the cout object. Instead, you have to use the AnsiString's c_str() function to temporarily acquire a pointer to the AnsiString's internal null-terminated character array. But if you #define VCL_IOSTREAM before including the vcl.h header file, you will be able to pass AnsiStrings directly to cout.

The following listing shows how to use AnsiStrings in C++Builder applications.

Listing 10-11: Using AnsiStrings

```
#include <iostream.h>
#include <conio.h>

#define VCL_IOSTREAM
#include <vcl.h>
#pragma hdrstop

#pragma argsused
```

```
int main(int argc, char* argv[])
{
   /* displaying strings */
   AnsiString s = "Borland AnsiString Class";
   cout << s.c_str() << endl;
   cout << s << endl;        // only if you've #defined VCL_IOSTREAM

   /* Find substring using Pos() */
   if (s.Pos("Borland") > 0)
      cout << "The string contains \"Borland\"" << endl;

   /* Find char in string, you can use Pos or do it manually */
   /* To determine the string's length, use the Length() method */
   for(int x = 1; x <= s.Length(); x++)
   {
      if(s[x] == 'A')
      {
         cout << "Found 'A' in the string." << endl;
         break;
      }
   }

   /* use the Insert method to insert substrings into the string */
   AnsiString s2 = "Windows,SysUtils,Forms;";
   for(int x = 1; x <= s2.Length(); x++)
   {
      if(s2[x] == ',')
         s2.Insert(' ', ++x);
   }
   cout << s2 << endl;

   /* to copy a part of a string, use the SubString method */
   AnsiString s3 = s.SubString(1, s.Pos(" Class"));
   cout << s3 << endl;       // "Borland AnsiString"

   /* deleting a part of a string */
   AnsiString s4 = s3;
   int pos = s4.Pos(' ');
   s4.Delete(pos, s4.Length() - pos);
   cout << s4 << endl; /* Borland */

   /* converting string to int */
   AnsiString s5 = "1234";
   long num = StrToInt(s5);
   cout << num << endl;

   /* convert int to string */
   AnsiString s6 = IntToStr(789);
   cout << s6.c_str() << endl;

   getch();
   return 0;
}
```

Basic File I/O in C++

To read or write data to files in a C++ application, you can use the ifstream and ofstream classes declared in the fstream.h header file. The ifstream class is used for reading from files and the ofstream class is used for writing to files.

Writing Text to a File

Working with files is the same in C++ and Delphi:

1. Open a file.
2. Write data to the file.
3. Close the file.

Before you start writing to a file, you need to include the fstream.h header file and create an instance of the ofstream class (declared in fstream.h):

```
ofstream myFile;
```

To start writing to a file, you only need to call the open method and pass at least the file name:

```
myFile.open("c:\\data.txt");
```

You have undoubtedly noticed the two backslash characters in the file name. They are necessary because the backslash character in C++ strings indicates an escape sequence. Table 10-2 shows some C++Builder escape sequences. Note that the table also contains the \\ escape sequence, which must be used in file names to produce the necessary backslash character.

Table 10-2: C++ Builder escape sequences

Escape Sequence	Description
\a	Bell
\b	Backspace
\f	Formfeed
\n	Newline
\r	Carriage return
\t	Tab
\\	Backslash
\'	Apostrophe
\"	Double quote
\?	Question mark

Once the file is opened, the file variable (instance of ofstream) can be used just like the cout object. Write a string to the file using something like this:

```
for(int i = 1; i <= 10; i++)
    myFile << "Line " << i << endl;
```

When you're done writing to the file, call the close() method to close the file:

```
myFile.close();
```

Reading Text from a File

To read text from a file you have to do the following:

- Create an instance of the ifstream class.
- Declare a buffer (a character array) to store the data while reading.
- Use the eof() function to determine if you've reached the end of the file.
- Use the getline() function to read a line of text and store it into the buffer (the getline function accepts a pointer to the buffer and the buffer's size — getline(char* _Str, int _Count)).
- Close the file when you're done.

Listing 10-12 shows how to write text to a file using the ofstream class and how to read text from the same file using the ifstream class.

Listing 10-12: Using ofstream and ifstream classes to read and write text to a file

```
#include <iostream.h>
#include <fstream.h>
#include <vcl.h>
#include <conio.h>
#pragma hdrstop

#pragma argsused
int main(int argc, char* argv[])
{
    const char* path = "c:\\data.txt";

    /* write some text to c:\data.txt */
    ofstream myFile;
    myFile.open(path);

    for(int i = 1; i <= 10; i++) {
        myFile << "Line " << i << endl;
    }
    myFile.close();

    /* display c:\data.txt */
    ifstream readFile;
    char buff[256];

    readFile.open(path);
    while(!readFile.eof()) {
        readFile.getline(buff, sizeof(buff));
        cout << buff << endl;
    }
    readFile.close();

    getch();
    return 0;
}
```

Chapter 11

Designing the User Interface

This chapter is the first in a series of chapters that shows how to build windowed applications using the VCL framework. The VCL (Visual Component Library) is Borland's class library that enables you to rapidly build high-quality Windows applications using either the Delphi for Win32 or the C++ language.

Other chapters that cover VCL Forms applications creation mostly use the Delphi language because C++Builder and Delphi VCL Forms applications only differ in syntax.

Creating a VCL Forms Application

To create a new VCL Forms application, double-click the VCL Forms Application item in the Delphi Projects category on the Tool Palette window or select File ➤ New ➤ VCL Forms Application - Delphi for Win32.

When the project is created, the IDE enables all the tools that can be used to design and develop VCL Forms applications (see Figure 11-1).

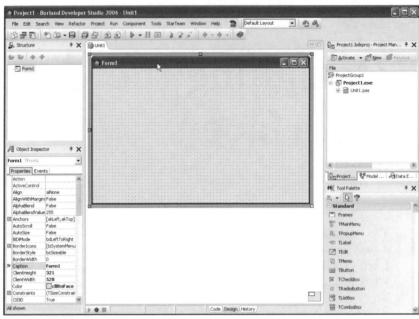

Figure 11-1: VCL Forms application project

The central point of a VCL Forms application is the main form, displayed on the Designer Surface. At design time, the Designer Surface enables you to resize the main form and to add additional objects (components) to it. Since currently only the main form exists, the form is automatically selected and its properties are displayed in the Object Inspector.

Before we thoroughly examine how VCL Forms applications function, let's change the title bar text of the main form to "My First VCL Application."

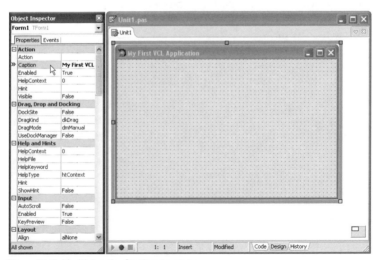

Figure 11-2: Modifying the Caption property

This requires modifying the form's Caption property in the Object Inspector. If the Object Inspector arranges properties by category, you can find the Caption property in the Action category (see Figure 11-2).

Before running the application, be sure to use the File ➢ Save All option to save the project files to disk. We have to use the Save All option because VCL Forms applications usually consist of more than just the main project file (.dpr). VCL Forms applications contain forms that are defined by two separate files: the Delphi form file (extension .dfm) and the form's unit (extension .pas). Accept the automatically generated names and run the application (see Figure 11-3).

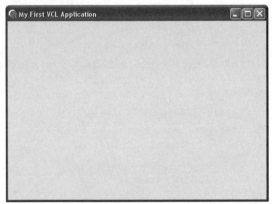

Figure 11-3: VCL Forms application at run time

As you can see, VCL Forms applications and console applications differ greatly. When you run a console application, the execution starts in the main block. The console application sequentially executes the statements in the main block and terminates when all statements have executed.

VCL Forms applications don't execute statements sequentially. They are idle most of the time and execute parts of the code randomly as a response to an event. VCL Forms applications are thus called event-driven applications.

Every time a user presses a key on the keyboard, moves the mouse cursor, activates another application — in general every time an event occurs — the operating system creates a message that describes exactly what happened and sends that message to the appropriate window. When developing VCL Forms applications, we see these messages as events, and all that we have to do is write code that responds to a specific event. The Events tab in the Object Inspector displays the list of events to which the main form can respond.

Figure 11-4: Events of the main form

If you run the VCL Forms application from the Delphi IDE, you won't be able to see the Object Inspector until you close the application.

The Main Form

Every VCL form is described by two separate files: the source file and the form file. The source file contains the source code of the form, that is, the class interface and the event responses. Listing 11-1 shows the source code of the main form generated by the Delphi IDE.

Listing 11-1: Source code of the main form

```
unit Unit1;

interface

uses
  Windows, Messages, SysUtils, Variants, Classes, Graphics, Controls, Forms,
  Dialogs;

type
  TForm1 = class(TForm)
  private
    { Private declarations }
  public
    { Public declarations }
  end;

var
  Form1: TForm1;

implementation

{$R *.dfm}

end.
```

The interface section of the unit contains the declaration of a new class: TForm1. Every form we create inherits the properties, methods, and events of the TForm class declared in the Forms unit.

```
TForm1 = class(TForm)
```

The TForm1 class declaration is somewhat different from the class declarations presented in the previous chapter because the TForm1 class declaration contains private and public sections. The reserved words private and public define the visibility of class members. Private class members can only be used in the unit where the class is declared. Public members, on the other hand, are globally visible.

The interface section of the unit also contains a variable declaration — the declaration of the Form1 object. At design time, Delphi automatically creates the Form1 object to be displayed by the Designer Surface. The Form1 variable is also used by the code in the main project file to create the Form1 object (the main form) when the application starts.

The implementation section of the unit currently contains a very important line of code:

```
{$R *.dfm}
```

The $R compiler directive is used to include a resource file into the executable at compile time. Resources are files like images, cursors, sounds, and Delphi form files.

In units, the * symbol replaces the unit name, and in the main project file, the * symbol replaces the project name. Currently, the main form is declared in Unit1.pas, and thus the form file has to be Unit1.dfm.

If you remove the $R compiler directive, the application will successfully compile but will not be able to run (see Figure 11-5).

Figure 11-5: Application compiled without the form file

The Delphi form file contains the list of properties and property values of the form and all objects that we placed on the form at design time. Unlike the Object Inspector that displays all properties of a selected object, the form file only contains properties that were modified at design time. Delphi doesn't have to write all object properties to the form file because all objects have default values and Delphi knows how to access these values. By not writing all object properties to the form file, Delphi reduces the amount of redundant data, thus reducing the size of both the form file and the final executable.

The Delphi IDE automatically updates both the source code and the form files when we add, remove, or modify components at design time. Although it's best to leave this job to the Delphi IDE, there are situations where you might have to modify the contents of the form file yourself. The form file can be easily modified because it is a text file that can easily be viewed inside the IDE. If you want to see the textual representation of the form, right-click anywhere on the Designer Surface and select the View as Text option from the context menu.

When you select the View as Text option, the Designer Surface is hidden and the form file is displayed in the Code Editor (see Figure 11-6). To return to the Designer Surface, right-click anywhere in the Code Editor and select the View as Form option on the context menu, or press Alt+F12.

```
E:\Delphi Book\Examples\CH11-01\Unit1.dfm                    _ □ X
Unit1
   1  object Form1: TForm1
   2    Left = 0
   3    Top = 0
   4    Caption = 'My First VCL application'
   5    ClientHeight = 320
   6    ClientWidth = 468
   7    Color = clBtnFace
   8    Font.Charset = DEFAULT_CHARSET
   9    Font.Color = clWindowText
  10    Font.Height = -11
  11    Font.Name = 'Tahoma'
  12    Font.Style = []
  13    OldCreateOrder = False
  14    PixelsPerInch = 96
  15    TextHeight = 13
  16  end
```

Figure 11-6: Contents of the Delphi form file

When you compile a VCL Forms application, the form's source file and the form file are compiled into a compiled unit file (.dcu).

Working with VCL Components

Components are classes that descend from the TComponent class and can be manipulated at design time on the Designer Surface.

The user interface is the most important part of an application, sometimes even more important than the code itself. To build a user interface in Delphi, you have to know how to add components to the Designer Surface and how to modify components using the Object Inspector.

The simplest way to add a component to the Designer Surface is by double-clicking the component on the Tool Palette window. Add a TLabel component to the Designer Surface by double-clicking the TLabel item in the Standard category on the Tool Palette window (see Figure 11-7).

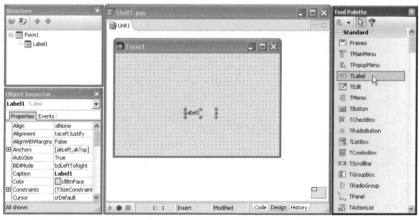

Figure 11-7: Adding a component to the Designer Surface

When you add a component to the Designer Surface, the new component is automatically selected and its properties are displayed in the Object Inspector. The Reference window is also updated to show the relationship between the components on the form.

The double-click method of adding components to the Designer Surface isn't extremely productive because we have to perform additional steps to move the component to the desired location.

Delphi also enables you to automatically place a component at the desired location on the form. To place a component at a specific location on the form, you have to select the component by clicking on it in the Tool Palette. The selected component is shown in purple (see Figure 11-8). Once the component is selected, you can add it to the Designer Surface by clicking at the desired location. You can also place a component at a specific location by dragging and dropping it from the Tool Palette to the Designer Surface.

Figure 11-8: Selected component

When you add components to the Designer Surface using any of the above methods, the components are placed at a default size. If you need a component that is bigger or smaller than the default sized component, you have to use yet another method.

To add a component to the Designer Surface and automatically adjust its size, you first have to select the component on the Tool Palette. Then click on the Designer Surface and draw the outline of the component. When you release the left mouse button, the component will be added at the position and size of the drawn outline (see Figure 11-9).

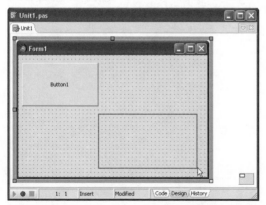

Figure 11-9: Drawing a component on the Designer Surface

The Tool Palette window also enables us to easily add a larger number of components to the Designer Surface. For instance, if we have to create the user interface for a calculator application, it would be tiresome to add all the necessary buttons one by one.

To add several components to the Designer Surface at once, you first have to select the component on the Tool Palette window by holding the Shift key and clicking on the desired component. A component thus selected appears highlighted with a dark outline (see Figure 11-10).

Figure 11-10: Multiple copy selection

After you have selected the component, you can click on the Designer Surface to add a component of the default size or draw an outline to create a resized component. Every time you click on the Designer Surface, another copy of the component is created. When you finish adding the components, deselect the selected component on the Tool Palette window by clicking on the mouse cursor button to the right of the Categories button on the Tool Palette (see Figure 11-11).

The Tool Palette window provides another tool: the Filter tool. Usually, to select a component, you have to know the component's category, scroll to the category, and select the component. The Filter tool enables you to quickly locate a component, regardless of the category. You only need to know the component's name. For instance, if you want to select the TButton component, click on the Filter button and start typing TButton. The Tool Palette filters the components and displays all components that start with the letters you typed (see Figure 11-12).

Figure 11-11: The deselect button

Figure 11-12: Filtering components on the Tool Palette

Standard Components and Properties

The Tool Palette window has a Standard category that contains components often used in VCL Forms applications. Among these are three components that are most often used: TLabel, TButton, and TEdit.

Each of these components has a very important job. TLabel is one of the simplest components and is used to display text on the form. The TLabel component is most often used to provide a name for a component that can't display its name on the form.

The purpose of the TButton component is to provide the user with a way of executing a piece of code. The TEdit component represents the standard text box and enables the user to enter some text.

The most important property of every component is the Name property. It is used in code to refer to the component.

Visual components like TLabel, TEdit, and TButton are also called controls. Controls are derived from the TControl class and have several standard properties that define their appearance on the form. The Top and Left properties define the position of the control, and the Width and Height properties define the size of the control.

Controls also have two standard properties that describe their functionality: Enabled and Visible. The Enabled property determines if the control can respond to events or execute code, and the Visible property determines if the control appears onscreen.

Responding to Events

To execute a piece of code in a VCL Forms application, you have to write a response to an event. The first application we'll create displays the user-entered text on the form's title bar.

To accept user input in VCL Forms applications, you cannot use the ReadLn procedure. Instead, you have to use the TEdit component. The Text property of the TEdit component enables you to read and write text displayed in the text box.

First, place a TEdit component on the form. This results in the component displaying its name on the form. Before we continue, remove the text from the TEdit component by clearing the Text property in the Object Inspector.

To copy the text from the TEdit component to the title bar, we have to write a response to an event. Without using a button, we can copy text from the TEdit component to the title bar in response to the OnChange event. The OnChange event occurs every time the user changes the contents of the text box.

To write a response to the OnChange event, select the Edit1 component on the Designer Surface and display the component's list of events in the Object Inspector. The OnChange event is the first event in the list.

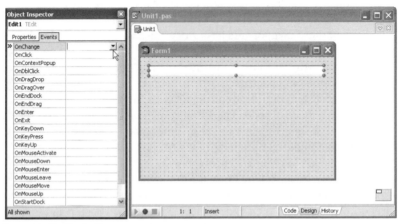

Figure 11-13: The OnChange event

Before you can write code, you have to create an empty event handler for the OnChange event. To create an empty event handler, double-click the right column in the Events page. Delphi creates an empty event handler in the Code Editor and adds the name of the event handler to the right column of the Events page (see Figure 11-14). The name of the event handler is always derived from the component and event names.

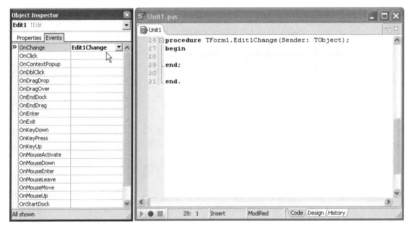

Figure 11-14: An empty event handler

As you can see, an event handler is nothing more than a procedure. Every time the user changes the contents of the Edit component, the Edit1Change procedure is called. To copy the text from the Edit1 component, you only have to write a single line of code:

```
procedure TForm1.Edit1Change(Sender: TObject);
begin
  Caption := Edit1.Text;
end;
```

The result of the OnChange event handler is displayed in Figure 11-15.

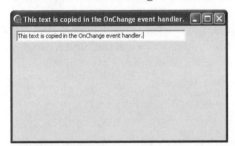

Figure 11-15:
The OnChange
event handler

Responding to the OnClick Event

The most frequently used event is the OnClick event. The following example enables the user to reverse a string. The example uses two TEdit components for input and output and a TButton component that reverses the string in the OnClick event handler (see Figure 11-16).

Figure 11-16:
The user interface
of the reverse
string application

Again, to provide the user with a more professional and nicer-looking user interface, you should delete the automatically generated text in the TEdit components. To be more productive, you should first select both TEdit components and then clear their Text properties in the Object Inspector. To select more components on the Designer Surface, first select a single component, then press and hold the Shift key and select other components.

When you select more components, the Object Inspector shows how many components you have selected and only displays the properties that exist in all selected components (see Figure 11-17).

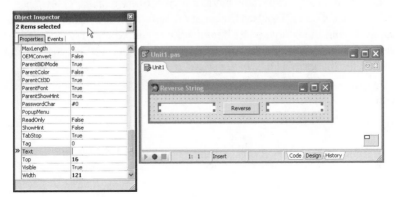

Figure 11-17: Multiple component selection

To write code for the OnClick event, you have to generate the empty event handler. Currently, there are two ways to achieve this because the OnClick event is the default event of the TButton component. The standard way of creating an event handler is to display the Events page in the Object Inspector and double-click the right column next to the event name. This is how you create empty event handlers for all events. But, if you want to create the event handler for the default event, you can simply double-click the component on the Designer Surface. After you double-click the Button1 component on the Designer Surface, Delphi creates the following event handler:

```
procedure TForm1.Button1Click(Sender: TObject);
begin

end;
```

To easiest way to reverse the string is to use a for-downto loop and copy characters from one TEdit component to the other. Note that this isn't the fastest way of reversing a string.

Listing 11-2: Reversing a string

```
procedure TForm1.Button1Click(Sender: TObject);
var
  i: Integer;
begin
  Edit2.Text := ''; { clear the old text }
  for i := Length(Edit1.Text) downto 1 do
    Edit2.Text := Edit2.Text + Edit1.Text[i];
end;
```

Figure 11-18: The reverse string application

Removing Event Handlers

Delphi's Code Editor has always been far superior to editors in other development environments, especially when it comes to code management. For instance, the Code Editor has the ability to automatically remove empty event handlers from the source code. If you, either deliberately or accidentally, double-click the Designer Surface, the Code Editor generates an empty event handler for the form's OnCreate event:

```
procedure TForm1.FormCreate(Sender: TObject);
begin

end;
```

If you don't have to respond to the OnCreate event, you will probably want to remove this unwanted piece of code. Although you can, you shouldn't remove the event handler manually because Delphi automatically removes all empty event handlers when you save the file or project to disk.

Removing an event handler that contains code involves some work. For instance, let's remove the OnClick handler of the reverse string button. Again, you should refrain from removing the method implementation manually. If you do, you will break your code and will be unable to compile the application (see Figure 11-19).

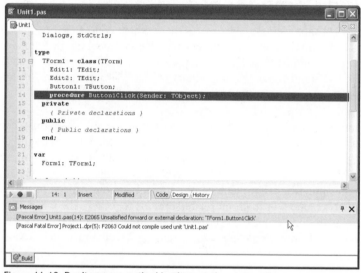

Figure 11-19: Don't remove method implementations manually.

If you've removed the method implementation manually, you then have to delete the method header in the interface section of the unit. The fastest way to delete a single line of code is to place the cursor anywhere in the line you want to delete and press Ctrl+Y.

The best way to remove an event handler from the source code is to only remove the code you added to it. In the case of the reverse string button, you have to remove the declaration of the variable and the code in the method block:

```
procedure TForm1.Button1Click(Sender: TObject);

begin

end;
```

When you're left with an empty event handler, you can remove the handler and all references to it by saving the project to disk.

The ability to remove empty event handlers is great and usually extremely useful. The only time this functionality can cause trouble is when we want to have empty event handlers as placeholders for future code. To trick the Code Editor into not removing the empty event handlers, write an empty comment in the method block:

```
procedure TForm1.Button1Click(Sender: TObject);
begin
  { }
end;
```

Grouping Components

In VCL Forms applications, the form is the ultimate container for components. Besides the form, Delphi provides several other components that are able to contain other components. These components are also known as container components. Standard container components are TGroupBox and TPanel in the Standard category, TScrollBox in the Additional category, and TPageControl in the Win32 category.

Components are usually grouped for two reasons. At design time, component groups increase productivity because we can treat a group of components as a single unit. At run time, groups improve the quality of the user interface. Some container components, like TGroupBox, also improve the visual appearance of the application. For instance, the Project Options dialog box uses the TGroupBox component to group related options together. The Code generation, Syntax options, Runtime errors, and Debugging frames visible in the dialog box are TGroupBox components that contain several check boxes each (see Figure 11-20).

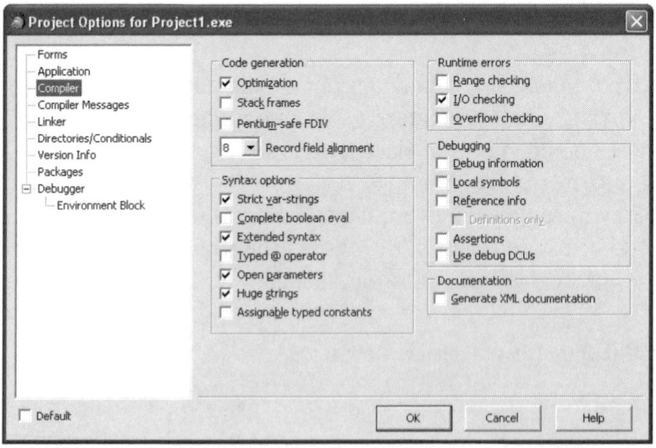

Figure 11-20: TGroupBox components in the Project Options dialog box

The best way to add child components to a container component is to first add the container component to the Designer Surface. When you add components to the Designer Surface, they are added to the container component under the mouse cursor. If there are no additional container components on the Designer Surface, the components are added to the form. When you have several container components on the form, the Structure window becomes an invaluable tool (see Figure 11-21).

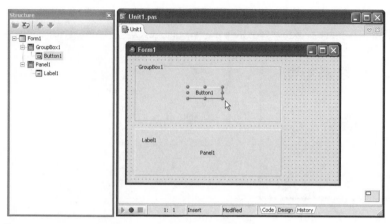

Figure 11-21: Parent-child relationships on the form

Parent and Owner Properties

The components that you work with at design time are real object instances. When you add a component from the Tool Palette window to the Designer Surface, the IDE calls the appropriate constructor to create an object instance.

The component constructor differs from the standard object constructor. The component constructor has a TComponent parameter:

```
constructor Create(AOwner: TComponent);
```

The AOwner parameter is used to define the owner of a component. The Owner component is responsible for freeing the memory occupied by the components it owns. When you design applications in the Delphi IDE, the form is automatically assigned as the owner of all components.

If you want to verify this, drop a button on the Designer Surface and write the following line in the OnClick event handler:

```
procedure TForm1.Button1Click(Sender: TObject);
begin
  Caption := 'The Owner of Button1 is ' + Button1.Owner.Name;
end;
```

While components only have the Owner property, controls (components derived from the TControl class) have both the Owner and Parent properties. The parent control is responsible for displaying the control onscreen. All container controls can be parents. If you add a component to the form, the form is both the owner and the parent. If you add the component to a container control like TPanel, the TPanel component becomes the Parent component.

To verify this, let's add a TPanel to the form and move the button to the TPanel. You can change the button's parent at design time by using the clipboard or the Structure window. To do so using the clipboard, do the following:

- Select the button and cut it to the clipboard using Edit ➤ Cut.
- Select the panel component on the Designer Surface.
- Use the Edit ➤ Paste option to add the previously cut button to the panel.

The Structure window provides an even easier way of moving the button to the panel — simple drag and drop.

Figure 11-22: Changing the component's parent at design time

Now that the button is located on the panel, we can, for instance, use the ShowMessage procedure to display the names of the Parent and Owner components. The ShowMessage procedure is a very simple message that accepts a single string parameter and displays a message box with an OK button (see Figure 11-23). The ShowMessage procedure is declared in the Dialogs unit.

Listing 11-3: Displaying parent and owner information

```
procedure TForm1.Button1Click(Sender: TObject);
begin
  ShowMessage('Owner: ' + Button1.Owner.Name);
  ShowMessage('Parent: ' + Button1.Parent.Name);
end;
```

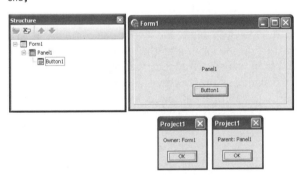

Figure 11-23: Displaying parent and owner information

The final note about container components concerns memory usage. Container controls are really useful and irreplaceable when it comes to grouping components, but they aren't meant to be used extensively as graphical decorations on the form.

For instance, the TPanel component is often used to create a frame around a group of components. With the BevelInner property set to bvRaised and the BevelOuter property set to bvLowered, the panel displays a beveled border. If you need the frame but don't need the container functionality of the TPanel component, you should use the TBevel component.

The TBevel component is a graphical component that can't contain other components and uses fewer system resources than the TPanel component. The TBevel component has only one purpose — to display a beveled frame on the form. To display the frame on the form, set the TBevel component's Shape property to bsFrame (see Figure 11-24). You can find the TBevel component in the Additional category on the Tool Palette window.

Figure 11-24: TPanel and TBevel frames

If you add a TBevel component to the form after you have added the components you wish to frame, the TBevel component will have a higher Z order and you won't be able to access the components "beneath" it. To access components beneath the TBevel component, right-click the TBevel component and select Control ➤ Send To Back from the context menu.

Aligning and Anchoring

Controls have two remarkable properties that enable us to create professional-looking, high-quality user interfaces that can be resized without losing their usefulness or ease of use.

The Align property enables us to align a control within its parent control. When you align a control to one of the sides of the parent control, the control is automatically resized when the parent's size changes. If the Align property is set to alNone, the control will not be moved or resized when the size of the parent changes.

The Align property is usually good for container controls that have to stretch from one side of the parent control to the other. But some controls, like TButton, TCheckBox, and the like, don't have the Align property. To align these controls, you have to use the Anchors property.

The Anchors property is a set of four values that define how the control holds on to the parent. The default value of the Anchors property is [akLeft, akTop]. Controls with this Anchors value don't change their position or size at run time. For instance, the Anchors property can be used if you need a button that always holds onto the right side of the form. To force the button to remain on the right side of the form even when the form is resized, set the Anchors property of the button to [akTop, akRight] (see Figure 11-25). To change the values in a set property, click the plus sign to the left of the property to expand it, and then modify the contents of the set.

Figure 11-25: The Anchors property

C++Builder VCL Forms Applications

To create a C++Builder VCL Forms application, either double-click the VCL Forms Application item in the C++Builder Projects category on the Tool Palette or select File ➢ New ➢ VCL Forms Application — C++ for Win32.

Project Files

When you create a new C++Builder VCL Forms application project, the IDE creates the necessary project files and displays the project's main form on the Designer Surface. The IDE creates six files — three project files and three files for the main form.

The three project files are .bdsproj, .cpp, and .res. The .bdsproj file contains project settings, the .cpp file with the project name contains the essential code that makes the VCL Forms application work, and the .res file contains the icon for the project's executable file.

The three files created for the main form are .cpp, .h, and .dfm. When you start working on the form, the .cpp file will contain event handlers, the .h file will contain the form's interface (the list of components added to the form at design time and the list of event handlers), and the .dfm file will contain properties of the components added to the form. Listings 11-4A and 11-4B show the .cpp and .h files created for the main form.

The Source File

Listing 11-4A: The main form's .cpp file

```
//$$---- Form CPP ----
//---------------------------------------------------------------------------

#include <vcl.h>
#pragma hdrstop

#include "Unit1.h"
//---------------------------------------------------------------------------
#pragma package(smart_init)
#pragma resource "*.dfm"
TForm1 *Form1;
//---------------------------------------------------------------------------
__fastcall TForm1::TForm1(TComponent* Owner)
    : TForm(Owner)
{
}
//---------------------------------------------------------------------------
```

The two #pragma directives after the #include directives are pretty important. The #pragma package directive ensures that units that reside in packages are properly initialized. All VCL components reside in packages.

The #pragma resource directive is used to link the .cpp, .h, and .dfm files together to make up a unit. The #pragma resource directive is the C++Builder equivalent of the {$R *.dfm} directive found in Delphi units. If you remove it, the .dfm will not be linked into the executable and the application won't be able to run.

Besides the #pragma directives and the Form1 variable, the .cpp file also contains the form's constructor:

```
__fastcall TForm1::TForm1(TComponent* Owner)
    : TForm(Owner)
{
}
```

In C++, the constructor is not called Create, as it is in Delphi, but instead has the same name as the class:

```
class MyClass {
public:
    MyClass(); // MyClass constructor
};
```

The Header File

Listing 11-4B: The main form's .h file

```
//$$---- Form HDR ----
//---------------------------------------------------------------------------

#ifndef Unit1H
#define Unit1H
//---------------------------------------------------------------------------
#include <Classes.hpp>
#include <Controls.hpp>
#include <StdCtrls.hpp>
#include <Forms.hpp>
//---------------------------------------------------------------------------
class TForm1 : public TForm
{
__published:    // IDE-managed components
private:         // User declarations
public:          // User declarations
    __fastcall TForm1(TComponent* Owner);
};
//---------------------------------------------------------------------------
extern PACKAGE TForm1 *Form1;
//---------------------------------------------------------------------------
#endif
```

The #ifndef and #define directives at the beginning of the header file are known as include guards. Include guards are put around the entire contents of the header file to make sure the contents of the file are only processed once at compile time, even if the header file is included in more than one unit in the project.

You should also consider protecting your own units with include guards. To protect your own unit, which in this example is called MyUnit.h, write this:

```
#ifndef MYUNIT_H
#define MYUNIT_H

// Contents of the MyUnit.h file

#endif
```

The form's header file also includes several VCL units (SysUtils, Classes, StdCtrls, and Forms) and contains the form's interface. Every component you drop onto the form at design time will be added to the __published section:

```
class TForm1 : public TForm
{
__published:      // IDE-managed components
    TButton *Button1;
    TLabel *Label1;
private:          // User declarations
public:           // User declarations
    __fastcall TForm1(TComponent* Owner);
};
```

Building a Simple VCL Forms Application

To see how to build VCL Forms applications using the C++ language, let's first create a very simple application that displays "My First C++Builder VCL Forms Application" on the form's title bar, as shown in Figure 11-26.

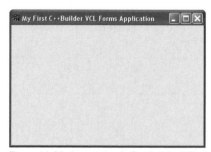

Figure 11-26: A very simple C++Builder VCL Forms application

You can create this application either by modifying the form's Caption property in the Object Inspector or by writing some code in the form's constructor. The following listing shows several ways of accessing the form's Caption property in code. Note that the following code always uses the indirect member selector (-> operator). This operator must be used because all VCL components are stored on the heap.

Listing 11-5: Accessing component properties in code

```
__fastcall TForm1::TForm1(TComponent* Owner)
  : TForm(Owner)
{
  this->Caption = "My First ";
  Form1->Caption = Form1->Caption + "C++Builder ";
  Caption = Caption + "VCL Forms Application";
}
```

The C++Builder Reverse String Application

There are two ways you can create a C++Builder version of a Delphi application. You can either translate the code to C++ or you can add a Delphi form to your C++ project.

First, let's create the C++Builder Reverse String application by adding the already created Delphi form to a C++Builder project. To add a Delphi form to a C++Builder VCL Forms application, first create a new C++Builder VCL Forms application. Before saving the project to disk, you need to remove the automatically created main form by selecting Project ➤ Remove from Project. When the Remove From Project dialog box appears, select Unit1.cpp in the list and click OK.

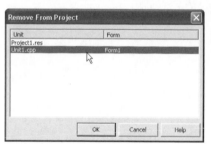

Figure 11-27:
Removing the
main form from
the project

Now that you've removed the main form, you can use Project ➤ Add to Project to add an existing form to the project (see Figure 11-28). To see Delphi units in the dialog box, you'll probably need to select the Pascal unit filter in the Files of type drop-down list.

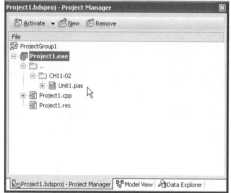

Figure 11-28:
A multi-language
VCL Forms project

When you add a Delphi form to a C++Builder project, Delphi will, at compile time, produce not only the .dcu file but will also generate a C++ header file for the Delphi form (with the .hpp extension) and produce an .obj file that can be used by the C++ compiler.

If you want, you can create a pure C++Builder VCL Forms application. The steps involved in creating a C++Builder and a Delphi VCL Forms application are the same. First you need to drop the necessary components on the Designer Surface (in this case you need two TEdit components and a TButton), then you have to double-click the button to have the IDE generate the event handler for the button's OnClick event:

```
void __fastcall TForm1::Button1Click(TObject *Sender)
{

}
```

Finally, you have to write the code to reverse the string:

```
void __fastcall TForm1::Button1Click(TObject *Sender)
{
    Edit2->Text = "";
    for(int i=Edit1->Text.Length(); i > 0; i--)
        Edit2->Text = Edit2->Text + Edit1->Text[i];
}
```

Runtime Packages

When you create a new Delphi VCL Forms application and compile it, the compiler will produce a 376 KB executable. But when you create a new C++Builder VCL Forms application and compile it, the compiler will produce a 29 KB executable file.

This enormous difference in the size of the executable is not because of the quality of the C++ compiler or defects in the Delphi compiler. The only reason this size difference exists is because of the default project settings.

By default, the Delphi compiler compiles all used VCL components and code into the executable file, which makes the file standalone and large. Such an executable file can be easily distributed because it doesn't require additional files to run.

Default C++Builder settings, however, tell the C++ compiler not to compile the VCL components into the executable but to use them from their runtime packages.

When you compile a C++ or a Delphi VCL Forms application with runtime packages, the executable file is no longer standalone and is much smaller. An executable file compiled with runtime packages cannot be distributed as easily as a standalone executable because, in addition to the executable file, you also have to distribute the runtime packages that contain components used by your application.

To compile a VCL Forms application with or without runtime packages, display the Project Options dialog box (Project ➢ Options), click on the Packages node on the left to display package-related options, and then check or uncheck the "Build with runtime packages" check box.

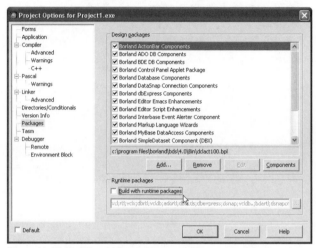

Figure 11-29: Building with or without runtime packages

Unless you're building an application suite with several executable files, you're better off building your applications without runtime packages, because the overall size of the application will be smaller.

Chapter 12

Using Forms

Forms are the most important container controls in VCL Forms applications because they represent main or secondary application windows and contain all other controls like buttons, images, and menus. Delphi's TForm class is an extremely powerful class that encapsulates an enormous number of properties, methods, and events.

Form Fundamentals

This part of the chapter deals with properties and events of the TForm class that enhance the quality of the user interface, either visually or practically.

Control Focus

The ActiveControl property can be used to specify which control should have the focus. When a control has focus, it can receive keyboard input. Only one control at a time can have the focus.

When you add controls to the Designer Surface, the focus may be given to a control that doesn't need it at application startup. For instance, the form shown in Figure 12-1 is designed to acquire the user's name, but instead of the more important text box, the Add button has the focus. In previous versions of the Windows operating system, or in XP and later versions that use the Classic visual style, the control that has the focus usually displays a dotted rectangle on its surface. Operating systems that use visual styles to display controls use the visual style's custom image to identify a focused control.

Figure 12-1: Control focus

To transfer the initial focus to the text box, select the Edit1 component from the drop-down list of the form's ActiveControl property.

Figure 12-2: Assigning a control to an object property

You can also change the focus of a control in code by using the SetFocus method. To change the initial focus of a control using the SetFocus method, place the SetFocus call in the OnShow event of the form.

Listing 12-1: Assigning focus to a control

```
procedure TForm1.FormShow(Sender: TObject);
begin
  Edit1.SetFocus;
end;
```

Alpha Blending

The AlphaBlend property specifies whether the form is translucent and is used in conjunction with the AlphaBlendValue property. The value of the AlphaBlendValue property is only relevant if the AlphaBlend property is set to True.

The AlphaBlendValue property accepts values in the 0 to 255 range. When the AlphaBlendValue property is set to 255, the form is opaque; when the AlphaBlendValue property is set to 0, the form is completely transparent.

Alpha-blended forms require more memory and more CPU power than standard forms. Besides using more resources, alpha-blended forms are only available in Windows NT 5.0 (Windows 2000) and later versions of the operating system.

You should think twice before enabling alpha blending on the main form because such forms are slower and the user may have trouble seeing the contents of the form.

Figure 12-3:
A translucent form

If you really want to have an alpha-blended form in your application, you should only enable alpha blending on forms that are used a short period of time, like the splash screen or the application's About box.

Form Style

To completely configure a form and make it look and work like you want it to, you usually have to modify three properties: BorderIcons, BorderStyle, and Position.

The Position property specifies the initial position of the form. You can use the Position property to, for instance, place the form exactly where you want it to be, allow the operating system to place the form where it wants the form to be, or center the form on the screen.

The BorderIcons property is a set property that specifies which icons appear on the title bar of the form. The most important value in the BorderIcons set is the biSystemMenu value. If biSystemMenu is included in the BorderIcons set, the title bar displays the application icon, the Close button, and the system menu when you click the application icon. The biMinimize and biMaximize values display the Minimize and Maximize buttons, respectively. If you only include the biMinimize value, the Maximize button is also displayed, but it is disabled. The biHelp value displays the Help button. The Help button is only intended to be displayed on dialog boxes and its purpose is to provide context-sensitive help for the controls on the form.

Figure 12-4:
Title bar buttons

The BorderStyle property specifies both the visual appearance of the form and the form's behavior. The default setting, bsSizeable, defines a form that has a thick border and enables the user to resize the form. The bsSingle value defines a form with a thin border that cannot be resized. The bsSizeToolWin and bsToolWindow values enable us to define toolbar windows, windows that look like standard windows but have thinner title bars.

The most extreme of all values is the bsNone value, which produces a non-resizable form that has no title bar and no borders (see Figure 12-5). This setting is very useful if you want to create a custom user interface.

Figure 12-5:
Form with
BorderStyle set
to bsNone

Although the bsNone value gives you complete control over the user interface, the form cannot be moved or resized. If you want to use a form without the system title bar in your applications, you need to write the code that allows the user to move your custom form on the screen. There are several ways to provide this functionality, and the way that requires the least technical knowledge is the one that uses the form's mouse events to move the form.

Basically, what we have to do is:

- Check whether the user pressed the left mouse button.
- Move the window while the left mouse button is pressed.
- Stop moving the window when the user releases the left mouse button.

When the user presses a mouse button over the form, the form fires the OnMouseDown event. An empty handler of the OnMouseDown event looks like this:

Listing 12-2: An empty OnMouseDown event handler

```
procedure TForm1.FormMouseDown(Sender: TObject; Button: TMouseButton;
  Shift: TShiftState; X, Y: Integer);
begin

end;
```

The OnMouseDown event handler provides a lot of information. The Sender parameter identifies the component that called the procedure. The Button parameter is an enumeration that identifies which button was pressed:

```
type TMouseButton = (mbLeft, mbRight, mbMiddle);
```

The Shift parameter is a set parameter that identifies which system keys and which mouse buttons were pressed when the event occurred, and the X and Y parameters hold pixel coordinates of the mouse pointer.

Inside the OnMouseDown event handler, you have to test whether the user pressed the left mouse button and save the X and Y coordinates for later use. To save the X and Y coordinates, you should declare two integer variables in the private section of the form. In addition to the integer variables, you have to declare a Boolean variable that will be used to identify whether or not the user can move the window.

Listing 12-3: Saving initial mouse coordinates

```
unit Unit1;

interface

uses
  Windows, Messages, SysUtils, Variants, Classes, Graphics, Controls, Forms,
  Dialogs;

type
  TForm1 = class(TForm)
    procedure FormMouseDown(Sender: TObject; Button: TMouseButton;
      Shift: TShiftState; X, Y: Integer);
  private
    { Private declarations }
    FOldX: Integer;
    FOldY: Integer;
    FMoving: Boolean;
  public
    { Public declarations }
  end;

var
  Form1: TForm1;

implementation

{$R *.dfm}

procedure TForm1.FormMouseDown(Sender: TObject; Button: TMouseButton;
  Shift: TShiftState; X, Y: Integer);
begin
  if Button = mbLeft then
  begin
    FMoving := True;
    FOldX := X;
    FOldY := Y;
  end;
end;

end.
```

The position of the window has to be updated every time the user moves the mouse pointer. Every time the position of the mouse changes while the mouse pointer is over the form, the form fires the OnMouseMove event.

Listing 12-4: An empty OnMouseMove event handler

```
procedure TForm1.FormMouseMove(Sender: TObject; Shift: TShiftState;
  X, Y: Integer);
begin

end;
```

In the OnMouseMove event handler, we have to test if the left mouse button is pressed and update the position of the form. Since the OnMouseMove event doesn't provide the button information, we have to use the FMoving variable to determine if we have to update the form's position. To calculate the new position of the form, we only have to get the difference between the old mouse coordinates and the new mouse coordinates provided in the X and Y parameters of the OnMouseMove event.

Listing 12-5: Moving the form in the OnMouseMove event

```
procedure TForm1.FormMouseMove(Sender: TObject; Shift: TShiftState;
  X, Y: Integer);
begin
  if FMoving = True then
  begin
    Left := Left + (X - FOldX);
    Top := Top + (Y - FOldY);
  end;
end;
```

Finally, we need to write code that stops moving the window when the user releases the left mouse button. When a button is released over a form, the form fires an OnMouseUp event. The OnMouseUp event provides the same parameters as the OnMouseDown event, but we actually don't need parameters. We only have to set the FMoving variable to False, and the user won't be able to move the window until he or she presses the left mouse button again.

Listing 12-6: Finishing the moving process

```
procedure TForm1.FormMouseUp(Sender: TObject; Button: TMouseButton;
  Shift: TShiftState; X, Y: Integer);
begin
  FMoving := False;
end;
```

Now that you can move the borderless form on the screen, you can create custom user interfaces, like the one displayed in Figure 12-6.

Figure 12-6:
A completely
customized form

It's actually pretty easy to create partially transparent forms like the one displayed in Figure 12-6. The first thing you need to have is the bitmap that you want to display on the form. Next, you need to define a transparent color, that is, a color that will be treated as transparent. In this example, magenta (fuchsia, RGB(255, 0, 255)) was selected as the transparent color.

Figure 12-7:
The original bitmap

Next, you have to place the bitmap on the form. The easiest way to display an image on the form is to use the TImage component, which can be found in the Additional category.

When you add a TImage component to the form, the TImage component is displayed as an empty frame. Set the TImage component's Left and Top properties to 0 and set the AutoSize property to True. When AutoSize is True, the component will be automatically resized when you assign an image to it. To assign an image to the Image component, you have to use the Picture property. When you select the Picture property in the Object Inspector, the Object Inspector displays a button with three dots. This button is only displayed for properties that have custom property editors. Click on the button to display the Picture Editor. You can use the Load button to select and load an image and the Clear button to remove the image from the form. Note that images assigned to the Picture property are saved in the form file and are included in the final executable.

Figure 12-08:
The Picture Editor

After you've loaded the image, you have to tell the form that you want to treat a color as transparent and you have to specify the exact color that is to be treated as transparent. You can do this by setting the form's TransparentColor property to True and the TransparentColorValue property to the color that identifies the transparent sections in the image. In this case, the color that identifies the transparent sections in the image is clFuchsia.

That's it. When you run the application, you should be able to see a partially transparent form. But if you try to move the form, you'll notice that the code no longer works. Actually, the code still works, but it's never called because the TImage component covers the surface of the form. When a mouse button is pressed or released, or when the mouse pointer is moved, the TImage component receives the notification of these events, not the form. Thus, the TImage component fires its OnMouseMove, OnMouseDown, and OnMouseUp events.

What we have to do now is move the form in response to the mouse events of the TImage component. But we don't have to rewrite the code that moves the form because Delphi enables us to assign a single event handler to more events. Thus, to enable the user to move the form, we have to call the existing event handlers in response to the TImage's mouse events. To do this, select the TImage component, display the Events tab on the Object Inspector, and assign appropriate event handlers to the OnMouseDown, OnMouseMove, and OnMouseUp events (see Figure 12-9).

Figure 12-9: Reusing existing event handlers

Useful Events

Most applications have to execute some code at application startup. This code usually includes reading user settings or something similar. The best event for code that needs to execute only once and only at application startup is the OnCreate event. For code that executes only once you should avoid the OnActivate event, since it fires every time the form regains focus (after losing it).

Usually, the OnCreate event is good enough for startup code. But there are some methods that may cause errors when called in the OnCreate event. One of them is the SetFocus method. For instance, if you try to focus a text box in the OnCreate event, you will receive an error, as shown in Figure 12-10.

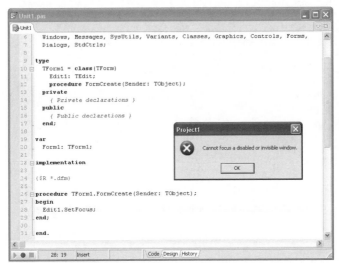

Figure 12-10: SetFocus causes an error because the form isn't visible.

The solution to this problem is really simple. If a method causes trouble in the OnCreate event, call the method inside the OnShow event.

Finally, to execute a piece of code when the application shuts down, write the code in the OnDestroy event handler.

The following example shows how to use the OnCreate and OnDestroy events. The application opens a text file in the OnCreate event and enables the user to add text to the file as long as the application is running. When the user closes the application, the application closes the file in the OnDestroy event. In this case, the OnClose event can also be used.

Figure 12-11: The user interface of the example application

Listing 12-7: Using the OnCreate and OnDestroy events

```
unit Unit1;

interface

uses
  Windows, Messages, SysUtils, Variants, Classes, Graphics, Controls, Forms,
```

```
    Dialogs, StdCtrls;

type
  TMainForm = class(TForm)
    Label1: TLabel;
    Edit1: TEdit;
    WriteButton: TButton;
    CloseButton: TButton;
    procedure WriteButtonClick(Sender: TObject);
    procedure FormDestroy(Sender: TObject);
    procedure FormCreate(Sender: TObject);
    procedure CloseButtonClick(Sender: TObject);
  private
    { Private declarations }
    FFile: TextFile;
  public
    { Public declarations }
  end;

var
  MainForm: TMainForm;

implementation

{$R *.dfm}

procedure TMainForm.CloseButtonClick(Sender: TObject);
begin
  Close;
end;

procedure TMainForm.FormCreate(Sender: TObject);
begin
  AssignFile(FFile, 'C:\Something.txt');
  {$I-}
  Rewrite(FFile);
  {$I+}
  { Disable the Write button if the file can't be opened. }
  if IOResult <> 0 then
    WriteButton.Enabled := False;
end;

procedure TMainForm.FormDestroy(Sender: TObject);
begin
  { If the Write button is enabled, the file is opened
    and it needs to be closed. }
  if WriteButton.Enabled then
    CloseFile(FFile);
end;

procedure TMainForm.WriteButtonClick(Sender: TObject);
begin
  if Edit1.Text <> '' then
```

```
    WriteLn(FFile, Edit1.Text);
end;

end.
```

Dynamic Component Creation

Let's say that we want to dynamically create a button that will be able to close the parent form. To create this button, we have to declare it in the private or public sections of the form.

```
type
  TForm1 = class(TForm)
  private
    { Private declarations }
  public
    { Public declarations }
    DynamicButton: TButton;
  end;
```

This code cannot be compiled because none of the units included by default in the uses list contain the declaration of the TButton class. The TButton class is declared in the StdCtrls unit, so add it to the uses list. When you add a TButton component to the Designer Surface, the IDE automatically adds the StdCtrls unit to the uses list. Since we're creating the button without the help of the Designer Surface, we have to add the reference to the StdCtrls unit manually.

```
uses
  Windows, Messages, SysUtils, Variants, Classes, Graphics, Controls, Forms,
  Dialogs, StdCtrls;
```

The best place to create this button is in the OnCreate event of the main form. To create the button, we have to call the TButton constructor.

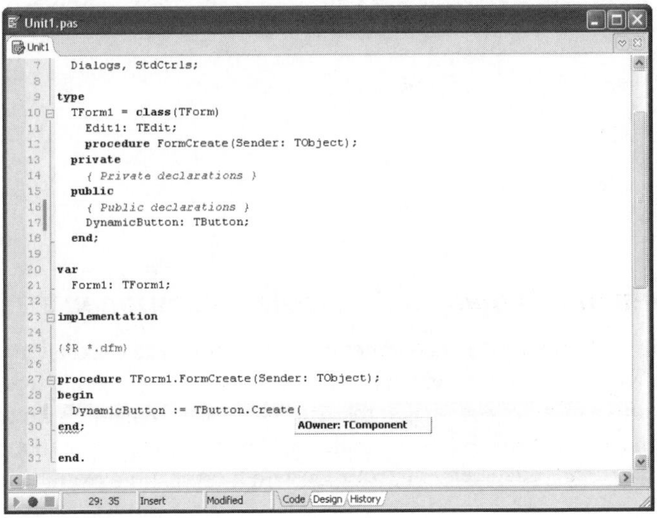

Figure 12-12: Calling the TButton constructor

As you can see in Figure 12-12, component constructors accept an AOwner parameter that is used to define the component's owner. Since we want to add the button to the main form, we can pass Self as the AOwner parameter. Since we're writing the code for the main form, Self references the main form.

```
DynamicButton := TButton.Create(Self);
```

The constructor only creates the button and defines the button's owner. If you run the application now, you won't be able to see the button because the button's parent component hasn't been defined. To display the button, you have to define the button's parent component.

```
{ Set form as the parent }
DynamicButton.Parent := Self;
```

Now that we've defined the button's parent, it will be displayed on the parent's surface. But it's hard to identify this control since it's situated in the top-left corner of the form and has no caption.

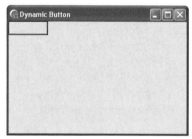

Figure 12-13: A dynamically created button

To completely define the button that will enable the user to close the form, set the Caption to "Close".

Listing 12-8: Dynamically creating a button

```
procedure TForm1.FormCreate(Sender: TObject);
begin
  DynamicButton := TButton.Create(Self);
  { Set form as the parent }
  DynamicButton.Parent := Self;
  DynamicButton.Caption := 'Close';
  DynamicButton.Top := 8;
  DynamicButton.Left := 8;
end;
```

Event Handlers and Dynamically Created Components

Currently, the DynamicButton component is only a graphical decoration on the form because none of its events have an event handler assigned. If you want to execute a piece of code when the user clicks the DynamicButton component, you have to assign an event handler to the OnClick event of the button. You can only assign an event handler with a compatible event list. If you take a look at the help file, you will notice that the OnClick event is declared like this:

```
[Delphi] property OnClick: TNotifyEvent;
```

TNotifyEvent is a custom type and defines a procedure that accepts a single TObject parameter.

```
type TNotifyEvent = procedure (Sender: TObject) of object;
```

So, a procedure that is compatible with the OnClick event has to accept a single TObject parameter.

Listing 12-9: A method compatible with the OnClick event

```
type
  TForm1 = class(TForm)
    procedure FormCreate(Sender: TObject);
  private
    { Private declarations }
  public
    { Public declarations }
    DynamicButton: TButton;
    procedure DynamicClick(Sender: TObject);
  end;

var
  Form1: TForm1;

implementation

{$R *.dfm}

procedure TForm1.DynamicClick(Sender: TObject);
begin
  ShowMessage('The form will now close.');
  Close;
end;
```

Finally, since the OnClick event and the DynamicClick method are compatible, to connect the DynamicClick method with the OnClick event you only have to write this:

```
DynamicButton.OnClick := DynamicClick;
```

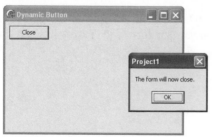

Figure 12-14: A dynamic component calling a dynamically assigned event handler

C++ Dynamic Component Creation

Dynamic component creation in Delphi and C++ is pretty much the same. The only difference between Delphi and C++ is that in C++ you have to use the new operator to create the component.

The first thing you have to do is declare an object variable in either the private or public section of the class. The component must be declared as a pointer because all VCL components must be heap allocated:

```
class TForm1 : public TForm
{
__published:
private:
   TButton* DynamicButton;
public:
   __fastcall TForm1(TComponent* Owner);
};
```

In Delphi, after we declared a TButton variable, we had to add the StdCtrls unit to the uses list in order to compile the code. In C++, we don't have to include the StdCtrls unit because it is included in all VCL Forms projects by default.

Now that you've declared the necessary variable, you can switch to the source code file and create the object dynamically in the form's constructor. To create the component, you have to use the following syntax:

```
ObjectVariable = new Class(Constructor_Parameters);
```

Here's the code that creates the DynamicButton button:

```
__fastcall TForm1::TForm1(TComponent* Owner)
   : TForm(Owner)
{
   // pass this in the constructor to make the form the Owner
   DynamicButton = new TButton(this);
   // set form as the Parent to make the button show
   // itself on the form
   DynamicButton->Parent = this;
   DynamicButton->Caption = "Close";
   DynamicButton->Top = 8;
   DynamicButton->Left = 8;
}
```

You don't have to worry about destroying the button because we passed this in the button's constructor, which means the form will destroy it when the application terminates.

Event Handlers and Dynamically Created Components in C++

To assign an event handler to a component's event, you need to create a method with a compatible parameter list. Since we're going to add an event handler to the button's OnClick event, you need to create a method that is compatible with the TNotifyEvent type. In C++, the TNotifyEvent type looks like this:

```
typedef void __fastcall (__closure *TNotifyEvent)(System::TObject* Sender);
```

As you can see from the above declaration, the TNotifyEvent type is a procedure that has only one parameter, an object pointer named Sender. The (__closure *TNotifyEvent) part of the declaration is the equivalent of Delphi's "of object" syntax, which is used to define a method pointer.

The __fastcall directive at the beginning of the declaration is a calling directive that makes sure the parameters are passed through CPU registers and in the appropriate order. To make your methods compatible with the VCL, you have to mark them with the __fastcall directive.

So, to add an event handler to the DynamicButton's OnClick event, first add the method's header to either the public or private section of the class:

```
class TForm1 : public TForm
{
__published:
private:
    TButton* DynamicButton;
    void __fastcall DynamicClick(TObject* Sender);
public:
    __fastcall TForm1(TComponent* Owner);
};
```

When you've added the method header to the class interface, write the method's implementation:

```
void __fastcall TForm1::DynamicClick(TObject* Sender)
{
    ShowMessage("The form will now close!");
    Close();
}
```

Finally, to have the button call the DynamicClick method in response to its OnClick event, assign the method to the button's OnClick event:

```
__fastcall TForm1::TForm1(TComponent* Owner)
    : TForm(Owner)
{
    DynamicButton = new TButton(this);
    DynamicButton->Parent = this;
    DynamicButton->Caption = "Close";
    DynamicButton->Top = 8;
    DynamicButton->Left = 8;

    DynamicButton->OnClick = DynamicClick;
}
```

Applications with Multiple Forms

To add a new form to the project, select File ➤ New ➤ Form - Delphi for Win32. The IDE automatically displays the second form on the Designer Surface. You can add components to the form and write code for the form, but you can't access the form from other units, at least not yet. To access the second form from the main form, you have to add the form to the uses list of the main form.

To add the second form's unit to the uses list of the main form, do the following:

1. Click on the tab of the main form to select it.

2. Select File ➤ Use Unit... to display the Use Unit dialog (see Figure 12-15).

3. In the Use Unit dialog box, select the unit and click OK to add it to the uses list of the selected form.

Figure 12-15: The Use Unit dialog box displays available units.

When you click OK in the Use Unit dialog box, the IDE adds the selected unit to the uses list of the main form. But that uses list resides in the implementation section of the unit. The IDE does this to avoid circular references between units. The uses list in the interface section of the unit should only contain references to essential units or units that contain code that you have to use in the interface section.

```
implementation

uses Unit2;

{$R *.dfm}

end.
```

If you're building a C++Builder VCL Forms application that has multiple forms, use the File ➤ Include Unit Hdr option to include another form's unit. The IDE will display the Use Unit dialog box, and when you click OK, it will add the #include directive after the #pragma hdrstop directive:

```
#include <vcl.h>
#pragma hdrstop

#include "Unit1.h"
#include "Unit2.h"
```

Displaying the Form

The TForm class provides two methods for displaying forms: Show and
ShowModal. The Show method simply displays the form. It is used when you
want to display and work with several forms at the same time.

The ShowModal method displays a modal form. A form displayed with the
ShowModal method allows the user to work with that form only. To access
other forms in the application, the user first has to close the modal form.

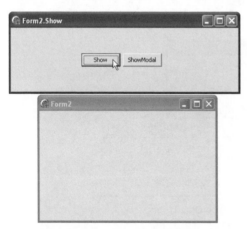

Figure 12-16: Second form displayed with the Show method

Here is the code for the Show and ShowModal buttons:

Listing 12-10: Displaying the form

```
procedure TForm1.ShowButtonClick(Sender: TObject);
begin
  Form2.Show;
  Caption := 'Form2.Show';
end;

procedure TForm1.ShowModalButtonClick(Sender: TObject);
begin
  Form2.ShowModal;
  Caption := 'Form2.ShowModal';
end;
```

When the user clicks the Show button to display the form, the form is displayed and the "Form2.Show" message is assigned to the Caption property of
the main form. But when the user clicks the ShowModal button to display the
form, the ShowModal method displays the form but doesn't return until the
user closes the form. Therefore, the "Form2.ShowModal" message is not displayed when the form is displayed but when the form closes.

Accessing components on another form is as simple as accessing components on the same form. The only difference is that when you access a
component on another form you have to write a fully qualified name:

```
FormName.ComponentName.Property
```

For instance, to copy the text typed in a text box to a text box on another form, we have to do the following:

1. Add a TEdit component to both forms.
2. Write the following code in the OnChange event of the TEdit component on the main form:

```
procedure TForm1.Edit1Change(Sender: TObject);
begin
  Form2.Edit1.Text := Edit1.Text;
end;
```

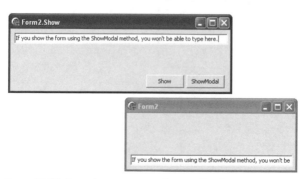

Figure 12-17: Accessing a component on another form

The Global Application Object

The global Application object represents the application and is the main reason we can work with forms without having to either create or destroy them. The Application object is an instance of the TApplication class that encapsulates methods, properties, and events related to the entire application.

When you add a form to the project at design time, the IDE creates the form and the code that automatically creates the form at application startup. That code resides in the main project file. To see the code that actually makes the application work, select Project ➤ View Source. Listing 12-11A shows the main project file of a Delphi VCL Forms application, and Listing 12-11B shows the main project file of a C++Builder VCL Forms application.

There are two differences between Delphi and C++Builder project files, apart from the syntax. The first difference is that execution in C++Builder project files doesn't begin in the main begin-end block but inside the WinMain function. The WinMain function replaces the main() function in Windows-based applications (VCL, generic, or other).

The second difference is that the C++Builder project file contains some exception handling code that checks for errors. Chapter 13 covers exception handling.

Listing 12-11A: The main project file of a Delphi VCL Forms application

```
program Project1;

uses
  Forms,
  Unit1 in 'Unit1.pas' {Form1},
  Unit2 in 'Unit2.pas' {Form2};

{$R *.res}

begin
  Application.Initialize;
  Application.CreateForm(TForm1, Form1);
  Application.CreateForm(TForm2, Form2);
  Application.Run;
end.
```

Listing 12-11B: The main project file of a C++Builder VCL Forms application

```
//$$---- EXE CPP ----
//---------------------------------------------------------------------------

#include <vcl.h>
#pragma hdrstop
//---------------------------------------------------------------------------
USEFORM("Unit1.cpp", Form1);
USEFORM("Unit2.cpp", Form2);
//---------------------------------------------------------------------------
WINAPI WinMain(HINSTANCE, HINSTANCE, LPSTR, int)
{
   try
   {
      Application->Initialize();
      Application->CreateForm(__classid(TForm1), &Form1);
      Application->CreateForm(__classid(TForm2), &Form2);
      Application->Run();
   }
   catch (Exception &exception)
   {
      Application->ShowException(&exception);
   }
   catch (...)
   {
      try
      {
         throw Exception("");
      }
      catch (Exception &exception)
      {
         Application->ShowException(&exception);
      }
   }
   return 0;
}
//---------------------------------------------------------------------------
```

The application uses the CreateForm method to create the forms automatically at startup. The CreateForm method accepts two parameters: the name of the class that is to be instantiated and the actual form variable. In C++Builder, the reserved word __classid must be used to work with classes directly.

When all forms are created, the application calls the Run method to start the application, and usually this involves displaying the main form. The main form of the application is the first form created with a call to the CreateForm method.

Creating Modal Forms

The ability to automatically instantiate forms at application startup enables us to quickly build application prototypes or, in some cases, to build entire applications without having to worry about creating and destroying the forms.

But in large applications that contain a large number of forms, automatic form creation is actually pretty undesirable. One of the reasons is application speed at startup. In an application that contains a large number of forms, it may take a while to create all the forms and display the main form on the screen. The longer it takes for an application to load, the less the users will like it.

Another, more serious reason why we should avoid automatic form creation in large applications is memory consumption. Since our application is only one of many that are concurrently executed in the OS, you should use system resources judiciously. Therefore, having all forms created at application startup is not the best solution.

If it's possible, you should create a form dynamically only when you need it and remove it from memory as soon as you're done with it. The following code shows how to dynamically create, display, and destroy a form.

Listing 12-12: Dynamically creating an empty form

```
procedure TForm1.Button1Click(Sender: TObject);
var
  F: TForm;
begin
  F := TForm.Create(Self);
  F.ShowModal;
  F.Free;
end;
```

To create a new form, you have to call the form's constructor and define the form's owner. The owner of the form is usually another form or the application itself. If you want to make the application the owner of the new form, pass the Application object to the constructor.

When you display the form using the ShowModal method, further statements aren't executed until the form is closed. When the form is closed, the Free method is called and the form is released from memory.

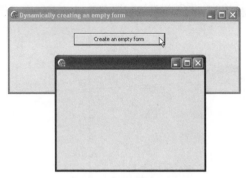

Figure 12-18: A dynamically created form

When you dynamically create a modal form, the owner component isn't absolutely necessary because the form gets immediately released from memory when the user closes it. Thus, you can pass nil to the form's constructor to create the form a bit faster.

Listing 12-13: Creating a form without an owner

```
procedure TForm1.Button1Click(Sender: TObject);
var
  F: TForm;
begin
  F := TForm.Create(nil);
  F.ShowModal;
  F.Free;
end;
```

The previous two examples show how to dynamically create a generic, empty form. But to dynamically create a form that belongs to the project, you first have to remove it from the auto-create list. There are two ways to remove a form from the auto-create list: by editing the main project file or by using the Project Options dialog box.

To manually remove the form from the auto-create list, do the following:

1. Open the main project file (Project ➤ View Source).

2. Remove the CreateForm call that creates the form you want to dynamically create later.

The Project Options dialog box provides a user-friendly way to manage auto-created and available forms. Forms listed under "Available forms" aren't automatically created at application startup, but they can be dynamically created.

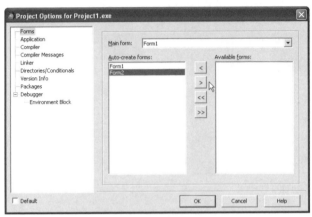

Figure 12-19: Managing auto-created forms

To dynamically create the second form, do the following:

1. Add the second form to the uses list of the main form (File ➤ Use Unit).

2. Add a button to the main form and write the following code in the OnClick event handler of the button.

Listing 12-14: Dynamically creating a modal form

```
procedure TForm1.Button1Click(Sender: TObject);
begin
  Form2 := TForm2.Create(Self);
  Form2.ShowModal;
  Form2.Free;
end;
```

Creating Modal Forms in C++

Forms, like all other components, have to be created using the new operator. To delete a dynamically created form (component), you don't call Free like you do in Delphi. Instead, you use the delete operator:

```
void __fastcall TForm1::CreateFormButtonClick(TObject *Sender)
{
   TForm* form = new TForm(this);
   form->ShowModal();
   delete form;
}
```

Creating Modeless Forms

Dynamic creation of a modeless form (a form displayed with the Show method) is more involved than the dynamic creation of a modal form.

To see how to dynamically create a modeless form, first create a new VCL Forms application project and add a second form to it. After you've added the second form, remove it from the auto-create list in the Project Options dialog box and add it to the uses list of the main form.

When creating a modeless form, you mustn't call the Free method after you call Show because modeless forms allow further statements to be executed. Thus, if you call Free immediately after Show, the modeless form will be created, displayed, and automatically released from memory.

Listing 12-15: Creating a modeless form

```
procedure TForm1.Button1Click(Sender: TObject);
begin
  Form2 := TForm2.Create(Self);
  Form2.Show;
end;
```

To release a modeless form from memory immediately after the user closes it, you have to do it in the form's OnClose event handler. Select the second form in the IDE and double-click the OnClose event in the Object Inspector to have Delphi generate the empty handler. To free the modeless form from memory, assign the value caFree to the Action parameter of the OnClose event.

Listing 12-16: Releasing a modeless form from memory

```
procedure TForm2.FormClose(Sender: TObject; var Action: TCloseAction);
begin
  Action := caFree;
end;
```

The caFree value is one of the values in the TCloseAction enumeration that enables us to define what should happen when a form is closed. When you assign caFree to the Action parameter, the form is closed and immediately released from memory.

Although the code that creates and destroys the modeless form works great, there is a small problem: Another instance of the TForm2 class is created every time the user clicks the button and the Form2 variable only points to the form that was created last.

If you only want to have a single copy of the modeless form (which is almost always the case), you have to determine whether the form exists before you call the constructor. The best way to see if a form (or any other object) is nil is to use the Assigned function, but you can also perform the test manually by comparing the form (object) variable to nil. Listings 12-17A and 12-17B show how to do this in both Delphi and C++.

Listing 12-17A: Creating the form only if it doesn't exist

```
procedure TForm1.Button1Click(Sender: TObject);
begin
  { if not created, create the form }
  if not Assigned(Form2) then
    Form2 := TForm2.Create(Self);

  Form2.Show;
end;
```

Listing 12-17B: Creating the form only if it doesn't exist, C++ version

```
void __fastcall TForm1::Button1Click(TObject *Sender)
{
```

```
if(Form2 == NULL)
   Form2 = new TForm2(this);

Form2->Show();
}
```

In this case, the constructor is called only when the form doesn't exist, but the Show method is always executed, regardless of the call to the constructor. This way, if the user tries to create the form after it's already been created, the constructor is skipped, but the Show method is called to display and activate the existing form.

We are still not finished. Currently, the code only works once. If you create the form once, then close it and try to create it again, you will get an error because when an object is destroyed, the object variable isn't set to nil. So, select the second form in the IDE and change the OnClose event handler to this:

Listing 12-18A: The proper way to destroy a modeless form

```
procedure TForm2.FormClose(Sender: TObject; var Action: TCloseAction);
begin
  Action := caFree;
  Form2 := nil;
end;
```

Listing 12-18B: The proper way to destroy a modeless form, C++ version

```
void __fastcall TForm2::FormClose(TObject *Sender, TCloseAction &Action)
{
   Action = caFree;
   Form2 = NULL;
}
```

Designing Dialog Boxes

Windows applications very often use dialog boxes to communicate with the user. You can either use one of the common dialogs or create your own. Common dialogs are described later in the book.

A dialog box is nothing more than a customized form. If you want to have a non-resizable dialog box without an icon on the title bar, you only have to set the BorderStyle property to bsDialog.

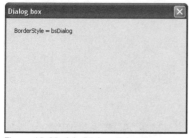

Figure 12-20: A bsDialog dialog box

If you want to have a dialog box that more closely resembles, for instance, the Project Options dialog box that can be resized or has an icon in the title bar, you have to do the following:

1. Set the BorderIcons property to [biSystemMenu].

2. Set the BorderStyle property to bsSizeable or bsSingle.

3. Optionally, set the Position property to poScreenCenter to position the form in the center of the screen.

Dialog boxes are usually modal forms that are used to retrieve additional information from the user. Dialog boxes must provide the user at least two buttons: OK and Cancel. The OK button is used to confirm the work in the dialog box is done, and the Cancel button is used to disregard the work done in the dialog box. Both buttons have to close the dialog box.

Now, let's create a dialog box that will enable the user to change the color of the main form. Add a TLabel component and two TButton components and modify them to resemble the ones displayed in Figure 12-21.

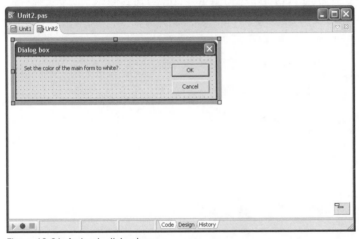

Figure 12-21: A simple dialog box

Now we have to modify the ModalResult property of the OK and Cancel buttons. Set the ModalResult property of the OK button to mrOK and the ModalResult property of the Cancel button to mrCancel. The ModalResult property enables us to do two things at the same time: close the dialog box and notify the caller whether the user selected OK, Cancel, or something else. When the user clicks a button with a modified ModalResult property, the value of the ModalResult property is automatically assigned to the ModalResult property of the dialog box. So, to see what button the user selected, we have to test the ModalResult property of the dialog box.

The following code shows how to use this dialog box to enable the user to modify the color of the main form.

Listing 12-19: Using the custom dialog box

```
procedure TForm1.Button1Click(Sender: TObject);
begin
  Form2.ShowModal;
  if Form2.ModalResult = mrOK then
  begin
    Caption := 'User selected OK.';
    Color := clWhite;
  end;
end;
```

To be technically and professionally correct, we have to do two more things. First, we have to enable the user to cancel the dialog box with the Esc key and to confirm the dialog box with the Enter key. Then, we have to remove the dialog box from the auto-create list and dynamically create it when necessary.

To fire the Cancel button's OnClick event when the user presses Esc on the keyboard, you have to set the button's Cancel property to True. To fire the OK button's OnClick event when the user presses Enter on the keyboard, set the button's Default property to True, and you're done.

Listing 12-20: Dynamically creating the dialog box

```
procedure TForm1.Button1Click(Sender: TObject);
begin
  Form2 := TForm2.Create(Self);
  Form2.ShowModal;
  if Form2.ModalResult = mrOK then
  begin
    Caption := 'User selected OK.';
    Color := clWhite;
  end;

  Form2.Free;
end;
```

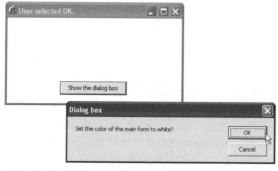

Figure 12-22: The finished application

Creating Splash Screens

A splash screen is a form that is displayed at application startup, typically while the application is busy creating other forms. The splash screen usually displays the company's name and logo and the application's name and version.

From a technical point of view, a splash screen is totally unnecessary in small applications because they often load very quickly. Splash screens are used in more complex applications to distract the user from counting the seconds (yeah, right) it takes for an application to load.

The first thing you have to do is add a new form to the project, name it SplashForm, and remove it from the auto-create list.

Splash forms are usually borderless and positioned in the center of the screen. So, set the BorderStyle property to bsNone and the Position property to poScreenCenter.

Now, open the main project file and dynamically create the SplashForm form. See Listing 12-21A for the Delphi version and Listing 12-21B for the C++ version. To use the SplashForm form in the main project file, don't forget to #include the form's header file.

Listing 12-21A: Creating the splash form

```
program Project1;

uses
  Forms,
  Unit1 in 'Unit1.pas' {Form1},
  Unit2 in 'Unit2.pas' {SplashForm};

{$R *.res}

begin
  Application.Initialize;
  { Create & display the splash screen }
  SplashForm := TSplashForm.Create(Application);
  SplashForm.Show;
  SplashForm.Update;

  Application.CreateForm(TForm1, Form1);

  { Destroy the splash screen }
  SplashForm.Free;
  Application.Run;
end.
```

Listing 12-21B: Creating the splash form, C++ version

```
#include <vcl.h>
#include <windows.h>
#pragma hdrstop
#include "Unit2.h" // SplashForm

USEFORM("Unit1.cpp", Form1);
USEFORM("Unit2.cpp", SplashForm);
```

```
WINAPI WinMain(HINSTANCE, HINSTANCE, LPSTR, int)
{
  try
  {
    Application->Initialize();

    SplashForm = new TSplashForm(Application);
    SplashForm->Show();
    SplashForm->Update();

    Application->CreateForm(__classid(TForm1), &Form1);

    delete SplashForm;
    Application->Run();
  }
  catch (Exception &exception)
  {
    Application->ShowException(&exception);
  }
  catch (...)
  {
    try
    {
      throw Exception("");
    }
    catch (Exception &exception)
    {
      Application->ShowException(&exception);
    }
  }
  return 0;
}
```

As you can see, the splash screen is a modeless form. If you display the splash screen as a modal form, the application will not run until you close it. The splash screen is displayed with two methods: Show and Update. The Update method actually displays the form in this case — it forces the form to display itself.

Since this example only creates the main form automatically, the splash screen will only be displayed for a short time. To see the splash screen a bit longer, you have to pause the application for a second or two by calling the Sleep procedure. The Sleep procedure is declared in the Windows unit (or windows.h if you're using C++Builder) and accepts a single integer value: the number of milliseconds the application should remain inactive. You should call the Sleep procedure before you release the splash screen.

Listing 12-22: Displaying the splash screen

```
program Project1;

uses
  { The Sleep procedure is declared in the Windows unit }
  Forms, Windows,
  Unit1 in 'Unit1.pas' {Form1},
  Unit2 in 'Unit2.pas' {SplashForm};

{$R *.res}

begin
  Application.Initialize;
  { Create & display the splash screen }
  SplashForm := TSplashForm.Create(Application);
  SplashForm.Show;
  SplashForm.Update;

  Application.CreateForm(TForm1, Form1);

  { Destroy the splash screen, but first wait 2 seconds. }
  Sleep(2000);
  SplashForm.Free;
  Application.Run;
end.
```

Figure 12-23: A splash screen

Chapter 13

Delphi and C++ Exception Handling

The examples we wrote in previous chapters, especially the ones that illustrate how to dynamically create objects, can be considered pretty unsafe. The reason is simple: The examples contain no or very little error-handling code. The only examples that check for errors extensively are the examples that use the IOResult function to see if an I/O error occurred.

This chapter deals with exception handling (also known as structured exception handling) — an error-handling mechanism that enables you to respond to errors in a uniform manner.

Exceptions and Exception Handling

When you develop applications, you have to write both the code that solves a particular problem and the code that checks for errors. Traditionally, the error-handling code is based around the if statement. The if statement is often used to test user input and function results. In simple cases, the if statement may be enough, but in GUI applications, where users have complete freedom, an error may occur anytime and anywhere. Using only the if statement to safeguard the application is not the best idea.

The exception handling mechanism is the best way to catch and respond to errors. When an error occurs in a Delphi application, the application automatically raises an exception. An exception is an object that describes the error that occurred. Raising an exception simply means that the application creates an exception object that describes the error in more detail.

If we don't handle the exception (if we don't write code that catches the exception), the application does it automatically. Usually, the application handles the exception by displaying a message box that notifies the user that an error occurred. For instance, if you pass a string that contains characters that can't be converted to a numerical value or an empty string to the StrToInt function, the function raises an exception (see Figure 13-1).

Figure 13-1: An exception handled by the application

To handle an exception raised by the StrToInt function, we have to put the call to the StrToInt function into a protected block. A protected block is a block that can respond to a certain exception. In Delphi, a protected block looks like this:

```
try
  statement(s);
except
end;
```

In C++, a protected block looks like this:

```
try
{
}
catch(...)
{
}
```

Statements that might raise an exception are placed in the try block, and any code that handles the exception is placed in the exception handler. The exception handler part of the protected block starts with the reserved word except in Delphi and the reserved word catch in C++.

If you pass a valid string to the StrToInt function and no exceptions occur, only the code in the try block is executed. The code in the exception block is only executed if a statement inside the try block raises an exception.

The following two examples show how to call the StrToInt function and catch any exception that might be raised by it. Listing 13-1A shows how to catch exceptions in a Delphi application, and Listing 13-1B shows how to catch exceptions in a C++Builder application.

Listing 13-1A: Catching an exception in Delphi

```
procedure TForm1.Button1Click(Sender: TObject);
var
  x: Integer;
begin
  try
    x := StrToInt(Edit1.Text);
  except
    ShowMessage('An error occurred.');
```

```
    end;
end;
```

Listing 13-1B: Catching an exception in C++

```cpp
void __fastcall TForm1::Button1Click(TObject *Sender)
{
    int x;
    try
    {
        x = StrToInt(Edit1->Text);
    }
    catch(...)
    {
        ShowMessage("An error occurred.");
    }
}
```

Figure 13-2: An exception handled by our exception handler

Handling Specific Exceptions in Delphi

Now, let's try to create a simple calculator that only enables you to divide two numbers. The user interface of the calculator is displayed in Figure 13-3.

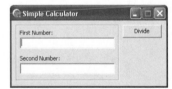

Figure 13-3: The simple calculator

To divide the values entered into the TEdit components we have to write code that first converts both numbers to integers and then divides them. This code can easily raise two exceptions. It can raise the EConvertError exception when a value in one of the TEdit components can't be converted, or it can raise the EDivByZero exception when you try to divide the first number by 0.

Listing 13-2: Dividing two values

```
procedure TForm1.Button1Click(Sender: TObject);
var
  Num1: Integer;
  Num2: Integer;
begin
```

```
  try
    Num1 := StrToInt(Edit1.Text);
    Num2 := StrToInt(Edit2.Text);
    ShowMessage('Result: ' + IntToStr(Num1 div Num2));
  except
    ShowMessage('You can''t divide these values.');
  end;
end;
```

Although you can write exception handlers that catch all exceptions, you should try to handle specific exceptions. The ability to handle a specific exception is provided by the reserved word on. The syntax of the reserved word on is:

```
on SomeException do HandleTheException;
```

The on-do construct can only be used inside the exception handler:

```
try
  statements(s);
except
  on Exception do HandleException;
  on AnotherOne do HandleThisOne;
end;
```

If possible, you should use the on-do construct to handle different exceptions in their own way. For instance, you can handle the EConvertError by displaying a message that displays the error, and you can handle the EDivByZero exception by telling the user that the second number can't be 0 and automatically changing it to 1. Listing 13-3A shows how to handle specific exceptions in Delphi. Listing 13-3B shows how to handle specific exceptions in C++.

Listing 13-3A: Handling specific exceptions

```
procedure TForm1.Button1Click(Sender: TObject);
var
  Num1: Integer;
  Num2: Integer;
begin
  try
    Num1 := StrToInt(Edit1.Text);
    Num2 := StrToInt(Edit2.Text);
    ShowMessage('Result: ' + IntToStr(Num1 div Num2));
  except
    on EConvertError do
      ShowMessage('One of the values is invalid.');

    on EDivByZero do
    begin
      ShowMessage('This value can''t be 0.');
      Edit2.Text := '1';
      Edit2.SetFocus;
    end; // on EDivByZero
  end;
end;
```

When you use the on-do construct to handle specific exceptions, you should also add code that deals with errors you know nothing about. To handle exceptions that you haven't handled specifically, you can add an else part to the exception handler.

```
try
  statement(s);
except
  on Exception do HandleIt;
  on AnotherOne do HandleThisOne;
  else
    HandleAllOtherExceptions;
end;
```

Handling Specific Exceptions in C++

To handle specific exceptions in C++, you have to write one or more catch blocks after the try block. When you use catch to catch a specific exception, you can't just specify the exception class as you can in Delphi. In C++, when you catch an exception you also have to specify the exception object and catch it by reference. In Delphi, you can catch an exception with or without catching the exception object. To see how to use the exception object in Delphi, see the "Using the Exception Object" section later in this chapter.

So, to handle specific exceptions in C++, you have to write this:

```
try
{
}
catch(ExceptionClass &Object)
{
}
catch(AnotherExceptionClass &Object)
{
}
/* if you want to catch other exceptions write catch(...) at the end */
catch(...)
{
}
```

Listing 13-3B: Handling specific exceptions in C++

```
void __fastcall TForm1::Button1Click(TObject *Sender)
{
    int Num1;
    int Num2;

    try
    {
        Num1 = StrToInt(Edit1->Text);
        Num2 = StrToInt(Edit2->Text);
        ShowMessage("Result = " + IntToStr(Num1 / Num2));
    }
    catch(EConvertError &e)
    {
        ShowMessage("One of the values is invalid.");
```

```
  }
  // instead of EDivByZero, division raises an
  // EAccessViolation exception in a C++Builder application
  catch(EAccessViolation &e)
  {
     ShowMessage("This value can't be 0!");
     Edit2->Text = "1";
     Edit2->SetFocus();
  }
}
```

Reraising Exceptions

When an error occurs, an exception object instance is created. When this exception is handled, the exception object is automatically freed. If you don't want to or don't know how to handle a specific exception, you should let Delphi handle it. To do that, you have to reraise the exception, that is, recreate the exception object instance. To reraise the exception in Delphi, you have to use the reserved word raise. In C++, you have to use the reserved word throw.

For instance, the following exception handler only handles the EConvertError exception. If any other exception is raised, the exception handler reraises it. This way the exception remains after the exception handler finishes, and another exception handler, usually the default one, has to handle it. Listing 13-4A shows how to reraise an exception in Delphi and Listing 13-4B shows how to reraise an exception in C++.

Listing 13-4A: Reraising exceptions in Delphi

```
procedure TForm1.Button1Click(Sender: TObject);
var
  Num1: Integer;
  Num2: Integer;
begin
  try
    Num1 := StrToInt(Edit1.Text);
    Num2 := StrToInt(Edit2.Text);
    ShowMessage('Result: ' + IntToStr(Num1 div Num2));
  except
    { Handle the EConvertError exception }
    on EConvertError do
      ShowMessage('One of the values is invalid.');

    { Reraise all other exceptions. }
    else raise;
  end;
end;
```

Listing 13-4B: Reraising exceptions in C++

```
void __fastcall TForm1::Button1Click(TObject *Sender)
{
   int Num1;
   int Num2;
```

```
try
{
   Num1 = StrToInt(Edit1->Text);
   Num2 = StrToInt(Edit2->Text);
   ShowMessage("Result = " + IntToStr(Num1 / Num2));
}
catch(EConvertError &e)
{
   ShowMessage("One of the values is invalid.");
}
catch(...)
{
   Caption = "Something wrong happened.";
   // reraise the exception
   throw;
}
}
```

So, if an EConvertError exception is raised, the exception handler handles it itself, and if any other exception occurs, like EDivByZero or EAccess-Violation, the exception handler reraises the exception and passes it to another handler (see Figure 13-4).

Figure 13-4: Local handler handling EConvertError and the default handler handling the reraised exception

Raising Exceptions

The reserved word `raise` is also used to raise exceptions. To raise an exception in Delphi, use the reserved word `raise` followed by an exception object instance. The exception object instance is usually a call to the exception constructor.

The syntax for raising an exception typically looks like this:

```
raise ExceptionClass.Create('Error message');
```

To raise an exception in C++, use the reserved word `throw`, also followed by a call to an exception's constructor:

```
throw ExceptionClass("Error message");
```

You can, for instance, create a custom version of the StrToInt function that raises the EConvertError exception with customized error messages when the string can't be converted. Listing 13-5A shows the Delphi version of the function and Listing 13-5B shows the C++ version.

Listing 13-5A: Raising exceptions in Delphi

```
unit Unit1;

interface

uses
  Windows, Messages, SysUtils, Variants, Classes, Graphics, Controls, Forms,
  Dialogs, ExtCtrls, StdCtrls;

type
  TForm1 = class(TForm)
    procedure Button2Click(Sender: TObject);
  private
    { Private declarations }
  public
    { Public declarations }
    function CustomStrToInt(const s: string): Integer;
  end;

var
  Form1: TForm1;

implementation

{$R *.dfm}

function TForm1.CustomStrToInt(const s: string): Integer;
var
  ErrorCode: Integer;
begin
  Val(s, Result, ErrorCode);

  if ErrorCode <> 0 then
  begin
    if s = '' then
      raise EConvertError.Create('An empty string can''t be used here.')
    else
      raise EConvertError.Create('Hello? You can''t convert "' +
        s + '" to an integer!');
  end;
end;

procedure TForm1.Button2Click(Sender: TObject);
var
  Num1: Integer;
  Num2: Integer;
begin
  Num1 := CustomStrToInt(Edit1.Text);
  Num2 := CustomStrToInt(Edit2.Text);
  ShowMessage(IntToStr(Num1 div Num2));
end;

end.
```

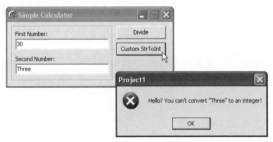

Figure 13-5: The EConvertError exception raised in the CustomStrToInt function

Listing 13-5B: Raising exceptions in C++

```cpp
int __fastcall TForm1::CustomStrToInt(const AnsiString s)
{
    int Result;

    if(s == "0")
        return 0;
    else {
        if(s == "")
            throw EConvertError("An empty string can't be used here.");
        else {
            // atoi returns 0 if it fails to convert the str to int
            Result = atoi(s.c_str());
            if(Result == 0)
                throw EConvertError("Hello? You can't convert \"" +
                    s + "\" to an integer!");
        }
        return Result;
    }
}
```

Using the Exception Object

The on-do construct enables us to temporarily acquire the actual exception object by using the following syntax:

```
on Identifier: Exception do HandleIt;
```

The identifier is usually the capital letter E. When you acquire the exception object, you can use it like any other object and access its properties and methods. The only thing that you really must not do is destroy the exception object because exception objects are automatically managed by the exception handler.

Listing 13-6: Using the exception object

```
procedure TForm1.Button1Click(Sender: TObject);
var
  x: Integer;
  y: Integer;
begin
  x := 20;
  y := 0;
```

```
try
  Caption := IntToStr(x div y);
except
  on E: EDivByZero do
    ShowMessage('Exception: ' + E.ClassType.ClassName +
      #13 + 'Exception Message: ' + E.Message);
end;
end;
```

Figure 13-6: Using the exception object

Creating Custom Exceptions in Delphi

Creating a custom exception is very simple and not that different from creating a custom class. Custom exceptions should descend from the Exception class or another descendant of the Exception class. The names of exception classes, by convention, always start with the capital letter E.

```
type
  EMyException = class(Exception);
```

Listing 13-7A shows how to raise and catch a custom exception in Delphi. Listings 13-7B and 13-7C that follow in the next section show how to raise and catch the same custom exception in C++.

Listing 13-7A: Working with a custom exception

```
unit Unit1;

interface

uses
  Windows, Messages, SysUtils, Variants, Classes, Graphics, Controls, Forms,
  Dialogs, StdCtrls;

type
  ENoUpperCaseLetters = class(Exception);

  TForm1 = class(TForm)
    Edit1: TEdit;
    Button1: TButton;
    Label1: TLabel;
    procedure Button1Click(Sender: TObject);
  private
    { Private declarations }
  public
```

```
    { Public declarations }
    function CountUpperCase(const s: string): Integer;
  end;

var
  Form1: TForm1;

implementation

{$R *.dfm}

function TForm1.CountUpperCase(const s: string): Integer;
var
  ch: Char;
begin
  Result := 0;
  for ch in s do
    if ch in ['A'..'Z'] then Inc(Result);

  { if there are no uppercase letters, raise the exception }
  if Result = 0 then
    raise ENoUpperCaseLetters.Create('No uppercase letters in the string.');
end;

procedure TForm1.Button1Click(Sender: TObject);
var
  Cnt: Integer;
begin
  try
    Cnt := CountUpperCase(Edit1.Text);
    Caption := IntToStr(Cnt) + ' uppercase letter';
    if Cnt > 1 then Caption := Caption + 's';
  except
    on E: ENoUpperCaseLetters do
      Caption := E.Message;
  end;
end;

end.
```

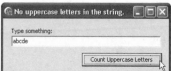

Figure 13-7: Working with a custom exception

Creating Custom Exceptions in C++

Creating a custom exception in C++ is only a bit more complicated than it is in Delphi. To create a custom exception, you have to derive a new class from Exception and create a constructor that accepts an AnsiString message and passes it to the Exception's constructor:

```
class EMyException: public Exception
{
public:
    EMyException(const AnsiString Msg) : Exception(Msg) {};
};
```

The : Exception(Msg) part of the constructor is known as the initializer list. In this case, it simply passes the Msg parameter to the Exception class's constructor.

Listings 13-7B and 13-7C show how to count uppercase letters in C++ and how to raise and catch the ENoUpperCaseLetters custom exception.

Listing 13-7B: Declaring a custom exception in C++

```
#ifndef Unit1H
#define Unit1H

#include <Classes.hpp>
#include <Controls.hpp>
#include <StdCtrls.hpp>
#include <Forms.hpp>

class ENoUpperCaseLetters: public Exception
{
public:
    ENoUpperCaseLetters(const AnsiString Msg): Exception(Msg) {};
};

class TForm1 : public TForm
{
__published:    // IDE-managed Components
    TButton *Button1;
    TEdit *Edit1;
    void __fastcall Button1Click(TObject *Sender);
private:         // User declarations
    int __fastcall CountUpperCase(const AnsiString s);
public:          // User declarations
    __fastcall TForm1(TComponent* Owner);
};

extern PACKAGE TForm1 *Form1;
#endif
```

Listing 13-7C: Working with a custom exception in C++

```
#include <vcl.h>
#pragma hdrstop
#include "Unit1.h"

#pragma package(smart_init)
#pragma resource "*.dfm"
TForm1 *Form1;

__fastcall TForm1::TForm1(TComponent* Owner)
    : TForm(Owner)
{
```

```
    }

int __fastcall TForm1::CountUpperCase(const AnsiString s)
{
    int cnt = 0;
    for(int i = 1; i <= s.Length(); i++)
    {
        if(s[i] >= 'A' && s[i] <= 'Z')
            cnt++;
    }

    if(cnt == 0)
        throw ENoUpperCaseLetters("No uppercase letters in the string.");

    return cnt;
}

void __fastcall TForm1::Button1Click(TObject *Sender)
{
    try
    {
        int Cnt = CountUpperCase(Edit1->Text);
        Caption = IntToStr(Cnt) + " uppercase letter";
        if(Cnt > 1) Caption = Caption + "s";
    }
    catch(ENoUpperCaseLetters &e)
    {
        Caption = e.Message;
    }
}
```

Securing Resource Allocations

The reserved word try enables us to construct two different blocks: the
exception handler block and the resource protection block. The exception
handler block is created with the reserved word except and the resource protection block is created with the reserved word finally. The syntax of the
resource protection block in Delphi is:

```
try
finally
end;
```

In C++, the resource protection block looks like this:

```
try
{
}
__finally
{
}
```

The exception handling and resource protection blocks are used differently
and act differently. While the statements in the exception handler execute
only if the statements in the try block raise an exception, the statements in

the finally block are always executed, even if no exceptions are raised by the statements in the try block. If an exception occurs in the try block, the control is passed to the finally block and cleanup code is executed. If no exceptions occur in the try block, the statements in the finally block are executed after the statements in the try block.

The proper way to use the resource protection block is to allocate or otherwise acquire the resource before the try block. After you have acquired the resource, write statements that use the resource inside the try block. When you're finished with the resource, you have to release it. The statements that release the resource should be placed in the finally block.

```
{ acquire the resource }
try
  { use the acquired resource }
finally
  { release the resource }
end;
```

The resource protection block is often used to ensure that dynamically created objects are released properly. For instance, you should always protect dynamic modal form creation with the try-finally block (see Listings 13-8A and 13-8B).

Listing 13-8A: Dynamically creating a form with resource protection, Delphi version

```
procedure TForm1.CreateFormClick(Sender: TObject);
var
  NewForm: TForm;
begin
  NewForm := TForm.Create(Self);
  try
    NewForm.ShowModal;
  finally
    NewForm.Free;
  end;
end;
```

Listing 13-8B: Dynamically creating a form with resource protection, C++ version

```
void __fastcall TForm1::CreateFormClick(TObject *Sender)
{
  TForm* NewForm = new TForm(this);
  try
  {
    NewForm->ShowModal();
  }
  __finally
  {
    delete NewForm;
  }
}
```

Listing 13-9 shows an even shorter way to dynamically create a form protected by the try-finally block.

Listing 13-9: Dynamically creating a form with resource protection, revisited

```
procedure TForm1.CreateFormShortClick(Sender: TObject);
begin
  with TForm.Create(Self) do
  try
    ShowModal;
  finally
    Free;
  end;
end;
```

The other difference between the exception handling and the resource handling blocks is that the resource handling block doesn't handle the exception. Thus, if an exception occurs, it will be passed to the first available exception handler. For instance, if you run the following code, the EDivByZero exception will cause the default exception handler to display the message box informing the user about the exception.

```
procedure TForm1.CreateFormShortClick(Sender: TObject);
begin
  with TForm.Create(Self) do
  try
    { raises EDivByZero because the Tag property = 0 }
    Caption := IntToStr(Top div Tag);
    ShowModal;
  finally
    Free;
  end;
end;
```

If you want to handle the EDivByZero exception (or any other exception) inside the resource protection block, you have to write a nested exception handler block. The following listing shows how to write a nested exception handler inside the resource protection block. You can also nest resource protection blocks inside other resource protection blocks or exception handling blocks.

Listing 13-10: Nested blocks

```
procedure TForm1.CreateFormClick(Sender: TObject);
begin
  with TForm.Create(Self) do
  try
    try
      Caption := IntToStr(Top div Tag);
    except
      on EDivByZero do Caption := 'Tag = 0';
    end;

    ShowModal;
  finally
    Free;
```

```
  end;
end;
```

Changing the Default Exception Handler

The global Application object is responsible for handling exceptions not handled by an exception handling block somewhere in the application. To change the default exception handler, we can use the TApplicationEvents component, found in the Additional category.

The TApplicationEvents component provides the OnException event that fires every time an unhandled exception occurs. The OnException event can be handled with a procedure of TExceptionEvent type. The procedure that handles the OnException event has to accept two parameters: the Sender object and the Exception object.

```
procedure TMainForm.AppEventsException(Sender: TObject; E: Exception);
begin

end;
```

Inside the OnException event handler you can write code that handles the exceptions in a different way than the default handler or you can leave the event handler empty. If you don't want anything to happen when an exception occurs, leave the event handler empty. In this case, you only have to write a comment inside the event handler block to disable the Code Editor's automatic code removal ability.

The OnException event handler can also be used for something more constructive. For instance, you can write code that logs all exceptions and saves them to a text file for later viewing. The following listing shows how to log exceptions inside the OnException event handler.

Listing 13-11: Logging unhandled exceptions

```
procedure TMainForm.AppEventsException(Sender: TObject; E: Exception);
var
  Log: TextFile;
  LogFilePath: string;
begin
  LogFilePath := 'c:\exceptions.log';

  AssignFile(Log, LogFilePath);
  try
    if not FileExists(LogFilePath) then
      Rewrite(Log)
    else
      Append(Log);

    WriteLn(Log, E.ClassType.ClassName,
      ' exception occurred with message "', E.Message, '".');
  finally
    CloseFile(Log);
  end;
end;
```

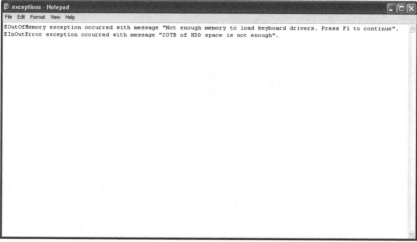

Figure 13-8: Logged exceptions

You can also modify the default exception handler manually (without the TApplicationEvents component) by creating a method that accepts the same parameters as the OnException event and assigning the method to the OnException event of the global Application object.

Listing 13-12: A custom OnException event handler

```
type
  TMainForm = class(TForm)
  private
    { Private declarations }
    procedure MyHandler(Sender: TObject; E: Exception);
  public
    { Public declarations }
  end;

var
  MainForm: TMainForm;

implementation

{$R *.dfm}

procedure TMainForm.MyHandler(Sender: TObject; E: Exception);
begin
  MessageDlg('Do you like the "' + E.Message + '" exception?',
    mtConfirmation, mbYesNo, 0);
end;
```

After you've created the OnException event handler, you have to assign it to the OnException event of the global Application object.

Listing 13-13: Assigning the event handler to the OnException event

```
procedure TMainForm.FormCreate(Sender: TObject);
begin
  Application.OnException := MyHandler;
end;
```

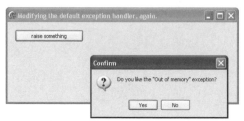

Figure 13-9: A customized default exception handler

Chapter 14

Using Components

So far, we have extensively used only three standard controls: TLabel, TButton, and TEdit. In order to build more complex applications, we have to see how and when to use other controls in the Standard category.

The TCheckBox Component

The TCheckBox component is used to present the user with an option that can be selected or deselected. The most important property of the TCheck-Box component is the Checked property, which specifies whether or not the check box is selected. The OnClick event handler is the best place for code that needs to be executed when the state of the check box control changes.

Now, we'll see how to use the TCheckBox component to enable the user to show/hide and enable/disable all buttons on the form. First, add several TButton components to the Designer Surface. Place them anywhere you like but don't modify their properties in the Object Inspector. Now add two TCheckBox components to the Designer Surface. Set the Caption property of the first check box to "Show" and the Caption property of the second check box to "Enable." Set the Checked property of both check boxes to True. You need to set the Checked property to True because the buttons on the Designer Surface are by default both visible and enabled and the check box controls have to show their true state (see Figure 14-1).

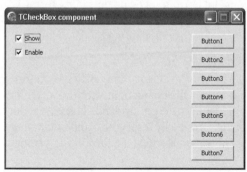

Figure 14-1: The user interface of the TCheckBox example

There are at least three possible ways to implement this functionality. The first way is the easiest but least sophisticated, more error-prone, and time consuming. It involves modifying the Enabled and Visible properties for every button on the form.

Listing 14-1: The least sophisticated way of working with a large number of components

```
procedure TMainForm.ShowButtons(Sender: TObject);
begin
  Button1.Visible := CheckBox1.Checked;
  Button2.Visible := CheckBox1.Checked;
  Button3.Visible := CheckBox1.Checked;
  Button4.Visible := CheckBox1.Checked;
  Button5.Visible := CheckBox1.Checked;
  Button6.Visible := CheckBox1.Checked;
  Button7.Visible := CheckBox1.Checked;
end;

procedure TMainForm.EnableButtons(Sender: TObject);
begin
  Button1.Enabled := CheckBox2.Checked;
  Button2.Enabled := CheckBox2.Checked;
  Button3.Enabled := CheckBox2.Checked;
  Button4.Enabled := CheckBox2.Checked;
  Button5.Enabled := CheckBox2.Checked;
  Button6.Enabled := CheckBox2.Checked;
  Button7.Enabled := CheckBox2.Checked;
end;
```

The FindComponent Method

The second and much better way of working with a larger number of components includes two things: default component names and the FindComponent method. Usually, the Designer Surface generates nonintuitive component names that we have to change if we want to have easily readable code. But the ComponentName + UniqueIndex naming style for components dropped on the Designer Surface is very useful here. It gives us the ability to easily reference the needed components by calling the FindComponent method in a loop.

Here is the declaration of the FindComponent method:

```
function FindComponent(const AName: string): TComponent;
```

The FindComponent method uses the AName parameter to search through the Components property and returns the component with the matching name. If no component is found, the function returns nil. The Components property is a list of all components owned by a specific component.

The following code shows how to determine if a form owns a component named "MyButton."

Listing 14-2: Searching for a specific component

```
procedure TMainForm.Button1Click(Sender: TObject);
begin
  if FindComponent('MyButton') <> nil then
    ShowMessage('The MyButton component exists');
end;
```

To show/hide or enable/disable all buttons on the form, we have to call the FindComponent method in a loop and use the loop counter to generate the needed component name. Since the FindComponent method always returns a TComponent, we have to typecast the resulting component to TButton before we can reference the Enabled and Visible properties (see Listing 14-3A for the Delphi version and Listing 14-3B for the C++ version).

Listing 14-3A: Using the FindComponent method

```
procedure TMainForm.ShowButtons(Sender: TObject);
var
  Cnt: Integer;
  Comp: TComponent;
begin
  for Cnt := 1 to 7 do
  begin
    Comp := FindComponent('Button' + IntToStr(Cnt));
    TButton(Comp).Visible := CheckBox1.Checked;
  end; // for Cnt
end;

procedure TMainForm.EnableButtons(Sender: TObject);
var
  Cnt: Integer;
  Comp: TComponent;
begin
  for cnt := 1 to 7 do
  begin
    Comp := FindComponent('Button' + IntToStr(Cnt));
    TButton(Comp).Enabled := CheckBox2.Checked;
  end;
end;
```

To typecast the TComponent returned by the FindComponent in a C++Builder application, you can use either the standard bracketed typecast or the C++ static_cast typecast, which has the following syntax:

```
static_cast<destination_type>(original_value)
```

The ShowButtons() method in Listing 14-3B shows how to use the bracketed typecast, and the EnableButtons() method shows how to use static_cast to typecast a TComponent to a TButton.

Listing 14-3B: Using the FindComponent method in a C++Builder VCL application

```
void __fastcall TForm1::ShowButtons(TObject *Sender)
{
  TComponent* Comp;
  for(int i = 1; i <= 7; i++)
```

```
   {
      Comp = FindComponent("Button" + IntToStr(i));
      ((TButton*)Comp)->Visible = CheckBox1->Checked;
   }
}

void __fastcall TForm1::EnableButtons(TObject *Sender)
{
   TComponent* Comp;
   for(int i = 1; i <= 7; i++)
   {
      Comp = FindComponent("Button" + IntToStr(i));
      static_cast<TButton*>(Comp)->Enabled = CheckBox2->Checked;
   }
}
```

The Delphi is Operator and C++ Dynamic Casting

The third way of working with a large number of components at run time is to browse through the Components property manually and find out if a component is of type TButton or any other component type that we need. To find out the component type at run time, we have to use the is operator. The syntax of the is operator is:

```
Object is Class
```

The is operator returns True if the object is an instance of the Class type or an instance of one of the class descendants. For example, the following test always evaluates to True because the main form is a descendant of TForm.

Listing 14-4A: Determining the object's class at run time

```
procedure TMainForm.Button1Click(Sender: TObject);
begin
  if Self is TForm then
    ShowMessage('The main form is really a form.');
end;
```

To determine the object's class in a C++Builder VCL Forms application, try to typecast it using the dynamic_cast typecast (see Listing 14-4B). If the typecast fails, it will return a NULL pointer.

Listing 14-4B: Determining the object's class in a C++Builder VCL Forms application

```
void __fastcall TForm1::Button1Click(TObject *Sender)
{
   if(dynamic_cast<TForm*>(this))
      ShowMessage("The main form is really a form.");
}
```

In order to find all buttons on a form, we have to browse through the Components property of the form. The ComponentCount property specifies the number of components in the Components list. The first component in the Components list has the index 0, and the last component has the index ComponentCount – 1.

Listings 14-5A and 14-5B show how to use the is operator in Delphi and dynamic casting in C++ applications to find and update all buttons on a form.

Listing 14-5A: Using the is operator to find and update all buttons on a form

```
procedure TMainForm.ShowButtons(Sender: TObject);
var
  Cnt: Integer;
begin
  for Cnt := 0 to Pred(ComponentCount) do
  begin
    if Components[Cnt] is TButton then
      TButton(Components[Cnt]).Visible := CheckBox1.Checked;
  end;
end;

procedure TMainForm.EnableButtons(Sender: TObject);
var
  Cnt: Integer;
begin
  for Cnt := 0 to Pred(ComponentCount) do
  begin
    if Components[Cnt] is TButton then
      TButton(Components[Cnt]).Enabled := CheckBox2.Checked;
  end;
end;
```

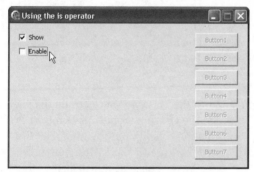

Figure 14-2: Using the is operator

Listing 14-5B: Using C++ dynamic casting to find and update all buttons on a form

```
void __fastcall TForm1::ShowButtons(TObject *Sender)
{
    for(int i = 0; i < ComponentCount; i++)
    {
        if(dynamic_cast<TButton*>(Components[i]))
            ((TButton*)Components[i])->Visible = CheckBox1->Checked;
    }
}
```

The TRadioButton Component

Like check boxes, radio buttons are used to present a set of options. The difference is that check boxes enable the user to select multiple options at the same time, while radio buttons work as a group and only allow a single radio button to be selected at a time. When the user selects a radio button, all other radio buttons in the same group are automatically deselected. Radio button groups are defined by their container. If you want to create more radio button groups, place the radio buttons in a separate container control (TGroupBox or TPanel).

The TRadioButton component is used just like the TCheckBox component. The Checked property defines whether or not the button is selected and the OnClick event enables us to execute code immediately after the radio button is selected.

Now, let's use the TRadioButton component to create an application that will enable the user to modify the message dialog box presented by the MessageDlg function. The MessageDlg function is typically used to display four standard message boxes: the warning, error, information, and confirmation dialog boxes.

Figure 14-3: Different dialog boxes displayed by the MessageDlg function

First, add a TGroupBox component to the Designer Surface and then add four TRadioButton components to it. Set the Caption properties of the radio buttons to "Warning," "Error," "Information," and "Confirmation." Set the Checked property of the Warning radio button to True. After you've defined the radio buttons, add a button to the form. This button will display the dialog box defined by the radio buttons.

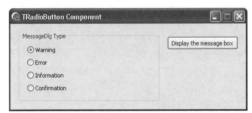

Figure 14-4: The user interface of the TRadioButton example

The message box type is defined by the TMsgDlgType enumeration declared in the Dialogs unit:

```
TMsgDlgType = (mtWarning, mtError, mtInformation, mtConfirmation, mtCustom);
```

The easiest way to change the message box type is to define a private TMsgDlgType variable and then assign the appropriate value to the variable in the OnClick event of every radio button.

Listing 14-6: Changing the message box type

```
private
  { Private declarations }
  FMessageType: TMsgDlgType;
public
  { Public declarations }
end;

var
  MainForm: TMainForm;

implementation

{$R *.dfm}

procedure TMainForm.WarningRadioClick(Sender: TObject);
begin
  FMessageType := mtWarning;
end;

procedure TMainForm.ErrorRadioClick(Sender: TObject);
begin
  FMessageType := mtError;
end;

procedure TMainForm.InformationRadioClick(Sender: TObject);
begin
  FMessageType := mtInformation;
end;

procedure TMainForm.ConfirmationRadioClick(Sender: TObject);
begin
  FMessageType := mtConfirmation;
end;

procedure TMainForm.DisplayButtonClick(Sender: TObject);
begin
  MessageDlg('MessageDlg function', FMessageType, [mbOK], 0);
end;
```

C++Builder Sets

In C++, sets are implemented as objects. To declare a new set type in C++, use the following syntax:

```
typedef Set<data_type, first_value, last_value> SetName;
```

For instance, here's how you can declare a Letters set in both Delphi and C++:

```
// Delphi
type
```

```
TLetters = set of 'a'..'z';

// C++
typedef Set<char, 'a', 'z'> Letters;
```

You can also create a new set based on an enumerated type. To create a new set based on an enumerated type in C++, use the following syntax:

```
typedef Set<enum_type, first_enum_value, last_enum_value> SetName;
```

Here's how you can create a TDays set based on the TDay enumeration in both Delphi and C++:

```
// Delphi
type
  TDay = (Monday, Tuesday, Wednesday,
    Thursday, Friday, Saturday, Sunday);

  TDays = set of TDay;

// C++
enum TDay {Monday, Tuesday, Wednesday,
    Thursday, Friday, Saturday, Sunday};

typedef Set<TDay, Monday, Sunday> TDays;
```

Working with Sets in C++

To add values to the set or remove them from the set, use the << and >> operators:

```
TDays days;

// add Monday-Wednesday to the set
days << Monday << Tuesday << Wednesday;

// remove Monday from the set
days >> Monday;
```

To determine if a value is included in the set, use the Contains method:

```
void __fastcall TForm1::Button1Click(TObject *Sender)
{
    TDays days;
    days << Monday << Tuesday << Wednesday;

    if(days.Contains(Monday))
    {
        ShowMessage("I don't want to work on Monday.");
        days >> Monday;
    }
}
```

Using the MessageDlg Function in C++

Now that you know a bit more about sets in C++, you can start using the MessageDlg function and other functions that accept set parameters in your C++ VCL Forms applications.

To pass a set as a parameter to a function or a procedure, you need to know the following:

■ The syntax for passing sets to functions

■ The name of the set

■ The values you need

The syntax for passing sets to functions looks like this:

```
SetName() << value_1 << value_2 << value_n
```

The MessageDlg function accepts only one set parameter: the Button parameter, of type TMsgDlgButtons. To display the MessageDlg dialog box with only the OK button, you need to add the mbOK value to the set.

Here's how you call the MessageDlg function in a C++ VCL Forms application:

```
MessageDlg("MessageDlg function", mtInformation,
    TMsgDlgButtons() << mbOK, 0);
```

The Sender Parameter

Another way to change the message box type is to merge the code from the existing event handlers into a single event handler. In the merged event handler we can use the Sender parameter to identify the radio button that called the event handler and then change the message box type accordingly. First, completely remove the OnClick event handlers of the Error, Information, and Confirmation radio buttons and then write the following code in the OnClick event handler of the Warning radio button.

Listing 14-7: Using the Sender parameter to identify the component that called the event handler

```
procedure TMainForm.WarningRadioClick(Sender: TObject);
begin
  if Sender = WarningRadio then
    FMessageType := mtWarning
  else if Sender = ErrorRadio then
    FMessageType := mtError
  else if Sender = InformationRadio then
    FMessageType := mtInformation
  else
    FMessageType := mtConfirmation;
end;

procedure TMainForm.DisplayButtonClick(Sender: TObject);
begin
  MessageDlg('MessageDlg function', FMessageType, [mbOK], 0);
end;
```

Now we have to assign this event handler to the OnClick event of all four radio buttons. The fastest way of assigning a single event handler to a larger number of components is to first select the components on the Designer Surface and then use the Object Inspector to assign the event handler to the appropriate event.

If the components you wish to select reside in a container control, you won't be able to select them as easily as you can select components that reside directly on the form. To select components that reside in a container control, press and hold the Ctrl key and then draw the selection rectangle. Another way to select components in a container control is to first select a single component by left-clicking on it, then press and hold the Shift key, and left-click all the other components you wish to select.

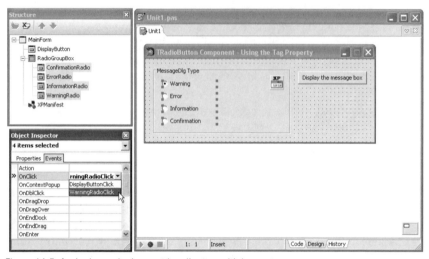

Figure 14-5: Assigning a single event handler to multiple events

The Tag Property

An even better way to change the message box type is to utilize the Tag property. The Tag property has no special purpose, except that it allows us to store an integer value and use it as we please. In this case, we can use the Tag property to completely remove the if-then statement from the event handler.

What we have to do is assign an integer value to the Tag property of the radio buttons to match the ordinal values of the mtWarning, mtError, mtInformation, and mtConfirmation constants. Thus, we can leave the Tag property of the Warning radio button unchanged since Ord(mtWarning) is 0, but we have to modify the Tag property of the other three radio buttons. So, set the Tag property of the Error radio button to 1, the Tag property of the Information button to 2, and the Tag property of the Confirmation button to 3.

Now that the Tag property of all four radio buttons contains the appropriate message type, we don't have to use the if-then statement to determine the message box type. We only have to typecast the Tag value of the Sender component to TMsgDlgType. We actually have to perform two typecasts. First, we have to typecast the Sender object to TComponent because the Tag property is defined in the TComponent class, and then we have to typecast the Tag property to TMsgDlgType.

Listing 14-8A shows how to use the Sender's Tag property in Delphi and Listing 14-8B shows how to use the Sender's Tag property in C++.

Listing 14-8A: Using the Tag property to change the message box type, Delphi version

```
procedure TMainForm.WarningRadioClick(Sender: TObject);
var
  SenderComp: TComponent;
begin
  SenderComp := TComponent(Sender);
  FMessageType := TMsgDlgType(SenderComp.Tag);
end;

procedure TMainForm.DisplayButtonClick(Sender: TObject);
begin
  MessageDlg('MessageDlg function', FMessageType, [mbOK], 0);
end;
```

As you can see, using the Tag property greatly reduces the amount of code needed to change the message box type. If you want to, you can also remove the SenderComp variable and perform both typecasts in the same line to reduce the amount of code even more.

```
procedure TMainForm.WarningRadioClick(Sender: TObject);
begin
  FMessageType := TMsgDlgType(TComponent(Sender).Tag);
end;
```

Listing 14-8B: Using the Tag property to change the message box type, C++ version

```
void __fastcall TMainForm::WarningRadioClick(TObject *Sender)
{
   TComponent* SenderComp = dynamic_cast<TComponent*>(Sender);
   FMessageType = static_cast<TMsgDlgType>(SenderComp->Tag);
}

void __fastcall TMainForm::DisplayButtonClick(TObject *Sender)
{
   MessageDlg("MessageDlg function", FMessageType,
      TMsgDlgButtons() << mbOK, 0);
}
```

The TListBox Component

The TListBox component displays a list of items. The most important property of the TListBox component is the Items property, which is an object property of type TStrings. The TStrings class represents a list of strings and enables us to manipulate the strings in the list. So, if you want to manipulate the items in the list box, you have to call the methods of the Items property. For instance, to add a new item to the list box, you have to call the Add method of the Items property. The Add method accepts a single string parameter — the string value that will be added to the end of the list.

Listing 14-9: Adding a new item to the list box

```
procedure TForm1.Button1Click(Sender: TObject);
begin
  ListBox1.Items.Add(Edit1.Text);
end;
```

Figure 14-6: The TListBox component

The Assign Method

In this section, we'll use the TListBox component to create an application that will enable us to view all installed fonts on the computer. The list of installed fonts is provided by yet another global object — the Screen object. The list of font names is contained in the Fonts property, which is also declared as a TStrings type property.

In order to display the font list in a list box, we have to copy the entire contents of the font list to the list box. Although we can manually copy the items from one list to another, there is a better way to do this — by using the Assign method. The Assign method is almost omnipresent in the VCL and is used to copy the contents of a source object to the destination object. In the case of a string list, the Assign method is used to copy all strings from a source string list to the destination list.

Now, add a TListBox component to the Designer Surface, double-click the form to create the empty event handler for the OnCreate event, and write the code to copy the contents of the font list to the list box.

Listing 14-10: Copying an entire string list

```
procedure TForm1.FormCreate(Sender: TObject);
begin
  ListBox1.Items.Assign(Screen.Fonts);
end;
```

Figure 14-7: Previewing installed fonts

To enable the user to preview the selected font, you first have to determine which item is selected. The selected string list item is specified by the ItemIndex property of the list box. The ItemIndex property is an integer property that contains –1 if no item is selected, 0 if the first item is selected, and Items.Count –1 if the last item in the list box is selected.

To preview the selected font, you have to do the following:

1. Add a TLabel component to the Designer Surface and rename it PreviewLabel.

2. Add an event handler for the OnClick event of the TListBox component.

3. Add the following code to the OnClick event handler of the list box.

Listing 14-11: Changing the label's font

```
procedure TForm1.ListBox1Click(Sender: TObject);
var
  SelectedFont: string;
begin
  { get selected item }
  SelectedFont := ListBox1.Items[ListBox1.ItemIndex];

  { change font & caption }
  PreviewLabel.Font.Name := SelectedFont;
  PreviewLabel.Caption := SelectedFont;
end;
```

Selecting Multiple Items

By default, the TListBox component enables us to select only one item from the list. If you want to select multiple items from the list box, you have to set the MultiSelect property to True. When you set the MultiSelect property to True, you won't be able to use the ItemIndex property to determine the selected items. In the case of a MultiSelect list box, the ItemIndex property only identifies the item that has the focus.

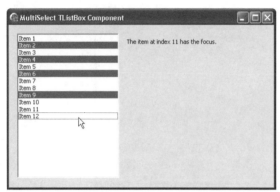

Figure 14-8: A MultiSelect TListBox component

To determine which items in a MultiSelect list box are selected, you have to use the Selected property. The Selected property is an indexed property that enables you to determine whether or not an item at the specified index is selected. For instance, the following code shows how to find out if the first item in a list box is selected:

```
if ListBox1.Selected[0] then
  Caption := 'The first item is selected.';
```

If you want to work with all selected items, you have to write a loop that tests each item to see if the item is selected or not.

Now, let's create a simple application that enables the user to select multiple items in one list and move them to another list. Drop two TListBox components to the Designer Surface. The ListBox1 component will serve as the source list and the ListBox2 component will be the target list.

To enable the user to select and move multiple items from the source to the destination list box, you have to first set the MultiSelect property of the ListBox1 component to True and then add several items to it. To add items to a TListBox component at design time, you have to use the String List Editor. The String List Editor is displayed by the Object Inspector when you click the (...) button next to the Items property of the selected list box.

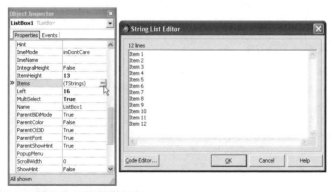

Figure 14-9: The String List Editor

Now, add a TButton component to the Designer Surface, place it somewhere between the two TListBox controls, and set its Caption property to ">>". We'll use the button's OnClick event to move the items from the source to the destination list box.

Listing 14-12: Moving multiple items from one list box to another

```
procedure TForm1.Button1Click(Sender: TObject);
var
  i: Integer;
begin
  { copy the selected items }
  for i := 0 to Pred(ListBox1.Items.Count) do
  begin
    if ListBox1.Selected[i] then
      ListBox2.Items.Add(ListBox1.Items[i]);
  end;

  { remove the selected items }
  for i := Pred(ListBox1.Items.Count) downto 0 do
  begin
    if ListBox1.Selected[i] then
      ListBox1.Items.Delete(i);
  end;
end;
```

We can copy the items from the source to the destination list box using the standard for loop because we aren't changing the contents of the source list box. But to delete the selected items from the source list box, we have to use the downto loop because the Delete method changes the contents (and the indexes) of the source list box.

Listing 14-12 shows how to manually remove the selected items from a list box. If you only have to remove the selected items, you can also use the DeleteSelected method.

```
procedure TForm1.Button1Click(Sender: TObject);
var
  i: Integer;
begin
  { copy the selected items }
  for i := 0 to Pred(ListBox1.Items.Count) do
  begin
    if ListBox1.Selected[i] then
      ListBox2.Items.Add(ListBox1.Items[i]);
  end;

  ListBox1.DeleteSelected;
end;
```

The BeginUpdate and EndUpdate Methods

Normally, every time you add a new item to a list box or otherwise change the contents of the list box, the list box repaints itself in order to display the new item. When you add items to a list box in a loop, you should consider using the BeginUpdate and EndUpdate methods of the Items property because they enable us to temporarily disable the repainting of the list box.

The BeginUpdate method temporarily disables repainting of the list box and the EndUpdate method forces the list box to repaint itself. BeginUpdate is usually called before the loop that modifies the contents of the list box, and EndUpdate is called after the loop to repaint the list box and display the changes made to the list box contents.

Listing 14-13: Using the BeginUpdate and EndUpdate methods to optimize list box operations

```
procedure TForm1.Button1Click(Sender: TObject);
var
  i: Integer;
begin
  { disable repainting }
  ListBox2.Items.BeginUpdate;

  for i := 0 to Pred(ListBox1.Items.Count) do
  begin
    if ListBox1.Selected[i] then
      ListBox2.Items.Add(ListBox1.Items[i]);
  end;

  { disable repaint before deleting }
  ListBox1.Items.BeginUpdate;
  ListBox1.DeleteSelected;
  ListBox1.Items.EndUpdate;

  { enable painting and refresh the list box }
  ListBox2.Items.EndUpdate;
end;
```

The BeginUpdate and EndUpdate methods really make a difference, especially in large loops. For instance, moving 5,000 selected items from one list box to another normally takes around 2 seconds on my machine. When the BeginUpdate and EndUpdate methods are used, the same loop takes about 0.2 seconds to finish.

Figure 14-10: Speed gained by using the BeginUpdate and EndUpdate methods

The IndexOf Method

The IndexOf method enables us to search for a string in a string list. This method accepts only one string parameter and returns the index of the passed string if the string is found. If the passed string doesn't exist in the string list, the IndexOf method returns –1.

The IndexOf method can be used, for instance, to allow the user to add only unique values to the list box. The following example illustrates not only how to use the IndexOf method, but also how to use the MessageDlg function to query the user. The MessageDlg function is used to ask the user if he or she wants to add a value to the list when the value already exists.

Before we continue, you'll need to add three components to the Designer Surface — TListBox, TEdit, and TButton components (see Figure 14-11).

Figure 14-11: Components used in the IndexOf example

Listing 14-14: Adding unique items to a list box

```
procedure TForm1.Button1Click(Sender: TObject);
begin
  if ListBox1.Items.IndexOf(Edit1.Text) = -1 then
    ListBox1.Items.Add(Edit1.Text)
  else begin
    if MessageDlg('This item already exists. Add anyway?',
      mtConfirmation, mbYesNo, 0) = mrYes then
        ListBox1.Items.Add(Edit1.Text);
  end;
end;
```

As you can see, the MessageDlg function can be used to get some kind of response from the user. The third parameter is a set parameter that enables you to define which buttons are displayed on the dialog box. You can either construct the set manually or use one of the predefined button sets. Listing 14-15 gives all the data types and constants that can be used to customize the MessageDlg dialog box.

Listing 14-15: MessageDlg related data types and constants

```
type
  TMsgDlgType = (mtWarning, mtError,
    mtInformation, mtConfirmation, mtCustom);
  TMsgDlgBtn = (mbYes, mbNo, mbOK, mbCancel, mbAbort, mbRetry,
```

```
   mbIgnore, mbAll, mbNoToAll, mbYesToAll, mbHelp);
  TMsgDlgButtons = set of TMsgDlgBtn;

const
  mbYesNo = [mbYes, mbNo];
  mbYesNoCancel = [mbYes, mbNo, mbCancel];
  mbYesAllNoAllCancel = [mbYes, mbYesToAll, mbNo, mbNoToAll, mbCancel];
  mbOKCancel = [mbOK, mbCancel];
  mbAbortRetryIgnore = [mbAbort, mbRetry, mbIgnore];
  mbAbortIgnore = [mbAbort, mbIgnore];
```

If you want, you can also take advantage of short-circuit evaluation here and rewrite Listing 14-14 like this:

Listing 14-16: Adding unique items to a list box, revisited

```
procedure TForm1.Button1Click(Sender: TObject);
begin
  if (ListBox1.Items.IndexOf(Edit1.Text) = -1) or
     (MessageDlg('This item already exists. Add anyway?',
      mtConfirmation, mbYesNo, 0) = mrYes) then
        ListBox1.Items.Add(Edit1.Text);
end;
```

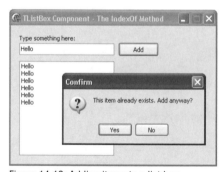

Figure 14-12: Adding items to a list box

The Names and Values Properties

The TStrings class defines two more properties that can be used to access strings in the string list. The Names and Values properties are indexed properties that allow us to access a part of a string that contains a name-value pair. By default, the character that separates the name part from the value part in a string is the equal sign (=). Figure 14-13 shows several name-value pairs that are used in the following example.

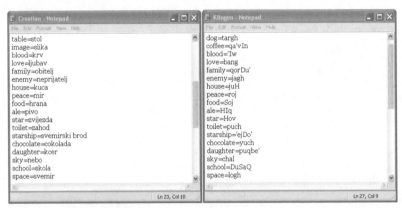

Figure 14-13: Name-value pairs

The Names and Values properties allow us to, for instance, easily create a simple dictionary. We'll now create a simple English-Croatian and English-Klingon dictionary using the Values property (see Figure 14-14).

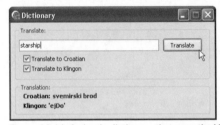

Figure 14-14: A simple dictionary that uses the Values property

The first thing we need to do is fill two separate text files with English-Croatian and English-Klingon name-value pairs. You can see a portion of these files in Figure 14-13. The best place to keep these data files is the root directory of the application. Name the files Croatian.txt and Klingon.txt.

In order to use the Values property to extract the value part of a string, we have to load the Croatian.txt and Klingon.txt text files into two string lists. If you don't need to display the string list on the form, you shouldn't use a TListBox component or any other control that can display a string list because you would unnecessarily waste system resources.

If you have to work with string lists in the background, you should use the TStringList class. We cannot use the TStrings class directly because it is an abstract class. An abstract class is a class that is never instantiated because at least one of its methods has no implementation, only the interface that needs to be implemented in a descendant class. One of the classes that implements the abstract methods of the TStrings class is the TStringList class.

Listing 14-17: Portions of the TStrings and TStringList class declarations

```
TStrings = class(TPersistent)
public
  destructor Destroy; override;
  function Add(const S: string): Integer; virtual;
  function AddObject(const S: string; AObject: TObject): Integer; virtual;
  procedure Append(const S: string);
  procedure AddStrings(Strings: TStrings); virtual;
  procedure Assign(Source: TPersistent); override;
  procedure BeginUpdate;
  procedure Clear; virtual; abstract;
  procedure Delete(Index: Integer); virtual; abstract;
  procedure EndUpdate;
  function IndexOf(const S: string): Integer; virtual;
  function IndexOfName(const Name: string): Integer; virtual;
  function IndexOfObject(AObject: TObject): Integer; virtual;
  procedure Insert(Index: Integer; const S: string); virtual; abstract;
  procedure InsertObject(Index: Integer; const S: string;
    AObject: TObject); virtual;
  procedure LoadFromFile(const FileName: string); virtual;
  procedure Move(CurIndex, NewIndex: Integer); virtual;
  procedure SaveToFile(const FileName: string); virtual;
  property Count: Integer read GetCount;
  property Names[Index: Integer]: string read GetName;
  property Values[const Name: string]: string read GetValue write SetValue;
  property Strings[Index: Integer]: string read Get write Put; default;
end;

TStringList = class(TStrings)
  function Add(const S: string): Integer; override;
  procedure Clear; override;
  procedure Delete(Index: Integer); override;
  function IndexOf(const S: string): Integer; override;
  procedure Insert(Index: Integer; const S: string); override;
end;
```

Our first job in this application is to dynamically create two TStringList objects and use them to load the Croatian.txt and Klingon.txt text files located in the root directory of the application. Although you can manually read the text file and use the TStringList.Add method to add strings to the list, the best way to load a text file into a string list is to call the TStringList.LoadFromFile method.

Listing 14-18: Loading the text files to TStringList objects

```
type
  TForm1 = class(TForm)
  private
    { Private declarations }
    Croatian: TStringList;
    Klingon: TStringList;
  public
    { Public declarations }
  end;
```

```
var
  Form1: TForm1;

implementation

{$R *.dfm}

procedure TForm1.FormCreate(Sender: TObject);
var
  AppPath: string;
begin
  { get root directory }
  AppPath := ExtractFilePath(Application.ExeName);

  { create lists }
  Klingon := TStringList.Create;
  Croatian := TStringList.Create;

  { load files from the root directory }
  Klingon.LoadFromFile(AppPath + 'Klingon.txt');
  Croatian.LoadFromFile(AppPath + 'Croatian.txt');
end;
```

The first line in the OnCreate event handler determines the root directory of the application by extracting the drive and directory parts from the ExeName property. The ExeName property of the global Application object always contains the fully qualified path (drive, directory, file name, and extension).

Notice how the TStringList objects are created. The constructor takes no parameters, which means that the TStringList class doesn't descend from the TComponent class and that the memory for the TStringList objects isn't automatically managed by an Owner component. Thus, we have to manually free all TStringList instances when we're done using them. In this case, we need to free the Klingon and Croatian TStringList instances in the OnDestroy event of the main form, at the end of application execution.

Listing 14-19: Releasing the string lists from memory

```
procedure TForm1.FormDestroy(Sender: TObject);
begin
  Croatian.Free;
  Klingon.Free;
end;
```

The last thing we have to do is write code that will use the Values property to translate from English to Klingon or Croatian, or both. This code is located in the OnClick event of the Translate button.

Listing 14-20: Locating a value using the Values property of the TStringList class

```
procedure TForm1.Button1Click(Sender: TObject);
begin
  if CroatianCheckBox.Checked then
    CroLabel.Caption := Croatian.Values[Edit1.Text]
  else
```

```
      CroLabel.Caption := '';

  if KlingonCheckBox.Checked then
    KlingLabel.Caption := Klingon.Values[Edit1.Text]
  else
    KlingLabel.Caption := '';
end;
```

The TComboBox Component

The TComboBox is a cross between the TEdit and TListBox components. The TComboBox has an edit box that enables the user to enter custom values and a drop-down list that enables the user to select a predefined value.

The two most important properties of the TComboBox component are the Items and Text properties. Like the Items property in the TListBox component, the Items property has a list of items displayed by the control. The only difference is that the items in a TComboBox are displayed only when the user presses the arrow button. The Text property contains the string displayed in the edit box of the TComboBox component.

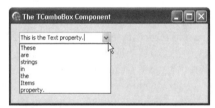

Figure 14-15:
The Text and Items
properties of the
TComboBox
component

Another often used property of the TComboBox component is the Style property, which modifies both the style and functionality of the combo box. The three standard styles are csDropDown, csDropDownList, and csSimple. The default csDropDown style enables the user to enter custom values in the edit box and select items from the drop-down list, if there are any. The csDropDownList style enables the user to only select predefined items from the drop-down list. This style is very useful when you don't want to write a lot of validation code. The csSimple style enables the user to both enter text into the edit box and select predefined values. The csSimple style also changes the appearance of the TComboBox component by displaying the list box underneath the edit box, as shown in Figure 14-16.

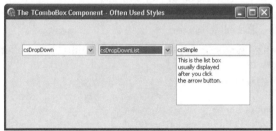

Figure 14-16:
Often used
TComboBox styles

The TRadioGroup Component

The TRadioGroup component is a perfect replacement for a TGroupBox component that only contains TRadioButton components. The main difference between the TGroupBox and the TRadioGroup components is that the TRadioGroup component can't act as a container. The TRadioGroup component can only contain radio buttons defined in its Items property.

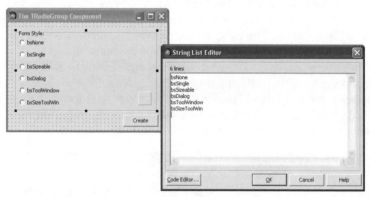

Figure 14-17: The TRadioGroup component

Normally, to see if a radio button is selected, you have to test its Checked property. Since the radio buttons in a TRadioGroup aren't real radio buttons, you cannot check the Checked property of a certain radio button. To determine which radio button is selected in a TRadioGroup component, use the ItemIndex property.

Listing 14-21: Using TRadioGroup radio buttons

```
procedure TForm1.Button1Click(Sender: TObject);
begin
  if RadioGroup1.ItemIndex = -1 then
  begin
    MessageDlg('Select a radio button first.', mtWarning, [mbOK], 0);
    Exit;
  end;

  with TForm.Create(Self) do
  try
    BorderStyle := TFormBorderStyle(RadioGroup1.ItemIndex);
    Caption := RadioGroup1.Items[RadioGroup1.ItemIndex];
    Position := poScreenCenter;
    ShowModal;
  finally
    Free;
  end;
end;
```

The TScrollBar Component

Although many controls have built-in scrolling capabilities, there are situations when we have to let the user scroll controls that don't support scrolling. The two most important properties of the TScrollBar component are the Kind and Position properties. The Kind property enables you to define whether the scroll bar is vertical or horizontal, and the Position property enables you to determine the position of the scroll bar.

Additionally, the Min and Max properties are used to limit the scrolling range of the scroll bar. The most important event is the OnChange event that fires every time the position of the scroll bar is modified.

The TScrollBar component, for instance, enables you to easily scroll an image on the form. To enable image scrolling, place a TImage component in a container component like TPanel and set the AutoSize property of the TImage component to True. Then add two TScrollBar components and set the Kind property of one TScrollBar component to sbVertical.

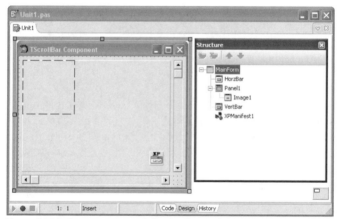

Figure 14-18: Components needed to implement image scrolling

In order to scroll an image, we have to load an image into the TImage component. To do this, use the TImage.Picture.LoadFromFile method. The Picture property enables the TImage component to load different file types like bitmaps, icons, and metafiles. The following example tries to load an image called image.bmp from the application root directory.

```
procedure TMainForm.FormCreate(Sender: TObject);
var
  ImagePath: string;
begin
  ImagePath := ExtractFilePath(Application.ExeName) + 'image.bmp';
  Image1.Picture.LoadFromFile(ImagePath);
```

```
{ define scroll range }
VertBar.Max := Image1.Height - Panel1.Height;
HorzBar.Max := Image1.Height;
end;
```

To scroll the image, write event handlers for the OnChange event of the two TScrollBar components and use their Position property to determine how much the image should be scrolled horizontally and vertically.

Listing 14-22: Scrolling an image

```
procedure TMainForm.HorzBarChange(Sender: TObject);
begin
  Image1.Left := -HorzBar.Position;
end;

procedure TMainForm.VertBarChange(Sender: TObject);
begin
  Image1.Top := -VertBar.Position;
end;
```

Figure 14-19: Scrolling an image with the TScrollBar component

Chapter 15

Standard VCL Components

This chapter covers some very important components and technologies that can be used in a plethora of applications. You'll see how to work with menus, add toolbars to the application, add images to both menus and toolbars, and use actions.

Creating and Using Menus

The main menu and the context menus are the most important parts of a user interface. Menus are centralized lists of options that enable the user to interact with the application. In VCL applications, menus are implemented using three components: TMainMenu, TPopupMenu, and TMenuItem.

The TMainMenu component is the main menu of a form, located below the caption bar. The TPopupMenu component is used to implement a pop-up (context) menu that appears when the user presses the right mouse button. Both the main menu and pop-up menus can contain multiple menu items. Each item in a menu is an actual TMenuItem instance.

The easiest way to add a main menu to an application is to drop a TMainMenu component on the Designer Surface and use the Menu Designer to add items to the menu at design time. To show the Menu Designer, simply double-click the TMainMenu component on the Designer Surface or right-click it and select the Menu Designer option from the context menu.

Figure 15-1: The Menu Designer

When we display it, the Menu Designer immediately creates an undefined
TMenuItem instance and thus enables us to start building the menu in no
time. This TMenuItem is also automatically selected and its properties and
events are listed in the Object Inspector.

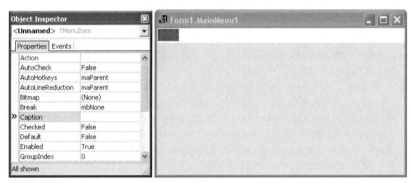

Figure 15-2: The undefined TMenuItem instance

The only thing that we have to do to create a valid menu item is type something in the Caption property of the selected TMenuItem instance and press
Enter.

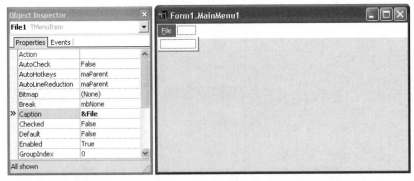

Figure 15-3: Adding a top-level menu

After we add a menu item to the selected menu, the Menu Designer automatically creates more undefined menu items and helps us quickly build a menu system for the application. The caption of the menu item we added is "&File". The optional ampersand character (&) is used to define the access (accelerator) key that enables the user to select the menu item with the keyboard using the Alt+access key combination. Access keys appear underlined in the menu. If you need to display the ampersand character in a menu item, you have to write the ampersand character twice.

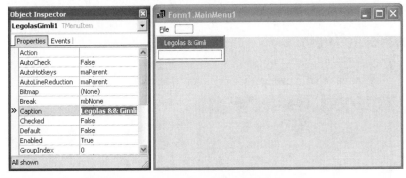

Figure 15-4: Menu item that contains an ampersand character

Normally, menu items are used in a similar fashion as buttons, but they can also emulate radio button and check box behavior. The Checked property can be used when you want the menu item to work like a check box or a radio button. If the RadioItem property is set to True, the checked menu item displays a round dot; otherwise, the checked menu item displays a check mark.

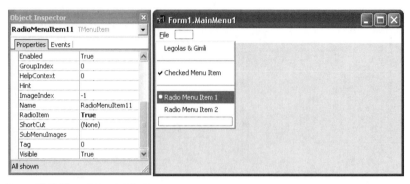

Figure 15-5: Menu item variations

Notice the lines that separate various menu items in Figure 15-5. These separators are menu items used to logically group other menu items in the menu. To create a separator, you simply type a hyphen (-) in the Caption property of the menu item.

The TMenuItem component has two more pretty useful properties: AutoCheck and ShortCut. Set the AutoCheck property to True to enable the menu item to automatically toggle its Checked property. Use the ShortCut property to select a keyboard shortcut combination that can be used to fire the menu item's OnClick event without having to select the item from the menu. Shortcut combinations appear on the right side of the menu item.

Displaying Hints

Hints (also known as tooltips) are short strings that appear onscreen while the user moves the mouse cursor over controls on the form.

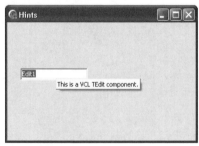

Figure 15-6: A hint

If you want to display hints in your application, you have to specify the hint text in the Hint property of all controls that should display the hint and then set the form's ShowHint property to True. When the ShowHint property of the form is set to True, the application displays hints for all child controls of the form. If the ShowHint property of the form is set to False (the default value), hints will only be displayed for specific controls whose ShowHint property is set to True.

In real-world applications, hints are also displayed in the status bar of the application, as shown in Figure 15-7.

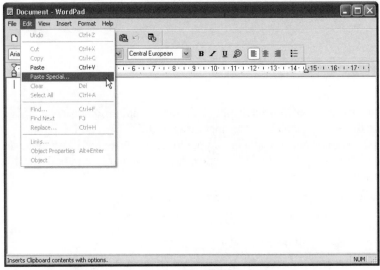

Figure 15-7: Displaying hints in the status bar of the application

Now, let's design a user interface that is able to display application hints in the status bar. First, design a small menu with several items and assign some text to their Hint properties.

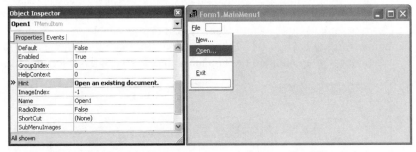

Figure 15-8: Assigning hints to menu items

In order to display hints in the status bar, we obviously need a status bar. The TStatusBar component is located in the Win32 category on the Tool Palette. Select the TStatusBar component and drop it anywhere on the Designer Surface. The component will automatically align itself to the bottom of the form.

There are actually two ways to make the TStatusBar component display application hints. The easier way simply requires you to set the AutoHint property of the TStatusBar component to True.

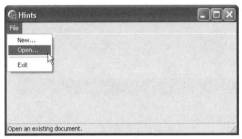

Figure 15-9: Showing hints in the status bar

If you want to control what happens when the application displays hints, you have to write a handler for the application's OnHint event. Drop the TApplicationEvents component on the form and write the following code in the OnHint event handler. The code displays the hint text in both the status bar and the title bar.

Listing 15-1: Displaying hints in the OnHint event

```
procedure TForm1.ApplicationEvents1Hint(Sender: TObject);
begin
  StatusBar1.SimpleText := Application.Hint;
  Caption := Application.Hint;
end;
```

The TPopupMenu Component

The only difference between building a pop-up menu and the main menu lies in the fact that the main menu is automatically assigned to the form (to the Menu property of the form) and therefore automatically used, whereas a pop-up menu has to be explicitly assigned to a control. Once we design a pop-up menu, using the same Menu Designer that enables us to design the main menu, we have to select the form or a control on the form and then assign our pop-up menu to the PopupMenu property of the selected control.

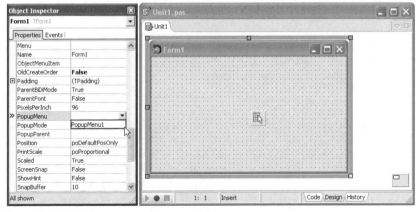

Figure 15-10: Assigning a pop-up menu to the form

The TImageList Component

The TImageList component is a nonvisual component that can contain a collection of glyphs, same-sized images used mainly in menus and toolbars. The TImageList component resides in the Win32 category on the Tool Palette window.

We have to use the TImageList component if we want to display images in the main menu, pop-up menus, or toolbars. The first thing that we have to do is drop a TImageList component to the Designer Surface. Then, we have to use the Image List Editor to add images to the TImageList component. To display the Image List Editor, double-click the TImageList component on the Designer Surface.

Figure 15-11: The Image List Editor

You don't have to worry if you have no 16x16 images that you can use in your applications — Delphi comes with a collection of standard glyphs. You can find these glyphs in the X:\Program Files\Borland Shared\Images directory. The Buttons subdirectory contains a collection of rather old but still useful glyphs. The GlyFX subdirectory, on the other hand, contains a collection of extremely nice, modern-looking glyphs. If your goal is to create a user-friendly interface, you should definitely use these glyphs.

When you add a glyph to the TImageList component, the glyph receives an index value, which is used to identify a particular glyph, as shown in Figure 15-12.

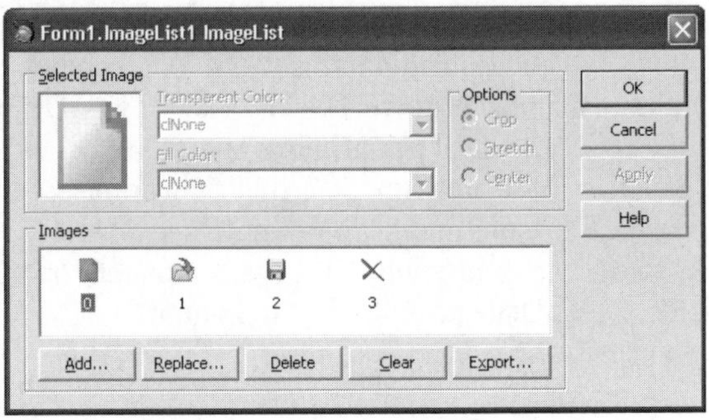

Figure 15-12: A TImageList component that contains several glyphs

In order to use the TImageList glyphs in the pop-up menu, we have to connect the image list with the pop-up menu. To do that, select the TPopupMenu component on the Designer Surface and then assign the ImageList1 component to the pop-up menu's Images property.

Finally, double-click the TPopupMenu component to display the Menu Designer and use the ImageIndex property to assign the appropriate glyph to a menu item.

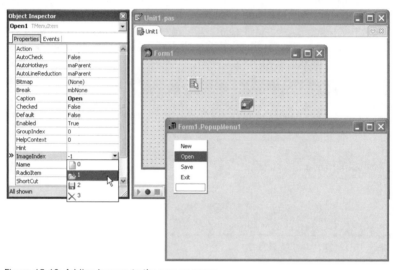

Figure 15-13: Adding images to the pop-up menu

NOTE By default, the TImageList component accepts 16x16 glyphs. If you want to work with glyphs of a different size, you have to modify the Width and Height properties before adding images to the image list because the image list is cleared when these properties are modified.

Common Dialog Controls

The Windows operating system provides several standard dialog boxes that are used by most applications to enable the user to perform standard tasks. These common dialog boxes are encapsulated into several VCL components. The most often used common dialog boxes are TColorDialog, TFindDialog (discussed in Chapter 16), TFontDialog, TOpenDialog, and TSaveDialog. All these components are nonvisual at design time, but they appear onscreen at run time after a call to the Execute method. If you want to see what a common dialog control looks like at run time, right-click the component on the Designer Surface and select Test Dialog from the context menu.

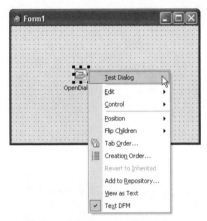

Figure 15-14: Testing a common dialog control at design time

The TColorDialog Component

The TColorDialog component enables the user to select a basic or custom color. The two most often used properties of the TColorDialog component are the Color and Options properties. The Color property contains the selected color, and the Options property enables you to customize the dialog box. For instance, if you include cdFullOpen in the Options property, the dialog box automatically displays not only the basic set of colors but also the section of the dialog box that enables you to select custom colors, as shown in Figure 15-15.

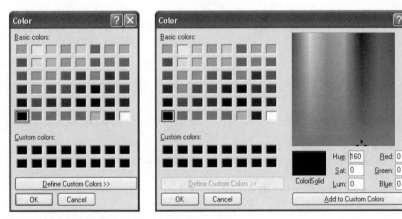

Figure 15-15: The TColorDialog component

To display a common dialog box onscreen, you have to use the Execute method. The Execute method is actually a function that returns True if the user clicks OK on the dialog box and False if the user closes the dialog box in any other manner. The following code shows how to change the background color of the form using the TColorDialog component.

Listing 15-2: Changing the background color of the form

```
procedure TForm1.Button1Click(Sender: TObject);
begin
  { select current color}
  ColorDialog1.Color := Color;

  { display and optionally change the color }
  if ColorDialog1.Execute then
    Color := ColorDialog1.Color;
end;
```

The TFontDialog Component

The TFontDialog component enables the user to select a font and define the font's style.

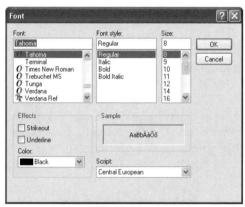

Figure 15-16: The TFontDialog component

In most cases, only the Font property of the TFontDialog component is used. Again, to display the Font dialog, call its Execute method; if the user clicks OK, assign the selected font to the target control (see Listing 15-3).

Listing 15-3: Modifying the Font property of a TLabel component

```
procedure TForm1.Button2Click(Sender: TObject);
begin
  FontDialog1.Font.Assign(Label1.Font);
  if FontDialog1.Execute then
    Label1.Font.Assign(FontDialog1.Font);
end;
```

The TOpenDialog and TSaveDialog Components

The TOpenDialog and TSaveDialog components enable you to select a file. The TOpenDialog component is suited for opening existing files, whereas the TSaveDialog is suited for creating (saving) new files. Figure 15-17 displays a TOpenDialog component.

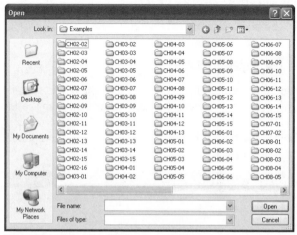

Figure 15-17: The TOpenDialog component

The most important properties of both components are the Filter, FileName, FilterIndex, and DefaultExt properties. The Filter property defines which file types are displayed in both dialog boxes. You can define the file filter manually or by using the Filter Editor (see Figure 15-18). The Filter Name column usually contains the file type description, and the Filter column contains one or more extensions. If more than one extension is associated with a particular file type description, separate the extensions with a semicolon.

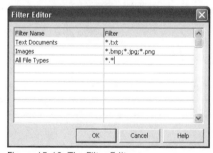

Figure 15-18: The Filter Editor

If you want to define the filter manually, use the vertical bar character. Here is a filter string that can be used to filter text and rich text documents:

```
Text Documents (*.txt)|*.txt|RichText Documents (*.rtf)|*.rtf
```

The FilterIndex property is very simple: It defines which filter is selected by default when the dialog box is displayed. The DefaultExt string property is only important in the TSaveDialog component. It defines the default extension that should be appended to file names. If you forget to define a default extension, the files saved by your application will have no extension. For instance, if you're creating a text editor, you should set the DefaultExt property to "txt" (without the quotes). This way, all documents saved by your application will have the necessary .txt extension.

The TMemo Component

The TMemo component is a multiline text box that enables us to load, edit, and save plain text files. The contents of the text file are stored in the Lines property.

Listing 15-4 shows how to use the TMemo and TListBox components to emulate Delphi's Code Editor and its code completion feature.

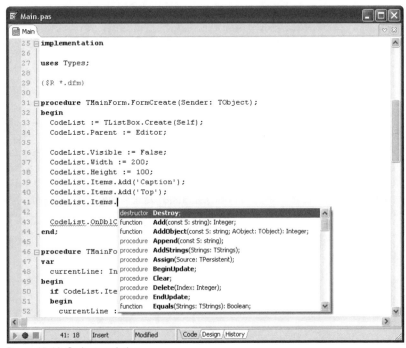

Figure 15-19: Code completion

Start by creating a new VCL Forms application project and then drop a TMemo component on the Designer Surface. Rename the TMemo component Editor.

The first thing that we have to do is dynamically create a TListBox component that will be displayed when the user types a period (full stop) in the editor.

Listing 15-4: Creating the code completion list

```
type
  TMainForm = class(TForm)
    Editor: TMemo;
    procedure FormCreate(Sender: TObject);
  private
```

```
  { Private declarations }
  public
  { Public declarations }
    CodeList: TListBox;
  end;

var
  MainForm: TMainForm;

implementation

{$R *.dfm}

procedure TMainForm.FormCreate(Sender: TObject);
begin
  CodeList := TListBox.Create(Self);
  CodeList.Parent := Editor;

  CodeList.Visible := False;
  CodeList.Width := 200;
  CodeList.Height := 100;
  CodeList.Items.Add('Caption');
  CodeList.Items.Add('Top');
  CodeList.Items.Add('Left');
end;
```

Now that we have the code completion list, we have to write code that displays it when the user types a period (full stop) in the editor. The best place for this code is the OnKeyPress event of the Editor component.

Listing 15-5: Displaying the code completion list

```
procedure TMainForm.EditorKeyPress(Sender: TObject; var Key: Char);
var
  CliPos: TPoint;
  ListX: Integer;
  ListY: Integer;
begin
  if Key = '.' then
  begin
    { get caret position }
    GetCaretPos(CliPos);

    { adjust list position }
    ListX := CliPos.X;
    ListY := CliPos.Y + CodeList.Canvas.TextHeight('W') + 4;

    if ListX + CodeList.Width >= Editor.Width then
      ListX := Editor.Width - CodeList.Width - 20;

    if ListY + CodeList.Height >= Editor.Height then
      ListY := Editor.Height - CodeList.Height - 20;

    CodeList.Top := ListY;
    CodeList.Left := ListX;
    CodeList.ItemIndex := 0;
```

```
      CodeList.Visible := True;
      CodeList.SetFocus;
    end else
      CodeList.Visible := False;
  end;
```

The most important thing when displaying the code completion list is to display it as close to the caret as possible. To get the position of the caret in pixels, we have to use the Windows API GetCaretPos function. After we read the caret's position with the GetCaretPos function, we have to adjust it so that the list appears beneath the line that contains the caret. This adjustment is done by calling the Canvas.TextHeight method to calculate the height of a line in the editor. In this case, we can call the CodeList's TextHeight method because both the Editor and CodeList components use the same font.

If you run the application now and type a period in the editor, you will see the custom code completion list.

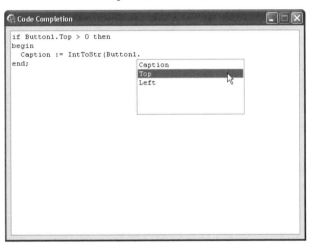

Figure 15-20: The code completion list

Finally, we have to write the code completion code — the code that adds the selected item from the code completion list to the editor.

Listing 15-6: Code completion

```
procedure TMainForm.CodeListClick(Sender: TObject);
var
  currentLine: Integer;
begin
  if CodeList.ItemIndex <> -1 then
  begin
    currentLine := Editor.CaretPos.Y;
    { add text from the list to the editor }
    Editor.Lines[currentLine] := Editor.Lines[currentLine] +
      CodeList.Items[CodeList.ItemIndex];
  end;
```

```
  CodeList.Visible := False;
  Editor.SetFocus;
end;
```

To determine the X and Y coordinates of the caret, we can use the TMemo's CaretPos property. The difference between the GetCaretPos function and the CaretPos property of the TMemo component is that the CaretPos property doesn't contain pixel values. The X value of the CaretPos property specifies the horizontal coordinate of the caret, in characters. The Y value of the CaretPos property specifies the vertical coordinate of the caret, the index of the line that contains the caret.

The last thing we have to do is assign the CodeListClick method to the OnDblClick event of the CodeList component in the OnCreate event handler.

Listing 15-7: Creating the code completion list, revisited

```
procedure TMainForm.FormCreate(Sender: TObject);
begin
  CodeList := TListBox.Create(Self);
  CodeList.Parent := Editor;

  CodeList.Visible := False;
  CodeList.Width := 200;
  CodeList.Height := 100;
  CodeList.Items.Add('Caption');
  CodeList.Items.Add('Top');
  CodeList.Items.Add('Left');

  CodeList.OnDblClick := CodeListClick;
end;
```

Actions

When you create VCL Forms applications, you usually have to do the following:

- Add user interface elements to the Designer Surface.
- Write code that enables or disables these elements depending on what the user can and cannot do at a given time.
- Write the actual application logic.

For instance, the following simple application enables the user to display the text entered in the text box if the check box is checked and the text box isn't empty (see Figure 15-21). If the check box is unchecked or if the text box is empty, the application has to disable the ShowMessage button. This way, the user will know when it's possible to use the button.

Figure 15-21: A simple VCL Forms application

In order to create this simple application, we have to write three different event handlers (see Listing 15-8):

- An event handler for the OnClick event of the check box to enable/disable the ShowMessage button

- An event handler for the OnChange event of the text box to enable/disable the ShowMessage button if the check box is checked and the text box isn't empty

- An event handler for the OnClick event of the ShowMessage button to display the text entered in the text box

Listing 15-8: The ShowMessage button related code

```
procedure TForm1.CheckBox1Click(Sender: TObject);
begin
  if CheckBox1.Checked then
    Button1.Enabled := Edit1.Text <> ''
  else
    Button1.Enabled := False;
end;

procedure TForm1.Button1Click(Sender: TObject);
begin
  ShowMessage(Edit1.Text);
end;

procedure TForm1.Edit1Change(Sender: TObject);
begin
  if CheckBox1.Checked then
    Button1.Enabled := Edit1.Text <> '';
end;
```

Now, let's create a main menu that enables the user to show the text from the text box by selecting Message ➤ ShowMessage. Add a TMainMenu component to the Designer Surface, create the Message menu, and add the ShowMessage item to the Message menu. Finally, assign the Button1Click method to the OnClick event of the ShowMessage menu item.

To complete the implementation of the ShowMessage menu item, we have to write validation code for it, just like we had to for the ShowMessage button.

Listing 15-9: Implementation of the ShowMessage user interface item

```
procedure TForm1.CheckBox1Click(Sender: TObject);
begin
  if CheckBox1.Checked then
  begin
    Button1.Enabled := Edit1.Text <> '';
    ShowMessage1.Enabled := Button1.Enabled;
  end else
  begin
    Button1.Enabled := False;
    ShowMessage1.Enabled := False;
  end;
end;

procedure TForm1.Button1Click(Sender: TObject);
begin
  ShowMessage(Edit1.Text);
end;

procedure TForm1.Edit1Change(Sender: TObject);
begin
  if CheckBox1.Checked then
  begin
    Button1.Enabled := Edit1.Text <> '';
    ShowMessage1.Enabled := Button1.Enabled;
  end;
end;
```

You can also write this validation code in a function and then call the function when necessary, as shown in Listing 15-10.

Listing 15-10: Moving the validation code to a function

```
type
  TForm1 = class(TForm)
  private
    { Private declarations }
    function ShowMessageUpdate: Boolean;
  public
    { Public declarations }
  end;

var
  Form1: TForm1;

implementation

{$R *.dfm}

function TForm1.ShowMessageUpdate: Boolean;
begin
  Result := CheckBox1.Checked and (Edit1.Text <> '');
end;

procedure TForm1.CheckBox1Click(Sender: TObject);
begin
```

```
  Button1.Enabled := ShowMessageUpdate;
  ShowMessage1.Enabled := ShowMessageUpdate;
end;

procedure TForm1.Button1Click(Sender: TObject);
begin
  ShowMessage(Edit1.Text);
end;

procedure TForm1.Edit1Change(Sender: TObject);
begin
  Button1.Enabled := ShowMessageUpdate;
  ShowMessage1.Enabled := ShowMessageUpdate;
end;

end.
```

When creating user interface commands, you should seriously consider using actions to implement their functionality. Actions are special components that allow us to write both validation and actual code for a user interface command in one place. Actions allow us to separate the application logic from the user interface. Once an action is completely defined, it can be assigned to one or more client controls.

Now, we'll recreate the previous example using actions. The first thing we need to do is add the necessary components to the Designer Surface. Add a TGroupBox component to the Designer Surface and then add TCheckBox, TEdit, and TButton components to the TGroupBox component (see Figure 15-22). Finally, change only the Caption property of the TCheckBox component to "Enable ShowMessage Button?".

Figure 15-22: The empty user interface

To use actions in an application we have to drop either the TActionList or the TActionManager component on the Designer Surface. Both components enable us to manage actions in the application.

Select the TActionList component in the Standard category on the Tool Palette window, drop it on the Designer Surface, and then double-click the TActionList component on the Designer Surface to display the Action List editor, shown in Figure 15-23.

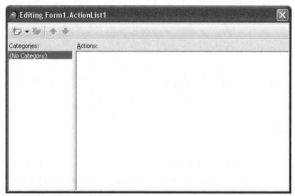

Figure 15-23: The Action List editor

Now, we'll use the Action List editor to create the ShowMessage action. To add a new item to the list, click the New Action button or click the drop-down arrow to the right of the New Action button and select New Action.

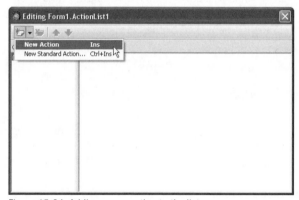

Figure 15-24: Adding a new action to the list

When you select the New Action item, the Action List editor creates a new action named Action1. To create the ShowMessage action, we need to change the Caption property of the Action1 component to "ShowMessage" and then give it a more descriptive name, like ShowAction.

Now that we have defined the action's properties, we can assign the action to a client control. Select the Button1 component on the Designer Surface and then assign the ShowAction action to its Action property. As you can see, when you assign an action to a client control, the properties of the action are copied to the client control.

Finally, we have to write code that displays the text entered in the text box and the code that disables the button when the message shouldn't or can't be shown. Display the Action List editor (if you've closed it), select the ShowAction action in the Actions list, and display the Events list in the Object Inspector.

The most important event is the OnExecute event. You should write the actual application logic in the OnExecute event handler. In this case, the OnExecute handler should only contain code that displays the text entered in the text box.

Listing 15-11: The OnExecute event handler

```
procedure TForm1.ShowActionExecute(Sender: TObject);
begin
  ShowMessage(Edit1.Text);
end;
```

Select the ShowMessage button and display its Events list in the Object Inspector. As you can see, the OnExecute event handler is automatically assigned to the OnClick event of the ShowMessage button. Thus, the action's OnExecute event gets fired when the user clicks the ShowMessage button.

The OnUpdate event can be used to update the action at run time. When an action is updated, all client targets are also automatically updated. Actions are usually updated when the application is idle, although you can explicitly update actions associated with a form by calling the UpdateActions method.

In this case, we can use the OnUpdate event to enable the action or disable it when the check box is unchecked or the text box contains no text.

Listing 15-12: Updating the ShowAction action

```
procedure TForm1.ShowActionUpdate(Sender: TObject);
begin
  ShowAction.Enabled := CheckBox1.Checked and (Edit1.Text <> '');
end;
```

That's it. If you run the application now, you'll see that the ShowMessage button is always properly updated even though we didn't write the event handlers for the OnClick event of the check box and the OnChange event of the text box.

To see just how easy it is to assign an action to a larger number of client controls, let's create the main menu that will enable the user to display the text by selecting Message ➤ ShowMessage. First, drop a TMainMenu component on the Designer Surface and then do the following:

1. Double-click the MainMenu1 component to display the Menu Designer.

2. Type "Message" in the Caption property of the unnamed menu item to create the Message menu.

3. Select the new unnamed menu item that appears beneath the Message menu.

4. Assign the ShowAction action to the Action property of the unnamed menu item.

When you assign an action to the unnamed menu item, the action automatically updates the necessary properties and events of the menu item. If you run the application now, you'll see that we don't have to write additional validation code to update the menu item because the action automatically updates all controls that use it, as shown in Figure 15-25.

Figure 15-25:
Using actions

Standard Actions

Besides being able to create new actions, the Action List editor enables you to add predefined actions to your application. Predefined actions are completely developed actions which contain their own code and have defined properties such as captions, hints, shortcuts, and even images. Predefined actions can be added to the application by clicking the drop-down arrow next to the New Action button in the Action List editor.

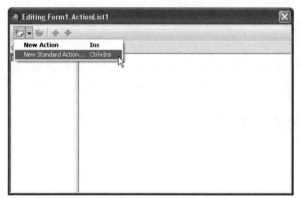

Figure 15-26: Adding standard actions to the application

If you want to use the predefined images contained in the standard actions, you have to drop a TImageList component on the Designer Surface and assign it to the action list's Images property before adding actions to the Actions list.

Add a TImageList component to the Designer Surface, assign it to the Images property of the TActionList component, and select New Standard Action in the Action List editor to display the list of available standard actions.

Figure 15-27: List of available standard actions

Select all actions in the Edit section and click OK to add them to the Actions list. These actions provide everything you need to manage text in TEdit and TMemo components, or any other TCustomEdit descendant.

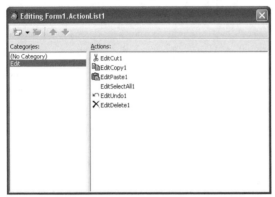

Figure 15-28: Standard Edit actions

To use these actions, add a TMainMenu component to the Designer Surface, and again, before creating menu items, assign the TImageList component to the Images property of the TMainMenu component. This way, when you assign an action to an unnamed menu item, the action also assigns the action's image to the menu item.

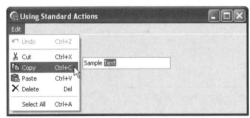

Figure 15-29: Standard Edit actions at run time

If you run the application now, you'll see that you are able to cut, copy, and paste text to and from the clipboard and undo changes in the text box without writing a single line of code.

The following chapter shows how to create a text editor application. You'll learn how to manually implement the functionality of these standard actions.

Chapter 16

Building a Text Editor

Almost every programmer tries to create a Notepad replacement at one time or another. With everything that is available in Delphi, building a great text editor is a pretty painless experience.

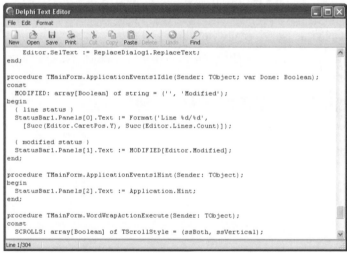

Figure 16-1: The text editor that we're going to create in this chapter

The first thing that we have to do is build the basic user interface of the application. To do that, drop TMainMenu, TMemo, TStatusBar (Win32 category), and TToolbar components on the Designer Surface.

After you have added the components to the Designer Surface, select the TMainMenu component and create the File, Edit, and Format menu groups (see Figure 16-2). Don't create any menu items; we're going to use actions to implement menu commands instead.

Figure 16-2: Main menu groups

Now select the TMemo component and do the following:

1. Rename it Editor.

2. Set the Align property to alClient to have the component fill the entire client area of the form.

3. Delete the Memo1 text from the Lines property.

4. Set the ScrollBars property to ssVertical to display the vertical scroll bar to enable the user to easily view long text files.

If you've done everything right, your Designer Surface should like the one in Figure 16-3.

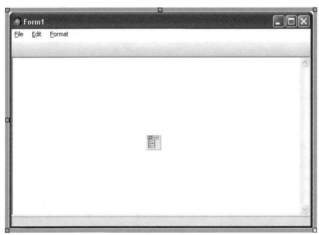

Figure 16-3: The basic user interface

The File Menu

The File menu should contain commands that enable the user to terminate the application and create, load, and save files as shown in Figure 16-4. We are not going to implement the Page Setup and Print commands in this chapter.

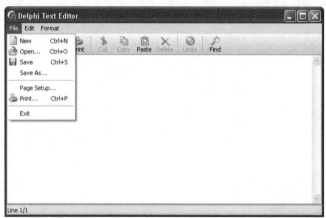

Figure 16-4: The File menu

To create the File menu commands, add a TActionList component to the Designer Surface and then double-click it to display the Action List editor.

First, we need to create the File ➢ Exit command. Click the New Action button to create a new action and then do the following:

1. Set the Caption property of the new action to E&xit.

2. Set the Hint property to "Exit the application."

3. Rename the action ExitAction.

4. Finally, assign the action to an unnamed menu item in the File menu.

To close the application, you only have to call the Close method of the form in the action's OnExecute event handler:

```
procedure TMainForm.ExitActionExecute(Sender: TObject);
begin
  Close;
end;
```

Loading Documents

Now we have to implement the File ➢ Open command to enable the user to open existing documents. First, we have to declare a private variable that will hold the file name of the opened document. This variable is required in the File ➢ Save command and in several other places, as you'll see in a moment.

```
type
  TMainForm = class(TForm)
  private
```

```
  FOpenedFile: string;
 public
 end;
```

To allow the user to select an existing document, you'll need to use the TOpenDialog component. Drop a TOpenDialog component on the Designer Surface and modify its Filter property to have the dialog box only display plain text files that have the .txt extension.

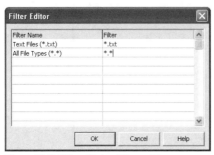

Figure 16-5: TOpenDialog Filter settings

It's always a good idea to add the All File Types filter because the user might have plain text documents that aren't saved under the .txt extension.

Now, add a new action to the action list and modify its settings as follows:

1. Set the Caption property of the new action to &Open…

2. Set the Hint property to "Open an existing document."

3. Rename the action OpenAction.

4. Set the Shortcut property to Ctrl+O.

To load a text document to a TMemo component, you have to do several things. First, you have to call the Execute method of the TOpenDialog component to allow the user to select a document. If the user clicks OK in the dialog box, the selected file name is written to the FileName property of the TOpenDialog component and the Execute method returns True. When the Execute method returns True, you have to copy the selected file name to the FOpenedFile variable and then call the LoadFromFile method to load the selected text document into the Lines property of the TMemo component (see Listing 16-1). Again, write this code in the action's OnExecute event handler.

Listing 16-1: Loading a text document

```
procedure TMainForm.OpenActionExecute(Sender: TObject);
begin
  if OpenDialog1.Execute then
  begin
    { save the selected file name }
    FOpenedFile := OpenDialog1.FileName;

    { load the selected document }
```

```
    Editor.Lines.LoadFromFile(FOpenedFile);
  end;
end;
```

The last thing that you have to do is create the Open command in the File menu. Here's how you do that:

1. Double-click the TMainMenu component to display the Menu Designer.

2. Select the Exit menu item in the File menu.

3. Press Insert on the keyboard to insert a new menu item before the Exit item.

4. Assign the OpenAction action to the Action property of the new menu item.

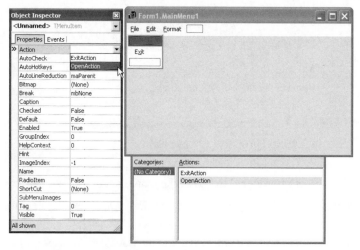

Figure 16-6: Inserting a menu item

Saving Documents

The majority of applications have two separate commands that allow the user to save a document: Save and Save As. The Save command is used to save changes to an existing document, and the Save As command is used to save a document that doesn't exist on disk or to save a copy of the existing document under a new name.

We'll first implement the File ➢ Save As command. The Save As command has to enable the user to select the directory and the file name for the document using the TSaveDialog component, so add a TSaveDialog component to the Designer Surface and then modify the following properties:

1. Set the DefaultExt property to "txt" (without the quotes) to have the dialog box automatically append the .txt extension to the file name.

2. Create the same filter as you did for the TOpenDialog component.

3. Expand the Options property and set the ofOverwritePrompt item to True.

When you include ofOverwritePrompt in the Options set, the TSaveDialog component automatically generates the following warning message if the user tries to use a file name that is already being used.

Figure 16-7: Result of the ofOverwritePrompt value

Now open the Action List editor and create the Save As action:

1. Set the Caption property to Save &As...

2. Rename the action SaveAsAction.

3. Set the Hint property to "Save the active document with a new name."

Finally, place the following code in the OnExecute event handler and then create the Save As command in the File menu.

Listing 16-2: Saving the document using the Save As dialog box

```
procedure TMainForm.SaveAsActionExecute(Sender: TObject);
begin
  if SaveDialog1.Execute then
  begin
    { remember the new file name }
    FOpenedFile := SaveDialog1.FileName;

    { save the document }
    Editor.Lines.SaveToFile(FOpenedFile);
    Editor.Modified := False;
  end;
end;
```

The Save action has to do two things — save changes made to the active document if the document exists or display the Save As dialog box (execute the Save As action) if the document doesn't exist.

To create the Save action, follow these steps:

1. Create a new action in the Action List editor.

2. Set the Caption property of the new action to &Save.

3. Set the Hint property to "Save the active document."

4. Rename the action SaveAction.

5. Set the ShortCut property to Ctrl+S.

Finally, here's the Save action's OnExecute event handler:

```
procedure TMainForm.SaveActionExecute(Sender: TObject);
begin
  { if the active document exists, save changes }
  if FOpenedFile <> '' then
  begin
    Editor.Lines.SaveToFile(FOpenedFile);
    Editor.Modified := False;
  end else
    { if the document doesn't exist, display the Save As dialog }
    SaveAsAction.Execute;
end;
```

Creating New Documents

The File ➢ New command is actually very simple because we only have to do two things:

■ Clear the FOpenedFile variable to let the application know that the active document doesn't exist.

■ Remove the existing text from the Editor component by calling Clear.

To create the New action, follow these steps:

1. Create a new action in the Action List editor.

2. Set the Caption property of the new action to &New.

3. Set the Hint property to "Create a new document."

4. Rename the action NewAction.

5. Set the ShortCut property to Ctrl+N.

6. Add the code in Listing 16-3 to the OnExecute event handler.

Listing 16-3: Creating a new document

```
procedure TMainForm.NewActionExecute(Sender: TObject);
begin
  Editor.Lines.Clear;
  FOpenedFile := '';
end;
```

Protecting User Data

Now that the entire File menu is finished, as shown in Figure 16-8, we have to write a bit more code that will protect the contents of the active document.

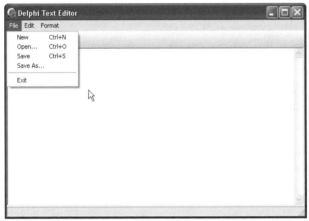

Figure 16-8: The File menu

A well-designed application must check whether the user modified the contents of the active document and ask the user if he or she wants to save the document before allowing the user to:

■ Create a new document

■ Open an existing document

■ Close the entire application

For instance, if you type some text in Notepad and then try to close it, Notepad automatically notifies you that you haven't saved the most recent changes to the document and allows you to either save or discard the changes in the active document.

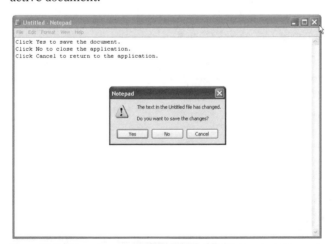

Figure 16-9: Notepad properly protects user data.

The best way to implement this behavior is to create a function that will check whether the user modified the text in the editor and ask the user if he or she wants to discard or save the changes.

Listing 16-4: The function that enables the user to save/discard changes

```
type
  TMainForm = class(TForm)
  private
    FOpenedFile: string;
    function CloseCurrentDocument: Boolean;
  public
    { Public declarations }
  end;

function TMainForm.CloseCurrentDocument: Boolean;
begin
  Result := True; { enable the user to close the current document }

  if Editor.Modified then
  begin
    case MessageDlg('Save changes to the current document?',
      mtWarning, mbYesNoCancel, 0) of
        mrYes: SaveAction.Execute;
        mrCancel: Result := False;
    end;    // case
  end;      // if Editor.Modified
end;
```

If the text displayed in the editor isn't modified, the function returns True, which allows us to either close the entire application or replace the text in the editor with an empty or an existing document. If the text in the editor is modified, the MessageDlg function is called to allow the user to save or discard the text displayed in the editor. If the user clicks Yes, the function first fires the Save action to save the document and returns True to notify us that we can now close the document. If the user clicks the No button, the function returns True because the user wants to discard the changes. Finally, if the user clicks the Cancel button, the function returns False to notify us that we can neither close the application nor replace the active document with another one.

Now, we have to call the CloseCurrentDocument function in the New and Open actions to actually ask the user what to do if there are changes in the text.

Listing 16-5: The updated New and Open actions

```
procedure TMainForm.NewActionExecute(Sender: TObject);
begin
  if CloseCurrentDocument then
  begin
    Editor.Clear;
    FOpenedFile := '';
  end;
end;

procedure TMainForm.OpenActionExecute(Sender: TObject);
```

```
begin
  if CloseCurrentDocument and OpenDialog1.Execute then
  begin
    FOpenedFile := OpenDialog1.FileName;
    Editor.Lines.LoadFromFile(FOpenedFile);
  end;
end;
```

Figure 16-10 shows what happens when you modify the text in the editor and then try to open another document.

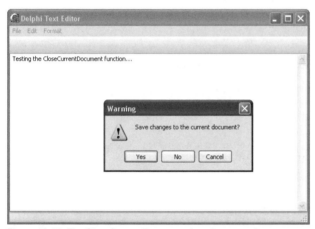

Figure 16-10: The CloseCurrentDocument function at work

The last thing we have to do now is write the handler for the form's OnCloseQuery event. This event occurs when the user tries to close the form. The CanClose parameter of the OnCloseQuery event enables us to specify whether or not the form can be closed.

The OnCloseQuery event handler is actually really simple. We only have to assign the result of the CloseCurrentDocument function to the CanClose parameter. This way, if the CloseCurrentDocument function returns True, the user can close the application. The only case when the closing of the form is stopped is when the text in the editor is modified and the user clicks Cancel in the MessageDlg dialog box.

Here's the OnCloseQuery event handler:

```
procedure TMainForm.FormCloseQuery(Sender: TObject; var CanClose: Boolean);
begin
  CanClose := CloseCurrentDocument;
end;
```

The Edit Menu

The Edit menu, shown in Figure 16-11, contains commands that work with the clipboard and enable the user to search and replace text in the editor.

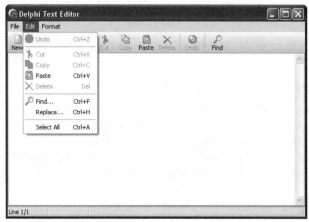

Figure 16-11: The Edit menu

All commands in the Edit menu, except Find and Replace, are so easy to implement that they're almost no fun. Actually, everything in the Edit menu can be implemented in about five seconds because there are standard actions for all the commands displayed in Figure 16-11. But we're not going to use standard actions here. Instead, we're going to implement all the Edit menu commands manually.

Undo

First, let's create the Undo action:

1. Create a new action.
2. Set the Caption property to &Undo.
3. Set the Hint property to "Undo the last action."
4. Rename the action UndoAction.
5. Set the ShortCut property to Ctrl+Z.

To undo changes in the editor, you have to call the Undo method. To determine if you can undo anything, you can call the CanUndo method. Better yet, you should call the CanUndo method in the action's OnUpdate event to disable the action when it's not possible to undo something, as shown in Listing 16-6.

Listing 16-6: The OnExecute and OnUpdate event handlers of the Undo action

```
procedure TMainForm.UndoActionExecute(Sender: TObject);
begin
  Editor.Undo;
end;

procedure TMainForm.UndoActionUpdate(Sender: TObject);
begin
  UndoAction.Enabled := Editor.CanUndo;
end;
```

Cutting and Copying to the Clipboard

The Cut and Copy actions are very similar. The Copy action copies the selected text to the clipboard, and the Cut action first copies the selected text to the clipboard and then deletes the text from the editor.

Because the Cut and Copy actions share the same OnUpdate event handler, let's create both actions first and then write the necessary event handlers.

To create the Cut action, follow these steps:

1. Create a new action in the Action List editor.

2. Set the Caption of the new action to Cu&t.

3. Set the Hint property to "Cut the selection to the clipboard."

4. Rename the action CutAction.

5. Set the ShortCut property to Ctrl+X.

To create the Copy action, follow these steps:

1. Create a new action in the Action List editor.

2. Set the Caption of the new action to &Copy.

3. Set the Hint property to "Copy the selection to the clipboard."

4. Rename the action CopyAction.

5. Set the ShortCut property to Ctrl+C.

Both OnExecute event handlers are easy to implement. To copy the text from the editor to the clipboard, you have to call the CopyToClipboard method. To cut the text to the clipboard, call the editor's CutToClipboard method.

Listing 16-7: Cut and Copy OnExecute event handlers

```
procedure TMainForm.CutActionExecute(Sender: TObject);
begin
  Editor.CutToClipboard;
end;

procedure TMainForm.CopyActionExecute(Sender: TObject);
begin
  Editor.CopyToClipboard;
end;
```

The code in the OnUpdate event handler needs to disable the action if there is no selected text in the editor. You can use the editor's SelLength property to determine how many characters are selected. If the value of the SelLength property is 0, there are no selected characters in the editor and we have to disable the action.

Now, write the following OnUpdate event handler for the Cut action and then assign it to the OnUpdate event of the Copy action:

```
procedure TMainForm.CutActionUpdate(Sender: TObject);
begin
  TAction(Sender).Enabled := Editor.SelLength > 0;
end;
```

Pasting from the Clipboard

The Paste action pastes the contents of the clipboard into the editor. To be completely professional, you should only allow the user to select Paste when the clipboard contains text. To find out the format of the data stored in the clipboard, call the clipboard's HasFormat method. To see if the clipboard contains plain text data that can be pasted into the editor, call the HasFormat method and pass the CF_TEXT constant as the parameter. To use the global Clipboard object, you have to add the Clipbrd unit to the uses list.

To create the Paste action, here's what you have to do:

1. Create a new action.

2. Set the Caption property to &Paste.

3. Set the Hint property to "Insert text from the clipboard."

4. Rename the action PasteAction.

5. Set the ShortCut property to Ctrl+V.

The implementation of the Paste action is displayed in Listing 16-8.

Listing 16-8: The Paste action

```
procedure TMainForm.PasteActionExecute(Sender: TObject);
begin
  Editor.PasteFromClipboard;
end;

procedure TMainForm.PasteActionUpdate(Sender: TObject);
begin
  PasteAction.Enabled := Clipboard.HasFormat(CF_TEXT);
end;
```

If you're building the text editor using the C++ langugage, you'll need to include the Clipbrd.hpp header file, in order to access the TClipboard class, and the Clipboard function, which returns the instance of the TClipboard class that we should use in our VCL Forms applications.

Here's how you call the HasFormat method in C++ to determine if the clipboard contains plain text data that can be pasted into the document:

```
void __fastcall TMainForm::PasteActionUpdate(TObject *Sender)
{
   PasteAction->Enabled = Clipboard()->HasFormat(CF_TEXT);
}
```

Deleting

The Delete action does pretty much the same thing as the Cut action. Just like Cut, the Delete action removes the selected text from the editor. The difference is that Delete doesn't copy the text to the clipboard before removing it from the editor.

To create the Delete action, follow these steps:

1. Create a new action.
2. Set the Caption property of the new action to De&lete.
3. Set the Hint property to "Erase the selection."
4. Rename the action DeleteAction.
5. Set the ShortCut property to Del.

To delete the text from the editor without changing the contents of the clipboard, use the ClearSelection method. Also, assign the Cut action's OnUpdate event handler to the OnUpdate event of the Delete action to enable the user to delete the selected text only if such text exists. The implementation of the Delete action is displayed in Listing 16-9.

Listing 16-9: The Delete action

```
procedure TMainForm.DeleteActionExecute(Sender: TObject);
begin
   Editor.ClearSelection;
end;
```

Selecting the Entire Document

Probably the simplest of all actions is Select All, which enables the user to select the entire contents of the editor. To create the Select All action, do the following:

1. Create a new action.
2. Set the Caption property to Select &All.
3. Set the Hint property to "Select the entire document."
4. Rename the action SelectAllAction.
5. Set the ShortCut property to Ctrl+A.

To select the entire contents of a TMemo component, you have to call the SelectAll method:

```
procedure TMainForm.SelectAllActionExecute(Sender: TObject);
begin
  Editor.SelectAll;
end;
```

Searching for Text in Delphi

To implement the Find command, first add the TFindDialog component to the Designer Surface. The TFindDialog component encapsulates the common Find dialog that enables the user to search for a string (see Figure 16-12). The string that the user wants to search for is stored in the FindText property.

Figure 16-12: The Find dialog

To enable the user to search for text, we have to create the Find action that displays the Find dialog and write a handler for the dialog's OnFind event to actually perform the search. Since the Find dialog enables the user to search for multiple instances of a string, we need to declare an Integer variable to store the last search position:

```
type
  TMainForm = class(TForm)
  private
    FLastSearch: Integer;
  public
  end;
```

Now, follow these steps to create the Find action:

1. Set the Caption property of the new action to &Find...

2. Set the Hint property to "Find the specified text."

3. Rename the action FindAction.

4. Set the ShortCut property to Ctrl+F.

5. Write the following code in the action's OnExecute event handler:

```
procedure TMainForm.FindActionExecute(Sender: TObject);
begin
  { start at the beginning of the document }
  FLastSearch := 0;

  { display the dialog }
  FindDialog1.Execute;
end;
```

The code that performs the search is displayed in Listing 16-10A. The C++ implementation is displayed in Listing 16-10B.

Listing 16-10A: Searching for text, Delphi version

```
procedure TMainForm.FindDialog1Find(Sender: TObject);
var
  memoText: string;
  searchPos: Integer;
  dialog: TFindDialog;
begin
  dialog := TFindDialog(Sender);

  memoText := Editor.Lines.Text;
  if FLastSearch <> 0 then Delete(memoText, 1, FLastSearch);

  searchPos := Pos(dialog.FindText, memoText);
  if searchPos = 0 then
    MessageDlg(Format('Cannot find "%s"', [dialog.FindText]),
      mtInformation, [mbOK], 0)
  else begin
    Inc(FLastSearch, searchPos);
    Editor.SelStart := Pred(FLastSearch);
    Editor.SelLength := Length(dialog.FindText);
    Editor.SetFocus;
  end;
end;
```

The first line (typecast of the Sender parameter to TFindDialog) is not necessary if you're only going to use this method in the Edit ➢ Find command. In this case, we need the typecast because it enables us to reuse this method in the OnFind event of the TReplaceDialog component.

The next two lines create a temporary copy of the entire document and remove the section of the document that the user previously searched. If we don't remove the previously searched section, the Pos function that is used to perform the search will always return the first instance of the search string.

If the Pos function finds an instance of the search string, we have to store the location of the found instance in the FLastSearch variable and then select the search string in the editor. To select the string in the editor, we have to modify the SelStart and SelLength properties. SelStart indicates the position of the cursor and SelLength specifies the number of selected characters. Finally, to display the selection we have to call the SetFocus method to focus the editor.

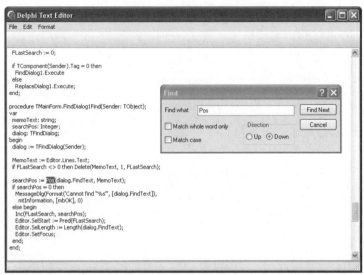

Figure 16-13: Using the Find dialog to search for text

Searching for Text in C++

Almost every line of code in Listing 16-10A can be easily translated into C++. The only problem lies in the line that calls the Format function to format the string displayed by the MessageDlg dialog box.

The problem is that the Format function accepts, as the second parameter, an array of const, which is the Delphi way of enabling the function to accept a variable number of parameters:

```
procedure TForm1.FormatPlay(Sender: TObject);
var
  x, y: Integer;
begin
  x := 1; y := 2;
  Caption := Format('%d + %d = %d', [x, y, x + y]); // 1 + 2 = 3
  Caption := Format('%s%s', ['Bor', 'land']);        // Borland
end;
```

To call the Format function (or other functions with variable parameter lists) in C++, you have to replace the open array constructor (brackets and statements inside the brackets) with the ARRAYOFCONST macro, which has the following syntax:

```
ARRAYOFCONST((value_1, value_2, value_n))
```

Here's an example of how to call the Format function in C++:

```
void __fastcall TForm1::FormatPlay(TObject *Sender)
{
    int x = 1, y = 2;
    Caption = Format("%d + %d = %d", ARRAYOFCONST((x, y, x + y)));
    Caption = Format("%s%s", ARRAYOFCONST(("Bor", "land")));
}
```

Listing 16-10B shows how to search for text using the C++ language.

Listing 16-10B: Searching for text, C++ version

```cpp
void __fastcall TMainForm::FindDialog1Find(TObject *Sender)
{
   AnsiString memoText = Editor->Lines->Text;
   int searchPos;
   TFindDialog* dialog = dynamic_cast<TFindDialog*>(Sender);

   if(FLastSearch != 0)
      memoText.Delete(1, FLastSearch);

   searchPos = memoText.Pos(dialog->FindText);
   if(searchPos == 0)
      MessageDlg(Format("Cannot find \"%s\"",
         ARRAYOFCONST((dialog->FindText))), mtInformation,
         TMsgDlgButtons() << mbOK, 0);
   else {
      FLastSearch += searchPos;
      Editor->SelStart = FLastSearch - 1;
      Editor->SelLength = dialog->FindText.Length();
      Editor->SetFocus();
   }
}
```

Replacing Text

To complete the Edit menu, we have to create the Replace action, which will enable us to search for and replace a string. To implement Replace, we have to do the following:

■ Drop a TReplaceDialog component on the Designer Surface (see Figure 16-14).

■ Create the action that will display the Replace dialog.

■ Write handlers for the OnFind and OnReplace events of the TReplaceDialog component.

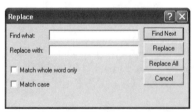

Figure 16-14: The TReplaceDialog component

To create the Replace action, do the following:

1. Set the Caption property of the new action to &Replace…

2. Set the Hint property to "Replace found text with different text."

3. Rename the action ReplaceAction.

4. Set the ShortCut property to Ctrl+H.

5. Set the Tag property to 1 or any other number not equal to 0.

6. Assign the OnExecute event handler of the Find action to the OnExecute event.

We have to change the Tag property to reuse the OnExecute event handler of the Find action. Once you've changed the Tag property of the Replace action, you can modify the OnExecute event handler of the Find action to display both dialogs:

```
procedure TMainForm.FindActionExecute(Sender: TObject);
begin
  FLastSearch := 0;

  if TComponent(Sender).Tag = 0 then
    FindDialog1.Execute
  else
    ReplaceDialog1.Execute;
end;
```

Finally, we have to write handlers for the OnFind event, which occurs when the user clicks the Find button, and the OnReplace event, which occurs when the user clicks the Replace or Replace All buttons.

Actually, we don't have to write a handler for the OnFind event, because we can use the already existing OnFind event handler of the TFindDialog component. We can use the existing OnFind event handler because of the initial typecast of the Sender parameter to a TFindDialog component and because TReplaceDialog descends from TFindDialog.

In the OnReplace event handler, we have to check if there is selected text in the editor (SelText <> "), and if there is, replace it with the string from the ReplaceText property.

Listing 16-11: The OnReplace event handler

```
procedure TMainForm.ReplaceDialog1Replace(Sender: TObject);
begin
  if Editor.SelText <> '' then
    Editor.SelText := ReplaceDialog1.ReplaceText;
end;
```

The Format Menu

The Format menu in our sample application is the simplest menu. It consists of only two commands: Word Wrap and Font.

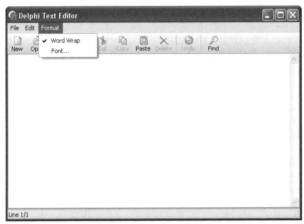

Figure 16-15: The Format menu

The Word Wrap command enables the user to wrap text at the right margin. If Word Wrap is checked, you should only enable vertical scrolling of the contents of the editor. If Word Wrap is unchecked, you have to display both scroll bars because long lines aren't wrapped at the right margin.

To create the Word Wrap action, follow these steps:

1. Create a new action and set its AutoCheck property to True to have it automatically toggle its Checked state.

2. Set the Caption property to &Word Wrap.

3. Set the Checked property to True because the WordWrap property of the editor is True by default.

4. Rename the action WordWrapAction.

Finally, write the following OnExecute event handler:

```
procedure TMainForm.WordWrapActionExecute(Sender: TObject);
const
  SCROLLS: array[Boolean] of TScrollStyle = (ssBoth, ssVertical);
begin
  Editor.WordWrap := WordWrapAction.Checked;
  Editor.ScrollBars := SCROLLS[Editor.WordWrap];
end;
```

To create the Format ➤ Font command, first drop a TFontDialog component on the Designer Surface and then create a new action. Set the Caption of the new action to &Font, rename the action FontAction, and then write the following code in its OnExecute event handler:

```
procedure TMainForm.FontActionExecute(Sender: TObject);
begin
  { display current font in the dialog box }
  FontDialog1.Font.Assign(Editor.Font);

  { change the font }
  if FontDialog1.Execute then
    Editor.Font.Assign(FontDialog1.Font);
end;
```

Displaying Hints and Status

If the SimplePanel property is set to True, the TStatusBar component can only display a single piece of information specified in the SimpleText property. But if the SimplePanel property is set to False, we can use the Panels property to create a multipanel status bar and display more information to the user.

Select the status bar component and then click the (...) button next to its Panels property to display the Collection Editor. Click the Add New button three times to create three status bar panels. Change the Width of the first two panels to 75 to make more room for text.

We'll use the first panel to display how many lines are in the document and which line is currently selected. The second panel will be used to display "Modified" if the contents of the editor are changed, and the last panel will be used to display the hint.

The best place for this code is in the OnIdle event of the application, so add a TApplicationEvents component to the Designer Surface and write the following code in the OnIdle event handler:

```
procedure TMainForm.ApplicationEvents1Idle(Sender: TObject; var Done: Boolean);
const
  MODIFIED: array[Boolean] of string = ('', 'Modified');
begin
  { line status }
  StatusBar1.Panels[0].Text := Format('Line %d/%d',
    [Succ(Editor.CaretPos.Y), Succ(Editor.Lines.Count)]);

  { modified status }
  StatusBar1.Panels[1].Text := MODIFIED[Editor.Modified];
end;
```

If you're using the C++ language, here's what your OnIdle event handler should look like:

```
void __fastcall TMainForm::ApplicationEvents1Idle(TObject *Sender, bool &Done)
{
  const AnsiString MODIFIED[] = {"", "Modified"};

  StatusBar1->Panels->Items[0]->Text = Format("Line %d/%d",
    ARRAYOFCONST((Editor->CaretPos.y + 1,
    Editor->Lines->Count + 1)));

  StatusBar1->Panels->Items[1]->Text = MODIFIED[Editor->Modified];
}
```

To display the hint in the last panel, write a handler for the OnHint event:

```
procedure TMainForm.ApplicationEvents1Hint(Sender: TObject);
begin
  StatusBar1.Panels[2].Text := Application.Hint;
end;
```

If you've done everything right, at run time your status bar should look like the one displayed in Figure 16-16.

Figure 16-16: The status bar

The Toolbar

There are only two things left to be done in this chapter: add glyphs to the most often used actions and then add these actions to the toolbar.

First, add a TImageList component to the Designer Surface, rename it Normal, and then add glyphs for the New, Open, Save, Undo, Cut, Copy, Paste, Delete, and Find actions (see Figure 16-17). After you add these images to the TImageList component, assign the TImageList component to the TActionList, TToolbar, and TMainMenu components and then open the Action List editor and assign the glyphs to the appropriate actions.

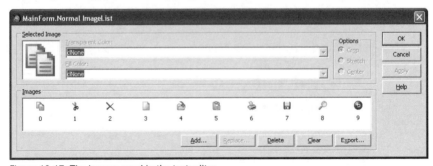

Figure 16-17: The images used in the text editor

When you're done assigning glyphs to the actions, select the toolbar and right-click it to display the toolbar's context menu. The context menu offers you the New Button option to create a new toolbar button and the New Separator option to create a separator item that enables you to visually group buttons. All that you have to do now is add several buttons to the toolbar and assign an action to the Action property of each button.

If you want, you can also modify the following two properties to make the toolbar more attractive:

1. Set the AutoSize property to True to remove the empty space on the toolbar.

2. Set the ShowCaptions property to True to display button captions (if you do this, you'll have to remove the ampersand characters and dots from the button captions).

Also, you can improve the look of the disabled toolbar buttons by adding another TImageList component to the Designer Surface to hold disabled glyphs. Here's what you have to do to add disabled glyphs to the toolbar:

1. Add another TImageList component to the Designer Surface.

2. Rename it Disabled.

3. Add disabled glyphs to the image list (the disabled glyphs in the GlyFX folder end with _d).

4. Make sure that the index of each disabled glyph matches the index of the normal glyph in the Normal image list (see Figure 16-18).

5. Assign the disabled image list to the toolbar's DisabledImages property.

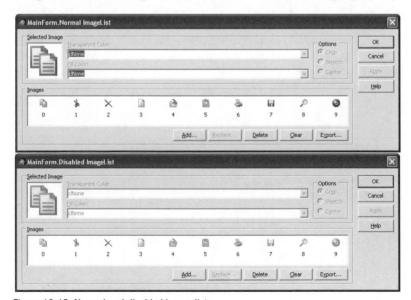

Figure 16-18: Normal and disabled image lists

After you've added the disabled glyphs to the toolbar, you're done. The text editor is completely finished. You can see the final product in Figure 16-19.

Figure 16-19: The best text editor in the galaxy

Chapter 17

The Multiple Document Interface

Generally, there are two types of user interface applications: SDI (single document interface) and MDI (multiple document interface). SDI applications have a single main form and enable us to view a single document at a time. Applications like Notepad, WordPad, Paint, and the Delphi Text Editor we built in the previous chapter are SDI applications.

Unlike SDI applications, MDI applications allow us to view more than one document at a time. An MDI application consists of a main (parent) form and none or many child window instances that are displayed within the parent form, as shown below.

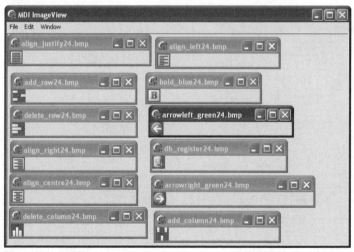

Figure 17-1: An MDI image viewer

Besides the SDI and MDI interface styles, there are two other styles that are often used: the Explorer-style interface (see Figure 17-2) and the tabbed interface (see Figure 17-3). Both of these styles are actually SDI interfaces built with complex components like TTreeView and TPageControl.

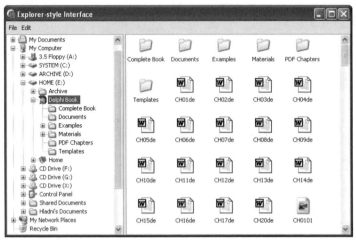

Figure 17-2: The Explorer-style interface

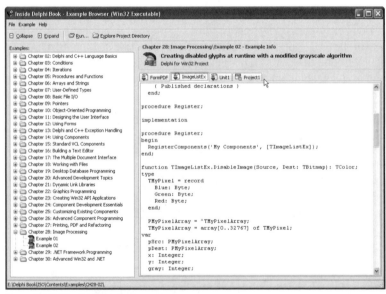

Figure 17-3: The tabbed interface

MDI Image Viewer

In this chapter, we are going to create an MDI image viewer application similar to the one displayed in Figure 17-1.

As you'll see in a moment, it's actually really easy to build MDI applications in Delphi, especially if you already know how to dynamically create modeless forms.

The first thing that you have to do, after you've created a new VCL Forms application project, is create the MDI parent form by setting the FormStyle property of the form to fsMDIForm.

Now that you've created the MDI parent form, you have to create the MDI child form by doing the following:

1. Add a new empty form to the project (File ➢ New ➢ Form - Delphi for Win32).

2. Set the FormStyle property of the form to fsMDIChild.

3. Optionally rename the form ChildForm or something similar.

If you run the application now, you'll see that the child form is automatically displayed inside the parent form.

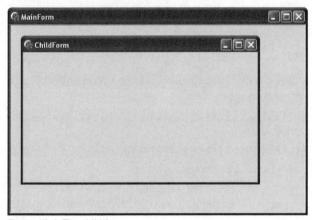

Figure 17-4: The child form

To finish the creation of the child form, we have to remove it from the auto-create list (Project ➢ Options). This way, the child form will not be automatically displayed when the application starts.

Also, we have to handle the form's OnClose event and tell the form to free itself when it's closed:

```
procedure TChildForm.FormClose(Sender: TObject; var Action: TCloseAction);
begin
  Action := caFree;
end;
```

We have to do this because, by default, child forms only get minimized when you try to close them, as shown in Figure 17-5.

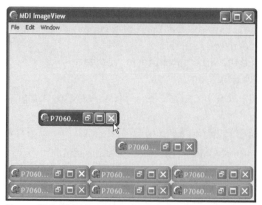

Figure 17-5: Child forms are, by default, only minimized when you try to close them.

Creating Child Forms

To display an image on the child window, add a TImage component to the child form and then do the following:

1. Set the Top and Left properties to 0 to move the image component into the top-left corner of the form.

2. Set the AutoSize property to True to enable the TImage component to resize itself when we load an image.

3. Switch to the main form, add a TMainMenu component to the form, and then create the File ≻ Open menu item to enable the user to select one or more images and open them.

NOTE   Besides bitmaps, icons, and metafiles, Delphi can also open JPEG images. To enable an application to work with JPEG images, you simply have to add jpeg to the uses list.

In the OnClick event handler of the Open item, we have to do the following:

1. Display the TOpenDialog dialog box to enable the user to select images.

2. Create an instance of the child form for every selected image.

3. Load the selected images.

First, let's create the TOpenDialog component dynamically and set its properties in code. To enable the user to select multiple items (in this case, multiple images), we have to create a filter that only displays image files in the dialog box and we have to include ofAllowMultiSelect in the Options set. Including ofAllowMultiSelect enables you to select multiple items and stores the selected items in the Files property.

Listing 17-1: Creating a common open dialog box that allows the user to select multiple files

```
procedure TMainForm.OpenItemClick(Sender: TObject);
var
  cnt: Integer;
begin
  with TOpenDialog.Create(Self) do
  try
    Filter := 'Images (*.bmp, *.jpg)|*.bmp;*.jpg;*.jpeg';
    Options := Options + [ofAllowMultiSelect];

  finally
    Free;
  end;              // try TOpenDialog.Create
end;
```

If the user clicks OK in the dialog box, we have to read the file names from the Files property and create a child form instance for each file (see Listing 17-2A for the Delphi version and Listing 17-2B for the C++ version).

Listing 17-2A: Creating child instances and loading selected images, Delphi version

```
procedure TMainForm.OpenItemClick(Sender: TObject);
var
  cnt: Integer;
begin
  with TOpenDialog.Create(Self) do
  try
    Filter := 'Images (*.bmp, *.jpg)|*.bmp;*.jpg;*.jpeg';
    Options := Options + [ofAllowMultiSelect];

    if Execute then
      for cnt := 0 to Pred(Files.Count) do
        with TChildForm.Create(Self) do
        begin
          // enable AutoSize temporarily to resize the window
          // to fit the loaded image
          AutoSize := True;

          // load the selected image
          Caption := ExtractFileName(Files[cnt]);
          Image1.Picture.LoadFromFile(Files[cnt]);

          // disable AutoSize so that we can resize the window
          AutoSize := False;
        end;      // with TChildForm
  finally
    Free;
  end;              // try TOpenDialog.Create
end;
```

Listing 17-2:B Creating child instances and loading selected images, C++ version

```cpp
void __fastcall TMainForm::OpenItemClick(TObject *Sender)
{
    AnsiString fName;
    TOpenDialog* dialog = new TOpenDialog(this);
    try
    {
        dialog->Filter = "Images (*.bmp, *.jpg)|*.bmp;*.jpg;*.jpeg";
        dialog->Options << ofAllowMultiSelect;

        if(dialog->Execute())
        {
            for(int cnt = 0; cnt < dialog->Files->Count; cnt++)
            {
                fName = dialog->Files->Strings[cnt];

                // don't forget to include the childform's unit
                // File -> Include Unit Hdr...
                TChildForm* frm = new TChildForm(this);
                frm->AutoSize = true;
                frm->Caption = ExtractFileName(fName);
                frm->Image1->Picture->LoadFromFile(fName);

                // disable AutoSize
                frm->AutoSize = false;
            }
        }
    }
    __finally
    {
        delete dialog;
    }
}
```

Managing Child Forms

MDI applications usually have a Window menu that contains commands like Tile Vertically, Tile Horizontally, Cascade, Arrange Icons, Minimize All, and Close All for managing child windows. The Window menu can also automatically display a list of all opened child windows, as shown in Figure 17-6. To have the Window menu automatically display the list of all opened child windows, assign the actual Window menu item to the WindowMenu property of the form.

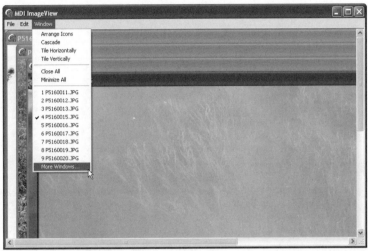

Figure 17-6: The Window menu

The implementation of all Window menu commands is displayed in Listing 17-3.

Listing 17-3: The Window menu commands

```pascal
procedure TMainForm.CloseAllItemClick(Sender: TObject);
var
  cnt: Integer;
begin
  for cnt := Pred(MDIChildCount) downto 0 do
    MDIChildren[cnt].Close;
end;

procedure TMainForm.ArrangeIconsItemClick(Sender: TObject);
begin
  ArrangeIcons;
end;

procedure TMainForm.CascadeItemClick(Sender: TObject);
begin
  Cascade;
end;

procedure TMainForm.TileHorizontallyItemClick(Sender: TObject);
begin
  TileMode := tbHorizontal;
  Tile;
end;

procedure TMainForm.TileVerticallyItemClick(Sender: TObject);
begin
  TileMode := tbVertical;
```

```
   Tile;
end;

procedure TMainForm.MinimizeAllItemClick(Sender: TObject);
var
   cnt: Integer;
begin
   for cnt := Pred(MDIChildCount) downto 0 do
     MDIChildren[cnt].WindowState := wsMinimized;
end;
```

Inverting Colors

To make this application a bit more fun, let's create the Edit ➢ Invert Colors command to enable the user to invert colors in the selected image (see Figure 17-7).

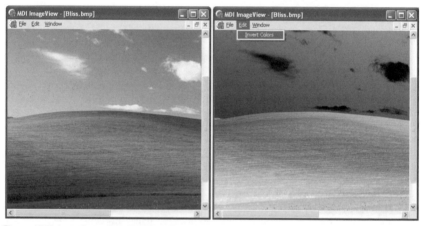

Figure 17-7: Inverting colors in an image

To invert colors in a bitmap image, you only have to call the Windows API InvertRect function. The InvertRect function accepts two parameters:

```
function InvertRect(hDC: HDC; const lprc: TRect): BOOL; stdcall;
```

The hDC parameter expects a valid device context handle — a handle of an object that supports drawing. In a VCL Forms application, you can pass the Canvas.Handle as the hDC parameter (to learn more about the Canvas property, see Chapter 22). The second parameter is a TRect record that defines the rectangle that should be inverted. To invert the entire image, pass the image's ClientRect rectangle as the lprc parameter.

If the user opens a JPEG image, we have to convert it to a bitmap before we can use the InvertRect function to invert colors in the image.

The implementation of the Edit ➢ Invert Colors command is displayed in the following thoroughly commented listing.

Listing 17-4: Inverting colors

```
procedure TMainForm.InvertColorsItemClick(Sender: TObject);
var
  ActiveView: TChildForm;
  NewBitmap: TBitmap;
begin
  if MDIChildCount = 0 then
  begin
    MessageDlg('Open an image first!', mtWarning, [mbOK], 0);
    Exit;
  end;

  // convert the active child form provided by the ActiveMDIChild
  // property to our child form type
  ActiveView := TChildForm(ActiveMDIChild);

  // if it's a bitmap - invert colors
  if ActiveView.Image1.Picture.Graphic is TBitmap then
  begin
    InvertRect(ActiveView.Image1.Canvas.Handle, ActiveView.Image1.ClientRect);
  end else if ActiveView.Image1.Picture.Graphic is TJPEGImage then
  begin
    // if it's a jpeg - first convert to bitmap, then invert colors
    NewBitmap := TBitmap.Create;
    try
      // to convert a jpeg image to a bitmap, you only have to assign
      // it to a bitmap
      NewBitmap.Assign(ActiveView.Image1.Picture.Graphic);

      // invert colors in the temporary bitmap
      InvertRect(NewBitmap.Canvas.Handle, ActiveView.Image1.ClientRect);

      // assign the temporary bitmap back
      ActiveView.Image1.Picture.Graphic.Assign(NewBitmap);
    finally
      NewBitmap.Free;
    end;
  end;

  // this is important - refresh the form
  ActiveView.Image1.Invalidate;
end;
```

Inverting Colors in C++

To invert colors in C++ you have to do the same thing as in Delphi: test if the image is a bitmap and invert its colors or convert the image to a bitmap if it's a JPEG and then invert its colors. To gain access to the TJPEGImage class you have to include the jpeg.hpp header file.

But if you try to typecast the image to a TBitmap using the following code, you'll get the "Ambiguity between TBitmap and 'Windows::TBitmap'" error message.

```
TGraphic* graphic = actChild->Image1->Picture->Graphic;

if(dynamic_cast<TBitmap *>(graphic)) // here's the problem
{
    InvertRect(actChild->Image1->Canvas->Handle, &imgRect);
}
```

This error results because two totally different TBitmap types exist and the compiler cannot determine which one you want to use.

One TBitmap type (a structure) exists in the Windows.hpp file, inside the Windows namespace, and the other TBitmap type (the VCL TBitmap class) exists in the Graphics.hpp file, inside the Graphics namespace.

Namespaces

Besides units, which are the default containers for data types, languages like C++, Delphi, and C# also store types in namespaces. A namespace is an additional container that groups types under a unique name and allows us to declare more classes with the same name.

For instance, the following code shows how to use namespaces to declare two completely different classes that are both called MyClass:

```
namespace This
{
    class MyClass {
    public:
        int x;
    };
}

namespace That
{
    class MyClass {
    public:
        char c;
    };
}
```

In order to access these two classes, you'll have to use the scope access operator (::) like this:

```
namespace::class
```

The following code shows how you can create an instance of the MyClass class from the This namespace and the MyClass class from the That namespace:

```
MyClass a;      // Error - Undefined Symbol
This::MyClass b;
That::MyClass c;
```

You can also use the reserved word using to access everything stored in a namespace. When you "open" a namespace with the reserved word using, you no longer have to use the scope access operator to access its types:

```
using namespace This;
MyClass mc;        // This::MyClass
mc.x = 5;
```

Everything will work properly as long as you're using only the This namespace. If you decide to use both the This and That namespaces, you'll receive exactly the same "Ambiguity..." error as we did with the TBitmap code:

```
using namespace This;
MyClass mc;        // This::MyClass
mc.x = 5;

using namespace That;
MyClass mc2;       // Ambiguity between MyClass and This::MyClass
mc2.c = 'A';
```

When both namespaces have been accessed with the reserved word using, you'll need to use the scope access operator to tell the compiler which class you're interested in:

```
using namespace This;
using namespace That;

This::MyClass mc;
mc.x = 5;

That::MyClass mc2;
mc2.c = 'A';
```

Now that you know a bit more about namespaces, you also know the solution to the TBitmap typecasting problem: You have to use the scope access operator to tell the compiler you want to use the VCL TBitmap class from the Graphics namespace:

```
if(dynamic_cast<Graphics::TBitmap *>(graphic))
{
    InvertRect(actChild->Image1->Canvas->Handle, &imgRect);
}
```

Invert Colors Implementation

Listing 17-5 shows how to implement the Edit ➢ Invert Colors command in C++Builder.

Listing 17-5: Inverting colors in C++

```cpp
void __fastcall TMainForm::InvertColorsItemClick(TObject *Sender)
{
   if(MDIChildCount == 0)
   {
      MessageDlg("Open an image first!", mtWarning,
         TMsgDlgButtons() << mbOK, 0);
      return;
   }

   TChildForm* actChild = dynamic_cast<TChildForm*>(ActiveMDIChild);
   TGraphic* graphic = actChild->Image1->Picture->Graphic;
   TRect imgRect = actChild->Image1->ClientRect;

   if(dynamic_cast<Graphics::TBitmap *>(graphic))
   {
      InvertRect(actChild->Image1->Canvas->Handle, &imgRect);
   }
   else if(dynamic_cast<TJPEGImage *>(graphic))
   {
      Graphics::TBitmap* NewBitmap = new Graphics::TBitmap;
      try
      {
         NewBitmap->Assign(graphic);
         InvertRect(NewBitmap->Canvas->Handle, &imgRect);
         graphic->Assign(NewBitmap);
      }
      __finally
      {
         delete NewBitmap;
      }
   }

   actChild->Invalidate();
}
```

Chapter 18

Working with Files

In this chapter, you'll learn how to search for files and how to store application settings in INI files or the Registry. You'll also see how to work with file streams.

Searching for Files

To search for files in Delphi, you have to use the TSearchRec record and the following three functions: FindFirst, FindNext, and FindClose. The TSearchRec record and the three functions are declared in the SysUtils unit.

To start searching a directory, you have to call the FindFirst function:

```
function FindFirst(const Path: string; Attr: Integer; var F: TSearchRec):
Integer;
```

When calling the FindFirst function to start searching for files, you have to pass both the directory path and the file mask in the Path parameter. Therefore, if you want to find all text files in the root directory of drive C, pass C:*.txt as the Path parameter.

The Attr parameter enables you to search for additional file types — system files, hidden files, and the like. The following constants, which are also declared in the SysUtils unit, can be passed as the Attr parameter: faReadOnly, faHidden, faSysFile, faDirectory, faArchive, and faAnyFile. There is also an faVolumeID constant, but it's not important anymore and has been marked as deprecated.

When calling both the FindFirst and FindNext functions, you have to pass a TSearchRec variable as the F parameter. Both functions store search results in the F parameter and both functions return 0 if a file was found or an error flag < > 0 if no matching files are found.

When FindFirst returns 0, you can call the FindNext function in a loop to try to find other files that match the given criteria. Finally, you have to call the FindClose function to release the memory allocated by the FindFirst function:

```
procedure FindClose(var F: TSearchRec);
```

Listing 18-1 shows how to search for all files in the root directory of drive C.

Listing 18-1: Searching for files

```
unit Unit1;

interface

uses
  Windows, Messages, SysUtils, Variants, Classes, Graphics, Controls,
  Forms, Dialogs, StdCtrls;

type
  TMainForm = class(TForm)
    ListBox1: TListBox;
    procedure FormCreate(Sender: TObject);
  private
    { Private declarations }
  public
    { Public declarations }
  end;

var
  MainForm: TMainForm;

implementation

{$R *.dfm}

procedure ReadDirectory(const APath: string; AList: TStrings);
var
  srec: TSearchRec;
begin
  AList.Clear;
  AList.BeginUpdate;

  if FindFirst(APath, faAnyFile, srec) = 0 then
  try
    repeat
      AList.Add(srec.Name);
    until FindNext(srec) <> 0;   // repeat until error flag
  finally
    FindClose(srec);
  end;                           // try FindFirst

  AList.EndUpdate;
end;

procedure TMainForm.FormCreate(Sender: TObject);
begin
  ReadDirectory('c:\*.*', ListBox1.Items);
end;

end.
```

Enumerating Available Drives

You can enumerate the available drives by calling either the GetLogicalDrives API function or the GetDriveType API function (both are declared in the Windows unit). The GetLogicalDrives function is a very simple function since it takes no parameters:

```
function GetLogicalDrives: DWORD; stdcall;
```

The drawback to the GetLogicalDrives function is that it requires us to know how to check whether a certain bit in the result value is on or off. It returns a bitmask in which the bit at position 0 represents drive A, the bit at position 1 represents drive B, and so on.

NOTE   The stdcall directive that follows the declaration of the GetLogicalDrives function is a calling convention. Calling conventions determine the order in which parameters are passed to a procedure or a function.

There are several calling conventions in Delphi. The default calling convention is register, which passes parameters from left to right. The default calling convention in the Windows OS, on the other hand, is stdcall, which passes parameters from right to left. Therefore, in order to accept parameters in the correct order, all Windows API functions have to be marked with the stdcall directive.

The EnumerateDrives procedure in Listing 18-2 illustrates how to use the GetLogicalDrives function to enumerate available drives.

Listing 18-2: Enumerating drives with the GetLogicalDrives function

```
procedure EnumerateDrives(AList: TStrings);
var
  Cnt: Integer;
  Disks: set of 0..25;
begin
  AList.Clear;

  Integer(Disks) := GetLogicalDrives;

  { loop through the Integer result and check each bit }
  for Cnt := 0 to 25 do
    if Cnt in Disks then
      AList.Add(Chr(Cnt + 65) + ':\');
end;
```

Code that is much easier to understand can be produced by using the GetDriveType function to enumerate the available drives. The GetDriveType function is actually meant to be used to determine whether a drive is fixed, removable, or other, but it can also be used to enumerate drives.

The GetDriveType function accepts a pointer to a null-terminated string that contains the root directory of the drive we want to check. The string that contains the root directory has to include the backslash: x:\.

```
function GetDriveType(lpRootPathName: PChar): UINT; stdcall;
```

When the function succeeds, it returns one of the constants from Table 18-1.

Table 18-1: GetDriveType function results

Constant	Description
DRIVE_UNKNOWN	An unknown drive type.
DRIVE_NO_ROOT_DIR	The root directory doesn't exist.
DRIVE_REMOVABLE	The drive is removable.
DRIVE_FIXED	The drive is fixed.
DRIVE_REMOTE	The drive is a network drive.
DRIVE_CDROM	The drive is a CD-ROM drive.
DRIVE_RAMDISK	The drive is a RAM drive.

The EnumerateDrives2 procedure in Listing 18-3 illustrates how to use the GetDriveType function to enumerate available drives.

Listing 18-3: Enumerating drives using the GetDriveType function

```
procedure EnumerateDrives2(AList: TStrings);
var
  c: Char;
begin
  AList.Clear;

  for c in ['A'..'Z'] do
    if GetDriveType(PChar(c + ':\')) <> DRIVE_NO_ROOT_DIR then
      AList.Add(c + ':\');
end;
```

Finally, you can now create a simple directory browser by adding a TCombo-Box component to the Designer Surface and adding the available drives to it in the OnCreate event of the form. You'll also have to set the Style property of the TComboBox component to csDropDownList to enable the user to only select existing items and write an event handler for its OnChange event to browse the root directory of the selected drive (see Figure 18-1):

```
procedure TMainForm.FormCreate(Sender: TObject);
begin
  with ComboBox1 do
  begin
    EnumerateDrives2(Items);
    ItemIndex := Items.IndexOf('C:\');
  end;

  ReadDirectory('c:\*.*', ListBox1.Items);
end;
```

```
procedure TMainForm.ComboBox1Change(Sender: TObject);
begin
  ReadDirectory(ComboBox1.Text + '*.*', ListBox1.Items);
end;
```

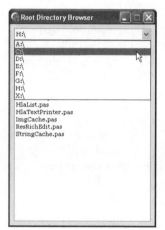

Figure 18-1:
The Root Directory
Browser

INI Files and the Registry

Although you can store application settings any way you like, developers typically use INI files or the Registry to store and retrieve application settings.

The TIniFile Class

The TIniFile class enables you to store application settings in an INI file. An
INI file is nothing more than a text file with a specific structure. The information in an INI file is stored in sections (strings in brackets) and the actual data
is stored in these sections as key=value pairs.

Here's an example of an INI file:

```
[Application]
Top=124
Left=142
Width=740
Height=520
Maximized=0
RollUp=0
LastFolder=C:\
[DefaultDisplay]
CompressionQuality=75
BackgroundColor=0
[UndoSettings]
MaxUndoSize=200
```

To use the TIniFile class in an application, you have to either add the IniFiles
unit to the uses list or include the IniFile.hpp header file if you're using C++.

The constructor of the TIniFile class is a bit different from the constructors we've used so far. The constructor of the TIniFile accepts a string that contains the path and file name of the INI file:

```
constructor TIniFile.Create(const FileName: string);
```

Methods that enable you to store data in the INI file begin with Write: WriteInteger, WriteString, WriteBool, and so on. These methods accept three parameters: section and key names, and the value that is to be stored in the INI file.

```
procedure WriteString(const Section, Ident, Value: String);
```

Methods that enable you to read data from the INI file begin with Read: ReadInteger, ReadString, ReadBool, and so on. These functions also accept three parameters. The first two parameters are identical, and the last parameter is used to specify a default value that will be used if the section, key, or value don't exist:

```
function ReadString(const Section, Ident, Default: String): String;
```

Listing 18-4 illustrates how to store and retrieve form settings from an INI file.

Listing 18-4: Using the TIniFile Class

```
unit Unit1;

interface

uses
  Windows, Messages, SysUtils, Variants, Classes,
  Graphics, Controls, Forms, Dialogs, IniFiles;

type
  TForm1 = class(TForm)
    procedure FormDestroy(Sender: TObject);
    procedure FormCreate(Sender: TObject);
  private
    { Private declarations }
    FIniPath: string;
  public
    { Public declarations }
  end;

var
  Form1: TForm1;

const
  MAIN_SECTION = 'MainForm';

implementation

{$R *.dfm}
```

```
procedure TForm1.FormCreate(Sender: TObject);
var
  Ini: TIniFile;
begin
  { store the ini file in the application directory }
  FIniPath := ChangeFileExt(Application.ExeName, '.ini');

  { read stored values }
  Ini := TIniFile.Create(FIniPath);
  try
    Left := Ini.ReadInteger(MAIN_SECTION, 'Left', 100);
    Top := Ini.ReadInteger(MAIN_SECTION, 'Top', 100);
    Color := Ini.ReadInteger(MAIN_SECTION, 'Color', clWhite);
    Caption := Ini.ReadString(MAIN_SECTION, 'Caption', 'TIniFile');
  finally
    Ini.Free;
  end;
end;

procedure TForm1.FormDestroy(Sender: TObject);
var
  Ini: TIniFile;
begin
  Ini := TIniFile.Create(FIniPath);
  try
    { store values }
    Ini.WriteInteger(MAIN_SECTION, 'Left', Left);
    Ini.WriteInteger(MAIN_SECTION, 'Top', Top);
    Ini.WriteInteger(MAIN_SECTION, 'Color', Color);
    Ini.WriteString(MAIN_SECTION, 'Caption', Caption);
  finally
    Ini.Free;
  end;
end;

end.
```

The TRegistry Class

The Registry is the main system database that can store operating system and application related data. It is a huge hierarchical tree that stores data in nodes (keys). Every key in the Registry can contain subkeys and values, as shown below.

Figure 18-2: The Registry

To access the Registry in Delphi, you can use either the TRegistry or the TRegistryIniFile class (both classes are declared in the Registry unit). The TRegistry class is normally used to access the Registry, but you can use the TRegistryIniFile class if you want to work with the Registry as if it were an INI file.

In order to read or write Registry values, you have to open one of the following predefined root keys:

- HKEY_CLASSES_ROOT
- HKEY_CURRENT_USER
- HKEY_LOCAL_MACHINE
- HKEY_USERS
- HKEY_CURRENT_CONFIG

By default, both the TRegistry and the TRegistryIniFile classes use the HKEY_CURRENT_USER key.

The TRegistryIniFile class, like the TIniFile class, accepts a file name parameter in the constructor. When using the TRegistryIniFile class to access the Registry, you have to pass the name of the key instead of a file name. The following example shows how to write a string to the Registry using the TRegistryIniFile class (see Listing 18-5). Don't forget to add the Registry unit to the uses list.

Listing 18-5: Writing to the Registry using the TRegistryIniFile class

```
procedure TForm1.FormCreate(Sender: TObject);
var
  Reg: TRegistryIniFile;
begin
  Reg := TRegistryIniFile.Create('MyApplication');
  try
```

```
    Reg.WriteString('Config', 'MyColor', 'Red');
  finally
    Reg.Free;
  end;
end;
```

The code in Listing 18-5 creates the MyApplication key under HKEY_
CURRENT_USER, adds a Config subkey to the MyApplication key, and writes
the MyColor value under Config, as shown in Figure 18-3.

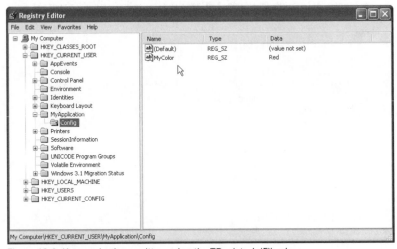

Figure 18-3: Keys and values written using the TRegistryIniFile class

When using the TRegistry class to access the Registry, you usually have to do
the following:

1. Select a root key if you don't want to use the HKEY_CURRENT_USER
    key.

2. Open the key that you want to access.

3. Read or write data to the opened key.

4. Close the opened key when you're done reading or writing data.

Selecting another root key is pretty easy. You only have to assign one of the
already mentioned root keys to the RootKey property of the TRegistry class.

To open a Registry key, use the OpenKey method. The OpenKey method
accepts two parameters: a string parameter that accepts the name of the key
that you want to open and a Boolean parameter that enables you to create the
key if it doesn't exist. To create the key if it doesn't exist, pass True as the
second parameter. Here's the declaraction of the OpenKey method:

```
function OpenKey(const Key: String; CanCreate: Boolean): Boolean;
```

To close the opened key, call the CloseKey method. The CloseKey method
accepts no parameters.

Listing 18-6 shows how you can use the TRegistry class in the Delphi Text Editor example to register the Delphi Text Editor as the default application for text documents.

Listing 18-6: Using the TRegistry class

```
procedure TMainForm.FormCreate(Sender: TObject);
var
  Reg: TRegistry;
begin
  if MessageDlg('Always use this application to open text documents?',
    mtConfirmation, mbYesNo, 0) = mrYes then
    begin
      Reg := TRegistry.Create;
      try
        { register the application }
        Reg.OpenKey('Software\Classes\Applications\Project1.exe' +
          '\shell\open\command', True);
        Reg.WriteString('', '"' + Application.ExeName + '" "%1"');
        Reg.CloseKey;

        { tell Windows to use the Delphi Text Editor
          to load text documents }
        Reg.OpenKey('Software\Microsoft\Windows\CurrentVersion\' +
          'Explorer\FileExts\.txt', True);

        Reg.WriteString('Application', 'Project1.exe');
        Reg.CloseKey;
      finally
        Reg.Free;
      end;        // try (Reg)
    end;        // if

  { open the file selected in the Explorer }
  FOpenedFile := ParamStr(1);
  if FOpenedFile <> '' then
    Editor.Lines.LoadFromFile(ParamStr(1));
end;
```

If you want to use this code in a real-world application, you'll have to change at least two things:

1. Change the file name from Project1.exe to something more meaningful.

2. Move the registration code from the OnCreate event handler to a specific option that will enable the user to register the application as the default application for a specific file type.

The TFileStream Class

The best tool for writing data to files and reading data from files is the TFileStream class (declared in the Classes unit). The TFileStream class enables you to:

■ Read or write any kind of data.

■ Read or write components.

■   Copy data to another stream.

To start reading or writing data to a file, you have to create an instance of the TFileStream class. The TFileStream constructor accepts two parameters:

```
constructor Create(const FileName: string; Mode: Word);
```

The first parameter is the file name and the second parameter indicates how the file should be opened — whether it be created, opened for reading, opened for writing, opened for reading and writing, etc. The following table contains the list of constants that can be passed as the Mode parameter.

Table 18-2: Common TFileStream open modes

Constant	Description
fmCreate	Create a new file or open for writing if the file exists
fmOpenRead	Open the file for reading only
fmOpenWrite	Open the file for writing only
fmOpenReadWrite	Open the file for both reading and writing

Reading and writing is done with the Read and Write methods. Both methods accept two parameters:

```
function Read(var Buffer; Count: Longint): Longint;
function Write(const Buffer; Count: Longint): Longint;
```

The Read method reads Count bytes from the file and places the data into the Buffer variable. The Write method writes Count bytes from the Buffer to the file. Both methods update the Position property, which indicates the position of the stream.

Listing 18-7 illustrates how to write a component and two values to a file using the TFileStream class.

Listing 18-7: Using the TFileStream class

```
procedure TForm1.WriteToFile(Sender: TObject);
var
  fs: TFileStream;
  n: Integer;
  s: string;
begin
  fs := TFileStream.Create('c:\test.txt', fmCreate);
  try
    fs.WriteComponent(Label1);

    n := 5650;
    fs.Write(n, SizeOf(Integer));

    { when writing strings, you have to tell Write to
      start writing from the first character }
    s := 'Some text';
    fs.Write(s[1], Length(s));
  finally
    fs.Free;
  end;      // try (fs)
end;
```

A lot of VCL components have the ability to load data from streams (LoadFromStream method) or save data to streams (SaveToStream method). The following example shows how to use the SaveToStream method to save the contents of two TMemo components to a single text file.

Listing 18-8: Saving TMemo contents to a stream

```
procedure TForm1.WriteMemosToFile(Sender: TObject);
var
  fs: TFileStream;
begin
  { write the contents of two TMemo components to a single text file }
  fs := TFileStream.Create('c:\test2.txt', fmCreate);
  try
    Memo1.Lines.SaveToStream(fs);
    Memo2.Lines.SaveToStream(fs);
  finally
    fs.Free;
  end;
end;
```

Copying data from one stream to another is done with the CopyFrom method. The CopyFrom method accepts two parameters: the source stream and the number of bytes that are to be copied from one stream to the other. The following example shows just how easy it is to copy a file using the TFileStream class.

Listing 18-9: Using the CopyFrom method to copy files

```
procedure TForm1.CopyingFiles(Sender: TObject);
var
  src, dest: TFileStream;
begin
  src := TFileStream.Create('c:\source.txt', fmOpenRead);
  try
    dest := TFileStream.Create('c:\dest.txt', fmCreate);
    try
      { copy the file }
      dest.CopyFrom(src, src.Size)
    finally
      dest.Free;
    end;        // try (dest)
  finally
    src.Free;
  end;          // try (src)
end;
```

Chapter 19

Desktop Database Programming

In this chapter, you'll see how to quickly and easily create a lightweight DVD Catalog application using the TClientDataSet component and Delphi's data-aware components. You'll also learn how to use the TActionManager component along with the TActionMainMenuBar and TActionToolbar components to create a modern-looking user interface, as shown in Figure 19-1.

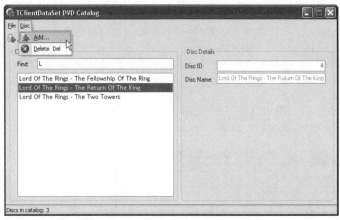

Figure 19-1: The TClientDataSet DVD Catalog application

The TClientDataSet Component

The TClientDataSet component (Data Access category) is a perfect choice for desktop database applications because of its following qualities:

■ It keeps table data in memory, which makes all operations extremely fast.

■ It can save data in CDS (binary files, smaller than XML) and XML formats.

- You only have to distribute the MIDAS.DLL dynamic link library (370 KB) with your application.
- You can also link the entire component into the executable file by including the MidasLib unit in the application's uses list (if you do this, the size of the executable will increase by 252 KB, but you won't need to distribute the MIDAS.DLL dynamic link library with your application).

To see just how easy it is to create a simple database application using the TClientDataSet component, we'll now create a simple application that will display data from the sample biolife.xml file on the form.

To create this application, you should first drop a TClientDataSet and a TDataSource component from the Data Access category on the Designer Surface. You need the TClientDataSet component to access the XML file and the TDataSource component to display database data in data-aware controls on the form.

To display data from the biolife.xml file on the form, you need to assign the biolife.xml file to the FileName property of the TClientDataSet component. To select the biolife.xml file, click the (...) button next to the FileName property in the Object Inspector to display the standard Open dialog. The biolife.xml (and other sample databases) is, by default, stored in the X:\Program Files\Common Files\Borland Shared\Data directory.

Before adding data-aware controls that will display database data on the form, you need to tell the TDataSource component from which database to read the data required by the data-aware controls. To do this, assign the TClientDataSet component to the DataSet property of the TDataSource component.

Now drop TDBGrid, TDBImage, and TDBNavigator components from the Data Controls category on the Designer Surface, as shown in Figure 19-2.

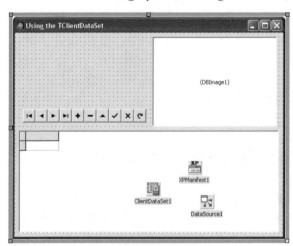

Figure 19-2: Several data-aware controls

The TDBGrid is used to display all records from the TClientDataSet, the TDBNavigator is used to enable the user to browse the database, and the TDBImage is used here to preview the images stored in the Graphic field of the biolife.xml database.

To enable these components to use data from the TClientDataSet component, you need to assign the TDataSource component to the DataSource property of all three components. To enable the TDBImage component to display images from the Graphic field, you need to assign the appropriate field to its DataField property, as shown below.

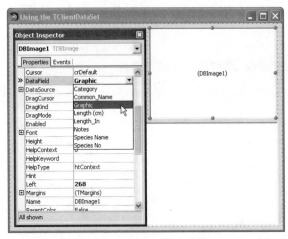

Figure 19-3: Selecting one of the available fields

Now that you've connected all components, you can set the Active property of the TClientDataSet component to True to see if you've done everything properly. If you have, the TDBGrid and TDBImage components should display data from the biolife.xml database.

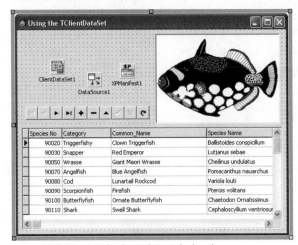

Figure 19-4: Viewing database data at design time

When you use TClientDataSet to access a database, you should not set the Active property to True at design time because the entire database will be linked into the executable file, which would in this case increase the executable by 1 MB. To display the data at run time, you need to open the database by either setting the TClientDataSet's Active property to True or calling its Open method:

```
procedure TForm1.FormCreate(Sender: TObject);
begin
  ClientDataSet1.Active := True;
  { or }
  { ClientDataSet1.Open; }
end;
```

The DVD Catalog Application

The DVD Catalog is a simple database application that illustrates how to do the following:

■ Define the structure of the TClientDataSet component
■ Load data from and save TClientDataSet data to XML files
■ Filter items in the database
■ Find a specific item in the database
■ Keep track of changes made to the database
■ Iterate through all records
■ Optimize the size of the database

Defining the Structure of the TClientDataSet

First, you need to drop the TDataSource and TClientDataSet components on the Designer Surface and link them by assigning the TClientDataSet component to the DataSet property of the TDataSource component. You can also rename the TClientDataSet component to CDS to reduce typing.

Now, select the TClientDataSet component on the Designer Surface, select the FieldDefs property in the Object Inspector, and click the (...) button to display the FieldDefs Collection Editor.

Figure 19-5: The FieldDefs Collection Editor

To add new fields to the table, click the Add New button or press Insert on the keyboard. Since we only need to store the movie's ID and name, click the Add New button twice to create two undefined fields.

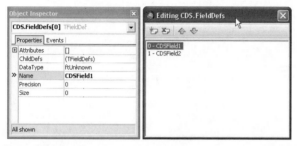

Figure 19-6: New fields

To complete the process of adding new fields to the TClientDataSet component, you need to change several properties of both fields. First, you should rename the first field MovieID and set its DataType property to ftInteger. Then, change the name of the second field to MovieName, set its DataType property to ftString, and, since movie names are sometimes pretty long, assign 100 to its Size property. Finally, close the FieldDefs Collection Editor, right-click the TClientDataSet component on the Designer Surface, and select Create DataSet to create the new dataset. You need to do this if you want to assign the TClientDataSet's fields to data-aware controls at design time, which is what we'll do in a moment.

Creating the Application's User Interface

To create the user interface of the DVD Catalog application displayed in Figure 19-1, you simply need to drop several components on the Designer Surface.

First, drop the TActionManager, TActionMainMenuBar, and TActionToolBar components from the Additional category. The TActionMainMenuBar and TActionToolBar components will automatically align themselves to the top of the form.

Then, drop two TGroupBox components from the Standard category, add a TEdit and a TListBox to the left TGroupBox component, and add two data-aware TDBEdit components to the right TGroupBox component. Finally, add as many TLabel components as you need to describe the purpose of these text boxes (see Figure 19-7).

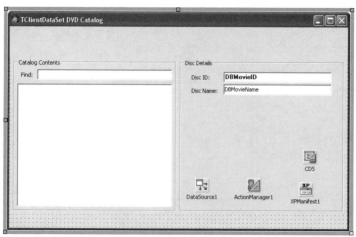

Figure 19-7: The application's user interface

Finally, drop a TStatusBar component from the Win32 category on the Designer Surface and set its SimplePanel property to True. Also, connect the data-aware components in the right TGroupBox with the TDataSource component, assign the MovieID field to the DataField property of the first TDBEdit, and assign the MovieName field to the DataField property of the second TDBEdit.

Utility Methods

Before adding actions to the TActionManager component, we need to create three utility methods for loading and saving data and for displaying all movie names in a TListBox. First, here's the DisplayDataset method that displays all movie names in a TListBox component:

```
procedure TMainForm.DisplayDataset;
begin
  MovieList.Clear;
  MovieList.Items.BeginUpdate;

  CDS.First;
  while not CDS.Eof do
  begin
    MovieList.Items.Add(CDS.FieldByName('MovieName').AsString);
    CDS.Next;
  end;

  MovieList.Items.EndUpdate;

  if MovieList.Items.Count = 0 then
    StatusBar.SimpleText := 'The disc catalog is empty.'
  else
    StatusBar.SimpleText := 'Discs in catalog: ' +
      IntToStr(MovieList.Items.Count);
end;
```

As you can see, the DisplayDataset method is pretty simple because its only job is to loop through all records in the TClientDataSet and copy anything stored in the MovieName field to the TListBox component.

To begin copying the data from the MovieName field, the DisplayDataset method calls the TClientDataSet's First method to move to the first record. Then it enters the while not Eof loop, which loops through all records in the TClientDataSet. The FieldByName method is used to find the MovieName field in the active record and then, in order to add the value of the MovieName field to a TListBox, the field's AsString property is used to treat the field's value as a string. Finally, the while loop calls the TClientDataSet's Next method, which moves to the next record in the table and makes it the active record.

The OpenCatalog and SaveCatalog methods for loading and saving data are likewise simple:

```
procedure TMainForm.OpenCatalog(const AFileName: string);
begin
  CDS.Close;
  CDS.FileName := AFileName;

  { call CreateDataSet to create an empty dataset }
  if not FileExists(AFileName) then CDS.CreateDataSet;
  CDS.Open;

  { call DisplayDataSet to automatically display the data
    when a file is opened or when a new file is created }
  DisplayDataset;
end;

procedure TMainForm.SaveCatalog(const AFileName: string);
begin
  CDS.FileName := AFileName;
  CDS.SaveToFile(CDS.FileName, dfXML);
end;
```

The TClientDataSet's SaveToFile method accepts two parameters: the destination file name and the format in which you want to save the TClientDataSet's data. You can save the data in any of the three formats provided by the TDataPacketFormat enumeration:

```
TDataPacketFormat = (dfBinary, dfXML, dfXMLUTF8);
```

The default dfBinary value is used to save data into binary CDS files, which are smaller than XML files but cannot be easily viewed and edited in a text editor. The two XML values allow you to save data in XML format.

Creating Actions and Menus

Now it's time to add several actions to the TActionManager component. Double-click the TActionManager component on the Designer Surface and then click the New Action button five times to add five new actions for the New, Open, Save, Save As, and Exit commands of the File menu, as shown in Figure 19-8.

Figure 19-8: Adding actions to the TActionManager

After you've created the five actions, it's time to define their categories. Since we're going to use these actions to implement the File menu commands, we need to select all five actions and set their Category properties to "File" (see Figure 19-9).

To select these five actions, first click on Action1, then press and hold Shift on the keyboard, and finally click on Action5. The selected actions will be placed into the File category after you type File in the Category property and press Enter.

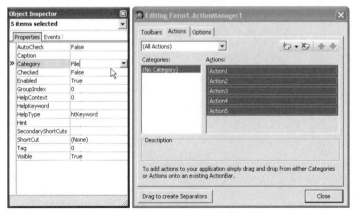

Figure 19-9: Placing the actions in a category

Categorizing actions in the TActionManager helps you to easily build the main menu. For instance, to create the entire File menu, you only have to select the File category in the TActionManager and drag and drop it to the TActionMain-MenuBar component on the Designer Surface. Note that Figure 19-10 shows a TMainMenuBar component on which the File category was already dropped from the TActionManager component.

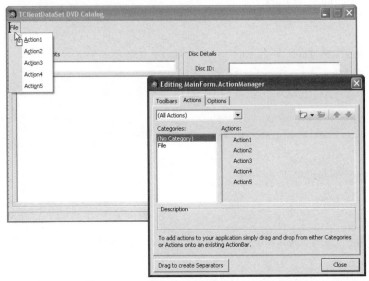

Figure 19-10: Creating a menu by dropping a category from the TActionManager to the TActionMainMenuBar

To completely implement these actions, you have to change their Caption properties, add a TOpenDialog and a TSaveDialog component to the Designer Surface, and create an OnExecute event handler for each action. These OnExecute event handlers are displayed in Listing 19-1.

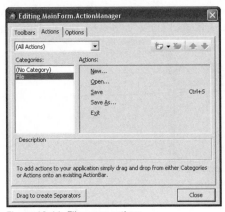

Figure 19-11: File menu actions

Since we're only going to work with XML files, set the DefaultExt property of both common dialogs to "xml" and the Filter property to "MyBase XML Table (*.xml)|*.xml".

Listing 19-1: OnExecute event handlers

```
procedure TMainForm.NewActionExecute(Sender: TObject);
begin
  if OpenDialog1.Execute then
    OpenCatalog(OpenDialog1.FileName);
end;

procedure TMainForm.OpenActionExecute(Sender: TObject);
begin
  if OpenDialog1.Execute then
    OpenCatalog(OpenDialog1.FileName);
end;

procedure TMainForm.SaveActionExecute(Sender: TObject);
begin
  if CDS.FileName <> '' then
    SaveCatalog(CDS.FileName)
  else
    SaveAsAction.Execute;
end;

procedure TMainForm.SaveAsActionExecute(Sender: TObject);
begin
  if SaveDialog1.Execute then
    SaveCatalog(SaveDialog1.FileName);
end;

procedure TMainForm.ExitActionExecute(Sender: TObject);
begin
  Close;
end;
```

Adding Records

To add new records to the TClientDataSet you need to create a simple dialog box to enable the user to enter the ID and name values for the new movie (see Figure 19-12).

Figure 19-12: The Add New Movie dialog box

The OK button's ModalResult property is set to mrNone because it must first check whether both the movie's name and ID are entered and only then return mrOK in ModalResult to let us know everything is OK. The Cancel button's ModalResult property can automatically be set to mrCancel to notify us when the user decides not to add a new record to the TClientDataSet.

The OK button's OnClick event handler, which checks if everything is entered, as well as the OnClick event handlers of the + and – buttons are displayed in the following listing.

Listing 19-2: The application logic of the Add New Movie dialog box

```
procedure TAddMovieForm.MinusButtonClick(Sender: TObject);
var
  Number: Integer;
begin
  Number := StrToInt(MovieID.Text) - 1;
  if Number < 1 then
  begin
    Number := 1;
    MessageDlg('Disc ID cannot be less than 1!', mtInformation, [mbOK], 0);
  end;
  MovieID.Text := IntToStr(Number);
end;

procedure TAddMovieForm.PlusButtonClick(Sender: TObject);
var
  Number: Integer;
begin
  Number := StrToInt(MovieID.Text) + 1;
  MovieID.Text := IntToStr(Number);
end;

procedure TAddMovieForm.OKButtonClick(Sender: TObject);
const
  ALLOW: array[Boolean] of TModalResult = (mrNone, mrOK);
begin
  { allow adding the item to the database only
    if both ID and name are properly defined }
  ModalResult := ALLOW[(MovieID.Text <> '') and (MovieName.Text <> '')];
  if ModalResult = mrNone then
    MessageDlg('Please enter both ID and disc name before clicking OK.',
      mtInformation, [mbOK], 0);
end;
```

Now that you have the dialog box, you can create the Add action that will display the dialog box to enable the user to enter the required data, check if the user pressed OK on the dialog box, and call the TClientDataSet's AppendRecord method to add the user's data to the TClientDataSet. After you create the Add action, you can drop it on the TActionToolBar component to create the Add button.

Here's the OnExecute event handler of the Add action:

```
procedure TMainForm.AddActionExecute(Sender: TObject);
begin
  with TAddMovieForm.Create(Self) do
  begin
    MovieID.Text := IntToStr(Succ(MovieList.Items.Count));
    ShowModal;

    if ModalResult = mrOK then
    begin
      CDS.AppendRecord([StrToInt(MovieID.Text), MovieName.Text]);
      FindEdit.Clear; { remove the filter to see all items }

      { refresh the list box }
      DisplayDataset;
    end;       // if ModalResult
    Free;
  end;         // with
end;
```

The following figure shows the Add New Movie dialog box and how the entire application looks and works at this stage.

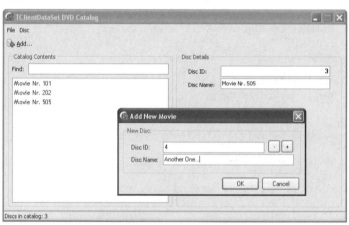

Figure 19-13: The Add New Movie dialog box at run time

Searching for Records

To search for records in a TClientDataSet, you can use the Locate method and pass the name of the field you want to search as the first parameter, the value you want to find as the second parameter, and search options as the last parameter:

```
function TCustomClientDataSet.Locate(const KeyFields: string;
  const KeyValues: Variant; Options: TLocateOptions): Boolean;
```

The TLocateOptions type is a set that enables you to perform a case-insensitive search and to search using only part of the value:

```
type
  TLocateOption = (loCaseInsensitive, loPartialKey);
  TLocateOptions = set of TLocateOption;
```

We need to call the Locate method in the OnClick event handler of the list box to activate the appropriate record in the TClientDataSet when the user selects an item in the list. Here's the OnClick event handler of the list box:

```
procedure TMainForm.MovieListClick(Sender: TObject);
begin
  if MovieList.ItemIndex <> -1 then
    CDS.Locate('MovieName', MovieList.Items[MovieList.ItemIndex], []);
end;
```

If you run the application now and click on an item in the list box, the Locate method will find and activate the appropriate record, and you'll be able to see the selected item's details in the data-aware components in the right group box, as shown in Figure 19-14.

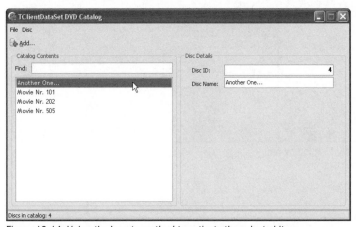

Figure 19-14: Using the Locate method to activate the selected item

Deleting Records

To delete the active record, we need to create the Delete action, which will call the TClientDataSet's Delete method to remove the active record only when a valid item is selected in the list.

Here are the OnExecute and OnUpdate event handlers of the Delete action:

```
procedure TMainForm.DeleteActionExecute(Sender: TObject);
const
  DELETE_MOVIE = 'Do you really want to delete disc:'#13;
begin
```

```
   if MessageDlg(DELETE_MOVIE +
     MovieList.Items[MovieList.ItemIndex] + '?',
     mtConfirmation, mbYesNo, 0) = mrYes then
   begin
     CDS.Delete;
     DisplayDataset;
   end; // if MessageDlg
end;

procedure TMainForm.DeleteActionUpdate(Sender: TObject);
begin
  DeleteAction.Enabled := MovieList.ItemIndex <> -1;
end;
```

The following figure shows the Delete action at run time.

Figure 19-15: Deleting records

Filtering

The two TClientDataSet properties that enable us to filter its records are Filter and Filtered. If you want to display only records that meet a certain condition, you have to set the Filtered property to True and write a filter string in the Filter property. For instance, if you want to display only the movie that's called "A" (without quotes), write the following filter:

```
MovieName = 'A'
```

We are now going to implement an incremental filter, which will filter the TClientDataSet's records as we type it in the Find edit box. To do this, we need to use the Substring method in the Filter string. For instance, to check if the first two characters in the movie name are "ab", we have to write the following filter:

```
Substring(MovieName, 1, 2) = 'ab'
```

The following listing shows the OnChange event handler of the Find edit box.

Listing 19-3: Incremental filtering

```
procedure TMainForm.FindEditChange(Sender: TObject);
const
  SUBSTRING = 'Substring(MovieName, 1, %d) = ''%s''';
var
  selectedMovie: string;
begin
  CDS.Filter := Format(SUBSTRING, [Length(FindEdit.Text), FindEdit.Text]);

  { enable filtering only if there's text in the FindEdit edit box }
  CDS.Filtered := FindEdit.Text <> '';

  { call DisplayDataSet to show only the filtered items }
  DisplayDataSet;

  selectedMovie := CDS.FieldByName('MovieName').AsString;
  MovieList.ItemIndex := MovieList.Items.IndexOf(selectedMovie);
end;
```

To see how filtering works, take a look at the following figure.

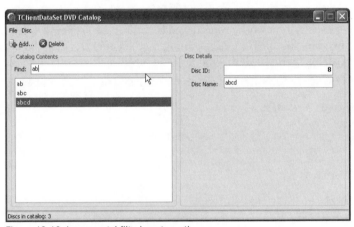

Figure 19-16: Incremental filtering at run time

Accepting and Discarding Changes

The TClientDataSet stores data in two separate packets called Data and Delta. The Data packet contains the current state of the data, and the Delta packet logs changes made to the TClientDataSet and holds inserted, updated, and deleted records. The Delta packet is very useful at run time since we can determine how many records were modified and we can select whether we want to accept or discard changes made to the data. However, the Delta packet, like normal data, is also written to the file, which increases the size of the file unnecessarily. The following figure shows a SampleDB.xml file that has both normal data and a change log (the PARAMS tag and the RowState attribute).

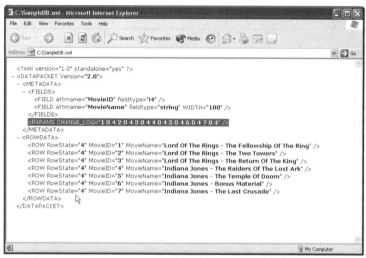

Figure 19-17: An XML file that contains both normal data and the change log

To have the application work properly and to reduce the size of the file on disk, we need to call the MergeChangeLog method before saving the data in the SaveCatalog method. Here's the updated SaveCatalog method:

```
procedure TMainForm.SaveCatalog(const AFileName: string);
begin
  CDS.FileName := AFileName;

  { call MergeChangeLog to apply changes to
    the database to reduce its size and to have the
    OnCloseQuery event handler work properly }
  CDS.MergeChangeLog;

  CDS.SaveToFile(CDS.FileName, dfXML);
end;
```

Finally, the last thing we have to do is write an OnCloseQuery event handler that will ask the user if he or she wants to save or discard changes made to the data. To see if the data was changed, check the TClientDataSet's ChangeCount property, which holds the number of changes in the change log. Note that in order to have this property report the correct number of changes, the file loaded from disk must not contain the change log (this is why we have to merge changes before saving the data to disk).

If the user wants to save changes made to the data, call the SaveAction's OnExecute handler. If the user wants to discard the changes, call the TClientDataSet's CancelUpdates method.

Here's the entire OnCloseQuery event handler:

```
procedure TMainForm.FormCloseQuery(Sender: TObject; var CanClose: Boolean);
begin
  if CDS.ChangeCount > 0 then
  begin
    case MessageDlg('Save changes to the database?',
      mtConfirmation, mbYesNoCancel, 0) of
        mrYes: SaveAction.Execute;
        mrNo: CDS.CancelUpdates;
        mrCancel: CanClose := False;
    end;        // case
  end;          // if
end;
```

Chapter 20

Advanced Development Topics

In this chapter, you'll see how to implement drag and drop between components on the form and how to accept dragged objects from Windows Explorer.

This chapter also includes a section that deals with Windows messages where you'll learn how to directly respond to messages your application receives, how to write event handlers from messages that aren't encapsulated in a VCL event, and how to create and use your own custom messages.

VCL Drag and Drop

Although drag and drop is a simple user interface interaction technique, the implementation of drag and drop in an application is not that simple.

To properly implement drag and drop in an application, we have to do the following:

1. Start the drag operation.
2. Check what is being dragged and either accept or decline the dragged item.
3. End the drag operation.

Dragging can be initiated automatically if we set the DragMode property of a control to dmAutomatic. Usually, automatically initiating the drag operation doesn't cause problems, but sometimes it can be a bit more difficult to use the control because it automatically changes the mouse cursor. We can also start and stop the drag and drop operation manually by calling the BeginDrag and EndDrag methods.

Now we'll create an application that enables the user to dynamically create controls by dragging the control's class name from a list box to the form (see Figure 20-1).

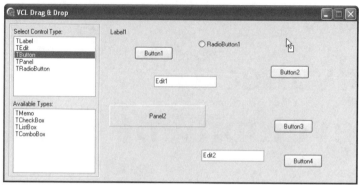

Figure 20-1: Simulating the Delphi Tool Palette

The list box in the upper-left corner contains the list of classes that can be instantiated, and the list box in the bottom-left corner contains additional classes that have to be dragged to the upper list box in order to be instantiated.

Rename the upper list box TypeList and set its DragMode property to dmAutomatic to enable it to initiate the drag operation automatically. Also add a TLabel, TEdit, and TButton to the list box using the String List Editor.

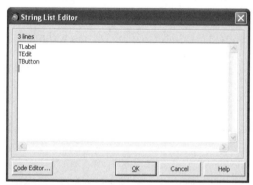

Figure 20-2: Add class names to the list box

After we've set the DragMode property to dmAutomatic, we have to write code that accepts or declines the dragged item. You can do this in the OnDrag-Over event handler. Since, we're dragging the items from the TypeList list box to the form, we have to write this in the form's OnDragOver event handler.

Listing 20-1: The OnDragOver event handler

```
procedure TMainForm.FormDragOver(Sender, Source: TObject;
  X, Y: Integer; State: TDragState; var Accept: Boolean);
begin
end;
```

In the OnDragOver event handler, we can use the Source parameter to see which control started the drag operation. The Accept parameter enables us to control the drag and drop operation. If we want to accept items from the Source control, we simply have to assign True to the Accept parameter. If an unsupported control started the drag and drop operation, we can set the Accept parameter to False to disable the form from accepting the dragged item. In this case, we also have to see if the user selected anything in the TypeList list box.

Listing 20-2: Accepting items from the TypeList list box

```
procedure TMainForm.FormDragOver(Sender, Source: TObject;
  X, Y: Integer; State: TDragState; var Accept: Boolean);
begin
  Accept := (Source = TypeList) and (TypeList.ItemIndex <> -1);
end;
```

Instantiating Controls

To finish the drag and drop operation (to accept the dragged item), we have to write a handler for the OnDragDrop event. The OnDragDrop event is fired only if the dragged item has been accepted in the OnDragOver event handler. The OnDragDrop event handler should contain code that instantiates the class selected in the TypeList list box.

The easiest way to write this code is to write an if-then test to see which class is selected and then create an instance of that specific class. This is actually not the way to do it, because each time you add a new class to the list, you have to write more code that instantiates the new class, as shown in Listing 20-3.

Listing 20-3: Not the best way to instantiate controls

```
procedure TMainForm.FormDragDrop(Sender, Source: TObject; X, Y: Integer);
var
  newLabel: TLabel;
  newButton: TButton;
  newEdit: TEdit;
  sel: string;
begin
  sel := TypeList.Items[TypeList.ItemIndex];
  if sel = 'TLabel' then
    newLabel := TLabel.Create(Self)
  else if sel = 'TEdit' then
    newEdit := TEdit.Create(Self)
  else
    newButton := TButton.Create(Self);
end;
```

Utilizing Polymorphism

The second (much better but not the best) way to dynamically create different controls is to use polymorphism. The code in Listing 20-4 utilizes the Control-Count property of the main form to create unique control names.

Listing 20-4: Using polymorphism to create controls

```
procedure TMainForm.FormDragDrop(Sender, Source: TObject; X, Y: Integer);
var
  newControl: TControl;
  sel: string;
begin
  sel := TypeList.Items[TypeList.ItemIndex];
  if sel = 'TLabel' then
    newControl := TLabel.Create(Self)
  else if sel = 'TEdit' then
    newControl := TEdit.Create(Self)
  else
    newControl := TButton.Create(Self);

  Inc(FControlCount);
  newControl.Name := newControl.ClassName +
    IntToStr(FControlCount);

  newControl.Parent := Self;
  newControl.Top := Y;
  newControl.Left := X;
end;
```

Class References (Metaclasses)

The best way to implement this functionality is to use class references (metaclasses). Class references enable us to work directly with classes, not with class instances. Class references are used extensively in all VCL Forms applications. For instance, the CreateForm method of the TApplication class uses class references to instantiate forms built at design time.

```
procedure CreateForm(FormClass: TFormClass; var Reference);
```

In order to reference a specific class in an application, that class has to be registered. Classes are registered automatically when an instance of a class is created at design time, but they can also be registered manually with the RegisterClasses procedure. In this case, we have to call the RegisterClasses procedure because we have to use classes that aren't instantiated on the Designer Surface. Place the RegisterClasses call in the OnCreate event handler.

Listing 20-5: Registering classes

```
procedure TMainForm.FormCreate(Sender: TObject);
begin
  RegisterClasses([TLabel, TEdit, TButton, TMemo, TCheckBox,
    TRadioButton, TListBox, TComboBox, TPanel]);
end;
```

Now that all necessary classes are registered, we have to obtain the class from the class name. We can obtain a registered class from its name by calling the GetClass function declared in the Classes unit. Since the GetClass function returns a TPersistentClass, we have to typecast its result to

TControlClass. The TControlClass enables us to reference any component that descends from TControl.

```
var
  selClass: TControlClass;
  selItem: string;
begin
  selItem := TypeList.Items[TypeList.ItemIndex];
  selClass := TControlClass(GetClass(selItem));
end;
```

After we've obtained the class, we have to instantiate it and define the properties of the new control. The property that requires the most work is the Name property because the name of the control has to be unique. To get a unique name like the Designer Surface generates, we have to count how many instances of a specific class already exist on the form. It is best to place this code in a separate function:

```
function TMainForm.GetControlCount(AClass: TControlClass): Integer;
var
  i: Integer;
begin
  Result := 0;
  for i := 0 to Pred(ControlCount) do
    if Controls[i] is AClass then Inc(Result);
end;
```

Listing 20-6 gives the entire OnDragDrop event handler.

Listing 20-6: Using class references to create controls

```
type
  TMainForm = class(TForm)
  private
    { Private declarations }
    function GetControlCount(AClass: TControlClass): Integer;
  public
    { Public declarations }
  end;

var
  MainForm: TMainForm;

implementation

{$R *.dfm}

function TMainForm.GetControlCount(AClass: TControlClass): Integer;
var
  i: Integer;
begin
  Result := 0;
  for i := 0 to Pred(ControlCount) do
    if Controls[i] is AClass then Inc(Result);
end;

procedure TMainForm.FormDragDrop(Sender, Source: TObject; X, Y: Integer);
```

```
var
  newControl: TControl;
  selClass: TControlClass;
  ctlName: string;
  selItem: string;
begin
  selItem := TypeList.Items[TypeList.ItemIndex];
  selClass := TControlClass(GetClass(selItem));

  newControl := selClass.Create(Self);
  newControl.Parent := Self;

  ctlName := newControl.ClassName +
    IntToStr(GetControlCount(selClass));
  Delete(ctlName, 1, 1); { remove "T" }

  newControl.Name := ctlName;
  newControl.Left := X;
  newControl.Top := Y;
end;
```

Drag and Drop between TListBox Components

Now it's time to enable the user to drag items from the Available Types list to the TypeList list box. The AvailableList list box should only be used as a container for classes that can be added to the TypeList list box.

Since we have to enable the user to drag and drop items from the AvailableList list box to the TypeList list box, we have to set the DragMode property of the AvailableList list box to dmAutomatic. Then we have to write the event handler for the OnDragOver event of the TypeList list box that will accept items dragged from the AvailableList list.

Listing 20-7: Accepting items from the AvailableList list box

```
procedure TMainForm.TypeListDragOver(Sender, Source: TObject;
  X, Y: Integer; State: TDragState; var Accept: Boolean);
begin
  Accept := (Source = AvailableList);
end;
```

When dragging an item to a list box, you can add the dragged item to the end of the list by calling the Add method of the Items property or you can be more professional and insert the dragged item at the position indicated by the mouse cursor. To do that, you have to call the ItemAtPos method of the list box to find out the index beneath the mouse cursor and then pass that index to the Insert method of the Items property, as shown in Listing 20-8.

Listing 20-8: Dragging an item from one list to another

```
procedure TMainForm.TypeListDragDrop(Sender,
  Source: TObject; X, Y: Integer);
var
  itemPos: Integer;
begin
  if AvailableList.ItemIndex = -1 then Exit;
```

```
itemPos := TypeList.ItemAtPos(Point(X, Y), False);
with AvailableList do
begin
  TypeList.Items.Insert(itemPos, Items[ItemIndex]);
  Items.Delete(ItemIndex);
end;
end;
```

Now that we have implemented drag and drop between two list boxes, the user can instantiate all available classes by first dragging them to the TypeList list box and then to the form (see Figure 20-3).

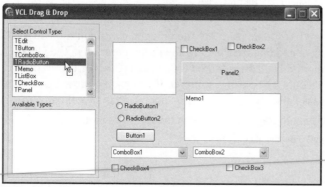

Figure 20-03: Drag and drop between components

BeginDrag and EndDrag Methods

The BeginDrag and EndDrag methods can be used to start and stop the dragging of a control when the DragMode property of the control is set to dmManual. We'll use the BeginDrag and EndDrag methods to enable the user to move controls on the form. First, create a new VCL Forms application project and then drop several controls to the form.

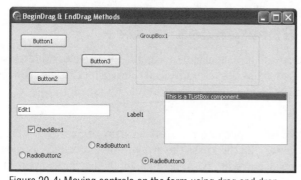

Figure 20-4: Moving controls on the form using drag and drop

The best place to put the BeginDrag call is in the OnMouseDown event handler. When calling the BeginDrag method, you have to pass a Boolean value to the Immediate parameter that defines whether the drag operation starts immediately or after the mouse cursor has been moved a short distance. To start the drag operation immediately, pass True; otherwise, pass False (see Listing 20-9). The Sender parameter is typecast to TWinControl so that we can assign the event handler to multiple controls.

Listing 20-9: Calling the BeginDrag method

```
procedure TForm1.ControlMouseDown(Sender: TObject;
  Button: TMouseButton; Shift: TShiftState; X, Y: Integer);
begin
  TWinControl(Sender).BeginDrag(True);
end;
```

Now, all that we have to do is accept the dragged control in the OnDragOver event of the form and finalize the drag and drop operation in the OnDragDrop event by calling the EndDrag method (see Listing 20-10). The EndDrag method also accepts a Boolean parameter. If you want to drop the control, pass True. If you pass False, the drag and drop operation is cancelled.

Listing 20-10: Ending drag and drop with the EndDrag method

```
procedure TForm1.FormDragDrop(Sender,
  Source: TObject; X, Y: Integer);
begin
  with TWinControl(Source) do
  begin
    Left := X;
    Top := Y;
    EndDrag(True); { drop the control }
  end;
end;

procedure TForm1.FormDragOver(Sender, Source: TObject;
  X, Y: Integer; State: TDragState; var Accept: Boolean);
begin
  Accept := True; { accept everything }
end;
```

Using Class References in C++

To build the VCL drag and drop application using C++ and class references, you first need to register the classes with a call to RegisterClasses. To acquire a class reference in C++, use the reserved word __classid:

```
__classid(class)
```

Since the RegisterClasses procedure registers an array of classes, it's best to create an array of classes and then pass the array to the procedure. Besides passing the array, you also need to pass the index of the last class in the array (class count − 1):

```
__fastcall TMainForm::TMainForm(TComponent* Owner)
  : TForm(Owner)
```

```
{
  TComponentClass classes[9] = {
    __classid(TLabel), __classid(TComboBox), __classid(TButton),
    __classid(TMemo), __classid(TCheckBox), __classid(TListBox),
    __classid(TRadioButton), __classid(TPanel), __classid(TEdit),
  };

  // the second parameter is the index of the last array item
  RegisterClasses(classes, 8);
}
```

The second thing that has to be done is to write the GetControlCount function
to calculate how many instances of a class already exist on the form. The function should accept a class reference, as it does in Delphi.

To determine the class type in Delphi, you can use the is operator. In
C++, you have to call the ClassType() method, which returns the class reference for the object:

```
int __fastcall TMainForm::GetControlCount(TControlClass AClass)
{
  int cnt = 0;
  for(int i = 0; i < ControlCount; i++)
  {
    // use ClassType() to get the class reference and
    // then compare the two class references
    if(Controls[i]->ClassType() == AClass)
      cnt++;
  }
  return cnt;
}
```

Instantiating Class References

Since there is no easy way to instantiate a class through a class reference in
C++, we need to create a Delphi function that will do that for us and then
simply add the Delphi unit to the C++ project.

This function should accept a control reference (TControlClass type),
because we are only going to use it to create controls. It should also accept an
owner parameter.

Here's the Delphi MetaUnit unit with the necessary function:

```
unit MetaUnit;

interface

uses Classes, Controls;

function CreateFromReference(AClassReference: TControlClass;
  AOwner: TControl): TControl;

implementation

function CreateFromReference(AClassReference: TControlClass;
  AOwner: TControl): TControl;
```

```
begin
  Result := AClassReference.Create(AOwner);
end;

end.
```

When you create the MetaUnit unit, add it to your C++ project and include it as MetaUnit.hpp; the compiler will generate the necessary header file from the Delphi unit:

```
// Borland C++ Builder
// Copyright (c) 1995, 2005 by Borland Software Corporation
// All rights reserved

// (DO NOT EDIT: machine generated header) 'Metaunit.pas' rev: 6.00

...

namespace Metaunit
{

extern PACKAGE Controls::TControl*
   __fastcall CreateFromReference(TMetaClass* AClassReference,
   Controls::TControl* AOwner);

} /* namespace Metaunit */

using namespace Metaunit;
```

Implementing Drag and Drop

Now that the biggest problem (instantiating class references) is solved, you can easily implement the same drag and drop behavior as you did in Delphi. The only difference is that instead of directly instantiating the class reference you call the CreateFromReference function to do the job.

Here's the entire OnDragDrop event handler:

```
void __fastcall TMainForm::FormDragDrop(TObject *Sender,
   TObject *Source, int X, int Y)
{
   TControl* newControl;
   TControlClass selClass;
   AnsiString ctlName;
   AnsiString selString;

   selString = TypeList->Items->Strings[TypeList->ItemIndex];
   selClass = GetClass(selString);

   // use the CreateFromReference function from MetaUnit.hpp
   newControl = CreateFromReference(selClass, this);
   newControl->Parent = this;

   ctlName = AnsiString(newControl->ClassName()) +
      IntToStr(GetControlCount(selClass));
```

```
ctlName.Delete(1, 1); // remove "T" from the name

newControl->Name = ctlName;
newControl->Left = X;
newControl->Top = Y;
}
```

Using and Creating Messages

The Windows operating system uses messages to notify the application that an event occurred. The operating system generates a message every time something happens — for example, when the user clicks the Start button, types something, or moves a window — and sends that message to the appropriate window.

Messages have several details, the most important of which are the window handle, the message identifier, and two message parameters. When a message occurs, its details are written to a TMsg record and then passed to the appropriate application. The TMsg record is declared in the Windows unit, shown in Listing 20-11.

Listing 20-11: Windows message details

```
tagMSG = packed record
  hwnd: HWND;
  message: UINT;
  wParam: WPARAM;
  lParam: LPARAM;
  time: DWORD;
  pt: TPoint;
end;

TMsg = tagMSG;
```

The hwnd field is the handle of the window to which the message is sent. In the Windows operating system, window handles are 32-bit integer values used to uniquely identify a window. Also, in the Windows operating system, all controls, like buttons, edit boxes, and list boxes, are windows and have a handle value that uniquely identifies them.

The message field is an integer value that identifies the message. For each Windows message there is a more descriptive constant in the Messages unit. All Windows message constants start with the WM_ prefix.

Listing 20-12: Several standard Windows messages

```
WM_MOVE          = $0003; { window has been moved }
WM_ENABLE        = $000A; { change window state }
WM_PAINT         = $000F; { repaint the window client area }
WM_CLOSE         = $0010; { close the window }
WM_KEYDOWN       = $0100; { a key is pressed }
WM_LBUTTONDOWN   = $0201; { the left mouse button is pressed }
```

The wParam and lParam fields are closely related to the message passed in the message field. Both values are used to further define the message. The time and pt values are rarely used. The time field specifies the time when the event occurred, and the pt field contains the X and Y coordinates of the mouse cursor at the time the event occurred.

The VCL encapsulates the majority of standard messages into events like OnClick and OnMouseDown, but it also gives you the ability to handle other messages. To handle a message that isn't encapsulated in a VCL event, you have to write a message method.

To create a message method, you have to create a method that accepts a single var TMessage (or a similar message-related record) parameter and you have to mark the method with the message directive followed by the constant that identifies the handled message. In VCL Forms applications, the TMessage record, rather than the TMsg record, is used when working with messages.

Handling Messages

Now let's try to handle the WM_MOVE message that is sent to the window after it has been moved. The message method that handles the WM_MOVE message should look like this:

```
procedure MyMoveHandler(var Message: TMessage); message WM_MOVE;
```

Listing 20-13 contains the entire message method that simply displays the top and left coordinates of the main form when the form is moved (see Figure 20-5).

Listing 20-13: The WM_MOVE message method

```
type
  TForm1 = class(TForm)
    Label1: TLabel;
  private
    { Private declarations }
  public
    { Public declarations }
    procedure WMMove(var Message: TMessage); message WM_MOVE;
  end;

var
  Form1: TForm1;

implementation

{$R *.dfm}

procedure TForm1.WMMove(var Message: TMessage);
begin
  Caption := Format('Top: %d - Left: %d', [Top, Left]);
end;
```

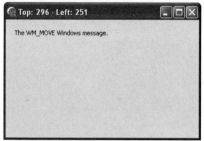

Figure 20-5: Handling the WM_MOVE message

The difference between VCL events and direct message handling is that we have to pass the message to the ancestor's message handler and, for some messages, notify the operating system that we've processed the message. The documentation for every message specifies what to return when we handle it.

```
procedure TForm1.WMMove(var Message: TMessage);
begin
  Caption := Format('Top: %d - Left: %d', [Top, Left]);
  inherited; { pass message to the ancestor's message handler }
end;
```

As said earlier, the lParam and wParam fields provide us with more information about the message. In the WM_MOVE message, lParam contains both X and Y coordinates of the window. The low-order word of the lParam value specifies the X coordinate and the high-order word specifies the Y coordinate.

Listing 20-14: Reading coordinates from the lParam value

```
procedure TForm1.WMMove(var Message: TMessage);
begin
  Caption := Format('X: %d - Y: %d', [Message.LParamLo, Message.LParamHi]);
  inherited;
end;
```

An even better way to handle a message is to use a record more related to the message than the generic TMessage record. The Messages unit contains a large collection of such records. Here's the record related to the WM_MOVE message:

```
TWMMove = packed record
  Msg: Cardinal;
  Unused: Integer;
  case Integer of
    0: (
      XPos: Smallint;
      YPos: Smallint);
    1: (
      Pos: TSmallPoint;
      Result: Longint);
end;
```

You should always use these message-related records, because if nothing else, they result in cleaner code, as shown in Listing 20-15.

Listing 20-15: Using a message-related record

```
type
  TForm1 = class(TForm)
  private
  public
    procedure WMMove(var Message: TWMMove); message WM_MOVE;
  end;

var
  Form1: TForm1;

implementation

{$R *.dfm}

procedure TForm1.WMMove(var Message: TWMMove);
begin
  Caption := Format('X: %d - Y: %d', [Message.XPos, Message.YPos]);
  inherited;
end;
```

Now that we know how to use messages, we can do something a bit more fun. For instance, we can create elastic windows that behave like the Main window and Playlist windows in Winamp and other media players. First, add another form to the project and then attach it to the main form in the WM_MOVE message handler, as shown in Listing 20-16.

Listing 20-16: Automatically moving another form in the WM_MOVE message handler

```
type
  TForm1 = class(TForm)
    procedure FormShow(Sender: TObject);
  private
  public
    procedure WMMove(var Message: TWMMove); message WM_MOVE;
  end;

var
  Form1: TForm1;

implementation

uses Unit2;

{$R *.dfm}

procedure TForm1.WMMove(var Message: TWMMove);
begin
  { we have to test if Form2 exists because the WM_MOVE message
    for the main form gets generated before the Form2 is created }
  if Assigned(Form2) then
  begin
```

```
    Form2.Top := Top + Height;
    Form2.Left := Left;
  end;
  inherited;
end;

procedure TForm1.FormShow(Sender: TObject);
begin
  Form2.Show;
end;
```

There is a section in Chapter 12 that describes how you can move a form that has no title bar. The implementation involved three different event handlers and a Boolean variable that was used to determine when the form should be moved. Although the code itself is not complicated, there is actually too much of it. A better way to implement this functionality is to catch and respond to the WM_NCHITTEST message.

The WM_NCHITTEST is sent to a window when a mouse button is pressed or released or when the mouse cursor is moved. The return value of this message indicates the position of the mouse cursor — whether the mouse is over the client area, the title bar, the menu, or any other window portion. The message result also determines what the operating system does with the window. So, the only thing that we have to do is trick Windows into believing that the mouse is always over the title bar by returning the HTCAPTION constant in the message result.

Listing 20-17: Enabling the user to move the form by clicking on its client area

```
type
  TForm1 = class(TForm)
  private
  public
    procedure WMNCHitTest(var Message: TWMNCHitTest); message WM_NCHITTEST;
  end;

var
  Form1: TForm1;

implementation

uses Unit2;

{$R *.dfm}

procedure TForm1.WMNCHitTest(var Message: TWMNCHitTest);
begin
  inherited;

  if Message.Result = HTCLIENT then
    Message.Result := HTCAPTION;
end;
```

The result of this code is displayed in Figure 20-6.

Figure 20-6: Moving both forms by clicking in the client area of the main form

Handling Messages in C++

The C++ language doesn't have a message directive that can be used to identify a method as a message handler. To handle a message in C++, you have to create a message method, which will be called in response to a message, and a message map in which you list your message handling methods.

For instance, to handle the WM_MOVE message in a C++Builder VCL Forms application, first create the message method:

```
class TMainForm : public TForm
{
__published:    // IDE-managed components
private:        // User declarations
public:         // User declarations
   void __fastcall WMMove(TWMMove &Message);
};

void __fastcall TMainForm::WMMove(TWMMove &Message)
{
   Caption = Format("X: %d - Y: %d",
      ARRAYOFCONST((Message.XPos, Message.YPos)));
}
```

When you're done with the method, you need to create the message map and add your method to the message map to notify the compiler that your method is a message handler.

To create a message map, you use two macros: BEGIN_MESSAGE_MAP and END_MESSAGE_MAP(BaseClass). The BaseClass is responsible for handling all other messages that aren't handled inside the message map.

To define your method as a message handler, you have to use the VCL_MESSAGE_HANDLER macro, which requires you to pass the message you are handling, the record (structure) that holds the message data, and the name of the message handler.

Here's how a message map looks:

```
BEGIN_MESSAGE_MAP
    VCL_MESSAGE_HANDLER(Message, Structure, Method)
END_MESSAGE_MAP(BaseClass)
```

So, to qualify the WMMove method as a message handler for the WM_MOVE message, you have to create the following message map (in the public section of the class):

```
class TMainForm : public TForm
{
__published:    // IDE-managed components
private:         // User declarations
public:          // User declarations
    __fastcall TMainForm(TComponent* Owner);
    void __fastcall WMMove(TWMMove &Message);
    BEGIN_MESSAGE_MAP
        VCL_MESSAGE_HANDLER(WM_MOVE, TWMMove, WMMove);
    END_MESSAGE_MAP(TForm)
};
```

If you have to pass the message to the base class, which is necessary in some cases, you cannot use the inherited reserved word. You have to call the Dispatch method of the base class:

```
BaseClass::Dispatch(&Message);
```

For instance, in order to work properly, the WM_NCHITTEST message handler needs to pass the message to the base class:

```
class TMainForm : public TForm
{
__published:    // IDE-managed components
private:         // User declarations
public:          // User declarations
    __fastcall TMainForm(TComponent* Owner);
    void __fastcall WMMove(TWMMove &Message);
    void __fastcall WMNCHitTest(TWMNCHitTest &Message);
    BEGIN_MESSAGE_MAP
        VCL_MESSAGE_HANDLER(WM_MOVE, TWMMove, WMMove);
        VCL_MESSAGE_HANDLER(WM_NCHITTEST,
            TWMNCHitTest, WMNCHitTest);
    END_MESSAGE_MAP(TForm)
};

void __fastcall TMainForm::WMNCHitTest(TWMNCHitTest &Message)
{
    // first call the base class handler
```

```
    TForm::Dispatch(&Message);

    if(Message.Result == HTCLIENT)
        Message.Result = HTCAPTION;
}
```

Creating Custom Messages

To create a custom message for use in an application, you only have to define an integer constant in the range of WM_USER to WM_USER + $7FFF (see Listing 20-18).

Listing 20-18: A custom message

```
uses
  Windows, Messages, SysUtils, Variants, Classes,
  Graphics, Controls, Forms, Dialogs;

const
  MM_CHANGECOLOR = WM_USER + 1;

type
  TForm1 = class(TForm)
  private
    { Private declarations }
  public
    { Public declarations }
  end;
```

After you've created a custom message, write a message method that will handle the message. Since this is a custom message, you can do whatever you want with it. You can, for instance, treat the wParam message field as a color value and use the MM_CHANGECOLOR message to change the color of the form, as shown in Listing 20-19.

Listing 20-19: Handling the custom message

```
type
  TForm1 = class(TForm)
  private
  public
    procedure MMChangeColor(var Message: TMessage);
      message MM_CHANGECOLOR;
  end;

procedure TForm1.MMChangeColor(var Message: TMessage);
begin
  Color := Message.wParam;
end;
```

The last thing to do is send the message to the form. In Delphi, there are three possible ways of sending a message. Besides the VCL Perform method, you can also use the SendMessage and PostMessage Windows API functions.

The SendMessage function is used when the message needs to be handled as soon as possible. When you use the SendMessage function, it doesn't return until the message is processed.

The PostMessage function is used to send the message when its processing isn't time-critical. A message sent using the PostMessage function is placed in the window's message queue and is handled later.

The most straightforward way to send a message in a VCL Forms application is to call the Perform method. You should use the Perform method when you know exactly which control should process the message.

Here's how you can send the MM_CHANGECOLOR message to the main form and instruct it to change its color to white (see Figure 20-7):

```
procedure TForm1.Button1Click(Sender: TObject);
begin
  Perform(MM_CHANGECOLOR, clWhite, 0);
end;
```

Figure 20-7: Using the MM_CHANGECOLOR custom message

If you want to use the SendMessage and PostMessage API functions to send messages, you'll have to pass the handle of the destination window as the first parameter. The window handle of the main form is specified in its Handle property.

```
SendMessage(Handle, MM_CHANGECOLOR, clWhite, 0);
```

The messaging system is very flexible and allows us to do whatever we want with our custom messages. For instance, we can even use messages to add text from a text box to a list box. This can be done by typecasting the components to integers and then sending them as the wParam and lParam fields in the message.

Listing 20-20: Playing with messages

```
const
  MM_ADDTOLIST = WM_USER + 2;

type
  TForm1 = class(TForm)
  public
    procedure MMAddToList(var Message: TMessage);
      message MM_ADDTOLIST;
  end;

var
  Form1: TForm1;
```

```
implementation

{$R *.dfm}

procedure TForm1.MMAddToList(var Message: TMessage);
var
  edit: TEdit;
begin
  edit := TEdit(Message.LParam);
  TListBox(Message.WParam).Items.Add(edit.Text);
end;

procedure TForm1.Button1Click(Sender: TObject);
begin
  SendMessage(Handle, MM_ADDTOLIST,
    Integer(ListBox1), Integer(Edit1));
end;
```

Drag and Drop from the Explorer

The ability to accept items dragged from the Windows Explorer is something that users today expect. The main reason is that the user is able to open a file much faster by dragging it from the Explorer than by using the common Open dialog box.

The first thing that we have to do in order to accept items from the Windows Explorer is register the window that should accept the dropped items. To do this, we have to call the DragAcceptFiles API function. The DragAcceptFiles function accepts two parameters: the handle of the window that should accept dropped items and a Boolean parameter that specifies whether or not the window should accept dropped items.

```
procedure DragAcceptFiles(Wnd: HWND; Accept: BOOL);
```

We actually have to call the DragAcceptFiles function twice. First, we have to call it in the OnCreate event handler to register the main form as the drop target, and then in the OnDestroy or OnClose event handlers to discontinue accepting dropped items. In order to use the DragAcceptFiles function, you have to add the ShellAPI unit to the uses list (see Listing 20-21).

Listing 20-21: Registering the main form as the drop target

```
unit Unit1;

interface

uses
  Windows, Messages, SysUtils, Variants, Classes, Graphics,
  Controls, Forms, Dialogs, ShellAPI;

type
  TForm1 = class(TForm)
    procedure FormDestroy(Sender: TObject);
    procedure FormCreate(Sender: TObject);
  private
```

```
  { Private declarations }
public
  { Public declarations }
end;

procedure TForm1.FormCreate(Sender: TObject);
begin
  DragAcceptFiles(Handle, True);
end;

procedure TForm1.FormDestroy(Sender: TObject);
begin
  DragAcceptFiles(Handle, False);
end;

end.
```

Once a window has been registered with the DragAcceptFiles function, it is able to process the WM_DROPFILES message. To accept the files dropped from the Explorer, we have to handle the WM_DROPFILES message.

```
type
  TForm1 = class(TForm)
  public
    procedure WMDropFiles(var Message: TWMDropFiles);
      message WM_DROPFILES;
  end;

procedure TForm1.WMDropFiles(var Message: TWMDropFiles);
begin

end;
```

Inside the WM_DROPFILES message handler, we have to do the following:

1. Determine how many files were dropped to the form.
2. Retrieve the file names of all dropped files.
3. Finish the drag and drop process by calling DragFinish.

To determine the number of dropped files, we have to call the DragQueryFile function:

```
function DragQueryFile(Drop: HDROP;
  FileIndex: UINT; FileName: PChar; cb: UINT): UINT;
```

The Drop parameter identifies the structure that contains the names of files dropped to the form. The value of the Drop parameter is always specified in the Drop field of the WM_DROPFILES message. The FileIndex parameter specifies the index of the file to query for the file name. If the value of the FileIndex parameter is between 0 and the number of dropped files, the DragQueryFile function writes the file name to the buffer specified in the File-Name parameter. If the value of the FileIndex parameter is $FFFFFFFF (or 0xFFFFFFFF in C++), the DragQueryFile function returns the total number of dropped files. When determining the number of dropped files, you can pass nil as the FileName buffer, as shown in Listing 20-22.

Listing 20-22: Determining the number of dropped files

```
procedure TForm1.WMDropFiles(var Message: TWMDropFiles);
var
  dropCount: Integer;
begin
  dropCount := DragQueryFile(Message.Drop, $FFFFFFFF, nil, 0);
  try

  finally
    DragFinish(Message.Drop);
  end;
end;
```

After we determine the number of dropped files, we have to write a loop that will read the file names of all dropped files and create a buffer large enough to hold long file names. The easiest way to create a file name buffer is to declare an array of characters. Since Windows XP with SP2 allows file names up to 2,048 characters long, you should declare an array that accepts that many characters plus one for the terminating null character.

Listing 20-23 shows the entire WM_DROPFILES message handler that adds the dropped file names to a TListBox component.

Listing 20-23: Working with items dropped from the Windows Explorer

```
procedure TForm1.WMDropFiles(var Message: TWMDropFiles);
var
  dropCount: Integer;
  nameBuffer: array[0..2048] of Char;
  i: Integer;
begin
  dropCount := DragQueryFile(Message.Drop, $FFFFFFFF, nil, 0);
  try
    for i := 0 to Pred(dropCount) do
    begin
      { process each file name }
      DragQueryFile(Message.Drop, i, nameBuffer, SizeOf(nameBuffer));
      ListBox1.Items.Add(string(nameBuffer));
    end;       // for
  finally
    DragFinish(Message.Drop);
  end;          // try..finally
end;
```

Figure 20-8: Dragging and dropping from the Windows Explorer

The TPageControl Component

Now, let's use the TPageControl (Win32 category) component to enhance the drag and drop example from the previous section and allow the user to preview plain text and rich text files and images.

To do that, we have to do the following:

1. Remove the TListBox component that was used in the previous section.

2. Add a TPageControl to the Designer Surface (and rename it PageControl).

3. Add the ExtCtrls unit to the uses list because we have to use the TImage component.

4. Create the OpenDroppedFile procedure that will load plain and rich text files and images and display them as pages in the TPageControl component.

The first thing we have to do in the OpenDroppedFile procedure is determine the file type, because we have to instantiate a different component for every file type: TMemo for plain text files, TRichEdit for rich text files, and TImage for images.

```
procedure TForm1.OpenDroppedFile(const AFileName: string);
var
  Extension: string;
  NewTab: TTabSheet;
  FileClass: TControlClass;
  NewControl: TControl;
```

```
begin
  Extension := LowerCase(ExtractFileExt(AFileName));

  { check the extension }
  if Extension = '.txt' then
    FileClass := TMemo
  else if Extension = '.rtf' then
    FileClass := TRichEdit
  else if Extension = '.bmp' then
    FileClass := TImage
  else
    Exit; { exit if an unsupported file is dropped }
```

After we've determined the file type, we have to create the page that will display the contents of the file. To create a new page, we have to create an instance of the TTabSheet class and then add it to the TPageControl by assigning the TPageControl component to the PageControl property of the TTabSheet.

```
{ create the new tab }
NewTab := TTabSheet.Create(PageControl);
NewTab.PageControl := PageControl;
NewTab.Caption := ExtractFileName(AFileName);
```

Now, we have to instantiate the component necessary to load the dropped file. To display a component in a TPageControl page, make the TTabSheet component its Parent.

```
{ create the required control }
NewControl := FileClass.Create(Self);
NewControl.Parent := NewTab;
NewControl.Align := alClient;
```

Finally, we have to open the file and activate the new page to display the freshly opened file. Because both TMemo and TRichEdit components descend from the TCustomMemo component, we can use polymorphism here to load both plain text and rich text files in a single line.

```
{ open the file }
if FileClass = TImage then
  TImage(NewControl).Picture.LoadFromFile(AFileName)
else
  TCustomMemo(NewControl).Lines.LoadFromFile(AFileName);

{ activate the new page }
PageControl.ActivePage :=
  PageControl.Pages[Pred(PageControl.PageCount)];
end;
```

Now that the OpenDroppedFile procedure is finished, replace the Items.Add call with the OpenDroppedFile procedure call in the WM_DROPFILES message handler:

```
for i := 0 to Pred(dropCount) do
begin
  DragQueryFile(Message.Drop, i, nameBuffer, SizeOf(nameBuffer));
  OpenDroppedFile(string(nameBuffer));
end;    // for
```

One last thing that we should enable the user to do is to close all opened files by selecting File ➤ Close All:

```
procedure TForm1.CloseAllClick(Sender: TObject);
var
  i: Integer;
begin
  for i := Pred(PageControl.PageCount) downto 0 do
    PageControl.Pages[i].Free;
end;
```

If you run the application now and drop several files to the form, the OpenDroppedFile procedure will open all supported files and display them as pages in the TPageControl component, as shown in Figure 20-9.

Figure 20-9: TPageControl pages

Chapter 21

Dynamic Link Libraries

Dynamic link libraries are compiled files very similar to the standard applications that you've been creating so far. Like standard applications, dynamic link libraries can contain routines, resources, or both, but they cannot be directly executed. Dynamic link libraries are meant to be used by other applications at run time.

Whether you know it or not, you've been using dynamic link libraries for some time now, ever since you called your first Windows API function. The entire Win32 API is a huge collection of dynamic link libraries, most of which are stored in the operating system's System (non-NT) or System32 (NT) directory. Among the most important dynamic link libraries are certainly kernel32.dll, gdi32.dll, user32.dll, shell32.dll, and comctl32.dll.

Just as you can compare dynamic link libraries to standard applications, you can compare them to Delphi units. The major difference between the two is that the routines contained in a unit are compiled into each executable in which they are used, whereas routines compiled in a dynamic link library only reside in that library and are called from outside applications. By having a single compiled copy of a routine, you save both disk space and memory at run time, especially if the user runs multiple copies of your application or if the user runs several applications that use the same dynamic link library.

DLLs also enable you to more efficiently reuse your common routines. If you change the implementation of a routine that resides in a unit, you'll have to recompile all applications that use that routine. If you add the same routine to a DLL, you'll be able to change the implementation of the routine without recompiling all applications; you only need to recompile the DLL. The calling applications will be able to use the updated routine as long as you don't change the routine's interface. If you change the routine's interface, you'll have to recompile all calling applications.

Like everything else, dynamic link libraries have advantages and disadvantages. Here are the advantages of dynamic link libraries:

■ You can share common routines among several applications.

■ You can save memory and disk space by maintaining a single compiled copy of the routine.

■ You can enable other developers to use your application logic without giving them your source code.

■ You can reuse your Delphi routines in other programming languages (or the other way around), as long as you mark the exported routines with the stdcall directive. (If you omit the stdcall directive, you'll be able to use the DLL in Delphi applications only.)

■ You can more easily update/upgrade applications that use one or more dynamic link libraries.

■ You can easily create multi-language applications.

■ You can create resource-only dynamic link libraries that contain commonly used images, icons, sounds, and animations (e.g., moricons.dll in the Windows\System directory).

And here are the disadvantages of using DLLs in Delphi:

■ You can't normally pass a Delphi string to a DLL (you can if you use the additional borlandmm.dll, which is something most developers don't want to do).

■ If you want to pass strings to a DLL, you can pass ShortStrings (which is mostly not good because of the 255-character limit) or PChars (which is better, but you have to handle the memory yourself).

Now it's time to create our first DLL. As you'll see in a moment, it's actually harder to use a DLL than it is to create it.

Creating a DLL

To create a new DLL in Delphi, select File ➢ New ➢ Other, then select the Delphi Projects node in the Item Categories tree, and finally double-click the DLL Wizard item at the right.

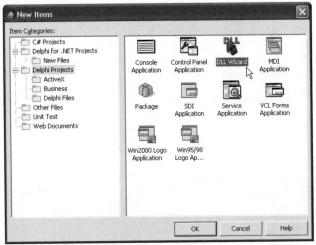

Figure 21-1: Selecting the DLL Wizard

The DLL Wizard creates the main source file for the DLL that looks almost exactly like the source code generated for a standard application. The only difference is that the file begins with the reserved word `library` instead of `program` (see Listing 21-1).

Listing 21-1: The basic source code for a DLL

```
library Project1;

{ Important note about DLL memory management: ShareMem must be the
  first unit in your library's uses clause AND your project's (select
  Project-View Source) uses clause if your DLL exports any procedures or
  functions that pass strings as parameters or function results. This
  applies to all strings passed to and from your DLL--even those that
  are nested in records and classes. ShareMem is the interface unit to
  the BORLNDMM.DLL shared memory manager, which must be deployed along
  with your DLL. To avoid using BORLNDMM.DLL, pass string information
  using PChar or ShortString parameters. }

uses
  SysUtils,
  Classes;

{$R *.res}

begin
end.
```

All that you have to do now is add a routine above the begin-end block and you're done. When you do that, you'll have an internal routine that you'll be able to use in the DLL but not from outside applications. If you want to call the routine from other applications and DLLs, you'll have to export it. To export a routine by name, add it to the exports list. The exports list has the same syntax as the uses list, except that in the exports list each item is a routine, not a unit.

The exports list is usually written immediately above the main begin-end block. Take a look at Listing 21-2 to see the source code of the simple FirstLib.dll that exports a single function.

Listing 21-2: A simple DLL

```
library FirstLib;

function Max3(Num1, Num2, Num3: Integer): Integer; stdcall;
begin
  Result := Num1;
  if Num2 > Result then Result := Num2;
  if Num3 > Result then Result := Num3;
end;

{ export the Max3 function }
exports
  Max3;

begin
end.
```

When you add a routine to the exports list, you are exporting the routine by name. You can also export the routine under a different name using the name directive or you can export the routine by ordinal value using the index directive. However, the use of the index directive is discouraged.

Here's how you can export a routine by ordinal value or under a different name:

```
exports
  Max3 name 'MyMax3Function',
  SaySomething index 1;
```

Static Loading

Static loading is the simpler of the two possible ways to load a dynamic link library. Static loading is also known as load-time dynamic linking, because the used DLLs get automatically loaded when the application starts.

To statically load a DLL, you have to copy the routine declaration to the calling application and mark it with the external directive, which tells the compiler that the routine resides in either an object file or a dynamic link library.

When you're importing routines from a dynamic link library, you have to mark the routine with the external directive followed by the name of the DLL that contains the routine's implementation. Here's how you can import the Max3 function from the FirstLib.dll:

```
function Max3(Num1, Num2, Num3: Integer): Integer;
  stdcall; external 'FirstLib.dll';
```

If you want, you can even rename the routine when importing it. To import a routine by renaming, declare the routine with a different name and specify the original name at the end of the declaration using the name directive:

```
function Max(Num1, Num2, Num3: Integer): Integer;
  stdcall; external 'FirstLib.dll' name 'Max3';
```

You can also import a function from a dynamic link library by creating an import unit and writing the standard routine header in the interface part of the unit and its external implementation in the implementation part of the unit. The following listing shows the entire FirstLib.dll import unit.

Listing 21-3: The FirstLib.dll import unit

```
unit FirstLibIntf;

interface

function Max3(Num1, Num2, Num3: Integer): Integer; stdcall;

implementation

const
  FirstLib = 'FirstLib.dll';

    { tell the compiler that the implementation of the
      Max3 function is in the FirstLib.dll }
    function Max3; external FirstLib;

end.
```

Once you've created the DLL and its import unit, you have to test the DLL to see if the routines work. Since you can't run the DLL, you have to create a test application that will use the DLL. The fastest way to create a test application is to create a project group by adding a new project to the current one. You can do this by right-clicking on the ProjectGroup1 item in the Project Manager and selecting Add New Project, as shown in Figure 21-2.

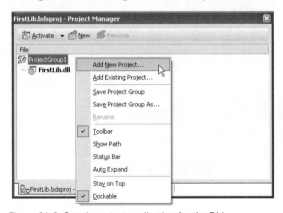

Figure 21-2: Creating a test application for the DLL

Now that you have the DLL, the import unit, and an empty VCL Forms application (or other) project, you can use the DLL's routines as you would all others — add the import unit to the uses list of the test application and call whichever routine you need (see Listing 21-3). The test application is displayed in Figure 21-3.

Listing 21-3: Testing the Max3 routine imported from the FirstLib.dll

```
unit Unit1;

interface

uses
  Windows, Messages, SysUtils, Variants, Classes, Graphics, Controls, Forms,
  Dialogs, StdCtrls, XPMan, FirstLibIntf;

type
  TMainForm = class(TForm)
    procedure Max3ButtonClick(Sender: TObject);
  private
    { Private declarations }
  public
    { Public declarations }
  end;

var
  MainForm: TMainForm;

implementation

{$R *.dfm}

procedure TMainForm.Max3ButtonClick(Sender: TObject);
var
  LargestNumber: Integer;
begin
  LargestNumber := Max3(StrToInt(Edit1.Text),
    StrToInt(Edit2.Text), StrToInt(Edit3.Text));

  MessageDlg(Format('The largest number is %d.', [LargestNumber]),
    mtInformation, [mbOK], 0);
end;

end.
```

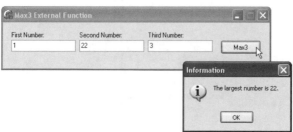

Figure 21-3: The FirstLib.dll test application

Dynamic Loading

Dynamic loading, also known as runtime dynamic linking, is a more versatile and more complex method of loading DLLs. Dynamic linking allows you to load and unload a dynamic link library whenever you want without having to create an import unit.

To dynamically load a DLL, you have to:

1. Declare a procedural variable or a procedural type that describes the routine that you want to call.

2. Call the LoadLibrary function to load the DLL.

3. Call the GetProcAddress function to retrieve a pointer to the routine in the DLL.

4. Call the routine.

5. Call the FreeLibrary function to unload the DLL.

Now we're going to create a new DLL that contains VCL forms and exports overloaded routines. First, create a new DLL (optionally name it FormLib) and then create and export a routine that dynamically creates and displays an empty form (see Listing 21-4). In case you forgot, you have to add the Forms unit to the DLL's uses list in order to work with VCL forms.

Listing 21-4: A DLL routine that creates and displays an empty form

```
library FormLib;

uses
  SysUtils, Classes, Forms;

{$R *.res}

procedure ShowDLLForm;
begin
  with TForm.Create(Application) do
  try
    ShowModal;
  finally
    Free;
  end;
end;

exports
  ShowDLLForm;

begin
end.
```

Now that you have the DLL, add a new VCL Forms project to the project group and drop a button on the Designer Surface. We're going to dynamically load the FormLib.dll in its OnClick event handler.

The first thing you have to do is declare a procedural variable that has the same parameter list as the routine you want to call. Since the ShowDLLForm routine in the FormLib.dll has no parameters, you have to declare a variable of type procedure. It does sound weird, but that is what you have to do. Here's the declaration of the procedural variable that we're going to use:

```
procedure TMainForm.ShowFormButtonClick(Sender: TObject);
var
  DLLRoutine: procedure;
begin
end;
```

To load the DLL, you have to call the LoadLibrary function and pass the DLL's file name as the lpLibFileName parameter. If the function succeeds, it returns the DLL's handle. You must store the function's return value because you can't unload the DLL or locate the routines in the DLL without its handle. Here's the portion of code that calls the LoadLibrary function:

```
procedure TMainForm.ShowFormButtonClick(Sender: TObject);
var
  DLLRoutine: procedure;
  DLLHandle: THandle;
begin
  DLLHandle := LoadLibrary('FormLib.dll');

end;
```

Before going any further, let's create a try-finally block that will make sure the DLL is unloaded even if an error occurs. To unload the DLL from memory, call the FreeLibrary function and pass the DLL's handle as the hLibModule parameter:

```
procedure TMainForm.ShowFormButtonClick(Sender: TObject);
var
  DLLRoutine: procedure;
  DLLHandle: THandle;
begin
  DLLHandle := LoadLibrary('FormLib.dll');
  try
  finally
    FreeLibrary(DLLHandle);
  end;     // try..finally
end;
```

The only thing left to do is to call the GetProcAddress function in the try block to retrieve the address of the ShowDLLForm routine. The GetProcAddress function accepts two parameters: the DLL's handle and the name of the routine you want to locate.

```
  DLLRoutine := GetProcAddress(DLLHandle, 'ShowDLLForm');
```

Before calling the routine pointed to by the DLLRoutine variable, you should check whether the DLLRoutine variable points to a valid address because GetProcAddress returns nil if it can't find the specified routine in the DLL.

The following listing shows how to call a routine from a dynamically loaded DLL.

Listing 21-5: Calling a procedure from a dynamically loaded DLL

```
procedure TMainForm.ShowFormButtonClick(Sender: TObject);
var
  DLLRoutine: procedure;
  DLLHandle: THandle;
begin
  DLLHandle := LoadLibrary('FormLib.dll');
  try
    { DLLRoutine points to ShowDLLForm in FormLib.dll' }
    DLLRoutine := GetProcAddress(DLLHandle, 'ShowDLLForm');

    { call the ShowDLLForm procedure }
    if Assigned(DLLRoutine) then
      DLLRoutine
    else
      MessageDlg('The specified routine cannot be found.',
        mtInformation, [mbOk], 0);
  finally
    FreeLibrary(DLLHandle);
  end;      // try..finally
end;
```

The result of the code in Listing 21-5 is shown in Figure 21-4.

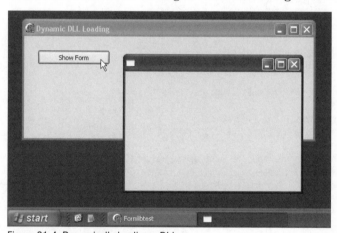

Figure 21-4: Dynamically loading a DLL

If you execute the code in Listing 21-5, you'll see that the ShowDLLForm procedure works properly and displays the empty form onscreen, but it also displays a Taskbar button for the form.

To remove the Taskbar button, you have to pass the calling application's Application.Handle (or the main form's handle) to the DLL and assign it to the DLL's Application.Handle property before creating the form in the DLL (see Listing 21-6).

Listing 21-6: Linking the DLL with the host application

```
library FormLib;

uses
  Windows, SysUtils, Classes, Forms,
  SampleFrm in 'SampleFrm.pas' {VCLForm};

{$R *.res}

procedure ShowDLLForm; overload;
begin
  with TForm.Create(Application) do
  try
    ShowModal;
  finally
    Free;
  end;
end;

procedure ShowDLLForm(HostHandle: THandle); overload;
var
  OrigHandle: THandle;
  DLLName: array[0..255] of Char;
begin
  OrigHandle := Application.Handle;
  try
    { link with the host application }
    Application.Handle := HostHandle;

    VCLForm := TVCLForm.Create(Application);
    try
      { extract the DLL's file name }
      GetModuleFileName(HInstance, DLLName, 255);

      { display the DLL and the host application's file names on the form }
      VCLForm.Label1.Caption := 'DLL: ' + ExtractFileName(DLLName);
      VCLForm.Label2.Caption := 'Host: ' +
        ExtractFileName(Application.ExeName);

      VCLForm.ShowModal;
    finally
      VCLForm.Free;
    end;
  finally
    Application.Handle := OrigHandle;
  end;       // try..finally
end;

exports
  ShowDLLForm,
  ShowDLLForm(HostHandle: THandle) name 'ShowDLLFormEx';

begin
end.
```

As you can see, the code in Listing 21-6 also illustrates how to export over-loaded routines. When exporting an overloaded routine, include its parameter list in the exports list and change its name using the name directive.

To call the overloaded ShowDLLForm routine that accepts the THandle parameter, you have to create another procedural variable with the same parameter list and call it by the name specified with the name directive (in this case, ShowDLLFormEx). This code is displayed in Listing 21-7.

Listing 21-7: The proper way to display a VCL form that resides in the DLL

```
procedure TMainForm.ShowFormButton2Click(Sender: TObject);
var
  DLLRoutine: procedure(HostHandle: THandle);
  DLLHandle: THandle;
begin
  DLLHandle := LoadLibrary('FormLib.dll');
  try
    { DLLRoutine points to ShowDLLFormEx in FormLib.dll' }
    DLLRoutine := GetProcAddress(DLLHandle, 'ShowDLLFormEx');

    { call the ShowDLLFormEx procedure }
    if Assigned(DLLRoutine) then
      DLLRoutine(Handle) { pass the form's handle }
    else
      MessageDlg('The specified routine cannot be found.',
        mtInformation, [mbOk], 0);
  finally
    FreeLibrary(DLLHandle);
  end;     // try..finally
end;.
```

The result of this updated code for displaying VCL forms that reside in a DLL is displayed in Figure 21-5.

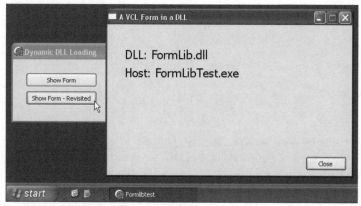

Figure 21-5: Properly displaying VCL forms

Passing Strings between the Application and the DLL

Now we're going to create a DLL that uses PChars to pass string data to the calling application. This application is displayed in Figure 21-6.

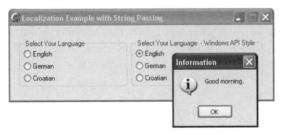

Figure 21-6: The MessageDlg text is from the DLL.

The first thing you have to do is create the host application:

1. Create a new VCL Forms application project.

2. Add two TRadioGroup components to the Designer Surface.

3. Add English, German, and Croatian items to both TRadioGroup components.

Once you've created the host application's user interface, you have to create a unit for the languages enumeration that will be used by the host application and the DLL and then add a new DLL project to the project group.

Here's the MyTypes unit that contains the languages enumeration:

```
unit MyTypes;

interface

type
  TMyLanguage = (mlEnglish, mlGerman, mlCroatian);

implementation

end.
```

There's only one decision that you have to make when you want to pass a PChar between the application and the DLL — how to manage the PChar's memory. Here's a list of things that you can and cannot do:

■ You can allocate and deallocate the PChar in the DLL.

■ You can allocate and deallocate the PChar in the calling application (this is the Windows API way).

■ You *cannot* allocate the PChar's memory in the DLL and release it in the host application, or vice versa (see Figure 21-7).

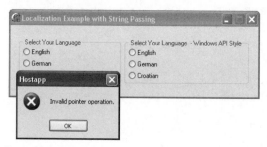

Figure 21-7: Bad things happen when the host application tries
to release memory allocated in the DLL.

The following listing shows how to allocate and deallocate the PChar's memory in the DLL. The listing contains two routines: the GetStringData function that allocates memory for and returns a localized string, and the FreeStringData procedure that must be used to release the memory allocated by the GetStringData function.

Listing 21-8: Routines that manage the memory in the DLL

```
library LanguageLib;

uses SysUtils, MyTypes;

const
  STRING_DATA: array[TMyLanguage] of string = ('Good morning.',
    'Guten Morgen.', 'Dobro jutro.');

{ return a localized string }
function GetStringData(Language: TMyLanguage): PChar;
begin
  { allocate the memory for the string and for the #0 character }
  GetMem(Result, Length(STRING_DATA[Language]) + 1);

  { the StrPCopy function copies a string to a null-terminated string }
  StrPCopy(Result, STRING_DATA[Language]);
end;

{ use this routine to release the PChars allocated with GetStringData }
procedure FreeStringData(Data: PChar);
begin
  FreeMem(Data);
end;

exports
  GetStringData,
  FreeStringData;

begin
end.
```

Listing 21-9 shows how to use the GetStringData and the FreeStringData routines in the host application.

Listing 21-9: Using the GetStringData and the FreeStringData routines to retrieve a localized string from the DLL

```
procedure TMainForm.RadioGroup1Click(Sender: TObject);
var
  DLLHandle: THandle;
  stringFunc: function(Language: TMyLanguage): PChar;
  freeProc: procedure (Data: PChar);
  buffer: PChar;
  selectedLang: TMyLanguage;
begin
  selectedLang := TMyLanguage(RadioGroup1.ItemIndex);

  DLLHandle := LoadLibrary('LanguageLib.dll');
  try
    { find both routines }
    stringFunc := GetProcAddress(DLLHandle, 'GetStringData');
    freeProc := GetProcAddress(DLLHandle, 'FreeStringData');

    if not Assigned(stringFunc) or not Assigned(freeProc) then
      MessageDlg('Error Loading DLL!', mtError, [mbOK], 0)
    else begin
      buffer := stringFunc(selectedLang);
      try
        MessageDlg(string(buffer), mtInformation, [mbOK], 0);
      finally
        { free the PChar's memory using the DLL's FreeStringData routine }
        freeProc(buffer);
      end;      // try..finally
    end;        // if not Assigned
  finally
    FreeLibrary(DLLHandle);
  end;          // try..finally
end;
```

If you really need to pass string data between the application and the DLL, you can do things the API way — allocate and deallocate PChars in the host application and design DLL functions to accept the PChar buffer and the maximum number of characters to copy. When doing things the API way, you also have to enable the developer to call the function with invalid parameters (like nil pointers) to determine how big the buffer should be.

The following listing shows the GetStringDataEx function, which expects the developer to pass both a pointer to a valid buffer and the length of the buffer. The GetStringDataEx function also allows the developer to pass nil to determine the appropriate length for the buffer.

Listing 21-10: Doing things the API way

```
library LanguageLib;

uses SysUtils, MyTypes;

const
  STRING_DATA: array[TMyLanguage] of string = ('Good morning.',
    'Guten Morgen.', 'Dobro jutro.');
```

```
{ the developer can pass nil to determine how big his/her buffer has to be }
{ if the developer passed a valid Buffer, StrPLCopy copies
  BufferLen bytes from a Delphi string to the Buffer }
function GetStringDataEx(Language: TMyLanguage;
  Buffer: PChar; BufferLen: Integer): Integer;
begin
  Result := Length(STRING_DATA[Language]);

  if Buffer <> nil then
    StrPLCopy(Buffer, STRING_DATA[Language], BufferLen);
end;

exports
  GetStringData,
  FreeStringData,
  GetStringDataEx;

begin
end.
```

Listing 21-11 shows how to use the GetStringDataEx function in the host application.

Listing 21-11: Calling the GetStringDataEx function

```
procedure TMainForm.RadioGroup2Click(Sender: TObject);
var
  DLLHandle: THandle;
  selectedLang: TMyLanguage;
  buffLen: Integer;
  buffer: PChar;
  stringProc: function(Language: TMyLanguage;
    Buffer: PChar; BufferLen: Integer): Integer;
begin
  selectedLang := TMyLanguage(RadioGroup2.ItemIndex);

  DLLHandle := LoadLibrary('LanguageLib.dll');
  try
    StringProc := GetProcAddress(DLLHandle, 'GetStringDataEx');
    if Assigned(StringProc) then
    begin
      { pass nil to the GetStringDataEx function to determine the
        appropriate size for the buffer }
      buffLen := StringProc(selectedLang, nil, 0);

      { allocate the buffer }
      GetMem(Buffer, buffLen + 1);
      try
        { call the GetStringDataEx function normally }
        StringProc(selectedLang, Buffer, buffLen);
        MessageDlg(string(Buffer), mtInformation, [mbOK], 0);
      finally
        { release the buffer }
        FreeMem(Buffer);
      end;     // try..finally (Buffer)
    end else
      MessageDlg('Cannot load the DLL!', mtWarning, [mbOK], 0);
```

```
  finally
    FreeLibrary(DLLHandle);
  end;      // try..finally (DLLHandle)
end;
```

Creating C++ DLLs

C++ also has a DLL wizard (the Dynamic-link Library item in the
C++Builder Projects category) that should be used to create a new DLL.
When you select to create a new dynamic link library, the IDE displays the
New Dynamic-link Library dialog box (see Figure 21-8) that allows you to
select which language you want to use, whether or not you'll be using VCL
components, and if you want the IDE to generate the DllMain function (Visual
C++ style) or the DllEntryPoint function (Borland C++ style).

Figure 21-8: The New Dynamic-link Library wizard

After you click OK, the IDE will generate the necessary files, and place the
main DLL function in the .cpp file (see Listing 21-12).

Listing 21-12: Basic source code of a C++Builder DLL

```
//---------------------------------------------------------------
#include <vcl.h>
#include <windows.h>
#pragma hdrstop
//---------------------------------------------------------------
//    Important note about DLL memory management when your DLL uses
//    the static version of the RunTime Library:
//
//    If your DLL exports any functions that pass String objects
//    (or structs/classes containing nested Strings) as parameter
//    or function results, you will need to add the library MEMMGR.LIB
//    to both the DLL project and any other projects that use the DLL.
//    You will also need to use MEMMGR.LIB if any other projects that
//    use the DLL will be performing new or delete operations on any
//    non-TObject-derived classes that are exported from the DLL.
//    Adding MEMMGR.LIB to your project will change the DLL and its
//    calling EXEs to use the BORLNDMM.DLL as their memory manager.
//    In these cases, the file BORLNDMM.DLL should be deployed along
//    with your DLL.
//
//    To avoid using BORLNDMM.DLL, pass string information using
//    "char *" or ShortString parameters.
//
//    If your DLL uses the dynamic version of the RTL, you do
//    not need to explicitly add MEMMGR.LIB as this will be done
```

```
//   implicitly for you
//------------------------------------------------------------------

#pragma argsused
int WINAPI DllEntryPoint(HINSTANCE hinst,
   unsigned long reason, void* lpReserved)
{
   return 1;
}
//------------------------------------------------------------------
```

The most notable difference between a Delphi and a C++Builder DLL is the DllEntryPoint function, which is called by the operating system when the library is loaded and unloaded. Unlike other "main" functions, you usually don't write code inside the DllEntryPoint function and you have to return a nonzero value to notify the system that everything is OK.

Exporting Functions

To see how to export functions from a C++ DLL, first add two simple functions that will display "Hello" and "Goodbye" messages using the Windows API MessageBox function (see Listing 21-13). The two functions also call the GetActiveWindow() function, which makes sure that the message dialog box is always displayed on top of the active window.

The default calling convention in C++ is cdecl, which allows functions to accept a variable number of parameters and also results in function names that start with an underscore. Just like the register (__fastcall) calling convention in Delphi, you should forget about cdecl in DLLs and use the default Windows calling convention, stdcall.

Listing 21-13: Two DLL functions (not counting DLLEntryPoint)

```
#pragma argsused
int WINAPI DllEntryPoint(HINSTANCE hinst,
   unsigned long reason, void* lpReserved)
{
   /* In DLLs, a nonzero value means that everything is OK */
   return 1;
}
//----------------------------------------------------------------------------
void __stdcall SayHello(void)
{
   MessageBox(GetActiveWindow(), "Hello",
      "C++ DLL", MB_OK | MB_ICONINFORMATION);
}

void __stdcall SayGoodbye(void)
{
   MessageBox(GetActiveWindow(), "Goodbye",
      "C++ DLL", MB_OK | MB_ICONINFORMATION);
}
```

These two functions can currently be used only inside the DLL. To use them in an application, you have to export them using the __declspec(dllexport) storage class specifier.

Here is how you export the SayHello() function from the DLL:

```
__declspec(dllexport) void __stdcall SayHello(void);
```

In a C DLL, the __declspec(dllexport) directive is all you need to successfully export a function from a DLL. In a C++ DLL, the __declspec(dllexport) directive is also enough to successfully export a function, but the results are different because the C++ compiler mangles function names. To retain the original function name, you also need to use the extern "C" directive.

To properly export a function from a C++ DLL, you should use both the extern and __declspec storage class specifiers to export functions from a DLL:

```
extern "C" __declspec(dllexport) void __stdcall SayHello(void);
```

If you have to export several functions, you don't have to mark them all with the extern directive. When you have to export several functions, you can open an extern "C" block and then export all of your functions inside it:

```
extern "C"
{
    __declspec(dllexport) void __stdcall SayHello(void);
    __declspec(dllexport) void __stdcall SayGoodbye(void);
};
```

When exporting functions, you should also make sure you only apply the extern "C" specifier when you compile the DLL as a C++ DLL. To do that, you can use the #ifdef conditional directive to check if the __cplusplus constant is defined. If the __cplusplus constant is defined, it means that the compiler is working in C++ mode:

```
#ifdef __cplusplus
extern "C"
{
#endif /* __cplusplus */

    __declspec(dllexport) void __stdcall SayHello(void);
    __declspec(dllexport) void __stdcall SayGoodbye(void);

#ifdef __cplusplus
};
#endif /* __cplusplus */
```

Creating a DLL Header File

In order to easily use the DLL in an application, you should move the export directives to a header file. When you move the exports to a header file, don't forget to include it in the main source file of the DLL.

Listings 21-14A and 21-14B show the current versions of the main source and header file.

Listing 21-14A: The DLL's source file (MainDLLUnit.cpp)

```
#include <vcl.h>
#include <windows.h>

#pragma hdrstop
#include "MainDLLUnit.h"   /* Include the DLL's header file */

#pragma argsused
int WINAPI DllEntryPoint(HINSTANCE hinst,
    unsigned long reason, void* lpReserved)
{
    return 1;
}

void __stdcall SayHello(void)
{
    MessageBox(GetActiveWindow(), "Hello",
        "C++ DLL", MB_OK | MB_ICONINFORMATION);
}

void __stdcall SayGoodbye(void)
{
    MessageBox(GetActiveWindow(), "Goodbye",
        "C++ DLL", MB_OK | MB_ICONINFORMATION);
}
```

Listing 21-14B: The DLL's header file (MainDLLUnit.h)

```
#ifndef MAIN_DLL_UNIT_H
#define MAIN_DLL_UNIT_H

#ifdef __cplusplus
extern "C"
{
#endif

    __declspec(dllexport) void __stdcall SayHello(void);
    __declspec(dllexport) void __stdcall SayGoodbye(void);

#ifdef __cplusplus
};
#endif /* __cplusplus */

#endif /* MAIN_DLL_UNIT_H */
```

Static Loading (Static Linking)

To test the previously created DLL and to see how to statically link a DLL, use the Project Manager to add a C++Builder VCL Forms application to the project group.

To statically link a DLL in a C++ application, you can't simply include the DLL's header file and compile the application. If you do that, you'll receive the "Unresolved external..." error because the compiler won't be able to find the functions listed in the header file.

To properly link a DLL, you need to include the DLL's header so you can call the functions it contains and you need to add the DLL's .lib file to the project. The .lib file is generated by the compiler when you compile the DLL, and you have to add it to client projects because it contains data the compiler needs to link the client application with the DLL.

You can add the .lib file to the client application by right-clicking it in the Project Manager and selecting the Add item on the context menu.

Figure 21-9: DLL and client application project files

When you include the necessary header files and add the .lib file to the project, you can use the functions exported from the DLL as easily as the ones that are in the same unit:

```
void __fastcall TMainForm::SayHelloButtonClick(TObject *Sender)
{
    SayHello(); // call the DLL SayHello() function
}
```

The result of the SayHello() call is displayed in Figure 21-10.

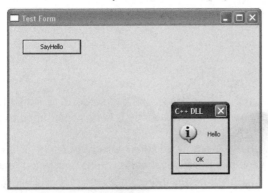

Figure 21-10: Testing the DLL

Functions exported from a DLL can also be used in a client application without including the header file. To do so, add the DLL's .lib file to the project and import the functions using the __declspec(dllimport) directive:

```
extern "C" __declspec(dllimport) void __stdcall SayHello(void);
extern "C" __declspec(dllimport) void __stdcall SayGoodbye(void);
```

The DllEntryPoint (DllMain) Function

The DllEntryPoint function is the main function in a DLL, called by the system on four occasions: when an application loads and unloads the DLL or when a thread loads and unloads the DLL.

You can easily determine why the DLL is used by checking the reason parameter of the DllEntryPoint function (see Listing 21-15). The reason parameter can be DLL_PROCESS_ATTACH, DLL_PROCESS_DETACH, DLL_THREAD_ATTACH, or DLL_THREAD_DETACH.

Listing 21-15: Executing code when the DLL is loaded and unloaded

```
#pragma argsused
int WINAPI DllEntryPoint(HINSTANCE hinst,
    unsigned long reason, void* lpReserved)
{
    if(reason == DLL_PROCESS_ATTACH)
        SayHello();
    else if(reason == DLL_PROCESS_DETACH)
        SayGoodbye();

    return 1;
}
```

The DllEntryPoint Function in a Delphi DLL

By default, the IDE doesn't generate the DllEntryPoint function for a DLL, but that doesn't mean a Delphi DLL can't execute code when a process loads or unloads the DLL.

To create a DllEntryPoint function in a Delphi DLL, you need to do the following three things:

1. Declare a procedure that only accepts the Reason parameter.

2. Pass this procedure, inside the main begin-end block, to the global DllProc variable to let Delphi know which procedure to call.

3. Call your procedure with the DLL_PROCESS_ATTACH reason when the DLL is loaded.

Listing 21-16 shows the Delphi version of the SayHello/SayGoodbye DLL we created in C++ in Listing 21-13.

Listing 21-16: DllEntryPoint in a Delphi DLL

```
library EntryDLL;

uses Windows;
```

```
{$R *.res}

procedure SayHello; stdcall;
begin
  MessageBox(GetActiveWindow, 'Hello',
    'Delphi DLL', MB_OK or MB_ICONINFORMATION);
end;

procedure SayGoodbye; stdcall;
begin
  MessageBox(GetActiveWindow, 'Goodbye',
    'Delphi DLL', MB_OK or MB_ICONINFORMATION);
end;

procedure DLLEntryPoint(Reason: Integer);
begin
  if Reason = DLL_PROCESS_ATTACH then
    SayHello
  else if Reason = DLL_PROCESS_DETACH then
    SayGoodbye;
end;

exports
  SayHello,
  SayGoodbye;

begin
  { Assign your DllEntryPoint function to the DllProc pointer }
  DllProc := DllEntryPoint;

  { Call DllProc with DLL_PROCESS_ATTACH when the DLL is loaded. }
  DllProc(DLL_PROCESS_ATTACH);
end.
```

Dynamic Loading in C++

To dynamically load a DLL in C++, you have to follow the same steps as you do in Delphi:

1. Create a new procedural type (a function pointer) that describes the routine you want to call (the return type, calling convention, parameters).

2. Load the DLL using the LoadLibrary function.

3. Call the GetProcAddress function to acquire a pointer to the routine in the DLL.

4. Call one or more routines from the DLL.

5. Remove the DLL from memory by calling FreeLibrary.

But before you see how to load functions from a DLL, you should create a DLL with a function or two. The following listing contains just that — a DLL with a simple function that displays an empty VCL form.

Listing 21-17: C++ DLL with VCL forms (MyDLL.dll)

```
#include <vcl.h>
#include <windows.h>
#pragma hdrstop

extern "C"
{
    __declspec(dllexport) void __stdcall VCL_Form(void);

};

#pragma argsused
int WINAPI DllEntryPoint(HINSTANCE hinst,
    unsigned long reason, void* lpReserved)
{
    return 1;
}
//---------------------------------------------------------------------------

void __stdcall VCL_Form(void)
{
    TForm* f = new TForm(Application);
    try
    {
        f->Caption = "VCL Form in a C++ DLL";
        f->ShowModal();
    }
    __finally
    {
        delete f;
    }
}
```

To call the VCL_Form function from MyDLL.dll, you need to create a function pointer type by using the following syntax:

```
typedef return_value (*function_name)(param_list);
```

or

```
typedef return_value (calling_convention *function_name)(param_list);
```

In this particular case, you have to declare the following type:

```
/* function pointer */
typedef void(__stdcall *PROC)(void);
/* you also need a variable of type PROC */
PROC proc;
```

Once you've declared the function pointer type, you're done with the hardest part. The only thing left to do now is to load the DLL and acquire the pointer to the VCL_Form function. To use the pointer returned by the GetProc-Address function, you need to typecast it to your pointer type. Listing 21-18 shows how to use the LoadLibrary, GetProcAddress, and FreeLibrary functions to dynamically load a DLL in C++.

Listing 21-18: Dynamically loading a DLL in C++

```cpp
void __fastcall TMainForm::ShowFormButtonClick(TObject *Sender)
{
   /* function pointer */
   typedef void(__stdcall *PROC)(void);
   /* you also need a variable of type PROC */
   PROC proc;

   HMODULE lib = LoadLibrary("MyDLL.dll");
   if(lib != 0)
   {
      proc = (PROC)GetProcAddress(lib, "VCL_Form");
      if(proc != NULL) {
         proc(); /* call the function */
      } else {
         ShowMessage("VCL_Host() cannot be found!");
      }

   FreeLibrary(lib);
   }
   else
   {
      ShowMessage("LoadLibrary failed!");
   }
}
```

Chapter 22

Graphics Programming

Graphics programming in Windows is based on the GDI, the Windows graphical device interface. The GDI is an API designed to enable us to draw graphics on screen and on the printer. In Delphi, you can use GDI objects and functions directly or you can use the VCL classes that encapsulate GDI functions and objects. In this chapter, we'll mostly work with VCL classes that encapsulate GDI functionality.

Using Colors

In Windows, colors are defined by three values: red, green, and blue. Each value specifies the intensity of the color component. If all the values are set to the minimum value 0, the resulting color is black. If all values are set to the maximum value 255, the resulting color is white. To create a color from these separate color components, you have to use the RGB function.

The RGB function accepts three byte parameters — one parameter for each color component — and returns a COLORREF value. The COLORREF value is a 32-bit unsigned integer value used to specify a color.

```
function RGB(r, g, b: Byte): COLORREF;
```

Listing 22-1 uses the RGB function to enable the user to select custom colors, as shown in Figure 22-1.

Figure 22-1: Creating custom colors with the RGB function

The application uses a TPanel component as a preview frame and three TScrollBar components that enable the user to modify the red, green, and blue color components. The Max property of all three TScrollBar components is set to the maximum value for each component: 255. All three TScrollBar components share a single, extremely simple OnChange event handler.

Listing 22-1: Using the RGB function

```
procedure TForm1.ScrollChange(Sender: TObject);
begin
  Panel1.Color := RGB(RedBar.Position,
    GreenBar.Position, BlueBar.Position);
end;
```

In Delphi, colors are automatically represented by 32-bit TColor values. The TColor type is declared in the Graphics unit, along with several useful color constants. These color constants cover:

- Standard colors like clWhite, clRed, clGreen, clBlue, clBlack, clMaroon
- System colors like clBtnFace, clScrollBar, clActiveBorder, clMenu, clWindow
- Named web colors like clWebBlueViolet, clWebGainsboro, clWebThistle

You can also specify colors as hexadecimal numbers. When doing so, remember to specify the components "backwards," that is, first specify the blue value, then green, and finally red:

```
Color := $000000; { black }
Color := $FF0000; { blue }
Color := $00FF00; { green }
Color := $0000FF; { red }
Color := $FFFFFF; { white }
```

The Canvas

The Windows GDI enables us to produce graphics by using GDI objects and by calling GDI functions that can draw lines, shapes, text, or images. The TCanvas class encapsulates most of the GDI functions and objects and provides the drawing surface on which we can draw. The three graphics objects that are used to do the drawing are Pen, Brush, and Font (discussed earlier).

The Pen

The Pen is used when you're drawing lines and shapes. When you're drawing shapes, Pen is used for the outline.

To draw a line, you have to use two Canvas methods: MoveTo and LineTo. The MoveTo method is used to set the beginning drawing position. The LineTo method is used to draw the line from the drawing position set by MoveTo to the point specified by its X and Y parameters. When finished, the LineTo method also updates the drawing position.

The following example shows how to draw a triangle using the MoveTo and LineTo methods. The result is displayed in Figure 22-2.

Listing 22-2: Drawing lines with MoveTo and LineTo

```
procedure TMainForm.DrawButtonClick(Sender: TObject);
begin
  Canvas.MoveTo(100, 100);
  Canvas.LineTo(200, 150);
  Canvas.LineTo(100, 200);
  Canvas.LineTo(100, 100);
end;
```

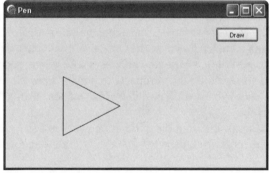

Figure 22-2: Drawing lines

The TPen class encapsulates these properties: Color, Width, and Style. The different Pen styles are displayed in Figure 22-3.

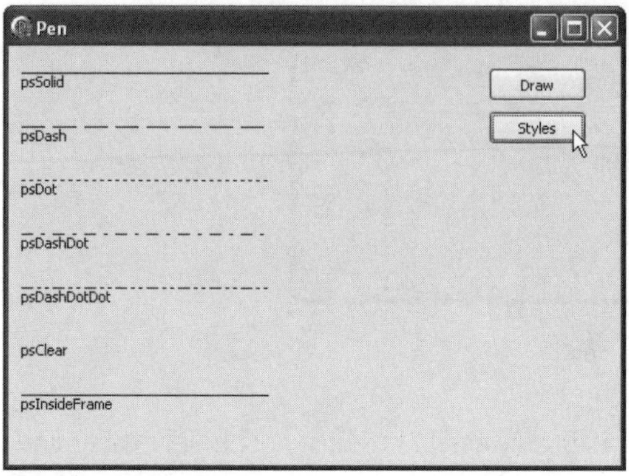

Figure 22-3: Pen styles

The StylesButtonClick method that produces the graphical output in Figure 22-3 is displayed in Listing 22-3.

Listing 22-3: Playing with styles

```
procedure TMainForm.StylesButtonClick(Sender: TObject);
const
  PEN_NAMES: array[TPenStyle] of string = ('psSolid', 'psDash', 'psDot',
    'psDashDot', 'psDashDotDot', 'psClear', 'psInsideFrame');
var
  i: Integer;
  y: Integer;
begin
  for i := 0 to Ord(psInsideFrame) do
  begin
    y := 20 + (i * 40);

    Canvas.Pen.Style := TPenStyle(i);
    Canvas.TextOut(10, y, PEN_NAMES[Canvas.Pen.Style]);
    Canvas.MoveTo(10, y);
    Canvas.LineTo(200, y);
  end;
end;
```

The TPen class has one more property that changes the appearance of lines on the canvas: Mode. The Mode property specifies the operation that is performed on the pixels when a line is drawn on the canvas. For instance, if you set the Mode property to pmWhite, all the drawn lines will be white, regardless of the Pen's color. If you set the Mode property to pmNotCopy, the Pen's color will be inverted. To see the list of all possible Mode values, search for TPenMode in Delphi's Help.

One of the Pen modes missing from the .NET framework is the pmNotXor mode, which is most often used to create the rubber-banding effect shown in Figure 22-4.

Figure 22-4: Rubber-banding

The rubber-banding effect is pretty easily produced. The only thing you have to do is draw the same line twice. The first time it's drawn, the pixels on the canvas are inverted to make the line visible. When you draw the line again using pmNotXor, the pixels on the canvas will be restored to their original values, thus erasing the line.

The code in Listing 22-4 enables you to draw lines on the canvas just as you would in Paint or any other application that supports drawing.

Listing 22-4: Drawing lines

```
unit Unit1;

interface

uses
  Windows, Messages, SysUtils, Variants, Classes, Graphics, Controls, Forms,
  Dialogs;

type
  TForm1 = class(TForm)
    procedure FormMouseMove(Sender: TObject; Shift: TShiftState;
      X, Y: Integer);
    procedure FormMouseUp(Sender: TObject; Button: TMouseButton;
      Shift: TShiftState; X, Y: Integer);
    procedure FormMouseDown(Sender: TObject; Button: TMouseButton;
      Shift: TShiftState; X, Y: Integer);
  private
    { Private declarations }
    FMouseDown: Boolean;
    FStart, FEnd: TPoint;
  public
    { Public declarations }
  end;

var
  Form1: TForm1;

implementation

{$R *.dfm}

procedure TForm1.FormMouseDown(Sender: TObject; Button: TMouseButton;
  Shift: TShiftState; X, Y: Integer);
begin
  if Button = mbLeft then
  begin
    FStart := Point(X, Y);
    FEnd := FStart;
    FMouseDown := True;
  end;      // if Button
end;

procedure TForm1.FormMouseUp(Sender: TObject; Button: TMouseButton;
  Shift: TShiftState; X, Y: Integer);
begin
  FMouseDown := False;
```

```
end;

procedure TForm1.FormMouseMove(Sender: TObject; Shift: TShiftState; X,
  Y: Integer);
begin
  if FMouseDown then
  begin
    { first erase the previous line }
    Canvas.Pen.Mode := pmNotXor;
    Canvas.MoveTo(FStart.X, FStart.Y);
    Canvas.LineTo(FEnd.X, FEnd.Y);

    { draw the new line }
    Canvas.MoveTo(FStart.X, FStart.Y);
    Canvas.LineTo(X, Y);

    { remember the new coordinates so that
      we can erase them next time an OnMouseMove occurs }
    FEnd := Point(X, Y);
  end;
end;

end.
```

The Brush

The Brush is used by methods that draw shapes to fill the interior of the drawn shape. Usually, the Brush only specifies the color of the shape, but it can also specify a pattern or a bitmap image that can be used as a pattern. Figure 22-5 displays the various Brush styles.

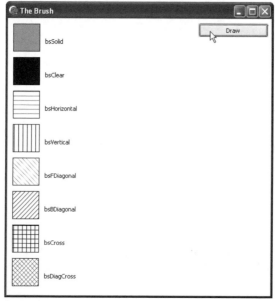

Figure 22-5: Brush styles

The following listing shows the code that displays the available Brush styles.

Listing 22-5: Working with Brush styles

```
procedure TMainForm.DrawButtonClick(Sender: TObject);
const
  RECT_SIZE = 50;
  BRUSH_NAMES: array[TBrushStyle] of string = ('bsSolid',
    'bsClear', 'bsHorizontal', 'bsVertical', 'bsFDiagonal',
    'bsBDiagonal', 'bsCross', 'bsDiagCross');
var
  y: Integer;
  style: TBrushStyle;
begin
  { erase the entire Canvas }
  Canvas.Brush.Style := bsSolid;
  Canvas.Brush.Color := clWhite;
  Canvas.FillRect(ClientRect);

  { draw rectangles }
  y := 10;
  for style := bsSolid to bsDiagCross do
  begin
    Canvas.Brush.Style := style;
    { select a random color }
    Canvas.Brush.Color := Random(High(TColor));

    Canvas.Rectangle(10, y, 10 + RECT_SIZE, y + RECT_SIZE);

    { temporarily change brush style to bsClear to
      draw text without a background color }
    Canvas.Brush.Style := bsClear;
    Canvas.TextOut(70, y + (RECT_SIZE div 2), BRUSH_NAMES[style]);

    Inc(y, RECT_SIZE + 10);
  end;     // for
end;
```

Drawing Text

The most straightforward method for drawing text on a canvas is the TextOut method. As you've already seen, the TextOut method accepts three parameters. The first two parameters are X and Y coordinates and the last is the string that is to be drawn on the canvas.

The TextOut method uses both the Brush and Font properties of the canvas when drawing the string. The Font property specifies the general characteristics of the text (font family and attributes) and the Brush property specifies the background color. If you want to draw text with a colored background, set Brush.Style to bsSolid. To draw the text without the colored background, set Brush.Style to bsClear.

Instead of using the Canvas's Brush property, you can also use the GDI API functions SetBkMode and SetBkColor to set the background color and mode (TRANSPARENT or OPAQUE):

```
function SetBkMode(DC: HDC; BkMode: Integer): Integer; stdcall;
function SetBkColor(DC: HDC; Color: COLORREF): COLORREF; stdcall;
```

Notice the first parameter in both functions. The first parameter accepts an HDC variable — a handle to a certain device context. At the API level, device contexts (data structures that contain screen or printer information) represent the drawing surface. The TCanvas class encapsulates the device context and the Handle property of the canvas is actually the handle of the GDI device context required by all GDI functions. So, when you need to call a GDI function directly, you can pass the Canvas's Handle property as the DC parameter (see Figure 22-6).

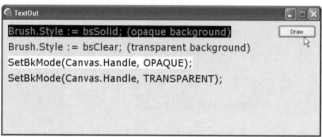

Figure 22-6: Drawing text

The following listing shows the code that produces the graphical output displayed in Figure 22-6.

Listing 22-6: Drawing text

```
procedure TMainForm.DrawButtonClick(Sender: TObject);
begin
  Canvas.Font.Name := 'Verdana';
  Canvas.Font.Size := 14;

  { VCL }
  Canvas.Brush.Color := clBlack;
  Canvas.Font.Color := clLime;
  Canvas.TextOut(10, 10, 'Brush.Style := bsSolid; (opaque background)');

  Canvas.Brush.Style := bsClear;
  Canvas.Font.Color := clBlue;
  Canvas.TextOut(10, 40, 'Brush.Style := bsClear; (transparent background)');

  { GDI API + VCL}
  SetBkMode(Canvas.Handle, OPAQUE);
  SetBkColor(Canvas.Handle, clWhite);
  SetTextColor(Canvas.Handle, clBlack);
  Canvas.TextOut(10, 70, 'SetBkMode(Canvas.Handle, OPAQUE);');
```

```
SetBkMode(Canvas.Handle, TRANSPARENT);
Canvas.TextOut(10, 100, 'SetBkMode(Canvas.Handle, TRANSPARENT);');
end;
```

To draw text on a canvas, you can also use the TextRect procedure, which writes a string inside a rectangle and clips the sections of the string that don't fit in the specified rectangle, as shown in Figure 22-7.

Listing 22-7: The TextRect method

```
procedure TMainForm.DrawButtonClick(Sender: TObject);
var
  rc: TRect;
begin
  rc := Rect(10, 10, 100, 40);
  Canvas.Brush.Color := clWhite;
  Canvas.Rectangle(rc);
  Canvas.TextRect(rc, 10, 10, 'TextRect displays text in a rectangle.');
end;
```

Figure 22-7: The TextRect method

The GDI API has yet another, really powerful text drawing function that isn't encapsulated in the TCanvas class and is often used by component developers: DrawText. The DrawText function can be used to display formatted text. It allows you to specify the rectangle that will be used for the formatting, the number of characters to draw, and the formatting options. Here's the declaration of the DrawText function:

```
function DrawText(hDC: HDC; lpString: PChar; nCount: Integer;
  var lpRect: TRect; uFormat: UINT): Integer; stdcall;
```

When you call the DrawText function, you have to do the following:

■ Pass the Canvas's handle as the hDC parameter.

■ Pass a string value as the lpString parameter. (If you're passing a string variable or a string property, you'll have to typecast it to PChar.)

■ Pass the length of the string as the nCount parameter. (If you pass –1, the DrawText function will display the entire string.)

■ Pass the rectangle in which the text is to be drawn as the lpRect parameter.

■ Pass one or more formatting constants as the uFormat parameter. (If you want to use several formatting styles, you have to combine them with the or operator.)

The most often used formatting values are listed in Table 22-1.

Table 22-1: Several text formatting values

Constant	Meaning
DT_SINGLELINE	Draw text on a single line.
DT_LEFT	Align text to the left.
DT_CENTER	Center text horizontally.
DT_RIGHT	Align text to the right.
DT_VCENTER	Align text vertically.
DT_WORD_ELLIPSIS	Truncate words that don't fit in the specified rectangle and display ellipses.
DT_WORDBREAK	Break words into new lines if they don't fit in the specified rectangle.
DT_CALCRECT	Use this value to calculate how big the rectangle has to be to accommodate the entire string. (If you use this value, the DrawText function will perform the calculation but won't display the string.)

The following figure shows several strings displayed with the DrawText function.

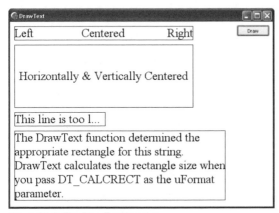

Figure 22-8: The DrawText function

The following listing contains the code that generates the graphical output displayed in Figure 22-8.

Listing 22-8: Using the DrawText function

```
unit Unit1;

interface

uses
```

```
  Windows, Messages, SysUtils, Variants, Classes, Graphics, Controls, Forms,
  Dialogs, XPMan, StdCtrls;

type
  TMainForm = class(TForm)
    DrawButton: TButton;
    XPManifest: TXPManifest;
    procedure DrawButtonClick(Sender: TObject);
  private
    { Private declarations }
  public
    { Public declarations }
  end;

var
  MainForm: TMainForm;

implementation

{$R *.dfm}

procedure ClearCanvas(ACanvas: TCanvas; AColor: TColor);
begin
  with ACanvas do
  begin
    Brush.Style := bsSolid;
    Brush.Color := AColor;

    { ClipRect identifies the section of the canvas that
      needs to be repainted. }
    FillRect(ClipRect);
  end;
end;

procedure TMainForm.DrawButtonClick(Sender: TObject);
var
  rc: TRect;
  msg: string;
begin
  { clear canvas }
  ClearCanvas(Canvas, clWhite);
  Canvas.Font.Name := 'Times New Roman';
  Canvas.Font.Size := 20;
  Canvas.Brush.Style := bsClear;

  { left, centered, and right text }
  rc := Rect(10, 10, 420, 10 + Canvas.TextHeight('W'));
  Canvas.Rectangle(rc);
  DrawText(Canvas.Handle, 'Left', -1, rc, DT_SINGLELINE or DT_LEFT);
  DrawText(Canvas.Handle, 'Centered', -1, rc, DT_SINGLELINE or DT_CENTER);
  DrawText(Canvas.Handle, 'Right', -1, rc, DT_SINGLELINE or DT_RIGHT);

  { center vertically and horizontally }
  rc := Rect(10, rc.Bottom + 10, 420, rc.Bottom + 150);
  Canvas.Rectangle(rc);
```

```
DrawText(Canvas.Handle, 'Horizontally && Vertically Centered', -1,
   rc, DT_SINGLELINE or DT_VCENTER or DT_CENTER);

{ truncate with ellipses }
msg := 'This line is too long and will be truncated.';
rc := Rect(10, rc.Bottom + 10, 220, rc.Bottom + 10 + Canvas.TextHeight('W'));
Canvas.Rectangle(rc);
DrawText(Canvas.Handle, PChar(msg), -1, rc, DT_WORD_ELLIPSIS);

{ draw multiline text }
msg := 'The DrawText function determined the appropriate ' +
   'rectangle for this string. DrawText calculates the ' +
   'rectangle size when you pass DT_CALCRECT as the uFormat parameter.';
rc := Rect(10, rc.Bottom + 10, 500, rc.Bottom + 20);

{ calculate the appropriate rectangle size }
DrawText(Canvas.Handle, PChar(msg), -1, rc, DT_CALCRECT or DT_WORDBREAK);

Canvas.Rectangle(rc);
DrawText(Canvas.Handle, PChar(msg), -1, rc, DT_WORDBREAK);
end;

end.
```

Measuring Text

The TCanvas class has three methods that allow you to determine the width
and height of a string: TextExtent, TextHeight, and TextWidth. While
TextHeight and TextWidth only return the height or width of the string, the
TextExtent function returns both width and height in a tagSize (TSize) record:

```
tagSIZE = record
   cx: Longint; { width }
   cy: Longint; { height }
end;
```

The following figure shows an example application that draws each character
in a string with a different font. This application uses the TextWidth function
to determine where it should draw each character. You can see the code in
Listing 22-9.

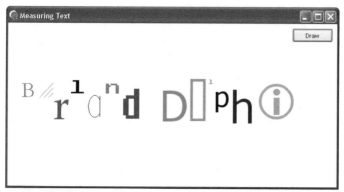

Figure 22-9: Using TextWidth to determine character width

Listing 22-9: Using the TextWidth function

```
procedure TMainForm.DrawButtonClick(Sender: TObject);
const
  s = 'Borland Delphi';
var
  c: Char;
  x: Integer;
begin
  Canvas.Brush.Color := clWhite;
  Canvas.FillRect(ClientRect);

  x := 25;
  for c in s do
  begin
    Canvas.Font.Name := Screen.Fonts[Random(Screen.Fonts.Count)];
    Canvas.Font.Size := Random(60) + 12;
    Canvas.Font.Color := Random(High(TColor));

    Canvas.TextOut(x, 100, c);
    Inc(x, Canvas.TextWidth(c));
  end;
end;
```

Using API Functions to Retrieve a Drawing Surface

Although it's best to use the Canvas to draw both on screen and to the printer, there are situations where you'll need to (or want to) do things the API way. To retrieve a device context, you can use the GetDC API function. The GetDC function accepts a window handle and returns a device context handle that enables you to draw in the client area of the specified window:

```
function GetDC(hWnd: HWND): HDC; stdcall;
```

When you use the GetDC function to retrieve a device context handle, you must release the acquired handle when you no longer need it. To release a device context, call the ReleaseDC function. This function requires you to pass both the device context handle and the handle of the window whose device context you're releasing:

```
function ReleaseDC(hWnd: HWND; hDC: HDC): Integer; stdcall;
```

When you draw using API functions, you'll notice that you have to do much more than when you're using TCanvas methods. For instance, if you want to draw a simple string, you can use the TextOut function, but you have to pass five parameters to the function, not three. Along with the X and Y coordinates and the string, the GDI TextOut function requires two more parameters: the device context handle and the length of the string. The following listing illustrates how to use GDI API functions to display a simple text message on the form.

Listing 22-10: Using API functions to draw on the form

```
procedure TMainForm.GetDCButtonClick(Sender: TObject);
var
  context: HDC;
  msg: string;
begin
  context := GetDC(Handle);
  try
    msg := 'Using GetDC & TextOut API functions.';
    TextOut(context, 20, 20, PChar(msg), Length(msg));
  finally
    { release the device context when you're done }
    ReleaseDC(Handle, context);
  end;
end;
```

You can see the result of the GetDCButtonClick method in Figure 22-10.

Figure 22-10: The result of all that code in Listing 22-10

The GetWindowDC function is another function that allows you to retrieve a device context. Unlike the TCanvas class and the GetDC function that enable you to draw only in the client area of the window, GetWindowDC returns the device context for the entire window including the title bar, menus, and window borders.

The following example shows how to paint in both the client and non-client areas of the window (see Listing 22-11 and Figure 22-11).

Listing 22-11: Using the GetWindowDC function

```
procedure TMainForm.GetWindowDCButtonClick(Sender: TObject);
var
  winContext: HDC;
begin
  winContext := GetWindowDC(Handle);
  try
    { erase the entire window, including borders & the title bar }
    Canvas.Brush.Color := clWebPaleGoldenrod;

    FillRect(winContext, Rect(0, 0, Width, Height),
      Canvas.Brush.Handle);
```

```
  finally
    ReleaseDC(Handle, winContext);
  end;
end;
```

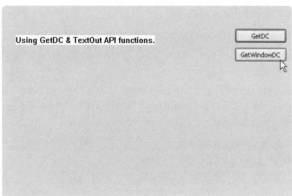

Figure 22-11: Painting in the non-client area of the window

The OnPaint Event

You might have noticed that the graphics displayed in the previous examples look fine as long as you don't move the window, minimize it, or cover it with another window. In fact, if you do almost anything that is either directly or indirectly related to the window, the graphics will either disappear entirely or get messed up (see Figure 22-12).

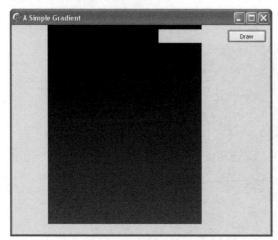

Figure 22-12: A messed-up gradient

To ensure that your graphics remain unscathed by other activities, you have to write your painting code in the OnPaint event handler because the OnPaint event occurs every time the operating system determines that either the entire window or only a portion of the window has to be repainted. You can also manually request a window repaint by calling Invalidate.

Listing 22-12 shows how to draw a simple gradient in the OnPaint event handler.

The easiest way to draw a gradient is to:

1. Draw a black-to-blue, black-to-red, or black-to-green gradient.

2. Draw the gradient in 256 steps, regardless of the width or height of the destination window.

3. Calculate the height or width of the rectangle that needs to be drawn for each color (if the form is 1,000 pixels high, you have to draw a 4-pixel high rectangle for each color).

Listing 22-12: Drawing a simple gradient

```
{ draw a black-to-blue gradient }
procedure TMainForm.FormPaint(Sender: TObject);
var
  rowHeight: Integer;
  i: Integer;
begin
  { calculate the height of each row }
  rowHeight := Succ(ClientHeight div 256);

  { draw 256 differently colored rectangles - the gradient}
  for i := 0 to 255 do
  begin
    Canvas.Brush.Color := RGB(0, 0, i);
    Canvas.FillRect(Rect(0, i * rowHeight, ClientWidth, Succ(i) * rowHeight));
  end;    // for
end;
```

The gradient drawn by the code in Listing 22-12 is displayed in Figure 22-13.

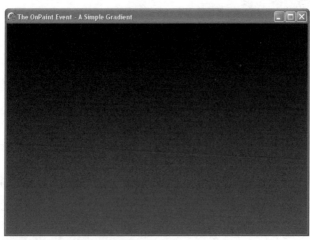

Figure 22-13: A simple gradient

The gradient in Figure 22-13 will be correctly displayed as long as you don't resize the window. If you want to display the gradient correctly while the user is resizing the window, call Invalidate in the form's OnResize event handler to repaint the entire form:

```
procedure TMainForm.FormResize(Sender: TObject);
begin
  Invalidate;
end;
```

When you run this code, you'll notice the flickering introduced by the Invalidate method when you try to resize the window. Some developers try to eliminate the flicker by calling Paint in the OnResize event handler or by assigning the same event handler to both OnPaint and OnResize. You should never do this, especially if your graphics are computationally expensive, because the OnPaint handler will be called twice.

The flickering occurs because Windows erases the background of the window before repainting. So, to avoid the flickering, you simply have to tell Windows to stop erasing the background of the window. To do that, you have to handle the WM_ERASEBKGND message and assign a nonzero value (usually 1) to the message's result. Listing 22-13 shows how to eliminate the flickering problem.

Listing 22-13: Handling WM_ERASEBKGND to eliminate flicker

```
type
  TMainForm = class(TForm)
    procedure FormResize(Sender: TObject);
    procedure FormPaint(Sender: TObject);
  private
    { Private declarations }
  public
    { Public declarations }
    procedure EraseBackground(var Message: TWMEraseBkgnd);
        message WM_ERASEBKGND;
  end;
procedure TMainForm.EraseBackground(var Message: TWMEraseBkgnd);
begin
  Message.Result := 1;
end;

procedure TMainForm.FormResize(Sender: TObject);
begin
  Invalidate;
end;
```

Now that you know how to draw a simple flicker-free gradient, we can create a better one. This "better" way is similar to the last one but uses floating-point values for better quality. It's also much faster because the MoveTo and LineTo procedures draw lines faster than FillRect.

Listing 22-14: Another way to draw gradients

```
type
  TMainForm = class(TForm)
    procedure FormResize(Sender: TObject);
    procedure FormPaint(Sender: TObject);
  private
    { Private declarations }
  public
    { Public declarations }
    procedure EraseBackground(var Message: TWMEraseBkgnd);
        message WM_ERASEBKGND;
  end;

var
  MainForm: TMainForm;

implementation

{$R *.dfm}

procedure TMainForm.FormPaint(Sender: TObject);
var
  colorHeight: Double;
  i: Integer;
begin
  if ClientHeight = 0 then Exit;

  { determine how much a single color should cover }
  colorHeight := 256 / ClientHeight;

  for i := 0 to ClientHeight do
  begin
    { draw a black-to-red gradient }
    Canvas.Pen.Color := RGB(Round(i * colorHeight), 0, 0);
    Canvas.MoveTo(0, i);
    Canvas.LineTo(ClientWidth, i);
  end;        // for i
end;

procedure TMainForm.FormResize(Sender: TObject);
begin
  Invalidate;
end;

procedure TMainForm.EraseBackground(var Message: TWMEraseBkgnd);
begin
  Message.Result := 1;
end;

end.
```

The gradient drawn by the code in Listing 22-14 is displayed in Figure 22-14.

Figure 22-14: Another gradient

Finally, let's create a real gradient that can use custom start and end colors.

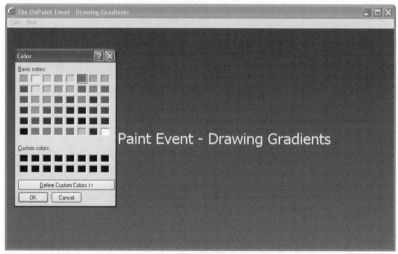

Figure 22-15: Drawing a real gradient with custom colors

The most important thing that you have to do if you want to draw a gradient that uses custom colors is determine how much red, green, and blue to add to the start color at each step. Listing 22-15 contains the source code of the application displayed in Figure 22-15.

Listing 22-15: Drawing gradients that support custom colors

```
unit Unit1;

interface

uses
  Windows, Messages, SysUtils, Variants, Classes, Graphics, Controls, Forms,
  Dialogs, ExtCtrls, XPMan, Menus;

type
  TMainForm = class(TForm)
  private
    { Private declarations }
  public
    { Public declarations }
    procedure EraseBackground(var Message: TWMEraseBkgnd);
        message WM_ERASEBKGND;
  end;

var
  MainForm: TMainForm;

implementation

{$R *.dfm}

procedure TMainForm.FormPaint(Sender: TObject);
var
  startColor: TColor;
  endColor: TColor;
  redStart, blueStart, greenStart: Integer;
  redStep, blueStep, greenStep: Double;
  i: Integer;
  rc: TRect;
begin
  if ClientHeight = 0 then Exit;

  { use colors from the two TColorDialogs }
  startColor := StartColorDialog.Color;
  endColor := EndColorDialog.Color;

  { extract R, G, and B value from the start color }
  redStart := GetRValue(startColor);
  greenStart := GetGValue(startColor);
  blueStart := GetBValue(startColor);

  { determine how much endColor you have to add to startColor each step }
  redStep := (GetRValue(endColor) - redStart) / ClientHeight;
  greenStep := (GetGValue(endColor) - greenStart) / ClientHeight;
  blueStep := (GetBValue(endColor) - blueStart) / ClientHeight;

  for i := 0 to ClientHeight do
  begin
```

```
    Canvas.Pen.Color := RGB(redStart + Round(i * redStep),
      greenStart + Round(i * greenStep), blueStart + Round(i * blueStep));

    Canvas.MoveTo(0, i);
    Canvas.LineTo(ClientWidth, i);
  end;

  { draw the Caption }
  rc := ClientRect;
  Canvas.Brush.Style := bsClear;
  Canvas.Font := FontDialog.Font;
  DrawText(Canvas.Handle, PChar(Caption), -1, rc,
    DT_SINGLELINE or DT_VCENTER or DT_CENTER);
end;

procedure TMainForm.StartColorItemClick(Sender: TObject);
begin
  if StartColorDialog.Execute then Invalidate;
end;

procedure TMainForm.EndColorItemClick(Sender: TObject);
begin
  if EndColorDialog.Execute then Invalidate;
end;

procedure TMainForm.SelectFontItemClick(Sender: TObject);
begin
  if FontDialog.Execute then Invalidate;
end;

procedure TMainForm.ExitItemClick(Sender: TObject);
begin
  Close;
end;

procedure TMainForm.FormResize(Sender: TObject);
begin
  Invalidate;
end;

procedure TMainForm.EraseBackground(var Message: TWMEraseBkgnd);
begin
  Message.Result := 1;
end;

end.
```

Bitmap Images

If you only have to display an image on the form, you can use the TImage component and load the bitmap into its Picture property. But if you want to do anything more complex with bitmap images, you should use the TBitmap class. The TBitmap class is a great class that enables you to load, save, and process bitmap images.

The TCanvas class has several methods that enable you to draw bitmap images. The three most often used methods are Draw, StretchDraw, and CopyRect. The Draw and StretchDraw methods enable you to draw entire images, while the CopyRect method enables you to draw portions of the bitmap, as shown in Figure 22-16.

Figure 22-16: Drawing bitmaps on the canvas

Carefully look at the comments (and the code, of course) in Listing 22-16 to see how to work with and draw bitmap images.

Listing 22-16: Drawing bitmaps

```
unit Unit1;

interface

uses
  Windows, Messages, SysUtils, Variants, Classes, Graphics, Controls, Forms,
  Dialogs;

type
  TMainForm = class(TForm)
    procedure FormPaint(Sender: TObject);
    procedure FormDestroy(Sender: TObject);
    procedure FormCreate(Sender: TObject);
  private
    { Private declarations }
```

```
    FImage: TBitmap;
  public
    { Public declarations }
  end;

var
  MainForm: TMainForm;

implementation

{$R *.dfm}

procedure TMainForm.FormCreate(Sender: TObject);
var
  imagePath: string;
begin
  { create and load the image here, actually - always do as
    much as you can outside of the OnPaint event handler, write
    only what's necessary in OnPaint }
  FImage := TBitmap.Create;
  imagePath := ExtractFilePath(Application.ExeName) + 'image.bmp';
  FImage.LoadFromFile(imagePath);
end;

procedure TMainForm.FormDestroy(Sender: TObject);
begin
  { don't forget to release the bitmap from memory }
  FImage.Free;
end;

procedure TMainForm.FormPaint(Sender: TObject);
var
  srcRect: TRect;
  destRect: TRect;
  txtHeight: Integer;
begin
  with Canvas do
  begin
    Font.Color := clYellow;
    Font.Size := 16;
    txtHeight := TextHeight('Wg');
  end;      // with Canvas

  { draw the entire image }
  Canvas.TextOut(10, 0, 'Draw');
  Canvas.Draw(10, txtHeight, FImage);

  { draw the image stretched in a 400x100 rect }
  Canvas.TextOut(10, FImage.Height + (txtHeight * 2), 'StretchDraw');
  srcRect := Rect(10, FImage.Height + txtHeight * 3,
    410, FImage.Height + (txtHeight * 3) + 100);
  Canvas.StretchDraw(srcRect, FImage);

  { draw the 100x100 top-left rect of the image }
  Canvas.TextOut(FImage.Width + 20, 0, 'CopyRect');
```

```
  srcRect := Rect(0, 0, 100, 100);
  destRect := Rect(FImage.Width + 20,
    txtHeight, FImage.Width + 120, txtHeight + 100);
  Canvas.CopyRect(destRect, FImage.Canvas, srcRect);
end;

end.
```

Simple Animation

The easiest way to perform something after a specific interval of time has passed is to use the TTimer component (System category). If the TTimer's Enabled property is set to True, the TTimer fires the OnTimer event after a specific amount of time has passed. The time interval (in milliseconds) is determined by the Interval property.

The following example uses the TTimer component to continuously display a series of colored rectangles.

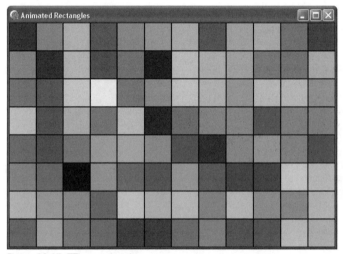

Figure 22-17: TTimer animation

The Interval property of the timer is set to 100 to have the OnTimer event occur every 100 milliseconds. Listing 22-17 shows the code that displays the rectangles displayed in Figure 22-17.

Listing 22-17: Randomly drawing colored rectangles

```
procedure TMainForm.AnimatedDraw(Sender: TObject);
var
  i,j: Integer;
begin
  for i := 0 to (ClientWidth div 50) do
    for j := 0 to (ClientHeight div 50) do
    begin
      Canvas.Brush.Color := RGB(Random(255), Random(255), Random(255));
      Canvas.Rectangle(i * 50, j * 50, (i + 1) * 50, (j + 1) * 50);
```

```
    end;
end;
```

The TTimer component is not suitable for high-quality, accurately timed animation because it has a resolution of ~50 milliseconds. One way to measure time more accurately is to use the Windows API GetTickCount function (declared in the Windows unit).

The GetTickCount function retrieves the number of milliseconds that have elapsed since the system was started. So all you have to do to determine a specific interval is to save the beginning time in a variable and simply wait until a desired amount of time has passed. In the following example, the FTick variable (of type Cardinal) holds the start value:

```
if GetTickCount > FTick + 40 {25 fps} then
begin
  { your code here }

  FTick := GetTickCount;
end;      // if GetTickCount
```

Drawing Snow

Now we're going to create a simple application that simulates snow falling (see Figure 22-18). Unfortunately, I didn't have a snowflake image, so I used a smiley.

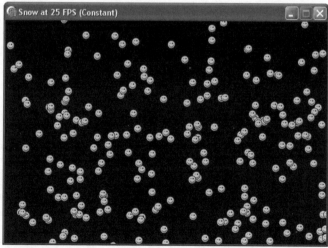

Figure 22-18: "Snow"

The application that we're going to create should work at 25 frames per second and use double-buffering to remove flickering. Double-buffering is a drawing technique that is often used, especially when drawing animated graphics, to eliminate flicker. Double-buffering involves drawing on two different surfaces: the back buffer and the screen. Double-buffering is implemented by:

■ Drawing everything on the back buffer (an off-screen image)

■ Displaying the back buffer onscreen when you're finished drawing

The first thing we have to do is declare the variables that we're going to use in this application. We need a back buffer bitmap, a snowflake bitmap, and an integer variable that will be used for timing. We also need a TPoint array to contain the coordinates of the snowflakes. Here are the variable declarations:

```
type
  TMainForm = class(TForm)
  private
    { Private declarations }
    Flake: TBitmap;                { the snowflake (smiley bitmap) }
    FBuffer: TBitmap;              { the back buffer }
    FTick: Cardinal;              { used for animation }
    Snow: array[1..255] of TPoint; { let's work with 255 snowflakes }
  public
    { Public declarations }
  end;
```

Now we have to create the back buffer and the snowflake images in the OnCreate event handler and also write an OnDestroy event handler to remove these images from memory when we're done.

Listing 22-18: Preparing the back buffer and randomizing the flakes

```
procedure TMainForm.FormCreate(Sender: TObject);
var
  i: Integer;
begin
  { create and set up the back buffer bitmap }
  FBuffer := TBitmap.Create;
  { make the back buffer the same size as the form - very important}
  FBuffer.Width := Self.ClientWidth;
  FBuffer.Height := Self.ClientHeight;

  { create and load the snowflake image }
  Flake := TBitmap.Create;
  Flake.LoadFromFile('flake.bmp');
  Flake.Transparent := True;

  { set random flake coordinates; Y coordinates have to
    be negative to have the flakes appear at the top
    of the form at startup }
  for i := Low(Snow) to High(Snow) do
  begin
    Snow[i].Y := -Random(Self.ClientHeight);
    Snow[i].X := Random(Self.ClientWidth) + Flake.Width;
  end;

  { start timing }
  FTick := GetTickCount;
end;

procedure TMainForm.FormDestroy(Sender: TObject);
begin
```

```
{ remove the sprite and the back buffer from memory }
Flake.Free;
FBuffer.Free;
end;
```

All we have to do now is create one procedure that will draw the snowflakes and another that will call this procedure every 40 milliseconds to achieve the desired 25 FPS animation.

Animating a snowflake is not hard at all. You only have to do the following:

■ Make the snowflake fall down by constantly increasing its Y coordinate by a couple of pixels (randomly is best).

■ Have the snowflake randomly move left or right.

■ When the snowflake reaches the ground, set its Y coordinate to 0 or less to make it fall again (if you want to, of course).

Listing 22-19 contains the DrawFlakes method that draws all flakes on the back buffer and the back buffer on screen. The DrawFlakes method uses a constant array of values to move the flakes, rather than the Random or RandomRange functions, because using the constant array results in better movement.

Listing 22-19: Drawing the snowflakes

```
procedure TMainForm.DrawFlakes;
const
  RANDOM_MOVES: array[0..5, 0..2] of Integer = ((1, -2, -1),
    (-1, 0, 1), (-1, 2, 1), (2, 1, -2), (-3, 1, 3), (2, 0, -2));
var
  i: Integer;
begin
  { clear the back buffer }
  FBuffer.Canvas.Brush.Color := Color;
  FBuffer.Canvas.FillRect(FBuffer.Canvas.ClipRect);

  Randomize;

  for i := Low(Snow) to High(Snow) do
  begin
    { select a new horizontal position for each snowflake }
    Snow[i].X := Snow[i].X + RANDOM_MOVES[Random(5), Random(2)];

    { use Abs to get positive values and to make the flakes fall }
    Snow[i].Y := Snow[i].Y + Abs(RANDOM_MOVES[Random(5), Random(2)]);

    { if a flake reaches the end, recycle it }
    if Snow[i].Y > Self.ClientHeight then
      Snow[i].Y := -(Random(ClientHeight) div 2);

    { don't let the snowflake leave the screen horizontally }
    if Snow[i].X < 0 then
      Snow[i].X := 0
    else if (Snow[i].X + Flake.Width) > Self.ClientWidth then
      Snow[i].X := Self.ClientWidth - Flake.Width;
```

```
  { draw the flake on the back buffer }
  FBuffer.Canvas.Draw(Snow[i].X, Snow[i].Y, Flake);
end;

{ finally, display the back buffer }
Canvas.Draw(0, 0, FBuffer);
end;
```

Now it's time to write the animation code. The best place for this code is in the application's OnIdle event handler. The OnIdle event is perfect because it allows us, by passing False to the Done parameter, to get as much CPU time as possible. Inside the OnIndle event handler, we can call the GetTickCount function to determine how much time has passed and call DrawFlakes to display the flakes.

First, drop a TApplicationEvents component on the Designer Surface and then write the code in Listing 22-20.

Listing 22-20: Animating the snowflakes

```
procedure TMainForm.ApplicationEventsIdle(Sender: TObject; var Done: Boolean);
begin
  { set Done to False to keep OnIdle working constantly }
  Done := False;

  { if enough time has passed, call DrawFlakes to update the screen }
  if GetTickCount > FTick + 40 {25 fps} then
  begin
    DrawFlakes;

    { remember the time the frame was drawn }
    FTick := GetTickCount;
  end;        // if GetTickCount
end;
```

Drawing on the Desktop

If you want to draw on the desktop, you'll have to use several GDI functions, especially if you want to do what we are about to do: update the previous example and draw the snowflakes on the desktop. In addition, we are going to use the snowflakes to draw an image on the desktop (see Figure 22-19).

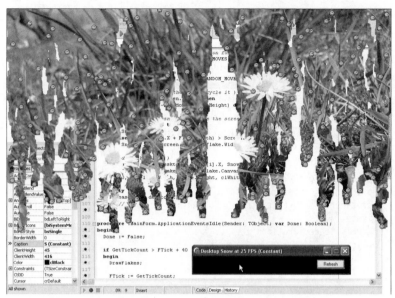

Figure 22-19: Drawing on the desktop

To successfully update the previous example, you have to know how do to the following:

- How to use the GetDC function to retrieve the desktop's device context
- How to use the BitBlt function to draw images on the screen
- How to use the TransparentBlt function to draw images transparently (works only on Win98, Win2K, and later versions)
- How to use the InvalidateRect function to refresh a window

To retrieve the desktop's device context, call the GetDC function and pass 0 as the hWnd parameter. Don't forget to call ReleaseDC to free the device context when you're done using it:

```
var
  desktopDC: HDC;
begin
  desktopDC := GetDC(0);
  try
  finally
    ReleaseDC(0, desktopDC);
  end; // try
end;
```

If you want to display a bitmap as fast as possible, you should use the BitBlt function. The BitBlt function requires you to pass a lot of parameters: handles for the destination and the source device contexts, four destination rectangle coordinates, two source coordinates, and the raster operation code:

```
function BitBlt(DestDC: HDC; X, Y, Width, Height: Integer;
  SrcDC: HDC; XSrc, YSrc: Integer; Rop: DWORD): BOOL; stdcall;
```

The Rop (raster operation code) parameter defines how the image pixels are combined with the source pixels (inverted, merged, etc.). There are several values that you can pass as the Rop parameter, but we're only going to use the SRCCOPY constant. The SRCCOPY constant is used when you want to copy the source pixels directly to the destination rectangle.

Here's a simple example that illustrates how to use the BitBlt function to display a bitmap image on the form.

Listing 22-21: Using the BitBlt function to draw bitmaps

```
type
  TMainForm = class(TForm)
    procedure FormPaint(Sender: TObject);
    procedure FormDestroy(Sender: TObject);
    procedure FormCreate(Sender: TObject);
  private
    { Private declarations }
  public
    { Public declarations }
    B: TBitmap;
  end;

var
  MainForm: TMainForm;

implementation

{$R *.dfm}

procedure TMainForm.FormCreate(Sender: TObject);
begin
  B := TBitmap.Create;
  B.LoadFromFile(ExtractFilePath(Application.ExeName) + 'image.bmp');
end;

procedure TMainForm.FormDestroy(Sender: TObject);
begin
  B.Free;
end;

procedure TMainForm.FormPaint(Sender: TObject);
begin
  { draw the entire image in the top-left corner of the form }
  BitBlt(Canvas.Handle, 0, 0, B.Width, B.Height,
    B.Canvas.Handle, 0, 0, SRCCOPY);
end;

end.
```

The parameter list of the TransparentBlt function is very similar to the parameter list of the BitBlt function. The only big difference is in the last parameter. The TransparentBlt function requires you to pass the color that will be treated as transparent rather than the raster operation code. Here's the declaration of the TransparentBlt function:

```
function TransparentBlt(DC: HDC; p2, p3, p4, p5: Integer; DC6: HDC;
  p7, p8, p9, p10: Integer; p11: UINT): BOOL; stdcall;
```

The InvalidateRect function can be used to invalidate a portion of or the entire window. This function accepts three parameters: the window's handle, a rectangle that defines the portion of the window that needs to be refreshed (pass nil to refresh the entire window), and a Boolean value that specifies whether or not the window's background should be erased. Here's the declaration of the InvalidateRect function:

```
function InvalidateRect(hWnd: HWND; lpRect: PRect; bErase: BOOL): BOOL;
stdcall;
```

Now that you know how these functions work, you can take a look at Listing 22-22 to see how to draw snowflakes on the desktop.

Listing 22-22: Drawing snowflakes on the desktop

```
unit Unit1;

interface

uses
  Windows, Messages, SysUtils, Variants, Classes, Graphics, Controls,
  Forms, Dialogs, ExtCtrls, AppEvnts, XPMan, StdCtrls;

type
  TMainForm = class(TForm)
    ApplicationEvents: TApplicationEvents;
    RefreshButton: TButton;
    XPManifest: TXPManifest;
    procedure RefreshButtonClick(Sender: TObject);
    procedure ApplicationEventsIdle(Sender: TObject; var Done: Boolean);
    procedure FormCreate(Sender: TObject);
    procedure FormDestroy(Sender: TObject);
  private
    { Private declarations }
    Flake: TBitmap;
    FBuffer: TBitmap;
  public
    { Public declarations }
    FTick: Cardinal;
    Snow: array[1..255] of TPoint;
    procedure DrawFlakes;
  end;

var
  MainForm: TMainForm;

implementation

{$R *.dfm}

procedure TMainForm.FormCreate(Sender: TObject);
var
  i: Integer;
```

```
begin
  { create the back buffer and use it to store
    the image the flakes will draw on the desktop }
  FBuffer := TBitmap.Create;
  FBuffer.LoadFromFile(ExtractFilePath(Application.ExeName) + 'back.bmp');

  { create and load the snowflake }
  Flake := TBitmap.Create;
  Flake.LoadFromFile('flake.bmp');

  for i := Low(Snow) to High(Snow) do
  begin
    Snow[i].Y := -Random(Screen.Height);
    Snow[i].X := Random(Screen.Width) + Flake.Width;
  end;

  { start timing }
  FTick := GetTickCount;
end;

procedure TMainForm.FormDestroy(Sender: TObject);
begin
  Flake.Free;
  FBuffer.Free;

  { refresh the desktop }
  InvalidateRect(0, nil, True);
end;

procedure TMainForm.DrawFlakes;
const
  RANDOM_MOVES: array[0..5, 0..2] of Integer = ((1, -2, -1),
    (-1, 0, 1), (-1, 2, 1), (2, 1, -2), (-3, 1, 3), (2, 0, -2));
var
  i: Integer;
  desktopDC: HDC;
begin
  { retrieve the desktop device context }
  desktopDC := GetDC(0);
  try
    for i := Low(Snow) to High(Snow) do
    begin
      { modify the portion of the desktop the flake passed }
        BitBlt(desktopDC, Snow[i].X, Snow[i].Y, Flake.Width,
        Flake.Height, FBuffer.Canvas.Handle, Snow[i].X, Snow[i].Y, SRCCOPY);

      { select a new horizontal position for the snowflake }
      Snow[i].X := Snow[i].X + RANDOM_MOVES[Random(5), Random(2)];

      { make the snowflake fall down }
      Snow[i].Y := Snow[i].Y + Abs(RANDOM_MOVES[Random(5), Random(2)]);
```

```
      { if flake reaches the end, recycle it }
      if Snow[i].Y > Screen.Height then
        Snow[i].Y := -(Random(Screen.Height) div 2);

      { don't let the snowflake leave the screen }
      if Snow[i].X < 0 then
        Snow[i].X := 0
      else if (Snow[i].X + Flake.Width) > Screen.Width then
        Snow[i].X := Screen.Width - Flake.Width;

      { draw the flake }
      TransparentBlt(desktopDC, Snow[i].X, Snow[i].Y,
        Flake.Width, Flake.Height, Flake.Canvas.Handle,
        0, 0, Flake.Width, Flake.Height, clWhite);
    end;        // for
  finally
    ReleaseDC(0, desktopDC);
  end;          // try
end;

procedure TMainForm.ApplicationEventsIdle(Sender: TObject; var Done: Boolean);
begin
  Done := False;

  if GetTickCount > FTick + 40 {25 fps} then
  begin
    DrawFlakes;
    FTick := GetTickCount;
  end;            // if GetTickCount
end;

procedure TMainForm.RefreshButtonClick(Sender: TObject);
begin
  InvalidateRect(0, nil, False);
end;

end.
```

Chapter 23

Creating Win32 API Applications

Not only does Delphi allow you to build applications using the VCL framework for Win32 and the VCL.NET framework for the .NET platform, but it also allows you to create pure Win32 API applications. In this chapter you'll see how to create and work with windows at the API level, which is something that you should at least begin to understand if you want to create your own components, great VCL applications, or multimedia applications and games using OpenGL or DirectX.

Creating an API Application

The easiest way to begin creating an API application in Delphi is to create a console application project and then make the following changes to the generated source code:

1. Remove the $APPTYPE compiler directive.

2. Change the uses list from "uses SysUtils;" to "uses Windows;".

Now that you've made these changes, you are ready to create your first API application. The simplest API application you can create is an application that displays a message box to the user. To display a message box in an API application, you should use the MessageBox function declared in the Windows unit:

```
function MessageBox(hWnd: HWND; lpText,
  lpCaption: PChar; uType: UINT): Integer; stdcall;
```

The following listing shows how to display a message box using the MessageBox function. Figure 23-1 shows how the API application looks at run time.

Listing 23-1: A very simple API application

```
program Generic;

uses
  Windows;

begin
  MessageBox(0, 'Hello from an API application!', 'Hello', MB_OK);
end.
```

Figure 23-1: Our first API application

Although a real API application is more complex than the one we just created, this application allows us to note several differences between VCL and API applications:

- The Designer Surface is not available when you're creating API applications, so you have to do everything in code.

- API applications require you to write a lot more code than VCL applications, as you'll see shortly.

- If you look at the produced executable, you'll notice that API applications are smaller in size than their VCL counterparts but immensely harder to write (an API application that displays an empty window compiles to 15 KB, while a VCL application that does the same compiles to 350 KB).

Now it's time to create a real API application by doing the following:

1. Create the main window.

2. Create a procedure that receives and processes all messages sent to the window.

3. Enter the message loop.

Windows are, at the API level, created with a call to the CreateWindow or the CreateWindowEx function. Window creation with these functions is very simple if you're creating child windows like buttons, list boxes, or other, already registered, window classes. But when you're creating the main window, you have to do the following:

1. Create the window's class by defining the window's properties like icon, background color, menu, etc.

2. Register the window's class since the CreateWindow function only works with registered classes.

3. Finally, call the CreateWindow or the CreateWindowEx function to create the window.

Defining and Registering the Window Class

Creating a window class is as easy as filling in a WNDCLASS record. The WNDCLASS record is declared in the Windows unit and looks like this:

```
WNDCLASSA = tagWNDCLASSA;

tagWNDCLASSA = packed record
    style: UINT;
    lpfnWndProc: TFNWndProc;
    cbClsExtra: Integer;
    cbWndExtra: Integer;
    hInstance: HINST;
    hIcon: HICON;
    hCursor: HCURSOR;
    hbrBackground: HBRUSH;
    lpszMenuName: PAnsiChar;
    lpszClassName: PAnsiChar;
  end;
```

Although the WNDCLASS record has a large number of fields, only two are extremely important: the lpfnWndProc and the lpszClassName fields. The lpfnWndProc field must point to the window procedure (the procedure that receives and processes messages) and the lpszClassName field is the name under which the window class is to be registered.

The style field is used to define the class's style. The constants that can be assigned to this field start with CS_. In the Windows unit, there are several of these constants, but you'll most often want to use CS_VREDRAW and CS_HREDRAW, which cause the window to be repainted when its size is updated. There are also three more pretty interesting, and sometimes useful, constants: CS_DBLCLKS, CS_NOCLOSE, and CS_DROPSHADOW. The CS_DBLCLKS constant enables the window to process double clicks; the CS_NOCLOSE constant disables the Close button on the window's title bar, the Close option on the window's menu, and the Alt+F4 shortcut; and the CS_DROPSHADOW constant displays the shadow under the window (note that the application will fail to run on Windows 98 if you use the CS_DROPSHADOW style). If you want to assign several styles to the window class, combine them with the Boolean or operator. Here's the code so far:

```
program Generic;

uses
  Windows, Messages;

var
  wc: WNDCLASS;

begin
  wc.style := CS_VREDRAW or CS_HREDRAW or CS_DROPSHADOW;
end.
```

The lpfnWndProc field is extremely important as it links the window with the window procedure that processes its messages. The window procedure is actually a function that must accept four parameters and return an integer result. The parameters are: the handle to the window, the message, and the wParam and LParam parameters of the message.

Here's the empty skeleton of the window procedure and the line of code that assigns the window procedure to the lpfnWndProc field of the window class:

```
function WindowProc(Wnd: HWND; Msg, WParam, LParam: LongInt): LongInt; stdcall;
begin
end;

wc.lpfnWndProc := @WindowProc;
```

The next two fields can be used to allocate extra bytes in the window class. Since this is rarely done, feel free to set both of these fields to 0:

```
wc.cbClsExtra := 0;
wc.cbWndExtra := 0;
```

The hInstance field needs to point to the application instance. You only have to assign the global HInstance variable to this field and you're done:

```
wc.hInstance := HInstance;
```

The hIcon field specifies the window's icon. If you set this value to 0, the operating system displays the default icon. You can also assign a custom or a standard icon to the window by using the LoadIcon function:

```
function LoadIcon(hInstance: HINST; lpIconName: PChar): HICON; stdcall;
```

To load a standard system icon, pass 0 as the hInstance parameter and pass one of the IDI_ constants as the lpIconName parameter:

```
IDI_APPLICATION = MakeIntResource(32512);
IDI_HAND = MakeIntResource(32513);
IDI_QUESTION = MakeIntResource(32514);
IDI_EXCLAMATION = MakeIntResource(32515);
IDI_ASTERISK = MakeIntResource(32516);
IDI_WINLOGO = MakeIntResource(32517);
IDI_WARNING = IDI_EXCLAMATION;
IDI_ERROR = IDI_HAND;
IDI_INFORMATION = IDI_ASTERISK;

wc.hIcon := LoadIcon(0, IDI_INFORMATION);
```

The hCursor field defines the mouse cursor that will be displayed when the mouse is over the window. To assign a standard cursor to the window, you need to call the LoadCursor function, pass 0 as the hInstance parameter, and pass one of the IDC_ constants as the second parameter. The following line loads the standard arrow cursor:

```
wc.hCursor := LoadCursor(0, IDC_ARROW);
```

The hbrBackground field is a handle to a brush that is used to fill the client area of the window (the background color). If you want to use system colors, you can use the COLOR_ constants like COLOR_BTNFACE or COLOR_

DESKTOP. If you use the COLOR_ constants, you have to add 1 to the selected color:

```
wc.hbrBackground := COLOR_BTNFACE + 1;
```

The operating system also has several stock brushes that you can use here. To do so, you have to call the GetStockObject function and pass the appropriate constant, such as WHITE_BRUSH or BLACK_BRUSH:

```
wc.hbrBackground := GetStockObject(BLACK_BRUSH);
```

The lpszMenuName field can be used to load a main menu from a resource file. Since we haven't yet created a resource file that contains a menu, you can set the lpszMenuName field to nil:

```
wc.lpszMenuName := nil;
```

Finally, to completely define the window class, you have to assign a class name to the lpszClassName field. Because we're going to use the same class name in the call to CreateWindow, it's best to create a constant for the class name. The class name can be anything you like, but you should at least try to give it a name that's somewhat related to the application you're creating:

```
const
  MY_CLASS = 'DelphiAPIWindow';
  ...

wc.lpszClassName := MY_CLASS;
```

Now that you've defined the window class, you have to register it by passing it to the RegisterClass function. If the RegisterClass function fails to register the class, it returns 0. So, before creating the main window based on your class, you should check the RegisterClass function's return value and terminate the application if the return value is 0:

```
if RegisterClass(wc) = 0 then Exit;
```

Creating and Displaying the Main Window

To create the window that you've described using the WNDCLASS record, you have to call the CreateWindow function. If you want to create windows with the CreateWindowEx function, you have to use the WNDCLASSEX record.

Here's the declaration of the CreateWindow function:

```
function CreateWindow(lpClassName: PChar; lpWindowName: PChar;
  dwStyle: DWORD; X, Y, nWidth, nHeight: Integer; hWndParent: HWND;
  hMenu: HMENU; hInstance: HINST; lpParam: Pointer): HWND;
```

And here's what you have to do when you're calling the CreateWindow function to create the window:

1. Pass the name of the registered class as the lpClassName parameter.
2. Pass the window's caption as the lpWindowName parameter.

3. Define the window style by passing one of the WS_ constants as the dwStyle parameter (for instance, the WS_OVERLAPPEDWINDOW constant creates a standard resizable window).

4. Set the location and the size of the window with the X, Y, nWidth, and nHeight parameters. (If you want, you can pass CW_USEDEFAULT to all four parameters to let the OS position and resize your window.)

5. Pass the handle of the parent window as the hWndParent parameter. (If you're creating the main window, pass 0.)

6. Pass 0 as the hMenu parameter since the window has no menu.

7. Pass the global HInstance variable as the hInstance parameter.

8. Pass nil as the lpParam parameter.

After a call to the CreateWindow function, you still have to call two functions to display the window: ShowWindow and UpdateWindow. The ShowWindow function is used to specify how the window is to be shown, and the UpdateWindow function updates the client area of the window and forces it to display itself:

```
MainWnd: HWND;
  ...

MainWnd := CreateWindow(MY_CLASS, 'Win32 API Application',
   WS_OVERLAPPEDWINDOW, Integer(CW_USEDEFAULT), Integer(CW_USEDEFAULT),
   Integer(CW_USEDEFAULT), Integer(CW_USEDEFAULT), 0, 0, HInstance, nil);

ShowWindow(MainWnd, SW_SHOWNORMAL);
UpdateWindow(MainWnd);
```

If you run the application now, you'll see the main window for a moment before the application closes and produces a memory leak (because we haven't yet written any code that destroys the main window). To create a completely functional API application, we still have to do two more things: create and enter the message loop, and fully implement the window procedure.

Entering the Message Loop

The message loop is a simple mechanism that retrieves messages and sends them to the application. It is an infinite while loop that keeps the application running until we close it. The message loop is actually terminated by a WM_QUIT message.

To create the message loop, you have to declare a variable of type TMsg to store the received message and then write the following while loop:

```
var
  Msg: TMsg;
  ...

while GetMessage(Msg, 0, 0, 0) do
```

```
begin
  TranslateMessage(Msg);
  DispatchMessage(Msg);
end;
```

The GetMessage function retrieves messages from the application's message queue and stores them in the Msg variable. If the GetMessage function retrieves a WM_QUIT message, the application terminates. If the GetMessage function retrieves any other message, the message is passed to the TranslateMessage and DispatchMessage functions for processing.

The TranslateMessage function actually does very little processing. It is simply meant to translate virtual keyboard codes to more understandable characters.

The DispatchMessage function is much more important. The job of this function is to dispatch the received message to the window procedure, where the application's logic resides. The application's window procedure is its heart, and everything that you've done so far is utility code that can be reused in all subsequent API applications.

The Window Procedure

Finally, the last thing to do is write the implementation of the window procedure. There are two things that you have to do in the window procedure:

1. Respond to whatever message you need.

2. Call the DefWindowProc function for messages that you didn't process. (This function provides default processing for messages not processed by the window procedure.)

To create a fully functional application, you'll have to process at least the WM_DESTROY message, which is sent to the application when the user selects Close to terminate the application. In response to the WM_DESTROY message, you have to call the PostQuitMessage function to post the WM_QUIT message and actually terminate the application:

```
function WindowProc(Wnd: HWND; Msg, WParam, LParam: LongInt): LongInt; stdcall;
begin
  { most messages require you to return 0 }
  Result := 0;

  case Msg of
    WM_DESTROY: begin
      PostQuitMessage(0);
    end;        // WM_DESTROY
  else
    Result := DefWindowProc(Wnd, Msg, WParam, LParam);
  end;          // case
end;
```

The Entire Application

Now that you've seen all the pieces that make up an API application, it's time to see the complete code for the API application. The source code is displayed in Listing 23-2.

Listing 23-2: The simple API application that only displays the main window

```
program Generic;

uses
  Windows, Messages;

const
  MY_CLASS = 'DelphiAPIWindow';

var
  Msg: TMsg;
  MainWnd: HWND;
  wc: WNDCLASS;

function WindowProc(Wnd: HWND; Msg, WParam, LParam: LongInt): LongInt; stdcall;
begin
  { most messages require you to return 0 }
  Result := 0;

  case Msg of
    WM_DESTROY: begin
      PostQuitMessage(0);
    end;       // WM_DESTROY
  else
    Result := DefWindowProc(Wnd, Msg, WParam, LParam);
  end;         // case
end;


begin
  wc.style := CS_VREDRAW or CS_HREDRAW;
  wc.lpfnWndProc := @WindowProc;
  wc.cbClsExtra := 0;
  wc.cbWndExtra := 0;
  wc.hInstance := HInstance;
  wc.hIcon := LoadIcon(0, IDI_INFORMATION);
  wc.hCursor := LoadCursor(0, IDC_ARROW);
  wc.hbrBackground := COLOR_BTNFACE + 1;
  wc.lpszMenuName := nil;
  wc.lpszClassName := MY_CLASS;

  if RegisterClass(wc) = 0 then Exit;

  { create the window }
  MainWnd := CreateWindow(MY_CLASS, 'Win32 API Application',
    WS_OVERLAPPEDWINDOW, Integer(CW_USEDEFAULT), Integer(CW_USEDEFAULT),
    Integer(CW_USEDEFAULT), Integer(CW_USEDEFAULT), 0, 0, HInstance, nil);
```

```
{ display the main window }
ShowWindow(MainWnd, SW_SHOWNORMAL);
UpdateWindow(MainWnd);

{ message loop }
while GetMessage(Msg, 0, 0, 0) do
begin
  TranslateMessage(Msg);
  DispatchMessage(Msg);
end;
end.
```

The API application is displayed in Figure 23-2.

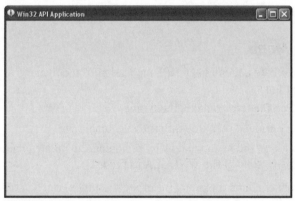

Figure 23-2: The API application

Working with Child Controls

In this portion of the chapter, we're going to use the API application template developed at the beginning of the chapter to create an API application that allows the user to view icons stored in executable files and dynamic link libraries. While creating this application, you'll learn how to do the following:

- Create resource files
- Specify a custom icon for the executable file
- Create a main menu
- Create child controls
- Use common dialog boxes
- Properly draw to the window in response to the WM_PAINT message
- Extract icons from other executables and dynamic link libraries
- Use an external manifest to enable child controls to use XP visual styles

Before we start creating the application, you should take a look at the final product. It is displayed in Figure 23-3.

Figure 23-3: The Icon Viewer

Creating the Main Menu

It's actually easy to create a menu in an API application. You only have to do these three simple things:

1. Create a resource file that contains the menu.
2. Link the aforementioned resource into the executable file.
3. Display the menu on the main window by assigning the menu's name to the lpszMenuName field of the WNDCLASS record.

The resource file that contains the menu (or other resources) can be created in any text editor, as long as you save the resource file with the .rc extension. The resource file that contains the main menu of the Icon Viewer is called Menu.rc and its contents are displayed in Listing 23-3.

Listing 23-3: The Menu.rc resource file

```
Main_Menu MENU
{
   POPUP "&File"
   {
      MENUITEM "&Open...", 101
      MENUITEM SEPARATOR
      MENUITEM "E&xit", 102
   }
}
```

It is clearly visible that the statements in the Menu.rc file define a simple File menu that has two commands (Open and Exit) and a separator between them. The numbers 101 and 102 at the end of the MENUITEM statements are ID numbers, which are used in the window procedure to identify the selected menu item.

Now that you've created the resource file, you have to compile it into a .res file so that it can be linked into the executable file. To compile the .rc file, you have to use the Resource Compiler (brcc32.exe). To avoid typing the command to compile the resource file over and over again, you should create a batch file to perform the compilation of the resource. Here are the contents of the CompileMenu.bat file that can be used to compile the Menu.rc resource file:

```
brcc32 Menu.rc
```

To use the menu from the compiled Menu.res file, you have to include the Menu.res file into the executable using the $R compiler directive and you have to assign the menu's name to the lpszMenuName field of the WNDCLASS:

```
{$R Menu.res}
wc.lpszMenuName := 'Main_Menu'; { load the menu from the resource }
```

If you've done everything correctly and recompiled the application, you should be able to see the File menu on your main window.

Figure 23-4: The main menu loaded from the resource file

Creating Buttons

Buttons, like all other windows, can be created with the CreateWindow function. Actually, there are several predefined classes that can be created with the CreateWindow function. These are: BUTTON, COMBOBOX, EDIT, LIST-BOX, RICHEDIT_CLASS, SCROLLBAR, and STATIC (label).

When you're creating buttons (or other windows), you have to declare an HWND variable that will hold the button's handle and preferably declare a constant with the unique ID value for the button. To create a standard button, you have to call the CreateWindow function and pass the following parameters:

- Pass "BUTTON" as the lpClassName parameter.
- Pass a WS_CHILD, WS_VISIBLE, BS_PUSHBUTTON, or BS_TEXT combination as the dwStyle parameter to create a child window that is initially visible, looks like a standard button, and displays text on its surface.
- Pass the MainWnd variable as the hWndParent parameter to create the button as a child window of the main window.
- Pass the unique ID value of the button as the hMenu parameter.

The following listing shows how to create the Previous and Next buttons shown in Figure 23-3.

Listing 23-4: Creating the Previous and Next buttons

```
const
  PREV_BUTTON = 103;
  NEXT_BUTTON = 104;

var
  prevButton: HWND; { handle of the Previous button }
  nextButton: HWND; { handle of the Next button }
...
  prevButton := CreateWindow('BUTTON', 'Previous', WS_CHILD or
    WS_VISIBLE or BS_PUSHBUTTON or BS_TEXT, 10, 115, 75, 25,
    MainWnd, PREV_BUTTON, HInstance, nil);

  nextButton := CreateWindow('BUTTON', 'Next', WS_CHILD or
    WS_VISIBLE or BS_PUSHBUTTON or BS_TEXT, 160, 115, 75, 25,
    MainWnd, NEXT_BUTTON, HInstance, nil);
```

Handling the WM_COMMAND Message

To implement the functionality of the File menu commands and the two buttons, we have to handle the WM_COMMAND message in the application's window procedure. The control that sends the WM_COMMAND message is specified in the wParam parameter of the message. Thus, to close the application when the user selects File ➢ Exit, you have to write something like this:

```
const
  FILE_EXIT = 102;
  {this must match the menu item ID specified in the .rc file }
...
function WindowProc(Wnd: HWND; Msg, WParam, LParam: LongInt): LongInt; stdcall;
begin
  Result := 0;

  case Msg of
    WM_COMMAND: begin
      case WParam of
        FILE_EXIT: SendMessage(MainWnd, WM_CLOSE, 0, 0);
      end;      // case WParam
    end;        // WM_COMMAND
  end;          // case
end;
```

Displaying the Open Dialog Box

To enable the user to extract icons from an EXE file or a DLL, we first have to display the Open dialog box to enable the user to select a file. The API way to display an Open dialog box is somewhat harder than using the TOpenDialog component. To display the Open dialog box in an API application, you have to do the following:

1. Add the CommDlg unit to the application's uses list to access the necessary records and functions.

2. Fill an OPENFILENAME record with the appropriate data.

3. Call the GetOpenFileName function to display the Open dialog box and retrieve the file name.

The following listing contains a function that displays the Open dialog box and returns the selected file name if the user selects OK or an empty string if the user selects Cancel.

Listing 23-5: Displaying the open dialog box

```
function OpenFileDialog: string;
var
  ofn: OPENFILENAME;
  fileName: array[0..MAX_PATH] of Char;
const
  FILTER = 'Executable Files' + #0 + '*.exe' + #0 +
    'Dynamic Link Libraries' + #0 + '*.dll' + #0#0;
begin
  fileName := '';
  ZeroMemory(@ofn, SizeOf(OPENFILENAME));
  ofn.lStructSize := SizeOf(OPENFILENAME);
  ofn.hWndOwner := MainWnd;
  ofn.lpstrFilter := FILTER;
  ofn.lpstrFile := fileName;
  ofn.nMaxFile := MAX_PATH;

  GetOpenFileName(ofn);
  Result := string(fileName);
end;
```

The OPENFILENAME record is pretty big and has a lot of fields that are not needed in this application. The ZeroMemory function is used here to set these unused fields to 0.

When displaying the Open dialog box you must specify a valid buffer in the lpstrFile parameter that will receive the file name and properly set the hWndOwner field. To hide unneeded items in the dialog box, you should also specify a valid filter string.

If you look at the local FILTER constant, you'll notice that the filter string in an API application differs from the filter string used by the VCL components. Each part of the filter has to be separated by a null character, not the vertical bar character. Also, the filter string in an API application must be terminated by two null characters.

The above code will only be able to display the Open dialog on NT 5.0 (Windows 2000) and later operating system versions because the OPENFILENAME record in the CommDlg unit contains three NT 5.0-specific fields:

```
pvReserved: Pointer;
dwReserved: DWORD;
FlagsEx: DWORD;
```

If you want to target Windows 98 as well, you cannot pass SizeOf(OPENFILENAME) to the lStructSize field. To have the Open dialog work on Windows 98, discard the size of these three fields from the lStructSize field:

```
ofn.lStructSize := SizeOf(OPENFILENAME) - SizeOf(ofn.pvReserved) -
  SizeOf(ofn.dwReserved) - SizeOf(ofn.FlagsEx);
```

Extracting Icons

The easiest way to extract icons from an executable file is to use the ExtractIcon function:

```
function ExtractIcon(hInst: HINST; lpszExeFileName: PChar;
  nIconIndex: UINT): HICON; stdcall;
```

The ExtractIcon function returns a handle to the icon, which must be released with a call to DestroyIcon. So, to prevent the possibility of a memory leak, we should create a function that automatically releases the extracted icon before extracting a new one. Since we're going to draw the extracted icon, the function should also refresh the window when a new icon is extracted. The window can be refreshed with a call to the InvalidateRect function.

The following listing displays the entire function that extracts icons from an executable file. Note that the fileName and the icon variables used in the function are global variables. The icon variable contains the handle of the extracted icon, and the fileName variable contains the path and file name of the selected executable.

Listing 23-6: Extracting icons

```
procedure DisplayIcon(IconIndex: Integer);
begin
  if icon <> 0 then
    DestroyIcon(icon); { remove the old icon from memory }

  if fileName <> '' then
    icon := ExtractIcon(HInstance, PChar(fileName), IconIndex);

  { refresh the window to display the newly extracted icon }
  InvalidateRect(MainWnd, nil, True);
end;
```

Now that you've created the necessary utility functions, you can implement the File ➢ Open command, as shown in Listing 23-7.

Listing 23-7: The File ➢ Open command

```
    FILE_OPEN: begin
      fileName := OpenFileDialog;  { select a new EXE or DLL }
      if fileName <> '' then       { if the user clicked OK }
      begin
        { pass -1 as the last parameter to get the icon count }
        iconCount := ExtractIcon(HInstance, PChar(fileName), Cardinal(-1));
        { if there are icons in the EXE, display the first one }
        if iconCount > 0 then
        begin
          currIcon := 0;
          DisplayIcon(currIcon);
```

```
        end else
        begin
          DisplayIcon(0); { call this to remove the old icon }
          MessageBox(MainWnd, 'The application or library ' +
            'contains no icons!', 'Message', MB_OK or MB_ICONINFORMATION);
        end;        // if iconCount
      end;        // if fileName
    end;        // FILE_OPEN
```

The only thing left to do now is handle the WM_PAINT message and draw the extracted icon on the window.

Handling the WM_PAINT message

The WM_PAINT message is sent to the window when all or part of the window should be repainted. If you want to draw in response to the WM_PAINT message, you should not use the GetDC and ReleaseDC functions but rather the BeginPaint and EndPaint functions:

```
function BeginPaint(hWnd: HWND; var lpPaint: TPaintStruct): HDC; stdcall;
function EndPaint(hWnd: HWND; const lpPaint: TPaintStruct): BOOL; stdcall;
```

The BeginPaint function prepares the window for drawing and returns a device context handle. When you call BeginPaint to begin drawing on a window, you must call EndPaint to finish drawing.

The following listing shows the WM_PAINT message handler of the Icon Viewer application.

Listing 23-8: Drawing icons and text in response to the WM_PAINT message

```
var
  selMessage: string;
  dc: HDC;
  ps: PAINTSTRUCT;

...

    WM_PAINT: begin
      dc := BeginPaint(MainWnd, ps);
      if icon <> 0 then { if we have a valid icon }
      begin
        SetBkMode(dc, TRANSPARENT);
        { select the default system font into the device context }
        SelectObject(dc, GetStockObject(DEFAULT_GUI_FONT));
        selMessage := Format('Icon %d of %d', [Succ(currIcon), iconCount]);
        { display the message using the previously selected system font }
        TextOut(dc, 10, 10, PChar(selMessage), Length(selMessage));

        { display the icon }
        DrawIcon(dc, 10, 40, icon);
      end;
      EndPaint(MainWnd, ps);
    end;        // WM_PAINT
```

The Icon Viewer Application

To fully understand how the Icon Viewer application works and where the previously described pieces of code go, you should take a closer look at Listing 23-9 since it contains the fully commented source code of the application.

Listing 23-9: The Icon Viewer

```
program Generic;

uses
  Windows, Messages, SysUtils, CommDlg, ShellAPI;

{$R Menu.res}

const
  MY_CLASS = 'DelphiAPIWindow';
  APP_CAPTION = 'Icon Viewer';
  FILE_OPEN = 101;
  FILE_EXIT = 102;
  PREV_BUTTON = 103;
  NEXT_BUTTON = 104;

var
  Msg: TMsg;
  MainWnd: HWND;              { the main window's handle }
  wc: WNDCLASS;              { the window class }
  prevButton: HWND;          { handle of the Previous button }
  nextButton: HWND;          { handle of the Next button }
  icon: HIcon;               { the selected icon's handle }
  iconCount: Integer;        { the number of icons in an EXE }
  currIcon: Integer;         { the currently selected item }
  fileName: string;          { the file name of the EXE we're viewing }
  screenWidth: Integer;
  screenHeight: Integer;

function OpenFileDialog: string;
var
  ofn: OPENFILENAME;
  fileName: array[0..MAX_PATH] of Char;
const
  FILTER = 'Executable Files' + #0 + '*.exe' + #0 +
    'Dynamic Link Libraries' + #0 + '*.dll' + #0#0;
begin
  fileName := '';
  ZeroMemory(@ofn, SizeOf(OPENFILENAME));
  ofn.lStructSize := SizeOf(OPENFILENAME);
  ofn.hWndOwner := MainWnd;
  ofn.lpstrFilter := FILTER;
  ofn.lpstrFile := fileName;
  ofn.nMaxFile := MAX_PATH;

  GetOpenFileName(ofn);
  Result := string(fileName);
end;
```

```
procedure DisplayIcon(IconIndex: Integer);
begin
  if icon <> 0 then
    DestroyIcon(icon); { remove the old icon from memory }

  if fileName <> '' then
    icon := ExtractIcon(HInstance, PChar(fileName), IconIndex);

  { refresh the window to display the newly extracted icon }
  InvalidateRect(MainWnd, nil, True);
end;

function WindowProc(Wnd: HWND; Msg, WParam, LParam: LongInt): LongInt; stdcall;
var
  selMessage: string;
  dc: HDC;
  ps: PAINTSTRUCT;
begin
  Result := 0;

  case Msg of
    WM_COMMAND: begin
      case WParam of
        FILE_EXIT: SendMessage(MainWnd, WM_CLOSE, 0, 0);

        FILE_OPEN: begin
          fileName := OpenFileDialog; { select a new EXE or DLL }
          if fileName <> '' then       { if the user clicked OK }
          begin
            { pass -1 as the last parameter to get the icon count }
            iconCount := ExtractIcon(HInstance, PChar(fileName), Cardinal(-1));
            { if there are icons in the EXE, display the first one }
            if iconCount > 0 then
            begin
              currIcon := 0;
              DisplayIcon(currIcon);
            end else
            begin
              { call DisplayIcon to remove
                the old icon and to refresh the screen }
              DisplayIcon(0);
              MessageBox(MainWnd, 'The application or library ' +
                'contains no icons!', 'Message', MB_OK or MB_ICONINFORMATION);
            end;    // if iconCount
          end;      // if fileName
        end;        // FILE_OPEN

        NEXT_BUTTON: begin
          if currIcon < Pred(iconCount) then
          begin
            Inc(currIcon);
            DisplayIcon(currIcon);
          end;
        end;        // NEXT_BUTTON
```

```
      PREV_BUTTON: begin
        if currIcon > 0 then
        begin
          Dec(currIcon);
          DisplayIcon(currIcon);
        end;
      end;        // PREV_BUTTON

    end;          // case WParam
  end;            // WM_COMMAND

WM_PAINT: begin
  dc := BeginPaint(MainWnd, ps);
  if icon <> 0 then { if we have a valid icon }
  begin
    SetBkMode(dc, TRANSPARENT);
    { select the default system font into the device context }
    SelectObject(dc, GetStockObject(DEFAULT_GUI_FONT));
    selMessage := Format('Icon %d of %d', [Succ(currIcon), iconCount]);
    { display the message using the previously selected system font }
    TextOut(dc, 10, 10, PChar(selMessage), Length(selMessage));

    { display the icon }
    DrawIcon(dc, 10, 40, icon);
  end;
  EndPaint(MainWnd, ps);
end;            // WM_PAINT

WM_CLOSE: begin
  if icon <> 0 then DestroyIcon(icon);  { release the icon }
  DestroyWindow(prevButton);            { destroy the Prev button }
  DestroyWindow(nextButton);            { destroy the Next button }
end;            // WM_CLOSE

WM_DESTROY: PostQuitMessage(0); { terminate the app }
else
  Result := DefWindowProc(Wnd, Msg, WParam, LParam);
  end;          // case
end;

begin
  wc.style := CS_DROPSHADOW;
  wc.lpfnWndProc := @WindowProc;
  wc.cbClsExtra := 0;
  wc.cbWndExtra := 0;
  wc.hInstance := HInstance;
  wc.hCursor := LoadCursor(0, IDC_ARROW);
  wc.hbrBackground := COLOR_BTNFACE + 1;
  wc.lpszMenuName := 'Main_Menu'; { load the menu from the resource }
  wc.lpszClassName := MY_CLASS;

  if RegisterClass(wc) = 0 then Exit;

  { create the window and emulate the poDesktopCenter form position }
  screenWidth := GetSystemMetrics(SM_CXSCREEN);
```

```
  screenHeight := GetSystemMetrics(SM_CYSCREEN);

MainWnd := CreateWindow(MY_CLASS, APP_CAPTION,
  WS_BORDER or WS_SYSMENU, screenWidth div 2 - 125,
  screenHeight div 2 - 100, 250, 200, 0, 0, HInstance, nil);

prevButton := CreateWindow('BUTTON', 'Previous', WS_CHILD or
  WS_VISIBLE or BS_PUSHBUTTON or BS_TEXT, 10, 115, 75, 25,
  MainWnd, PREV_BUTTON, HInstance, nil);

nextButton := CreateWindow('BUTTON', 'Next', WS_CHILD or
  WS_VISIBLE or BS_PUSHBUTTON or BS_TEXT, 160, 115, 75, 25,
  MainWnd, NEXT_BUTTON, HInstance, nil);

{ use system font on the buttons }
SendMessage(prevButton, WM_SETFONT, GetStockObject(DEFAULT_GUI_FONT), 0);
SendMessage(nextButton, WM_SETFONT, GetStockObject(DEFAULT_GUI_FONT), 0);

{ display the main window }
ShowWindow(MainWnd, SW_SHOWNORMAL);
UpdateWindow(MainWnd);

{ message loop }
while GetMessage(Msg, 0, 0, 0) do
begin
  TranslateMessage(Msg);
  DispatchMessage(Msg);
end;
end.
```

Custom Application Icon and the Manifest File

Once you've finished the application, you should take care of two user inter-face details: replacing the default application icon with a custom one, and creating the external manifest file to enable the child controls to use XP visual styles.

To change the main icon of the application, open the Menu.rc file and write the following statement to define the MAINICON resource:

```
MAINICON ICON "Factory.ico"
```

The above statement uses the Factory icon that can be found in the X:\Pro-gram Files\Common Files\Borland Shared\Images\Icons directory.

After you've added the above statement to the Menu.rc resource file, you should recompile both the resource file and the application. The Delphi com-piler will replace the default white application icon with your custom one, but the custom icon won't be displayed on the title bar of the main window. To dis-play the icon on the main window's title bar, you have to use the LoadIcon function to load the icon from the resource file and assign the result of the LoadIcon function to the hIcon field of the WNDCLASS record:

```
wc.hIcon := LoadIcon(HInstance, 'MAINICON');
```

By passing the global HInstance variable as the first parameter in the LoadIcon function, you're telling the function that the requested resource is stored in the executable file.

The final step in the creation of the Icon Viewer is the manifest file that will render the child controls using the XP visual styles. You actually don't have to create the manifest because the sample manifest file already exists in the X:\Program Files\Borland\BDS\4.0\source\Win32\vcl directory under the name sample.manifest. You only have to copy it to the application directory and rename it as follows:

```
ApplicationName.exe.manifest
```

Since the Icon Viewer's executable is Generic.exe, you must rename the manifest file to Generic.exe.manifest, and you're done. The child controls will be rendered using XP visual styles.

C++ Generic Applications

There is almost no difference between C++ and Delphi API applications. The only two differences are:

- Syntax differences between Delphi and C++ languages
- Since the main begin-end block doesn't exist in C++ applications, the window class registration, creation of the main window, and the message loop is written inside the WinMain function.

To create a generic C++ application in C++Builder, select the Console Application item to start creating a new console application project and uncheck the Console Application radio button on the New Console Application dialog box. When you uncheck the Console Application radio button, the IDE will generate the appropriate WinMain function instead of the main function:

```
#include <windows.h>
#pragma hdrstop

#pragma argsused
WINAPI WinMain(HINSTANCE hInstance,
    HINSTANCE hPrevInstance, LPSTR lpCmdLine, int nCmdShow)
{
    return 0;
}
```

To create the API application, you have to register and create the window in the WinMain function and add a WindowProc function that will handle messages for the window. The following listing shows the complete source code for a simple C++ API application.

Listing 23-10: A simple C++ API application

```cpp
#include <windows.h>
#pragma hdrstop

const char* GENERIC_WNDCLASS = "CppBuilderWindow";
HWND hMainWindow;

LRESULT CALLBACK WindowProc(HWND hwnd,
  UINT uMsg, WPARAM wParam, LPARAM lParam) {
    switch(uMsg) {
        case WM_DESTROY: {
            PostQuitMessage(0);
            return 0;
        }
    }
    return DefWindowProc(hwnd, uMsg, wParam, lParam);
}

#pragma argsused
WINAPI WinMain(HINSTANCE hInstance, HINSTANCE hPrevInstance,
    LPSTR lpCmdLine, int nCmdShow)
{
    MSG msg;
    WNDCLASS wClass;

    wClass.cbClsExtra = 0;
    wClass.cbWndExtra = 0;
    wClass.hbrBackground = (HBRUSH)(COLOR_BTNFACE + 1);
    wClass.hCursor = LoadCursor(NULL, IDC_ARROW);
    wClass.hIcon = LoadIcon(NULL, IDI_APPLICATION);
    wClass.hInstance = hInstance;
    wClass.lpszClassName = GENERIC_WNDCLASS;
    wClass.lpfnWndProc = WindowProc;
    wClass.lpszMenuName = NULL;
    wClass.style = CS_HREDRAW | CS_VREDRAW;
    RegisterClass(&wClass);

    // create the main window
    hMainWindow = CreateWindow(GENERIC_WNDCLASS,
        "C++ Win32 API Application", WS_OVERLAPPEDWINDOW,
        CW_USEDEFAULT, CW_USEDEFAULT, CW_USEDEFAULT,
        CW_USEDEFAULT, NULL, NULL, hInstance, NULL);

    ShowWindow(hMainWindow, SW_SHOWNORMAL);
    UpdateWindow(hMainWindow);

    // enter the message loop
    while(GetMessage(&msg, NULL, 0, 0)) {
        TranslateMessage(&msg);
        DispatchMessage(&msg);
    }

    return msg.wParam;
}
```

Chapter 24

Component Development Essentials

There are a number of reasons for creating new components. You might want to create a new component to encapsulate and reuse an important piece of code, to enhance an existing component, in order to gain profit and prestige, or even when the sole purpose of creating a component is pure and simple fun. Whatever the reason, this chapter (and the following two chapters) will try to give you all the information you need to successfully create components.

From a theoretical standpoint, it's extremely easy to create a new component, given that you know how to create a new class:

```
type
  TMyClass = class(TObject)
  end;
```

In order to create a component that can be used in the IDE, you have to derive the new class from the ultimate ancestor of all components: the TComponent class or any of its descendants:

```
type
  TMyComponent = class(TComponent)
  end;
```

The TComponent class has the following traits:

- It can be added to the Tool Palette.
- It can be dropped on the Designer Surface and manipulated at design time.
- It can own other components and manage them at run time.
- It is a persistent object, meaning that it has the ability to save and load its properties to and from a DFM file (the TComponent class inherits this ability from the TPersistent class).

Components that inherit directly from the TComponent class (like the main menu and the common dialogs) are nonvisual components that have no user interface and are, at design time, displayed as an icon.

Ancestor Classes

After you've made the decision to create a new component, you still have to decide the class from which you need to derive your new component. You can find out which class you need to derive from by answering these simple questions:

1. Should the component be available at design time?

    If you want to use the component at design time, you have to derive your component from TComponent or one of its descendants. If you don't need to use the component at design time, you shouldn't create a component. A better solution in this case is to derive a new class from TObject.

2. Is it a nonvisual component like the TMainMenu and the TXPManifest components?

    If you need a component that lacks a user interface but needs to be available at design time, you should derive it from TComponent. If you need a visual component, you should derive your new component from TControl or, better yet, from one of TControl's descendant classes.

3. Should the new component be a visual component (a control)?

    If you need to create a new control, you can choose between the TGraphicControl and TCustomControl classes. By deriving your component from TGraphicControl, you are creating a graphic control. By deriving your component from TCustomControl, you are creating a windowed control.

    Graphic controls are lightweight controls. They use fewer system resources than windowed controls and are able to respond to mouse events. However, graphic controls have no window handle and therefore cannot be passed to API functions, cannot respond to keyboard events, cannot receive focus, and cannot respond to Windows messages.

    Windowed controls, unlike graphic controls, have a window handle that makes them much more powerful than graphic controls. The window handle allows windowed controls to be passed to API functions, to receive input focus and keyboard events, to respond to Windows messages, and even to contain other windowed and graphic controls.

4. Should the new component be a completely new component or a customized version of an existing one?

    If you want to create a completely new component, you should use the TComponent, TGraphicControl, or TCustomControl class as the ancestor class. But if you want to customize an existing component, it is best to derive your new component from the component you wish to customize. For instance, if you want to customize the behavior or appearance of the

TListBox component, you can derive your new component from TListBox.

The VCL also contains a number of TCustomComponentName components that can be used when you want to customize an existing component. For instance, you can use either the TListBox class or the TCustomListBox class to create a customized list box component. You can do this because the TCustomListBox and the TListBox components are essentially the same. The TListBox component is derived from the TCustomListBox component and the only difference between the two is that the TListBox component publishes all of TCustomListBox's properties, making them available in the Object Inspector at design time.

Creating a New Component

In order to use the new component, you have to add it to a package. A package is a special dynamic link library with a .bpl (Borland Package Library) extension that can be used by the IDE at design time and by applications at run time.

There are two types of packages:

- Design-time packages — contain components and property editors that are used by the IDE at design time
- Run-time packages — contain functionality that is used at run time

Packages can also be both run-time and design-time. These run-time/design-time packages usually contain components that have the minimum amount of design-time specific code. This type of package is automatically created by the IDE, as you can see in Figure 24-1.

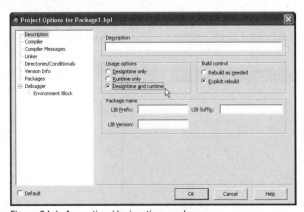

Figure 24-1: A run-time/design-time package

So, before creating a new component, you have to either open an existing package or create a new one. To create a new package, select File ➢ New ➢ Package - Delphi for Win32. If you have created a new package, you should save it before going any further.

Now that you have a package opened in the IDE, you can create a new component by selecting Component ➢ New VCL Component. The New VCL Component dialog box that appears first asks you to select the ancestor class of your new component. The first component that we are going to build will be a simple nonvisual component, so select the TComponent class from the list and then press Next (see Figure 24-2).

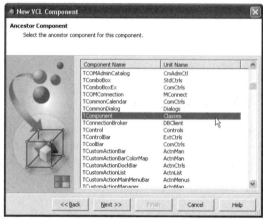

Figure 24-2: Selecting the ancestor class

Now that you have selected the ancestor class, you have to name the class, select or type the name of the Tool Palette category in which to place the component, and click the (...) button next to the Unit name text box to define the file name of the component's unit. You should now create a component called TSimple, place it in the "My Components" category (you can, of course, type anything you want here), and save it in the package's directory under the name Simple.pas (see Figure 24-3). Make sure you don't forget the .pas extension in the unit's file name.

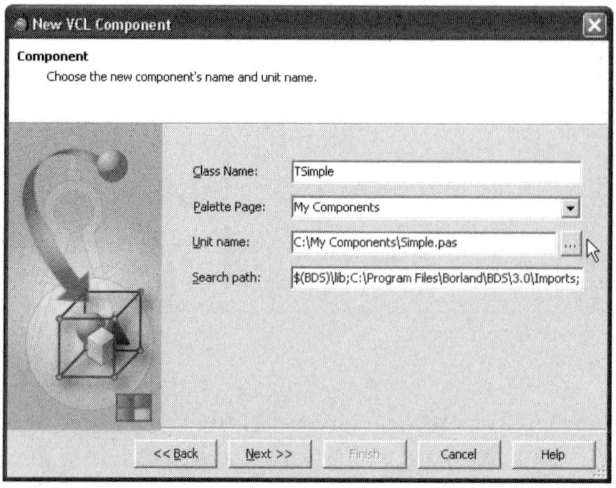

Figure 24-3: Defining the component's class name

In the final step, the New VCL Component dialog box enables you to create the unit and add it to an existing package. Select the Add unit to PackageName.bdsproj project button and click Finish to create the TSimple component.

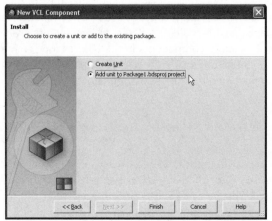

Figure 24-4: Adding the new component to the opened package

Listing 24-1 shows the source code generated by the New VCL Component dialog box.

Listing 24-1: The source code of the TSimple component

```
unit Simple;

interface

uses
  SysUtils, Classes;

type
  TSimple = class(TComponent)
  private
    { Private declarations }
  protected
    { Protected declarations }
  public
    { Public declarations }
  published
    { Published declarations }
  end;

procedure Register;

implementation

procedure Register;
begin
  RegisterComponents('My Components', [TSimple]);
```

```
end;
```

```
end.
```

The only thing not seen before is the Register procedure. The Register procedure is the only case-sensitive procedure in Delphi and it has only one purpose: to register one or a set of components in the IDE. To register the components, the Register procedure calls the RegisterComponents procedure that is able to register one or more components in the IDE, as long as they all appear in the same Tool Palette category. Here's an example of how you can register a set of components using the RegisterComponents procedure:

```
procedure Register;
begin
  RegisterComponents('My Components', [TSimple, TSecondComponent]);
end;
```

The last thing that we have to do in order to add the new component to the Tool Palette is install the package. To install the entire package, right-click the package icon in the Project Manager and select Install. A message box will appear that will notify you if the package was successfully installed or not.

Figure 24-5: Successful installation of the package

If the package was successfully installed, all the components passed to the RegisterComponents procedure will be registered in the IDE.

To test the new component, you can add a new VCL Forms application project to the project group (right-click the ProjectGroup1 icon in the Project Manager and select Add New Project) and then use your component as you would any other.

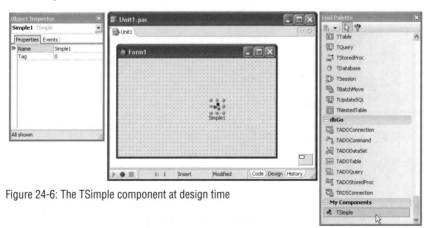

Figure 24-6: The TSimple component at design time

Creating Properties

If you need to store additional data in a component, you can create new fields or new properties. If you create a new field, you will be able to work with the data stored in the field, but you won't be able to control how the field is accessed. However, if you create a new property, you will be able to control how the property's value is accessed and modified.

To create a new property, do the following:

1. Create a new field to hold the property's value (usually in the private section).

2. Define the property's name, type, and read and write access using the reserved word `property` (usually in the public or published sections).

Here's how to declare a simple property:

```
property PropertyName: Type read FieldName write FieldName;
```

The read and write specifiers enable you to define how the underlying field is accessed. The field can be accessed directly if you specify the field's name or through a method if you specify a valid method in either the read or the write specifier (you'll see this shortly).

Here's how to add a simple string property to the TSimple component:

```
type
  TSimple = class(TComponent)
  private
    { Private declarations }
    FMyString: string;
  protected
    { Protected declarations }
  public
    { Public declarations }
  published
    { Published declarations }
    property MyString: string read FMyString write FMyString;
  end;
```

Visibility of Class Fields

The fields that hold the property data are usually added to the private section of the class. The private section is perfect for field declarations because it enables you to hide fields from the outside world. By hiding a field in the private section, you allow access to the field only through the property, which is usually declared in one of the other three sections and perhaps has a write method that controls how the field is accessed.

NOTE   Although it's not necessary, you should always begin the field's name with the letter F and the component's name with the letter T.

The `private`, `protected`, `public`, and `published` reserved words define the visibility of class members. Private members are generally inaccessible from the outside world, although they can be accessed by code that resides in the same unit. If you want to have a really private field, one that can't be accessed in the same unit or from other units, place it in the strict private section:

```
type
  TSomeClass = class(TAnotherClass)
  strict private
    { strict private fields can only be accessed inside the class }
    FMyString: string;
  private
    { private fields can be used by code
      inside the class and in the same unit }
end;
```

To an application developer, the protected section is the same as the private section, since protected members, like private members, cannot be accessed from outside units. The protected section and the protected members are only useful to component developers because you can access all protected class members in a descendant class, regardless of the unit in which the descendant class is declared. Like private fields, protected fields can be used by code that resides in the same unit. To have a field that can be used in a descendant class but not by code in the same unit, place it in the strict protected section.

At the beginning of your component development career, you'll mostly create public and published properties, simply because they can be used throughout the application. If you declare a public member, it will be available wherever the object is available.

Properties are added to the published section of the class when you want them to appear in the Object Inspector at design time. Published properties are similar to public properties because they are globally accessible. The difference between public and published properties is that the Delphi compiler generates run-time type information (RTTI) for published properties, which enables them to be displayed in the Object Inspector and saved to and loaded from .dfm files.

Simple Properties

Now that we've covered the visibility of class fields, it's time to finish the TSimple component. Since you've already declared the MyString property in the published section of the TSimple component, you can now recompile the package and then drop a TSimple component on the Designer Surface (if you haven't done that already) to see what your first property looks like in the Object Inspector.

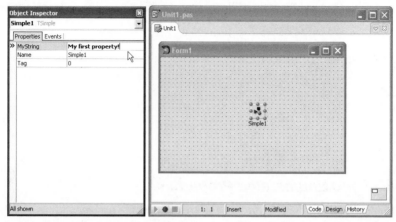

Figure 24-7: The MyString string property

Besides string properties, the Object Inspector considers character and numerical properties to be simple properties. All simple property types are displayed as directly editable strings in the Object Inspector.

The following listing shows the TSimple component with four different properties.

Listing 24-2: Simple properties

```
type
  TSimple = class(TComponent)
  private
    { Private declarations }
    FMyChar: Char;
    FMyDouble: Double;
    FMyInteger: Integer;
    FMyString: string;
  protected
    { Protected declarations }
  public
    { Public declarations }
  published
    { Published declarations }
    property MyChar: Char read FMyChar write FMyChar;
    property MyDouble: Double read FMyDouble write FMyDouble;
    property MyInteger: Integer read FMyInteger write FMyInteger;
    property MyString: string read FMyString write FMyString;
  end;
```

Figure 24-8 shows how the Object Inspector displays all simple properties.

Figure 24-8:
Simple properties

Boolean and Enumerated Properties

Boolean and enumerated properties are, like simple property types, displayed as directly editable strings. However, the Object Inspector also allows you to select one of the possible values from a drop-down list.

The following listing shows the TSimple component with a Boolean and an enumerated property. The four simple properties displayed in Listing 24-2 were removed to save space and also to illustrate what happens in the IDE when you remove published properties.

Listing 24-3: Boolean and enumerated properties

```
type
  TDaysEnum = (deMonday, deTuesday, deWednesday, deThursday,
    deFriday, deSaturday, deSunday);

  TSimple = class(TComponent)
  private
    { Private declarations }
    FEnumeration: TDaysEnum;
    FBool: Boolean;
  protected
    { Protected declarations }
  public
    { Public declarations }
  published
    { Published declarations }
    property Bool: Boolean read FBool write FBool;
    property Enumeration: TDaysEnum read FEnumeration write FEnumeration;
  end;
```

After you remove a published property from a component and recompile the package where the component resides, you will receive the error shown in Figure 24-9 when you try to display a form that uses an older version of your component. The error occurs because the IDE tries to load a value from the .dfm file into a property that no longer exists.

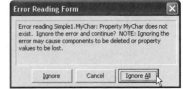

Figure 24-9: This happens when you delete published properties

Since you've deleted the properties, it must mean that you have no need for them and thus the best thing to do is to click the Ignore All button to have the IDE remove the old property values from the .dfm file and display the Designer Surface.

The following figure shows how the Object Inspector displays Boolean and enumerated properties.

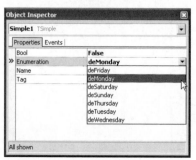

Figure 24-10:
Boolean and enumerated properties

Set Properties

Set properties are displayed in the Object Inspector the same way they are in the code, as a comma-delimited list of values inside square brackets. Set values can also be expanded and treated as a list of Boolean values. By setting a specific value to True, you include it in the set.

The following listing shows the TSimple class with the previously created Boolean and enumerated properties along with the new set property, WorkDays.

Listing 24-4: A set property

```
type
  TDaysEnum = (deMonday, deTuesday, deWednesday, deThursday,
    deFriday, deSaturday, deSunday);

  TDays = set of TDaysEnum;

  TSimple = class(TComponent)
  private
    { Private declarations }
    FEnumeration: TDaysEnum;
    FBool: Boolean;
    FWorkDays: TDays;
  protected
    { Protected declarations }
  public
    { Public declarations }
  published
    { Published declarations }
    property Bool: Boolean read FBool write FBool;
    property Enumeration: TDaysEnum read FEnumeration write FEnumeration;
    property WorkDays: TDays read FWorkDays write FWorkDays;
  end;
```

The following figure shows how set properties are displayed in the Object Inspector and how you can manage individual set values.

Figure 24-11: A set property

Default Property Values

You might have noticed that the values of the Bool and Enumeration properties are always displayed boldfaced, which means that the values of these properties are modified and that they will eventually be saved to the .dfm file.

These properties are displayed as modified in the Object Inspector because we haven't marked them with the default directive. The default directive is a storage specifier that allows us to tell Delphi which value is the default value. When saving components to the .dfm file, Delphi uses the default value to see whether or not it should save the property's value to the .dfm file. If the property's value differs from the default value, it will be saved to the .dfm file. If the current property value matches the default value, Delphi will not save the property to the .dfm file, thus reducing the size of both the .dfm file and the final executable (especially if you have a large number of components with non-default property values).

To define a default value for a property, simply add the default directive to the end of the property declaration, followed, of course, by an appropriate constant. The following listing shows how to set default values for the Bool and Enumeration properties of the TSimple component.

Listing 24-5: Default property values

```
property Bool: Boolean read FBool write FBool default False;
property Enumeration: TDaysEnum read FEnumeration
  write FEnumeration default deMonday;
```

Currently, the default directive will only work properly if you specify the default type values that are automatically assigned by Delphi to all properties

— 0 for numbers, empty string for strings, nil for pointers, the first enumeration value for enumerations, etc.

To specify a default value that differs from the automatically assigned property value, you have to change the property's value in the component's constructor (you'll see how to do this shortly).

The following figure shows the .dfm file and the Object Inspector without the default directive and after the default directive has been added to the Bool and Enumeration properties.

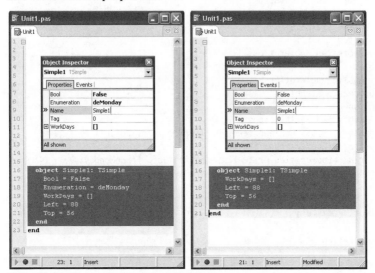

Figure 24-12: The result of the default directive

Methods

In component development, you will mostly be creating public and protected methods — public methods for everyday use and protected methods for use in descendant classes.

At this point in the book, it shouldn't be necessary to tell you how to create a new method, but for the sake of completeness, the following listing shows the TSimple class with a simple SayHello method. Note that the SayHello method was created as an example of a simple method, not one that is very optimized.

Listing 24-6: A simple method

```
unit Simple;

interface

uses
  SysUtils, Classes, Dialogs;
```

```
type
  TDaysEnum = (deMonday, deTuesday, deWednesday, deThursday,
    deFriday, deSaturday, deSunday);

  TDays = set of TDaysEnum;

  TSimple = class(TComponent)
  private
    { Private declarations }
    FEnumeration: TDaysEnum;
    FBool: Boolean;
    FWorkDays: TDays;
  protected
    { Protected declarations }
  public
    { Public declarations }
    procedure SayHello;
  published
    { Published declarations }
    property Bool: Boolean read FBool write FBool default False;
    property Enumeration: TDaysEnum
      read FEnumeration write FEnumeration default deMonday;
    property WorkDays: TDays read FWorkDays write FWorkDays;
  end;

procedure Register;

implementation

procedure Register;
begin
  RegisterComponents('My Components', [TSimple]);
end;

procedure TSimple.SayHello;
var
  msg: string;
  cnt: Integer;
  day: TDaysEnum;
const
  NAMES: array[TDaysEnum] of string = ('Monday', 'Tuesday',
    'Wednesday', 'Thursday', 'Friday', 'Saturday', 'Sunday');
begin
  if WorkDays = [] then
    msg := 'I don''t have to work this week.'
  else begin
    msg := 'I have to work on ';
    cnt := 0;
    for day in WorkDays do
    begin
      Inc(cnt);
      if cnt > 1 then
        msg := msg + ', ' + NAMES[day]
      else
        msg := msg + NAMES[day];
```

```
    end;    // for
    msg := msg + '.';
  end;      // if WorkDays

  { add Dialogs to the uses list to use MessageDlg }
  MessageDlg(msg, mtInformation, [mbOK], 0);
end;

end.
```

To see what the SayHello method does, take a look at Figure 24-13.

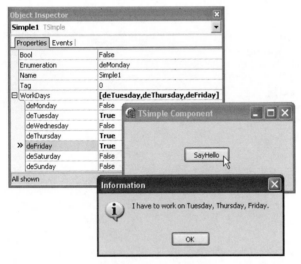

Figure 24-13: The output of the SayHello method

The SayHello method shown in Listing 24-6 is a static method. Static methods are methods not marked with either the virtual or the dynamic directive. The primary advantage of static methods is that they are faster than other method types. The primary disadvantage of static methods is that they cannot be overridden in descendant classes.

Unlike static methods, both virtual and dynamic methods can be overridden using the override directive. Overriding gives us the ability to change a method in a descendant class. It takes a bit longer to execute virtual and dynamic methods because the appropriate method must be determined at run time. When you have to create a non-static method, it is usually best to create a virtual method rather than a dynamic method, because they are faster than dynamic methods.

The following listing shows three different classes that illustrate how to create a virtual method and how to override it in descendant classes.

Listing 24-7: Overriding virtual methods

```
unit Animals;

interface

uses Dialogs;

type
  TAnimal = class
  public
    procedure Hello; virtual;
  end;

  TDog = class(TAnimal)
    procedure Hello; override;
  end;

  TCat = class(TAnimal)
    procedure Hello; override;
  end;

implementation

procedure TAnimal.Hello;
begin
end;

procedure TDog.Hello;
begin
  ShowMessage('Class = ' + ClassName);
end;

procedure TCat.Hello;
begin
  MessageDlg('Does the word Polymorphism ring a bell?',
      mtInformation, [mbOK], 0);
end;

end.
```

To see how virtual methods work, write the code displayed in Listing 24-8 and see what happens. The result of calling the virtual method Hello is displayed in Figure 24-14.

Listing 24-8: Calling a virtual method

```
procedure TForm1.Button1Click(Sender: TObject);
var
  A: TAnimal;
begin
  A := TCat.Create;
  A.Hello; { calls TCat.Hello }
  A.Free;
end;
```

Figure 24-14: Calling the virtual method Hello

After this short escapade, it's time to return to our TSimple component. The last thing that you should learn in this section is how to properly set default property values. To set, for instance, the deWednesday value as the default value for the Enumeration property, you have to mark the Enumeration property with the default directive, override the component's constructor, and assign the same value to the Enumeration property in the constructor. The following listing shows how this is done. Note that you must always call the inherited constructor first and only then can you do anything else in the constructor.

Listing 24-9: Properly defining default property values

```
unit Simple;

interface

uses
  SysUtils, Classes, Dialogs;

type
  TDaysEnum = (deMonday, deTuesday, deWednesday, deThursday,
    deFriday, deSaturday, deSunday);

  TDays = set of TDaysEnum;

  TSimple = class(TComponent)
  private
    { Private declarations }
    FEnumeration: TDaysEnum;
    FBool: Boolean;
    FWorkDays: TDays;
  protected
    { Protected declarations }
  public
    { Public declarations }
    constructor Create(AOwner: TComponent); override;
  published
    { Published declarations }
    property Bool: Boolean read FBool write FBool;
```

```
    property Enumeration: TDaysEnum
      read FEnumeration write FEnumeration default deWednesday;
    property WorkDays: TDays read FWorkDays write FWorkDays;
  end;

procedure Register;

implementation

procedure Register;
begin
  RegisterComponents('My Components', [TSimple]);
end;

constructor TSimple.Create(AOwner: TComponent);
begin
  inherited Create(AOwner); { you must call the inherited constructor first! }
  FEnumeration := deWednesday;
end;

end.
```

Property Access Methods

Properties with direct access are the easiest to write and, of course, slightly faster than properties that use methods to read values from and write values to underlying fields (if there are such). The downside of direct-access properties is that they are less flexible than properties that use read and/or write methods, since they have no control over what's happening with the property's value.

To illustrate how to create a write method, let's create a new integer property named Limited that will only allow the user to enter numbers from 0 to 100. Since the Limited property is an integer property, the write method must be a procedure that accepts a single integer parameter. To enable yourself, or other developers, to update the Limited property in the future, you should create the write method in the protected section of the class and mark it with the virtual directive:

```
protected
  { Protected declarations }
  procedure SetLimited(Value: Integer); virtual;
published
  { Published declarations }
  { use the SetLimited method to write values to the Limited property }
  property Limited: Integer read FLimited write SetLimited;
end;
```

The following listing shows the entire TSimple class with the Limited property. All other properties were removed so that you can focus on the code related to the Limited property.

Listing 24-10: The Limited property's write method

```
unit Simple;

interface

uses
  SysUtils, Classes, Dialogs;

type
  TSimple = class(TComponent)
  private
    { Private declarations }
    FLimited: Integer;
  protected
    { Protected declarations }
    procedure SetLimited(Value: Integer); virtual;
  published
    { Published declarations }
    property Limited: Integer read FLimited write SetLimited;
  end;

procedure Register;

implementation

procedure Register;
begin
  RegisterComponents('My Components', [TSimple]);
end;

procedure TSimple.SetLimited(Value: Integer);
begin
  if (Value >= 0) and (Value <= 100) then
    FLimited := Value
  else
    raise ERangeError.Create('Give me a number from 0 to 100!');
end;

end.
```

The SetLimited method is now implicitly called every time anyone tries to change the value of the Limited property. Figure 24-15 shows what happens when you try to assign an invalid value in the Object Inspector.

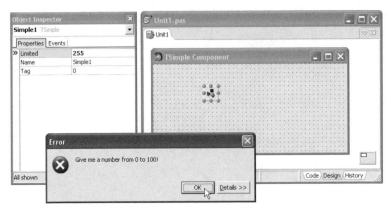

Figure 24-15: Using the Limited property

Just as you can create the write method to control what happens when someone tries to write a new value to the property, you can create a read method to control what happens when someone reads the existing value of the property. Read methods have to be parameterless functions whose result type matches that of the property.

To illustrate how to create a read method, let's create a new property called AccessCount that will be updated by the read method of the Limited property every time someone reads its value. The AccessCount property can be both public and read-only. It can be public because its value only changes at run time and it can be read-only because its value is automatically updated by the Limited property. To create a read-only property, you only have to omit the write directive.

Listing 24-11 shows the TSimple component with the new AccessCount property and the updated Limited property.

```
unit Simple;

interface

uses
  SysUtils, Classes, Dialogs;

type
  TSimple = class(TComponent)
  private
    { Private declarations }
    FLimited: Integer;
    FAccessCount: Integer;
  protected
    { Protected declarations }
    function GetLimited: Integer; virtual;
    procedure SetLimited(Value: Integer); virtual;
```

```
public
  property AccessCount: Integer read FAccessCount; { read-only }
published
  { Published declarations }
  property Limited: Integer read GetLimited write SetLimited;
end;

procedure Register;

implementation

procedure Register;
begin
  RegisterComponents('My Components', [TSimple]);
end;

procedure TSimple.SetLimited(Value: Integer);
begin
  if (Value >= 0) and (Value <= 100) then
    FLimited := Value
  else
    raise ERangeError.Create('Give me a number from 0 to 100!');
end;

function TSimple.GetLimited: Integer;
begin
  Inc(FAccessCount);
  Result := FLimited;
end;

end.
```

The following figure shows the value of the AccessCount property after accessing the Limited property several times.

Figure 24-16:
The result of
accessing the
Limited property

Creating Events

We can also take the Limited property to the next level by firing an event each
time the value of the property is read. The simplest event type that we can
create is a notification, using the TNotifyEvent type:

```
type TNotifyEvent = procedure (Sender: TObject) of object;
```

To create the OnAccess event, you have to add a TNotifyEvent field to the
private section and the event's declaration in the published section (see Figure 24-17). Although you can name your events anything you like, event
names usually begin with "On":

```
private
  FOnAccess: TNotifyEvent;
published
  property OnAccess: TNotifyEvent read FOnAccess write FOnAccess;
```

Figure 24-17:
The new OnAccess
event

Now that the interface part of the event is done, you have to write the event's
implementation. The implementation of events is actually quite simple. Since
the TNotifyEvent type (like all other procedures of object) is a method
pointer, you only have to check whether the method pointer points to a valid
memory location and call it:

```
if Assigned(FOnAccess) then
  FOnAccess(Self); { pass Self as the Sender parameter }
```

The best way to implement an event is to create a protected virtual method.
By creating a method to fire the event, you'll have less typing to do if you
decide later on that you want to fire the event somewhere else:

```
procedure DoAccess; virtual;
  ...
procedure TSimple.DoAccess;
begin
  if Assigned(FOnAccess) then
    FOnAccess(Self); { pass Self as the Sender parameter }
end;
```

The following listing shows the entire TSimple component. The OnAccess
event is fired by calling the DoAccess method in the read method of the
Limited property.

Listing 24-12: The TSimple component with the OnAccess event

```
unit Simple;

interface

uses
  SysUtils, Classes, Dialogs;

type
  TSimple = class(TComponent)
  private
    { Private declarations }
    FLimited: Integer;
    FAccessCount: Integer;
    FOnAccess: TNotifyEvent;
  protected
    { Protected declarations }
    function GetLimited: Integer; virtual;
    procedure SetLimited(Value: Integer); virtual;
    procedure DoAccess; virtual;
  public
    property AccessCount: Integer read FAccessCount; { read-only }
  published
    { Published declarations }
    property Limited: Integer read GetLimited write SetLimited;
    property OnAccess: TNotifyEvent read FOnAccess write FOnAccess;
  end;

procedure Register;

implementation

procedure Register;
begin
  RegisterComponents('My Components', [TSimple]);
end;

procedure TSimple.SetLimited(Value: Integer);
begin
  if (Value >= 0) and (Value <= 100) then
    FLimited := Value
  else
    raise ERangeError.Create('Give me a number from 0 to 100!');
end;

function TSimple.GetLimited: Integer;
begin
  Inc(FAccessCount);
  Result := FLimited;
  { fire the OnAccess event }
  DoAccess;
end;

procedure TSimple.DoAccess;
begin
```

```
  if Assigned(FOnAccess) then
    FOnAccess(Self); { pass Self as the Sender parameter }
end;

end.
```

The following event handler shows that the OnAccess event indeed works (see Figure 24-18):

```
procedure TForm1.Simple1Access(Sender: TObject);
begin
  ListBox1.Items.Add('The Limited property was last accessed on: ' +
    DateTimeToStr(Now));
end;
```

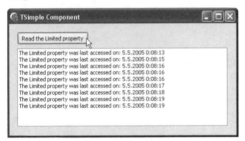

Figure 24-18: Using the OnAccess event

Object Properties

Although it requires a bit more work, you can also add object properties to your components. To create an object property, you have to do the following:

1. Add the object field to the component.

2. Define the object property.

3. Create the object in the component's constructor.

4. Destroy the object in the component's destructor.

Now we are going to create a new component called TStringsCache. The TStringsCache component will be useful not only because it shows how to create an object property, but also because it will enable you to easily add strings or even entire text files to the executable.

First, you have to create the TStringsCache component using the New VCL Component dialog box. To create the TStringsCache component, select the TComponent class as the ancestor class, save the component's unit, preferably StringsCache.pas, in the same directory where you have previously saved the TSimple component, and finally add the TStringsCache component to your package.

When the wizard is finished, you can start creating the component by adding the Strings property to the interface part of the class. Note that when you're creating subcomponents you must use a write method for the property because you aren't changing the object, just its properties:

```
type
  TStringsCache = class(TComponent)
  private
    { Private declarations }
    FStrings: TStrings;
  protected
    { Protected declarations }
    procedure SetStrings(Value: TStrings); virtual;
  public
    { Public declarations }
  published
    { Published declarations }
    property Strings: TStrings read FStrings write SetStrings;
  end;
```

The TStringsCache component is actually almost finished. To finish it, you
have to override the component's destructor and constructor to create and
destroy the FStrings object, and you have to write the implementation of the
SetStrings method, which only calls Assign to copy the properties of the Value
parameter to the FStrings object. Also note that in order to create the
FStrings object, you have to create an instance of the TStringList class, not
the TStrings class, because the TStrings class cannot be directly instantiated.

The following listing shows the entire TStringsCache component.

Listing 24-13: The TStringsCache component

```
unit StringsCache;

interface

uses
  SysUtils, Classes;

type
  TStringsCache = class(TComponent)
  private
    { Private declarations }
    FStrings: TStrings;
  protected
    { Protected declarations }
    procedure SetStrings(Value: TStrings); virtual;
  public
    { Public declarations }
    constructor Create(AOwner: TComponent); override;
    destructor Destroy; override;
  published
    { Published declarations }
    property Strings: TStrings read FStrings write SetStrings;
  end;

procedure Register;

implementation

procedure Register;
```

```
begin
  RegisterComponents('My Components', [TStringsCache]);
end;

constructor TStringsCache.Create(AOwner: TComponent);
begin
  inherited Create(AOwner);
  FStrings := TStringList.Create;
end;

destructor TStringsCache.Destroy;
begin
  FStrings.Free;
  { always call the inherited destructor, and always call it last }
  inherited Destroy;
end;

procedure TStringsCache.SetStrings(Value: TStrings);
begin
  FStrings.Assign(Value);
end;

end.
```

The following figure shows the TStringsCache component on the Designer Surface.

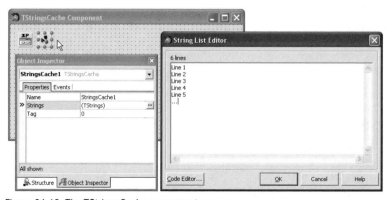

Figure 24-19: The TStringsCache component

Creating the Component's Tool Palette Icon

The following figure shows our two components (TSimple and TStringsCache) on the Designer Surface. But how do you really know that Figure 24-20 shows both a TSimple and a TStringsCache component?

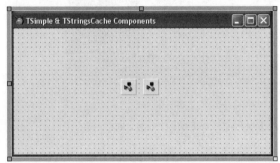

Figure 24-20: The TSimple and TStringsCache components on the Designer Surface

Although the default component icon isn't ugly, you should always change it when you create a new component.

The following steps show how to create a Tool Palette icon for the TStringsCache component:

1. Open the Image Editor by selecting Tools ➢ Image Editor.

2. Create a new component resource file by selecting File ➢ New ➢ Component Resource File (.dcr) in the Image Editor.

3. Save the new .dcr file in the component's directory. The file name of the .dcr file must match the file name of the component. So, if the TStringsCache component's unit is StringsCache.pas, you have to save the .dcr file under StringsCache.dcr.

4. Now right-click the Contents node in the StringsCache.dcr window and select New ➢ Bitmap to display the Bitmap Properties dialog box (see Figure 24-21).

5. The Tool Palette icon should be a 24x24 bitmap, so update the Width and Height text boxes. You should also select the SuperVGA option if you want to have a nice-looking icon.

6. When you click OK to create the new bitmap, it will be named Bitmap1. You must change the bitmap's name to match the class name of the component. In this case, you have to rename the bitmap TStringsCache (the Image Editor will automatically convert the name to uppercase).

7. Now you need to draw a nice component icon.

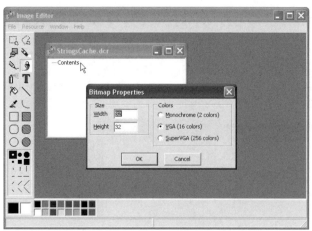

Figure 24-21: Creating a Tool Palette icon in the Image Editor

8. Finally, when you're done drawing or pasting the image from an external source, save the .dcr file and return to the Project Manager.

9. Right-click the StringsCache.pas file in the Project Manager and select Remove from Project to temporarily remove the TStringsCache component from the package.

10. Right-click the package icon (Package1.bpl, or whatever it's called), select Add…, and add the StringsCache.pas file back to the package. Since the directory now contains both the .pas file and the .dcr file, the IDE will automatically add both files to the package.

11. Finally, recompile the package and you're done. (If you cannot see the new icon, try restarting Delphi to reload the package.)

Figure 24-22 shows the new component icon in the IDE.

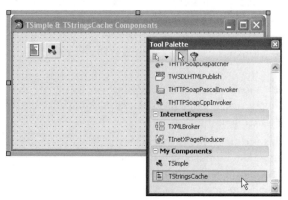

Figure 24-22: The new component icon

Grouping Related Properties

Standard Delphi components like TForm and TShape display related properties as groups of properties. For instance, the Brush, Pen, and Constraints
properties of the TShape component are simply groups of related properties
(see Figure 24-23).

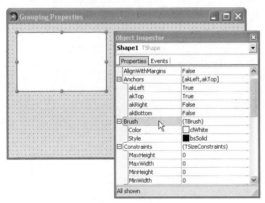

Figure 24-23: Grouped properties

Grouped properties, like the Color and Style properties in the Brush group,
actually don't belong directly to the TShape component but to a
subcomponent of type TBrush.

To create a property group, you first have to derive a new class from
TPersistent (for instance, TMyProperties) and add your properties to the published section of that class. When you're done with the TPersistent
descendant, add the property group to the main component by creating a
TMyProperties object property.

The following listing shows both the TPersistent descendant class and a
main component that uses it.

Listing 24-14: Creating a property group

```
unit PropertyGroup;

interface

uses
  SysUtils, Classes, Graphics;

type
  TMyProperties = class(TPersistent)
  private
    FColor: TColor; { needs Graphics in the uses list }
    FID: Integer;
    FText: string;
  published
    property Color: TColor read FColor write FColor;
    property ID: Integer read FID write FID;
```

```
    property Text: string read FText write FText;
  end;

  TPropertyGroup = class(TComponent)
  private
    { Private declarations }
    FMyProperties: TMyProperties;
  protected
    { Protected declarations }
    procedure SetMyProperties(Value: TMyProperties); virtual;
  public
    { Public declarations }
    constructor Create(AOwner: TComponent); override;
    destructor Destroy; override;
  published
    { Published declarations }
    property MyProperties: TMyProperties
      read FMyProperties write SetMyProperties;
  end;

procedure Register;

implementation

procedure Register;
begin
  RegisterComponents('My Components', [TPropertyGroup]);
end;

constructor TPropertyGroup.Create(AOwner: TComponent);
begin
  inherited Create(AOwner);
  FMyProperties := TMyProperties.Create;
end;

destructor TPropertyGroup.Destroy;
begin
  FMyProperties.Free;
  inherited Destroy;
end;

procedure TPropertyGroup.SetMyProperties(Value: TMyProperties);
begin
  FMyProperties.Assign(Value);
end;

end.
```

Finally, recompile the package and drop a TPropertyGroup component on the Designer Surface to see the MyProperties property group.

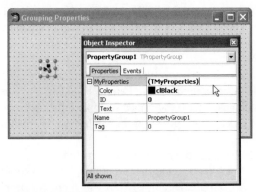

Figure 24-24: The MyProperties property group

Building VCL Components with C++Builder

If you don't have an existing package that you use, the first thing that you need to do, in both Delphi and C++, is to create a new package. To create a C++ package, select File ➢ New ➢ Package - C++ for Win32.

Once you've created the package, save it to disk, and then select Component ➢ New VCL Component to start building your new component. The IDE will, based on the package that you've created earlier, know that you want to create a C++ VCL component. If you don't open a package before starting to create a new component, the first page on the New VCL Component wizard will ask you to select the language you want to use and the platform you wish to target.

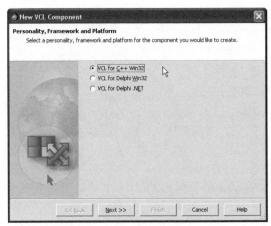

Figure 24-25: Building a component without an opened package

But when you first open a package and then select to create a new VCL component, the first page in the New VCL Component wizard will ask you to select the ancestor class of your new component. Select TComponent as the ancestor class and press Next.

On the Component page of the wizard, type TCPPSimple in the Class Name text box and My CPP Components in the Palette Page text box, and press Next to go to the final page. Since the final page only informs you that a unit will be created for the component, press the Finish button to finish building the component.

The New VCL Component wizard will create a source and a header file for the component. Before you add any code to the component, you should save it, in this case under CPPSimple. Delphi will use this name for both the source and the header file. Listings 24-15A and 24-15B show the component's source and header files.

Listing 24-15A: TCPPSimple component's source file

```
#include <vcl.h>

#pragma hdrstop
#include "CPPSimple.h"

#pragma package(smart_init)
//----------------------------------------------------------
// ValidCtrCheck is used to assure that the components
// created do not have any pure virtual functions.
//
static inline void ValidCtrCheck(TCPPSimple *)
{
    new TCPPSimple(NULL);
}
//----------------------------------------------------------
__fastcall TCPPSimple::TCPPSimple(TComponent* Owner)
    : TComponent(Owner)
{
}
//----------------------------------------------------------
namespace Cppsimple
{
    void __fastcall PACKAGE Register()
    {
        TComponentClass classes[1] = {__classid(TCPPSimple)};
        RegisterComponents("My CPP Components", classes, 0);
    }
}
//----------------------------------------------------------
```

Listing 24-15B: TCPPSimple component's header file

```
//----------------------------------------------------------

#ifndef CPPSimpleH
#define CPPSimpleH
//----------------------------------------------------------
#include <SysUtils.hpp>
```

```
#include <Classes.hpp>
//----------------------------------------------------
class PACKAGE TCPPSimple : public TComponent
{
private:
protected:
public:
    __fastcall TCPPSimple(TComponent* Owner);
__published:
};
//----------------------------------------------------
#endif
```

Finally, when you've saved the component's files to disk, right-click the package file (CppPackage.bpl) in the Project Manager and select Add on the context menu to add the component to the package. If you want, you can right-click the page file again and select Install on the context menu to add the newly created component to the Tool Palette, as shown in Figure 24-26.

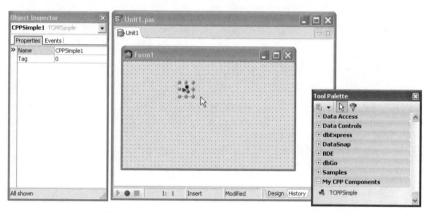

Figure 24-26: A simple C++Builder VCL component

Creating Properties

Properties in C++Builder VCL components are created with the reserved word __property, using the following syntax:

```
/* Read-only property */
__property DataType PropertyName = {
   read = Variable or Function
};

/* Complete property that can be read
   from and written to. */
__property DataType PropertyName = {
   read = Variable or Function,
   write = Variable or Function
};
```

Based on the above syntax, here's the MyString property in C++:

```
class PACKAGE TCPPSimple : public TComponent
{
private:
   AnsiString FMyString;
protected:
public:
   __fastcall TCPPSimple(TComponent* Owner);
__published:
   __property AnsiString MyString = {
      read = FMyString,
      write = FMyString
   };
};
```

To give the property a default value, you have to use the reserved word default inside the property block and also assign the same value to the underlying field in the component's constructor. Here's the MyInteger property with a default value of 20:

```
class PACKAGE TCPPSimple : public TComponent
{
private:
   int FMyInteger;
protected:
public:
   __fastcall TCPPSimple(TComponent* Owner);
__published:
   __property int MyInteger = {
      read = FMyInteger,
      write = FMyInteger,
      default = 20
   };
};

__fastcall TCPPSimple::TCPPSimple(TComponent* Owner)
   : TComponent(Owner)
{
   FMyInteger = 20;
}
```

Methods and Events

Adding methods and events to a C++ VCL component is as simple as it is in Delphi. To see how to create methods and events, let's implement the OnAccess event we implemented in the Delphi TSimple class.

To implement the OnAccess event, you'll need to add a TNotifyEvent field to the private section of the class and create a read method for the MyInteger property that will actually fire the OnAccess event when the property value is read:

```
class PACKAGE TCPPSimple : public TComponent
{
private:
```

```
    int FMyInteger;
    TNotifyEvent FOnAccess;
public:
    int __fastcall GetMyInteger(void);
__published:
    __property int MyInteger = {
        // use the GetMyInteger read method
        read = GetMyInteger,
        write = FMyInteger,
        default = 20
    };

    __property TNotifyEvent OnAccess = {
        read = FOnAccess,
        write = FOnAccess
    };
};

//------------------------------------------------------------
int __fastcall TCPPSimple::GetMyInteger(void)
{
    /* fire the OnAccess event */
    if(FOnAccess != NULL)
        FOnAccess(this);

    return FMyInteger;
}
```

Object Properties

To create an object property in a VCL component, you need to declare an object field, instantiate the object in the component's constructor, and delete the object in the component's destructor. To see how to add object properties to a C++ VCL component, let's recreate the TStringsCache component.

First, add the TStringList field to the private section of the component, and then create the object in the component's constructor:

```
class PACKAGE TCPPStringsCache : public TComponent
{
private:
    TStringList* FStrings;
    ...
};

__fastcall TCPPStringsCache::TCPPStringsCache(TComponent* Owner)
    : TComponent(Owner)
{
    FStrings = new TStringList;
}
```

All objects that are created in the constructor should be deleted in the component's destructor. In C++, the destructor isn't called Destroy. Instead, it is denoted by a tilde followed by the class name:

```
TClass::~TClass() {
}
```

Since we only need to delete the FStrings object, we can inline the destructor to reduce typing. Here's the TCPPStringCache component's destructor:

```
class PACKAGE TCPPStringsCache : public TComponent
{
private:
   TStringList* FStrings;
public:
   __fastcall TCPPStringsCache(TComponent* Owner);

   /* inlined destructor */
   virtual __fastcall ~TCPPStringsCache()
   {
      delete FStrings;
   }
};
```

To finish the property, we still need to create the SetStrings write method to allow us to change the contents of the TStringList (this should preferably be a protected virtual method if you plan on changing it in the future), and we need to define the property in the published section of the class:

```
class PACKAGE TCPPStringsCache : public TComponent
{
protected:
   virtual void __fastcall SetStrings(TStringList* Value);
__published:
   __property TStringList* Strings = {
      read = FStrings,
      write = SetStrings
   };
};

//----------------------------------------------------------------------
void __fastcall TCPPStringsCache::SetStrings(TStringList* Value)
{
   FStrings->Assign(Value);
}
```

Chapter 25

Customizing Existing Components

The first thing you are going to learn in this chapter is how to use the Object Repository to reuse your custom forms in other projects. Then you'll learn how to create a TRichEdit descendant that can load rich text documents from resource-only DLLs and, of course, how to create such DLLs.

Creating a Custom Form

The main goal of this part of the chapter is to show how to save a form to the Object Repository and how to reuse it in other projects. To illustrate this, we are going to create a form that will fade in or slide in when displayed and fade out or slide out when closed. These effects can be easily implemented using the AnimateWindow API function.

First, you should create a new VCL Forms application project and rename the main form AnimatedForm. Then, create the TAnimationType enumeration and the AnimationType public property to enable the users to select whether they want the form to fade or slide:

```
type
  TAnimationType = (atSlide, atFade);

  TAnimatedForm = class(TForm)
  private
    { Private declarations }
    FAnimationType: TAnimationType;
  public
    { Public declarations }
    property AnimationType: TAnimationType
      read FAnimationType write FAnimationType;
  published
  end;
```

Next, you have to call the AnimateWindow function in the OnShow and
OnClose event handlers to run the selected effect when the form is displayed
and closed. AnimateWindow is a simple function that accepts three parameters: the handle of the window to be animated, the duration of the animation in
milliseconds, and one of the AW_* constants that specifies the animation type:

```
function AnimateWindow(hWnd: HWND; dwTime: DWORD; dwFlags: DWORD): BOOL;
stdcall;
```

The AW_* constants that can be used in the dwFlags parameter are declared
in the Windows unit. To slide the window from the center outward or to slide
inward toward the center, we are going to use the AW_CENTER constant. To
fade the window, we're going to use the AW_BLEND constant. To animate the
window in the OnClose event when the form is closed, combine (using the or
operator) one of the above constants with the AW_HIDE constant.

Since the animation messes up the display of the child controls on the
form, we have to do two more things in the OnShow event handler: Call
SetFocus to properly display the form in front of other forms (if the form is not
the main form) and repaint all child controls. To repaint all child controls, we
can use the Controls and ControlCount properties of the form in a loop that
will repaint all child controls by calling their Repaint method.

The following listing displays the AnimatedForm's implementation.

Listing 25-1: The AnimatedForm

```
unit Unit1;

interface

uses
  Windows, Messages, SysUtils, Variants, Classes, Graphics, Controls, Forms,
  Dialogs;

type
  TAnimationType = (atSlide, atFade);

  TAnimatedForm = class(TForm)
    procedure FormClose(Sender: TObject; var Action: TCloseAction);
    procedure FormShow(Sender: TObject);
  private
    { Private declarations }
    FAnimationType: TAnimationType;
  public
    { Public declarations }
    property AnimationType: TAnimationType
      read FAnimationType write FAnimationType;
  end;

const
  DURATION = 200; { ms }
```

```
var
  AnimatedForm: TAnimatedForm;

implementation

{$R *.dfm}

procedure TAnimatedForm.FormShow(Sender: TObject);
var
  cnt: Integer;
begin
  if FAnimationType = atSlide then
    AnimateWindow(Handle, DURATION, AW_CENTER)
  else
    AnimateWindow(Handle, DURATION, AW_BLEND);

  { focus the form and repaint the form's child controls }
  SetFocus;
  for cnt := 0 to Pred(ControlCount) do
    if Controls[cnt].Visible then Controls[cnt].Repaint;
end;

procedure TAnimatedForm.FormClose(Sender: TObject; var Action: TCloseAction);
begin
  if FAnimationType = atSlide then
    AnimateWindow(Handle, DURATION, AW_CENTER or AW_HIDE)
  else
    AnimateWindow(Handle, DURATION, AW_BLEND or AW_HIDE);
end;

end.
```

Now that the form is finished, you should save it (only the form, using the File ➤ Save As command) to a dedicated object repository directory. You can either create your own or use Delphi's Object Repository (BDS\4.0\Objrepos\ DelphiWin32). Save the form as Anim.pas.

Saving the form to a custom directory only makes it project independent. To reuse the form in other projects, you still have to add it to the Object Repository by right-clicking the form and selecting Add To Repository on the context menu. The Add to Repository dialog box that appears allows you to define basic repository item properties like category, name, and description.

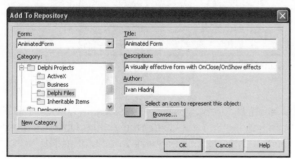

Figure 25-1:
Adding the form
to the Object
Repository

You can now close the current project and create a new VCL Forms application project to test the new form. After you've created the new project, select Project ➤ Remove from Project to display the Remove From Project dialog box, which allows us to remove forms from a project (see Figure 25-2). To remove the Form1 form from the project, select it in the Remove From Project dialog box and click OK. When you click OK to remove the form, Delphi will ask you to confirm the removal, so you'll have to click another OK button to completely remove the form from the project.

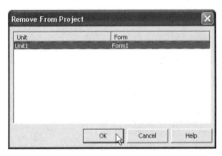

Figure 25-2:
Removing a form
from the project

The reason we removed the main form should be obvious: to replace it with the animated form we created earlier. To add an instance of the animated form to the project, select File ➤ New ➤ Other to display the New Items dialog box. You should be able to see the Animated Form item immediately, if you added the form to the Delphi Files category.

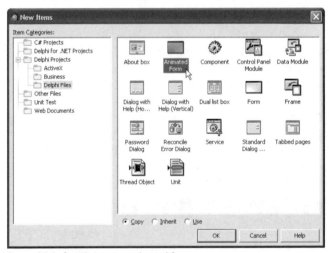

Figure 25-3: Creating a new animated form

Before creating a new animated form, you have to choose how to use it. There are three ways to use the animated form (and other similar Object Repository items) in a project. You can copy the form, inherit from it, or use it. Notice the

three radio buttons that allow you to make this choice at the bottom of the
New Items dialog box.

If you select Copy, the original animated form unit will be copied to your
project. If you use this option, changes made to the form in this project will
not be available in other projects, and changes made to the original animated
form won't be available in the current project.

If you select Use, you will be able to use the original animated form. This
is something you shouldn't do if you want to use the animated form in other
projects. If you use this option, make sure the changes made to the animated
form can be successfully reused in other projects.

If you select Inherit, the New Items dialog box will derive a new form
from the original animated form (this is known as visual form inheritance). If
you inherit the original animated form, future changes made to the animated
form will be immediately available in the project (you'll only have to recompile
it). This is the best choice most of the time.

So, to use the animated form in your projects, select Inherit to derive a
new form from the original animated form and click OK. When you derive a
new form from an Object Repository form, Delphi also adds the reference to
the original form to your project (see Figure 25-4), so be careful what form
you're changing until you get used to using visually inherited forms.

Figure 25-4:
Visually inheriting
a form

Finally, the following example shows how to animate a form that covers the
entire desktop (using the wsMaximized WindowState property doesn't work
properly):

```
procedure TMainForm.FormCreate(Sender: TObject);
begin
  AnimationType := atFade;
  SetBounds(Screen.WorkAreaLeft, Screen.WorkAreaTop,
    Screen.WorkAreaWidth, Screen.WorkAreaHeight);
end;
```

Figure 25-5 shows an animated form that uses the above code.

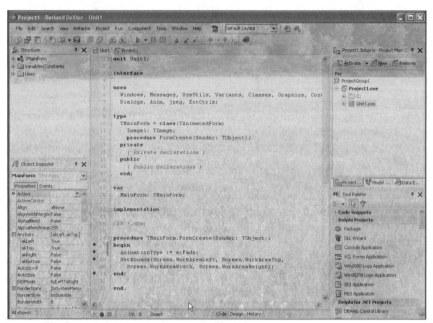

Figure 25-5: The animated form caught in the middle of the fade effect

TRichEdit Descendant

In this section, you learn how to create a TRichEdit descendant that can load rich text documents from resource-only DLLs. But before learning how to create the TRichEdit descendant, let's see how to create resource-only DLLs (without using the IDE).

Creating the Resource-Only DLL

Since we're going to create and compile the DLL without using the IDE, you should first create a new project directory and two subdirectories called Data and Bin. The Data subdirectory will be used to store rich text documents, and Bin will be used as the destination directory for the compiled resource file and the DLL. These additional subdirectories are by no means a necessity, but they can help you keep data, code, and binary files separated and more manageable.

Now that the directories are done, create a rich text document (see Figure 25-6) in WordPad (or any other application that can save .rtf documents) and save the document to the Data subdirectory under the name SampleDoc.rtf.

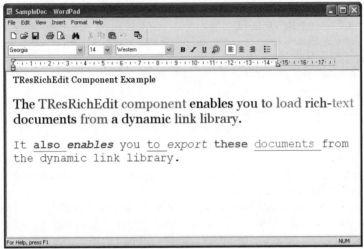

Figure 25-6: The sample rich text document

Now we have to create the .rc file in order to compile the rich text document into a .res file that can be linked into the DLL. Open Notepad (or any other application that saves plain text files) and write the following:

```
SAMPLE_DOCUMENT RCDATA "Data\SampleDoc.rtf"
```

The above line defines a custom resource called SAMPLE_DOCUMENT. The RCDATA statement is used to add any type of data to a resource file. The last part tells the resource compiler to use the SampleDoc.rtf file from the Data subdirectory. Since you're telling the resource compiler that the SampleDoc.rtf document is in the Data subdirectory, you must save this text document in the project's root directory. Save the text document as Data.rc.

Now, let's create the main project file for the DLL. Again, open Notepad and then write the following:

```
library ResLib;

{$R Data.res}

begin
end.
```

The above code is actually the entire DLL! The reason this DLL is called a resource-only DLL is now obvious: There's no code in it.

Before creating the batch file that will compile both the resource file and the DLL, you have to save the DLL to the root directory of the project under ResLib.dpr.

The only thing left to do is create the batch file that will compile the resource file and the DLL. Open Notepad one last time, write the statements that follow, and save the file in the project's root directory under Compile.bat:

```
@brcc32 -foBin\Data.res Data.rc
@dcc32 ResLib.dpr -RBin -EBin
@PAUSE
```

The first line in the Compile.bat file calls the resource compiler. The -fo option is used to tell the resource compiler where to put the output file and how to name it. In this case, the resource compiler is told to create the Data.res file in the Bin subdirectory. The Data.rc part tells the compiler that the Data.rc file contains the statements that specify which resources should be compiled into the Data.res file.

The second line calls the Delphi for Win32 compiler (dcc32.exe). The first part of the line after @dcc32 identifies which project file should be compiled. The -RBin option tells the compiler that the project's resources reside in the Bin directory (the Data.res file compiled by the previous line). The -EBin option tells the compiler to place the final EXE or DLL in the Bin directory.

Finally, the @PAUSE statement, which is a standard batch file statement, is used to keep the console window visible until we close it manually (see Figure 25-7). You shouldn't remove this line because it enables you to view compilation errors, if any occur.

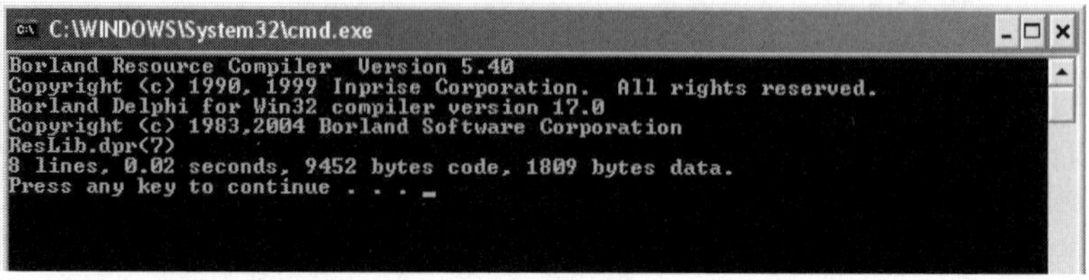

Figure 25-7: Running Compile.bat

Creating the TResRichEdit Component

To create the TResRichEdit component, go back to the Delphi IDE and then do the following:

1. Open the package you created in the last chapter (or create a new one, whichever suits you better).

2. Select Component ➢ New VCL Component to display the New VCL Component dialog box.

3. Select TRichEdit as the ancestor component.

4. Save the TResRichEdit component in the package's directory under ResRichEdit.pas.

5. Proceed to the final step and add the new component to the opened package.

To enable the TResRichEdit component to load rich text documents from any DLL we create, we have to create a public method that accepts two constant string parameters: the name of the DLL and the name of the resource we want to load.

```
procedure LoadLibrary(const LibraryName, ResourceName: string);
```

The best way to load a resource-only DLL is by using the LoadLibraryEx API function. To use this function, you must add the Windows unit to the component's uses list.

Here's the declaration of the LoadLibraryEx function:

```
function LoadLibraryEx(lpLibFileName: PChar;
  hFile: THandle; dwFlags: DWORD): HMODULE; stdcall;
```

When you pass the LOAD_LIBRARY_AS_DATAFILE constant as the dwFlags parameter, the LoadLibraryEx function simply sucks the DLL into memory, without executing additional code that usually gets executed for normal DLLs.

DLLs loaded with the LoadLibraryEx function must be released from memory with a call to FreeLibrary, like DLLs loaded using the LoadLibrary function.

After we load the resource-only DLL into memory, we have to load the resource into the TRichEdit component. Since there's no way the TRichEdit component can load a rich text document stored as a resource in a dynamic link library, we have to extract the rich text resource from the DLL into something the TRichEdit component can use — a memory stream.

Delphi has a specialized stream class that can be used to load resources into memory: the TResourceStream class. The constructor of the TResourceStream class is all that we have to call:

```
constructor Create(Instance: THandle; const ResName: string; ResType: PChar);
```

To load resources from the DLL, pass the DLL's handle (returned by the LoadLibraryEx function) as the Instance parameter. ResName is obviously the name of the resource we wish to load. Finally, we must pass the resource type as the ResType parameter. The Windows unit contains several RT_ constants that can be passed, but since we're using rich text documents, which are custom RCDATA resources, we have to use the RT_RCDATA constant.

After the TResourceStream loads the rich text document from the DLL into memory, the TRichEdit component can load the data from the stream using the LoadFromStream method. The following listing shows the entire LoadLibrary method.

Listing 25-2: The LoadLibrary method for loading rich text documents from a DLL

```
procedure TResRichEdit.LoadLibrary(const LibraryName, ResourceName: string);
var
  LibraryHandle: THandle;
  ResourceStream: TResourceStream;
begin
  LibraryHandle := LoadLibraryEx(Pointer(LibraryName),
```

```
    0, LOAD_LIBRARY_AS_DATAFILE);
  try
    ResourceStream := TResourceStream.Create(LibraryHandle,
      ResourceName, RT_RCDATA);
    try
      Lines.LoadFromStream(ResourceStream);
    finally
      ResourceStream.Free;
    end;        // try..finally
  finally
    FreeLibrary(LibraryHandle);
  end;          // try..finally
end;
```

To test the new component, make sure the component is registered by right-clicking the package and selecting Install. Then add a new VCL Forms application project to the project group and drop the TResRichEdit component and a button on the Designer Surface.

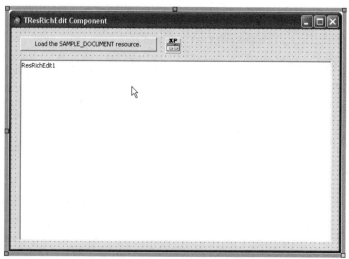

Figure 25-8: The TResRichEdit component

To load the sample document from the DLL we created earlier, you need to do two things:

1. Copy ResLib.dll from the Bin subdirectory to the root directory of this test application (to avoid having to specify a path or use the TOpenDialog component to locate the DLL).

2. Call the LoadLibrary method of the component to load the SAMPLE_DOCUMENT resource from the ResLib.dll.

Here's the code that you have to write to make things work:

```
procedure TForm1.Button1Click(Sender: TObject);
begin
  ResRichEdit1.LoadLibrary('ResLib.dll', 'SAMPLE_DOCUMENT');
end;
```

The result of using the LoadLibrary method to load a rich text document into the component is displayed in Figure 25-9.

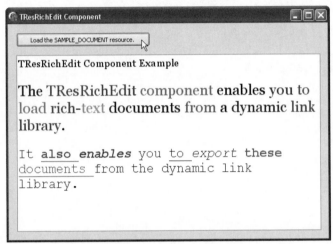

Figure 25-9: Loading the sample document from the DLL

The last thing left to do is to create a second method that enables us to export documents from the DLL. This method is painfully similar to the LoadLibrary method. The only difference is that instead of calling TRichEdit.LoadFromStream, we call the SaveToFile method of the TResourceStream class to write the contents of the memory stream to the disk. You can see the entire ExportResource method in the following listing.

Listing 25-3: The ExportResource method for exporting individual resources from the DLL to the disk

```
procedure TResRichEdit.ExportResource(const LibraryName,
  ResourceName, DestFileName: string);
var
  LibraryHandle: THandle;
  ResourceStream: TResourceStream;
begin
  LibraryHandle := LoadLibraryEx(Pointer(LibraryName),
    0, LOAD_LIBRARY_AS_DATAFILE);
  try
    ResourceStream := TResourceStream.Create(LibraryHandle,
      ResourceName, RT_RCDATA);
```

```
      try
        ResourceStream.SaveToFile(DestFileName);
      finally
        ResourceStream.Free;
      end;
    finally
      FreeLibrary(LibraryHandle);
    end;
  end;
end;
```

Chapter 26

Advanced Component Programming

In this chapter, you're going to see how to create two fairly complex components. The first component is a customized list box that displays Latin-1 characters from the XHTML 1.0 Character Entity Set (see Figure 26-1). The second component is a TComponent descendant that allows you to save multiple images to a single file.

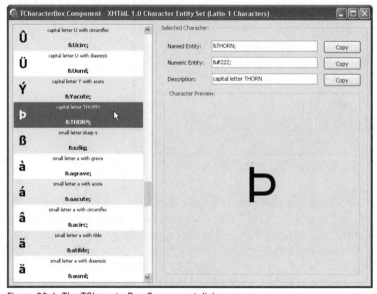

Figure 26-1: The TCharacterBox Component dialog

Custom List Control

In Chapter 24, it was mentioned that you can derive a new list control from TCustomListBox, since the TCustomListBox is really the same thing as TListBox, except that the majority of the properties are protected or public.

The TCustomListBox component is the perfect ancestor for the TCharacterBox component that we are going to create because, among other things, the TCustomListBox doesn't publish the Items property. There is no need to enable the user to change or even access the Items property of the TCharacterBox component at design time, because the component's data is constant (it always has 96 items) and dynamically generated in the component's constructor (well, almost).

To create the basic skeleton of the TCharacterBox component, open your component package and select Component ➤ New VCL Component. On the New VCL Component dialog box, select the TCustomListBox component as the ancestor component, name the new component TCharacterBox, add it to your Tool Palette category, and save it to your component directory under CharacterBox.pas.

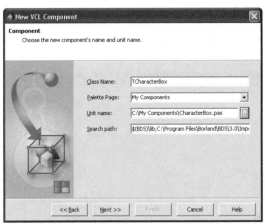

Figure 26-2: Creating the TCharacterBox component

The TCharacterBox is specific not only because it is derived from a "TCustomComponentName" class, but also because it surfaces data stored in a two-dimensional array declared in the implementation part of the unit. This array contains symbol descriptions (like "small letter a with tilde") and named entities (like "nbsp") that can be added to HTML/XHTML pages to display a particular symbol. In fact, valid named entities begin with an ampersand and end with a semicolon ( ), but this is not important in the array. We'll generate valid named entities when we copy the data from the array to the Items property of the list.

The following listing displays the entire CHARACTERS array used by the TCharaterBox component. The array is declared in the implementation part of the unit, beneath the reserved word implementation and above the implementation of the Register procedure.

Listing 26-1: The entire character list

```
const
  { Description | Named Entity  }
  CHARACTERS: array[0..95, 1..2] of string = (
    ('non-breaking space', 'nbsp'), ('inverted exclamation mark', 'iexcl'),
    ('cent sign', 'cent'), ('pound sign', 'pound'),
    ('currency sign', 'curren'), ('yen sign', 'yen'),
    ('broken bar', 'brvbar'), ('section sign', 'sect'), ('diaresis', 'uml'),
    ('copyright sign', 'copy'), ('feminine ordinal indicator', 'ordf'),
    ('left-pointing double angle quotation mark', 'laquo'),
    ('not sign', 'not'), ('soft hyphen', 'shy'), ('registered sign', 'reg'),
    ('macron', 'macr'), ('degree sign', 'deg'), ('plus-minus sign', 'plusmn'),
    ('superscript two', 'sup2'), ('superscript three', 'sup3'),
    ('acute accent', 'acute'), ('micro sign', 'micro'),
    ('pilcrow sign', 'para'), ('middle dot', 'middot'),
    ('cedilla', 'cedil'), ('superscript one', 'sup1'),
    ('masculine ordinal indicator', 'ordm'),
    ('right-pointing guillemet', 'raquo'), ('fraction one quarter', 'frac14'),
    ('fraction one half', 'frac12'), ('fraction three quarters', 'frac34'),
    ('inverted question mark', 'iquest'),
    ('capital letter A grave', 'Agrave'),
    ('capital letter A with acute', 'Aacute'),
    ('capital letter A with circumflex', 'Acirc'),
    ('capital letter A with tilde', 'Atilde'),
    ('capital letter A with diaresis', 'Auml'),
    ('capital letter A with ring above', 'Aring'),
    ('capital letter AE', 'AElig'),
    ('capital letter C with cedilla', 'Ccedil'),
    ('capital letter E with grave', 'Egrave'),
    ('capital letter E with acute', 'Eacute'),
    ('capital letter E with circumflex', 'Ecirc'),
    ('capital letter E with diaeresis', 'Euml'),
    ('capital letter I with grave', 'Igrave'),
    ('capital letter I with acute', 'Iacute'),
    ('capital letter I with circumflex', 'Icirc'),
    ('capital letter I with diaresis', 'Iuml'),
    ('capital letter ETH', 'ETH'), ('capital letter N with tilde', 'Ntilde'),
    ('capital letter O with grave', 'Ograve'),
    ('capital letter O with acute', 'Oacute'),
    ('capital letter O with circumflex', 'Ocirc'),
    ('capital letter O with tilde', 'Otilde'),
    ('capital letter O with diaresis', 'Ouml'),
    ('multiplication sign', 'times'),
    ('capital letter O with stroke', 'Oslash'),
    ('capital letter U with grave', 'Ugrave'),
    ('capital letter U with acute', 'Uacute'),
    ('capital letter U with circumflex', 'Ucirc'),
    ('capital letter U with diaresis', 'Uuml'),
    ('capital letter Y with acute', 'Yacute'),
    ('capital letter THORN', 'THORN'), ('small letter sharp s', 'szlig'),
    ('small letter a with grave', 'agrave'),
    ('small letter a with acute', 'aacute'),
```

```
    ('small letter a with circumflex', 'acirc'),
    ('small letter a with tilde', 'atilde'),
    ('small letter a with diaeresis', 'auml'),
    ('small letter a with ring above', 'aring'), ('small letter ae', 'aelig'),
    ('small letter c with cedilla', 'ccedil'),
    ('small letter e with grave', 'egrave'),
    ('small letter e with acute', 'eacute'),
    ('small letter e with circumflex', 'ecirc'),
    ('small letter e with diaeresis', 'euml'),
    ('small letter i with grave', 'igrave'),
    ('small letter i with acute', 'iacute'),
    ('small letter i with circumflex', 'icirc'),
    ('small letter i with diaeresis', 'iuml'), ('small letter eth', 'eth'),
    ('small letter n with tilde', 'ntilde'),
    ('small letter o with grave', 'ograve'),
    ('small letter o with acute', 'oacute'),
    ('small letter o with circumflex', 'ocirc'),
    ('small letter o with tilde', 'otilde'),
    ('small letter o with diaeresis', 'ouml'), ('division sign', 'divide'),
    ('small letter o with stroke', 'oslash'),
    ('small letter u with grave', 'ugrave'),
    ('small letter u with acute', 'uacute'),
    ('small letter u with circumflex', 'ucirc'),
    ('small letter u with diaeresis', 'uuml'),
    ('small letter y with acute', 'yacute'), ('small letter thorn', 'thorn'),
    ('small letter y with diaeresis', 'yuml')
  ); // CHARACTERS
```

Now that we have the data, we have to override the component's constructor in order to do two things: change the size of the items in the list and change the list's style. To display all relevant data (the symbol, its description, and its named entity), we have to set the ItemHeight property to 50 (you can set the ItemHeight property to whatever you want, but 50 gives good results and the rest of the code is based on the assumption that the ItemHeight is 50).

We also have to change the component's Style property. The Style property is an enumerated property of type TListBoxStyle, with the default value lbStandard, which results in a list that only displays strings and has items of the same height.

Here's the declaration of the TListBoxStyle type:

```
type TListBoxStyle = (lbStandard, lbOwnerDrawFixed, lbOwnerDrawVariable,
  lbVirtual, lbVirtualOwnerDraw);
```

To customize the drawing of the list's items, we are going to use the lbOwnerDrawFixed style. A list box with this style uses the ItemHeight property to determine the height of all items and it fires the OnDrawItem event for each item that has to be displayed. You can also use the lbOwnerDraw-Variable style if you want to have items of varying heights. A list box with the lbOwnerDrawVariable style fires the OnMeasureItem event first, which enables you to specify the height for an item. After the OnMeasureItem, the list box fires the OnDrawItem event to display the item.

Here's the component's constructor:

```
type
  TCharacterBox = class(TCustomListBox)
  private
    { Private declarations }
  protected
    { Protected declarations }
  public
    { Public declarations }
    constructor Create(AOwner: TComponent); override;
  published
    { Published declarations }
  end;

implementation
...
constructor TCharacterBox.Create (AOwner: TComponent);
begin
  inherited Create (AOwner);
  Style := lbOwnerDrawFixed;
  ItemHeight := 50;
end;
```

Now we have to populate the Items property with the named entities from the CHARACTERS array. The problem with this part of the component development ment process is not how to do it, because you are now able to copy items from a string array to a string list blindfolded and half asleep:

```
{ generate and add named entities to the Items property }
{ named entities begin with & and end with ; =>   }
Items.BeginUpdate;
for cnt := 0 to 95 do
  Items.Add('&' + CHARACTERS[cnt, 2] + ';');
Items.EndUpdate;
```

The problem is where to put this code, because you definitely can't put it in the component's constructor. If you try to access the Items property in the constructor, you'll break your component because the Items property isn't properly initialized at that point. If you access the Items property in the constructor, you'll be able the compile the component but you'll receive the "Control " has no parent window" error when you try to drop the component on the Designer Surface (see Figure 26-3).

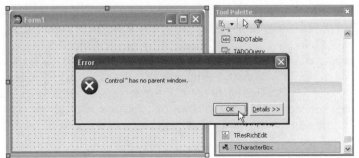

Figure 26-3: Trying to do things that can't be done in the constructor

There is a deceptively simple solution to the "Control " has no parent window" error. Simply typecast the constructor's AOwner parameter to TWinControl and assign the result to the component's Parent property:

```
constructor TCharacterBox.Create (AOwner: TComponent);
var
  cnt: Integer;
begin
  inherited Create (AOwner);
  Parent := TWinControl(AOwner);
  { ... }
end;
```

This simple assignment successfully solves the "no parent window" problem, but it creates another very serious problem: The IDE *always* sets the form as the component's parent, which means you can only add the component to the form and you *cannot* add your component to any other container control!

The following figure shows what happens when you try to drop the TCharacterBox component on a TPanel. Notice (in the Structure window) that the TButton component is properly added to the TPanel component and that the TCharacterBox component is, because of the parent assignment, erroneously added to the form.

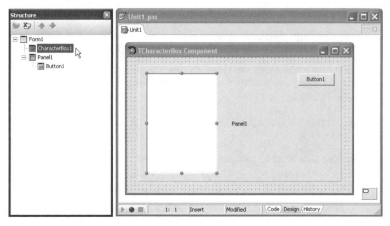

Figure 26-4: The IDE cannot properly create your component if you modify the Parent property in the constructor.

Note that you can move the component to a container control once you've added it to the Designer Surface, but this is by no means something that you can or should tolerate.

To properly initialize the component, we have to override the Loaded procedure and move the initialization code into that procedure. The Loaded procedure is perfect for this job because it is called when the component is fully loaded into memory to execute code that depends on other objects. You should override the Loaded method in the protected section of the component; there's no need to promote the method to the public section because it's of no use (possibly even harmful) to component users.

Here's the implementation of the Loaded method:

```
type
  TCharacterBox = class(TCustomListBox)
  private
    { Private declarations }
  protected
    { Protected declarations }
    procedure Loaded; override;
  public
    { Public declarations }
    constructor Create(AOwner: TComponent); override;
  published
    { Published declarations }
  end;

...
constructor TCharacterBox.Create (AOwner: TComponent);
begin
  inherited Create (AOwner);
  Style := lbOwnerDrawFixed;
  ItemHeight := 50;
end;

procedure TCharacterBox.Loaded;
var
  cnt: Integer;
begin
  inherited Loaded;

  { generate and add named entities to the Items property }
  { named entities begin with & and end with ; =>   }
  Items.BeginUpdate;
  for cnt := 0 to 95 do
    Items.Add('&' + CHARACTERS[cnt, 2] + ';');
  Items.EndUpdate;
end;
```

Now that the initialization code resides in the Loaded method, we can successfully add the component to the appropriate control on the Designer Surface. The following figure shows what the TCharacterBox component should look like currently.

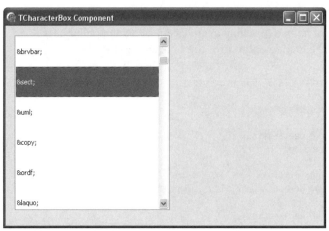

Figure 26-5: The TCharacterBox component still without custom drawing

Creating Array Properties

The TCharacterBox component should, for each item in the list, be able to return four different values: the symbol, the named entity, the numeric entity, and the symbol's description. The named entity part is already solved because we generated the named entities in the Loaded method and placed them in the Items property.

After named entities, the easiest value to return is the symbol's description. To enable the user to acquire a symbol's description, we need to create a simple public function that accepts the symbol's index and simply reads it from the CHARACTERS array:

```
type
  TCharacterBox = class(TCustomListBox)
  private
    { Private declarations }
  protected
    { Protected declarations }
  public
    { Public declarations }
    function GetDescription(CharIndex: Integer): string;
  published
    { Published declarations }
  end;

...

function TCharacterBox.GetDescription(CharIndex: Integer): string;
begin
  if (CharIndex >= 0) and (CharIndex <= 95) then
    Result := CHARACTERS[CharIndex][1]
  else
    Result := '';
end;
```

We can now use this function to create the Descriptions array property. An array property is nothing more than a standard property that has a parameter list, which enables it to represent more complex items, like elements of an array or items in a list. The Descriptions property needs an index parameter to access a particular symbol in the CHARACTERS array and a read method that will read the character at the specified index from the CHARACTERS array. Since we've already created the read method, we only have to declare the property in the public section of the class (array properties cannot be declared in the published section):

```
property Descriptions[CharIndex: Integer]: string read GetDescription;
```

Now that we've created the public property that enables the user to access the stored descriptions, we should move the declaration of the GetDescription function to the protected section and mark it as virtual, because the GetDescription function should now only be a dedicated read method for the Descriptions property.

After creating the Descriptions property, write something like this so the user can now easily view the selected item's description:

```
procedure TForm1.Button1Click(Sender: TObject);
begin
  with CharacterBox1 do
    MessageDlg(Descriptions[ItemIndex], mtInformation, [mbOK], 0);
end;
```

Returning the symbol is also not very difficult. To create the desired symbol, you have to increase the symbol's array index by 160 and pass it to the standard Chr function. You do this because the symbols contained in the CHARACTERS array are ANSI characters. The non-breaking space character's index in the ANSI character table is 160, the inverted exclamation mark's index in the ANSI table is 161, and so on.

Here are both the Descriptions and the new Symbols array properties:

```
type
  TCharacterBox = class(TCustomListBox)
  private
    { Private declarations }
  protected
    { Protected declarations }
    function GetDescription(CharIndex: Integer): string; virtual;
    function GetSymbol(CharIndex: Integer): string; virtual;
  public
    { Public declarations }
    property Descriptions[CharIndex: Integer]: string read GetDescription;
    property Symbols[CharIndex: Integer]: string read GetSymbol;
  published
    { Published declarations }
  end;

...

function TCharacterBox.GetDescription(CharIndex: Integer): string;
```

```
begin
  if (CharIndex >= 0) and (CharIndex <= 95) then
    Result := CHARACTERS[CharIndex][1]
  else
    Result := '';
end;

function TCharacterBox.GetSymbol(CharIndex: Integer): string;
begin
  if (CharIndex >= 0) and (CharIndex <= 95) then
    Result := Chr(CharIndex + 160)
  else
    Result := '';
end;
```

Finally, the last property to implement is the NumericEntities property, which should return a string formatted like this: for the non-breaking space character, ¡ for the inverted exclamation mark character, and so on. Here's the implementation of the NumericEntities property:

```
protected
  { Protected declarations }
  function GetEntity(CharIndex: Integer): string; virtual;
public
  { Public declarations }
  property NumericEntities[CharIndex: Integer]: string read GetEntity;
end;

...

function TCharacterBox.GetEntity(CharIndex: Integer): string;
begin
  if (CharIndex >= 0) and (CharIndex <= 95) then
    Result := '&#' + IntToStr(CharIndex + 160) + ';'
  else
    Result := '';
end;
```

Sharing Property Access Methods

If you take a closer look at the Descriptions, Symbols, and NumericEntities properties and their read methods, you'll notice that they're almost identical, except for the return value. When you have several properties of the same type that use either read or write methods (or both), you can create a single read or write method that can be used by all properties.

To use such a method that can serve multiple properties, you must mark the properties with the index directive to give each property a unique index:

```
property PropertyName: DataType index IndexValue read Method write Method;
```

When you mark the properties with the index directive, you can no longer use your current read and/or write methods. You have to create another method with an additional index parameter that is used to determine which property called the method. This index parameter must be the last parameter in read methods.

The following listing contains the updated code of the TCharacterBox component. The GetEntityData method replaces all three functions that we created earlier. Its first parameter is the character index and its second parameter is the index of the property that called it.

Listing 26-2: The updated TCharacterBox component that shares a single read method among all three custom properties

```
unit CharacterBox;

interface

uses
  Windows, SysUtils, Classes, Controls, StdCtrls;

  { unique indexes of the three custom public properties }
const
  ID_DESCRIPTION = 1;
  ID_NUMERIC = 2;
  ID_SYMBOL = 3;

type
  TCharacterBox = class(TCustomListBox)
  private
    { Private declarations }
  protected
    { Protected declarations }
    function GetEntityData(Index, PropertyIndex: Integer): string; virtual;
    procedure Loaded; override;
  public
    { Public declarations }
    constructor Create(AOwner: TComponent); override;

    property Descriptions[CharIndex: Integer]: string
      index ID_DESCRIPTION read GetEntityData;

    property NumericEntities[CharIndex: Integer]: string
      index ID_NUMERIC read GetEntityData;

    property Symbols[CharIndex: Integer]: string
      index ID_SYMBOL read GetEntityData;

  published
    { Published declarations }
  end;

implementation

{ Index is the the index of the character in the CHARACTERS array }
{ PropertyIndex is the index of the property that called the method }
function TCharacterBox.GetEntityData(Index, PropertyIndex: Integer): string;
begin
  if (Index >= 0) and (Index <= 95) then
```

```
begin
  case PropertyIndex of
    ID_DESCRIPTION: Result := CHARACTERS[Index, 1];
    ID_NUMERIC: Result := '&#' + IntToStr(Index + 160) + ';';
    ID_SYMBOL: Result := Chr(Index + 160);
  end;
end else
  Result := '';
end;

end.
```

Default Array Properties

The default directive can be used with array properties to create a default array property. The advantage of a default array property is that you no longer have to type the property's name to access it. For instance, without marking the Descriptions property as the default property, you have to type the following line to access its first item:

```
TCharacterBoxObject.Descriptions[0]
```

But if you mark the Descriptions property with the default directive:

```
property Descriptions[CharIndex: Integer]: string
    index ID_DESCRIPTION read GetEntityData; default;
```

you'll be able to access the items in the Descriptions property by writing the index value in brackets immediately after the object's name:

```
TCharacterBoxObject[0]
```

Publishing Inherited Properties

Currently, the TCharacterBox component is not really usable in an application because most of its properties and all of its events are not displayed in the Object Inspector. To display such properties as Anchors and Align, and events like OnClick and OnDrawItem, you don't have to recreate them because they already exist in the TCustomListBox class. To display the currently protected properties and events of the TCustomListBox class, you only have to publish them by listing them in the published section of the class.

The following code shows how easy it is to publish inherited properties:

```
type
  TCharacterBox = class(TCustomListBox)
  published
    { Published declarations }
    property Style;
    property Align;
    property Anchors;
    property OnClick;
    property OnDrawItem;
    property OnMeasureItem;
    property OnMouseDown;
```

```
    property OnMouseMove;
    property OnMouseUp;
  end;
```

Drawing Items

Before overriding the DrawItem method to draw the items, add the Windows unit to the component's uses list. The Windows unit is required because the code in the DrawItem method uses the ANSI_CHARSET constant to change the font's character set. We must use ANSI_CHARSET in order to draw the correct symbols in the list. In order to use the TColor type and other graphics-related types and routines, you also have to add the Graphics unit to the uses list.

To display its items, an owner-drawn list box calls the DrawItem method and passes three parameters to it: the item's index, a TRect parameter with the item's coordinates, and a state parameter of type TOwnerDrawState that specifies the item's state (we only need the odSelected value that indicates the item is selected).

The DrawItem method is protected in the TCustomListBox class because the component user doesn't have to call the method directly. You should also override the DrawItem method in the protected section of the class.

Here's the declaration of the DrawItem method:

```
procedure DrawItem(Index: Integer; Rect: TRect; State: TOwnerDrawState);
```

To display three different strings (symbol, named entity, and description) at three different locations, the DrawItem method relies heavily on two API functions: DrawText to display the strings, and OffsetRect to update the coordinates of the display rectangle used by the DrawText function.

Here's the declaration of the OffsetRect function:

```
function OffsetRect(var lprc: TRect; dx, dy: Integer): BOOL; stdcall;
```

Besides the DrawText and OffsetRect API functions, the DrawItem method also uses the Canvas's DrawFocusRect method to erase the automatically drawn focus rectangle. DrawFocusRect can be used to display and to erase the focus rectangle because it uses the same xor trick we used in Chapter 22 to implement the rubber-banding effect.

Finally, here's how the TCharacterBox component displays its items:

- Changes the character set of the Canvas's font to ANSI_CHARSET to correctly display the symbols
- Fills the item's background with a color — standard window color if the item is even, 3D light color if the item is odd, or the standard highlight color if the item is selected
- Draws the three strings
- Calls the DrawFocusRect method to remove the automatically drawn focus rectangle
- Finally, calls the inherited DrawItem method to enable the component to fire the OnDrawItem event but only if the user assigned an event handler

> to the OnDrawItem event (We have to see if there's an event handler
> present because the inherited DrawItem method performs its own
> drawing if there's no event handler.)

The following listing shows the entire DrawItem method.

Listing 26-3: The DrawItem method of the TCharacterBox component

```
type
  TCharacterBox = class(TCustomListBox)
  protected
    { Protected declarations }
    procedure DrawItem(Index: Integer; Rect: TRect; State: TOwnerDrawState);
      override;

...

procedure TCharacterBox.DrawItem(Index: Integer; Rect: TRect; State:
  TOwnerDrawState);
const
  ITEM_COLOR: array[Boolean] of TColor = (clWindow, cl3DLight);
begin
  { we must use ANSI_CHARSET for valid symbol display }
  Canvas.Font.Charset := ANSI_CHARSET;

  if odSelected in State then
  begin
    { if the item is selected, use the system's highlight color for
      both the background and the text }
    Canvas.Brush.Color := clHighlight;
    Canvas.Font.Color := clHighlightText;
  end else
    Canvas.Brush.Color := ITEM_COLOR[Odd(Index)];

  { fill the background with the selected Brush color }
  Canvas.FillRect(Rect);

  { draw the symbol, 10px towards the center, horizontally }
  Canvas.Font.Style := [fsBold];
  Canvas.Font.Size := 18;
  OffsetRect(Rect, 10, 0);
  DrawText(Canvas.Handle, PChar(Symbols[Index]),
    -1, Rect, DT_LEFT or DT_VCENTER or DT_SINGLELINE);

  { draw the named entity center at the bottom of the item,
    call OffsetRect with x = -10 to restore x coordinate and
    with y = 32 to move the rect's top coordinate 32px down }
  Canvas.Font.Size := 8;
  OffsetRect(Rect, -10, 32);
  DrawText(Canvas.Handle, PChar('&' + Items[Index]),
    -1, Rect, DT_CENTER or DT_SINGLELINE);

  { draw the small description at the top of the item,
    by moving the rect back to the top, actually 4px lower }
  Canvas.Font.Size := 7;
  Canvas.Font.Style := [];
```

```
  OffsetRect(Rect, 0, -28);
  DrawText(Canvas.Handle, PChar(Descriptions[Index]),
    -1, Rect, DT_CENTER or DT_SINGLELINE);

  { restore original item rect to successfully remove the
    automatically drawn focus rect }
  OffsetRect(Rect, 0, -4);
  if odSelected in State then
    Canvas.DrawFocusRect(Rect);

  { call the inherited DrawItem method to fire the OnDrawItem event,
    but only if an event handler is assigned to it }
  if Assigned(OnDrawItem) then
    inherited DrawItem(Index, Rect, State);
end;
```

Figure 26-6 shows the final TCharacterBox component with and without an additional user-created OnDrawItem event handler.

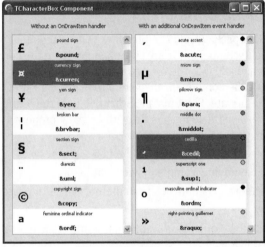

Figure 26-6: The TCharacterBox component

The TImageCache Component

The TImageCache component is a TComponent descendant that can save and load multiple images to a single file. It's a pretty interesting component because it shows how to use the TFileStream and TMemoryStream classes to work with files and memory, and how to use the TList class to maintain a list of objects in memory.

The TList Class

The TList class is a very powerful and very addictive class that is declared in the Classes unit and enables you to manage a list of pointers in memory. Its addictiveness arises from the fact that it can be used to store anything you want: objects, records, integers, strings, and even methods. For instance, the following code adds a pointer to the ShowMessage procedure to a TList and then calls the ShowMessage procedure through the pointer stored in the list:

```
procedure TForm1.Button1Click(Sender: TObject);
var
  Lst: TList;
type
  TStringProc = procedure(const S: string);
begin
  Lst := TList.Create;
  try
    Lst.Add(@ShowMessage);
    TStringProc(Lst[0])('An awkward Hello!');
  finally
    Lst.Free;
  end;       // try..finally
end;
```

Creating the TImageCache Component

Now, open your component package and run the New VCL Component wizard to derive the TImageCache component from TComponent. Save the component as ImageCache.pas and add it to the opened package.

To give the TImageCache component the ability to manage a list of bitmaps, we have to use a private TList instance that will hold the bitmap images and we have to surface these images through an array property. The component should also have the following methods:

■ One or more methods for adding images to the list

■ A Delete method for removing a single image from the list

■ A Clear method for releasing all images from memory once they are no longer needed

First, we have to override the component's constructor and destructor to create and destroy the TList instance:

```
unit ImageCache;

interface

uses
  SysUtils, Classes;

type
  TImageCache = class(TComponent)
  private
    { Private declarations }
    FImages: TList;
  protected
    { Protected declarations }
  public
    { Public declarations }
    constructor Create(AOwner: TComponent); override;
```

```
    destructor Destroy; override;
  published
    { Published declarations }
  end;

procedure Register;

implementation

procedure Register;
begin
  RegisterComponents('My Components', [TImageCache]);
end;

constructor TImageCache.Create(AOwner: TComponent);
begin
  inherited Create(AOwner);
  FImages := TList.Create;
end;

destructor TImageCache.Destroy;
begin
  FImages.Free;
  inherited Destroy;
end;

end.
```

To surface the images stored in the FImages list, we have to create a
read-only array property called Images. Since this property has to return a
TBitmap, add the Graphics unit to the uses list.

The read method of this property should check whether the Index parameter is in the valid range (0 -> FImages.Count – 1) and typecast the stored
pointer to a TBitmap when returning the image:

```
type
  TImageCache = class(TComponent)
  protected
    { Protected declarations }
    function GetImage(Index: Integer): TBitmap; virtual;
  public
    { Public declarations }
    property Images[Index: Integer]: TBitmap read GetImage; default;
  published
    { Published declarations }
  end;
...
function TImageCache.GetImage(Index: Integer): TBitmap;
begin
  if (Index >= 0) and (Index <= Pred(FImages.Count)) then
    Result := TBitmap(FImages[Index])
  else
    Result := nil;
end;
```

To make the component more user-friendly, let's create the following three overloaded Add methods:

■ One method should accept a TBitmap parameter to enable the programmer to add an already loaded bitmap to the list.

■ The second method should accept a string parameter to enable the programmer to load a bitmap from file and add it to the list.

■ The final method should accept a TStrings parameter to allow the programmer to add a larger number of images to the list.

Here are the three overloaded public Add methods:

```
type
  TImageCache = class(TComponent)
  public
    { Public declarations }
    procedure Add(ABitmap: TBitmap); overload;
    procedure Add(const AFileName: string); overload;
    procedure Add(AStrings: TStrings); overload;
end;
...
procedure TImageCache.Add(ABitmap: TBitmap);
begin
  FImages.Add(ABitmap);
end;

procedure TImageCache.Add(const AFileName: string);
var
  B: TBitmap;
begin
  B := TBitmap.Create;
  B.LoadFromFile(AFileName);
  FImages.Add(B);
end;

procedure TImageCache.Add(AStrings: TStrings);
var
  item: string;
begin
  for item in AStrings do
    Add(item);
end;
```

Now that we have the ability to add images to the list, we should also create the methods that remove these images from memory. To delete an image from memory, you cannot just call the TList's Delete method because that would only delete the pointer to the TBitmap in memory. You should first typecast the pointer to a bitmap and call Free to delete the image, and only then call the TList's Delete method to remove the pointer from the list. For the Clear method, which needs to remove all bitmaps from memory, you don't have to call the TList's Delete method to remove every bitmap's pointer from the list. You should first delete all images in a loop and then call the TList's Clear method to remove all pointers from the list.

Here are the Clear and Delete methods:

```
type
  TImageCache = class(TComponent)
  protected
    { Protected declarations }
    procedure Clear;
    procedure Delete(Index: Integer); virtual;
end;
...
procedure TImageCache.Delete(Index: Integer);
begin
  if (Index >= 0) and (Index <= Pred(FImages.Count)) then
  begin
    TBitmap(FImages[Index]).Free;
    FImages.Delete(Index);
  end;      // if Index
end;

procedure TImageCache.Clear;
var
  cnt: Integer;
  bmp: TBitmap;
begin
  { first delete all TBitmaps }
  for cnt := 0 to Pred(FImages.Count) do
  begin
    bmp := TBitmap(FImages[cnt]);
    bmp.Free;
  end;

  { remove all pointers from the list since they now point
    to invalid memory locations }
  FImages.Clear;
end;
```

Now that we have the Clear method, we must update the component's destructor and first call the Clear method to remove the images from memory when the component is destroyed:

```
destructor TImageCache.Destroy;
begin
  Clear;
  FImages.Free;
  inherited Destroy;
end;
```

Saving and Loading Images

The most important methods of the TImageCache class are the SaveToFile and LoadFromFile methods that enable us to store images to and load images from a cache file. Let's start by creating the SaveToFile method.

Here's how the TImageCache component stores multiple images to a single file:

- First, the SaveToFile method needs to instantiate the TFileStream class to create the destination file.
- The first piece of data that is written to the file is the number of images that exist in the list (this helps us read the images from the file more easily).
- To save the image from the list to the file and to read the image's size, the SaveToFile method copies the bitmap to a TMemoryStream.
- For every image, the SaveToFile method stores two values: the bitmap's size and the bitmap itself.

The following listing shows the TImageCache component's SaveToFile method.

Listing 26-4: The SaveToFile method

```
type
  TImageCache = class(TComponent)
  public
    { Public declarations }
    procedure SaveToFile(const AFileName: string);
end;
...
procedure TImageCache.SaveToFile(const AFileName: string);
var
  cnt: Integer;
  fs: TFileStream;
  buffer: TMemoryStream;
  imgSize: Integer;
  imgCount: Integer;
begin
  fs := TFileStream.Create(AFileName, fmCreate);
  try
    { create the TMemoryStream before the loop because there's no need
      to create a new instance of the TMemoryStream for every image }
    buffer := TMemoryStream.Create;
    try
      { write image count }
      imgCount := FImages.Count;
      fs.Write(imgCount, SizeOf(Integer));

      for cnt := 0 to Pred(FImages.Count) do
      begin
        { save the image to the memory stream, but first call Clear
          to remove the old image and to reset the stream's position }
        buffer.Clear;
        TBitmap(FImages[cnt]).SaveToStream(buffer);

        { write the bitmap's size to the file }
        imgSize := buffer.Size;
        fs.Write(imgSize, SizeOf(Integer));

        { finally, write the image to the file }
```

```
      fs.CopyFrom(buffer, 0);
    end;    // for cnt
  finally
    buffer.Free;
  end;       // try..finally (TMemoryStream.Create)
finally
  fs.Free;
end;         // try..finally (TFileStream.Create)
end;
```

To implement the LoadFromFile method, you have to do the opposite of what you did in the SaveToFile method (and a bit more):

■ First, you have to call the Clear method to remove the existing images from memory.

■ Instantiate the TFileStream to access the file.

■ Read the number of images stored in the file.

■ Use the read image count in a loop to read all images.

When loading the image from the file, you have to do the following:

■ Read the size of the bitmap stored in the file by the SaveToFile method.

■ Call the Clear method of the memory stream to remove the old data and to restore the stream's Position to 0.

■ Load the image to the memory stream.

■ To read the entire image using the TBitmap.LoadFromStream method, you must set the stream's Position to 0 (after you load the image into the memory stream, the Position property points to the end of the stream, and this is not good because the TBitmap's LoadFromStream method reads the stream's data from Position to the stream's end).

■ After resetting the stream's Position, create a new TBitmap instance and call its LoadFromStream method to load the image from the memory stream into the TBitmap.

■ Finally, call the TImageCache's Add method and pass it the new TBitmap to add it to the list.

The following listing shows the TImageCache component's LoadFromFile method.

Listing 26-5: The LoadFromFile method

```
type
  TImageCache = class(TComponent)
  public
    { Public declarations }
    procedure LoadFromFile(const AFileName: string);
end;
...
procedure TImageCache.LoadFromFile(const AFileName: string);
var
  fs: TFileStream;
  imgCount: Integer;
  buffer: TMemoryStream;
```

```
  imgSize: Integer;
  cnt: Integer;
  bmp: TBitmap;
begin
  Clear; { remove existing data from memory }

  { pass fmOpenRead if you only want to open the file }
  fs := TFileStream.Create(AFileName, fmOpenRead);
  try
    { create the TMemoryStream helper object that will load images from
      the file to a memory stream that can then be used by the TBitmap }
    buffer := TMemoryStream.Create;
    try
      { read the number of bitmaps stored in the file }
      fs.Read(imgCount, SizeOf(Integer));

      { now that you have the image count, read them from the file }
      for cnt := 1 to imgCount do
      begin
        { first read the size of the bitmap }
        fs.Read(imgSize, SizeOf(Integer));

        { now read imgSize bytes to the memory stream }
        buffer.Clear;
        buffer.CopyFrom(fs, imgSize);
        { reset the buffer's position before calling LoadFromStream }
        buffer.Position := 0;

        { finally, create the image }
        bmp := TBitmap.Create;
        bmp.LoadFromStream(buffer);
        FImages.Add(bmp);
      end;     // for cnt
    finally
      buffer.Free;
    end;       // try..finally (TMemoryStream.Create)
  finally
    fs.Free;
  end;         // try..finally (TFileStream.Create)
end;
```

Final Touches

To complete the TImageCache component, we have to create two public properties and an event. In order to use the TImageCache component in an
application, we need a Count property to tell us how many images there are in
the list and an ImageIndex property to tell us which one is currently being
used (displayed) by the client application.

To create the Count property, you only have to surface the Count property of the FImages list:

```
type
  TImageCache = class(TComponent)
  protected
    { Protected declarations }
```

```
    function GetImageCount: Integer; virtual;
  public
    { Public declarations }
    property Count: Integer read GetImageCount;
end;
...
function TImageCache.GetImageCount: Integer;
begin
  Result := FImages.Count;
end;
```

The ImageIndex property is an integer property with a write method that makes sure we can't enter a value that's outside the 0 to FImages.Count – 1 range. Here's the implementation of the ImageIndex property:

```
type
  TImageCache = class(TComponent)
  private
    { Private declarations }
    FImageIndex: Integer;
  protected
    { Protected declarations }
    procedure SetImageIndex(Value: Integer); virtual;
  public
    { Public declarations }
    property ImageIndex: Integer read FImageIndex write SetImageIndex;
end;
...
procedure TImageCache.SetImageIndex(Value: Integer);
begin
  if Value < 0 then
    FImageIndex := 0
  else if Value > Pred(FImages.Count) then
    FImageIndex := Pred(FImages.Count)
  else
    FImageIndex := Value;
end;
```

Now that you have the ImageIndex property, you should update the LoadFromFile method to have it "select" the first image in the cache by setting the FImageIndex field to 0 at the end of the method:

```
procedure TImageCache.LoadFromFile(const AFileName: string);
...
  finally
    fs.Free;
  end;      // try..finally (TFileStream.Create)
  FImageIndex := 0; { "select" the first image }
end;
```

Finally, to justify the creation of a component, we need to create the OnRead event, which should occur every time an image is accessed. To correctly implement the OnRead event, you have to update the implementation of the GetImage read method to have it fire the OnRead event if the user passes a valid bitmap index. The following code shows how to implement the OnRead event:

```
type
  TImageCache = class(TComponent)
  private
    { Private declarations }
    FOnRead: TNotifyEvent;
  protected
    { Protected declarations }
    procedure DoRead; virtual;
  published
    { Published declarations }
    property OnRead: TNotifyEvent read FOnRead write FOnRead;
  end;
...
function TImageCache.GetImage(Index: Integer): TBitmap;
begin
  if (Index >= 0) and (Index <= Pred(FImages.Count)) then
  begin
    Result := TBitmap(FImages[Index]);
    DoRead; { fire the OnRead event }
  end else
    Result := nil;
end;

procedure TImageCache.DoRead;
begin
  if Assigned(FOnRead) then FOnRead(Self);
end;
```

Testing the Component

The easiest way to test the TImageCache component is to create two simple applications: an editor application to create the cache files and a viewer application that can view the images stored in a cache file.

To create a simple editor application (see Figure 26-7), you only have to do the following:

1. Use the TOpenDialog component to enable the user to add bitmaps to a TListBox.

2. Pass the TListBox component's Items to the Add method of the TImageCache component to load the images.

3. Call the TImageCache component's SaveToFile method to save the selected images to a cache file.

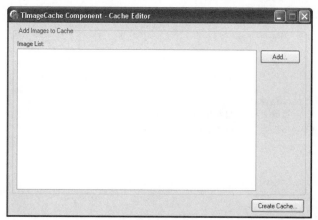

Figure 26-7:
The Cache Editor

Here's the complete source code of the Cache Editor application:

```
procedure TMainForm.CreateCacheButtonClick(Sender: TObject);
begin
  if SaveDialog1.Execute then
  begin
    ImageCache.Add(ListBox1.Items);
    ImageCache.SaveToFile(SaveDialog1.FileName);
    MessageDlg('Cache created', mtInformation, [mbOK], 0);
  end;
end;

procedure TMainForm.AddImagesButtonClick(Sender: TObject);
begin
  if OpenDialog1.Execute then
    ListBox1.Items.AddStrings(OpenDialog1.Files);
end;
```

To create a simple viewer application (see Figure 26-8), you need to drop three buttons on the Designer Surface, use the LoadFromFile method to load the images from the cache file, and use the Images and ImageIndex properties to browse the cache.

Figure 26-8:
The Cache Viewer

Here's the complete source code of the Cache Viewer application:

```
procedure TMainForm.LoadButtonClick(Sender: TObject);
begin
  if OpenDialog1.Execute then
  with ImageCache do
  begin
    LoadFromFile(OpenDialog1.FileName);
    { the following line fires the OnRead event }
    Image1.Picture.Bitmap := Images[ImageIndex];
  end;
end;

procedure TMainForm.PrevButtonClick(Sender: TObject);
begin
  with ImageCache do
  begin
    ImageIndex := ImageIndex - 1;
    { the following line fires the OnRead event }
    Image1.Picture.Bitmap := Images[ImageIndex];
  end;
end;

procedure TMainForm.NextButtonClick(Sender: TObject);
begin
  with ImageCache do
  begin
    ImageIndex := ImageIndex + 1;
    { the following line fires the OnRead event }
    Image1.Picture.Bitmap := Images[ImageIndex];
  end;
end;

{ this is the TImageCache component's OnRead event handler }
procedure TMainForm.ImageCacheRead(Sender: TObject);
const
  STATUS = 'Viewing image %d of %d';
begin
  with ImageCache do
    StatusBar1.SimpleText := Format(STATUS, [Succ(ImageIndex), Count]);
end;
```

Chapter 27

Printing, Creating PDF Documents, and Refactoring

In this chapter, you'll first learn the basics of printing and then you'll learn how to create a pretty complex component: TTextPrinter. The TTextPrinter component is a TComponent descendant able to print both plain text documents and Delphi source files. The TTextPrinter component even prints syntax highlighting: reserved words, directives, and comments, both single-line and block. However, several details are not implemented because the discussion of the component would be too long to fit into a single chapter, but feel free to implement these details yourself.

This chapter also shows how to use the Refactoring commands available in Delphi to restructure several parts of the TTextPrinter component in order to make it more readable and more robust.

The chapter ends with a description of the PDF file format and shows how to print, or more precisely, how to export text files to a PDF document.

AssignPrn Printing

One of the easiest ways to output text to the printer is to use the AssignPrn procedure, which enables you to assign a text file to the printer and use the WriteLn procedure to print text on the printer. When you assign a text file to the printer, you must call the Rewrite procedure to begin printing. When you're done printing, close the printer by calling CloseFile. Finally, to use the AssignPrn procedure and other printing related types, classes, and routines, you have to add the Printers unit to the uses list.

Here's an example of how you can use the AssignPrn procedure to output text to the printer:

```
procedure TMainForm.AssignPrintingClick(Sender: TObject);
var
  F: TextFile;
begin
  AssignPrn(F); { you need the Printers unit for this }
  try
    Rewrite(F); { must Rewrite when using AssignPrn }
    WriteLn(F, 'Hello from Delphi.');
  finally
    CloseFile(F);
  end;
end;
```

Figure 27-1 shows the output of the above code.

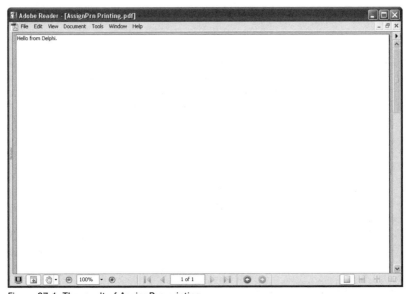

Figure 27-1: The result of AssignPrn printing

TRichEdit Printing

An even easier way to print both rich text and plain text documents is to use the Print method of the TRichEdit component. The Print method accepts a string parameter that you can use to name your current print job. This name appears in the print manager.

Here's an example of how to use the Print method:

```
RichEdit1.Print('TRichEdit Print Job');
```

Printer Settings and the TPageSetupDialog Component

The TPageSetupDialog component (Dialogs category) is a nonvisual component that encapsulates the common Windows Page Setup dialog. This component is really useful because it shows the default printer settings in its properties. The TPageSetupDialog component and its published properties are displayed in the following figure.

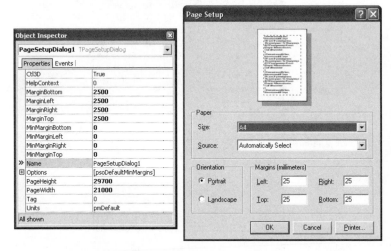

Figure 27-2: The TPageSetupDialog component at run time and its properties

As you can see in Figure 27-2, the TPageSetupDialog component very effectively answers the standard set of questions we need answered in order to start printing:

- What is the size of the paper?
- What measurement units are used?
- What are the margin dimensions?

The most important property by far is the Units property, which specifies the units used by the user. The Units property is a TPageMeasureUnits enumeration, which allows you to use one of the following three values:

- pmDefault — The user must specify values in units defined by locale settings.
- pmMillimeters — The user must specify values in millimeters.
- pmInches — The user must specify values in inches.

The default value of the Units property is pmDefault. When the Units property is set to pmDefault, the TPageSetupDialog component uses locale settings to determine the paper and margin settings (the TPageSetupDialog component expresses these values in thousandths of an inch or thousandths of a centimeter).

Since my machine uses the metric system (see Figure 27-3), the TPageSetupDialog component sets all margins to 2500 (2.5 cm, roughly one inch). On a machine that uses the U.S. measurement system, the TPageSetupDialog component sets margins to 1000 (one inch).

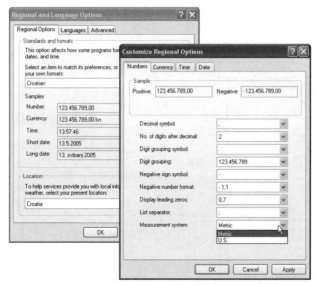

Figure 27-3: Locale settings

The TPrinter Class

If you want to print text or graphics and have full control over the printing process, you should use the TPrinter class declared in the Printers unit.

In order to print with the TPrinter class, here's what you usually have to do:

1. Call the Printer function to obtain the global TPrinter instance.
2. Call the Printer BeginDoc method to begin a new print job.
3. Draw anything you want on the Printer Canvas.
4. Call the Printer NewPage method if you need to continue printing on a new page.
5. Call the Printer EndDoc method to end printing and to send the print job to the printer.

What follows is a short example of how to print a rectangle and a string using the TPrinter class and the global Printer object. The code uses the Printer PageWidth and PageHeight properties to determine the paper size so it can draw the page border.

```
procedure TMainForm.SimplePrintClick(Sender: TObject);
begin
  Printer.BeginDoc;
  try
    Printer.Canvas.Font.Size := 36;
    Printer.Canvas.Rectangle(100, 100,
      Printer.PageWidth - 100, Printer.PageHeight - 100);

    Printer.Canvas.TextOut(150, 150, 'Printing with the TPrinter class!');
  finally
    Printer.EndDoc;
  end;
end;
```

The output of the above code is displayed in Figure 27-4.

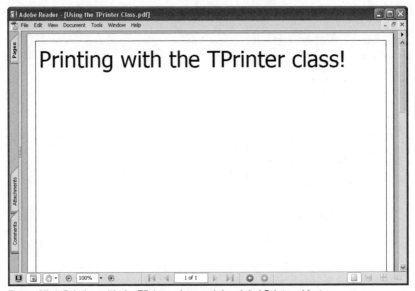

Figure 27-4: Printing with the TPrinter class and the global Printer object

Now that you know how printing works, we can do something a bit more complex — print the entire contents of a TMemo component. This is actually a pretty simple feat, since you only have to do the following:

1. Determine the height of each line by calling the TextHeight method of the Printer Canvas.

2. Print all TMemo lines in a loop, using the simple TextOut method.

3. After a line is printed, test if the next line can be printed on the current page.

4. If the line cannot be printed on the current page, call the Printer NewPage method to create a new page and to continue printing on it.

The following listing shows how to print the entire contents of a TMemo, using the TMemo's font. Don't forget to read the comments because they explain in detail what's happening.

Listing 27-1: Printing the contents of a TMemo component

```
procedure TMainForm.MemoPrintClick(Sender: TObject);
var
  i: Integer;
  yPos: Integer;
  lineHeight: Integer;
begin
  { use the TMemo's font }
  Printer.Canvas.Font := Memo1.Font;

  { determine the line height }
  lineHeight := Printer.Canvas.TextHeight('W');

  { start printing at the top of the page }
  yPos := 0;

  { start printing }
  Printer.BeginDoc;
  try
    for i := 0 to Pred(Memo1.Lines.Count) do
    begin
      { display the line at yPos }
      Printer.Canvas.TextOut(0, yPos, Memo1.Lines[i]);
      { increment the vertical position }
      Inc(yPos, lineHeight);

      { check if we can fit the next line into the page,
        and if we can't, create a new empty page }
      if yPos + lineHeight > Printer.PageHeight then
      begin
        { reset yPos to 0 to start painting at the top of the new page }
        yPos := 0;
        Printer.NewPage;
      end;     // if yPos + lineHeight
    end;       // for i
  finally
    Printer.EndDoc;
  end;         // try..finally (Printer.BeginDoc)
end;
```

The following figure shows the result of the above code.

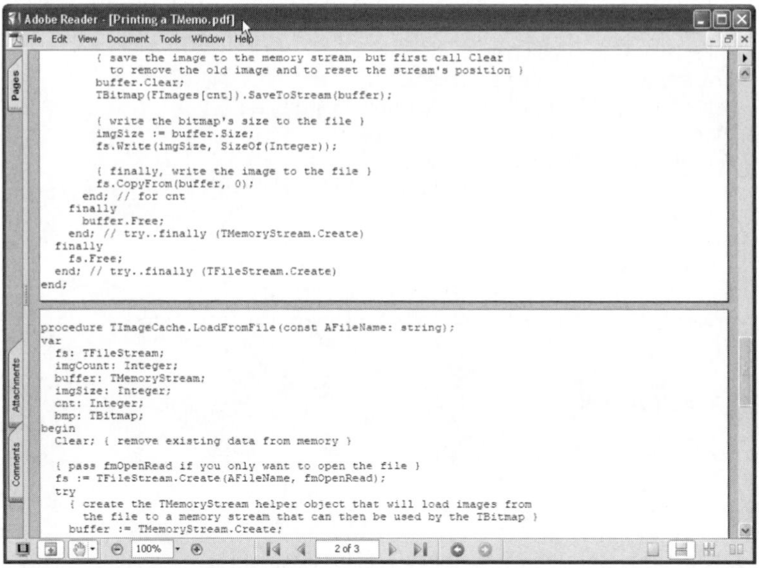

Figure 27-5: Printing the contents of a TMemo component

Now that you know how to print an entire plain text file, we can start creating the TTextPrinter component, which supports margins and syntax highlighting.

The TTextPrinter Component

First, you need to derive the TTextPrinter component from TComponent using the New VCL Component wizard. Save the TTextPrinter component under TextPrinter.pas and add it to your component package.

To enable the user to print multiple lines of text using whatever font is available and supported by the printer, we have to create two properties: Font and Strings. In order to use the TFont class, you have to add the Graphics unit to the component's uses list.

Here's the initial code of the component that sets up these two object properties:

```
unit TextPrinter;

interface

uses
  SysUtils, Classes, Graphics;

type
  TTextPrinter = class(TComponent)
  private
    { Private declarations }
```

```
    FFont: TFont;
    FStrings: TStrings;
  protected
    { Protected declarations }
    procedure SetFont(Value: TFont); virtual;
    procedure SetStrings(Value: TStrings); virtual;
  public
    { Public declarations }
    constructor Create(AOwner: TComponent); override;
    destructor Destroy; override;
  published
    { Published declarations }
    property Font: TFont read FFont write SetFont;
    property Strings: TStrings read FStrings write SetStrings;
  end;

procedure Register;

implementation

procedure Register;
begin
  RegisterComponents('My Components', [TTextPrinter]);
end;

constructor TTextPrinter.Create(AOwner: TComponent);
begin
  inherited Create(AOwner);
  FFont := TFont.Create;
  FStrings := TStringList.Create;
end;

destructor TTextPrinter.Destroy;
begin
  FFont.Free;
  FStrings.Free;
  inherited Destroy;
end;

procedure TTextPrinter.SetStrings(Value: TStrings);
begin
  FStrings.Assign(Value);
end;

procedure TTextPrinter.SetFont(Value: TFont);
begin
  FFont.Assign(Value);
end;

end.
```

Measurement System and Resolution

Now it's time to duplicate a portion of the TPageSetupDialog component's functionality. We have to determine which measurement system the user is using and we have to create the Margins and the Units properties, which will contain either 2500 if the user uses the metric system or 1000 if the user uses the U.S. measurement system. We also have to determine the printer's pixels per inch values, both horizontal and vertical.

We can determine the measurement system by calling the GetLocaleInfo API function, declared in the Windows unit:

```
function GetLocaleInfo(Locale: LCID; LCType: LCTYPE;
  lpLCData: PChar; cchData: Integer): Integer; stdcall;
```

When calling the GetLocaleInfo function to determine the measurement system, you have to do the following:

1.   Pass the LOCALE_SYSTEM_DEFAULT constant as the Locale parameter to get the information about the system's default locale settings.

2.   Get the measurement system information by passing the LOCALE_IMEASURE constant as the LCType parameter.

3.   Accept the information about the measurement system by declaring an array of two characters and passing the array's pointer as the @lpLCData parameter (you have to use a two-character array, which is the maximum allowed number of characters).

4.   Finally, you have to pass the size of the buffer as the cchData parameter, which is 2 in this case.

The following code shows the TTextPrinter's private method called GetLocaleUnit, which uses the GetLocaleInfo API function to determine the measurement system (don't forget to add the Windows unit to the uses list):

```
// -------------------------------------------------------------------------
// Name: GetLocaleUnit
// Desc: Returns 0 for mm (metric system) and 1 for inch (U.S. system).
// -------------------------------------------------------------------------
function TTextPrinter.GetLocaleUnit: Integer;
var
  localeData: array[0..1] of char;
begin
  GetLocaleInfo(LOCALE_USER_DEFAULT, LOCALE_IMEASURE, @localeData, 2);
  Result := StrToInt(localeData);
end;
```

Now that we know which measurement system is used, we need to find out the printer's resolution in order to correctly convert inches and millimeters into pixels. To determine the number of pixels per inch, both horizontally and vertically, we need to call the GetDeviceCaps API function:

```
function GetDeviceCaps(DC: HDC; Index: Integer): Integer; stdcall;
```

To determine the pixels per inch values of the printer, we have to call the GetDeviceCaps function twice. We have to pass the LOGPIXELSX constant as the Index parameter to determine the number of pixels per inch horizontally, and then pass the LOGPIXELSY constant as the Index parameter to determine the number of pixels per inch vertically. Both times, we have to pass the Printer's handle as the DC parameter.

Since we're going to need these values later, we should store them in two public read-only properties: PXPerInchX and PXPerInchY. The best place to call the GetDeviceCaps function is in the component's constructor. Here's the code related to the pixels per inch properties (don't forget to add the Printers unit to the uses list, because the code in the constructor uses the global Printer object):

```
type
  TTextPrinter = class(TComponent)
  private
    { Private declarations }
    FPXPerInchX: Integer;
    FPXPerInchY: Integer;
  public
    { Public declarations }
    property PXPerInchX: Integer read FPXPerInchX;
    property PXPerInchY: Integer read FPXPerInchY;
end;
...
constructor TTextPrinter.Create(AOwner: TComponent);
begin
  inherited Create(AOwner);
  FFont := TFont.Create;
  FStrings := TStringList.Create;

  { Get pixels per inch }
  FPXPerInchX := GetDeviceCaps(Printer.Handle, LOGPIXELSX);
  FPXPerInchY := GetDeviceCaps(Printer.Handle, LOGPIXELSY);
end;
```

Margins and Units Properties

Let's solve the easier problem first and create the Units property. The Units property is a simple direct-access published property of type TPageMeasure-Units. In order to use the TPageMeasureUnits enumeration, you have to add the Dialogs unit to the component's uses list.

Here's the declaration of the Units property, which is, like the same property in the TPageSetupDialog component, set by default to the pmDefault value:

```
TTextPrinter = class(TComponent)
private
  { Private declarations }
  FUnits: TPageMeasureUnits;
published
  { Published declarations }
  property Units: TPageMeasureUnits
```

```
      read FUnits write FUnits default pmDefault;
    end;
```

The TTextPrinter component has eight (yes, eight) properties that define the margins. Four properties are read-only and public, and specify margin values in pixels. The other four properties are published and specify margin values like the TPageSetupDialog component — in thousandths of an inch or thousandths of a millimeter, depending on the measurement system.

Here are the declarations of the simple read-only properties:

```
TTextPrinter = class(TComponent)
private
  { Private declarations }
  FPXMarginBottom: Integer;
  FPXMarginLeft: Integer;
  FPXMarginRight: Integer;
  FPXMarginTop: Integer;
public
  { Public declarations }
  property PXMarginBottom: Integer read FPXMarginBottom;
  property PXMarginLeft: Integer read FPXMarginLeft;
  property PXMarginRight: Integer read FPXMarginRight;
  property PXMarginTop: Integer read FPXMarginTop;
end;
```

The four margin-related published properties are a bit more complex than the above read-only properties. The published properties are indexed properties that share a single write method called SetMarginValue, which not only updates the published property that called it, but also automatically calculates the margin value in pixels for the appropriate PXMargin property.

Here are the declarations of the four margin-related published properties:

```
TTextPrinter = class(TComponent)
private
  { Private declarations }
  FMarginBottom: Integer;
  FMarginLeft: Integer;
  FMarginRight: Integer;
  FMarginTop: Integer;
published
  { Published declarations }
  property MarginBottom: Integer
    index 1 read FMarginBottom write SetMarginValue;
  property MarginLeft: Integer
    index 2 read FMarginLeft write SetMarginValue;
  property MarginRight: Integer
    index 3 read FMarginRight write SetMarginValue;
  property MarginTop: Integer
    index 4 read FMarginTop write SetMarginValue;
end;
```

To automatically calculate the margin values in pixels, the SetMarginValue method must first check the Units property to see which measurement unit is used. If the U.S. measurement system is used, the method must divide the margin value by 1000 to get inches instead of thousandths of an inch and then multiply by PXPerInchX or PXPerInchY to get the margin value in pixels. If the metric system is used, the method must divide the margin value by 1000 to get millimeters instead of thousandths of millimeters, then it must divide the millimeters by 2.54 to get inches, and finally it must multiply that value by PXPerInchX or PXPerInchY to get the margin value in pixels.

Here's the SetMarginValue method:

```
type
  TTextPrinter = class(TComponent)
  protected
    { Protected declarations }
    procedure SetMarginValue(Index, Value: Integer); virtual;
end;
...
procedure TTextPrinter.SetMarginValue(Index, Value: Integer);
var
  conv: Double;
begin
  case FUnits of
    { if we're using the metric system, use 2.54 to get inches }
    pmMillimeters: conv := 2.54;
    { if we're using the U.S. system, set conv to 1.0,
      to use the original margin value }
    pmInches: conv := 1.00;
    else begin
      if GetLocaleUnit = 0 then
        conv := 2.54
      else
        conv := 1.00;
    end;    // pmDefault
  end;      // case FUnits

  case Index of
    1: begin
      FMarginBottom := Value;
      FPXMarginBottom := Round(FMarginBottom / conv / 1000 * pxPerInchY);
    end;    // bottom
    2: begin
      FMarginLeft := Value;
      FPXMarginLeft := Round(FMarginLeft / conv / 1000 * pxPerInchX);
    end;    // left
    3: begin
      FMarginRight := Value;
      FPXMarginRight := Round(FMarginRight / conv / 1000 * pxPerInchX);
    end;    // right
    4: begin
      FMarginTop := Value;
      FPXMarginTop := Round(FMarginTop / conv / 1000 * pxPerInchY);
    end;    // top
  end;      // case Index
end;
```

The TTextPrinter component also has two public overloaded methods that enable us to easily change margin values. One method accepts a TPageSetupDialog parameter and copies the margin settings from the passed component. The other method accepts a single integer value and assigns that value to all four margins.

Here are both SetMargins overloads:

```
type
  TTextPrinter = class(TComponent)
  public
    { Public declarations }
    procedure SetMargins(ADialog: TPageSetupDialog); overload;
    procedure SetMargins(SingleValue: Integer); overload;
end;
...
procedure TTextPrinter.SetMargins(ADialog: TPageSetupDialog);
begin
  FUnits := ADialog.Units;
  MarginBottom := ADialog.MarginBottom;
  MarginLeft := ADialog.MarginLeft;
  MarginRight := ADialog.MarginRight;
  MarginTop := ADialog.MarginTop;
end;

procedure TTextPrinter.SetMargins(SingleValue: Integer);
begin
  MarginBottom := SingleValue;
  MarginLeft := SingleValue;
  MarginRight := SingleValue;
  MarginTop := SingleValue;
end;
```

Finally, in order to set default margin values when the component is created, we have to update the component's constructor and set all margins to 2500 if the metric system is used or 1000 if the U.S. system is used.

Here's the final version of the constructor, which calls the GetLocaleUnit function to determine the measurement system and updates all margins appropriately:

```
constructor TTextPrinter.Create(AOwner: TComponent);
const
  DEFAULT_MARGINS: array[0..1] of Integer = (2500, 1000);
begin
  inherited Create(AOwner);
  FFont := TFont.Create;
  FStrings := TStringList.Create;

  { Get pixels per inch. }
  FPXPerInchX := GetDeviceCaps(Printer.Handle, LOGPIXELSX);
  FPXPerInchY := GetDeviceCaps(Printer.Handle, LOGPIXELSY);

  { Set default Units value. }
  FUnits := pmDefault;

  { Set default margins. These are the same as in the TPageSetupDialog. }
  SetMargins(DEFAULT_MARGINS[GetLocaleUnit]);
end;
```

Syntax Highlighting Utility Functions

Before writing the printing code, we need to create two functions to determine if a word is a reserved word or not. The IsReservedWord function, which determines whether or not the passed string is a reserved word, is pretty simple: It has a large array that contains all reserved words and directives of the Delphi language and returns True if it can find the passed string in the array and False if the passed string cannot be found.

Here's the IsReservedWord function:

```
{ returns True if the AReservedWord is a reserved word or a directive }
function IsReservedWord(const AReservedWord: string): Boolean;
const
  RESERVED: array[1..116] of string = ('and', 'else', 'inherited',
    'packed', 'then', 'array', 'end', 'end;', 'end.', 'initialization',
    'procedure', 'threadvar', 'as', 'except', 'inline', 'program', 'to',
    'asm', 'exports', 'interface', 'property', 'try', 'begin', 'file',
    'is', 'raise', 'type', 'case', 'final', 'label', 'record', 'unit',
    'class', 'finalization', 'library', 'repeat', 'unsafe', 'const',
    'finally', 'mod', 'resourcestring', 'until', 'constructor', 'for',
    'nil', 'sealed', 'uses', 'destructor', 'function', 'not', 'set',
    'var', 'dispinterface', 'goto', 'object', 'shl', 'while', 'div',
    'if', 'of', 'shr', 'with', 'do', 'implementation', 'or', 'static',
    'xor', 'downto', 'in', 'out', 'string', 'absolute', 'dynamic',
    'local', 'platform', 'requires', 'abstract', 'export', 'message',
    'private', 'resident', 'assembler', 'external', 'name', 'protected',
    'safecall', 'automated', 'far', 'near', 'public', 'stdcall', 'cdecl',
    'forward', 'nodefault', 'published', 'stored', 'contains',
    'implements', 'overload', 'read', 'varargs', 'default', 'index',
    'override', 'readonly', 'virtual', 'deprecated', 'package',
    'register', 'write', 'dispid', 'library', 'pascal', 'reintroduce',
    'writeonly');
var
  lcaseWord: string;
  reservedWord: string;
begin
  lcaseWord := LowerCase(Trim(AReservedWord));
  Result := False;

  { see if it's a reserved word }
  for reservedWord in RESERVED do
    if reservedWord = lcaseWord then
    begin
      Result := True;
      Exit;
    end;
end;
```

The second function solves a part of the problem that occurs with the array and class reserved words. Since these words are closely followed by a left parenthesis or the left square bracket plus additional text, the above IsReservedWord function can't identify them successfully. So, in order to solve this problem, the following SpecialCases function tests whether the passed string contains the "class(" or "array[" strings:

```
{ check if the word contains "class(" or "array[" }
function SpecialCases(const AReservedWord: string): Boolean;
var
  lowWord: string;
begin
  lowWord := LowerCase(AReservedWord);
  Result := (Pos('class(', lowWord) > 0) or (Pos('array[', lowWord) > 0);
end;
```

Printing

The printing code is separated into two procedures: the public Print method that does 99% of the printing, and the private NewLine method that increments the vertical line position and creates a new page if the line doesn't fit on the current page.

Here's the NewLine method:

```
type
  TTextPrinter = class(TComponent)
  private
    procedure NewLine(var YPos: Integer; LineHeight: Integer);
  end;
  ...
procedure TTextPrinter.NewLine(var YPos: Integer; LineHeight: Integer);
begin
  Inc(YPos, LineHeight);
  if YPos + LineHeight > Printer.PageHeight - PXMarginBottom then
  begin
    YPos := PXMarginTop;
    Printer.NewPage;
  end;
end;
```

The Print method is the largest and most complex of all TTextPrinter methods because it must print the entire text document word by word in order to break a line if it doesn't fit inside the margins and to determine whether or not one of the words is a reserved word. Even more complexity arises from the fact that it also supports comments, both single-line and block comments. To manage the comments, the TTextPrinter component uses a custom TCommentType enumeration because it has to manage each comment type differently.

Here's the TCommentType enumeration:

```
TCommentType = (ctNoComment, ctSingleLine, ctBlockComment);
```

The following list describes the most important parts of the Print method:

1. The method enters a global for loop that loops though all strings stored in the Strings property.

2. Then it enters a second inner loop that breaks each line into individual words.

3. Each acquired word is first tested for the two special cases — "array["
   and "class(" — because they must be handled differently from all other
   words.

4. The word is then tested for reserved words and comments and the Canvas Font is updated appropriately to display either boldfaced reserved
   words or italicized comments.

5. After the syntax highlighting code determines how the word should be
   printed, the NewLine method is called before printing if the word cannot
   fit in the current line.

6. At the end of the inner loop, the method tests whether an opened block
   comment should be closed.

7. Finally, the method exits to the outer loop and calls NewLine to move to
   the next line.

8. If there are more strings in the Strings property, the method again enters
   the inner loop and prints the new line word by word.

The following listing displays the fully commented Print method. Be sure to
carefully read the comments since they describe in detail what's going on with
each word that is printed.

Listing 27-2: The Print method of the TTextPrinter component

```
procedure TTextPrinter.Print;
var
  i: Integer;
  fntHeight: Integer;
  yPos: Integer;
  xPos: Integer;
  maxWidth: Integer;
  currLine: string;
  oneWord: string;
  wordWidth: Integer;
  spacing: Integer;
  comment: TCommentType;
begin
  comment := ctNoComment;
  { assign the selected font to the printer }
  Printer.Canvas.Font.Assign(Font);

  { determine the line height }
  fntHeight := Printer.Canvas.TextHeight('W');

  { see how much horizontal space is available }
  maxWidth := Printer.PageWidth - PXMarginRight;

  { start printing }
  Printer.BeginDoc;
  try
    yPos := PXMarginTop;
```

```
{ print all lines }
for i := 0 to Pred(FStrings.Count) do
begin
  { add a space to the end of the string to simplify the process
    of breaking the string into separate words }
  currLine := FStrings[i] + ' ';
  xPos := PXMarginLeft;

  { find the end of the first word }
  spacing := Pos(' ', currLine);
  while spacing <> 0 do
  begin
    { get one word }
    oneWord := Copy(currLine, 1, spacing);

    { see if the line contains "class(" or "array[" }
    if SpecialCases(oneWord) then
    begin
      { use only the first 5 chars, "class" or "array" }
      oneWord := Copy(oneWord, 1, 5);
      Delete(currLine, 1, 5);
    end else
      { if the word doesn't contain "class(" or "array[",
        then delete the entire word from the current line }
      Delete(currLine, 1, spacing);

      { check if we're dealing with a comment of any type }
      if Pos('//', oneWord) > 0 then
        comment := ctSingleLine
      else if Pos('{', oneWord) > 0 then
        comment := ctBlockComment;

      with Printer.Canvas.Font do
      begin
        { assume we're printing "normal text" }
        Style := [];
        Color := clBlack;

        { check for a reserved word, but only if neither a
          single-line nor a block comment are opened }
        if (comment = ctNoComment) and IsReservedWord(oneWord) then
        begin
          Style := Style + [fsBold];
          Color := clNavy;
        end;

        { check if the word is inside a block or a single-line
          comment and render appropriately }
        if comment <> ctNoComment then
        begin
          Style := Style + [fsItalic];
          Color := clGreen;
        end;
      end;        // with Printer.Canvas.Font
```

```
        { get the word's width }
        wordWidth := Printer.Canvas.TextWidth(oneWord);

        { if the word doesn't fit in the current line,
          move to the next line and print it in the next line }
        if xPos + wordWidth > maxWidth then
        begin
          xPos := PXMarginLeft;
          NewLine(yPos, fntHeight);
        end;     // if xPos

        { display the word and update the print position }
        Printer.Canvas.TextOut(xPos, yPos, oneWord);
        Inc(xPos, wordWidth);

        { if a block comment is opened, close it if end char is found }
        if (comment = ctBlockComment) and (Pos('}', oneWord) > 0) then
          comment := ctNoComment;

        { update the loop to print the next word }
        spacing := Pos(' ', currLine);
      end;       // while spacing

    { when the entire FStrings[n] line is printed,
      move to the next line }
    NewLine(yPos, fntHeight);

    { if there's a single-line comment,
      reset comment status before printing the next line}
    if comment = ctSingleLine then comment := ctNoComment;

    if Printer.Aborted then Exit;
  end;           // for i
  finally
    Printer.EndDoc;
  end;            // try
end;
```

Final Touches

If you try to print the contents of a TMemo component that doesn't use
WordWrap, you'll have no problems. But when the WordWrap property is set
to True, the TMemo component breaks lines at the right margin in a way that
messes up printing. So, in order to print a TMemo properly, we shouldn't
assign the contents of the TMemo to the Strings property directly. We need a
method that will first disable the TMemo's WordWrap, then copy the
TMemo's Lines to the TTextPrinter's Strings property, and finally restore the
TMemo's original WordWrap property.

Here's the code of the GetText method that does exactly that:

```
procedure TTextPrinter.GetText(AMemo: TMemo);
begin
  oldWordWrap := AMemo.WordWrap;
  try
```

```
    AMemo.WordWrap := False; { temporarily disable wrapping }
    FLines.Assign(AMemo.Lines);
  finally
    AMemo.WordWrap := oldWordWrap;
  end;      // try..finally
end;
```

The GetText method does exactly what it's supposed to do, but it doesn't compile because it uses an undeclared identifier: oldWordWrap. Although you can resolve this problem by declaring the variable manually, we are going to use one of the Refactoring commands to declare the oldWordWrap variable. To declare the oldWordWrap variable, right-click the oldWordWrap identifier in the Code Editor, point to Refactoring on the context menu, and select the Declare Variable command, as shown in Figure 27-6.

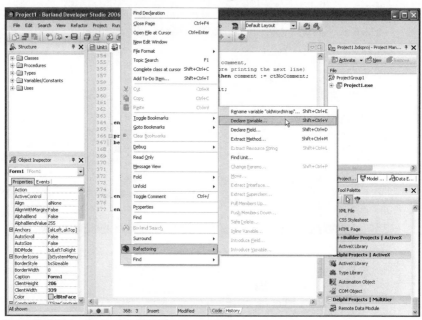

Figure 27-6: Using the Declare Variable command

After you select the Declare Variable command, the refactoring engine displays the Declare Variable dialog box, which automatically determines the appropriate data type for the new variable.

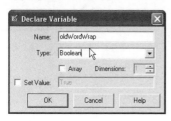

Figure 27-7:
The Declare
Variable dialog
box

To declare the local oldWordWrap Boolean variable you only have to click the OK button:

```
procedure TTextPrinter.GetText(AMemo: TMemo);
var
  oldWordWrap: Boolean;
begin
  oldWordWrap := AMemo.WordWrap;
  try
    AMemo.WordWrap := False; { temporarily disable wrapping }
    FLines.Assign(AMemo.Lines);
  finally
    AMemo.WordWrap := oldWordWrap;
  end;        // try..finally
end;
```

Now the entire component is finished, and you can drop it on the Designer Surface and use it by writing something as simple as this:

```
procedure TMainForm.TextPrinterPrintClick(Sender: TObject);
begin
  if PageSetupDialog.Execute then
  with TextPrinter do
  begin
    Font.Assign(Memo1.Font); { use the TMemo's Font }
    GetText(Memo1); { get the contents of the TMemo }
    Print;
  end;
end;
```

The following figure shows how the TTextPrinter component prints Delphi units.

Figure 27-08: Printing with the TTextPrinter component

Refactoring the TTextPrinter Component

In the last section, you saw how to use the Declare Variable command to refactor the GetText method and create a new variable from an undeclared identifier. In this portion of the chapter, you'll learn a bit more about refactoring.

Refactoring is the name of a set of commands that enable you to restructure your source code without changing its functionality. Besides the Declare Variable refactoring that you've already used, you're going to see how to use the following refactorings:

- Rename Symbol
- Extract Resourcestring
- Extract Method

Renaming Symbols

Rename Symbol refactoring enables you to rename an identifier and all its references. For instance, to rename the Font property PrinterFont, right-click the Font identifier in the Code Editor and select Refactoring ➤ Rename property 'Font'. Selecting the Rename property 'Font' command displays the following dialog box.

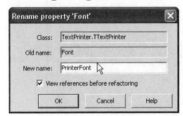

Figure 27-9:
The Rename
symbol dialog
box

If the View references before refactoring check box is checked, two things occur:

- The IDE displays the Refactorings window (see Figure 27-10), which contains the list of all code portions that are affected by the selected refactoring.
- The refactoring itself is postponed until you choose to either apply or discard it.

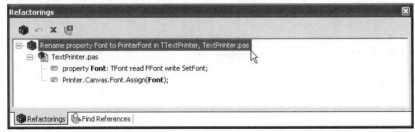

Figure 27-10: The Refactorings window

When you apply the refactoring by clicking the Refactor button on the Refactorings window, the refactoring remains in the list, in case you opt to undo it. If you don't plan to undo the applied refactoring, you can remove it by clicking either the Remove Refactoring or Remove All Refactorings buttons.

Sync Edit

Delphi's Code Editor also allows you to rename an identifier by switching to the Sync Edit mode. If the identifier is local and you can easily select it, you should rename it using the Sync Edit feature. If the identifier you wish to rename is a field, a property, or a similar identifier that is used throughout the unit, you should rename it using Rename Symbol refactoring.

To enter the Sync Edit mode, you first have to select a portion of source code in the Code Editor. When you select a block of code, the Code Editor's left margin displays the Sync Edit icon as shown in Figure 27-11.

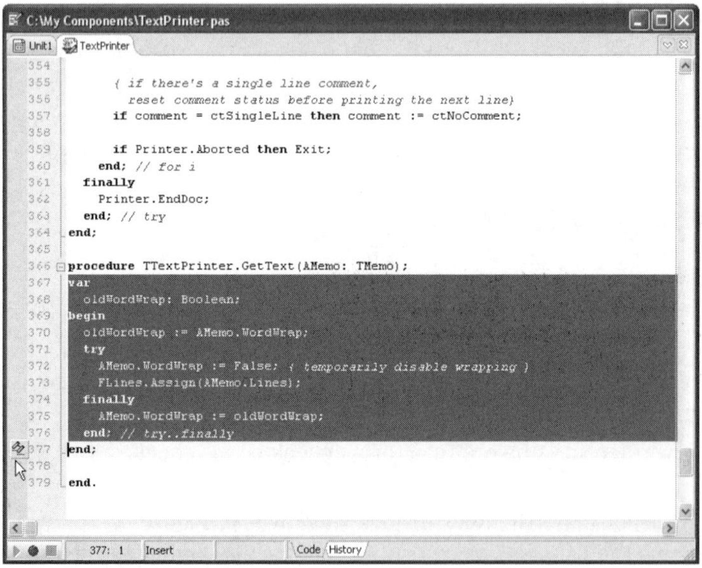

Figure 27-11: The Sync Edit icon

To enter the Sync Edit mode, click the Sync Edit icon in the Code Editor's left margin. When you enter the Sync Edit mode, the Code Editor outlines all duplicate identifiers that can be renamed (see Figure 27-12). To rename an identifier and all of its occurrences in the selected portion of the code, simply type over the existing identifier.

```
☞ C:\My Components\TextPrinter.pas                              _ □ X
📄 Unit1  🔧 TextPrinter
354
355              { if there's a single line comment,
356                reset comment status before printing the next line}
357              if comment = ctSingleLine then comment := ctNoComment;
358
359              if Printer.Aborted then Exit;
360            end; // for i
361          finally
362            Printer.EndDoc;
363          end; // try
364      end;
365
366   procedure TTextPrinter.GetText(AMemo: TMemo);
367   var
368     EDITED_WORDWRAP: Boolean;
369   begin
370     EDITED_WORDWRAP := AMemo.WordWrap;
371     try
372       AMemo.WordWrap := False; { temporarily disable wrapping }
373       FLines.Assign(AMemo.Lines);
374     finally
375       AMemo.WordWrap := EDITED_WORDWRAP;
376     end; // try..finally
377   end;
378
379   end.

▶ ● ■   368: 18   Insert      Modified      Code  History
```

Figure 27-12: The Sync Edit mode

Extracting Resource Strings

Extract Resource String refactoring enables you to extract a string from the source code and create a resource string in the resourcestring section of the unit. Extract Resource String refactoring also creates the resourcestring section if one doesn't exist. Modifying the strings in the resourcestring section doesn't require you to recompile the application.

For instance, if you want to extract the 'class(' string from the Special-Cases function, right-click on the string and select Refactoring ➢ Extract Resource String 'class(' on the context menu. The Extract Resource String dialog box that appears allows you to define the resourcestring's name.

Figure 27-13:
Extracting resource
strings

If you click OK in the Extract Resource String dialog box, it will make the following changes to the source code:

```
implementation

resourcestring
  StrClass = 'class(';
```

```
...
function SpecialCases(const AReservedWord: string): Boolean;
var
  lowWord: string;
begin
  lowWord := LowerCase(AReservedWord);
  Result := (Pos(StrClass, lowWord) > 0) or (Pos('array[', lowWord) > 0);
end;
```

Extracting Methods

The refactoring that you are most likely to use is Extract Method. It allows you to select a portion of a routine and extract it to another one. The TTextPrinter's Print method is the perfect target for Extract Method refactoring, because it is large and contains a code segment that can very successfully be extracted to another method. This code segment deals with applying the font settings for comments and reserved words.

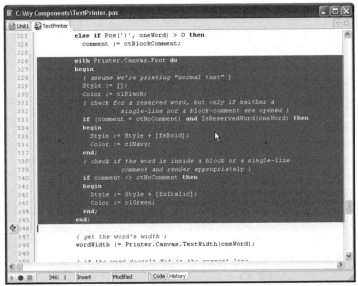

Figure 27-14: The code segment that should be extracted with Extract Method refactoring

To extract the selected code segment from the Print method to another method, right-click the selected code segment and select Refactoring ➢ Extract Method on the context menu. The Extract Method dialog box that appears (see Figure 27-15) allows you to see what the new method will look like and to rename it. You should name the new method ApplyFormatting and press OK to have Extract Method refactoring create it.

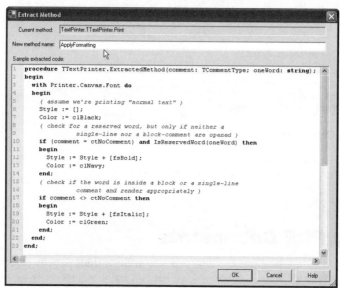

Figure 27-15: The Extract Method dialog box

Extract Method refactoring makes the following changes to the source code:

```
TTextPrinter = class(TComponent)
private
  { Private declarations }
  procedure ApplyFormatting(comment: TCommentType; oneWord: string);
end;
...
procedure TTextPrinter.ApplyFormatting(comment: TCommentType;
  oneWord: string);
begin
  with Printer.Canvas.Font do
  begin
    { assume we're printing "normal text" }
    Style := [];
    Color := clBlack;
    { check for a reserved word, but only if neither a
              single-line nor a block comment are opened }
    if (comment = ctNoComment) and IsReservedWord(oneWord) then
    begin
      Style := Style + [fsBold];
      Color := clNavy;
    end;
    { check if the word is inside a block or a single-line
              comment and render appropriately }
    if comment <> ctNoComment then
    begin
      Style := Style + [fsItalic];
      Color := clGreen;
    end;
```

```
    end;
end;

procedure TTextPrinter.Print;
begin
    ...
      else if Pos('{', oneWord) > 0 then
        comment := ctBlockComment;

      ApplyFormatting(comment, oneWord);

      { get the word's width }
      wordWidth := Printer.Canvas.TextWidth(oneWord);
    ...
end;
```

Creating PDF Documents

It is common for applications to allow users to archive their data by printing it. However, it may also be useful to archive data digitally, and the best way to do this is to store them as PDF documents because the PDF (Adobe Portable Document Format) file format is designed to be portable among platforms and operating systems.

Document Structure

For instance, to convert text to an HTML page, you need to write a fairly simple piece of code that generates the basic HTML skeleton and then goes through a string list appending <br> for line breaks and <p> for paragraphs.

Creating a PDF document is much more difficult because a PDF document consists of a collection of objects that describe various pieces of the document: a page, a page's contents, a font, etc.

Essentially, a PDF document consists of the following four parts:

- The document header, which specifies the document version (PDF specification conformance)
- The document itself (the document body), which contains various objects that define the document and its contents
- The cross-reference table, which is a table of objects present in the document. The cross-reference table allows applications to access any object in the document without having to read the entire file. As a result, applications can easily manage both small and large documents, even ones that contain thousands of pages.
- The document trailer, which points to the location of the cross-reference table. The document trailer and the cross-reference table are very important parts of PDF documents because PDF documents are meant to be read from the end, through the document trailer and the cross-reference table.

To learn more about the structure of PDF documents, you should take a look at the source of a simple PDF document. Listing 27-3 shows the source of a very simple PDF document, and Figure 27-16 shows what the document looks like in a PDF reader application.

The document header is the %PDF-1.2 line. Everything between the first line and the line that contains only the PDF reserved word xref is the document body. The cross-reference table begins with the reserved word xref and ends with the reserved word trailer. Not surprisingly, the document trailer begins with the reserved word trailer and ends with the end of file marker, %%EOF.

Listing 27-3: A simple PDF document

```
%PDF-1.2
1 0 obj
<<
/Author (Santa Claus)
/Producer (Inside Delphi Book - TPDFExport Component)
/Subject ()
/Title (Christmas Presents)
>>
endobj
2 0 obj
<< /Type /Font
/Subtype /Type1
/Name /F1
/BaseFont /Courier
/Encoding /WinAnsiEncoding
>>
endobj
3 0 obj
<< /ProcSet [ /PDF /Text]
/Font <<
/F1 2 0 R
>>
>>
endobj
4 0 obj
<< /Length 76
>>
stream
BT
/F1 12 Tf
72 720 Td
(A very simple PDF document...) Tj
0 -12 TD
ET
endstream
endobj
5 0 obj
<< /Type /Pages
/Kids [
6 0 R
]
```

```
/Count 1
>>
endobj
6 0 obj
<< /Type /Page
/Parent 5 0 R
/MediaBox [0 0 612 792]
/Contents 4 0 R
/Resources 3 0 R
>>
endobj
7 0 obj
<< /Type /Catalog
/Pages 5 0 R
>>
endobj
xref
0 8
0000000000 65535 f
0000000010 00000 n
0000000156 00000 n
0000000269 00000 n
0000000342 00000 n
0000000473 00000 n
0000000540 00000 n
0000000652 00000 n
trailer
<< /Size 9
/Root 7 0 R
/Info 1 0 R
>>
startxref
706
%%EOF
```

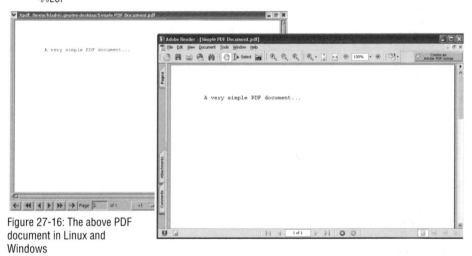

Figure 27-16: The above PDF document in Linux and Windows

Creating the TPDFExport Component

The first thing that you need to do is derive the TPDFExport component from TComponent and add it to your package. Once you've created the component, we should override the constructor and destructor and introduce several basic properties, like PageHeight and PageWidth.

In this component, we are going to use the TMemoryStream class to store the PDF document, although the TStringList class can also be used, because, as you've already seen, a PDF document can be represented as text. While a TStringList-oriented implementation would be a bit easier to write, we would lose the ability to compress pieces of the PDF document using the zlib/flate compression.

To create a PDF document, we need to create and use three objects: the TMemoryStream object for storing the PDF document and two string lists. One string list will be used for the component's Strings property, so that we can add text to the TPDFExport component at design time (and run time). The second string list must be created because we have to build the cross-reference table while we're generating other pieces of the document. The cross-reference table must contain byte offsets of every object found in the document, and the best way to construct the table is to have it available at all times and add the objects' offsets to the table as soon as we create them.

Besides the three objects, let's define four basic properties: Compress, FontSize, PageWidth, and PageHeight. The Compress property allows the user to select whether to compress the contents of the document using zlib compression or to leave the contents uncompressed.

Even though PDF documents are able to use any number of fonts, the TPDFExport component only uses the Courier New font, simply to help you understand how to work with fonts and because we'll only be generating documents that contain plain text. The only thing the TPDFExport component allows you to do with the font is to change its size.

Every page in a PDF document can have its own size, but again, to keep things simple, TPDFExport uses only one size, specified in the PageHeight and PageWidth properties, for all pages in the document. Default values of 792 for PageHeight and 612 for PageWidth are expressed in units called points, where 72 points equals one inch, and define an 8.5 x 11-inch page (lettersize). Table 27-1 shows typical page sizes in centimeters, inches, and points.

Table 27-1: Letter and A4 page sizes

Paper Type/Size	Centimeters	Inches (cm / 2.54)	Points (inches * 72)
Letter Width	21.59	8.5	612
Letter Height	27.94	11	792
A4 Width	21	8.27	596
A4 Height	29.7	11.7	842

Listing 27-4 shows the TPDFExport component's constructor and destructor and the above-mentioned four properties.

Listing 27-4: TPDFExport component, the beginning

```
unit PDFExport;

interface

uses
  SysUtils, Classes;

type
  TPDFExport = class(TComponent)
  private
    { Private declarations }
    PDF: TMemoryStream;
    FOffsetList: TStringList;
    FStrings: TStrings;
    FPageWidth: Integer;
    FPageHeight: Integer;
    FFontSize: Integer;
    FCompress: Boolean;
  protected
    { Protected declarations }
  public
    { Public declarations }
    constructor Create(AOwner: TComponent); override;
    destructor Destroy; override;
  published
    { Published declarations }
    property Compress: Boolean
      read FCompress write FCompress default False;
    property FontSize: Integer
      read FFontSize write FFontSize default 12;
    property PageHeight: Integer
      read FPageHeight write FPageHeight default 792;
    property PageWidth: Integer
      read FPageWidth write FPageWidth default 612;
  end;

procedure Register;

implementation

procedure Register;
begin
  RegisterComponents('My Components', [TPDFExport]);
end;

constructor TPDFExport.Create(AOwner: TComponent);
begin
  inherited;
  PDF := TMemoryStream.Create;
  FOffsetList := TStringList.Create;
  FStrings := TStringList.Create;

  FPageWidth := 612;
  FPageHeight := 792;
```

```
    FFontSize := 12;
    FCompress := False;
  end;

destructor TPDFExport.Destroy;
begin
  FStrings.Free;
  FOffsetList.Free;
  PDF.Free;
  inherited;
end;

end.
```

You've probably noticed that the way the inherited constructor and destructor are called in TPDFExport is different from the way we've been calling inherited constructors in previous components. When you only write inherited in a method, Delphi will call the ancestor method that has the same name and the same parameter list. In these two cases, the reserved word inherited will result in a call to TComponent.Create and TComponent.Destroy.

Utility Methods and the Document Header

The simplest part of the PDF document, and the easiest to create, is the document header:

```
%PDF-1.2
```

The TPDFExport component should conform to at least PDF 1.2, because this enables the user to compress data using zlib compression, which was introduced in PDF version 1.2.

Every line of text (the ones that contain PDF commands) must be terminated with the end of line marker: carriage return (CR, #13) and line feed (LF, #10) characters. If we were using the TStringList class to generate the PDF, things would be simpler because the TStringList class ends every string it contains with the abovementioned end of line marker. But since we're using the TMemoryStream class, we have to add the end of line marker to the stream manually.

To write strings to the memory stream and to automatically end them with the end of line marker, we need a simple method that will do the job for us. Here is the TPDFExport's overloaded Write method that allows us to write a string directly to the PDF or another stream:

```
type
  TPDFExport = class(TComponent)
  private
    procedure Write(const S: string); overload; inline;
    procedure Write(AStream: TStream; const S: string); overload;
  end;

procedure TPDFExport.Write(const S: string);
begin
  Write(PDF, S);
```

```
end;

procedure TPDFExport.Write(AStream: TStream; const S: string);
const
  EOLN = #13#10;
var
  pdfString: string;
begin
  pdfString := S + EOLN;
  AStream.Write(pdfString[1], Length(pdfString));
end;
```

Now that the Write method is done, we have to create two more methods: StartDocument and SaveToFile. The SaveToFile method is the most important method because it calls all other methods and actually generates the document. We also need an FCurrentObject private integer field to help us keep track of the object we're working with. For now, simply declare the field and set it to 0 in the StartDocument method.

Here are the StartDocument and SaveToFile methods:

```
type
  TPDFExport = class(TComponent)
  private
    FCurrentObject: Integer;
    procedure StartDocument;
  public
    procedure SaveToFile(const AFileName: string);
  end;

procedure TPDFExport.SaveToFile(const AFileName: string);
begin
  { 1. Write the document header. }
  StartDocument;

  { Finally, save the stream to disk. }
  PDF.SaveToFile(AFileName);
end;

procedure TPDFExport.StartDocument;
begin
  { remove the old pdf document from the stream
    and reset the cross-reference (offset) list }
  PDF.Clear;
  FOffsetList.Clear;
  FCurrentObject := 0;

  { Write the PDF document header. }
  Write('%PDF-1.2');
end;
```

Indirect Objects

Indirect objects in PDF are objects with a unique identifier (a positive integer) and a generation number. In new PDF documents, the generation number is 0, but in updated documents, the generation number can be larger than 0. In this component, we'll only be creating objects with a generation number of 0.

Indirect objects are extremely useful because they can reference each other in the document. As you'll see in a moment, almost everything we write to the PDF document will be an indirect object or an indirect object reference.

The syntax for creating an indirect object looks like this:

```
UniqueID GenerationNumber obj
  ObjectData
endobj
```

Here's a real indirect object from a PDF document:

```
1 0 obj
<<
/Author (Santa Claus)
/Producer (Inside Delphi Book - TPDFExport Component)
/Subject ()
/Title (Christmas Presents)
>>
endobj
```

Each time an indirect object is created, like the document information dictionary above, the TPDFExport component has to create its entry in the cross-reference table. To solve these two problems, let's create the StartObject function. The StartObject function should first add the offset of the new object to the reference list, acquire a unique number for the new object, and then write the object's header to the PDF stream.

Entries in the cross-reference table are strictly defined. Each entry in the table has to be 20 bytes long (18 bytes of data and the end of line marker). The format of the cross-reference table entry is:

```
nnnnnnnnnn ggggg n eoln
```

The nnnnnnnnnn part is a 10-digit byte offset, the ggggg part is the 5-digit generation number (which in the TPDFExport component is always 00000), and the n part is actually the letter "n". The letter "n" is used to specify that this object is in use. In PDF documents, you can also use an "f" letter here. The letter "f" specifies that the location is free, but we aren't going to be using or creating free entries in the TPDFExport component.

The Format function can help us generate the required 10-digit offset string. When you pass a %10d format string to the Format function, the function will convert the number into a 10-character string. However, the function will fill the string with spaces, so we need to change the spaces into zeros after the Format call. The FormatOffset function, which follows, is used by the TPDFExport component to generate the 10-digit object offset:

```
function FormatOffset(Index: Integer): string;
var
```

```
    i: Integer;
begin
  Result := Format('%10d', [Index]);
  { replace spaces with zeros }
  for i := 1 to Length(Result) do
    if Result[i] = ' ' then Result[i] := '0';
end;
```

Now that the biggest problem is solved, we can create the StartObject and EndObject methods. The TPDFExport component uses these two methods and the Write method to generate the PDF document. Note that the EndObject procedure only outputs the endobj reserved word to the PDF stream and that its only purpose beyond outputting the reserved word is to improve the readability of the source code that generates PDF objects.

Listing 27-5: StartObject and EndObject methods

```
type
  TPDFExport = class(TComponent)
  private
    function StartObject: Integer;
    procedure EndObject;
  end;

function TPDFExport.StartObject: Integer;
const
  NEW_OBJECT = '%d 0 obj';
begin
  { Remember the offset of the object and
    automatically create its entry in the xref list }
  FOffsetList.Add(FormatOffset(PDF.Size) + ' 00000 n');

  { Increment object count and write the object's
    header to the PDF stream }
  Inc(FCurrentObject);
  Write(Format(NEW_OBJECT, [FCurrentObject]));

  { return the object's ID }
  Result := FCurrentObject;
end;

procedure TPDFExport.EndObject;
begin
  Write('endobj');
end;
```

Document Information Dictionary

The document information dictionary is one of the simplest objects you can create in a PDF. Even though this dictionary is completely optional, we're going to create it as the very first one because this dictionary allows us to add metadata to the PDF document, such as the document's title, the name of the author, etc. Dictionaries are sequences of key-value pairs enclosed in "<<" and ">>".

Again, here is what the document information dictionary looks like:

```
1 0 obj
<<
/Author (Santa Claus)
/Producer (Inside Delphi Book - TPDFExport Component)
/Subject ()
/Title (Christmas Presents)
>>
endobj
```

To allow the user to customize the PDF document's metadata, you need to at least create the Author, Producer, Subject, and Title string properties and use the StartObject, Write, and EndObject methods to generate the document information dictionary from this data. Listing 27-6 shows the CreateInfoObject method that generates the document information dictionary. To create the information dictionary as the first object, call the CreateInfoObject method in the SaveToFile method, immediately after the StartDocument method that generates the document header.

Listing 27-6: Generating the document information dictionary

```
type
  TPDFExport = class(TComponent)
  private
    FAuthor: string;
    FProducer: string;
    FSubject: string;
    FTitle: string;
    procedure CreateInfoObject;
  published
    property Author: string read FAuthor write FAuthor;
    property Producer: string read FProducer write FProducer;
    property Subject: string read FSubject write FSubject;
    property Title: string read FTitle write FTitle;
  end;

procedure TPDFExport.CreateInfoObject;
begin
  StartObject;
    Write('<<');
    Write('/Author (' + FAuthor + ')');
    Write('/Producer (' + FProducer + ')');
    Write('/Subject (' + FSubject + ')');
    Write('/Title (' + FTitle + ')');
    Write('>>');
  EndObject;
end;

procedure TPDFExport.SaveToFile(const AFileName: string);
begin
  { 1. Write the document header. }
  StartDocument;
  { 2. Create the info object, always 1 }
  CreateInfoObject;
```

```
{ Other objects will be generated here. }

{ Finally, save the stream to disk. }
PDF.SaveToFile(AFileName);
end;
```

The metadata from the information dictionary can be viewed in any PDF reader, such as Adobe Reader or Foxit Reader (see Figure 27-17).

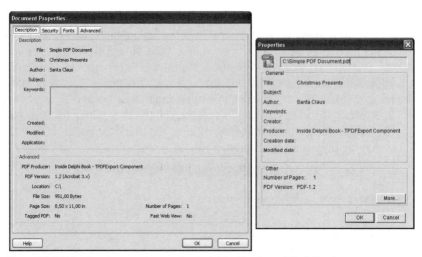

Figure 27-17: Viewing document properties in Adobe Reader and Foxit Reader

Creating the Font Object

The PDF specification requires viewer applications to support 14 standard (Type 1) fonts. Thus, you can freely use these 14 fonts without having to worry about the document size or how the document will be displayed. PDFs can also use non-standard fonts. Applications that support non-standard fonts embed them in the document, which increases the size of the PDF document but enables it to be displayed on machines that don't have the specific font.

The following table shows the 14 standard fonts that can be safely used in PDF documents.

Table 27-2: Standard fonts

Times-Roman	Helvetica	Courier	Symbol
Times-Bold	Helvetica-Bold	Courier-Bold	Zapf-Dingbats
Times-Italic	Helvetica-Oblique	Courier-Oblique	
Times-BoldItalic	Helvetica-BoldOblique	Courier-BoldOblique	

The TPDFExport component uses only one font — Courier — for several reasons:

■ Since we are only working with plain text files, we don't need to use more than one font.

- Courier is one of the standard fonts, which means that every PDF document created by the component will be small and will look almost the same on different operating systems and in different viewers.

- Every character in the Courier font has the same width, which allows us to create simple algorithms for text output. Other standard fonts, not to mention non-standard ones, have variable character widths. To find out about character widths in other standard fonts, take a look at the Adobe font metrics (AFM) files (available on the companion CD). Figure 27-18 shows a piece of the Helvetica.afm file, which contains information about the Helvetica font. The WX column, in which the value 278 is highlighted, contains character widths of the Helvetica font.

```
☞ C:\Program Files\Wordware Publishing\Inside Delphi\CH27-02\Core14_AFMs\Helvetica.afm
Unit1   Helvetica.afm
 1   StartFontMetrics 4.1
 2   Comment Copyright (c) 1985, 1987, 1989, 1990, 1997 Adobe Systems Incorporated.
 3   Comment Creation Date: Thu May  1 12:38:23 1997
 4   Comment UniqueID 43054
 5   Comment VMusage 37069 48094
 6   FontName Helvetica
 7   FullName Helvetica
 8   FamilyName Helvetica
 9   Weight Medium
10   ItalicAngle 0
11   IsFixedPitch false
12   CharacterSet ExtendedRoman
13   FontBBox -166 -225 1000 931
14   UnderlinePosition -100
15   UnderlineThickness 50
16   Version 002.000
17   Notice Copyright (c) 1985, 1987, 1989, 1990, 1997 Adobe Systems Incorporated.  A
18   EncodingScheme AdobeStandardEncoding
19   CapHeight 718
20   XHeight 523
21   Ascender 718
22   Descender -207
23   StdHW 76
24   StdVW 88
25   StartCharMetrics 315
26   C 32 ; WX 278 ; N space ; B 0 0 0 0 ;
27   C 33 ; WX 278 ; N exclam ; B 90 0 187 718 ;
28   C 34 ; WX 355 ; N quotedbl ; B 70 463 285 718 ;
29   C 35 ; WX 556 ; N numbersign ; B 28 0 529 688 ;
30   C 36 ; WX 556 ; N dollar ; B 32 -115 520 775 ;
31   C 37 ; WX 889 ; N percent ; B 39 -19 850 703 ;
32   C 38 ; WX 667 ; N ampersand ; B 44 -15 645 718 ;

                26: 11      Insert                    Code │ History
```

Figure 27-18: The Helvetica font's font metrics file

To use a font in a PDF document, you have to describe it in a dictionary and then reference the font object when you need it. When creating a font object, you need to give the font a name (in this case the name of the font is F1, for font1), use the BaseFont key to specify the name of the font you want to use (in this case it's Courier), and optionally specify the encoding like MacRomanEncoding, MacExpertEncoding, or WinAnsiEncoding.

The following listing shows the CreateFontObject method that creates the Courier font object. In the TPDFExport component, the font object is assumed to be the second object.

Listing 27-7: Generating the font object

```
procedure TPDFExport.CreateFontObject;
begin
  StartObject;
    Write('<< /Type /Font');
    Write('/Subtype /Type1');
```

```
      Write('/Name /F1');
      Write('/BaseFont /Courier');
      Write('/Encoding /WinAnsiEncoding');
      Write('>>');
  EndObject;
end;

procedure TPDFExport.SaveToFile(const AFileName: string);
begin
  ...
  { 3. Create the font object, always 2 }
  CreateFontObject;
  ...
end;
```

The Resource Dictionary

To use the indirect font object we created earlier, we need to create a resource dictionary that will contain a reference to the font. The pages that use the font (and other resources) will then reference the resource dictionary.

A resource dictionary looks like this:

```
3 0 obj
<< /ProcSet [ /PDF /Text]
/Font <<
/F1 2 0 R
>>
>>
```

To create the resource dictionary in this component, you pretty much only have to output what you see above. The ProcSet key in the resource dictionary is an array that holds PostScript procedure sets, which are only used when the PDF document is sent to a PostScript output device to allow the device to understand PDF operators.

Besides the procedure sets, the above resource dictionary also contains a reference to the F1 font. The syntax for an object reference in PDF is ObjectID GenerationNumber and the letter "R" for reference.

Here's the TPDFExport component's CreateResourcesObject method that generates the resource dictionary:

```
{ The resource dictionary is always 3 in this component. }
procedure TPDFExport.CreateResourcesObject;
begin
  { The font object (F1) is always 2 in this component. }
  StartObject;
    Write('<< /ProcSet [ /PDF /Text]');
    Write('/Font <<');
    Write('/F1 2 0 R');
    Write('>>');
    Write('>>');
  EndObject;
end;
```

```
procedure TPDFExport.SaveToFile(const AFileName: string);
begin
  ...
  { 4. Create resources object, always 3 }
  CreateResourcesObject;
  ...
end;
```

Preparing Strings for Output

Before we can store text into a PDF document using the TPDFExport component, we need to finish the implementation of the Strings property. The write
method of the Strings property must not blindly assign the strings it acquires
to the Strings property. To reduce the amount of code that needs to be written
to actually generate PDF output, the write method of the Strings property
should also reformat the strings to fit inside the margins.

To find out how many characters fit inside the margins, we need to divide
the space inside the margins by the character width. Since the character width
in PDF is specified in units that are the thousandth part of the default unit, we
need to divide the result by 1000 to get the number of characters.

Here's how the TPDFExport component determines how many characters fit inside the margins (this is an excerpt from the Strings property's write
method):

```
var
  charCount: Integer;
begin
  { 144 are left and right one-inch margins }
  { 600 is the constants width of all Courier characters }
  charCount := Round((FPageWidth - 144) / (600 * FFontSize / 1000));
end;
```

Once the number of characters per line is known, the SetStrings method
needs to search for delimiter characters that can't be directly written to the
PDF: (,), \, and the tab character (#9). The (,), and \ characters need to be
escaped with another \ character to create a sequence that can be written to
the PDF stream. So, to display a left parenthesis, you need to output \(to the
PDF stream, and to display the \ character, you need to output \\ to the PDF
stream. The tab character (#9) should be replaced with \t, although not
replacing the tab character wreaks much less havoc on the PDF than the
above three characters do.

Listing 27-8 shows the SetStrings write method that reformats the
strings while assigning them to the Strings property. The code is thoroughly
commented so you should have no problems in figuring out what's going on.

Listing 27-8: Reformatting the strings in the component's Strings property

```
type
  TPDFExport = class(TComponent)
  private
    procedure SetStrings(Value: TStrings);
```

```
published
  property Strings: TStrings read FStrings write SetStrings;
end;

procedure TPDFExport.SetStrings(Value: TStrings);
var
  charCount: Integer;
  line: string;
  i: Integer;
  lastSpace: Integer;
  delimiter: Integer;
  lineFits: Boolean;
begin
  { 144 are left and right one-inch margins }
  { 600 is the constants width of all Courier characters }
  charCount := Round((FPageWidth - 144) / (600 * FFontSize / 1000));
  FStrings.Clear;

  for i := 0 to Pred(Value.Count) do
  begin
    if Value[i] = '' then
      FStrings.Add('')
    else begin
      line := Value[i] + ' ';
      { if line fits into margins, copy the entire line into
        FStrings, but after the treatment of delimiter characters }
      lineFits := Pred(Length(line)) <= charCount;

      { if one of the special characters is found, replace it
        with its escape sequence, which can be used in the string }
      delimiter := 1;
      while delimiter < Length(line) do
      begin
        if line[delimiter] in ['\', '(', ')'] then
        begin
          Insert('\', line, delimiter);
          Inc(delimiter);    // skip inserted char
        end else if line[delimiter] = #9 {Tab} then
        begin
          { remove tab }
          Delete(line, delimiter, 1);
          { insert the proper tab marker }
          Insert('\t', line, delimiter);
          Inc(delimiter);    // skip "\t"
        end;
        Inc(delimiter);
      end;                   // while delimiter

      { if the line fits into margins, copy the
        entire line and move to the next one }
      if lineFits = True then
      begin
        FStrings.Add(line);
        Continue;
      end;
```

```
    { if the line doesn't fit into the margins, try to
      find the last space and break the line there }
    while line <> '' do
    begin
      { start at max length char }
      lastSpace := charCount;
      while (lastSpace > 1) and
        (line[lastSpace] <> ' ') do Dec(lastSpace);

      { if there are no spaces, break the string at charCount }
      if lastSpace = 1 then
      begin
        FStrings.Add(Copy(line, 1, charCount));
        Delete(line, 1, charCount);
      end else
      begin
        { if space is found, break it at the last full word }
        FStrings.Add(Copy(line, 1, lastSpace - 1));
        Delete(line, 1, lastSpace);
      end;       // if lastSpace = 1
    end;         // while line <> ''
  end;           // the main if, if value[i] <> ''
  end;           // for i
end;
```

Generating Page Contents (Content Streams)

An interesting thing about PDF documents is that they store pages and page contents as separate objects. The TPDFExport component first generates all page contents objects and then creates all page objects with references to the appropriate contents stream.

Here is a very simple page contents object (content stream):

```
4 0 obj
<< /Length 76
>>
stream
BT
/F1 12 Tf
72 720 Td
(A very simple PDF document...) Tj
0 -12 TD
ET
endstream
endobj
```

Every stream has to have a Length entry that tells the viewer application how many bytes the stream contains. If the stream is compressed, Length should specify the compressed size. The length of the stream is the amount of data between the stream and endstream reserved words.

The BT operator in PDF documents is used to start text output. The end of text output is marked with the ET operator. Between the two operators are additional PDF commands that display text.

The /F1 12 Tf line shows how to use the Tf operator to select a font and define the font's size. In this case, this line tells the viewer application to use our F1 font and to display the text in size 12.

The 72 720 Td line marks the beginning of text output; these are the coordinates of the first line. The Td operator is a text-positioning operator used to specify where the text should be displayed. These two values result in text being displayed in the top-left corner of the page, next to the left margin (72) and beneath the top margin (720, page height – top margin (72)).

The (A very simple PDF document...) Tj line uses the Tj operator to display the text in parentheses on the page. Now that you've seen that parentheses are used in PDF to contain strings, you understand why these characters had to be escaped with \ in the SetStrings write method.

The final line inside the stream, 0 –12 TD, uses the TD operator to offset text from the current location. In this case, the horizontal coordinate isn't modified (0). The –12 value moves text to the next line; actually it moves the text by FontSize toward the bottom of the page.

To create page contents objects, the TPDFExport component uses the CreatePageContents method that is able to create both uncompressed and zlib compresssed streams.

Compressing data in Delphi cannot be simpler. To compress a stream that contains uncompressed data, you have to use the TCompressionStream class declared in the ZLib unit. The actual compression of data occurs when you copy data from an uncompressed stream to the compression stream.

The constructor of the TCompressionStream class accepts two parameters: the level of compression and the destination stream where the compressed data will be written. The following excerpt shows how to compress a stream using the TCompressionStream class. In the excerpt, the buff variable is a TMemoryStream that contains uncompressed data, C is the TCompressionStream used to compress data, and destStream is another TMemoryStream whose purpose is to accept the compressed output of the TCompressionStream object:

```
{ create the dest stream to hold compressed data }
destStream := TMemoryStream.Create;
try
  C := TCompressionStream.Create(clDefault, destStream);
  try
    { compress data by copying it from another stream }
    C.CopyFrom(buff, 0);
  finally
    C.Free;
  end;       // C
finally
  destStream.Free;
end;          // destStream
```

Listing 27-9 shows the entire CreatePageContents method. Notice that the method has two out parameters (which are only used to output values from the method to the outside world). FirstObject returns the ID of the first page

contents object and the ObjectCount parameter returns the number of page
contents objects created. These two values are later used by the method that
creates page objects.

Listing 27-9: Generating page contents objects

```
unit PDFExport;

interface

uses SysUtils, Classes, ZLib;

type
  TPDFExport = class(TComponent)
  private
    procedure CreatePageContents(out FirstObject,
      ObjectCount: Integer);
  end;

procedure TPDFExport.SaveToFile(const AFileName: string);
var
  contentsFirst: Integer;
  contentsCount: Integer;
begin
  { 5. Create contents objects }
  CreatePageContents(contentsFirst, contentsCount);
end;

procedure TPDFExport.CreatePageContents(out FirstObject,
  ObjectCount: Integer);
var
  i, j: Integer;
  linesPerPage: Integer;
  index: Integer;
  buff: TMemoryStream;
  destStream: TMemoryStream;
  C: TCompressionStream;
const
  CONST_LENGTH = '<< /Length %d';
begin
  { determine how many lines fit on a page by dividing
    the space between top and bottom margins by FontSize }
  { to get some white space and reduce the possibility of
    overlaping characters, increment the font size internally by 1 }
  { finally, because of the way PDF outputs text, we can fit
    two more lines inside the margins, so increment the result by 2 }
  linesPerPage := ((FPageHeight - 144) div (FFontSize + 1)) + 2;

  { return FirstObject and ObjectCount values because
    they are needed to create page objects later }
  FirstObject := Succ(FCurrentObject);
  { ObjectCount is actually page count }
  ObjectCount := Succ(FStrings.Count div linesPerPage);

  buff := TMemoryStream.Create;
  try
```

```
{ create the contents }
for i := 0 to ObjectCount - 1 do
begin
  buff.Clear;
  Write(buff, 'BT');
  Write(buff, '/F1 ' + IntToStr(FFontSize) + ' Tf');
  Write(buff, '72 ' + IntToStr(FPageHeight - 72) + ' Td');

  for j := 0 to linesPerPage - 1 do
  begin
    index := (i * linesPerPage) + j;
    if index > Pred(FStrings.Count) then Break;
    Write(buff, '(' + FStrings[index] + ') Tj');
    { move to next line, -FontSize }
    Write(buff, '0 -' + IntToStr(FFontSize + 1) + ' TD');
  end;        // for i

  Write(buff, 'ET'); { finish text output }

  { create the page }
  if FCompress then
  begin
    { create the dest stream to hold compressed data }
    destStream := TMemoryStream.Create;
    try
      C := TCompressionStream.Create(clDefault, destStream);
      try
        { compress data by copying it from another stream }
        C.CopyFrom(buff, 0);
      finally
        C.Free;
      end;    // C

      { Write the compressed object to the PDF stream }
      StartObject;
        Write(Format(CONST_LENGTH, [destStream.Size]));
        Write('/Filter [/FlateDecode]');
        Write('>>');
        Write('stream');
        destStream.SaveToStream(PDF);
        Write('endstream');
      EndObject;
    finally
      destStream.Free;
    end;      // destStream
  end else
  begin
    { Write uncompressed object to the PDF stream }
    StartObject;
      Write(Format(CONST_LENGTH, [buff.Size]));
      Write('>>');
      Write('stream');
      buff.SaveToStream(PDF);
      Write('endstream');
    EndObject;
```

```
      end;       // if FCompressed
    end;         // for i
  finally
    buff.Free;
  end;
end;
```

Creating the Page Tree and the Page Objects

The page tree is a very important object that contains the number of pages available in the document (the Count key) and the references to all document pages (the Kids array). The page tree is used by viewer applications to quickly access any page in the document, no matter how many pages there are.

Here's what a page tree object looks like in a document that has only one page (with ID 6):

```
5 0 obj
<< /Type /Pages
/Kids [
6 0 R
]
/Count 1
>>
endobj
```

Among other things, a page object needs to reference the page tree object, and because of that, the TPDFExport component first generates the page tree object (based on the count of page contents objects from the CreatePage-Contents method) and then creates the page objects.

Besides having to reference the page tree (Parent) object, a page object must have a MediaBox key that defines the page size, a Contents key that references the page contents object for the page, and a Resources key that references the resource dictionary.

Here's what a page object looks like:

```
6 0 obj
<< /Type /Page
/Parent 5 0 R
/MediaBox [0 0 612 792]
/Contents 4 0 R
/Resources 3 0 R
>>
endobj
```

The TPDFExport component uses the CreatePages method to generate both the page tree object and all document pages. To achieve this, the method has to accept the ID of the first page contents object and the number of page contents objects available in the document (both values are returned by the CreatePageContents method). The method must also return the ID of the page tree object because it's needed later. Listing 27-10 shows the CreatePages method.

Listing 27-10: Generating the page tree and the page objects

```
procedure TPDFExport.SaveToFile(const AFileName: string);
var
  PageTreeID: Integer;
begin
  { 6. Create page tree and actual page objects }
  CreatePages(contentsFirst, contentsCount, PageTreeID);
end;


procedure TPDFExport.CreatePages(FirstRef,
  CountRef: Integer; out PageTreeID: Integer);
var
  i: Integer;
begin
  { First create the page tree object }
  PageTreeID := StartObject;
    Write('<< /Type /Pages');
    Write('/Kids [');

    for i := 1 to CountRef do
      Write(IntToStr(PageTreeID + i) + ' 0 R');

    Write(']');
    Write('/Count ' + IntToStr(CountRef)); { page count }
    Write('>>');
  EndObject;

  { Then create page objects }
  for i := 0 to CountRef - 1 do
  begin
    StartObject;
      Write('<< /Type /Page');
      Write('/Parent ' + IntToStr(PageTreeID) + ' 0 R');
      Write('/MediaBox [0 0 ' +
        IntToStr(FPageWidth) + ' ' + IntToStr(PageHeight) + ']');
      Write('/Contents ' + IntToStr(FirstRef + i) + ' 0 R');

      { Resource object is always 3 in this component. }
      Write('/Resources 3 0 R');
      Write('>>');
    EndObject;
  end;       // for i
end;
```

Creating the Document Catalog

The document catalog is the root object whose main purpose is to reference other objects that define the contents of the document. In this case, the document catalog only needs to reference the page tree object.

Here's what a document catalog looks like:

```
7 0 obj
<< /Type /Catalog
/Pages 5 0 R
>>
endobj
```

To generate the document catalog, the CreateCatalog method needs to accept the ID of the page tree object. The CreateCatalog method also needs to return the document catalog's ID:

```
procedure TPDFExport.SaveToFile(const AFileName: string);
var
  CatalogID: Integer;
begin
  { 7. Create the catalog object }
  CatalogID := CreateCatalog(PageTreeID);
end;

function TPDFExport.CreateCatalog(PageTreeRef: Integer): Integer;
begin
  Result := StartObject;
    Write('<< /Type /Catalog');
    Write('/Pages ' + IntToStr(PageTreeRef) + ' 0 R');
    Write('>>');
  EndObject;
end;
```

The Cross-Reference Table and the File Trailer

At this point, it's extremely easy to finish the cross-reference table because most of it has already been constructed with every call to the StartObject method. To finish the cross-reference table, we need to output the `xref` reserved word to the PDF stream. The `xref` reserved word has to be followed by two numbers: the ID of the first object (0) and the number of objects in the table. The ID of the first object in the following cross-reference table is 0, and there are eight objects in the table. The "0000000000 65535 f" entry is an obligatory placeholder for other entries:

```
xref
0 8
0000000000 65535 f
0000000010 00000 n
0000000156 00000 n
0000000269 00000 n
0000000342 00000 n
0000000473 00000 n
0000000540 00000 n
0000000652 00000 n
```

The file trailer starts with the trailer dictionary and enables viewer applications to quickly find the cross-reference table and objects like the document catalog. The trailer dictionary should have a Size key that specifies the total number of entries in the xref table + 1. It also must point to the document catalog and optionally to the info object, if there is one. The trailer dictionary has to be followed by the startxref reserved word, which must be followed by a number that is the byte offset of the xref table. The only thing that should follow this byte offset is the end of file marker, %%EOF.

Here's what a file trailer looks like:

```
trailer
<< /Size 9
/Root 7 0 R
/Info 1 0 R
>>
startxref
706
%%EOF
```

Listing 27-11 shows the EndDocument method that generates both the cross-reference table and the file trailer.

Listing 27-11: Generating the cross-reference table and the file trailer

```
procedure TPDFExport.SaveToFile(const AFileName: string);
begin
  { 8. Write the cross-reference table and the trailer }
  EndDocument(CatalogID);
end;

procedure TPDFExport.EndDocument(CatalogRef: Integer);
var
  xrefOffset: Integer;
  refCount: Integer;
begin
  xrefOffset := PDF.Size;
  Write('xref');

  // refCount = objectCount + the constant xref entry
  refCount := Succ(FCurrentObject);
  Write('0 ' + IntToStr(refCount));
  Write('0000000000 65535 f');
  FOffsetList.SaveToStream(PDF);

  // Write the trailer
  Write('trailer');
  Write('<< /Size ' + IntToStr(refCount + 1));
  Write('/Root ' + IntToStr(CatalogRef) + ' 0 R');
  Write('/Info 1 0 R');
  Write('>>');
  Write('startxref');
  Write(IntToStr(xrefOffset));
  Write('%%EOF');
end;
```

Testing the Component

The TPDFExport component is really easy to use. The only thing you have to remember is to set all component properties like page height, page width, and font size before assigning strings to the Strings property. Listing 27-12 shows an example of how to use the TPDFExport component. The code first displays a simple dialog box (see Figure 27-19) that allows the user to customize the PDF document and then generates the document based on the user's settings.

Listing 27-12: Using the TPDFExport component to save TMemo text to PDF

```
procedure TMainForm.ExportPDFActionExecute(Sender: TObject);
var
  origWordWrap: Boolean;
begin
  PDFForm := TPDFForm.Create(Self);
  try
    if PDFForm.ShowModal = mrOK then
    begin
      origWordWrap := Editor.WordWrap;
      try
        Editor.WordWrap := False;
        if PDFSaveDialog.Execute then
        begin
          PDF.Title := PDFForm.TitleEdit.Text;
          PDF.Author := PDFForm.AuthorEdit.Text;
          PDF.Producer := PDFForm.ProducerEdit.Text;
          PDF.Subject := PDFForm.SubjectEdit.Text;
          PDF.Title := PDFForm.TitleEdit.Text;
          PDF.Compress := PDFForm.CompressLabel.Checked;
          PDF.FontSize := StrToInt(PDFForm.FontCombo.Text);

          PDF.Strings := Editor.Lines;
          PDF.SaveToFile(PDFSaveDialog.FileName);
        end;   // if PDFSaveDialog
      finally
        Editor.WordWrap := origWordWrap;
      end;     // try..finally (Editor.WordWrap)
    end;       // if ShowModal
  finally
    PDFForm.Free;
  end;         // try..finally (PDFForm)
end;
```

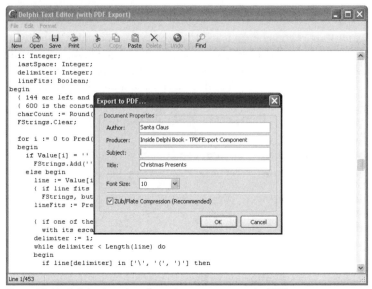

Figure 27-19: A dialog box that allows the user to customize PDF output

Chapter 28

Image Processing

In this chapter, you'll see how to implement several simple effects like converting an image to grayscale and inverting colors using the TCanvas.Pixels and TBitmap.ScanLine properties. You'll also learn how to create an extremely useful TImageList descendant that can generate disabled glyphs at run time, thus saving development time since you won't need to find or create disabled glyphs that match the normal glyph. Even better, using this component reduces the size of the executable significantly since you won't have to add disabled glyphs to the form at design time.

Before we can start writing the graphics related code, we have to create a new VCL Forms application and write a small amount of utility code for opening and displaying bitmaps on the form. The following figure shows the test application at run time.

Figure 28-1: The test application

To enable us to easily test various effects, this application does the following:

- Creates a TBitmap instance in the OnCreate event handler
- Releases the TBitmap instance from memory in the OnDestroy event handler

- Uses the TOpenDialog component to enable us to select a bitmap
- Draws the selected bitmap in the OnPaint event handler

Listing 28-1 shows everything required for the subsequent graphics code.

Listing 28-1: The utility code

```
unit Unit1;

interface

uses
  Windows, Messages, SysUtils, Variants, Classes, Graphics, Controls, Forms,
  Dialogs, Menus;

type
  TMainForm = class(TForm)
  private
    { Private declarations }
    FImage: TBitmap;
  public
    { Public declarations }
  end;

var
  MainForm: TMainForm;

implementation

{$R *.dfm}

procedure TMainForm.FileExitClick(Sender: TObject);
begin
  Close;
end;

procedure TMainForm.FormCreate(Sender: TObject);
begin
  FImage := TBitmap.Create;

  { if your resolution is high enough, resize the form to
    display the entire 800x600 flower.bmp image that comes
    with this example }
  if Screen.Width >= 1024 then
  begin
    ClientWidth := 800;
    ClientHeight := 600;
  end;
end;

procedure TMainForm.FormDestroy(Sender: TObject);
begin
  FImage.Free;
end;

procedure TMainForm.FormPaint(Sender: TObject);
```

```
begin
  if OpenDialog.FileName <> '' then
    Canvas.Draw(0, 0, FImage);
end;

procedure TMainForm.FileOpenClick(Sender: TObject);
begin
  if OpenDialog.Execute then
  begin
    FImage.LoadFromFile(OpenDialog.FileName);
    Invalidate; { Display the image }
  end;
end;

end.
```

The Canvas.Pixels Property

The Pixels property of the TCanvas class provides the easiest way to access pixels on a surface. It enables you to read and write the color value of a pixel at the specified location:

```
property Pixels[X, Y: Integer]: TColor;
```

Inverting Colors

To see how to use the Pixels property and how to write a simple effect, let's first create a duplicate of the InvertRect API function, which we used in Chapter 17 to enable the user to invert colors in an image.

Here are three ways to invert the pixel's color:

```
NewPixel = not OldPixel
NewPixel = OldPixel xor 1
NewPixel = 1 - OldPixel
```

To implement any of the above formulas, we must first extract the pixel's red, green, and blue values and then apply the formula to each value separately. Since the "1" in the formula represents the "maximum value," it becomes 255 in the implementation because 255 is the maximum value of a color component.

The following listing shows how to implement the NewPixel = 1 – OldPixel formula.

Listing 28-2: Inverting colors using the Pixels property

```
procedure TMainForm.PixelsInvertColorsClick(Sender: TObject);
var
  x: Integer;
  y: Integer;
  oldColor: TColor;
  newRed, newGreen, newBlue: Integer;
begin
  for y := 0 to Pred(FImage.Height) do
  begin
    for x := 0 to Pred(FImage.Width) do
```

```
begin
  { extract original color at x,y }
  oldColor := FImage.Canvas.Pixels[x, y];

  { invert the color }
  newRed := 255 - GetRValue(oldColor);
  newGreen := 255 - GetGValue(oldColor);
  newBlue := 255 - GetBValue(oldColor);

  { assign the inverted color to x,y }
  FImage.Canvas.Pixels[x, y] := RGB(newRed, newGreen, newBlue);
  end;        // for x
 end;         // for y

 Invalidate; { Invalidate the form to display the image. }
end;
```

The result of this code is displayed in Figure 28-2.

Figure 28-2: The result of the Invert Colors effect

The Solarize Effect

The Solarize effect is probably the closest relative of the Invert Colors effect. To solarize an image, you have to invert a pixel's component if its value is larger than half the maximum value (127). If the value of a pixel's component is less than 127, you have to use the original value.

Here's the pseudocode of the Solarize effect:

```
if OldPixel > 1/2 then
  NewPixel = 1 - OldPixel
else
  NewPixel = OldPixel
```

The following listing shows how to solarize an image.

Listing 28-3: The Solarize effect

```
procedure TMainForm.PixelsSolarizeClick(Sender: TObject);
var
  x: Integer;
  y: Integer;
  oldColor: TColor;
  newRed, newGreen, newBlue: Integer;
begin
  for y := 0 to Pred(FImage.Height) do
  begin
    for x := 0 to Pred(FImage.Width) do
    begin
      { extract original color at x,y }
      oldColor := FImage.Canvas.Pixels[x, y];

      { invert the color }
      newRed := GetRValue(oldColor);
      if newRed > 127 then newRed := 255 - newRed;

      newGreen := GetGValue(oldColor);
      if newGreen > 127 then newGreen := 255 - newGreen;

      newBlue := GetBValue(oldColor);
      if newBlue > 127 then newBlue := 255 - newBlue;

      { assign the inverted color to x,y }
      FImage.Canvas.Pixels[x, y] := RGB(newRed, newGreen, newBlue);
    end;       // for x
  end;         // for y

  Invalidate; { Invalidate the form to display the image. }
end;
```

You can see the solarized image in the following figure.

Figure 28-3: The Solarize effect

Now that you've seen and learned how to write simple effects, it's time to say goodbye to the Pixels property because it is, as you've undoubtedly noticed, extremely slow and totally inappropriate for this job.

The ScanLine Property

The TBitmap.ScanLine property is an indexed property that returns a pointer to a row of pixels. The way we use the result of the ScanLine property differs greatly, depending on the bitmap's format. To determine or specify the format of a TBitmap, use its PixelFormat property. The PixelFormat property is a TPixelFormat enumeration, declared in the Graphics unit:

```
TPixelFormat = (pfDevice, pf1bit, pf4bit, pf8bit,
  pf15bit, pf16bit, pf24bit, pf32bit, pfCustom);
```

If the bitmap's PixelFormat doesn't match the way we access the bitmap's pixels, the result is usually very ugly. For instance, the following figure shows an Invert Colors effect that failed because the code tried to treat a pf8bit bitmap as if it were a pf24bit bitmap.

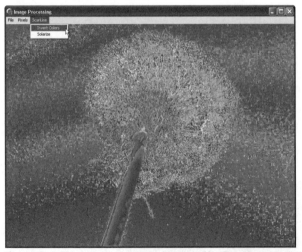

Figure 28-4: This happens when the bitmap's PixelFormat and code aren't compatible

Since this is not a graphics book, we'll only be using the standard 24-bit (true-color) bitmaps. To achieve this, we have to change the PixelFormat of the image after it's loaded to pf24bit. So, here's how the File ➢ Open command should look:

```
procedure TMainForm.FileOpenClick(Sender: TObject);
begin
  if OpenDialog.Execute then
  begin
    FImage.LoadFromFile(OpenDialog.FileName);

    { always treat the bitmap as a 24-bit bitmap }
```

```
    FImage.PixelFormat := pf24bit;
    Invalidate; { Display the image }
  end;
end;
```

As you already know, each pixel in a 24-bit bitmap is described by three values of red, green, and blue. What you might have forgotten is that these values are stored in reverse order in memory. The pixel's blue component is stored first, then the green, and finally the red component. So, when you use the ScanLine property to access a row of pixels in an image, you get a pointer to an array of bytes that looks like this:

BlueGreenRed | BlueGreenRed | BlueGreenRed | BlueGreenRed | BlueGreenRed...

To get the above result, you have to assign the value of the ScanLine property to a PByteArray variable, which enables us to treat a memory block as if it were an array:

```
var
  p: PByteArray;
begin
    p := FImage.ScanLine[0];
end;
```

The following example uses the ScanLine property to access the first row of pixels and then sets the first pixel to black and the second pixel to white.

```
procedure TMainForm.ChangeTwoPixels(Sender: TObject);
var
  p: PByteArray;
begin
  p := FImage.ScanLine[0];
  { change first pixel to clBlack }
  p[0] := 0;
  p[1] := 0;
  p[2] := 0;

  { change second pixel to clWhite }
  p[3] := 255;
  p[4] := 255;
  p[5] := 255;

  Invalidate;
end;
```

When you use the PByteArray type to access the pixels in an image, the first pixel is located at offset 0, the second at offset 3, the third at offset 6, the fourth at offset 9, and so on. So if you want to modify all pixels in a row, you can't use the following code because it only changes the first third of the pixels to black:

```
procedure TMainForm.ChangeTwoPixels(Sender: TObject);
var
  p: PByteArray;
  x: Integer;
begin
```

```
  p := FImage.ScanLine[0];
  for x := 0 to Pred(FImage.Width) do
    p[x] := 0;

  Invalidate;
end;
```

To correctly access the x pixel, you have to multiply it by 3 to get its offset in the scan line. The byte at location x*3 is actually the pixel's blue component. The pixel's green component is located at offset x*3+1 and the pixel's red component is located at offset x*3+2.

So, here's what you have to write in order to change all pixels in an image to black:

```
procedure TMainForm.Blackness(Sender: TObject);
var
  p: PByteArray;
  x: Integer;
  y: Integer;
begin
  { loop through all lines }
  for y := 0 to Pred(FImage.Height) do
  begin
    p := FImage.ScanLine[y];

    for x := 0 to Pred(FImage.Width) do
    begin
      p[x*3]   := 0;
      p[x*3+1] := 0;
      p[x*3+2] := 0;
    end;   // for x
  end;     // for y

  Invalidate;
end;
```

Now that you know how to use the ScanLine property, you can write new versions of the Invert Colors and Solarize effects to see the enormous speed difference gained by using the ScanLine property and the PByteArray type.

Here's the ScanLine version of the Invert Colors effect:

```
procedure TMainForm.ScanLineInvertColorsClick(Sender: TObject);
var
  p: PByteArray;
  x: Integer;
  y: Integer;
begin
  for y := 0 to Pred(FImage.Height) do
  begin
    { get the pointer to the y line }
    p := FImage.ScanLine[y];

    for x := 0 to Pred(FImage.Width) do
    begin
      { modify the blue component }
```

```
      p[x*3] := 255 - p[x*3];

      { modify the green component }
      p[x*3+1] := 255 - p[x*3+1];

      { modify the red component }
      p[x*3+2] := 255 - p[x*3+2];
    end;     // for x
  end;       // for y

  Invalidate; { display the image }
end;
```

Here's the ScanLine version of the Solarize effect:

```
procedure TMainForm.ScanLineSolarizeClick(Sender: TObject);
var
  p: PByteArray;
  x: Integer;
  y: Integer;
begin
  for y := 0 to Pred(FImage.Height) do
  begin
    p := FImage.ScanLine[y];
    for x := 0 to Pred(FImage.Width) do
    begin
      if p[x*3] > 127 then
        p[x*3] := 255 - p[x*3];

      if p[x*3+1] > 127 then
        p[x*3+1] := 255 - p[x*3+1];

      if p[x*3+2] > 127 then
        p[x*3+2] := 255 - p[x*3+2];
    end;     // for x
  end;       // for y

  Invalidate;
end;
```

Before you start creating a bunch of routines that use the PByteArray type,
you might want to consider creating your own pixel description type. You can,
for instance, use the following type and array to treat the pixels in the image
as an array of TMyPixelDescriptor records:

```
type
  { the order of fields must match the BGR order of bytes in memory }
  TMyPixelDescriptor = record
    Blue: Byte;
    Green: Byte;
    Red: Byte;
  end;

  PMyPixelArray = ^TMyPixelArray;
```

```
{ use an array of 32768 pixels if you want to make sure
  you'll be able to use extra large images sometime in the future }
TMyPixelArray = array[0..32767] of TMyPixelDescriptor;
```

Here's the much more readable Solarize effect written using the PMyPixelArray type:

```
procedure TMainForm.ScanLineSolarizeClick(Sender: TObject);
var
  p: PMyPixelArray;
  x: Integer;
  y: Integer;
begin
  for y := 0 to Pred(FImage.Height) do
  begin
    p := FImage.ScanLine[y];
    for x := 0 to Pred(FImage.Width) do
    with p[x] do
    begin
      if Blue > 127 then Blue := 255 - Blue;
      if Green > 127 then Green := 255 - Green;
      if Red > 127 then Red := 255 - Red;
    end;    // with p[x]
  end;      // for y

  Invalidate;
end;
```

Converting the Image to Grayscale

One of the easiest ways to convert a color image to grayscale is to use the following formula:

```
Gray = (Red * 3 + Blue * 4 + Green * 2) div 9
```

When you get the gray value, you have to assign it to all three components. Here's the entire conversion to grayscale, again using the PMyPixelArray type:

```
procedure TMainForm.ScanLineGrayscaleClick(Sender: TObject);
var
  p: PMyPixelArray;
  x: Integer;
  y: Integer;
  gray: Integer;
begin
  for y := 0 to Pred(FImage.Height) do
  begin
    p := FImage.ScanLine[y];
    for x := 0 to Pred(FImage.Width) do
    with p[x] do
    begin
      gray := (Red * 3 + Blue * 4 + Green * 2) div 9;
      Blue := gray;
      Red := gray;
      Green := gray;
    end;    // with p[x]
```

```
end;      // for y

  Invalidate;
end;
```

Adjusting Brightness

Adjusting the brightness of an image is likewise a pretty easy task. To darken or lighten the image, you can use the following formula:

```
NewPixel = OldPixel + (1 * Percent) div 100
```

To darken the image, pass a negative Percent value; to lighten it, pass a positive Percent value. If you pass –100 as the Percent, you'll get a black image, and if you pass +100 as the Percent value, you'll get a white image. If you want your brightness algorithm to produce the same output as, for instance, Adobe Photoshop or other image editors, simply divide the NewPixel value by 200 to halve the user's ability to darken or lighten the image:

```
NewPixel = OldPixel + (1 * Percent) div 200
```

To properly implement the Adjust Brightness effect, you have to create a simple function that will make sure the new values are in the allowable 0 to 255 range:

```
function IntToByte(AInteger: Integer): Byte; inline;
begin
  if AInteger > 255 then
    Result := 255
  else if AInteger < 0 then
    Result := 0
  else
    Result := AInteger;
end;
```

You should also implement the effect as a separate method that accepts the Percent parameter and then call this method inside the ScanLine ➢ Adjust Brightness command's OnClick event handler:

```
{ Percent must be a number from -100 to 100 }
procedure TMainForm.AdjustBrightness(Percent: Integer);
var
  p: PMyPixelArray;
  x: Integer;
  y: Integer;
  amount: Integer;
begin
  amount := (255 * Percent) div 200;

  for y := 0 to Pred(FImage.Height) do
  begin
    p := FImage.ScanLine[y];
    for x := 0 to Pred(FImage.Width) do
    with p[x] do
    begin
      Blue := IntToByte(Blue + amount);
```

```
      Green := IntToByte(Green + amount);
      Red := IntToByte(Red + amount);
    end;
  end;

  Invalidate;
end;
```

Finally, to enable the user to enter a value from –100 to 100 before calling AdjustBrightness, the OnClick event handler calls the InputBox function, which displays a small input dialog box and allows the user to enter a string value:

```
procedure TMainForm.ScanLineBrightnessClick(Sender: TObject);
var
  amount: Integer;
begin
  amount := StrToInt(InputBox('Brightness Level',
    'Enter a value from -100 to 100:', '50'));

  AdjustBrightness(amount);
end;
```

The following figure shows both the input dialog box and the result of passing 75 to the AdjustBrightness method.

Figure 28-5: Adjusting the brightness of the image

The TImageListEx Component

The TImageListEx component is a TImageList descendant that can use the images from another image list to generate disabled images, which can be used on toolbars and other user interface elements.

There are several benefits of the TImageListEx component:

■ It eliminates the need for creating disabled glyphs.

■ It eliminates the need for adding the disabled glyphs to an additional TImageList component at design time.

■ It can drastically reduce the size of the .dfm file and of the entire application, especially in large applications that use a lot of glyphs.

■ It's extremely fast, taking only milliseconds to disable all images in an image list, even when there are number of images.

■ It's extremely lightweight. (If you add it to an application that already uses the standard TImageList component, it won't increase the size of the executable at all, and if you add it to an application that doesn't use the standard TImageList component, the overhead is only 2 KB.)

To create the TImageListEx component, you have to derive it from the standard TImageList component and then create the DisableImage function for disabling an image and the AcquireDisabled procedure that uses the DisableImage function to disable all images from another image list.

The DisableImage function is not really complex. It first determines the "transparent" color by extracting the bottom-right pixel of the source image. Then it uses the "transparent" pixel to determine which pixels should be converted to grayscale and which should be copied. All pixels that match the "transparent" pixel are directly copied to the destination bitmap and all other pixels are first converted to grayscale and then copied to the destination image. Finally, it returns the "transparent" pixel as Result because we have to pass this value to the AddMasked method of TImageList component when adding images to the image list.

The following listing shows the entire DisableImage function.

Listing 28-4: Disabling an image

```
type
  TImageListEx = class(TImageList)
  private
    { Private declarations }
  protected
    { Protected declarations }
    function DisableImage(Source, Dest: TBitmap): TColor;
  end;
...
function TImageListEx.DisableImage(Source, Dest: TBitmap): TColor;
type
  TMyPixel = record
    Blue: Byte;
```

```
      Green: Byte;
      Red: Byte;
    end;

  PMyPixelArray = ^TMyPixelArray;
  TMyPixelArray = array[0..32767] of TMyPixel;
var
  pSrc: PMyPixelArray;
  pDest: PMyPixelArray;
  x: Integer;
  y: Integer;
  gray: Integer;

  { these will hold the transparent color }
  tr: Integer;
  tg: Integer;
  tb: Integer;
begin
  { first, make sure both are pf24bit }
  Source.PixelFormat := pf24bit;
  Dest.PixelFormat := pf24bit;

  { pixel at [W-1,H-1] in the Source is treated as "transparent" }
  pSrc := Source.ScanLine[Pred(Source.Height)];
  with pSrc[Pred(Source.Width)] do
  begin
    tr := Red;
    tg := Green;
    tb := Blue;
  end;

  for y := 0 to Pred(Source.Height) do
  begin
    pSrc := Source.ScanLine[y];
    pDest := Dest.ScanLine[y];

    for x := 0 to Pred(Source.Width) do
    begin
      { if px <> transparent then grayscale it }
      if (pSrc[x].Red <> tr) or (pSrc[x].Green <> tg) or
        (pSrc[x].Blue <> tb) then
      begin
        gray := (pSrc[x].Red * 3 +
          pSrc[x].Blue * 4 + pSrc[x].Green * 2) div 9;

        pDest[x].Red := gray;
        pDest[x].Green := gray;
        pDest[x].Blue := gray;
      end else
      begin
        { if transparent then copy it }
        pDest[x].Red := pSrc[x].Red;
        pDest[x].Green := pSrc[x].Green;
        pDest[x].Blue := pSrc[x].Blue;
      end; // if pSrc
```

```
  end;    // for x
end;      // for y

{ return the color used as transparent; we need to pass this
  to the AddMasked method when adding images to the image list }
Result := RGB(tr, tg, tb);
end;
```

The AcquireDisabled procedure accepts a source TCustomImageList object as the sole parameter and simply loops through its images, converting them to grayscale using the DisableImage function we created above.

To access a particular bitmap in a TImageList, you have to call the GetBitmap method, which accepts the image's index and a TBitmap where the GetBitmap method will store the requested image:

```
function GetBitmap(Index: Integer; Image: TBitmap): Boolean;
```

Finally, after you've acquired the original glyph from the source list and converted it to grayscale using the DisableImage function, you have to call the TImageList's AddMasked method to add the new glyph to the list. When calling the AddMasked method, you have to pass the glyph's transparent color as the MaskColor parameter to have the TImageList component generate the glyph's mask, which is used to draw the glyph transparently.

The following listing shows the AcquireDisabled procedure.

Listing 28-5: The AcquireDisabled procedure

```
procedure TImageListEx.AcquireDisabled(AList: TCustomImageList);
var
  cnt: Integer;
  newImage: TBitmap;
  tempSource: TBitmap;
  transparent: TColor;
begin
  { use AList's image size }
  Width := AList.Width;
  Height := AList.Height;

  { make sure there are no old images in the list }
  Clear;

  tempSource := TBitmap.Create;
  try
    newImage := TBitmap.Create;
    try
      for cnt := 0 to Pred(AList.Count) do
      begin
        { erase the old images because the GetBitmap method doesn't }
        tempSource.Assign(nil);
        newImage.Assign(nil);

        { resize the new image }
        newImage.Width := Width;
        newImage.Height := Height;
```

```
        { get image from the source image list }
        AList.GetBitmap(cnt, tempSource);

        { generate the new image }
        transparent := DisableImage(tempSource, newImage);

        { add the new image to the list }
        AddMasked(newImage, transparent);
      end;
    finally
      newImage.Free;
    end;
  finally
    tempSource.Free;
  end;
end;
```

Using the TImageListEx Component

To use the TImageListEx component in an application, you have to do three things:

- Remove an existing TImageList component that contains disabled glyphs.
- Add the TImageListEx component to the Designer Surface and assign it to the appropriate Disabled properties of the components that used the original TImageList component.
- Call the TImageListEx component's AcquireDisabled method in the main form's OnCreate event handler and pass the TImageList that contains normal glyphs to create appropriate disabled glyphs.

For instance, you can use the Delphi Text Editor example that we created earlier to test this component. First, remove the original disabled TImageList component and drop a TImageListEx component on the Designer Surface. Then, assign the TImageListEx component to the DisabledImages property of the main toolbar and write the following line in the OnCreate event handler of the main form:

```
procedure TMainForm.FormCreate(Sender: TObject);
begin
  ImageListEx1.AcquireDisabled(Normal);
end;
```

The TImageListEx will correctly create all disabled glyphs, except for the Delete button. The original Delete glyph cannot be successfully converted because this glyph, unlike almost all other GlyFX glyphs, treats the bottom-right pixel as a part of the image instead of as the "transparent" pixel. The following figure shows the original (erroneous) glyph and the updated glyph that can be successfully converted to grayscale by the TImageListEx component.

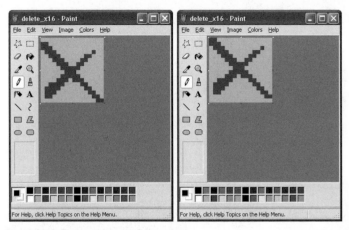

Figure 28-6: The troublesome Delete glyph

The toolbar in the following figure shows what the disabled glyphs generated by the TImageListEx component look like.

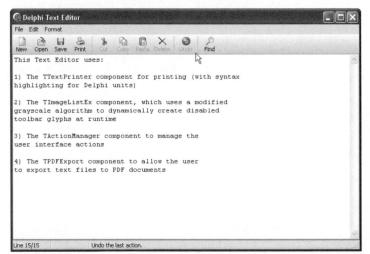

Figure 28-7: The final version of the Delphi Text Editor that uses the TImageListEx component

Finally, Figure 28-8 shows the impact of the TImageListEx component on the size of the Delphi Text Editor's executable. Although the Delphi Text Editor only had 10 disabled glyphs, the TImageListEx component managed to reduce the size of the executable by 17,408 bytes (17 KB).

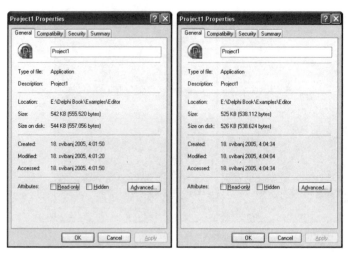

Figure 28-8: The difference in the size of the executable after using the TImageListEx component

Chapter 29

.NET Framework Programming

This chapter introduces the .NET Framework and shows how to build .NET applications using both C# and Delphi for .NET languages. Besides learning the basics of the .NET framework and the C# language, you'll see how to create cross-language and Windows.Forms GUI applications and learn about differences between Windows.Forms and VCL.NET frameworks.

Overview of the .NET Platform

The .NET platform is a managed, language-independent platform for building and running applications. There are two primary components of the .NET platform: CLR and FCL, the Common Language Runtime and the .NET framework class library.

The Common Language Runtime

Standard Win32 applications, like VCL applications built with Delphi for Win32, are compiled to machine code that is directly executable on x86 processors. Unlike Win32 applications, .NET applications are compiled to what is known as CIL — the common intermediate language. The common intermediate language is also known as MSIL — Microsoft intermediate language.

To actually run a .NET application, the machine must have the .NET framework installed. The .NET framework is required because the CIL instructions of the .NET applications are JIT (just-in-time) compiled by the CLR to machine instructions when a .NET application is run.

The JIT compilation has advantages and disadvantages. The disadvantage of JIT compilation of .NET applications is that they execute a little slower than the equivalent Win32 applications the first time they are run.

The advantages of JIT compilation are:

- The JIT compiler doesn't compile the entire application, but only the parts that have to be executed.

- To improve the performance of .NET applications, the JIT compiler compiles a section of code only once and then caches the resulting native code.

- Since the JIT compiler compiles the application on the client machine, not on the developer's machine, it could optimize code for the processor available on the client machine.

- During the compilation of CIL to native code, the CIL code is verified for type safety, which ensures, among other things, that the code cannot access parts of memory that it isn't authorized to access.

Besides the JIT compilation, here are several more benefits of the CLR:

- The CLR allows you to compile the application once to CIL and then run it on different CPUs and operating systems.

- The CLR supports cross-language development (not only can you develop an application using several .NET languages, but you can also create a class in one language and inherit it in another one).

- Objects created in .NET applications are managed by the CLR and garbage collected to prevent memory leaks. (The garbage collector also improves productivity because you don't have to worry about or write code to release objects from memory.)

The .NET Framework Class Library

The .NET framework class library (FCL) contains thousands of types divided into numerous namespaces. The FCL contains classes and data types that can and are used by developers that use any .NET language like Delphi for .NET, C#, VB.NET, Managed Extensions for C++, and JScript.NET.

The main namespace in the FCL is the System namespace. The System namespace contains all base classes of the .NET framework, including the root class of the framework, System.Object. The System.Object class is the base class for everything in the .NET framework, including primitive data types such as Boolean, integer, and string.

Table 29-1 shows several basic FCL types and their C# and Delphi for .NET equivalents. C# and Delphi for .NET types are merely aliases that help you write more C-like code in C# and more Delphi-like and Delphi for Win32-compatible code in Delphi for .NET.

The biggest difference lies in the way the string type is interpreted in Delphi for Win32 and Delphi for .NET. In Delphi for Win32, the string type is an alias for the AnsiString type. In Delphi for .NET, the string type is an alias for the System.String type, which is a Unicode string type, like the WideString type in Delphi for Win32.

Table 29-1: Basic FCL data types

FCL Class Name	Delphi for .NET Type	C# Type
Byte	Byte	byte
Int16	Smallint	short
Int32	Integer	int
Int64	Int64	long
Single	Single	float
Double	Double	double
Boolean	Boolean	bool
String	String	string
Object	TObject	object

Besides the System namespace, there are several more commonly used FCL namespaces:

■ System.Data — Contains ADO.NET classes for accessing and manipulating data

■ System.Drawing — Contains GDI+ classes for creating graphical output

■ System.Collections — Contains lists, arrays, hashtables, and dictionaries

■ System.IO — Contains classes for file and stream I/O

■ System.Windows.Forms — Contains classes for building GUI applications

■ System.Web.UI — Contains basic ASP.NET classes

■ System.Web.UI.WebControls — Contains ASP.NET server controls

■ System.Web.Services — Contains classes for building web services

The VCL.NET Framework

The VCL.NET framework is the .NET version of the VCL framework, and is currently only available for Delphi developers. One of the biggest advantages of the VCL.NET framework over the FCL is that existing Win32 applications can be easily ported to .NET, with none or only minor changes to the code. The VCL.NET framework allows Delphi developers to continue using their Win32 Delphi experience and develop applications that can be, with a bit of help from the IFDEF compiler directive, recompiled to run on both Windows and Linux, and on the .NET platform.

By developing applications using VCL.NET you are not distancing yourself from the .NET framework; you can actually write Delphi applications that use both frameworks. For instance, Listing 29-1 shows a simple Delphi for .NET console application that uses the WriteLn procedure from the Delphi Runtime Library and the WriteLine method of the FCL's Console class (from the System namespace) to display text in the console window.

Listing 29-1: Using both the Delphi RTL and the FCL in a Delphi for .NET console application

```
program Project1;

{$APPTYPE CONSOLE}

uses SysUtils;

begin
  WriteLn('Delphi Runtime Library - WriteLn');
  System.Console.WriteLine('FCL - Console.WriteLine');

  Console.ReadLine; { FCL equivalent of the Readln procedure }
end.
```

Both FCL and VCL.NET are implemented as a set of DLLs, which are like .NET executables, known as assemblies. The FCL assemblies, such as System.Drawing.dll and System.Windows.Forms.dll, are stored in the Windows directory, under Microsoft .NET\Framework\<Framework Version>\. VCL.NET assemblies, such as Borland.VclRtl.dll and Borland.VCL.dll, are stored in the Program Files directory, under Common Files\Borland Shared\BDS\Shared Assemblies\<Delphi Version>\.

VCL.NET assemblies can be used as external libraries or they can be, like packages, linked into the .NET executable to produce a "standalone" executable that only requires the .NET runtime to be installed on the target machine.

C# and Delphi for .NET Languages

The C# language is the "default" language of the .NET framework (the FCL is written in C#). It is a .NET-only, case-sensitive, and fully object-oriented language that in many ways resembles C++, Delphi, and Java programming languages. If you've read the C++ portions of this book or if you already know C++ or Java, you'll have no trouble learning the C# language since it is syntactically closest to these two languages.

To learn more about the C# language, let's create a C# console application project. When you select the Console Application item to create a C# console application project, the IDE will first ask you to name the project (see Figure 29-1) and then will automatically save all project files to disk. The code generated for the C# console application is displayed in Listing 29-2.

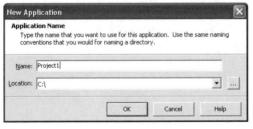

Figure 29-1:
Creating a C#
console application

Listing 29-2: The source code of a C# console application

```
using System;

namespace Project1
{
    /// <summary>
    /// Summary description for Class.
    /// </summary>
    class Class
    {
        /// <summary>
        /// The main entry point for the application.
        /// </summary>
        [STAThread]
        static void Main(string[] args)
        {
            //
            // TODO: Add code to start application here
            //
        }
    }
}
```

Besides the project code, the list of references in a project is extremely important. In order to use a specific class, we must first reference the assembly in which the class is implemented. For instance, to use the Console class (declared in the System namespace), we have to reference the System assembly. If you look at the References node in the Project Manager (see Figure 29-2), you'll notice that the console application already references not only the most important System but also the System.Data and System.XML assemblies.

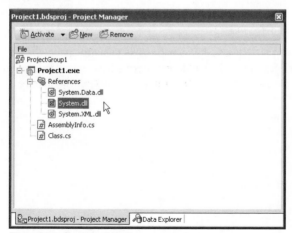

Figure 29-2: Project references

To reference other assemblies, right-click the References node in the Project Manager and select Add Reference to display the Add Reference dialog box (see Figure 29-3). The Add Reference dialog box allows you to reference standard and custom .NET assemblies.

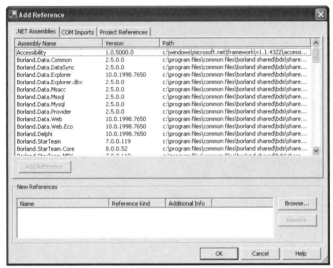

Figure 29-3: The Add Reference dialog box

The purpose of the first directive in the code, the using directive, is to allow us to use the types in a specific namespace without having to specify the namespace. In this case, we can use the Console class and its methods without having to specify the System namespace before the Console class:

```
// without using System;
System.Console.WriteLine("Hello from C#!");
// with using System;
Console.WriteLine("Hello from C#!");
```

The using directive can also be used to create class or namespace aliases, which reduce typing even more. For instance, here's how you can create an alias for the System.Console class and use the class through the alias:

```
using System;
using Con = System.Console;

namespace Project1
{
    class Class
    {
        [STAThread]
        static void Main(string[] args)
        {
            Con.WriteLine("Hello from C#");

            Con.WriteLine("Press any key to continue...");
            Con.ReadLine();
```

```
      }
    }
}
```

Each project also gets its own namespace. The syntax of a C# namespace is:

```
namespace namespaceName
{
}
```

or

```
namespace name1.name2.nameN
{
}
```

If you don't like the generated namespace name, you can either change it manually or use Rename Namespace refactoring. When naming namespaces, you should use the CompanyName.TechnologyName format:

```
namespace Wordware.InsideDelphi
{
}
```

Since C# is completely object-oriented, the source code of the console applications also contains a class and a static method called Main. The Main method is the most important method in a C# project, as it is the entry point of the program.

The summary comments in the code are special comments that can be used by the compiler to generate XML documentation for the project. To have the compiler generate the documentation, check Generate XML documentation in the Code generation group box on the Project Options dialog box, as shown in Figure 29-4. Generated XML documentation for a simple console application is displayed in Figure 29-5.

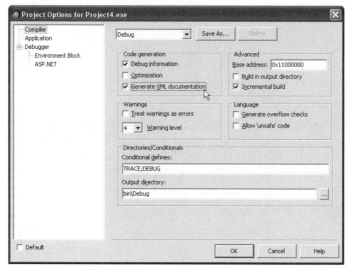

Figure 29-4: C# Project Options dialog box

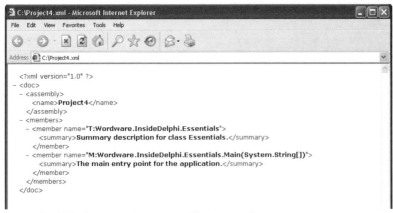

Figure 29-5: XML documentation generated by the compiler

C# Essentials (Variables, Constants, and Casting)

Variables in C# are declared as they are in C++: data type followed by an identifier and a semicolon. Variables declared in C++ can be initialized, but they don't have to be; if they aren't initialized, they contain random values. In C#, you can declare a variable, but you cannot use it until you initialize it:

```
static void Main(string[] args)
{
    int x;
    // Error: Use of unassigned local variable 'x'
    Console.WriteLine(x);
}
```

You can initialize a variable in C# at the same time you declare it or, of course, by using the assignment operator after the variable is declared:

```
int x = 1;
int y;
y = 2;
```

Constants in C# are defined with the reserved word `const`, followed by the data type, identifier, assignment operator, and value:

```
const int ConstValue = 2005;
```

Explicit typecasts in C# are written as they are in C++, by writing the target data type in parentheses before the value. All objects in the .NET framework can be converted to string by calling the ToString() method.

Here's an example of an explicit typecast and the usage of the ToString() method:

```
static void Main(string[] args)
{
    int x = (int)1.2;
    /* since 2005 is an int object, we can
       call its ToString() method */
    string s = 2005.ToString();
```

```
    string s2 = x.ToString();

    Console.WriteLine("x = {0}", x);
    Console.WriteLine("s = {0} and s2 = {1}", s, s2);
    Console.ReadLine();
}
```

The above example also illustrates how to use the WriteLine method to output several values to the console. The {0} and {1} parts of the string are placeholders for values, just like %d and %s values are placeholders for values in the Delphi Format function.

Value and Reference Types

The .NET framework supports two categories of types: value types and reference types. Value types are derived from the System.ValueType class; they are allocated on the stack and directly contain their data. Value types in the .NET framework are numeric data types; Boolean, Char, and Date types; enumerations; and structures (records).

Reference types are derived directly from the System.Object class, contain a pointer to the data allocated on the heap, and are managed by the framework's garbage collector. Reference types are string, arrays, classes, and delegates (covered in the next chapter).

The .NET framework also allows us to convert value to reference and reference to value types. The process of converting a value type to a reference type is known as boxing. The process of converting a reference type to a value type is known as unboxing.

Boxing

When boxing occurs, a new object is allocated on the managed heap and the variable's value is copied into the managed object stored on the heap.

The following code illustrates when boxing occurs. In this case, boxing is done implicitly by the C# compiler:

```
static void Main(string[] args)
{
   char c = 'A';
   object o = c; /* implicit boxing */

   Console.WriteLine(o);
   Console.ReadLine();
}
```

Here's the same code in Delphi for .NET, which also results in implicit boxing of the c variable:

```
program Boxing;

{$APPTYPE CONSOLE}

var
  c: Char = 'A';
```

```
  o: System.Object;

begin
  o := c; { implicit boxing in Delphi for .NET }
  Console.WriteLine(o);
  Console.ReadLine();
end.
```

The .NET SDK includes an extremely useful tool that allows us to view the IL code produced by a .NET compiler — the IL Disassembler (ILDASM). ILDASM can show us how things work in the .NET framework, which is great, because the .NET framework, unlike Delphi's RTL and VCL, doesn't ship with its source code.

In this case, we can use ILDASM to confirm that boxing actually occurs in the object o = c line. The ildasm.exe file is located in the Program Files directory under \Microsoft.NET\SDK\v1.1\Bin. When you run it and load the appropriate assembly (in this case the project's exe file), ILDASM shows not only the IL code but also the namespaces, classes, types, and methods to which the code belongs.

Figure 29-6 shows what ILDASM looks like and also shows the disassembled C# version of the above code that contains an implicit box operation.

Figure 29-6: Using ILDASM to view assembly contents

Unboxing

Unboxing occurs when a reference type is explicitly typecast to a value type. The unboxing operation first checks whether the typecast value is a boxed value and then copies the value from the object instance to a value type variable.

The following C# code shows when boxing and unboxing operations occur and Figure 29-7 shows the results:

```
static void Main(string[] args)
{
    int x = 2005;
    object o = x; /* box */
    int y = (int)o; /* unbox */

    Console.WriteLine(x);
    Console.ReadLine();
}
```

```
Unboxing::Main : void(string[])
.method private hidebysig static void  Main(string[] args) cil managed
{
  .entrypoint
  .custom instance void [mscorlib]System.STAThreadAttribute::.ctor() = ( 01 00 00 00 )
  // Code size       34 (0x22)
  .maxstack  1
  .locals init (int32 V_0,
           object V_1)
  IL_0000:  ldc.i4     0x7d5
  IL_0005:  stloc.0
  IL_0006:  ldloc.0
  IL_0007:  box        [mscorlib]System.Int32
  IL_000c:  stloc.1
  IL_000d:  ldloc.1
  IL_000e:  unbox      [mscorlib]System.Int32
  IL_0013:  ldind.i4
  IL_0014:  pop
  IL_0015:  ldloc.0
  IL_0016:  call       void [mscorlib]System.Console::WriteLine(int32)
  IL_001b:  call       string [mscorlib]System.Console::ReadLine()
  IL_0020:  pop
  IL_0021:  ret
} // end of method Unboxing::Main
```

Figure 29-7: Boxing and unboxing

Conditions

The C# language provides us with the if and switch statements for testing conditions. The syntax of both statements and the relational and logical operators that are used with them are the same in C++ and C#.

Although syntactically the same, the switch statement in C# differs from the C++ switch statement. The C# switch statement doesn't allow fall-through (all cases must be followed by the break statement) and it supports string cases.

The following listing shows both statements in action and also shows how to use the System.Convert class to convert types in .NET (in this case, how to convert a string to an integer).

Listing 29-3: if and switch statements

```
using System;

namespace Wordware.InsideDelphi
{
    class Conditions
    {
        [STAThread]
```

```
static void Main(string[] args)
{
    Console.Write("Enter a number: ");
    string userValue = Console.ReadLine();

    // convert string to int using the Convert class
    int num = Convert.ToInt32(userValue);

    if ((num < 1) || (num > 5))
        Console.WriteLine("Invalid number");
    else {
        /* C# switch doesn't allow fall through */
        switch(num)
        {
            case 1: Console.WriteLine("One");
                    break;
            case 2: Console.WriteLine("Two");
                    break;
            case 3: Console.WriteLine("Three");
                    break;
            default: Console.WriteLine("Four or five");
                    break;
        }
    }

    Console.ReadLine();
}
}
}
```

Arrays and Loops

Arrays in C# are reference types, and because of that, they cannot be declared as simply as variables of primitive types like integer.

To declare an array in C#, the following syntax is used:

```
data_type[] array_name;
```

To actually use an array, it must be instantiated with the reserved word new:

```
data_type[] array_name = new data_type[nr_of_elements];
```

Arrays can also be automatically initialized using the following syntax:

```
type[] array = new type[nr] {val1, val2, valn};
```

The following listing illustrates both how to declare and automatically initialize a one-dimensional array in C# and how to loop through the array using all four C# iteration statements: for, while, do, and foreach (C# version of Delphi's for-in loop). The for, while, and do loops work as they do in C++, so only the foreach loop needs to be described.

Like Delphi's for-in loop, the foreach loop is used to loop through arrays and collections. The syntax of the C# foreach loop is:

```
foreach(data_type identifier in array_or_collection) statement;
```

The listing also shows how to determine the length of the array using its Length property. C# arrays inherit the Length property from the System.Array class.

Listing 29-4: Arrays in C#

```
using System;

namespace Wordware.InsideDelphi
{
   class Arrays
   {
      [STAThread]
      static void Main(string[] args)
      {
         int[] arr = new int[10] {1, 2, 3, 4, 5, 6, 7, 8, 9, 10};
         int i;

         /* for */
         for(i = 0; i < arr.Length; i++)
            Console.WriteLine(arr[i]);

         /* while */
         i = 0;
         while (i < arr.Length)
            Console.WriteLine(arr[i++]);

         /* do..while */
         i = 0;
         do {
            Console.WriteLine(arr[i++]);
         } while (i < arr.Length);

         /* foreach */
         foreach(int x in arr) {
            Console.WriteLine(x);
         }

         Console.ReadLine();
      }
   }
}
```

When you're building .NET applications, you can either declare an array as you always do, or you can create an instance of the System.Array class. To instantiate the System.Array class, you need to call its CreateInstance method and pass the element type and the number of elements you want the array to have.

When calling the CreateInstance method, you can't directly pass a type like string to the method; you need to use the typeof operator (TypeOf in Delphi for .NET), which returns the required System.Type object that describes a data type.

Listing 29-5 shows how to create an instance of the System.Array class in Delphi for .NET.

Listing 29-5: Instantiating and using the System.Array class

```
program Project1;

{$APPTYPE CONSOLE}

uses
  SysUtils;

var
  arr: System.Array;
  s: string;
  i: Integer;

begin
  { array[0..9] of string }
  arr := System.Array.CreateInstance(TypeOf(string), 10);
  arr[0] := 'Using the ';
  arr[1] := 'System.Array ';
  { the SetValue method can be used to assign a value to an element }
  arr.SetValue('class...', 2);

  for s in arr do
  begin
    { if s <> '' can also be used }
    if s <> nil then
      Console.Write(s);
  end;

  { the GetValue method can also be used to read element values }
  for i := 0 to Pred(arr.Length) do
    Console.Write(arr.GetValue(i));

  Console.ReadLine();
end.
```

Besides the System.Array class, which can be used to create arrays with a known number of elements, we can also use the ArrayList class, which allows us to dynamically increase or decrease the number of elements in the array. The ArrayList class exists in the System.Collections namespace. Listing 29-6 shows how to use the ArrayList class in Delphi for .NET.

Listing 29-6: Using the ArrayList class

```
program Project1;

{$APPTYPE CONSOLE}

uses System.Collections;

var
  list: ArrayList = ArrayList.Create;
  i: Integer;

begin
  list.Add('Item 1');
  list.Add('Item 2');
```

```
list.Add('Item 3');

for i := 0 to Pred(list.Count) do
  Console.WriteLine(list[i]);

Console.ReadLine();
end.
```

Methods

Since C# is entirely object-oriented, it doesn't allow developers to create global methods, that is, methods that don't belong to a class. Delphi for .NET supports global methods, but only syntactically; the Delphi for .NET compiler compiles units as classes and global routines as their methods.

The syntax of a C# method is:

```
return_type method_name(parameter_list)
{
}
```

Using a C# Class Library in a Delphi for .NET Application

To see how to create and use methods in C# and to illustrate how easy it is to create cross-language applications in .NET, let's create a simple class library (a .NET assembly with the .dll extension) and then use it in a Delphi for .NET console application.

To create a C# class library, double-click the Class Library item in the C# Project category. The only difference between a C# console application project and the class library project is that the compiler will produce a .dll, not an .exe file.

The HelloClass class in the library also has two methods: a normal and a static method. The standard ConsoleHello() method illustrates how to create a method that can only be called when an instance of a class is created. The static method StaticConsoleHello() illustrates how to create a static method that can be called without having to instantiate the class first. For instance, the WriteLine method that we've used constantly is a static method. If it weren't, we would have to create an instance of the Console class first and then call the WriteLine() method through the instance.

Since C# methods are private by default, both methods need to be marked as public in order to use them outside of the class. Listing 29-7 shows the source code of the entire class library.

Listing 29-7: A very simple C# class library

```
using System;

namespace TestLib
{
  public class HelloClass
  {
    private const string MSG = "Hello from C#.";
    private const string STATIC = "Static Hello from C#.";
```

```
/* constructor currently does nothing */
public HelloClass()
{
}

/* a simple C# method */
public void ConsoleHello()
{
    Console.WriteLine(MSG);
}

/* can be called without creating a HelloClass instance */
public static void StaticConsoleHello()
{
    Console.WriteLine(STATIC);
}
}
}
```

After you've compiled the class library, create a new Delphi for .NET console application project. To use the C# TestLib class library in the console application, right-click the References node in the Project Manager window to reference it. To add a reference to a custom assembly, use the Browse button in the lower part of the Add Reference dialog box, as shown in Figure 29-8.

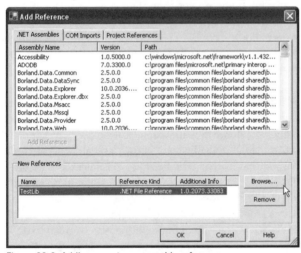

Figure 29-8: Adding a custom assembly reference

When you add an assembly reference in a Delphi for .NET application, the IDE adds a {%DelphiDotNetAssemblyCompiler} directive that references the assembly to the source code:

```
{%DelphiDotNetAssemblyCompiler '..\testlib\bin\debug\TestLib.dll'}
```

When you add a custom assembly to either a C# or a Delphi for .NET project, the IDE checks the Copy Local option. When Copy Local is checked (see Figure 29-9), the assembly is copied to the directory of the executable file when the executable is compiled. Local copies of custom assemblies greatly reduce development and deployment issues because everything (except the standard assemblies from the .NET runtime) is stored in the application directory.

Figure 29-9: Custom assemblies are copied to the application directory

If you don't know which namespaces, types, or classes are available in the assembly, you don't have to launch ILDASM; you can double-click the assembly (in this case, TestLib.dll) in the Project Manager to display its contents.

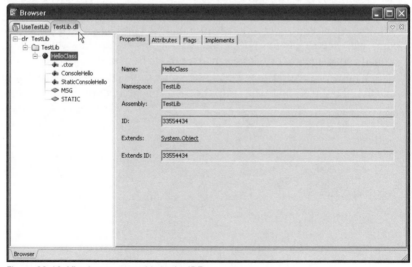

Figure 29-10: Viewing an assembly in the IDE

Finally, to use the HelloClass class, you only have to add the TestLib namespace to the uses list. Listing 29-8 shows the entire console application that illustrates how to call both normal and static methods.

Listing 29-8: Using HelloClass from the C# TestLib class library

```
program UseTestLib;

{$APPTYPE CONSOLE}
{%DelphiDotNetAssemblyCompiler '..\testlib\bin\debug\TestLib.dll'}

uses TestLib;

var
  HC: HelloClass;

begin
  { static methods can be called without an instance }
  TestLib.HelloClass.StaticConsoleHello;

  HC := HelloClass.Create;
  HC.ConsoleHello;
  { no need to free the HC object; it gets
    destroyed by the garbage collector }

  Console.ReadLine;
end.
```

Using a Delphi for .NET Package in a C# Application

Now that you know how to build applications using both C# and Delphi for .NET languages, let's create a Delphi for .NET package (Delphi .NET DLL) with a unit that contains a single global procedure, and then use it in a C# console application. The rationale for building a package with a global procedure is to see Delphi for .NET compiler magic — to see how the compiler constructs namespaces, classes, and methods from units and procedures.

When you create a new Delphi for .NET package, add to it a new unit named About.pas and then create the following procedure:

```
unit About;

interface

procedure ShowAbout;

implementation

procedure ShowAbout;
begin
  Console.WriteLine('Built with Delphi for .NET.');
end;

end.
```

After you create the procedure, compile the package to create the necessary
DLL file and then open it with ILDASM (see Figure 29-11). The compiler
uses the unit name to both create the namespace and name the class. The
namespace created by the compiler has the UnitName.Units format, so in this
case, it's About.Units. The class name in this case is About. The ShowAbout
procedure from the unit is converted into a public static method of the About
class.

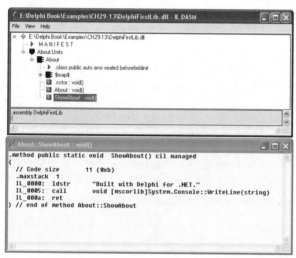

Figure 29-11: Delphi for .NET compiles units as classes.

All these internal changes have no effect on Delphi for .NET code that uses
the package and the ShowAbout procedure from the unit. To use the Delphi
for .NET package in a Delphi for .NET application, you have to reference the
package, and then you can use the unit and the procedure as if they are part of
the current project:

```
program Project1;

{$APPTYPE CONSOLE}

{%DelphiDotNetAssemblyCompiler '..\delphinet_firstlib\DelphiFirstLib.dll'}

uses About;

begin
  ShowAbout;
  ReadLn;
end.
```

Although Delphi allows you to use the unit and the procedure as you do in
Delphi for Win32, the compiler has to play around with the emitted CIL code
and call the appropriate method of the appropriate class (see Figure 29-12).

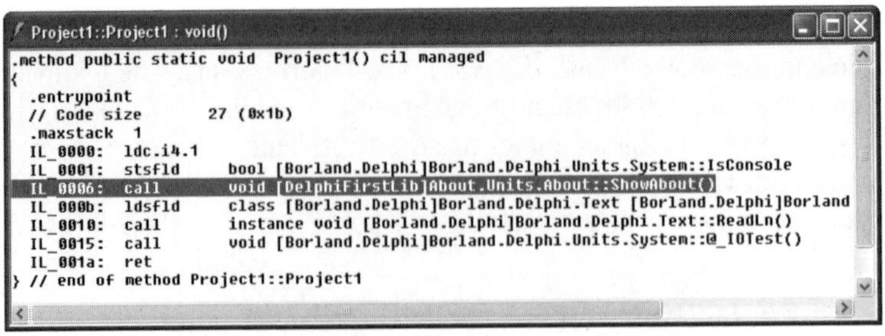

Figure 29-12: CIL code emitted for the ShowAbout procedure call

When you have to use a Delphi for .NET package in another language, like C# or VB.NET, you need to reference the package and import the appropriate namespace manually.

Listings 29-9A and 29-9B show how to use the Delphi for .NET package in a C# and a VB.NET console application (you can find the VB.NET console application project item in the Other Files category on the Tool Palette). VB.NET applications can be built in Delphi because the vbc.exe (VB.NET compiler) is included in the .NET Framework SDK.

Listing 29-9A: Using a Delphi for .NET package in a C# application

```
using System;

/* About.Units is the namespace,
   final About is the class name */
using DelphiClass = About.Units.About;

namespace CSharpUsesDelphi
{
   class UserClass
   {
      [STAThread]
      static void Main(string[] args)
      {
         DelphiClass.ShowAbout();
         Console.ReadLine();
      }
   }
}
```

Listing 29-9B: Using a Delphi for .NET package in a VB.NET application

```
Imports System
Imports DelphiClass = About.Units.About

Module VBNETUser

   Sub Main()
      DelphiClass.ShowAbout()
      Console.ReadLine()
   End Sub

End Module
```

Method Parameters

Methods can accept none, one, or many parameters, and they can return none, one, or many values. As in Delphi, methods in C# can be overloaded, can be static, and can accept a variable number of parameters. By default, methods in C# are private (in C++ they are also private, but in Delphi they are public).

When you want to create a method that accepts no parameters, write an empty pair of parentheses as in Listing 29-10.

Listing 29-10: A method without parameters

```
public void NoParams()
{
    return; /* you can but don't have to write return */
}
```

When you want to create a method that accepts a single parameter, declare it inside the parameter list's parentheses as you would a variable but without the semicolon:

Listing 29-11: Method that accepts a single parameter by value

```
public void OneStringParam(string UserName)
{
    System.Console.WriteLine(UserName);
}
```

When you want to create a method that accepts several parameters, separate the parameters with commas:

Listing 29-12: Accepting a larger number of parameters

```
public void SeveralParams(int One, string Two, char Three)
{
}
```

To return a single value from the method, use the function syntax:

```
public int RetIntegerSum(int One, int Two)
{
    return One + Two;
}
```

To modify values passed as parameters (if they are not constant values), have the method accept parameters by reference using the reserved word ref. C# ref parameters are equivalent to Delphi's var parameters (see Listing 29-13).

Listing 29-13: Passing parameters by reference

```
public void PassByReference(ref string Name, ref bool Changed)
{
    if(Name == "")
    {
        Name = "The string can't be empty.";
        Changed = true;
    }
}
```

You won't be able to test the PassByReference method in the Main method because non-static methods cannot be called in a static method. To test the PassByReference method, either declare the method as static or create an instance of the class inside the Main method and then call the PassByReference method on that instance. When you have a method that accepts ref parameters, you also have to use the reserved word ref when you call the method as shown in Listing 29-14.

Listing 29-14: Calling a method that accepts parameters by reference

```
using System;

namespace Parameters
{
    class ParamsClass
    {
        public void PassByReference(ref string Name, ref bool Changed)
        {
            if(Name == "")
            {
                Name = "The string can't be empty.";
                Changed = true;
            }
        }

        [STAThread]
        static void Main(string[] args)
        {
            ParamsClass pc = new ParamsClass();
            bool b = false;
            string s = "";

            pc.PassByReference(ref s, ref b);
            Console.WriteLine(s); /* writes "The string ... */

            Console.ReadLine();
        }
    }
}
```

C# also supports out parameters, which, like Delphi out parameters, allow us to pass uninitialized parameters and modify the passed value inside the method. When calling a method that accepts an out parameter, the reserved word out must also be used.

Listing 29-15: C# out parameters

```
public void ModifyValues(out string Text)
{
    Text = "Initializing...";
}

[STAThread]
static void Main(string[] args)
{
    ParamsClass pc = new ParamsClass();
```

```
        bool b = false;
        string s = "";

        pc.PassByReference(ref s, ref b);
        Console.WriteLine(s); /* writes "The string ... */

        /* uninitialized string variable */
        string noInit;
        pc.ModifyValues(out noInit); /* no error! */
        Console.WriteLine(noInit);

        Console.ReadLine();
}
```

If you've read the Delphi for Win32 portions of this book, you'll know that objects in Delphi don't have to be passed as var parameters in order to change their fields. If you do pass objects as var parameters, nothing bad will happen, but you'll unnecessarily be passing a pointer to pointer. The same is true for C# ref parameters. If you need to pass an object to a method, pass it by value, as shown in Listing 29-16.

Listing 29-16: Passing objects to methods

```
using System;

namespace Parameters
{
    class FieldClass {
        public string TestField = "";
    }

    class ParamsClass
    {
        public void AcceptAnObject(FieldClass fc)
        {
            fc.TestField = "Changed in the AcceptAnObject method.";
        }

        [STAThread]
        static void Main(string[] args)
        {
            ParamsClass pc = new ParamsClass();

            /* object parameters don't have to be ref */
            FieldClass fld = new FieldClass();
            Console.WriteLine(fld.TestField);  // empty string
            pc.AcceptAnObject(fld);            // change fld.TestField
            Console.WriteLine(fld.TestField);

            Console.ReadLine();
        }
    }
}
```

There is no special syntax involved in method overloading in C#. To create an overloaded version of a method, you have to create a method with the same name but with a different parameter list.

Listing 29-16: Overloaded methods

```
/* overloaded method */
public void AcceptAnObject(FieldClass fc)
{
    fc.TestField = "Changed in the AcceptAnObject method.";
}

/* overloaded method */
public void AcceptAnObject(FieldClass fc, string s)
{
    fc.TestField = s;
}
```

To have a C# method accept a variable number of parameters, have it accept an array and mark the array parameter with the reserved word params.

Listing 29-17: Passing a variable number of parameters to a method

```
public void VariableParamNum(params string[] names)
{
    foreach(string name in names)
        Console.WriteLine(name);
}

[STAThread]
static void Main(string[] args)
{
    /* passing a variable number of parameters to a method */
    pc.VariableParamNum("Anders");
    pc.VariableParamNum("Danny", "Allen");
    pc.VariableParamNum("Michael", "Lino", "Steve", "David");

    Console.ReadLine();
}
```

Enumerations

In C#, enumerations are declared with the reserved word enum, which has the following syntax (you can end the declaration with a semicolon, but it isn't required like it is in C++):

```
enum enumeration_name {enumerator_list}
```

To use an enumerated value in C#, you have to write the fully qualified name of the value, that is, the enumeration name followed by the dot operator and the enumerated value.

Listing 29-18: C# enumerations

```
using System;

namespace Enumerations
{
```

```
enum Days {Monday, Tuesday, Wednesday, Thursday, Friday}
enum Weekend {Saturday = 10, Sunday = 20}

class EnumerationClass
{
    [STAThread]
    static void Main(string[] args)
    {
        Console.WriteLine(Days.Monday);          // Monday
        Console.WriteLine((int)Days.Monday);     // 0

        Console.WriteLine(Weekend.Sunday);       // Sunday
        Console.WriteLine((int)Weekend.Sunday);  // 20

        Console.ReadLine();
    }
}
}
```

Exception Handling

C# exception handling is very similar to Delphi exception handling. C# allows you to catch exceptions in a try-catch block and to protect resource allocations with the try-finally block. Unlike Delphi, C# allows you to catch multiple exceptions after a single try block and lets you add a finally block after one or more exception handling blocks.

All exceptions in Delphi are derived from the Exception class (the SysUtils unit). In C#, all exceptions are derived from the System.Exception class. In Delphi for .NET, the Exception type is mapped to the FCL's System.Exception class. As in Delphi, all exceptions are objects, and you can use the properties of the exception object to find out more about the exception.

To catch all exceptions that a piece of code can throw ("raise" in Delphi parlance), write a "plain" try-catch block:

```
private void CatchAllExceptions()
{
    try
    {
        int i = 2, j = 0;
        Console.WriteLine("Result = {0}", i / j);
    }
    catch  /* all exceptions */
    {
        Console.WriteLine("I caught an error, but I " +
            "have no idea what happened.");
        Console.ReadLine();
    }
}
```

To catch specific exceptions, use the following syntax:

```
try
{
}
```

```
catch (AnException)
{
}
```

Listing 29-19 shows how to catch specific exceptions in C#. The try block is followed by two catch blocks. The first catch block tries to catch the Divide-ByZeroException, which gets thrown when you try to divide a number by zero. The second catch block tries to catch all other exceptions (except the DivideByZeroException) that might be thrown by code from the try block.

Listing 29-19: Catching several exceptions

```
private void CatchSpecificException()
{
   try
   {
      int i = 2, j = 0;
      Console.WriteLine("Result = {0}", i / j);
   }
   catch (System.DivideByZeroException)
   {
      Console.WriteLine("Cannot divide by zero!");
      Console.ReadLine();
   }
   catch(System.Exception)
   {
      Console.WriteLine("Something wrong happened.");
      Console.ReadLine();
   }
}
```

To catch an exception and use the exception object, use the following syntax:

```
catch (AnException ExceptionInstance)
```

Use the reserved word throw to throw or rethrow an exception. When you want to rethrow an exception, write the throw reserved word, followed by a semicolon. When you want to throw an exception, use the following syntax:

```
throw new ExceptionName();
```

Listing 29-20 shows how to use exception object instances and how to throw and rethrow exceptions in C#. The result of the code displayed in Listing 29-20 is displayed in Figure 29-13.

Listing 29-20: Using exception objects, throwing and rethrowing exceptions

```
using System;

namespace csharp_exceptions
{
   class Exceptions
   {
      private void ThrowOneForFun()
      {
         // pass the text to the exception's Message property
```

```
            throw new System.Exception("Catch me if you can!");
        }

        private void Rethrow()
        {
            Exceptions exceptions = new Exceptions();
            try
            {
                ThrowOneForFun();
            }
            catch(Exception e)
            {
                Console.WriteLine("Exception \"{0}\" " +
                    "caught and rethrown in Rethrow().", e.Message);
                throw; /* rethrow the exception */
            }
        }

        [STAThread]
        static void Main(string[] args)
        {
            Exceptions exc = new Exceptions();
            try
            {
                exc.Rethrow();
            }
            catch(Exception e)
            {
                Console.WriteLine("Exception with message \"{0}\" " +
                    "caught after rethrow in Main().", e.Message);
                Console.ReadLine();
            }

            Console.WriteLine("Press any key to continue...");
            Console.ReadLine();
        }
    }
}
```

```
C:\csharp_exceptions\bin\Debug\csharp_exceptions.exe                    _ □ x
Exception "Catch me if you can!" caught and rethrown in Rethrow().
Exception with message "Catch me if you can!" caught after rethrow in Main().
```

Figure 29-13: Throwing and rethrowing exceptions in C#

The System.IO Namespace

To see how to work with files in .NET, and to see how easily we can catch
exceptions thrown by another .NET language, we'll now use the Stream-
Reader and File classes from the System.IO namespace to build a simple
"type" program that displays text files, screen by screen, in the console
window.

The File class provides various methods for working with files, including the static Exists method, which can be used to test whether or not a file exists.

The System.IO namespace provides the StreamReader class to read data from text files, and the StreamWriter class to write data to text files. Reading text files with the StreamReader class is extremely easy: After you open the file by calling the StreamReader's contructor, you read the file by calling the ReadLine() method until it returns an empty string (a null object).

When you're done with the StreamReader object, you'll need to destroy it manually because the StreamReader class uses resources that should be released as soon as possible. .NET classes that allocate resources always provide Close() or Dispose() methods for releasing these resources when you're done using them. The StreamReader class, for instance, provides the Close() method, which then calls Dispose() internally to free the stream used by the StreamReader class.

Listing 29-21, which follows, shows the entire source of a C# class library, which uses the System.IO.File and System.IO.StreamReader classes to implement the functionality of the command prompt's "type" command. The DisplayFile() method either throws the System.IO.FileNotFound-Exception exception if the file is not found or instantiates the StreamReader class and displays the contents of the file if the file exists.

Listing 29-21: Reading text files with the StreamReader class

```
using System;
using System.IO;

namespace Wordware.IOLibrary
{
    public class TextFileReader
    {
        public static void DisplayFile(string FileName)
        {
            if(!File.Exists(FileName))
            {
                // pass the message to the Message property
                // pass the file name to the FileName property
                throw new FileNotFoundException("File not found!",
                    FileName);
            }

            string line;
            int counter = 1;

            StreamReader sr = new StreamReader(@FileName);
            try
            {
                line = sr.ReadLine();
                while(line != null)
                {
                    Console.WriteLine(line);
                    // stop after the screen is filled
```

```
            if(counter == 24)
            {
               Console.WriteLine("-- More --");
               Console.ReadLine();
               counter = 1;
            }              // if (counter)

            line = sr.ReadLine();
            counter++;
         }                 // while
      }
      finally
      {
         sr.Close();    // close the StreamReader
      }
   }

   public TextFileReader()
   {
      // constructor does nothing
   }
}
}
```

If you've read the code carefully, you've undoubtedly noticed the @ operator in front of the FileName string passed to the StreamReader's constructor:

```
StreamReader sr = new StreamReader(@FileName);
```

By default, C# strings support escape sequences (\\, \n, etc.), and thus file names like "c:\Folder\SubFolder\Data.txt" aren't properly interpreted. The proper way to write this path in C# is "c:\\Folder\\SubFolder\\Data.txt." However, by using the @ operator in front of the string, you can disable escape sequence processing, and thus you can write file paths normally, i.e., @"C:\Folder\SubFolder\Data.txt."

To use the Wordware.IOLibrary.TextFileReader class, create a new Delphi for .NET console application and add the reference to the library. To display a text file using the TextFileReader class, you need to call the DisplayFile method, preferably in a try block, and display an error message if you catch the System.IO.FileNotFoundException exception.

Listing 29-22 shows the source code of a Delphi for .NET console application that uses the Wordware.IOLibrary.TextFileReader class. Figure 29-14, which follows the listing, shows how the TextFileReader class displays text files.

Listing 29-22: Using the Wordware.IOLibrary.TextFileReader class to view text files

```
program Project1;

{$APPTYPE CONSOLE}

{%DelphiDotNetAssemblyCompiler '..\io_library\bin\debug\io_library.dll'}
```

```
uses System.IO, Wordware.IOLibrary;

const
  FNAME: string = 'C:\My Components\PDFExport.pas';

begin
  try
    TextFileReader.DisplayFile(FNAME);
  except
    // catch the exception thrown in a C# class library
    on e: System.IO.FileNotFoundException do
    begin
      Console.WriteLine('File "{0}" does not exist!', e.FileName);
      Console.WriteLine;
    end;    // on Exception
  end;      // try

  Console.WriteLine;
  Console.WriteLine('Press any key to continue...');
  Console.ReadLine();
end.
```

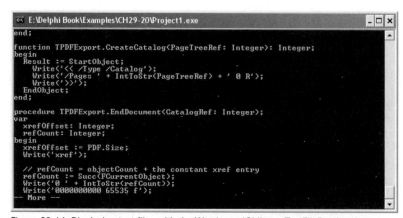

Figure 29-14: Displaying text files with the Wordware.IOLibrary.TextFileReader class

VCL.NET and Windows.Forms

Controls located in the Windows.Forms namespace are to .NET languages the same thing VCL is to Delphi and C++Builder languages — a collection of controls that allow us to build GUI applications.

Building Windows.Forms and VCL.NET applications inside the IDE is pretty much the same. Figure 29-15 and the following points illustrate this:

■ The center of a VCL.NET application is the TForm class (located in the Borland.VCL.Forms unit), and the center of a Windows.Forms application (either Delphi for .NET or C#) is the Form class, located in the System.Windows.Forms namespace, and physically in the System.Windows.Forms assembly.

- Both VCL.NET and Windows.Forms applications are built by dropping components on the Designer Surface (form).
- To build either VCL.NET or Windows.Forms applications, you have to write code in response to various events fired by the components.
- Both frameworks are built on top of the Win32 API.

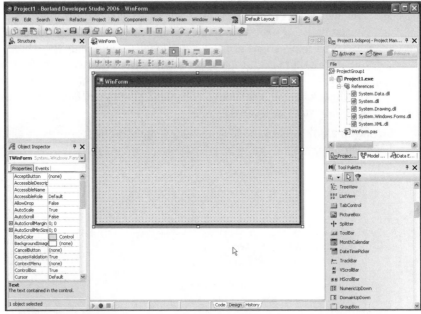

Figure 29-15: Building Windows.Forms applications in Delphi

There are also differences between the two frameworks:

- The VCL framework can be used to build applications that run on Windows and Linux (if you install CrossKylix you can build both Windows and Kylix applications on Windows), while Windows.Forms applications only run on the .NET platform.
- With minor changes, VCL applications can be converted to VCL.NET and target the .NET platform. Windows.Forms applications cannot target any platform besides .NET.
- VCL applications can currently be built only by Delphi and C++Builder developers, and VCL.NET applications can only be built by Delphi developers. Windows.Forms applications can be created with any .NET language.
- Custom VCL/VCL.NET components can only be created by Delphi and C++Builder developers (Win32 version). .NET components can be created in any .NET language.
- VCL objects are stored in separate files (*.dfm files in VCL, *.nfm files in VCL.NET). Windows.Forms controls are stored in the main source file as

a series of statements that create them and initialize their properties. (Listing 29-23 shows the source code of the main form from a Delphi for .NET Windows.Forms application.)

■   Windows.Forms does not have anything similar to actions and the TActionList/TActionManager components; however, VCL doesn't have an ErrorProvider component. :)

■   Windows.Forms applications are easier to deploy because the System.Windows.Forms assembly ships with the .NET framework. VCL.NET applications can be "standalone" (require only the .NET framework) but take up approximately 2 MB, or they can reference VCL assemblies and be much smaller (in this case, you'll have to deploy Borland.Delphi.dll, Borland.Vcl.dll, and Borland.VclRtl.dll assemblies alongside your application).

Listing 29-23: The source code of a basic Windows.Forms form with a single Label component

```
unit MainForm;

interface

uses
  System.Drawing, System.Collections, System.ComponentModel,
  System.Windows.Forms, System.Data;

type
  TMainForm = class(System.Windows.Forms.Form)
  { $REGION 'Designer Managed Code' }
  strict private
    /// <summary>
    /// Required designer variable.
    /// </summary>
    Components: System.ComponentModel.Container;
    Label1: System.Windows.Forms.Label;
    /// <summary>
    /// Required method for Designer support - do not modify
    /// the contents of this method with the code editor.
    /// </summary>
    procedure InitializeComponent;
  { $ENDREGION }
  strict protected
    /// <summary>
    /// Clean up any resources being used.
    /// </summary>
    procedure Dispose(Disposing: Boolean); override;
  private
    { Private Declarations }
  public
    constructor Create;
  end;

[assembly: RuntimeRequiredAttribute(TypeOf(TMainForm))]
```

```
implementation

{ $AUTOBOX ON }

{ $REGION 'Windows Form Designer generated code' }
/// <summary>
/// Required method for Designer support -- do not modify
/// the contents of this method with the code editor.
/// </summary>
procedure TMainForm.InitializeComponent;
begin
  Self.Label1 := System.Windows.Forms.Label.Create;
  Self.SuspendLayout;
  //
  // Label1
  //
  Self.Label1.Location := System.Drawing.Point.Create(32, 32);
  Self.Label1.Name := 'Label1';
  Self.Label1.TabIndex := 0;
  Self.Label1.Text := 'Label1';
  //
  // TMainForm
  //
  Self.AutoScaleBaseSize := System.Drawing.Size.Create(5, 13);
  Self.ClientSize := System.Drawing.Size.Create(448, 270);
  Self.Controls.Add(Self.Label1);
  Self.Name := 'TMainForm';
  Self.Text := 'Delphi for .NET Windows.Forms Application';
  Self.ResumeLayout(False);
end;
{ $ENDREGION }

procedure TMainForm.Dispose(Disposing: Boolean);
begin
  if Disposing then
  begin
    if Components <> nil then
      Components.Dispose();
  end;
  inherited Dispose(Disposing);
end;

constructor TMainForm.Create;
begin
  inherited Create;
  //
  // Required for Windows Form Designer support
  //
  InitializeComponent;
  //
  // TODO: Add any constructor code after InitializeComponent call
  //
end;

end.
```

Windows.Forms Application's Entry Point

As in .NET console applications, the entry point of a Windows.Forms application is the Main method. With Windows.Forms applications, the Main method contains a single line of code that creates the main form and calls the Run method of the global .NET Application object (instance of System.Windows.Forms.Application) to start the application and display the main form on screen. Listings 29-24A and 29-24B show the Main methods from a Delphi for .NET Windows.Forms application and a C# Windows.Forms application.

Listing 29-24A: The entry point of a Delphi for .NET Windows.Forms application

```
[STAThread]
begin
  Application.Run(TWinForm.Create);
end.
```

Listing 29-24B: The entry point of a C# Windows.Forms application

```
[STAThread]
static void Main()
{
    Application.Run(new WinForm());
}
```

Multicast Events

Among other differences, Windows.Forms and VCL frameworks differ in the fact that Windows.Forms controls can call multiple handlers in response to an event, while VCL components traditionally only fire a single event handler in response to an event.

In VCL applications, you can assign event handlers to an event using the assignment operator. If you assign the nil value to an event handler, you are removing the event handler from the event.

In Windows.Forms applications, you can add and remove multiple event handlers from an event using the Include and Exclude procedures. To see how this is done, take a look at Figure 29-16 and the example in Listing 29-25.

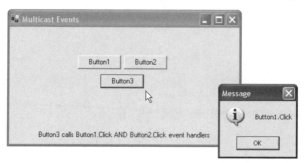

Figure 29-16: Windows.Forms application that illustrates multicast events

The Button1 and Button2 components in this example have their own event handlers that use the Show method of the MessageBox class to display a message dialog box. Button3 doesn't have its own Click event handler but calls the Click event handlers of Button1 and Button2.

The two event handlers are added to the Click event using the Include procedure in the form's OnLoad event (equivalent to the OnCreate event in VCL applications).

Listing 29-25: Assigning multiple event handlers to an event in a Delphi for .NET Windows.Forms application

```
procedure TWinForm.TWinForm_Load(sender: System.Object; e: System.EventArgs);
begin
  // add event handlers of Button1 and Button2 to the
  // Click event of Button3
  Include(Button3.Click, Button1_Click);
  Include(Button3.Click, Button2_Click);
end;

procedure TWinForm.Button2_Click(sender: System.Object; e: System.EventArgs);
begin
  MessageBox.Show('Button2.Click', 'Message',
    MessageBoxButtons.OK, MessageBoxIcon.Information);
end;

procedure TWinForm.Button1_Click(sender: System.Object; e: System.EventArgs);
begin
  MessageBox.Show('Button1.Click', 'Message',
    MessageBoxButtons.OK, MessageBoxIcon.Information);
end;
```

In C#, you use the += to add event handlers to an event and −= to remove an event handler from an event (see Listing 29-26). Besides using these two operators, you have to instantiate the System.EventHandler delegate (delegates are covered in the next chapter) and pass to the EventHandler's constructor the name of the event handler you wish to add to the event.

Listing 29-26: Assigning multiple event handlers to an event in a C# Windows.Forms application

```
private void button1_Click(object sender, System.EventArgs e)
{
  MessageBox.Show("button1.Click", "Message",
    MessageBoxButtons.OK, MessageBoxIcon.Information);
}

private void button2_Click(object sender, System.EventArgs e)
{
  MessageBox.Show("button2.Click", "Message",
    MessageBoxButtons.OK, MessageBoxIcon.Information);

}

private void WinForm_Load(object sender, System.EventArgs e)
{
  button3.Click += new System.EventHandler(button1_Click);
  button3.Click += new System.EventHandler(button2_Click);
}
```

Creating Windows.Forms Controls Dynamically

When creating controls dynamically, you have to manually set the control's parent, because the control is displayed on its parent control. In VCL, you display a control by setting a container control, like the main form, to its Parent property. In Windows.Forms applications, you add the component to the container control by calling the Add method of the container control's Controls collection.

Listing 29-27 shows how to dynamically create a Windows.Forms.Button control and how to display it on the main form. Figure 29-17 shows the result of the code in Listing 29-27.

Listing 29-27: Dynamically creating a Windows.Forms.Button control

```
procedure TWinForm.DynamicEvent(sender: System.Object; e: System.EventArgs);
begin
  System.Windows.Forms.MessageBox.Show('The form will now close.',
    'Message', MessageBoxButtons.OK, MessageBoxIcon.Information);
  Self.Close;
end;

procedure TWinForm.TWinForm_Load(sender: System.Object; e: System.EventArgs);
var
  btn: Button;
begin
  btn := Button.Create;
  btn.Location := System.Drawing.Point.Create(10, 10); // top and left
  btn.Size := System.Drawing.Size.Create(100, 25);     // width and height
  btn.Text := 'Close';
  Include(btn.Click, DynamicEvent);

  // equivalent to "Button.Parent := Self" in VCL
  Self.Controls.Add(btn);
end;
```

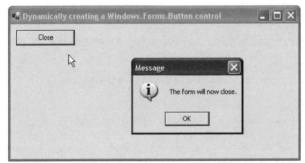

Figure 29-17: A dynamically created Windows.Forms.Button calling a dynamically assigned event handler

Windows Forms MDI Essentials

Figure 29-18 shows a very simple Windows.Forms MDI application that we are going to build in this section.

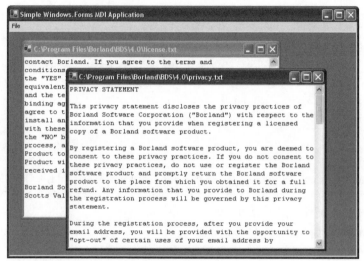

Figure 29-18: A Windows.Forms MDI application

To have a Windows.Forms form act as an MDI parent, set its IsMDIContainer property to True. Then add a MainMenu and an OpenFileDialog component from the components category to it. To allow users to select multiple files with the OpenFileDialog component, set its MultiSelect property to True.

Now add another Windows Form to the project and drop a TextBox component on it. The Windows.Forms.TextBox control can act as the TEdit and TMemo component. To display an entire text file in the TextBox control, set its Multiline property to True and its Dock property to Fill, to have it cover the entire form.

To load an entire text file into the TextBox control, you have to use the System.IO.StreamReader class. Listing 29-28 shows how to load a text file into a TextBox control.

Listing 29-28: Loading an entire text file into a Windows.Forms.TextBox control

```
unit Child;

interface

uses
  System.Drawing, System.Collections, System.ComponentModel,
  System.Windows.Forms, System.Data, System.IO;

type
  TChildForm = class(System.Windows.Forms.Form)
  public
```

```
    constructor Create;
    procedure LoadFile(FileName: string);
  end;

implementation

procedure TChildForm.LoadFile(FileName: string);
var
  sr: System.IO.StreamReader;
begin
  sr := System.IO.StreamReader.Create(FileName);
  try
    TextBox1.Text := sr.ReadToEnd;
  finally
    sr.Close;
  end;
end;
```

The last tasks you have to do are create a File menu and the File ➢ Open item and write code that displays the OpenFileDialog and creates child forms. This code is displayed in Listing 29-29.

Listing 29-29: Creating child forms

```
procedure TWinForm.FileOpenItem_Click(sender: System.Object; e:
System.EventArgs);
var
  fileName: string;
  childForm: TChildForm;
begin
  // display the OpenFileDialog
  if OpenFileDialog1.ShowDialog =
    System.Windows.Forms.DialogResult.OK then
  begin
    // browse through the selected files
    for fileName in OpenFileDialog1.FileNames do
    begin
      childForm := TChildForm.Create;
      // this changes the form to an mdi child form
      childForm.MdiParent := Self;
      childForm.Text := fileName;
      childForm.LoadFile(fileName);
      childForm.Show;
    end;    // for
  end;      // if ShowDialog
end;
```

Chapter 30

Advanced Win32 and .NET Programming

In this chapter, you'll learn about object-oriented programming in C# and Delphi for .NET, and about several new features added to the Delphi for Win32 language. Specifically, you'll learn how to add to your Win32 and .NET classes the ability to be used with the foreach loop (C#) and the for-in loop (Delphi for Win32 and Delphi for .NET), how to create lightweight classes (records/structures with methods and properties), how to overload operators in Delphi (both flavors) and C#, how to create and use delegates, and how to implement single-cast and multicast events in Delphi and C# classes.

Adding for-in Enumeration Functionality to a Delphi Class

The for-in loop is, by default, supported by arrays, strings, sets, and the following classes: TList, TCollection, TStrings, TInterfaceList, TComponent, TMenuItem, TCustomActionList, TFields, TListItems, TTreeNodes, and TToolbar.

To use a class with the for-in loop, you first need to create a collection class, that is, a class like the TList component or the TImageCache component that has items that we can loop through. This section uses the TImageCache component we created in Chapter 26 to illustrate how to implement for-in enumeration functionality in a class. When you're done, you (and other developers) will be able to use the for-in loop to browse through the Images property of the TImageCache class.

To use a class with the for-in loop, you need to create another class, an enumerator class, which is used by the for-in loop to loop through the main class. In this case, the TImageCacheEnumerator enumerator class is created for the main TImageCache class:

```
TImageCacheEnumerator = class(TObject)
end;

TImageCache = class(TComponent)
  ...
end;
```

At this stage, these classes are completely unrelated. One of the easiest ways to link the enumerator class with the main class is to create a custom constructor that accepts an instance of the main class. Here's how you can link the enumerator and the main class:

```
TImageCacheEnumerator = class(TObject)
private
  FImageCache: TImageCache;
public
  constructor Create(AImageCache: TImageCache);
end;

TImageCache = class(TComponent)
end;

implementation

constructor TImageCacheEnumerator.Create(AImageCache: TImageCache);
begin
  inherited Create;      // call TObject's constructor
  // link the enumerator with a TImageCache instance
  FImageCache := AImageCache;
end;
```

If you try to compile the code now, you'll receive an undeclared identifier error in the FImageCache: TImageCache line. This error occurs because the TImageCache class is declared after the TImageCacheEnumerator class. It cannot be resolved by declaring the TImageCacheEnumerator class after the TImageCache class because the TImageCache class also has to reference the TImageCacheEnumerator class. If you declare the TImageCacheEnumerator class after the TImageCache, you'll later receive an error that will tell you the TImageCacheEnumerator identifier is undeclared.

When two classes are mutually dependent, like the TImageCache and TImageCacheEnumerator classes are, you have to make a forward class declaration. When you create a forward class declaration, mutually dependent classes are possible and the code successfully compiles because the identifier is no longer undeclared.

The syntax of a forward class declaration is extremely simple:

```
type TClassName = class;
```

So, to enable the TImageCacheEnumerator class to have a TImageCache field, create a forward declaration of the TImageCache class, as shown in Listing 30-1.

Listing 30-1: Forward class declaration

```
type
  { forward declaration of the TImageCache class }
  TImageCache = class;

  TImageCacheEnumerator = class(TObject)
  private
    FImageCache: TImageCache;
  public
    constructor Create(AImageCache: TImageCache);
  end;

  TImageCache = class(TComponent)
  end;
```

The only thing the main class must have in order to be used by the for-in loop is the public GetEnumerator method that returns an instance of the enumerator class. When the for-in loop begins, it calls the GetEnumerator method of the object to acquire an instance of the enumerator class and then uses the methods of the enumerator object to loop through the main object.

In the case of the TImageCache class, the GetEnumerator method has to return an instance of the TImageCacheEnumerator class (see Listing 30-2). The for-in loop will then use the TImageCacheEnumerator object to loop through the Images property of the TImageCache object (this isn't implemented yet).

Listing 30-2: Instantiating the enumerator class in the GetEnumerator method

```
  TImageCache = class(TComponent)
  public
    { Public declarations }
    function GetEnumerator: TImageCacheEnumerator;
  end;

implementation

function TImageCache.GetEnumerator: TImageCacheEnumerator;
begin
  // passing Self links the TImageCache instance with
  // the enumerator object used by the for-in loop
  Result := TImageCacheEnumerator.Create(Self);
end;
```

Although the enumerator and the main class are now linked, the enumerator class is pretty much worthless to the for-in loop. In order to be successfully used by the for-in loop, an enumerator class must have two things: a public read-only property called Current that provides access to the currently selected element in the collection, and a public function called MoveNext, which must advance the loop to the next element in the collection and return a Boolean value to tell the loop whether or not the end of the collection is reached.

Listing 30-3 shows the complete and thoroughly commented TImageCacheEnumerator class.

Listing 30-3: The TImageCacheEnumerator class

```
type
  { forward declaration of the TImageCache class }
  TImageCache = class;

  TImageCacheEnumerator = class(TObject)
  private
    FImageCache: TImageCache;
    FIndex: Integer;
    function GetCurrent: TBitmap;
  public
    constructor Create(AImageCache: TImageCache);
    function MoveNext: Boolean;
    property Current: TBitmap read GetCurrent;
  end;

  TImageCache = class(TComponent)
  public
    { Public declarations }
    function GetEnumerator: TImageCacheEnumerator;
  end;

implementation

constructor TImageCacheEnumerator.Create(AImageCache: TImageCache);
begin
  inherited Create;     // call TObject's constructor
  // link the enumerator with a TImageCache instance
  FImageCache := AImageCache;
  // enumerators are always initialized to -1
  FIndex := -1;
end;

function TImageCacheEnumerator.MoveNext: Boolean;
begin
  // if the currently selected image is not the last one,
  // return True and move to the next image
  Result := FIndex < Pred(FImageCache.Count);
  if Result then Inc(FIndex);
end;

function TImageCacheEnumerator.GetCurrent: TBitmap;
begin
  // return the currently selected image from the Images property
  Result := FImageCache.Images[FIndex];
end;

// ----------------------------------------------------------------------------
```

```
function TImageCache.GetEnumerator: TImageCacheEnumerator;
begin
  // passing Self links the TImageCache instance with
  // the enumerator object used by the for-in loop
  Result := TImageCacheEnumerator.Create(Self);
end;
```

Now that we've created the enumerator class for the TImageCache component, we need to test it to see if it works. Let's test the for-in loop by adding an Export Images option to the Cache Viewer application that was built in Chapter 26.

The Export Images option needs to allow the user to select a directory and then export all images from the cache file to the selected directory. To allow users to select a directory, you should use the Browse for Folder dialog box.

Figure 30-1:
The Browse for
Folder dialog box

To display the Browse for Folder dialog box in a Delphi application, add a TBrowseForFolder standard action to a TActionList or a TActionManager component. The Execute method of the action displays the dialog box, and if the user presses OK to select a directory, the selected directory is stored in the action's Folder property and the OnAccess event is fired. So, to export the images from an image cache file, add the TBrowseForFolder action to the Cache Viewer application and then write the export code in the action's OnAccess event (see Listing 30-4). The result of the export code is displayed in Figure 30-2.

Listing 30-4: Exporting images

```
procedure TMainForm.BrowseForFolderActionAccept(Sender: TObject);
var
  folder: string;
  image: TBitmap;
  prefix: string;
  startIndex: Integer;
const
  FILENAME = '%s%d.bmp';
begin
  folder := BrowseForFolderAction.Folder;
  { if the final "\" is missing, add it }
  if folder[Length(folder)] <> '\' then
```

```
      folder := folder + '\';

  startIndex := 100;
  prefix := 'Image';
  for image in ImageCache do
  begin
    image.SaveToFile(folder + Format(FILENAME, [prefix, startIndex]));
    Inc(startIndex);
  end;

  MessageDlg('Finished!', mtInformation, [mbOK], 0);
end;
```

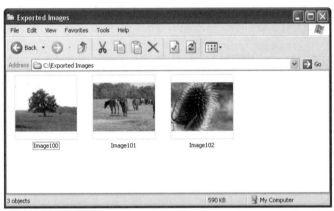

Figure 30-2: Images exported using the for-in loop and the TImageCacheEnumerator class

Adding foreach Enumeration Functionality to a C# Class

Now that you know how the for-in loop works, you should have no problems implementing the same functionality in a C# class.

To see how to add enumeration support to a custom C# class, we first need to create a class, in this case a Library class that will only contain five books. Each book in the library is a structure (Book structure) that has three public fields: Author, PageCount, and Title.

To declare a structure (record) in C#, you have to use the reserved word `struct`, followed by the structure's name, and list the structure's fields in its block. The fields you want to use from the outside world need to be marked as public, just like fields in a class.

Here's the Book structure used by the Library class:

```
using System;

namespace Wordware.ForEachSupport
{
  struct Book
  {
```

```
    public string Author;
    public int PageCount;
    public string Title;
  }
}
```

The Library class is a very simple class that has methods for changing and displaying book data. The entire Library class is displayed in Listing 30-5.

Listing 30-5: The Library class

```
class Library
{
    public int Count = 5;
    private Book[] books = new Book[5];

    /* this method displays a book */
    public void Show(Book aBook)
    {
        if(aBook.Title == null) return;

        Console.WriteLine("Title: {0}", aBook.Title);
        Console.WriteLine("Author: {0}", aBook.Author);
        Console.WriteLine("Page Count: {0}", aBook.PageCount);
        Console.WriteLine();
    }

    /* this method can be used to modify a book */
    public void Set(int bookID, string title,
        string author, int pageCount)
    {
        if((bookID >= 0) && (bookID <= books.Length - 1))
        {
            books[bookID].Author = author;
            books[bookID].Title = title;
            books[bookID].PageCount = pageCount;
        }
    }

    /* this method is used by the LibraryEnumerator class */
    public Book GetBook(int bookID)
    {
        return books[bookID];
    }

    [STAThread]
    static void Main(string[] args)
    {
        Library library = new Library();
        library.Set(0, "The Art of War", "Sun Tzu", 260);
        library.Set(1, "Amber Chronicles", "Roger Zelazny", 1200);

    }
}
```

To loop through the books stored in a Library object with the foreach statement, we need to create the LibraryEnumerator class. In C#, we also have to link the main class with the enumerator class (in the constructor), create the public function MoveNext() to advance to the next element in the collection, create the public property Current to return the currently selected element, and create a Reset method that resets the loop to its initial position (–1). We also have to create the GetEnumerator() public method in the main class to create and return a new instance of the enumerator class.

But before we create the enumerator class, we need to see how to create a property in a C# class. Properties in C# are implemented with the following syntax:

```
access_modifier data_type PropertyName
{
   get {
      // place code that reads the property value here
   }
   set {
      // place code that changes the property value here
   }
}
```

The above syntax is used to create properties that can be read from and written to. If you want to (or have to) create a read-only property, you can create it by simply not implementing the set part of the property.

Here's what the Current read-only property of the LibraryEnumerator class looks like:

```
// public read-only property that returns a Book structure
// lib is a Library instance
public Book Current
{
   get {
      return lib.GetBook(index);
   }
}
```

Listing 30-6 shows the entire LibraryEnumerator class, the GetEnumerator() public method of the Library class, and the updated Main() method that uses the foreach statement to loop through the books stored in a Library instance.

Listing 30-6: The LibraryEnumerator class

```
using System;

namespace Wordware.ForEachSupport
{
   class Library
   {
      public LibraryEnumerator GetEnumerator()
      {
         return new LibraryEnumerator(this);
      }
```

```
        [STAThread]
        static void Main(string[] args)
        {
            Library library = new Library();
            library.Set(0, "The Art of War", "Sun Tzu", 260);
            library.Set(1, "Amber Chronicles", "Roger Zelazny", 1200);

            foreach(Book book in library)
            {
                library.Show(book);
            }

            Console.WriteLine("Press any key to continue...");
            Console.ReadLine();
        }
    }

// ------------------------------------------------------------------------

    class LibraryEnumerator
    {
        private Library lib;
        private int index = -1;

        /* the constructor */
        public LibraryEnumerator(Library library)
        {
            lib = library;
        }

        public bool MoveNext()
        {
            bool Result = index < lib.Count - 1;
            if(Result == true) index++;
            return Result;
        }

        public Book Current
        {
            get {
                return lib.GetBook(index);
            }
        }

        public void Reset()
        {
            index = -1;
        }
    } // LibraryEnumerator class

}    // namespace
```

Records

Besides being collections of fields, records in Delphi and structures in C# can also have properties, methods, constructors, and operator overloads. While classes in Delphi and C# are always allocated on the heap, records, even those with methods and overloaded operators, are stored on the stack. Because records are allocated on the stack, your code is more efficient since stack allocation is faster than heap allocation. Since records in .NET aren't allocated on the managed heap, they are also not garbage collected, which again results in better overall performance.

Besides the allocation difference, there are several more differences between classes and records:

■ Classes support inheritance; records don't.

■ Classes support polymorphism; records don't.

■ Classes can have parameterless (default) constructors; records cannot. (In C#, records have an implicit parameterless constructor that is called to initialize record fields when you use the new operator. In Delphi, fields get initialized automatically, so there's no need to call the default constructor Create, and actually, you cannot call it.)

■ In Delphi for Win32 only records support operator overloading; classes don't. (In C# and Delphi for .NET, both classes and records support operator overloading.)

■ Records don't have destructors; classes do.

Listings 30-7 and 30-8 show how records with fields, properties, methods, and constructors work in Delphi (both flavors) and C#.

Listing 30-7: Records in Delphi for Win32 and Delphi for .NET

```
program Project1;

{$APPTYPE CONSOLE}

uses
  SysUtils;

type
  TMyRecord = record
  private
    FX: Integer;
    FY: Integer;
    procedure SetX(Value: Integer);
    procedure SetY(Value: Integer);
  public
    constructor Create(newX, newY: Integer);
    procedure Display(const Prefix: string);
    property X: Integer read FX write SetX;
    property Y: Integer read FY write SetY;
  end;
```

```
constructor TMyRecord.Create(newX, newY: Integer);
begin
  // assign to properties to call SetX and SetY
  // to take care of negative values
  X := newX;
  Y := newY;
end;

procedure TMyRecord.SetX(Value: Integer);
begin
  if Value >= 0 then
    FX := Value
  else
    FX := 0;
end;

procedure TMyRecord.SetY(Value: Integer);
begin
  if Value >= 0 then
    FY := Value
  else
    FY := 0;
end;

// Prefix is used only to get more meaningful output
procedure TMyRecord.Display(const Prefix: string);
begin
  WriteLn(Prefix, 'X = ', Self.X);    // or just X
  WriteLn(Prefix, 'Y = ', Self.Y);    // or just Y
  WriteLn;
end;

var
  a: TMyRecord;
  b: TMyRecord;
  c: TMyRecord;

begin
  { fields are initialized to 0, displays X = 0, Y = 0 }
  a.Display('a.');

  { using the custom constructor to initialize fields }
  b := TMyRecord.Create(100, 200);
  b.Display('b.');

  { copies the entire record, not a reference (pointer) }
  c := b;
  c.X := 1;
  c.Display('c.');     // c.X is 1
  b.Display('b.');     // b.X remains 200

  ReadLn;
end.
```

Listing 30-8: Structures in C#

```csharp
using System;

namespace Wordware.Records
{
    struct MyRecord
    {
        private int fx;
        private int fy;

        // x property
        public int X
        {
            get {
                return fx;
            }
            set {
                fx = value >= 0 ? value : 0;
            }
        }

        // y property
        public int Y
        {
            get {
                return fy;
            }
            set {
                fy = value >= 0 ? value : 0;
            }
        }

        /* custom constructor */
        public MyRecord(int newX, int newY)
        {
            fx = newX;
            fy = newY;
        }

        /* another constructor that accepts strings */
        public MyRecord(string newX, string newY)
        {
            fx = System.Int32.Parse(newX);
            fy = System.Int32.Parse(newY);
        }

        // there's no need for const when passing strings in .NET
        public void Display(string prefix)
        {
            Console.WriteLine("{0}X = {1}", prefix, fx);
            Console.WriteLine("{0}Y = {1}", prefix, fy);
            Console.WriteLine();
        }
    }
}
```

```
class RecordUser
{
   [STAThread]
   static void Main(string[] args)
   {
      /* if you don't use the new operator, the fields are
      unassigned, and Console.WriteLine doesn't compile */

      // MyRecord a;
      // Console.WriteLine(a.X);

      /* initialized to default values */
      MyRecord b = new MyRecord();
      b.Display("b.");

      /* call the custom (int, int) constructor */
      MyRecord c = new MyRecord(1, 2);
      c.Display("c.");

      /* call the custom (string, string) constructor,
         System.Int32.Parse understands spaces */
      MyRecord d = new MyRecord(" 2  ", "10");
      d.Display("d.");

      /* struct assignment */
      MyRecord e = new MyRecord(1000, 1001);
      MyRecord f = e;      // only if "e" is completely initialized
      f.Display("f.");

      Console.ReadLine();
   }
}
}
```

Operator Overloading in Delphi and C#

Overloading an operator in Delphi is as simple as creating a function. The only difference is that instead of the reserved word function, you have to use the reserved words class and operator in the following way:

```
type
  TMyRecordOrClass = record|class
    class operator OperatorName(RequiredParameters): ResultType;
  end;
```

The following table shows several operators that can be overloaded in Delphi. To see a complete list of operators that can be overloaded in Delphi, open Delphi's Help and load the "Operator Overloading" topic (ms-help://borland.bds4/bds4ref/html/OperatorOverloads.htm).

Listing 30-9 shows how to overload the Explicit and Add operators in a record.

Table 30-1: Several overloadable operators in Delphi

Operator	Operator Syntax	Overloaded Symbol
Explicit	Explicit(A: SrcType): ResultType	(Explicit Typecast)
Equal	Equal(A: Type; B: Type): ResultType	=
Add	Add(A: Type; B: Type): ResultType	+

Listing 30-9: Overloading operators in Delphi

```
program Project1;

{$APPTYPE CONSOLE}

uses Types;      // for TRect type

type
  TMyPoint = record
  public
    X: Integer;
    Y: Integer;
    constructor Create(AX, AY: Integer);
    class operator Add(A, B: TMyPoint): TMyPoint;
    class operator Explicit(A: TRect): TMyPoint;
  end;

constructor TMyPoint.Create(AX, AY: Integer);
begin
  X := AX;
  Y := AY;
end;

class operator TMyPoint.Add(A, B: TMyPoint): TMyPoint;
begin
  Result.X := A.X + B.X;
  Result.Y := A.Y + B.Y;
end;

class operator TMyPoint.Explicit(A: TRect): TMyPoint;
begin
  Result.X := A.Left;
  Result.Y := A.Top;
end;

var
  RecOne, RecTwo: TMyPoint;
  RecResult: TMyPoint;
  Exp: TMyPoint;
  RC: Types.TRect;

begin
  RecOne := TMyPoint.Create(10, 20);
  RecTwo := TMyPoint.Create(100, 200);
  RecResult := RecOne + RecTwo;
  WriteLn(RecResult.X);    // 110
```

```
RC := Rect(1, 1, 10, 10);
// without the overloaded Explicit operator,
// this typcast would produce a compiler error
Exp := TMyPoint(RC);
WriteLn(Exp.X);          // 1

  ReadLn;
end.
```

When overloading operators in C#, you need to remember that all operator overloads must be both public and static. You should also notice that there are syntactical differences between an operator and a conversion overload. Here's the syntax for overloading operators and the explicit typecast:

```
public static ReturnType operator Symbol(Type a, Type b)
{
}

public static explicit operator ReturnType(SourceType)
{
}
```

Listing 30-10 shows how to overload the + operator and explicit typecast. It is the C# version of the Delphi example in Listing 30-9.

Listing 30-10: Overloading operators in C#

```
using System;

namespace Wordware.OperatorOverloading
{
   struct Rect
   {
      public int Left;
      public int Top;
      public int Right;
      public int Bottom;
      public Rect(int newLeft, int newTop,
         int newRight, int newBottom)
      {
         Left = newLeft;
         Top = newTop;
         Right = newRight;
         Bottom = newBottom;
      }
   }

   struct MyPoint
   {
      public int X;
      public int Y;

      public MyPoint(int newX, int newY)
      {
         X = newX;
```

```
        Y = newY;
    }

    // + operator overload
    public static MyPoint operator + (MyPoint a, MyPoint b)
    {
        return new MyPoint(a.X + b.X, a.Y + b.Y);
    }

    // explicit typecast overload
    public static explicit operator MyPoint(Rect a)
    {
        return new MyPoint(a.Left, a.Top);
    }
}

class OverloadUser
{
    [STAThread]
    static void Main(string[] args)
    {
        MyPoint RecOne = new MyPoint(10, 20);
        MyPoint RecTwo = new MyPoint(100, 200);
        MyPoint RecResult = RecOne + RecTwo;   // + overload
        Console.WriteLine(RecResult.X);        // 110

        Rect RC = new Rect(1, 1, 10, 10);
        MyPoint Exp = (MyPoint)RC;             // explicit overload
        Console.WriteLine(Exp.X);              // 1

        Console.ReadLine();
    }
}
```

C# Indexers

If you read Chapter 26, which covers array properties in Delphi, you already know almost everything about C# indexers — they are a C# language construct that allows you to access classes and records as if they were arrays.

To declare an indexer, you have to use the following syntax:

```
public ReturnType this[Type Identifier]
/* for instance */
public string this[int index]
```

Listing 30-11 shows a simple Languages class that contains a private string array and allows access to the array through two indexers. One indexer accepts an integer value and returns the string at the specified index. The other indexer accepts a string and returns the index of the string if it exists in the array.

Listing 30-11: C# indexers

```
using System;

namespace Wordware.Indexers
{
   class Languages
   {
      private string[] langArray = {"Delphi", "<empty>", "C++",
         "IL", "Assembler", "JScript.NET", "VB.NET" };

      public string this[int index]
      {
         get {
            // index is available in get and set blocks
            if(index >= 0 && index <= langArray.Length - 1)
               return langArray[index];
            else
               throw new IndexOutOfRangeException();
         }

         set {
            // value is only available in the set block
            if(index < 0)
               langArray[0] = value;
            else if(index > langArray.Length - 1)
               langArray[langArray.Length - 1] = value;
            else
               langArray[index] = value;
         }
      }

      /* return the index of a language, read-only */
      public int this[string index]
      {
         get {
            for(int cnt=0; cnt<langArray.Length - 1; cnt++)
            {
               if(langArray[cnt] == index)
                  return cnt;
            }
            // if not found return -1
            return -1;
         }
      }
   }

   class IndexersUser
   {
      [STAThread]
      static void Main(string[] args)
      {
         Languages lg = new Languages();
         try
         {
            // display Delphi
```

```
              Console.WriteLine(lg[0]);

              // find the "<empty>" item and replace it with "C#"
              int empty = lg["<empty>"];
              if(empty != -1)
              {
                 lg[empty] = "C#";
                 Console.WriteLine(lg[empty]);
              }

              // throw the invalid index exception
              Console.WriteLine(lg[-1]);
           }
           catch(Exception e)
           {
              Console.WriteLine();
              Console.WriteLine("Exception thrown by the indexer:");
              Console.WriteLine(e.ToString());
           }

           Console.ReadLine();
        }
     }
}
```

Delegates and Single-cast and Multicast Events

Delegates, single-cast events, and multicast events are names for language constructs that you have been using for quite some time now.

Although there are some differences between C# and Delphi events, delegates in all three languages — C#, Delphi for Win32, and Delphi for .NET — are simply methods that are called in response to an event.

Single-cast events are events that call only one event handler in response to themselves. They are used by the VCL. Delphi for Win32 only supports single-cast events.

Multicast events are events that can call multiple event handlers. Windows.Forms controls use multicast events. Delphi for .NET language supports both single-cast and multicast events.

Delegates and Single-Cast Events in Delphi for Win32

A delegate in Delphi is a procedure of object like, for instance, the TNotifyEvent and TMouseEvent types, which looks like this:

```
type TNotifyEvent = procedure (Sender: TObject) of object;
type TMouseEvent = procedure (Sender: TObject; Button: TMouseButton;
  Shift: TShiftState; X, Y: Integer) of object;
```

Single-cast events are created with the read and write reserved words:

```
FOnClick: TNotifyEvent;
...
property OnClick: TNotifyEvent read FOnClick write FOnClick;
```

Now it's time to see how to create and use a custom delegate in Delphi for Win32. We are going to derive a new component from TGraphicControl, draw randomly colored rectangles on the component's surface, and fire a custom event of type TSelectColor when the user clicks on the component, as shown in Figure 30-3.

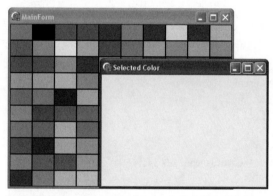

Figure 30-3: Using a custom delegate in Delphi for Win32

Besides the Sender parameter, which tells us the component that called the method, the TSelectColor delegate has another parameter, SelectedColor, which tells us what color is selected. Here's the TSelectColor delegate:

```
type
  TSelectColor = procedure(Sender: TObject;
    SelectedColor: TColor) of object;
```

The TGraphicControl descendant, the TColorMix component, needs to override two methods of the TGraphicControl to do its job: Paint and MouseUp. It needs to override the Paint method to paint on the component's surface and it needs to override the TGraphicControl's MouseUp method to fire the custom OnSelectColor event when the user releases a mouse button over the component.

Listing 30-12 shows the source of the TColorMix component and the source of the main form that uses the component.

Listing 30-12: Using a custom delegate in Delphi for Win32

```
unit Unit1;

interface

uses
  Windows, Messages, SysUtils, Variants, Classes,
  Graphics, Controls, Forms, Dialogs;
```

```
type
  TSelectColor = procedure(Sender: TObject;
    SelectedColor: TColor) of object;

  TColorMix = class(TGraphicControl)
  private
    FOnSelectColor: TSelectColor;
  public
    constructor Create(AOwner: TComponent); override;
    procedure Paint; override;
    procedure MouseUp(Button: TMouseButton;
      Shift: TShiftState; X, Y: Integer); override;
    property OnSelectColor: TSelectColor read
      FOnSelectColor write FOnSelectColor;
  end;

  TMainForm = class(TForm)
    procedure FormCreate(Sender: TObject);
  private
    { Private declarations }
    Mix: TColorMix;
  public
    { Public declarations }
    procedure SelectColorDelegate(Sender: TObject;
      SelectedColor: TColor);
  end;

var
  MainForm: TMainForm;

implementation

{$R *.dfm}

constructor TColorMix.Create(AOwner: TComponent);
begin
  inherited;
  Align := alClient;        // automatically fill the form
end;

{ Paint 100 rectangles on the component's surface }
procedure TColorMix.Paint;
var
  i, j: Integer;
  rcWidth: Integer;
  rcHeight: Integer;
begin
  inherited;
  rcWidth := Width div 10;
  rcHeight := Height div 10;

  // paint random rects
  for i := 0 to 10 do
    for j := 0 to 10 do
    begin
```

```
      Canvas.Brush.Color := RGB(Random(255),
        Random(255), Random(255));
      Canvas.Rectangle(i * rcWidth, j * rcHeight,
        (i + 1)* rcWidth, (j + 1) * rcHeight);
    end;
end;

procedure TColorMix.MouseUp(Button: TMouseButton;
  Shift: TShiftState; X, Y: Integer);
var
  selectedColor: TColor;
begin
  inherited;
  if Assigned(FOnSelectColor) then
  begin
    selectedColor := Canvas.Pixels[X, Y];
    // Fire the OnSelectColor event, and pass Self as the Sender
    // parameter and the selected color as the SelectedColor param.
    FOnSelectColor(Self, selectedColor);
  end;
end;

// ----------------------------------------------------------

procedure TMainForm.FormCreate(Sender: TObject);
begin
  // display the TColorMix component on the form
  Mix := TColorMix.Create(Self);
  Mix.Parent := Self;
  Mix.OnSelectColor := SelectColorDelegate;
end;

// this is called by the OnSelectColor event
procedure TMainForm.SelectColorDelegate(Sender: TObject;
  SelectedColor: TColor);
var
  Frm: TForm;
begin
  // if user didn't click on border (black)
  if SelectedColor <> clBlack then
  begin
    Frm := TForm.Create(Self);
    try
      Frm.Caption := 'Selected Color';
      Frm.Position := poScreenCenter;
      Frm.Color := SelectedColor;
      Frm.ShowModal;
    finally
      Frm.Free;
    end;
  end;
end;

end.
```

Delegates and Multicast Events in Delphi for .NET

Multicast events can be implemented with great ease in Delphi. The only thing that you have to do is use the reserved words add and remove, instead of read and write:

```
property OnClick: TNotifyEvent
  add FCustomOnClick remove FCustomOnClick;
```

The above OnClick event is from a custom button class, displayed in Listing 30-13. In order to create a multicast version of the OnClick event, you have to override the TButton's Click procedure and, instead of the inherited behavior, call FCustomOnClick. Figure 30-4 shows what happens when you click on a TMultiClickButton.

Listing 30-13: A TButton descendant with a multicast OnClick event

```
unit Unit1;

interface

uses
  Windows, Messages, SysUtils, Variants, Classes, Graphics,
  Controls, Forms, Dialogs, System.ComponentModel,
  Borland.Vcl.StdCtrls, Borland.Vcl.XPMan;

type
  TMultiClickButton = class(TButton)
  private
    FCustomOnClick: TNotifyEvent;
  public
    procedure Click; override;
  published
    property OnClick: TNotifyEvent
      add FCustomOnClick remove FCustomOnClick;
  end;

  TMainForm = class(TForm)
    XPManifest: TXPManifest;
    procedure FormCreate(Sender: TObject);
  private
    { Private declarations }
    mcb: TMultiClickButton;
  public
    { Public declarations }
    procedure ChangeCaption(Sender: TObject);
    procedure ShowMyMessage(Sender: TObject);
  end;

var
  MainForm: TMainForm;

implementation

{$R *.nfm}
```

```
procedure TMultiClickButton.Click;
begin
  if Assigned(FCustomOnClick) then FCustomOnClick(Self);
end;

// ----------------------------------------------------------------

procedure TMainForm.FormCreate(Sender: TObject);
begin
  mcb := TMultiClickButton.Create(Self);
  mcb.Parent := Self;
  mcb.SetBounds(10, 10, 200, 25);
  mcb.Caption := 'Click to call two handlers!';
  // add TWO methods to the OnClick event
  Include(mcb.OnClick, ChangeCaption);
  Include(mcb.OnClick, ShowMyMessage);
end;

// another sample method
procedure TMainForm.ChangeCaption(Sender: TObject);
begin
  Caption := 'Hello from method #1!';
end;

// another sample method
procedure TMainForm.ShowMyMessage(Sender: TObject);
begin
  MessageDlg('Hello from method #2!', mtInformation, [mbOK], 0);
end;

end.
```

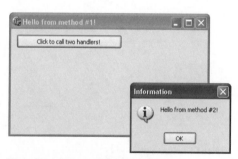

Figure 30-4: Using a TMultiClickButton

Delegates and Events in C#

Delegates can be used to anonymously call methods and to implement events in C# classes. To create a delegate in C# (procedure of object equivalent), you have to use the following syntax:

```
public delegate ReturnType DelegateName(Parameters)
```

To use a delegate, you then have to create a method with the same return type and the same parameter list. When you have both the delegate and a method with the appropriate return type and parameter list, you can call the method through the delegate, using the following syntax:

```
delegate InstanceName = new delegate(MethodName);
delegate(MethodParameters);
```

Listing 30-14 illustrates how to use the above syntax to declare, instantiate, and call a method through a delegate.

Listing 30-14: Using delegates

```
using System;

namespace Wordware.Delegates
{
    public delegate void MathOperation(int value);

    class DelegateUser
    {
        public static int x = 0;

        public static void Add(int value)
        {
            x += value;
        }

        public static void Subtract(int value)
        {
            x -= value;
        }

        public static void Show()
        {
            Console.WriteLine("x = {0}", x);
        }

        [STAThread]
        static void Main(string[] args)
        {
            MathOperation a = new MathOperation(Add);
            a(100);
            Show();      // 100

            MathOperation b = new MathOperation(Subtract);
            b(50);
            Show();      // 50

            Console.ReadLine();
        }
    }
}
```

Now that you know the syntax involved in the creation and usage of a delegate, it's time to see how to implement events in C# classes.

Once you've created a delegate, you declare an event using the reserved word event:

```
public event DelegateType EventName;
```

Events in C# are fired like events in Delphi: you first check whether an event has event handlers assigned to it and then call the handlers:

```
if(Event != null)
    Event(ParameterList);
```

Finally, you need to assign an event handler to an event, using the following syntax:

```
Object.Event += new DelegateType(EventHandler);
```

Listing 30-15 shows the MyFileReader class that can read text files. The class has four events: OnNoFile (error), OnOpen, OnReadLine, and OnClose. The OnReadLine event is the most complex and the most important event because it allows other classes to do whatever they want with the strings read from the file. In this example, the DelegateUser class's OnReadLine event handler only reads the interface part of a Delphi unit and displays it in the console window. The OnReadLine event handler of the FormUser class shows how to use the same MyFileReader class and read the file into a ListBox.

Figure 30-5 shows how the event handlers of the DelegateUser class work.

Listing 30-15: Delegates and events in C#

```
using System;
using System.IO;
using System.Windows.Forms;

namespace Wordware.Delegates
{
    /* three different delegates */
    public delegate void Notification();
    public delegate void ErrorNotification(string file);
    public delegate void BreakEvent(string line, ref bool Break);

    class MyFileReader
    {
        /* events */
        public event Notification OnOpen;
        public event Notification OnClose;
        public event ErrorNotification OnNoFile;
        public event BreakEvent OnReadLine;

        /* this method fires all four events */
        public void ReadFile(string FileName)
        {
            if(!File.Exists(FileName) && (OnNoFile != null))
            {
                OnNoFile(FileName);
```

```
            return;
        }

        StreamReader sr = new StreamReader(FileName);
        try
        {
            if(OnOpen != null)
                OnOpen();

            string line;
            bool Break = false;
            while((line = sr.ReadLine()) != null)
            {
                if(OnReadLine != null) {
                    OnReadLine(line, ref Break);
                }
                /* if Break == true, the caller wants to
                    stop reading from the file */
                if(Break == true) return;
            }
        }
        finally
        {
            sr.Close();
            if(OnClose != null)
                OnClose();
        }
    }
} // MyFileReader class

// -------------------------------------------------------------

class DelegateUser
{
    public static void OpenHandler()
    {
        Console.WriteLine("File opened...");
        Console.WriteLine("--------------");
    }

    public static void CloseHandler()
    {
        Console.WriteLine("--------------");
        Console.WriteLine("File closed...");
    }

    public static void ErrorHandler(string file)
    {
        Console.WriteLine("Cannot load file \"{0}\".", file);
    }

    public static void ReadInterfaceOnly(string line,
        ref bool Break)
    {
        if(line == "implementation")
```

```
            Break = true;
        else
            Console.WriteLine(line);
    }

    [STAThread]
    static void Main(string[] args)
    {
        string fileName = @"C:\My Components\StringsCache.pas";
        MyFileReader mfr = new MyFileReader();

        /* Passing handlers to all four events */
        mfr.OnOpen += new Notification(OpenHandler);
        mfr.OnClose += new Notification(CloseHandler);
        mfr.OnNoFile += new ErrorNotification(ErrorHandler);
        mfr.OnReadLine += new BreakEvent(ReadInterfaceOnly);

        // displays the file and fires the events
        mfr.ReadFile(fileName);

        // display the file on a form by using a
        // different OnReadLine event handler
        FormUser fu = new FormUser();
        fu.DisplayFile();

        Console.ReadLine();
    }
}

// ---------------------------------------------------------------

class FormUser
{
    private string fileName = @"C:\My Components\StringsCache.pas";
    private Form f;
    private ListBox fileList;
    private MyFileReader fr;

    public void ReadFileToList(string line, ref bool Break)
    {
        fileList.Items.Add(line);

        // after the unit's name has been displayed,
        // remove the display unit name handler; this
        // works because the OnOpen event first assigns
        // the DisplayUnitName handler, and then the
        // main code assigns the ReadFileToList handler
        // to the OnReadLine event
        fr.OnReadLine -= new BreakEvent(DisplayUnitName);
    }

    public void OpenHandler()
    {
        // add another handler to the OnReadLine event;
        // this handler needs to execute only once and its
```

```
            // purpose is to display the unit name on the form
            fr.OnReadLine += new BreakEvent(DisplayUnitName);
        }

        public void DisplayUnitName(string line, ref bool Break)
        {
            f.Text = line;
        }

        // display the file in a listbox
        public void DisplayFile()
        {
            f = new Form();
            try
            {
                fileList = new ListBox();
                try
                {
                    f.Controls.Add(fileList);
                    fileList.Dock = DockStyle.Fill;

                    fr = new MyFileReader();
                    // assign the handler that reads the unit name
                    fr.OnOpen += new Notification(OpenHandler);
                    // assign the main handler that reads the
                    // file into the list box
                    fr.OnReadLine += new
                        BreakEvent(ReadFileToList);
                    fr.ReadFile(fileName);

                    f.ShowDialog();
                }
                finally
                {
                    fileList.Dispose();
                }
            }
            finally
            {
                f.Dispose();
            }
        }
    }
}
```

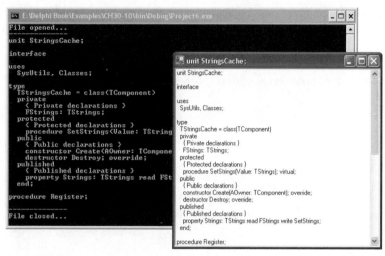

Figure 30-5: Reading a text file using delegates and events

GDI+ Programming

Just as GDI is the default graphics interface in the Win32, GDI+, the successor of GDI, is the default graphics interface in .NET. GDI+ is physically stored in the System.Drawing assembly and split into several System.Drawing namespaces:

- System.Drawing — the main namespace that contains classes aimed at graphics rendering
- System.Drawing.Design — contains classes for developers that are developing design-time user interfaces
- System.Drawing.Drawing2D — contains more advanced graphics classes
- System.Drawing.Imaging — contains classes that allow us to work with images
- System.Drawing.Printing — contains printing-related classes
- System.Drawing.Text — contains additional font-related classes

The central object in GDI+ is the Graphics object, which allows the production of graphics output. Unlike the Canvas property, which is always available, the Graphics object must be explicitly created with a call to CreateGraphics(), or you have to write the graphics code in an OnPaint event handler, in which case, the e parameter provides the Graphics object:

```
private void WinForm_Paint(object sender,
    System.Windows.Forms.PaintEventArgs e)
{
    Graphics g = e.Graphics;
}
```

The CreateGraphics method is not part of the Graphics class. Instead, it is a part of the Control class, and you call it on the control on which you want to paint.

For instance, if you want to paint on the form, you can write this:

```
Graphics g = this.CreateGraphics();
try
{
}
finally
{
   g.Dispose();
}
```

or

```
using(Graphics gr = this.CreateGraphics())
{
}
```

Notice the usage of the reserved word using. Besides its use as a namespace importer, the reserved word using can be used to create a special block at the end of which the Dispose method of the used object will be called. Essentially, the above try-finally and using block do the same thing: dispose of the Graphics object once it is no longer needed.

To draw shapes and lines in GDI+, you have to use pens and brushes and the methods available in the Graphics class. Again, GDI+ does not provide a constant Pen or Brush object like VCL's Canvas does, so if you want a custom pen or brush, you'll need to create a custom pen or brush object. But if you need a plain pen or brush, like a 1px wide black pen, you can use the static pens and brushes from the System.Drawing.Pens and the System.Drawing.Brushes classes.

The following listing shows how to produce simple graphics output with GDI+ in a C# Windows.Forms application. It shows how to paint inside the OnPaint event, create a new Graphics object with a call to CreateGraphics, use static pens and brushes, create custom pen objects, and use the using block to release graphics object when you're done with them.

You can see the result of the code from Listing 30-16 in Figure 30-6.

Listing 30-16: GDI+ essentials

```
private void WinForm_Paint(object sender,
   System.Windows.Forms.PaintEventArgs e)
{
   Graphics g = e.Graphics;
   Rectangle rc = new Rectangle(20, 20, 200, 200);

   // create and use a custom pen (Color, Width)
   using(Pen p = new Pen(Color.Blue, 2))
   {
      // use the static White brush from the Brushes class
```

```
            g.FillRectangle(Brushes.White, rc);
            // use the custom pen
            g.DrawRectangle(p, rc);
        }
    }

    private void WinForm_MouseMove(object sender,
        System.Windows.Forms.MouseEventArgs e)
    {
        if(e.Button != MouseButtons.Left) return;

        using(Graphics g = this.CreateGraphics())
        {
            // top, left, width, height
            g.FillRectangle(Brushes.Chocolate,
                e.X - 2, e.Y - 2, 4, 4);
        } // the g object gets disposed here
    }
```

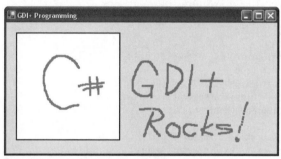

Figure 30-6: GDI+ essentials

Besides being able to display shapes, lines, and curves, GDI+ allows us to, for instance, draw gradients and semitransparent shapes, and work with a larger number of image formats.

The following example shows how to load and display images, use the System.Drawing.Drawing2.LinearGradientBrush class to draw gradients, fill text with a texture using the System.Drawing.Drawing2D.TextureBrush class, and antialias the text with the help of the TextRenderingHint property. The example is thoroughly commented and not very complex, so there should be no problem understanding how it works. Figure 30-7 shows the graphics output produced by the code in Listing 30-17.

Listing 30-17: Working with images, text, texture, and gradient brushes

```
private string dir;
private System.Drawing.Image img;
private System.Drawing.Image texture;

[STAThread]
static void Main()
```

```
{
    Application.Run(new WinForm());
}

private void WinForm_Load(object sender, System.EventArgs e)
{
    // System.IO.Path class, get app path
    dir = Path.GetDirectoryName(Application.ExecutablePath);
    // load the image and resize the form
    // to see the entire image
    img = Image.FromFile(dir + @"\Rijeka.jpg");
    this.ClientSize = new Size(img.Width, img.Height);

    // load the texture image
    texture = Image.FromFile(dir + @"\Texture.jpg");
}

private void WinForm_Paint(object sender,
    System.Windows.Forms.PaintEventArgs e)
{
    Graphics g = e.Graphics;

    // System.Drawing.Drawing2D.LinearGradientBrush
    LinearGradientBrush grad =
        new LinearGradientBrush(this.ClientRectangle,
            Color.White, Color.Transparent,
            LinearGradientMode.Horizontal);

    // System.Drawing.Drawing2D.TextureBrush
    TextureBrush tex = new TextureBrush(texture);

    Font myFont = new Font("Impact", 66, FontStyle.Bold);

    try
    {
        g.DrawImage(img, 0, 0, img.Width, img.Height);
        g.FillRectangle(grad, this.ClientRectangle);

        // System.Drawing.Text namespace,
        // use RenderingHint to display antialiased text
        g.TextRenderingHint = TextRenderingHint.AntiAlias;

        g.DrawString("The Adriatic Sea", myFont, tex, 20, 20);
    }
    finally
    {
        grad.Dispose();
        tex.Dispose();
        myFont.Dispose();
    } // try..finally
}   // OnPaint
```

Figure 30-7: Using more advanced GDI+ classes

Index

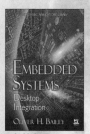

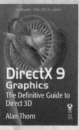

About the CD

The companion CD contains the code and compiled executables for every example in the book, and two tools that help you view the contents of the CD. You can use the Autorun application to browse the contents of the CD, run the Example Browser application to see the book's examples, or install the book's examples to your hard drive.

The files on the CD are stored in three folders. The Autorun Source folder contains the source code of the Autorun application, the Examples folder contains the book's examples and the Example Browser application (also comes with full source code), and the Setup directory contains the setup application for installing the examples to the hard drive.

WARNING: By opening the CD package, you accept the terms and conditions of the CD/Source Code Usage License Agreement. Additionally, opening the CD package makes this book nonreturnable.

CD/Source Code Usage License Agreement

Please read the following CD/Source Code usage license agreement before opening the CD and using the contents therein:

1. By opening the accompanying software package, you are indicating that you have read and agree to be bound by all terms and conditions of this CD/Source Code usage license agreement.
2. The compilation of code and utilities contained on the CD and in the book are copyrighted and protected by both U.S. copyright law and international copyright treaties, and is owned by Wordware Publishing, Inc. Individual source code, example programs, help files, freeware, shareware, utilities, and evaluation packages, including their copyrights, are owned by the respective authors.
3. No part of the enclosed CD or this book, including all source code, help files, shareware, freeware, utilities, example programs, or evaluation programs, may be made available on a public forum (such as a World Wide Web page, FTP site, bulletin board, or Internet news group) without the express written permission of Wordware Publishing, Inc. or the author of the respective source code, help files, shareware, freeware, utilities, example programs, or evaluation programs.
4. You may not decompile, reverse engineer, disassemble, create a derivative work, or otherwise use the enclosed programs, help files, freeware, shareware, utilities, or evaluation programs except as stated in this agreement.
5. The software, contained on the CD and/or as source code in this book, is sold without warranty of any kind. Wordware Publishing, Inc. and the authors specifically disclaim all other warranties, express or implied, including but not limited to implied warranties of merchantability and fitness for a particular purpose with respect to defects in the disk, the program, source code, sample files, help files, freeware, shareware, utilities, and evaluation programs contained therein, and/or the techniques described in the book and implemented in the example programs. In no event shall Wordware Publishing, Inc., its dealers, its distributors, or the authors be liable or held responsible for any loss of profit or any other alleged or actual private or commercial damage, including but not limited to special, incidental, consequential, or other damages.
6. One (1) copy of the CD or any source code therein may be created for backup purposes. The CD and all accompanying source code, sample files, help files, freeware, shareware, utilities, and evaluation programs may be copied to your hard drive. With the exception of freeware and shareware programs, at no time can any part of the contents of this CD reside on more than one computer at one time. The contents of the CD can be copied to another computer, as long as the contents of the CD contained on the original computer are deleted.
7. You may not include any part of the CD contents, including all source code, example programs, shareware, freeware, help files, utilities, or evaluation programs in any compilation of source code, utilities, help files, example programs, freeware, shareware, or evaluation programs on any media, including but not limited to CD, disk, or Internet distribution, without the express written permission of Wordware Publishing, Inc. or the owner of the individual source code, utilities, help files, example programs, freeware, shareware, or evaluation programs.
8. You may use the source code, techniques, and example programs in your own commercial or private applications unless otherwise noted by additional usage agreements as found on the CD.

WARNING: By opening the CD package, you accept the terms and conditions of the CD/Source Code Usage License Agreement. Additionally, opening the CD package makes this book nonreturnable.